Recht und Verfassung in Afrika – Law and Constitution in Africa

Band/Volume 38

Patricia Kameri-Mbote | Alexander Paterson
Oliver C. Ruppel | Bibobra Bello Orubebe
Emmanuel D. Kam Yogo (eds.)

Law | Environment | Africa

Publication of the 5th Symposium | 4th Scientific Conference | 2018 of the Association of Environmental Law Lecturers from African Universities in cooperation with the Climate Policy and Energy Security Programme for Sub-Saharan Africa of the Konrad-Adenauer-Stiftung and UN Environment

Nomos

ASSELLAU
Association of Environmental Law Lecturers in African Universities

Konrad Adenauer Stiftung

Disclaimer
The contents of the articles, including any errors or omissions are solely the responsibility of the authors. Opinions expressed by the different authors, do not necessarily reflect those of the editors or of the Konrad-Adenauer-Stiftung. The editors did their best to acknowledge the usage of copyright protected material. In case any copyright violation should be detected, please contact the editors and any such error or omission will be rectified in a reprint or 2nd edition.

The Deutsche Nationalbibliothek lists this publication in the Deutsche Nationalbibliografie; detailed bibliographic data are available on the Internet at http://dnb.d-nb.de

ISBN 978-3-8487-5287-4 (Print)
978-3-8452-9460-5(ePDF)

British Library Cataloguing-in-Publication Data
A catalogue record for this book is available from the British Library.

ISBN 978-3-8487-5287-4 (Print)
978-3-8452-9460-5 (ePDF)

Library of Congress Cataloging-in-Publication Data
Kameri-Mbote, Patricia / Paterson, Alexander / Ruppel, Oliver C. /
Orubebe, Bibobra Bello / Kam Yogo, Emmanuel D.
Law | Environment | Africa
Publication of the 5th Symposium | 4th Scientific Conference | 2018 of the Association of Environmental Law Lecturers from African Universities in cooperation with the Climate Policy and Energy Security Programme for Sub-Saharan Africa of the Konrad-Adenauer-Stiftung and UN Environment
Patricia Kameri-Mbote / Alexander Paterson / Oliver C. Ruppel /
Bibobra Bello Orubebe / Emmanuel D. Kam Yogo (eds.)
724 p.
Includes bibliographic references and index.

ISBN 978-3-8487-5287-4 (Print)
978-3-8452-9460-5 (ePDF)

1st Edition 2019

Table of contents

PART III: WATER GOVERNANCE, MANAGEMENT AND USE

PART IV: REGULATING SOCIAL AND ENVIRONMENTAL IMPACTS

Foreword

One of the great privileges in being an academic is in learning new ways of approaching issues. Another is in collaborating with colleagues from our own and other countries. As Chair of the IUCN Academy of Environmental Law (the Academy), I have been privileged to meet and become friends with many of the contributors to this book. They have introduced me to many aspects of the interactions of law and the environment in Africa and, as this edited collection amply demonstrates, there is so much more for all of us to learn.

Our mission in the Academy is to advance understanding of, and capacity to research and teach environmental law across the world. Our annual colloquia and our open access, peer reviewed, eJournal along with our many edited collections on aspects of environmental law and on line teaching materials include contributions from African colleagues. Through these contributions, our colleagues have introduced many Academy members to the rich scholarship of African environmental lawyers. We have also learnt of the gaps in African literature and of the need to develop materials with which to educate the next generation of African environmental lawyers. The substantive volume that is 'Law | Environment | Africa' provides a rich contribution to this body of scholarship and a contribution that extends beyond the continent of Africa.

The volume addresses a range of issues which are common to every legal system. Questions such as how innovative new legislation actually is in practice, what the role of law is in developing a cultural of environmental respect and what the best policy, regulatory or governance frameworks might look like, arise across the globe. The areas of focus – climate change, natural resource governance, water governance and social and environmental impacts are pertinent to all corners of the globe.

While the impacts of climate change, for example, may vary across the continents, common lessons are evident from the experiences of all countries. Contributions in this collection which address climate change demonstrate, for example, the required legislative changes if ambitious targets to reduce greenhouse gases while continuing development are to be met. The potential severity of climate change impacts in Africa serve to highlight the types of legal measures necessary to mitigate that impact, or to help communities adapt to it. It is also clear that the measures needed to address these impacts include some that pose significant challenges to the way we currently organise ourselves, be that in terms of infrastructure planning (for example for transport) or in how we address particular sections of the population, such as marginalised groups.

Contributions in this collection thus highlight discourses that are echoed around the world. For example, the analysis of private and community rights addressed in chapters dealing with natural resource governance and water governance reflect broader legal and political discourse of how rights should be organised. Those on public participation, access to benefits and environmental justice raise issues germane to both national and international law across the globe.

The relative dearth of globally available publications on environmental law in Africa compared to the physical presence and population of Africa in itself makes this volume extremely important. More than that, however, the volume holds lessons for environmental lawyers from across the globe and highlights areas in which inter-continental collaborations on environmental law may be beneficial.

Prof. Elizabeth A. Kirk
Chair, IUCN Academy of Environmental Law
Professor of International Environmental Law
Nottingham Trent University

Nottingham, October 2018

Preface

Many African countries have signed international treaties governing the environment and natural resources and have constitutional provisions on environmental law. Framework environmental laws and sectoral statutes on diverse aspects of the environment and natural resource management at the national level complement these. The need for analysis and critique of the content, implementation and enforcement of the laws cannot be overemphasised in such a dynamic field. The fodder for research and academic writing is readily available and it is gratifying to note that African scholars have taken up the challenge and provided much needed leadership in this regard.

This book is a celebration of the development of environmental law scholarship in Africa. Coming from a dearth of universities teaching environmental law in Africa until the early 2000s, the array of authors, diversity of subjects and representation of universities in the book demonstrates the power of dreams. This book's genesis is traceable to Professor Charles Odidi Okidi's dream to have an environmental law scholars from African universities network within the Association of Environmental Law Lecturers in African Universities (ASSELLAU). Prof. Okidi leveraged his networks and sought support of the United Nations Environment Programme to bring together a group of researchers and scholars from different African countries in 2004. These scholars decried the paucity of environmental law scholarship and research from Africa and resolved to establish ASSELLAU with the main objective of popularizing the teaching of environmental law in African universities. As the person charged to run with Prof. Okidi's dream, I must confess that this was a daunting challenge and I had no idea how to execute the task and what direction the dream would lead.

It is therefore my great joy and pride to observe the remarkable success recorded by the Association in both getting environmental law into the undergraduate and graduate curricula of African universities and growing the discipline in the region in less than two decades. This book is testament to that success. It illustrates the Association's prowess in enlisting committed law researchers working on diverse aspects of the environment – climate change; natural resource governance; water management and use; and regulation of social and environmental impacts. The capacity and agility of the scholars in the region is demonstrated in the variety and complexity of the subjects tackled in the book. They range from case studies of specific ecosystems and species within countries to broader natural resource governance issues applicable across different countries. The book also includes chapters dealing with innovations in national laws dealing with environment dispute resolution and interdisciplinary issues such as the human right to water and sanitation; natural resource management and indigenous communities; gender and environment; and resource management and development.

The authors include members of ASSELLAU and younger scholars who have taken up the discipline more recently, some under the tutelage of older members of the Association. The engagement of scholars across different generations sets a solid foundation for sustained research going forward. It is my expectation that this book will: promote environmental law scholarship in the continent, the sub-regions, the individual countries and institutions of higher learning in Africa; promote exchange of ideas within countries; contribute to policy discourses globally, regionally and nationally; and inform global scholarship and developments in environmental law.

I applaud the audacity of Professor Oliver Ruppel, the Founding Director of the Climate Policy and Energy Security Programme for Sub-Saharan Africa (CLESAP) of the Konrad-Adenauer-Stiftung for supporting the conference at which drafts of the papers included in this book were presented in Yaoundé, Cameroon in January 2018. As a founder member of ASSELLAU, Prof. Ruppel has also modelled leadership as an environmental law scholar and researcher.

Finally, I would be remiss not to acknowledge the mentorship and friendship of Prof. Okidi who has been rightly named the 'father of environmental law in Africa', in steering ASSELLAU forward over the years. While always throwing me into the deep end of things, he has been a great source of encouragement and inspiration, ensuring that I keep afloat when all forces seemed to conspire to get me to sink under the weight of things.

Prof. Dr. Patricia Kameri-Mbote (on behalf of the Editors)
Chairperson ASSELLAU

Nairobi, August 2018

Acknowledgements

Law | Environment | Africa is a publication of the Proceedings of the 5th Symposium and the 4th Scientific Conference of the Association of Environmental Law Lecturers from African Universities (ASSELLAU) in cooperation with the Climate Policy and Energy Security Programme for Sub-Saharan Africa of the Konrad-Adenauer-Stiftung (KAS), the United Nations Environment Programme (UNEP) and the University of Douala. This high level event was held at the Hilton Hotel in Yaounde, Cameroon from 11-12 January 2018. At the occasion, the participants hailed the conference as an historic one in Africa. The conference was held in both official languages of Cameroon, namely English and French, with parallel sessions. It was an opportunity for more than 50 legal experts from all over Africa to present their papers and discuss the latest issues pertaining to environmental law on the continent.

Selected presentations have now been captured in this remarkable book publication. The book's object is to explore, review and analyse recent developments located at the nexus of law and the environment in Africa. The collection comprises 32 chapters from legal experts from central, eastern, southern and western Africa. It is a great achievement to have the book published in the renowned legal series "Law and Constitution in Africa (*Recht und Verfassung in Afrika*)" with Nomos Law Publishers in Germany. The series is known to intensify existing efforts in strengthening and deepening scientific knowledge of legal and constitutional issues in Africa and to contribute to a lively cooperation of academia and practice on both continents – Africa and Europe.

A multi-authored publication such as this one is a great team effort. Therefore, special thanks go to my fellow editors and to all the distinguished contributors. Thanks also go to the Konrad-Adenauer-Stiftung (KAS) for making this publication financially possible. As a longstanding member of ASSELLAU, I herewith congratulate the association and Professor Patricia Kameri-Mbote (who is the chair of ASSELLAU) for the enormous impact on the development of environmental law in Africa over the past 15 years of ASSELLAU's existence.

Prof. Dr. Oliver C. Ruppel
Founding Director
Climate Policy and Energy Security Programme for Sub-Saharan Africa (CLESAP)
Konrad-Adenauer-Stiftung (KAS)

Yaounde, August 2018

The editors

Prof. Dr. Patricia Kameri-Mbote
Professor of Law, Former Dean, School of Law, University of Nairobi, Kenya; Chair: Association of Environmental Law Lecturers in African Universities (ASSELLAU).

Prof. Dr. Alexander Ross Paterson
Professor of Law and Director, Institute of Marine and Environmental Law, Faculty of Law, University of Cape Town, South Africa.

Prof. Dr. Oliver C. Ruppel
Professor of Law and Director, Development and Rule of Law Programme (DROP), Stellenbosch University, South Africa; Founding Director, Climate Policy and Energy Security Programme for sub-Saharan Africa (CLESAP), Konrad-Adenauer-Stiftung, Yaounde, Cameroon; Distinguished Fellow Fraunhofer Center for International Management and Knowledge Economy (IMW), Leipzig, Germany; Professor Extraordinaire, University of Central Africa (UCAC), Yaounde, Cameroon; Strathmore Law School, Nairobi, Kenya; and European Faculty of Law, Nova University, Slovenia.

Prof. Dr. Bibobra Bello Orubebe
Professor of Law, Provost and Dean, College of Law, Novena University Ogume, Delta State, Nigeria.

Prof. Dr. Emmanuel D. Kam Yogo
Professor of Law, Department of Public Law, Faculty of Legal and Political Sciences, University of Douala, Cameroon and Associate Professor, Faculty of Law, Laval University, Canada.

The contributors

Dr. Oluwatoyin Adejonwo-Osho
Lecturer, Department of Public Law, Faculty of Law, University of Lagos, Nigeria.

Dr. Lanre Aladeitan
Senior Lecturer, Energy, Oil and Gas and Environmental Law; previously Head of Department, Department of Public and International Law, Faculty of Law, University of Abuja, Gwagwalada, Nigeria.

Dr. Jean-Claude Ashukem
Postdoctoral Fellow, North-West University, Potchefstroom Campus, South Africa.

Dr. Godard Busingye
Senior Lecturer of Public International Law, School of Law, Kampala International University, Uganda.

Prof. Dr. Mark B. Funteh
Associate Professor of Peace Studies, University of Maroua, Cameroon.

Dr. Elizabeth Gachenga
Deputy Vice Chancellor, Academic and Student Affairs, Strathmore University, Kenya.

Prof. Dr. Patricia Kameri-Mbote
Professor of Law; Former Dean, School of Law, University of Nairobi, Kenya; Chair: Association of Environmental Law Lecturers in African Universities (ASSELLAU).

Prof. Dr. Emmanuel D. Kam Yogo
Professor of Law, Department of Public Law, Faculty of Legal and Political Sciences, University of Douala, Cameroon and Associate Professor, Faculty of Law, Laval University, Canada.

Prof. Dr. Emmanuel Kasimbazi
Professor of Law and Chair, Environmental Law Centre, School of Law, Makerere University, Kampala, Uganda.

Prof. Dr. Michael Kidd
Professor of Law, School of Law, University of Kwazulu-Natal, South Africa.

Gift Dorothy Makanje
Lecturer in Law, Department of Foundational Law, University of Malawi.

Amanda Mkhonza
Lecturer in Law, Department of Public Law, University of Cape Town, South Africa.

Prof. Dr. Ayoade Morakinyo Adedayo
Associate Professor, Department of Jurisprudence and International Law, Faculty of Law, University of Lagos, Akoka, Nigeria.

Dr. Kariuki Muigua
Senior Lecturer, School of Law, University of Nairobi, Kenya; Senior Partner: Kariuki Muigua & Co. Advocates; Member of the National Environment Tribunal, Kenya.

Dr. Phiona Muhwezi Mpanga
Lecturer, School of Law, Makerere University, Kampala, Uganda.

Andrew Muma
Lecturer, School of Law, University of Nairobi, Kenya; Senior Partner: Muma & Kanjama Advocates.

Dr. Joseph Magloire Ngang
Senior Lecturer, University of Yaounde II – Soa, Cameroon.

Dr. Marie Ngo Nonga
Senior Lecturer, Faculty of Juridical Sciences and Politics, University of Yaounde II – Soa, Cameroon.

Chidinma Therese Odaghara
Lecturer, Environmental and Planning Law, Sub-Coordinator, Law Clinic, Faculty of Law, University of Abuja, Nigeria.

Edna Odhiambo
Tutorial Fellow, School of Law, University of Nairobi, Kenya.

Dr. Collins Odote
Senior Lecturer, Centre for Advanced Studies in Environmental Law and Policy (CASELAP), University of Nairobi, Kenya.

Dr. Irekpitan Okukpon
Research Fellow, Nigerian Institute of Advanced Legal Studies (NIALS), University of Lagos Campus, Yaba, Lagos State, Nigeria.

Dr. Erimma Gloria Orie
Senior Lecturer, National Open University of Nigeria, Lagos, Nigeria.

Prof. Dr. Bibobra Bello Orubebe
Professor of Law, Provost and Dean, College of Law, Novena University Ogume, Delta State, Nigeria.

Daniel Armel Owona Mbarga
Lawyer and Doctoral Candidate, Catholic University of Central Africa (UCAC), Yaounde, Cameroon.

Prof. Dr. Alexander Ross Paterson
Professor of Law and Director, Institute of Marine and Environmental Law, Faculty of Law, University of Cape Town, South Africa.

Olivia Rumble
Senior Lecturer, Environmental Law, University of Cape Town, South Africa; Director, Climate Legal.

Prof. Dr. Oliver C. Ruppel
Professor of Law and Director of the Development and Rule of Law Programme (DROP), Stellenbosch University, South Africa; Founding Director, Climate Policy and Energy Security Programme for sub-Saharan Africa (CLESAP), Konrad-Adenauer-Stiftung, Yaounde, Cameroon; Distinguished Fellow at the Fraunhofer Center for International Management and Knowledge Economy (IMW), Leipzig, Germany; Professor Extraordinaire, University of Central Africa (UCAC), Yaounde, Cameroon; Strathmore Law School, Nairobi, Kenya; and European Faculty of Law, Nova University, Slovenia.

Dr. Esther Effundem Njieassam
Post-Doctoral Research Fellow, South African Research Chair in International Law, University of Johannesburg, South Africa.

Dr. Pamela Towela Sambo
Lecturer; immediate past Assistant Dean (Undergraduate), School of Law, University of Zambia.

Prof. Dr. Christopher Funwie Tamasang
Associate Professor, Vice-Dean in charge of Research and Cooperation, Faculty of Laws and Political Science, University of Yaounde II, Cameroon; Member: IUCN Academy of Environmental Law; Member: World Commission on Environmental Law; Vice Chair: ASSELLAU in charge of the Central African Region.

Prof. Mekete Bekele Tekle
Associate Professor of Law, School of Law, Addis Ababa University, Ethiopia.

Robert Alex Wabunoha
Regional Coordinator, Environment Government, United Nations Environment (UNEP), Nairobi, Kenya; visiting Lecturer; formerly, senior environment lawyer, National Environment Management Authority, Uganda; Principle State Attorney, Ministry of Justice, Uganda.

Nerima Akinyi Were
Tutorial Fellow, School of Law, University of Nairobi, Kenya.

Hadijah Yahyah
Lecturer, School of Law, Kampala International University, Kampala, Uganda.

Chapter 1: Law, environment, Africa: introducing the imperatives, parameters and trends

Alexander Paterson

1 The context

> Fundamentally we all depend on nature: the ecological infrastructure of the planet that provides the flow of goods and services upon which our livelihoods and economies are built. Yet Africa's ecosystems are changing faster than ever before through the combined impact of global and local pressures. Loss of ecosystem services is compromising future security, health and well-being and effects are being borne disproportionately by the poor.[1]

This telling reality highlighted in the Africa Ecological Footprint Report (2012)[2] is mimicked in several more recent regional reports comprehensively canvassing both the state of the environment in Africa and the range of factors leading to its deterioration. These reports include the African Environment Outlook 3 (2013),[3] Climate Change 2014: Impacts, Adaptation, and Vulnerability (2014)[4] and most recently the Global Environmental Outlook GEO-6 – Regional Assessment for Africa (2016).[5] Repeating the numerous statistics exhaustively outlined in these reports serves no purpose here as several realities are clearly indicated. The deficit between what the continent's ecological infrastructure can sustain and is being expected to sustain is growing rapidly. The range of factors contributing to the growing deficit is diverse. The current negative impacts associated with the growing deficit on the continents' inhabitants' security, health and well-being are vast and expanding.

Recognising this ecological fragility, Agenda 2063 outlines the continent's development agenda for the next 45 years. It includes a prosperous Africa based on inclusive growth, sustainable development, peace, security, resilience, good governance, democracy, respect for human rights, justice and the rule of law amongst its express aspirations.[6] Agenda 2063 coincides with the post-2015 global development agenda reflected in Transforming our World: the 2030 Agenda for Sustainable Development,[7]

1 WWF (2012: 6).
2 Ibid.
3 UNEP (2013: 3).
4 Niang et al. (2014: 1199-1265).
5 UNEP (2016).
6 See generally: African Union (2015).
7 UNGA Res. 70/1 (2015).

adopted by the United Nations General Assembly in September 2015. In seeking to fulfil the Agenda 2063 aspirations, African states are also seeking to promote the attainment of the 17 sustainable development goals (SDGs) and associated targets. The SDGs envisage a world, and accordingly an African continent: devoid of poverty, hunger and inequity; ensuring the health and well-being of its inhabitants and the sustainable provision and management of water, sanitation and energy; promoting sustained, sustainable and inclusive economic growth, cities and human settlements resting on resilient infrastructure; governed by peaceful, inclusive, democratic and accountable institutions; undertaking urgent action to combat climate change; and protecting, restoring and promoting the sustainable use of its terrestrial and marine ecosystems.

Realising Africa's desired development trajectory within the constraints of the realities facing the continent's valuable yet fragile ecological infrastructure is a tricky balancing act clearly requiring a multi-disciplinary approach. Within this context, the critical role of law has been increasingly recognised. This role includes the manner in which law constructs and regulates the functioning of key institutions; regulates and promotes the equitable and sustainable use and consumption of natural resources; creates mechanisms to inform and control pollution; constrains environmentally harmful actions; fashions tools to promote sustainable land-use planning and development; and provides processes through which the impacts associated with the foregoing can be prudently considered and mitigated.

In seeking to encourage this role for law in Africa, and in keeping with the spirit of forging African solutions to African challenges, scholars from across the continent formed the Association of Environmental Law Lecturers from African Universities (ASSELLAU) in 2004. Its specific objectives include promoting the generation and dissemination of environmental law research to assist Africa's law and policymakers to craft and implement legal frameworks that achieve the tricky balance referred to above through conferences and symposia. In partial fulfilment of this mandate, ASSELLAU held its 4th Scientific Conference in Yaoundé, Cameroon, from 10-13 January 2018. This book comprises of selected papers presented at the conference. Divided into four parts, its object is to explore, review and analyse several recent issues and developments located at the nexus of law, the environment and Africa.

2 Climate change and energy

Part I of the book focuses on climate change and energy issues and comprises of eight chapters. In Chapter 2 titled "Climate change legislative developments on the African continent", Olivia Rumble discusses the role of law in responding to climate change, the meaning of 'climate change legislation' and the status of this legislation in Africa. She then turns to consider in detail the recent legal reform in two African countries, namely South Africa and Kenya, teasing out possible trends and lessons which may provide guidance to other African countries in assessing the adequacy of their existing laws to deal with climate change and amending or introducing new laws in response. In Chapter 3, Oluwatoyin Adejonwo-Osho explores the issue from a Nigerian perspective, specifically "Nigeria's commitments under the climate change Paris Agreement: legislative and regulatory imperatives towards ensuring sustainable development". Acknowledging the absence of dedicated climate change legislation in Nigeria, she considers the impacts of climate change in Nigeria, provides an overview of the country's nationally determined contribution (NDC) under the Paris Agreement, and the existing domestic laws and policies of relevance to giving effect to the NDC (including the establishment of a Department of Climate Change and a proposed new bill to establish a National Climate Change Commission). She concludes by exploring key gaps and contradictions in these existing relevant laws and policies and options for reform. Dayo Ayoade builds on this analysis in Chapter 4, titled "Bridging the gap between climate change and energy policy options: what next for Nigeria?". He specifically focuses on the manner in which Nigeria's current law and policy addresses climate change and energy issues separately and argues for the need for a more holistic and integrated approach comprising of what he terms a tripartite structure comprising of a Nigerian Climate Change and Energy Policy, a National Climate Change and Energy Act and a Climate Change and Energy Agency.

Oliver Ruppel and Marc Funteh's Chapter 5 shifts to a more regional perspective focusing on the Lake Chad Basin region. In their chapter titled "Climate change, human security and the humanitarian crisis in the Lake Chad Basin region: selected legal and developmental aspects with a special focus on water governance", they adopt a transdisciplinary approach in exploring the many factors characterising and fuelling the crisis in the region including: diverse and changing climatic conditions, hydrological cycles and biophysical environments; shifting livelihoods; human security, conflict and migration; water scarcity and regional security; and poor water governance. They conclude that climate change has been a sustaining force for the existing humanitarian crises in the region and that human security predicaments of the Lake Chad Basin region have been exacerbated by environmental shifts. They further highlight that public international, regional and domestic law and policy could more effectively foster the integration of climate change adaptation, water governance and conflict management; with the SDGs, the Paris Agreement and NDCs providing feasibly important entry points.

The following two chapters focus on climate change issues relevant to Cameroon. In Chapter 6, Christopher Tamasang considers "Forests, forest rights, benefit-sharing and climate change implications under Cameroonian law". He assesses the various forest types extant in Cameroon, the bundle of rights attached thereto, the formula for allocating and sharing benefits under the country's forestry legislation, and analyses their implications specifically in the context of climate change mitigation. He argues that although Cameroon's forestry legislation establishes a bundle of rights attached to each forest type and mechanisms for facilitating benefit-sharing, the forest rights are not adequate for some relevant stakeholders involved in forest management and the mechanisms are plagued with inherent flaws which ultimately undermine their role in contributing to climate change mitigation in the country. In Chapter 7, Daniel Mbarga considers the specific nexus between "Indigenous peoples and climate change in Cameroon", highlighting the fact that although indigenous peoples are among those who produce the least carbon emissions, they are the most vulnerable to the effects of climate change. He critically reviews the legal measures undertaken in Cameroon to protect indigenous people from the effects of climate change and proposes solutions where they are viewed as inadequate. Continuing the focus on the link between forests and climate change, Chapter 8 explores "REDD+ and benefit sharing: an examination of the legal framework in Uganda". In this chapter, Hadijah Yahyah begins by exploring the theoretical nexus between REDD+ initiatives and benefit-sharing mechanisms before critically reviewing Uganda's relevant law and policy framework. She concludes that although benefit-sharing is a vital component of Uganda's REDD+ programme the necessary legal guidance to implement it is lacking, and proposes several reforms to fill the current legal vacuum.

In the final chapter of this part of the book, Edna Odhiambo shifts the climate change focus to the transport sector and the Kenya context in Chapter 9 titled "Regulatory preparedness on non-motorised transport in Nairobi". Founded on the premises that if car-oriented planning continues to dominate, a lock into unsustainable carbon-intensive infrastructure will result and exacerbate adverse climate change. The chapter considers the link between global climate change and the transport sector, before introducing the concept and benefits of non-motorised transport. It then turns to investigate whether Kenya's national and local regulatory framework currently prioritises non-motorised transport as a low-carbon mobility option, concluding that whilst much has been done at the county level, significant options exist for prioritising and implementing non-motorised transport as a climate mitigation strategy in the transport sector at the national level.

3 Natural resource governance

Part II of the book is dedicated to several issues falling under the rubric of natural resource governance. It comprises of nine chapters canvassing a broad array of issues relating to different natural resources including terrestrial wildlife, oil, wetlands and marine resources. In Chapter 10, Patricia Kameri-Mbote considers "Wildlife conservation and community property rights in Kenya". She assesses the extent to which the contemporary Community Land Act (2016), read together with the Wildlife Conservation and Management Act (2013), jointly support wildlife conservation on community lands in Kenya. This, she argues, is a vital issue given that 66% of Kenya's total land mass comprises of community land. She considers the conceptual framework relevant to wildlife conservation and land rights before outlining and assessing Kenya's relevant legal framework. She ultimately concludes that the enabling legal and policy framework is in place to enable and encourage wildlife conservation on community land and that the National Land Use Policy (2017) provides an opportunity to further synergise land tenure and land use. Following the wildlife theme, Marie Nonga considers "Criminal law protection of wildlife reserves in Cameroon" in Chapter 11. She begins the chapter by decrying the current state of the country's biological resources before engaging in an extensive analysis of the nature and efficacy of the criminal remedies prescribed in Cameroon's legal framework seeking to protect these biological resources situated in the country's wildlife reserves. Within this analysis, she highlights concerning ambiguities and outdated provisions and provides options for necessary reform.

Chapter 12 shifts sectors and is titled "Harnessing oil as natural resource wealth: a focus on the legal frameworks of Nigeria and Uganda". In this chapter, Lanre Aladeitan, Robert Wabunoha and Odaghara Therese examine the correlation between the resource-rich state and the content of its law focusing on performance level under three key components in the 2017 Resource Governance Index Report, namely: value realisation; revenue management; and enabling environment. Focusing on the resource of oil, and undertaking a comparative approach, the chapter outlines in detail the relevant legal frameworks of Nigeria and Uganda, before comparing, contrasting and evaluating them against the abovementioned three components of the 2017 Resource Governance Index Report. The authors conclude that their assessment confirms that a governance deficit exists in the decision-making chain in the extractive industry in Nigeria and Uganda, which urgently require legal reform.

Andrew Muma turns to consider "Access and benefit sharing: beyond the Nagoya Protocol and its ideals" in Chapter 13. He analyses the utility of the Nagoya Protocol in the conservation and subsequent sustainable use of biodiversity resources, and argues that one of the causes of what he views as a problematic current state of affairs is that the crusade for private land ownership has led to the neglect of values and principles of communitarianism that were geared toward sustainable resource use. In coming to this conclusion, the author firstly considers an array of conceptual issues relating to community-based participation models in the context of biodiversity conservation, purported misunderstandings of customary tenure, and the link between property rights and biodiversity conservation. He then engages in a thorough critical analysis of the relevant international, regional and Kenyan legal framework of relevance to the issue, concluding by proposing a set of sui generis rights which he argues are yet to be given rightful attention in policy-making processes.

In Chapter 14, titled "Ecosystem services: legal issues relevant to Nigeria's wetlands", Erimma Orie provides a comprehensive critical review of Nigeria's legal framework of relevance to wetlands. She highlights the absence of a dedicated legal framework governing wetlands, the inadequacy of piecemeal complementary laws and regulations on land management to fill the void, and problematic institutional and governance arrangements – proposing a swathe of legal reform options to overcome the current regulatory and institutional vacuum. This is followed in Chapter 15 by a critical review of the "The role of the Environment and Land Court in governing natural resources in Kenya". In this chapter, Collins Odote reviews the successes of the Environment and Land Court, established following constitutional reform in Kenya in 2010, in improving natural resource governance in the country. In doing so, he reviews the court's jurisprudence and argues that despite recent court decisions clarifying that court's status and jurisdiction, and also granting magistrates' courts powers to determine land and environmental matters, there is a need for reform particularly relating to the appointment of its judges and the nature of its decision-making processes. He also notes that the number of environmental cases brought before the court has been limited with the bulk of the cases relating to land issues.

Jean-Claude Ashukem moves in Chapter 16 to consider whether public participation in environmental decision-making in Cameroon is a myth or reality. Through a comprehensive review of the relevant domestic legal framework, he assesses whether it empowers local communities to effectively participate in environmental decision-making processes; and whether or not their views and aspirations are taken into account in the decisions to emanate from these processes. He ultimately concludes that the rules, procedures and processes governing public participation in Cameroon are flawed and do not often align with governance practices that provide for the effective involvement and participation of local communities during decision-making processes; thereafter providing certain reform proposals to overcome this problematic reality.

Marine resources form the focus of Chapter 17, titled "Utilising Kenya's marine resources for national development". In this chapter, Kariuki Muigua discusses how Kenya can take advantage of its rich marine resources to boost national economic development while empowering the coastal communities whose livelihoods mainly depend on these resources. The discourse canvassed in this chapter goes beyond legal and institutional arrangements to offer practical solutions based on principles such as public participation, empowerment, sustainable development and inclusiveness.

The final chapter in this part of the book, Chapter 18, considers whether the environmental Management Act (2017) and natural resource regulation in Malawi provide opportunities for or limitations to effective enforcement in the natural resource sector, particularly relating to forest, fish and wildlife resources. Gift Makanje critically evaluates the enforcement mechanisms provided for in the relevant legal framework, highlighting outstanding barriers to enforcement and opportunities for reform.

4 Water governance, management and use

With water scarcity and insecurity characterising vast parts of Africa, Part III of the book focuses on a broad array of legal issues relating generally to water governance, management and use. It begins with Chapter 19 titled "Pollution of water in South Africa by untreated sewage: addressing the governance issues". In this chapter, Michael Kidd begins by describing the pervasive problem of the pollution of South Africa's water resources by untreated sewage over recent years. He describes the country's governance structure in relation to water treatment, focussing specifically on legal aspects of governance, and evaluates how water governance is failing in the country. Elizabeth Gachenga turns in Chapter 20 to discuss an issue of water governance in Kenya, specifically whether the country's contemporary water legislation, the Water Act (2016), provides for real devolution or simply the 'same script, different cast'. She critically analyses the Water Act (2016) to specifically determine the extent to which it aligns with the spirit of devolution enshrined in Kenya's Constitution (2010). She concludes her chapter with several recommendations on the basic tenets that the water governance framework should address in order to achieve the desired delicate balance between sustainable development of water resources and the principle of subsidiarity so critical to devolved governments.

With vast parts of South Africa currently suffering severe drought, Amanda Mkhonza considers improving the legal protection of strategic water source areas in Chapter 21. Described as the 'crown jewels' of South Africa's water resources, these strategic water source areas comprise only 8% of the country's landscape, yet provide more than 50% of its surface water. She begins her analysis by briefly outlining South Africa's current environmental regime with a view to identifying and evaluating possible area-based management measures which could be used to fill the current apparent regulatory vacuum when it comes to managing, conserving and protecting the country's strategic water source areas. Realising their limitations, she then turns to consider the Australian context, specifically New South Wales' state laws, with a view to scoping possible legal reform for South Africa's water legislation relevant to improving the plight of these important areas.

This is followed by three additional domestic legal perspectives focusing on Uganda, Kenya and Ethiopia. In Chapter 22, titled "Institutional and legal challenges to realising clean and safe water for all in Uganda", Phiona Mpanga interrogates the legislative and institutional frameworks relating to water and sanitation service delivery, recommending a more decentralised approach. In Chapter 23, Nerima Were considers "The Conflict between privatisation and the realisation of the right to water in Kenya". With the Kenyan Constitution (2010) prescribing the right to water, the author interrogates whether the model of water governance promoted in the Water Act (2016) is adequate to meet the fulfilment of the right. She argues that privatisation as a model of water supply, whether systemic or inadvertent, is not sufficient to guarantee the right to water and offers a critique of the model and its use in Kenya. Finally, Mekete Tekle grapples with "Policy, regulatory and institutional frameworks relevant to Ethiopian water governance" in Chapter 24. He provides both an extensive overview and critique of the existing relevant legal and institutional regime and identifies options for improved implementation and legal reform.

The final three chapters in this part of the book take a more regional and comparative perspective to water governance. Joseph Ngang addresses "Water resources management and environmental sustainability in west and central Africa" (Chapter 25); Irekpitan Okukpon "Water security and environmental justice in Nigeria and South Africa: achievable concord or discordant alliance?" (Chapter 26); and Emmanuel Kam Yogo "The Lake Chad Basin Water Charter: strengths and weaknesses" (Chapter 27). In each of these chapters, the authors highlight the inherent strengths and fragilities of the relevant regional and domestic legal regimes.

5 Regulating social and environmental impacts

Part IV of the book is dedicated to considering several diverse issues relevant to the role of the law in regulating social and environmental impacts associated with human activity. Godard Busingye begins in Chapter 28 by "Making the case for gender and environmental considerations in the regulatory framework relating to the Uganda-Tanzania crude oil pipeline project". Using the East African Crude Oil Project undertaken by Uganda and Tanzania as a case study, he reviews the relevant legal framework applicable to the project in both countries and concludes that it is inadequate to forestall the environmental and gender 'evils' associated with the construction of the project. In Chapter 29, Orubebe Bello considers the challenges and prospects of "Integrating climate change in the environmental impact assessment process" in Nigeria. Having undertaken a comprehensive analysis of Nigeria's relevant law and policy framework, he bemoans the fact that climate change impacts are not currently adequately integrated into the environmental impact assessment process and calls for urgent legal reform.

Pamela Sambo then undertakes a review of Zambia's Environmental Management Act (2011) in Chapter 30, in order to determine whether it provides a basis for the growth of an environmental ethos and good environmental governance in the country. She begins by analysing the historical development of the now repealed Environmental Protection and Pollution Control Act (1990) and its successor the Environmental Management Act (2011). The purpose of this analysis is to identify the key environmental themes that these two laws embody, which she then uses as the structure against which to assess whether the more contemporary legislation has led to the development of an environmental ethos in Zambia. The author concludes that while the Environmental Management Act (2011) 'gifted' Zambia a robust and forward-looking environmental regime, the absence of a constitutionally entrenched environmental right constrains the development of a meaningful environmental ethos in the country.

In Chapter 31, titled "Regulating environmental impacts associated with mining in Uganda", Emmanuel Kasimbazi critically analyses the effectiveness of the regulatory and institutional framework for the protection of the environment in the mining sector in Uganda. He concludes that while the regulatory framework has been developed, there is a limited level of enforcement which results in mining authorities and companies not adhering to the legal requirements.

The final chapter of the book (Chapter 32) considers the social and environmental impacts associated with the exploitation of timber on indigenous communities in Cameroon. Titled "An analysis of environmental impacts of timber exploitation on indigenous communities' land in Cameroon", Esther Njieassam argues that despite the government's efforts in signing several international, regional and national environmental legal instruments seeking to protect the rights of indigenous peoples, incoherent government policies, weak provisions for ensuring adequate public participation, and inefficient monitoring and enforcement mechanisms have resulted in gross environmental and human rights violations. She argues further that the government in collaboration with multinational extractive companies undermine and ignore indigenous peoples' right to a safe and healthy environment.

6 Conclusion

The Global Environmental Outlook GEO-6 – Regional Assessment for Africa (2016) highlighted that "Africa faces both enormous challenges in relation to environmental management, and equally huge opportunities for 'doing this better'".[8] Considering the content contained in the chapters of this book canvassing a broad range of legal issues across several jurisdictions, the same appears true for the role of law. The legal challenges are plenty, but the opportunities to improve the laws and governance arrangements equally are plenty. It is hoped that the analysis and solutions proposed in the covers of this book provide some additional and useful food for thought to those engaged in formulating, refining and implementing legal frameworks central to Africa's tricky quest in attaining its desired development trajectory within the confines of the continent's valuable yet fragile ecological infrastructure.

8 UNEP (2016: 8).

References

African Union (2015) *Agenda 2063: framework document.*

Niang, I, OC Ruppel, MA Abdrabo, A Essel, C Lennard, J Padgham & P Urquhart (2014) "Africa" in VR Barros, CB Field, DJ Dokken, MD Mastandrea, KJ Mach, TE Bilir, M Chatterjee, KL Ebi, YO Estrada, RC Genova, B Girma, ES Kissel, AN Levy, S MacCracken, PR Mastrandrea & LL White (eds) *Climate change 2014: impacts, adaptation, and vulnerability: contribution of Working Group II to the Fifth Assessment Report of the Intergovernmental Panel on Climate Change* 1199-1265.

UNGA / United Nations General Assembly (2015) *Transforming our world: the 2030 Agenda for Sustainable Development* (21 October 2015 UN Doc. A/RES/70/1).

UNEP / United Nations Environment Programme (2013) *African environmental outlook.*

UNEP / United Nations Environment Programme (2016) *GEO-6 Regional assessment for Africa.*

WWF / World Wide Fund For Nature (2012) *Africa ecological footprint report.*

PART I:

CLIMATE CHANGE AND ENERGY

Chapter 2: Climate change legislative development on the African continent

Olivia Rumble

1 Introduction

Global warming as a result of climate change is no longer a future threat, but an experienced reality in many countries. Partly because of its lower adaptive capacity, some of the worst impacts of climate change will be experienced in Africa, even though its contribution to the problem is disproportionately low.[1] Anticipated impacts include more intense and frequent droughts, heat stress, tropical cyclones, and flooding. The sectors which are particularly vulnerable to its many impacts include water, agriculture and human health. Not only does climate change have the potential to affect the realisation of human rights negatively,[2] it is also expected to be a significant disruptor to developmental aspirations such as poverty reduction, job creation, and inclusive and equitable macroeconomic growth. As a threat multiplier, climate change also has wide-reaching economic and security impacts on governance through its ability to exacerbate existing trends, tensions and instability, for example in the form of increased tensions over scarce resources, border disputes, energy conflicts and conflict prompted by migration.[3] For these reasons, adaptation is a priority area for policymakers on the continent, and the African Union has urged all member states to put in place systems

1 UNECA (2017). The article comments on investigations which suggest that the public expenditure on adaptation as a percentage of the overall adaptation costs for African countries is approximately 20% of total needs, ranging between 2 and 9% of the GDP. This demonstrates that African countries are already investing a higher percentage of finances in adaptation spending than international financial support. It confirms that these countries are already making major contributions to adaptation efforts and related expenditure.

2 There are numerous studies on the linkages between climate change and human rights. See for example OHCHR (2009) and Knox (2009). The OHCHR noted that climate change threatens the enjoyment of a wide array of human rights, although it does not in itself necessarily violate human rights. That notwithstanding, human rights law places duties on states concerning climate change and those duties include an obligation of international cooperation. Examples of affected human rights include the right to life, health, privacy, property as well as components of the right to an adequate standard of living.

3 See IPCC (2014: 1203) where it is stated that "climate change and climate variability have the potential to exacerbate or multiply existing threats to human security including food, health, and economic insecurity, all being of particular concern for Africa...Many of these threats are known drivers of conflict".

and structures to take full advantage of the global mechanisms in support of climate change mitigation and adaptation.[4]

The extent of the current and anticipated impacts necessitates the implementation of comprehensive and costly adaptive measures by national governments in Africa. These have been proven to be difficult. The most recent Intergovernmental Panel on Climate Change Fifth Assessment Report (AR5), highlights that national governments across the continent have initiated governance systems for adaptation responses, however, as of yet, evolving institutional frameworks are unable to coordinate the range of adaptation initiatives being implemented effectively.[5] It was concluded that whilst there had been progress on national and subnational strategies and policies in starting to mainstream adaptation into sectoral planning, there was "incomplete, under-resourced, and fragmented institutional frameworks and overall low levels of adaptive capacity" to manage highly complex socio-ecological changes.[6] This resulted in reform being driven by reactive, ad-hoc and project orientated approaches, which were donor-funded in many cases.[7]

Not only must governments plan for adaptive measures, but they must mitigate greenhouse gases (GHGs). The Paris Agreement now requires all countries to participate in a global mitigation effort to reduce the impacts of GHG emissions and to achieve a long-term temperature goal of below 2 degrees centigrade.[8] All parties are required to make a fair contribution to this effort and must submit Nationally Determined Contributions (NDCs), which address both adaptation and mitigation actions, successive versions of which must be increasingly more ambitious. The NDCs must set out what these national contributions entail, and governments are obliged to pursue domestic GHG mitigation measures with the aim of achieving the objectives of these contributions.[9] The Paris Agreement specifically provides that developing countries, which includes most of Africa, are required to continue enhancing their GHG mitigation efforts and are encouraged to move over time towards economy-wide GHG emissions reduction or limitation targets.[10]

While African countries collectively have a relatively low GHG emissions profile, many countries on the continent have a wealth of opportunities for the deployment of

---

4 CAHOSCC (2014). This framework programme was adopted at the 23rd Ordinary Session of the Summit of the African Union in Malabo, Equatorial Guinea, and it reaffirms that adaptation is a priority in all actions on climate change in Africa.

5 IPCC (2014: 1203).

6 Ibid.

7 Ibid. It was found that "[d]isaster risk reduction, social protection, technological and infrastructural adaptation, ecosystem-based approaches, and livelihood diversification are reducing vulnerability, but largely in isolated initiatives".

8 In addition to this goal it was agreed that countries would pursue efforts to limit the temperature increase to 1.5 degrees Celsius (Article 2(1)(a) of the Paris Agreement).

9 Article 4(2) of the Paris Agreement.

10 Article 4 of the Paris Agreement. This is subject to the qualification that this obligation is subject to different national circumstances.

renewable energy and related co-benefits, given the maturity of their energy sectors.[11] Indeed, 53 of the 54 African NDCs submitted under the Paris Agreement included renewable energy as part of their mitigation ambitions.[12] Whilst low carbon development is indeed an opportunity, the effective implementation of a medium to long-term low carbon development strategy is often underpinned by a host of strategic, financial and legal considerations which governments need to be attuned to. Similarly, decisions related to the exploitation of the continent's abundant natural resources, many of which result in the release of GHGs, will need to be guided by domestic financial, legal and related strategic considerations, taking into account the country's relevant commitments under its NDC.

These challenges, opportunities and interactions paint a complex picture of the scale and complexity of responding to climate change at a national level. An effective response will require a nationally led and coordinated effort which goes beyond what has traditionally been perceived as the terrain of 'environmental' governance, to almost every sector of national government, including energy and industry, transport, trade, human settlements and migration, health, agriculture and fisheries, mining and water. This precipitates the need for cross-sectoral governance, levels of cooperation, and forward planning at a national, regional and international level at a hitherto unknown scale. In the midst of this response, the law plays an important mediating and empowering role.

To date, policy and strategy have largely directed government action on the continent. This may be symptomatic of the equivocality in the international legal regime over the past decade. The finalisation and adoption of the Paris Agreement at the 21st Session of the Conference of the Parties to the United National Framework Convention on Climate Change (UNFCCC), however, constitute a turning point in the international negotiations. For the first time in history, all countries have publicly committed to taking action on mitigating GHG emissions and responding to the impacts of climate change. The domestic legal systems of each member state will play a critical role in implanting the commitments made by each party.[13]

Interestingly, since the conclusion of the Paris Agreement, many African countries have developed, or are in the process of developing, dedicated climate change laws, or amendments to existing laws that take into account climate change considerations. Most of these initiatives build on existing climate change policies and the NDCs devised in accordance with the Paris Agreement. Current legislative initiatives include

---

11 In other words, they are not subject to the same technological and energy development "lock-in" that other more developed countries are.

12 Phillips (2016) quoting Abdalla Hamdok, Chief Economist and Deputy Executive Secretary of the United Nations Economic Commission for Africa. It has been speculated that the Paris Agreement could be the catalyst for new investment drivers for structural transformation in Africa to achieve low carbon development.

13 Averchenkva & Matikamen (2017: 193).

the Kenyan Climate Change Act 11 of 2016, which was promulgated in May 2016, and the regulations under the South African National Environmental Management: Air Quality Act 39 of 2004, published in 2017. South Africa is also in the process of finalising a draft Carbon Tax Bill and a separate draft Climate Change Bill. In addition, Uganda, Zambia, Rwanda and Nigeria are all either in the process of debating in parliament legislative mechanisms to respond to climate change or have also implemented partial legislative reforms to respond to climate change impacts.

To date, there has been little academic discussion of these developments and what they might mean for African countries in particular. This chapter seeks to provide an overview of some of these legislative reforms, specifically those in South Africa and Kenya, to distil whether there are any lessons or examples of best practice for other African countries currently debating whether to introduce such reforms.

The chapter begins with a discussion on the role of law in responding to climate change, the meaning of 'climate change legislation' and the status of this legislation in Africa. This discussion is followed by an overview of how two African countries, Kenya and South Africa, have approached this challenge and the different legal frameworks they have adopted or are in the process of adopting to address their unique domestic needs. The analysis considers whether there are any possible lessons to be learnt from these legislative responses which will aid other African countries in assessing the adequacy of their existing laws to respond to climate change, and amending or introducing new laws in response. The complexity of the required legal response cannot be ignored. The need for tailored legislative responses to unique domestic situations cannot be overridden by simplistic 'quick fix' legislative solutions. Baring this in mind, the purpose of this chapter is to provide examples of possible legal options to African countries who wish to introduce climate change legislation, in a nascent area of law that is rapidly evolving.

2 The nature and function of climate change legislation

Compared to the dynamic and evolving policy and strategic climate change responses developed by governments to date, the law is a relatively cumbersome and static medium to address climate change. It is often reactive, responding to different challenges and impacts as they arise, typically in response to defined and known problems. In the case of climate change, the extent of the challenge is only now being experienced, and the required response is anticipatory in nature. Yet legislative mechanisms can and do play a critical role in empowering governments to take action, creating certainty; powerful incentives and disincentives; structures; institutions; and mechanisms to facilitate a more co-ordinated, effective and mandatory response.

The importance of law in regulating a climate change response is evident in the upswing of climate change laws over the last two decades. This is partially attributable to the dynamism in the international negotiations on climate change (domestic laws typically follow the enactment of international agreements in order to support implementation) but also a growing appreciation of the crucial role that domestic laws and measures play.[14] The first law to expressly regulate climate change was passed by Japan in 1998.[15] Since then there was a slow increase in laws with a flurry in 2009 and 2010,[16] likely ascribable to the international political factors around the Copenhagen negotiations in 2009. The introduction of such laws then fell again, largely as a result of inertia in the international negotiations, challenging macroeconomic environments and the fact that most developed (Annex 1) countries had introduced relatively comprehensive climate change laws.[17] Since then, the legislative momentum moved towards developing (non-Annex 1) countries.[18]

The Grantham Institute's annal on the status of climate change legislation and litigation has been a consistent gauge of the rise of climate laws worldwide. Its latest publication in 2017 posited that there were now more than 1,200 climate change or climate change-relevant laws across the world, which according to their records was a twenty-fold increase in the last twenty years.[19] Approximately 44% of the instruments used in their research are legislative acts of parliament.[20]

While many have sought to track this development, it is difficult to arrive at a consensus of what exactly 'climate change legislation' is. Low carbon and climate resilient development require a combination of technical, social, cultural and management change, and the law plays a fundamental role in facilitating these changes. The peculiar nature of climate change, its complexity, uncertainty, relative novelty as a global phenomenon and scale in terms of space and time, make it challenging to regulate. Climate change has been described as a 'wicked' problem: it has enormous interdependencies, uncertainties, and conflicting stakeholders resulting in the inability to formulate a single problem or solution.[21] Furthermore, the more time it takes to address the more difficult it becomes, while those who are well placed to respond have the least incentive to act, making its governance a complex reality. Climate change is also interlinked with numerous policy issues which are often already regulated by other laws, such as energy, transport, industrial policy, forestry and land use, biodiversity, water, air quality, poverty and food security.[22] Any legislative response needs to take into account these linkages, either by adding further layers to existing legislation or through

14 Oulu (2015: 230).
15 Japan's Law Concerning the Promotion of the Measures to Cope with Global Warming (1998).
16 Townshend et al. (2013: 430).
17 Ibid.
18 Fankhauser et al. (2014).
19 Nachmany et al. (2017: 5).
20 Ibid: 8.
21 Lazarus (2008: 1153).
22 Nachmany et al. (2017: 10). Sectors of biodiversity and water have been added to the list set out by the Grantham Institute.

enacting a separate climate change law.[23] In sum, there are no basic minimum requirements which climate change legislation is required to address, and there is no easy definition of what it entails.

In 2011, Townshend et al. used the term climate change 'Flagship Laws' to mean "a key piece of legislation through which lawmakers have attempted to put their stamp on climate change policy",[24] and again used the term in 2013 to mean "a piece of legislation or regulation with equivalent status that serves as a comprehensive unifying basis for climate change policy".[25] Such flagship laws were described as "often [being] integrative laws that bring together the various strains of pre-existing and new climate change regulation under one legislative umbrella, as has occurred in Brazil, France, South Korea and the United Kingdom".[26] Townshend argued that the five-year plans in China and India served a similar purpose.[27] The Grantham Research Institute has expanded upon this definition of 'Flagship Laws' to retain its original scope but to add to its content and rename it as 'framework laws'. The latter represents a law or regulation with an equivalent status which serves as a comprehensive, unifying basis for climate change policy which addresses multiple aspects or areas of climate change mitigation or adaptation (or both) in a holistic and overarching manner.[28] Typical examples provided in their study include the United Kingdom's Climate Change Act (2008); Bulgaria's Climate Change Mitigation Act (2014); Denmark's Climate Change Act (2014) and Mexico's General Law on Climate Change (2012). The database, however, also includes much wider policy instruments under the 'framework laws' heading, such as Slovakia's National Adaptation Strategy (2014) and Germany's Action Programme on Climate Protection (2014).[29] This chapter does not seek to address the appropriateness of the inclusion of policy in this working definition.[30] For the purpose of this analysis, the author uses the term 'framework law' to represent an act of parliament or equivalent authority having binding legal effect at a national (as opposed to provincial or local) level, which does not include policies, strategies, plans

23 Ibid.
24 Townshend et al. (2011: 6).
25 Townshend et al. (2013: 430).
26 Townshend et al. (2011: 9).
27 Ibid.
28 Nachmany et al. (2015: 20).
29 Ibid: 17.
30 The Grantham Research Institute justifies the approach on the basis that different countries use different routes to address climate change and they have different regulatory traditions and local contexts. For example, China has a strong executive branch which governs by policy whilst the UK has a strong Parliamentary tradition. They also acknowledge that executive activity may reflect an early phase in climate policy development where policies have not yet matured into formal legislation or legislative capacities are insufficient. Their reports distinguish between legislative acts passed by a parliament or equivalent legislative authority and executive instruments (e.g. presidential degrees, executive orders, government policies or plans) passed or decreed by the government, president or equivalent executive authority. Where both existed, prominence was devoted to legislative acts, see Nachmany et al. (2015: 30).

or similar documents. The reason for doing so is the author's belief that not only is legislation in certain cases more appropriate, for example where it relates to decisions which curtail or limit existing rights, but also because of the binding and enduring nature of legislation over policy.

So-called framework laws, or 'overarching' legislative approaches are not the only means of regulating climate change. As mentioned above, legislators have also followed an approach which focuses on specific areas of law and the statutes which directly regulate those areas of law. This approach is referred to in this chapter as the 'sectoral' approach.[31] For example, legislators can 'climate proof' existing energy legislation, by adding further layers to it which speak directly to the mitigation of GHGs only. Surveys of these amendments indicate that amendments to energy law frameworks are the most popular.[32] A further distinction under the sectoral approach is that some prefer a process of statutory amendment through parliament or equivalent authority, whilst other countries prefer to use a regulative approach, i.e. through the executive. For example, after failing to pass bespoke legislation the United States' executive government developed regulations under the Clean Air Act 1970 for GHG emissions.

While there is no best practice set of climate change legislative principles, there are some compelling arguments on both sides on whether a framework law or a sectoral approach is more effective or appropriate. On the one hand, as Oulu argues, despite being constrained by time and resource requirements, a stand-alone framework law is preferable to piecemeal amendments to relevant laws.[33] He draws this conclusion on the basis that –[34]

> (i) the 'wicked' nature of climate change requires strategies and policy instruments that go beyond what existing sectoral legislation might have been conceived to deal with, and
>
> (ii) the nature and degree of potential amendments to existing sectoral laws are so extensive that they are best captured in comprehensive stand-alone legislation.

As an example, he cites the experience in the United Kingdom of the initially limited Climate Change and Sustainable Energy Act (2006) which was expanded to become the more comprehensive Climate Change Act (2008).

In support of this approach, the Grantham Institute holds the view that not all laws are equal in importance and scope, and framework laws (which admittedly also includes overarching policies under their definition) have been shown to "encourage a strategic approach to climate policy and to generate further policy action".[35]

31 Nachmany et al. (2015: 10).

32 88% of countries in 2017 had an integration of climate change issues in energy policy, mostly focused on electrification, energy efficiency and conservation and renewable energy, see Nachmany et al. (2017: 12).

33 Nachmany et al. (2015: 22).

34 Oulu (2015: 245).

35 Nachmany et al. (2015: 17); and Fankhauser et al. (2014).

Highlighting the important political statement that such laws can make and their resilience to political flux, Williams also notes that after Brexit in the United Kingdom, the domestic Climate Change Act (2008) was a robust instrument in the light of policy uncertainty, by providing a "continuous and consistent overarching framework which requires no primary amendment".[36]

It can also be more politically challenging to incorporate amendments across a broad suite of laws that address different sectors of the economy as it requires numerous Ministers to champion the passage of multiple amendments to the legislation applicable to their respective mandates. This makes framework laws more appetising from a parliamentary economy perspective.

An overarching framework law is also particularly conducive to the introduction of mechanisms and institutions to achieve specific climate change objectives. For example, the creation of a climate change institution such as a committee or forum (which is typical of many framework laws) depending on its powers and functions, can be a compelling platform for ensuring that cross-cutting, harmonised and coordinated decision making is made at the highest levels of government, and integrated across sectors. Whilst it is not always necessary to have laws to create or regulate these types of bodies, if they are to have meaningful powers and functions with statutory accountability, it is certainly preferable to empower and direct them through framework laws.

On the other hand, there are compelling arguments which support a sectoral approach where climate change considerations are incorporated into existing decision making and empowering provisions. Much of this turns on how mainstreaming is best achieved. The cross-cutting nature of climate change has seen mainstreaming being widely advocated as an important approach to its management.[37] This recognises the need for climate change considerations to be included within the prevailing direction or processes adopted by government. This supports an approach whereby climate change considerations are 'layered' into existing processes through the inclusion of specific climate change considerations within relevant statutes and regulations. This can be achieved through a framework law or under a sectoral approach. Purely from a pragmatic perspective, a sectoral approach may better facilitate the mainstreaming since relevant authorities are often typically appraised of their powers and duties under sectoral laws relevant to their spheres of governance. It may be challenging to get administrators to learn a new set of laws, and for this reason alone it may be easier to incorporate climate considerations into statutes which they are familiar with implementing. Where there are capacity restraints, it can be particularly challenging to educate both the public and the administration on a new climate change law, in addition to the suite of laws the public and the administration are already required to abide by or implement. These challenges can be mitigated if existing and familiar laws are

36 Williams (2017).

37 Oulu (2011: 375).

amended to take climate change considerations into account (i.e. to use a sectoral approach).

There are numerous benefits to both approaches which warrant further discussion and consideration. For the purpose of this chapter, the advantages of framework laws appear to outweigh a sectoral approach. However, the author is cognisant of the fact that each country will have individual requirements and unique climate change considerations which will require it to consider these merits and disadvantages. Perhaps, true to the so-called 'bottom-up'[38] approach of the Paris Agreement, it is up to each country to tailor its legislative response to fit national circumstances, mindful that framework laws are a particularly useful approach. This chapter seeks to demonstrate the prevalence of national framework laws and related regulations on the continent in order to provide guidance on the possible options available to national governments of what they might address.

Before turning to this overview, and mindful of the nationally determined nature of such responses, it is also useful to consider some of the key objectives which climate change laws can address. The next section accordingly briefly discusses the way in which law can address the two key issues in climate change: the mitigation of GHG emissions; and the increase of resilience to the impacts of climate change (adaptation).

2.1 Mitigation law

Much of the public discourse relating to climate change governance has related to mitigation.[39] The law can play a particularly important role in incorporating the mitigation aspects of NDCs under the Paris Agreement. It can do this by prescribing a binding emissions reduction target for the country (such as in the case of the United Kingdom's Climate Change Act).[40] Alternatively, it can prescribe a process for determining this target and how it is to be achieved domestically. The latter may be a more appropriate approach mindful that the Paris Agreement envisages a 'ratcheting up' mechanism to require increasingly more ambitions contributions over time.

According to the Intergovernmental Panel on Climate Change (IPCC),[41] the law plays a particularly important role in enabling governments to limit GHGs by Land Use (AFOLU), and land use planning where activity is often strongly influenced by

38 In terms of which domestic contributions to the international effort are determined based on country's nationally determined contributions instead of being prescribed at an international level.

39 Osofsky & McAllister (2012).

40 The United Kingdom's Climate Change Act (2008) requires the Secretary of State to ensure that the United Kingdom's net carbon account of GHGs by the year 2050 is at least 80% lower than the 1990 baseline.

41 IPCC (2014: 1168).

planning and provision, regulations/statutes. The law can also promote the diffusion and innovation of emerging technologies, and it can remove barriers to energy efficiency. Indeed, an effective mitigation response requires fundamental changes to domestic and international energy systems, bringing an entirely distinct field, energy law, into the discussion.[42]

2.2 Adaptation law

Often, traditional models of environmental, planning and related laws either do not address the complexities and uncertainties of climate change or behave as barriers to adequate adaptation.[43] This has implications for a broad spectrum of sectoral laws such as land use planning regimes, human health systems, biodiversity conservation and the exploitation of natural resources.

In commenting on this issue, McDonald and Styles[44] promote the incorporation of adaptive management in legal frameworks as a means of recognising the dynamism of natural systems and the importance of monitoring, review, and modification of projects, plans and activities in response to new understanding, as a result of climate change.[45] They propose five mechanisms to achieving it: namely changing statutory objectives; requiring monitoring and evaluation of projects, plans and activities; staged approvals processes; conditional approvals and statutory triggers; and proportionate resource allocation models. In their view, the use of these flexibility mechanisms facilitates decision making to respond to the impacts of climate change, while continuing to provide a level of legal certainty.

In addition to principles of adaptive management generally, climate change impacts will require the state to develop new strategies and policies for avoiding and recovering from these negative effects and seizing and harnessing the benefits of adaptation actions.[46] The development of such plans and strategies can be facilitated through statutes and regulations which require administrators and developers to undertake climate change vulnerability assessments at various junctures in the development and governance process and to develop plans to respond to these risks. This applies not only in the context of an Environmental Impact Assessments (EIAs) but across a wide spectrum of planning processes. For this reason, these can be individual plans, or there can be statutory requirements to undertake such assessments as part of existing planning

42 Klass (2013: 182).

43 McDonald & Styles (2014: 25) and Craig (2010: 9).

44 McDonald & Styles (2014: 25).

45 Ibid. They noted in 2014, that, even though it is a dominant approach in natural resource management, it finds very little express mention in legal frameworks.

46 Rumble (2016).

requirements, such as local development plans for municipalities, national sector strategies, or in the EIA process itself.

Countries will, in any event, have to communicate in their NDCs under the Paris Agreement, a description of their adaptation goals, priorities, actions and needs. The Agreement also calls on countries to initiate processes to prepare and implement national adaptation plans. A priori, this will require countries to undertake vulnerability assessments across a wide range of vulnerable sectors, and the law can play an important role in ensuring that the requisite information is available to make submissions under the Paris Agreement. It can also play a guiding role in determining the content, timing and form of local assessments and plans.

3 Status of climate change laws in Africa

The upswell of climate change laws internationally has also been experienced in Africa. An increasing number of African countries are in the process of developing or have already developed framework laws or sectoral amendments. Many of these initiatives advance the objectives and strategies in existing climate change policies and NDCs under the Paris Agreement.[47]

One of the more notable developments has been the Kenyan Climate Change Act which was promulgated in May 2016, as discussed in the sections which follow. In the same year, Zambia amended its Constitution to impose a duty on the State to "...establish and implement mechanisms that address climate change".[48] The Zambian Green Party has petitioned Parliament to present a Bill on implementing Zambia's climate change commitments.[49] In 2017, the party submitted a draft Bill to Parliament for consideration.[50]

In 2015, Uganda's Cabinet directed the Ministry of Water and Environment to create a framework law on climate change. Members of parliament were concerned about the delay in the enactment of legislation, which prompted them to give notice to government that further delay would result in draft legislation being introduced to parliament via a private member's Bill.[51] In 2017, the Ministry published a call for proposals for a service provider to assist with the drafting of a Climate Change Bill, which included a complex scope of work as well as stakeholder consultation.[52]

In Nigeria, the House of Representatives initiated a Bill in 2017 which sought to establish a legal framework for the national climate change response and the formation

47 This summary is largely drawn from Gilder & Rumble (2017: 268).
48 Gilder & Rumble (2017: 268).
49 Arounusi (2017).
50 Ibid. Copies of this draft Bill are not publicly available for review by the author.
51 Gilder & Rumble (2017: 268).
52 Ibid.

of a National Council on Climate Change.[53] According to reports, the proposed law is intended to be "holistic and overarching as it seeks to address both mitigation and adaptation efforts towards meeting NDC [objectives]". [54] Furthermore, it will "pave way for a set of laws that will take care of sectoral challenges and targets".[55] Recent reports suggest that trade unions, civil society organisations and academia have reviewed and been making inputs into a draft Climate Change Framework Bill.[56]

In addition to these framework laws, countries have also been adopting regulations and statues to address specific narrower climate change related issues. The Rwandan Parliament has enacted a law to improve the functioning of the Rwanda Green Fund (FONERWA) and its ability to mobilise climate finance.[57] The law determines FONERWA's mission and organisation and defines how the climate financing institutional aspects will function.

In South Africa, regulations have also been developed to declare GHGs as priority pollutants under the National Environmental Management Air Quality Act[58] 39 of 2004 (NEMAQA), and emitters are required to develop GHG mitigation plans and comply with GHG emissions reporting regulations. These regulations are discussed in further detail in the sections which follow. The Department of Environmental Affairs is also in the process of developing a Climate Change Bill which will ultimately incorporate these regulations and will also serve as a framework statute for the management of climate change impacts. In October 2017, the South African Parliamentary Environmental Affairs Portfolio Committee issued a statement confirming its support of a Climate Change Bill to be introduced in parliament.[59] The National Treasury also published a draft Carbon Tax Bill for comment in December 2017 and stated that the actual date of implementation of the carbon tax would be determined through a separate and later process by the Minister of Finance through an announcement during 2018 or 2019, taking into account the state of the economy.

The sections which follow provide a brief overview of the Kenyan and South African examples in order to highlight their salient features and discuss similarities and useful provisions.

53 Iroanusi (2017).

54 A copy of the draft Bill was not available for review at the time of drafting this chapter. All information has been obtained from Uwaegbulam (2016).

55 Uwaegbulam (2016).

56 Danmaryam (2017).

57 Tashobya (2017).

58 Act 39 of 2004.

59 Parliamentary Communication Services (2017).

4 South Africa's climate change regulatory framework

For more than a decade, South Africa has been formulating a comprehensive climate change response. The overarching policy directive is found in the White Paper on the National Climate Change Response Policy 2011 (NCCRP). The NCCRP builds on a series of policy statements and strategies including the National Climate Change Response Strategy (September 2004)[60] and the Long-Term Mitigation Scenarios Document (2007).[61] Since its publication, the NCCRP has been complemented by a range of related documents including the Mitigation Potential Analysis (2014);[62] the Long-Term Adaptation Scenarios Report (LTAS, 2013 and 2015)[63]; the Intended Nationally Determined Contribution (2015)[64] which has become the country's NDC under the Pairs Agreement; and two important draft documents, namely the Draft National Adaptation Strategy (2016)[65] and the Draft Post-2020 Mitigation Scenarios Systems Report (2017).[66] A series of regulations to address mitigation of GHGs have also been published (as discussed below). The Department of Environmental Affairs (Department) has also expressed an intention to develop a Climate Change Bill which will be in the form of a framework law. Since the Climate Change Bill has not been formally published for public comment yet, it is not possible to discuss its contents in detail for the purpose of this chapter. However, where possible, key elements of its likely content will be discussed.

Besides, the National Treasury also expressed its intention to implement a national carbon tax and to this end, it published a series of policies and strategies outlining the reason for the tax and proposing its intended content and scope, followed by two draft Carbon Tax Bills. Again, it is not possible to address the extensive detail of these regulatory provisions within the confines of this chapter. However, it is helpful to outline their key elements and how they are likely to relate to each other and evolve as they come into effect sequentially over the next five years.

4.1 Mitigation framework

In respect of mitigation, the South African Department of Environmental Affairs intends to address low carbon development in five distinct ways, entailing:

60 South African Department of Environmental Affairs (2004).
61 Winkler (2007).
62 South African Department of Environmental Affairs (2014).
63 South African Department of Environmental Affairs (2013) and Department of Environmental Affairs (2015).
64 Government of South Africa South Africa (2015).
65 South African Department of Environmental Affairs (2016a).
66 South African Department of Environmental Affairs (2017).

- the establishment of a National Greenhouse Gas Emissions Reduction Trajectory;
- using the trajectory to inform the imposition of sectoral emissions targets for certain government departments (i.e. for overall sectors such as 'energy' and 'transport') and legally binding individual carbon budgets for individual entities which have high GHG emissions;
- a carbon tax implemented through the National Treasury;
- a monitoring and evaluation regime for GHGs; and
- plans to mitigate GHGs: the formal declaration of six GHGs under the existing legislation as priority pollutants which triggers the obligation on individual high emitting industries to create pollution prevention plans, describing how emissions will be controlled and reduced, over time.

Concerning the National Greenhouse Gas Emissions Reduction Trajectory, various trajectories have been established in terms of the abovementioned policies and South Africa's NDC, but its development and implementation are currently not contemplated by any existing legislation. It is likely that this issue will be addressed in the proposed Climate Change Bill. Similarly, the sectoral emissions targets and carbon budgets require legislation to be implemented as the existing legal regime does not cater for them. Conerning the carbon tax, legislation to bring it into effect has been drafted and the second iteration of a Carbon Tax Bill was published for public comment in December 2017. With regard to GHG monitoring, evaluation and mitigation, several relevant regulations have been published under NEMAQA including: the National Greenhouse Gas Emission Reporting Regulations,[67] which came into operation on 3 April 2017 (as read with the technical guideline);[68] the Declaration of Greenhouse Gases as Priority Pollutants;[69] and the National Pollution Prevention Plans Regulations.[70] The intention is for these regulations to apply as an interim measure until 2020, after which time a final Climate Change Act will have ideally been promulgated by Parliament. The intention is then for the above regulations promulgated under NEMAQA to be revised and re-promulgated under the future Climate Change Act. The above five components are discussed in more detail below.

67 *Government Gazette* 40762 GN 275 of 3 April 2017.
68 South African Department of Environmental Affairs (2016b).
69 *Government Gazette* 40996 GNR 710 of 21 July 2017.
70 *Government Gazette* 40996 GNR 712 of 21 July 2017.

4.1.1 Emissions reduction trajectory, sectoral emissions targets and carbon budgets

According to the Draft Post-2020 Mitigation Systems Report (2017), it is intended for a national emissions trajectory to be set.[71] It is likely that the legal mechanisms to support the setting and subsequent use of the trajectory in decision making will be dealt with under the Climate Change Bill.

The emissions trajectory will then be translated into sectoral emissions targets –[72]

> that cover all GHG emissions within the South Africa economy and represents the cumulative amount of emissions that can be emitted within a specific time period (i.e. the area under the curve for the emissions trajectory).

Relevant national government departments will be responsible for ensuring these targets are achieved. According to the Draft Post-2020 Mitigation Systems Report (2017), these departments are likely to do so through the development of policies and measures (PAMs) which are to be set out in a plan. Again, it is envisaged that the empowering provisions and relevant rights and duties regarding these plans will be contained in the Climate Change Bill. Provinces and municipalities will also be required to develop plans which support the achievement of these targets.[73]

It is understood that carbon budgets will, effectively, operate as a cap on GHG emissions from a particular installation. It is likely that legislative mechanisms will make it an offence to exceed the cap and to impose a related penalty in the event of conviction. Again, the empowering provisions for carbon budgets (which effectively take away existing rights) will need to be prescribed in law and are likely to be in a proposed Climate Change Bill. There is still considerable debate whether and how, after 2020, the carbon tax and carbon budgets will be aligned. It is possible that instead of a criminal penalty that the carbon tax is used as a compliance mechanism for exceeding a carbon budget. However, this remains to be clarified by the Department and National Treasury.

---

71 At present, the National Benchmark Emissions Trajectory is based on the 'Peak, Plateau and Decline' trajectory defined in 2010. The final emissions trajectory has not yet been set but will most likely be aligned to South Africa's commitments under the Paris Agreement. The Department's *Draft Post-2020 Mitigation Systems Report* (2017) defines emission trajectories as "…alternative computations of the likely quantity and trend of greenhouse gas emissions released for a given period, including variances related to levels of economic growth, the structural makeup of an economy, demographic development and the effect of emission reduction policies". Under this analysis, projections were made for 2020, 2030 and 2050 with projected GHG emissions trajectories categorised by the sectors, energy, transport (as a subcategory of energy), industrial processes and products use, agriculture forestry and other land use, and waste.

72 South African Department of Environmental Affairs (2017: 56).

73 Ibid.

4.1.2 Carbon tax

For many years, National Treasury has insisted that it intends to implement a carbon tax in order to reduce South Africa's GHG emissions. On 2 November 2015, following a series of policies and related documents on the topic,[74] the first draft of a Carbon Tax Bill was published for public comment. This was later accompanied by a set of Draft Carbon Offsets Regulations.[75] A revised Carbon Tax Bill was published on 14 December 2017. In early 2018, it was announced that the tax would come into effect in January 2019.[76]

The tax is intended to be implemented in phases with the first phase designed to be revenue-neutral.[77] The tax is a tax on fossil fuel inputs. Entities which conduct listed activities in the schedule to the Bill which emit GHGs above a prescribed threshold (also in the schedule) are tax liable. The proposed headline carbon tax (which is subject to review) is R120 per ton of CO_2e for emissions above the tax-free thresholds.[78] The intention was to introduce the tax at a relatively low rate and increase it incrementally over time to reduce its impact on the economy whilst simultaneously giving certainty to the industry with time to adjust. Liable entities can reduce their tax liability by making use of various allowances available under the Bill.[79] The total amount of allowances can be as high as 95% in the first phase (which is likely to run until 2022). The Explanatory Memorandum to the revised Carbon Tax Bill (2017) anticipates that as a result, the effective tax rate will be as low as R6 to R48 per ton CO_2e. It is intended for the South African Revenue Authority to implement the tax. However, their systems will be aligned with the Department's in order to verify reported emissions.

Unfortunately, notwithstanding much deliberation between the Department and National Treasury, there is still no certainty as to how the carbon tax and carbon budgets

74 South African National Treasury (2006, 2010, 2013, 2014 and 2017); South African Department of Environmental Affairs (2011 and 2017); Partnership for Market Readiness (2014, 2016 and 2017); South African National Treasury Draft Carbon Tax Bill (2015); Davis Tax Committee (2015); National Treasury Draft Carbon Offsets Regulations (2016); Van Heerden et al. (2016: 714).

75 South African National Treasury (2016, the proposed draft Regulations have not yet been published in the Gazette).

76 South African National Treasury (2018: 47).

77 Revenues are likely to be recycled by way of reducing the current electricity generation levy, credit rebate for the renewable energy premium, and a tax incentive for energy efficiency savings.

78 The carbon tax liability will be calculated as the tax base (total quantity of GHG emissions from combustion, fugitive and industrial processes proportionately reduced by the tax-free allowances) multiplied by the rate of the carbon tax.

79 A basic tax-free allowance of 60%; an additional tax-free allowance of 10% for process emissions; an additional tax-free allowance of 10% for fugitive emissions; a variable tax-free allowance for trade-exposed sectors (up to a maximum of 10%); a maximum tax-free allowance of 5% for above average performance; a 5% tax-free allowance for companies with a carbon budget; and a carbon offset allowance of either 5% or 10%.

will be aligned. The former is a fiscal instrument using the market to drive behaviour and prescribing, in advance, the financial value associated with mitigating GHG emissions. In other words, it creates a carbon price of approximately R120/CO_2e *ab initio*, taking into account allowances. Carbon budgets, on the other hand, do not establish a carbon price directly, but rather use the threat of punitive regulatory sanctions to incentivise behaviour, and the cost of compliance as compared to the quantum of the criminal penalty then creates a parallel financial value for reducing GHG emissions. Although not impossible to implement simultaneously, it is a highly unique regime combining both a regulatory and fiscal instruments to achieve a reduction in the same set of GHG emissions. This design will require careful harmonisation to avoid unwanted or unanticipated macroeconomic and environmental impacts.

4.1.3 Monitoring, evaluation and planning

Pending the finalisation of the post-2020 carbon budget/sectoral emissions target regime, the Department is building the architecture of the monitoring and reporting regime for GHGs. This will enable a more accurate determination of GHG emissions at a national level and will likely also be used as a basis to determine carbon budgets and potentially to support South Africa's position in the international negotiations on climate change. To this end, the Department published National Greenhouse Gas Emissions Reporting Regulations,[80] which came into effect on 3 April 2017. They were published under NEMAQA, South Africa's air quality management legislation. They apply to private sector GHG emitting entities that: (i) fall into the sectors specified in the annexure to the Regulations; and (ii) which have an installed capacity above a prescribed capacity threshold. The Regulations require these entities to register, monitor and report certain prescribed information regarding their GHG emissions, specifically information regarding process, fugitive and combustion emissions from all GHG emission sources and source streams.

The Department has also used NEMAQA to require emitters to manage GHG emissions, pending the finalisation of the Climate Change Bill. On 21 July 2017, the Minister declared six GHGs originally identified under the Kyoto Protocol as necessitating reduction, as 'priority pollutants' under NEMAQA (the Declaration).[81] NEMAQA enables the Minister to declare priority pollutants if they are substances which 'contribute to air pollution'.[82] Upon declaring a substance a priority pollutant, identified entities are required to submit pollution prevention plans under NEMAQA.[83] In terms of the

80 *Government Gazette* 40762 GN 275 of 3 April 2017.

81 Declaration of Greenhouse Gases as Priority Air Pollutants (Government Gazette 40996 GN 710 of 21 July 2017).

82 Section 29(1)(a) of NEMAQA.

83 Section 21(1)(b) of NEMAQA.

Declaration, entities which undertake the production processes set out in its annexure, which emit more than 0.1 Mt of CO_2e, are required to submit a pollution prevention plan to the Minister for approval and must subsequently monitor and report on its implementation.[84] It is up to the emitting entity to propose its own set of 'mitigation measures'[85] in the plan, subject to the qualification that the Minister can reject the plan and require revision if these are considered inadequate.

The Declaration was published together with the National Pollution Prevention Plan Regulations (2017)[86] which set out the prescribed scope and content of a pollution prevention plan, and requirements for the submission of an annual progress report. It is only an offence to fail to comply with the obligation to submit a plan or an annual progress report or to submit false and misleading information, with a fine of up to ZAR5 million and/or five years imprisonment. It is not, however, an offence to fail to implement the mitigation measures approved in the plan itself. As such this system will ultimately be replaced by the carbon budgets regime in 2020, at which time the non-binding mitigation measures in the pollution prevention plan will be replaced by an effective legislated cap on emissions.

4.2 Adaptation

At present, there are no existing draft or final laws which regulate adaptation in South Africa. It is intended for these issues to be addressed in the proposed Climate Change Bill, where it is likely that the primary responsibility for increasing resilience and reducing vulnerability will fall upon identified government sectors, provinces and municipalities. It is anticipated that these sectors and spheres of government will have to undertake vulnerability assessments and devise plans in order to respond to the impacts anticipated in these assessments. It is also likely that the Climate Change Bill will to some degree facilitate the realisation of the adaptation related commitments made by South Africa in its NDC under the Paris Agreement. These include the development of a National Adaptation Plan (a draft plan has already been circulated for public comment); the inclusion of climate change considerations in sub-national and cross-sector policy frameworks; the building of institutional capacity; and the development of an early warning, vulnerability and adaptation monitoring system. The NDC also contemplates the creation of various assessments and frameworks including a national

84 Regulation 4 and 5.

85 Specifically, it must contain a "description of migration measures, based on the best information available at [the] time, that will be implemented and result in [a] deviation from the greenhouse gas emissions baseline over the pollution prevention plan's period, and the projected emissions reductions that will be achieved" (Regulation 3(1)(f)).

86 National Pollution Prevention Plan Regulations (Government Gazette 40996 GN 712 of 21 July 2017).

vulnerability assessment, and adaptation needs framework as well as an adaptation communication, education and awareness framework. As noted earlier in this chapter, the Bill can play an empowering role by mandating the prescribed contents of such plans and frameworks, identifying the responsible state actors for their creation, specifying their period of review and requiring a public participation process.

5 Kenya's climate change regulatory framework

Like South Africa, Kenya's climate change regulatory framework grew from a robust set of policies setting out Government's intention on how to manage the county's emissions and adapt to anticipated impacts. The most important of these is the 2010 National Climate Change Response Strategy (NCCRS) [87] which was operationalised by the National Climate Change Action Plan 2013-2017 (NCCAP) [88] and the National Adaptation Plan 2015-2030 (National Adaptation Plan). [89] One of the key focuses of the NCCRS developed in 2010, was the mainstreaming of climate change considerations into policies and plans. It recommended the development of a comprehensive climate change policy which would serve as a platform for the development of a climate change statute. It proposed that this could be either in the form of amendments to existing laws or the development of a framework law, with a preference expressed for the latter.[90] In March 2013, an Action Plan was developed to operationalise this policy, covering a wide array of issues such as low carbon development; strategies; adaptation and mitigation measures; climate finance; and a policy, legislative, and institutional framework to support the mainstreaming of climate change considerations.[91]

Kenya's NDC under the Paris Agreement[92] contains a number of mitigation and adaptation objectives as well. The country is seeking to reduce GHG emissions by 30% by 2030 relative to the business as usual scenario of 143 $MtCO_2eq$, and the NDC proposes various actions to achieve this target. To enhance resilience, one of the focal adaptation actions is to 'mainstream' climate change adaptation into medium-term plans and implement adaptation actions. Priority adaptation actions are elaborated upon in the National Adaptation Plan. Climate change actions are also currently being considered under the medium-term planning process to implement Kenya's national

87 Kenyan Ministry of Environment and Natural Resources (2010).
88 Kenyan Ministry of Environment and Natural Resources (2013).
89 Kenyan Ministry of Environment and Natural Resources (2015a).
90 Kenyan Ministry of Environment and Natural Resources (2010: 6). See also the summary provided by Oulu (2015: 230).
91 Oulu (2015: 230).
92 Kenyan Ministry of Environment and Natural Resources (2015b: 2-6).

planning instrument: Vision 2030, which guides the implementation of Kenya's NDC.[93]

In May 2016, soon after the conclusion of the Paris Agreement, Kenya passed the Kenyan Climate Change Act. The Act is primarily focused on the creation of institutional structures and the 'mainstreaming' of climate change actions within government. It creates three institutional mechanisms. The first is the National Climate Change Council which is chaired by the President, with the Cabinet Secretary responsible for Climate Affairs as its Secretary. The Secretary is supported by the Climate Change Directorate. This leadership role demonstrates the cross-cutting nature of climate change and is a useful example of how the elevation of governance functions to the level of the Presidency, can serve to overcome sectoral challenges within climate change governance. This Council is responsible for "ensuring the mainstreaming of climate change functions by the national and county governments" and must "approve and oversee the implementation of the National Climate Change Action Plan".[94] By extension, this also includes the oversight and mainstreaming of adaptation and mitigation functions and also the implementation of the National Adaptation Plan.[95] It is also required to provide "guidance on [the] review, amendment and harmonisation of sectoral laws and policies in order to achieve the objectives of [the] Act" and to set targets for the regulation of GHGs.[96]

The Cabinet Secretary has various powers and duties, including the provision of technical assistance on climate change actions and responses to County Governments. The Cabinet Secretary is also obliged to develop, review and update the NCCAP, and to report biennially to Parliament on the status of implementation of international and national obligations, and progress achieved towards attaining low carbon and climate resilient development.[97] The Act also creates the Climate Change Directorate as the lead agency of government on national climate change plans, and which reports to the Cabinet Secretary.[98] It also plays a coordinating role and will provide technical assistance on climate change actions and responses to County Governments. It has a relatively wide responsibility for "set[ting] targets and coordinat[ing] actions for building resilience to climate change and enhancing adaptive capacity, and the undertaking of a biennial review of the implementation of the NCCAP and reporting to the Council".[99] Lastly, the Act creates the Kenya Climate Fund to be a financing mechanism for

93 Statement by Wakhungu, Ministry of Environment and Natural Resources, Kenya to the UNFCCC, at <http://unfccc.int/files/meetings/bonn_nov_2017/statements/application/pdf/kenya_cop23cmp13cma1-2_hls.pdf> (accessed 20-12-2017).

94 Section 6(a) and (b).

95 Kenyan Ministry of Environment and Natural Resources (2016: 10).

96 Section 6(f) of the Climate Change Act (2016).

97 Section 8 of the Climate Change Act (2016).

98 Section 9 of the Climate Change Act (2016).

99 Section 9(8) of the Climate Change Act (2016).

prioritised climate change actions and interventions that have been approved by the Council.[100]

The Act prescribes the content of the NCCAP,[101] with relatively general objectives, mostly towards increasing resilience, low carbon sustainable development and the mainstreaming of climate change actions. The Council also has the power to impose 'climate change duties' on the public sector.[102] State departments and other national entities also have a duty to mainstream climate change considerations into existing strategies and plans, to report on sectoral GHG emissions for a national inventory, to create a designated unit within each department to coordinate the mainstreaming of climate change in that body, with related functions for monitoring and reporting. In particular, there is a detailed process for performance review of climate change functions by these bodies, ultimately involving the National Assembly. [103] The Act also empowers the Council to impose "climate change obligations on private entities",[104] and to make regulations regarding monitoring and the evaluation of compliance with such obligations. The Act does not specify what such obligations may be, but presumably, they entail limitations on GHG emissions and potentially also adaptation actions. The Act also places a duty upon the National Environmental Management Authority, on behalf of the Council, to monitor and report on compliance by public and private entities on their assigned climate change duties, and the extent of "compliance on levels of greenhouse gas emissions as set by the Council under this Act".[105]

Lastly, there are extensive provisions on how 'mainstreaming' is to be achieved by other spheres of government, including: the mainstreaming of climate change considerations into 'functions and budgets' of relevant state departments and entities; the performance of all functions by County Governments; Country Integrated Development Plan and Country Sectoral Plans; the integration of climate risk and vulnerability assessments into all forms of assessments (e.g. EIAs); and into the national education curriculum.[106]

6 Common themes and useful provisions

Whilst it would be simplistic to assume that the above regulatory and statutory references serve as a measure of best practice for the continent, it is useful to consider

100 Section 25 of the Climate Change Act (2016).
101 Section 13(3) of the Climate Change Act (2016).
102 Section 15 of the Climate Change Act (2016).
103 Section 15(6)-(10) of the Climate Change Act (2016).
104 Section 16 of the Climate Change Act (2016).
105 Section 17 of the Climate Change Act (2016).
106 Section 18-21 of the Climate Change Act (2016).

common themes and some examples which are, in the author's view, elements of good practice.

Clearly, both countries have sought to pursue framework laws instead of sectoral amendments. This seems to be the prevalent theme for other African countries in any event, as discussed in Part 3 above, where Uganda, Zambia and Nigeria are all in the process of considering the development of framework laws. The Kenyan example is easier to illustrate, simply because it has been able to crystallise climate policy in a framework law before South Africa was able to. In each instance, however, the benefits of a framework law become immediately apparent.

The framework law can create an institution to guide the development and implementation of climate change policy and 'mainstreaming', with a view to harmonising state action and ensuring a coordinated response. Kenya's escalation of this function to the level of the Presidency is a particularly useful example of the need to prioritise climate change actions across sectors and to afford it the necessary gravitas of political will. As Oulu suggests, fragmentation, conflicting mandates and capacity challenges plague many developing country institutions, and for this reason, the creation of climate change specific institutions (notably at this level) is particularly useful.[107]

The detailed function of the Kenyan Council and the focus on the need for appropriately technically qualified experts across a wide array of disciplines (for example in the Directorate)[108] create a politically and technically balanced forum that is sufficiently robust against political flux.

Commentators have argued that successful climate change legislation must be simultaneously flexible in certain respects and steadfast in others.[109] This means that it should incorporate institutional design features that significantly insulate implementation from vested political and economic interests. The Kenyan example is a useful example of such legislation. Oulu puts the argument well when he argues for design features such as "pre-commitment strategies which deliberately make it hard, though not impossible, to change the law in response to emerging concerns and insights, as well as those intended to keep the statute on course over time".[110] One way in which this is achieved in Kenya is through the deep mainstreaming of climate change considerations across sectors and spheres of government in a way that makes it difficult to reverse because of its scope and depth. Similarly, the elevated quasi-legislative status of the Kenyan NCCAP and its prescribed content makes it less vulnerable to political whim and neglect.

Oulu also cites other examples of best practice such as "requirements for consultation with other agencies, scientific advisory committees, and stakeholders; judicial

107 Oulu (2015: 230).
108 See for example the qualification requirements in Section 9(4).
109 Lazarus (2008: 1153).
110 Oulu (2015: 231).

review provisions; and pre-emption triggers that accommodate competing interests while exploiting the resulting tension to further climate change policy".[111] Kenya achieves some of this through the appointment of technically qualified staff in the Directorate (as specified in the Act), public consultation provisions,[112] and the right to approach the Environmental and Land Court for climate change specific complaints with a reduced burden of proof.[113]

A common theme across the Kenyan Climate Change Act is also the need for mainstreaming. If the Act had to be summarised in one word it would probably be that. South Africa's NCCRP, the National Adaptation Plan and related government policies also place a particular emphasis on mainstreaming climate change considerations, and it is likely to play an important role in the South African Climate Change Bill. As discussed above, not only does mainstreaming protect against political inaction or a change in policy, but it also overcomes some of the cross-sectoral and intra-governmental challenges which beset any government when addressing climate change. It ensures that there is an uptake in action by all relevant spheres and sectors, ensuring buy-in and coordination, and it also recognises the need for climate change responses to be driven by a multitude of actors in both the private and public sphere. Whilst mitigation can, to some degree, be driven by one state department through, for example, the South African approach of creating sectoral GHG targets and carbon budgets, adaptation requires a much wider array of actors to be effective. Mainstreaming is possibly one of the most useful instruments to include in a Climate Change Act particularly in Africa where adaptation is a pressing and urgent priority. The way that this has been achieved in the Kenyan Climate Change Act and its detailed provisions identifying the specific planning instruments requiring mainstreaming, together with its definition of mainstreaming is considered particularly useful.

One issue the Kenyan Climate Change Act is relatively unclear on is the nature and process for imposing limitations on GHG emissions. The Act speaks of the Council needing to set targets for the regulation of GHGs, state departments reporting on sectoral GHGs, and a general reference to 'climate change obligations' which can be imposed on private entities. Potentially this issue may be captured in regulations under the Act. By comparison, the South African regulatory regime, including the proposed carbon tax, the current monitoring and reporting regulations for the purposes of a GHG inventory, coupled with the duty to create a pollution prevention plan, as well as the extensive architecture for the emissions trajectory, carbon budgets and sectoral emissions targets is a relatively more advanced example of GHG mitigation regulation.

111 Oulu (2015: 231).

112 Section 24 of the Climate Change Act (2016).

113 Section 23 of the Climate Change Act (2016). There is no need to demonstrate loss or injury in such complaints.

This is likely symptomatic of the fact that South Africa emits considerably more GHGs per capita than Kenya,[114] and accordingly, there is a greater impetus to regulate these emissions in the near future. Whilst this approach may seem premature for many African countries, many of which have similarly low emissions profiles to Kenya, the author believes that it is a useful and necessary legislative regime to at least consider when developing a Climate Change Act, mindful that instituting early action on the regulation of GHGs will not only facilitate the achievement of African country commitments under their NDCs, but it will facilitate the adoption of low carbon technologies within the earlier phases of development thereby reducing future retrofit and compliance costs. The costs of low carbon technologies are also becoming increasingly competitive and as such may not in themselves always be an impediment to development if adopted at an early phase.

This is not to suggest that African countries should pursue the extensive and complicated carbon budget/carbon tax scheme proposed by South Africa, but it is helpful to consider the development of an inventory, implementing monitoring and reporting requirements in regulations and an architecture for GHG emissions targets/allowances within the empowering legislation at an early stage. As the Grantham Institute suggests:[115]

> ... a good evidence base for informed climate policy requires data about both emissions and climate risks, as well as about options to reduce emissions and improve resilience to climate change. A key plank of good climate change legislation is therefore a detailed greenhouse gas inventory consisting of compulsory, timely and systematic reporting for greenhouse gases from all sectors as well as regular climate change risk assessments that can inform adaptation measures.

Similarly, they advocate the use of GHG emissions targets as a means to "set a long-term trajectory and send a signal of political intent to business and civil society".[116]

Lastly, one common theme is that both regulatory developments grew from a sound, well researched and detailed set of policies and strategies. In both cases, there were more than just one policy or strategy addressing climate change, and both countries had drafted a national adaptation plan underpinned by comprehensive vulnerability assessments. The usefulness of this approach is that it enables detailed and extensive public input into policy (and ultimately regulatory) objectives, ensuring that the law, once developed, is tailored to national circumstances and also has public and political buy-in. This is typically the case in many countries which enact framework laws, and it finds equal relevance on the African continent. As such the first step in the development of any climate change law ideally is the development of a national framework climate change policy or strategy underpinned by a well-informed vulnerability and needs assessment, ideally coupled with an action or implementation plan.

---

114 In 2014, South Africa emitted 9 Mt/capita, compared to Kenya which emitted 0.3 Mt/capita, see <https://data.worldbank.org/indicator/EN.ATM.CO2E.PC.> (accessed 20-12-2017).

115 Nachmany et al. (2015).

116 Ibid.

7 Conclusion

Climate change legislation plays an important role in spurring action, operationalising climate change policy and also shielding it from policy change. Certainly, it has its challenges, and its nature varies greatly. The risk of subsequent amendments, budgetary limitations, delays in bringing regulations into effect, vested interests, and a lack of enforcement can render a seemingly strong legal mandate mere symbolic aspirational statement.[117] Nevertheless, if appropriately crafted and with the necessary political will, climate change laws can play an important and meaningful role in driving a national response.

Countries across Africa are in the process of developing climate change laws, primarily in framework form, to address the anticipated impacts of climate change and to facilitate low carbon development. Framework laws have proven to be durable instruments with the advantage that they facilitate mainstreaming and the development of cross-sectoral institutions. The Kenyan example is a useful prototype of how both of these objectives can be achieved, and it is anticipated that South Africa will follow a similar route. The South African example is also a helpful demonstration of how to create a relatively detailed regulatory architecture for the management of GHG emissions and the related mechanisms to develop an inventory, trajectory and ultimately GHG emissions thresholds.

It would not be appropriate to simply duplicate these examples when developing national legislation and regulations. However, it is encouraging to see national responses that are relatively advanced and nuanced on the continent and which speak to immediate challenges. It has been shown that the propensity to legislate is heavily influenced by the passage of similar laws elsewhere, suggesting a strong role for peer pressure or learning effects.[118] This will hopefully be the case for climate change legislation in Africa where national influences can foster regional growth in climate change laws. Going forward, and mindful of the relative youth of this field of law, it is hoped that these developments will cross-pollinate each other and build a robust set of laws to drive climate change action nationally, regionally and across the continent.

References

Arounusi, Q (2017) "Green party petitions to present a Bill on implementation of zambia's commitments on climate change" *Lusaka Times* (8-1-2017), at <https://www.lusakatimes.com/2017/01/08/green-party-petitions-parliament-present-bill-implementation-zambias-commitments-climate-change/> (accessed 20-12-2017).

117 Oulu (201: 231).

118 Fankhauser et al. (2014).

Averchenkva, A & S Matikamen (2017) "Climate legislation and international commitments" in A Averchenkova, S Fankhauser & M Nachmeny (eds) *Trends in climate change legislation.*

CAHOSCC / Committee of African Heads of States and Governments on Climate Change (2014) *Work programme on climate change action in Africa.*

Craig, R (2010) "Stationarity is dead – long live transformation: five principles for climate change adaptation law" 34 *Harvard Environmental Law Review* 9-75.

Danmaryam, H (2017) "Trade unions, CSOs, academia, make input into Climate Change Bill" *EnviroNews* Nigeria (20-7-2017), at <http://www.environewsnigeria.com/trade-union-csos-academia-make-input-climate-change-bill/> (accessed 20 December 2017).

Davis Tax Committee (2015) *First interim report on the proposed carbon tax for South Africa.*

Fankhauser, S, C Gennaioli & M Collins (2014) *Domestic dynamics and international influence: What explains the passage of climate change legislation?* Policy Working Paper No. 156 Grantham Research Institute on Climate Change and the Environment and Centre for Climate Change Economics, at <http://www.lse.ac.uk/GranthamInstitute/wp-content/uploads/2014/05/Wp156-Domestic-dynamics-and-international-influence-what-explains-the-passage-of-climate-change-legislation.pdf> (accessed 20-7-2017).

Gilder, A & O Rumble (2017) "Africa, current developments in carbon and climate law" 3 *Climate and Carbon Law Review* 268-271.

Government of South Africa (2015) *South Africa's intended nationally determined contribution under the Paris Agreement.*

IPCC / Intergovernmental Panel on Climate Change (2014) *Climate change 2014: impacts, adaptation, and vulnerability: contribution of Working Group II to the Fifth Assessment Report of the Intergovernmental Panel on Climate Change* [VR Barros, CB Field, DJ Dokken, MD Mastandrea, KJ Mach, TE Bilir, M Chatterjee, KL Ebi, YO Estrada, RC Genova, B Girma, ES Kissel, AN Levy, S MacCracken, PR Mastrandrea & LL White (eds)].

Iroanusi, Q (2017) "Nigeria: house moves to establish Climate Change Council" *Premium Times* (20-7-2017), at <http://allafrica.com/stories/201707210026.html> (accessed 20 December 2017).

Kenyan Ministry of Environment and Natural Resources (2010) *National climate change response strategy.*

Kenyan Ministry of Environment and Natural Resources (2013) *National climate change action plan 2013-2017.*

Kenyan Ministry of Environment and Natural Resources (2015a) *National adaptation plan 2015-2030.*

Kenyan Ministry of Environment and Natural Resources (2015b) *Kenya's intended nationally determined contribution (INDC)* (23-6-2015), at <http://www4.unfccc.int/ndcregistry/Published Documents/Kenya%20First/Kenya_NDC_20150723.pdf> (accessed 20-12-2017).

Klass, A (2013) "Climate change and the convergences of environmental and energy law" XXIV *Fordham Environmental Law Review* 180-275.

Knox, J (2009) "Linking human rights and climate change at the United Nations" 33(2) *Harvard Environmental Law Review* 477-498.

Lazarus, R (2008) "Super wicked problems and climate change: restraining the present to liberate the future" 94 *Cornell Law Review* 1153-1233.

McDonald, J & M Styles (2014) "Legal strategies for adaptive management under climate change" 26(1) *Journal of Environmental Law* 25-53.

Nachmany, M, S Fankhauser, J Davidová, N Kingsmill, T Landesman, H Roppongi, P Schleifer, J Setzer, A Sharman, C Stolle Singleton, J Sundaresan & T Townshend (2015) *The 2015 global climate legislation study*, at <http://www.lse.ac.uk/GranthamInstitute/wp-content/uploads/2015/05/Global_climate_legislation_study_20151.pdf> (accessed 17-7-2018).

Nachmany M, S Fankhauser, J Setzer & A Averchenkova (2017) *Global trends in climate change legislation and litigation: 2017 update*, at <http://www.lse.ac.uk/GranthamInstitute/wp-content/uploads/2017/04/Global-trends-in-climate-change-legislation-and-litigation-WEB.pdf> (accessed 20-12-2017).

OHCHR / Office of the United Nations High Commissioner for Human Rights (2009) *Report of the Office of the United Nations High Commissioner for Human Rights on the relationship between climate change and human rights* (U.N. Doc. A/HRC/10/61 (15-1-2009)), at <http://www.ohchr.org/Documents/Press/AnalyticalStudy.pdf> (accessed 20-12-2017).

Osofsky, H & L McAllister (2012) *Climate change law and policy*.

Oulu, M (2011) "Mainstreaming climate adaptation in Kenya" 2(3) *Climate Law* 375-394.

Oulu, M (2015) "Climate change governance: emerging legal and institutional frameworks for developing countries" in W Filhou (ed.) *The handbook of climate change adaptation* 227-250.

Parliamentary Communication Services (2017) "Environmental Affairs Portfolio Committee encouraged to hear that climate change legislation will soon be introduced in Parliament" (10-10-2017), at <https://www.parliament.gov.za/press-releases/environmental-affairs-portfolio-committee-encouraged-hear-climate-change-legislation-will-soon-be-introduced-parliament> (accessed 20-12-2017).

Partnership for Market Readiness (2014) *Emissions intensity benchmarks for the South African carbon tax – technical support study*.

Partnership for Market Readiness (2016) *Modelling the impact on South Africa's economy of introducing a carbon tax*.

Partnership for Market Readiness (2017) *Integration of the carbon tax and carbon budgets in South Africa*.

Phillips, G "Paris Agreement on climate change places Africa at the fulcrum of renewable energy deployment, experts agree" *African Development Bank Group* (29-03-2016), at <https://www.afdb.org/en/news-and-events/paris-agreement-on-climate-change-places-africa-at-the-fulcrum-of-renewable-energy-deployment-experts-agree-15531/> (accessed 20-12-017).

Rumble, O (2016) "Water resource management and climate change" in T Humby, L Kotze, O Rumble & O Gilder (eds) *Climate change law and governance in South Africa* 9(1)-9(31).

South African Department of Environmental Affairs (2004) *National climate change response strategy*.

South African Department of Environmental Affairs (2011) *National climate change response white paper*.

South African Department of Environmental Affairs (2013) *Long-term adaptation scenarios flagship research programme (LTAS) – Phase 1*.

South African Department of Environmental Affairs (2014) *South Africa's greenhouse gas (GHG) mitigation potential analysis*.

South African Department of Environmental Affairs (2015) *Long-term adaptation scenarios flagship research programme (LTAS) – Phase 2*.

South African Department of Environmental Affairs (2016a) *South Africa's draft national adaptation strategy*.

South African Department of Environmental Affairs (2016b) *Technical guidelines for monitoring, reporting and verification of greenhouse gas emissions by industry – a companion to the South African National GHG reporting regulations* (Version No. TG-2016.1).

South African Department of Environmental Affairs (2017) *Development of South Africa's post-2020 climate change mitigation system draft report.*

South African National Treasury (2006) *A framework for considering the use of market-based instruments to support environmental fiscal reform in South Africa.*

South African National Treasury (2010) *reducing greenhouse gas emissions: the carbon tax option.*

South African National Treasury (2013) *Carbon tax policy paper: reducing greenhouse gas emissions.*

South African National Treasury (2014) *Carbon offsets.*

South African National Treasury (2016) *Proposed regulations: carbon offsets* (not yet published in the *Gazette*).

South African National Treasury (2018) *Budget review.*

Tashobya, A (2017) "Rwanda: revised law equips climate fund to mobilise resources" *The New Times* (25-8-2017), at <http://allafrica.com/stories/201708250012.html> (accessed 20-12-2017).

The World Bank (2017) "CO_2 emissions (metric tons per capita)", at <https://data.worldbank.org/indicator/EN.ATM.CO2E.PC.> (accessed 20-12-2017).

Townshend, T, S Frankhauser, A Matthews, A Feger, J Liu & T Narciso (2011) "Legislating climate change on a national level" 53(5) *Environment: Science and Policy for Sustainable Development* 5-17.

Townshend, T, S Fankhauser, R Aybar, M Collins, T Landesman, M Nachmany & C Pavese (2013) "How national legislation can help to solve climate change" 3 *Nature Climate Change* 430-432.

UNECA / United Nations Economic Commission for Africa (2017) "Africa spending more than its fair share for adaptation" (06-11-2017), at <https://www.uneca.org/stories/africa-spending-more-its-fair-share-climate-adaptation-new-study-reveals> (accessed 20-12-2017).

Uwaegnulam, C (2016) "Legislators plan new law to unify climate change policies" *The Guardian* (15-11-2016), at <https://guardian.ng/news/legislators-plan-new-law-to-unify-climate-change-policies/> (accessed 20-12-2017).

Van Heerden, J, J Blignaut, H Bohlmann, A Cartwright, N Diederichs & M Mander (2016) "The economic and environmental effects of a carbon tax in South Africa: a dynamic CGE modelling approach" 19(5) *South African Journal of Economic and Management Sciences* 714-732.

Williams, R (2017) "The UK Climate Change Act: standing strong in a time of change" (6-04-2017), at <https://sandbag.org.uk/2017/04/06/uk-climate-change-act-standing-strong-time-change/> (accessed 20-12-2017).

Winkler, H (2007) (ed.) *Long term mitigation scenarios: technical report*, Prepared by the Energy Research Centre for Department of Environment Affairs and Tourism.

Chapter 3:
Nigeria's commitments under the climate change Paris Agreement: legislative and regulatory imperatives towards ensuring sustainable development

Oluwatoyin Adejonwo-Osho

1 Introduction

The United Nations Framework Convention on Climate Change (UNFCCC) was signed at the 1992 Rio Earth Summit when countries agreed to limit their emissions of greenhouse gases (GHGs). Years after this historic treaty was opened for signature there have been far-reaching changes in the understanding of, response to, and governance of climate change. The latest report by the Intergovernmental Panel on Climate Change (IPCC) indicates that human-induced climate change is already taking place with significant adverse effects on the environment and the earth systems.[1] In response to this phenomenal threat to humanity, there are increasing and sometimes comprehensive international, regional, and national climate change policies and programmes from governments, business and civil society. For instance, many countries have developed comprehensive legislation on climate change. The UK was the first country, with its historic 2008 Climate Change Act.[2] Other countries have followed the UK's footsteps.[3] Altogether, 99 countries, consisting of 33 developed and 66 developing countries, which represent around 93% of global emissions, have national laws or policies directly related to climate change mitigation and adaptation.[4]

The foundation for the Paris Climate Change Agreement, 2015 was laid during the 2011 Durban climate change rounds of negotiation in Durban, South Africa. The Durban Outcome is significant because it heralded a new climate change regime that finally culminated in the Paris Agreement. One of the key characteristics of the Paris Agreement is that it applies to all, both developed, emerging economies, developing and least developed countries, unlike the UNFCCC's Kyoto Protocol of 2005 which

1 IPCC (2014).
2 Climate Change Act 2008, CAP 27.
3 According to the Globe climate legislation study, by the end of 2014 there were 804 climate change laws and policies. See Nachmany et al. (2015). Also see the UK Climate Change Act of 2008, the Philippines Climate Change Act of 2009 and most recently the Mexico General Law on Climate Change of 2012 and Kenya's Climate Change Authority Bill of 2012.
4 Nachmany et al. (2015).

made a distinction amongst nations based on their capabilities and the international law principle of common but differentiated responsibilities.[5]

The success of the Paris Agreement can be linked to its bottom-up approach, different from the Kyoto Protocol which adopted a top-down approach adopted by the UN and influential powers for decades.[6] Basically, the negotiations were focused on what each country and region, whether developed, developing, or least developed, is willing to contribute to the 2°C target. More importantly, it is hoped that these joint efforts will collectively contribute to what is required to stem catastrophic climate change in the future, such that we can restrict and keep warming under 2°C pre-industrial levels.

The Paris Agreement still retains the founding principle of the UNFCCC such as the international principle of sustainable development,[7] the precautionary principle and the principle of common but differentiated responsibility (CBDR).[8] For instance, the country-specific pledges required applied the principle of CBDR. In addition, the Paris Agreement acknowledges and introduces new concepts that were not captured in the UNFCCC such as human rights obligations, climate justice, the rights of women, vulnerable groups, and indigenous peoples.[9]

The key elements of the Paris Agreement include the goal of holding global warming below 2°C; a system of national pledges to reduce emissions referred to in the Paris Agreement as 'nationally determined contributions' (NDCs);[10] the non-binding character of these contributions, the reliance on transparency rather than legal enforcement to promote accountability and effectiveness; the shift away from the Annex I and non-Annex I differentiation in terms of emission reduction commitments towards a more flexible approach that encompasses all countries, whether developed or developing; the pledge to mobilise climate finance from public and private sources, and, perhaps most importantly, the bottom-up approach of the agreement. The Paris Agreement

---

5 The Kyoto Protocol made a fine distinction between developed and developing countries in terms of having binding emission reduction commitment. Under the Kyoto Protocol, based on the international law principle of common but differentiated responsibilities, only developed countries, tagged as Annex I countries, have binding emission reduction commitments while developing countries, tagged as non-Annex I countries, did not have binding emission reduction commitments but were enjoined to work towards achieving the 'ultimate objective of the Convention. Article 2 of the UNFCCC states that the ultimate objective of the Convention and any related instrument is to achieve stabilisation of greenhouse gas concentrations in the atmosphere at a level that would prevent dangerous anthropogenic interference with the climate system. Such a level should be achieved within a time-frame sufficient to allow ecosystems to adapt naturally to climate change, to ensure that food production is not threatened and to enable economic development to proceed in a sustainable manner.

6 Although Van Asselt and Zelli (2018: 31) disagree with this description and stated that the Protocol never fitted neatly into the top-down description. Rather, that the Kyoto climate regime was a hybrid of top-down and bottom-up elements. See also Hare et al. (2010).

7 Article 2(1) of the Paris Agreement.

8 Article 2(2) of the Paris Agreement.

9 Preamble para. 6 of the Paris Agreement.

10 Article 4 para. 2 of the Paris Agreement.

entered into force on 4 November 2016, thirty days after the date on which the minimum of 55 Parties to the Convention accounting in total for at least an estimated 55% of the total global greenhouse gas emissions had deposited their instruments of ratification, acceptance, approval or accession with the Depositary.[11]

2 The impacts of climate change in Nigeria

The IPCC's Fourth Assessment Report 2007 stated that of all the continents, Africa would be severely hit by the impacts of climate change, strengthened by Africa's weak capacity for adaptation and mitigation.[12] According to the IPCC Report, Africa is one of the most vulnerable continents to climate change and climate variability. Africa's major economic sectors are vulnerable to current climate sensitivity, with huge economic impacts. The Fifth Assessment Report of the IPCC confirms that this vulnerability is exacerbated by existing developmental challenges such as endemic poverty, complex governance and institutional dimensions, limited access to capital, including markets, infrastructure and technology, ecosystem degradation, and natural disasters and conflicts. These, in turn, have contributed to Africa's weak adaptive capacity, increasing the continent's vulnerability to projected climate change.[13]

Many scientists studying the potential impact of climate change have predicted that Africa is likely to experience higher temperatures, rising sea levels, changing rainfall patterns and increased climate variability with consequential impacts on its population.[14] The Food and Agriculture Organisation (FAO) of the United Nations predicts negative impacts of climate change on agricultural production and food security in large parts of sub-Saharan Africa, higher temperatures, the drying-up of soils, increased pest and disease pressure, and shifts in suitable areas for growing crops and livestock.[15] Unmitigated climate change could create risks of major disruption to economic and social activity similar in scale to those experienced during the great wars and the economic depression of the first half of the 20th century.[16]

At present and in the long term, Nigeria remains vulnerable to climate change and its negative impacts. For example, certain activities in Nigeria are directly and indirectly associated with long-term adverse environmental impacts which contribute to global warming. These include gas flaring, deforestation due to cutting forests for biomass products, and emission of GHGs due to the use of fossil fuels. Many elements of the environment and human society are sensitive to climate change, such as the

11 Article 21 of the Paris Agreement.
12 Parry et al. (2007: 433-435).
13 IPCC (2014).
14 Tadesse (2010: 1).
15 FAO (2008).
16 Stern (2006: ii).

ecosystem, agriculture, water needs and supply, and food production among others. Nigeria's 2011 National Adaptation Strategy and Plan of Action on Climate Change for Nigeria (NASPA-CCN)[17] identifies 13 sectors as having climate change impacts. These are agriculture (Crops and Livestock); freshwater resources; coastal water resources and fisheries; forests; biodiversity; health and sanitation; human settlements and housing; energy; transportation and communications; industry and commerce; disaster migration and security; livelihoods; and vulnerable groups and education.[18]

Many developing countries located in tropical areas are already enduring climate extremes, such as very high temperatures, heat waves, droughts, hurricanes, floods, and variability in rainfall.[19] The continued increase in global temperature will intensify these incidences of extreme weather conditions. For example, in recent years, Nigeria has been experiencing very high temperatures, heat waves, droughts, and variability in rainfall.[20] These extreme weather conditions result in several adverse effects such as poor air quality which increases air-borne diseases, and it increases the incidences of respiratory-related illness. Similarly, sea level rise threatens small islands, low-lying coastal areas such as Lagos State in Nigeria and other major world cities such as New York and London.[21] It threatens Nigeria's coastal regions. For example, although the Niger Delta is the source of oil wealth, its low-lying terrain, crisscrossed with waterways makes it extremely vulnerable to flooding and salinisation.[22] Furthermore, half of the 15 million population of the city of Lagos live less than six feet above sea level; Victoria Island is particularly vulnerable along with the several slum settlements around it.[23] According to the News Agency of Nigeria (NAN),[24] there are fears that no fewer than 25 million Nigerians living along coastal communities of Rivers Niger, Benue, Sokoto, Katsina Lagos, Ondo, Delta, Akwa Ibom, Bayelsa and the Cross River States in Nigeria are exposed to possible displacement and devastation due to flooding.

---

17 This Report was prepared for the Special Climate Change Unit of Nigeria's Federal Ministry of Environment by the Building Nigeria's Response to Climate Change (BNRCC) project, a project funded by the Canadian International Development Agency.

18 National Adaptation Strategy and Plan of Action on Climate Change for Nigeria (NASPA-CCN) 2011 <http://nigeriaclimatechange.org/naspa.pdf> (accessed 11-12-2017).

19 Stern (2006: 106-107).

20 Abaje et al. (2014). Also see Tunde (2011).

21 For example, Tuvalu, a Polynesian island nation located in the Pacific Ocean, midway between Hawaii and Australia, is particularly susceptible to the adverse impacts of climate change and rising sea level, and there are fears that Tuvalu will be uninhabitable or may vanish entirely within a few decades. According to its Prime Minister, SaufatuSapo'aga, the sea level rise as a result of climate change and global warming is no different from "a slow and insidious form of terrorism against us". See Mansbach & Taylor (2012).

22 Fatile (2012: 78).

23 Ibeabuchi et al. (2018).

24 The National Emergency Management Agency (NEMA) also confirms that about 25 million people living in coastal regions of the country were at risk of the devastation of floods.

Communities have been displaced in Kano, Jigawa, Cross River, Taraba, Adamawa, Niger, and the Anambra States.[25]

As a result of climate change, droughts will become more severe in some areas, particularly in Africa.[26] A key example is the vanishing Lake Chad in West Africa.[27] Lake Chad was once Africa's largest water reservoir in the Sahel region, covering an area of about 26,000 km^2. However, by 2000, the lake covered less than one-fifth of that area.[28] According to Salkida[29], the FAO describes the state of the lake as an ecological catastrophe, and has predicted that the lake could disappear this century. The ecological catastrophe has led to drought-induced famine and locusts, and an increase in the number of extremely hot days in the Sahel and northern Nigeria. Climate change will lead to increased incidence of death from climate-related diseases such as diarrhoea, malaria, meningitis, and malnutrition.[30] The distribution and abundance of disease vectors are closely linked to temperature and rainfall patterns. Changes to mosquito distributions and abundance will have profound impacts on malaria prevalence in developing countries such as Nigeria. The World Health Organisation (WHO) estimates that since the 1970s, climate change has been responsible for over 150,000 deaths each year from diarrhoea, malaria, and malnutrition, predominantly in Africa, and other developing regions.[31] If effective mitigation and adaptation strategies are not observed, the numbers are expected to double to 300,000 deaths each year by 2030.[32] According to the NASPA-CCN, climate change has a direct and indirect impact on the health of Nigerians. Direct health impacts of climate change stem from extreme events such as heat waves, floods, droughts, windstorms, and wildfires. Indirect effects of climate change on health may arise from malnutrition due to reduced food production, from a spread of infectious disease on food and water-borne illness, and from increased air pollution.[33]

Also, the various impacts of climate change will likely result in migration.[34] Some of these impacts are land degradation, droughts, deforestation, water scarcity, floods,

25 National Adaptation Strategy and Plan of Action on Climate Change for Nigeria (NASPA-CCN), 2.

26 Conway (2009).

27 "As you approach the Lake Chad basin from Maiduguri… the atmosphere of despair is telling. The air is dusty, the wind is fierce and unrelenting, the plants are wilting and the earth is turning into sand dunes…. The lives of herdsmen, fishermen and farmers are teetering on the edge as the lake dries up before their eyes" Salkida (2012). Lake Chad is located in the far west of Chad and the northeast of Nigeria. The lake also extends to Niger and Cameroon. It is fed mainly by the Chari River. See the Lake Chad Basin Commission at <http://www.lakechadbc.org/.> (accessed 11-12-2017).

28 See Salkida (2012).

29 Ibid.

30 African Climate Policy Centre (2011).

31 Stern (2006: 75).

32 Ibid.

33 NASPA-CCN, 19.

34 Raleigh et al. (2008).

storms and famines linked to food shortages and insecurity.[35] Furthermore, climate change-induced migration, which is likely to be more frequent as a result of increased flooding and extreme weather conditions in Nigeria, can create and intensify violent conflicts over scarce resources such as water and land for farming.[36]

Climate change threatens Nigeria's oil and gas investment.[37] This investment is at risk from the negative impacts of climate change, including rising sea levels, heavy storms, floods, high winds and shoreline erosion.[38] It is also expected to negatively impact the already limited electrical power supply through impacts on hydroelectric and thermal generation.[39] There is no gainsaying that these impacts will add pressures on limited resources and they are a threat to the sustainable development goals. In Africa and other developing regions of the world, climate change is a threat to economic growth, long-term prosperity, as well as the survival of already vulnerable populations. Consequences of this include persistence of economic, social and environmental inequalities and vulnerabilities.

3 Highlights of Nigeria's Nationally Determined Contribution

Nigeria's contribution to global emissions as of 2010 is estimated to be 1% of total total emission.[40] Nevertheless, Nigeria is committed to tackling climate change. NDCs are country-specific pledges to cut carbon emissions, thereby, 'contributing' to the net global carbon emission index which is aimed at an overall reduction of global warming. The Intended Nationally Determined Contributions (INDCs) become Nationally Determined Contributions as countries ratify the Paris Agreement. Nigeria's INDCs became the NDCs in March 2017 after the ratification of the Paris Agreement by the Federal Government of Nigeria. The approved NDCs emphasise the delivery of direct development benefits and sustainable growth of the economy through policy measures that help to alleviate poverty, increase social welfare and inclusion, as well as improve individual well-being and promote a healthy environment. The NDCs aim to achieve a reduction in GHG emissions from the business as usual (BAU) scenario using historical emissions data between 2010 and 2014 for predicting 2015 to 2030 emissions scenario.[41]

35 Bob & Bronkhorst (2010).
36 Fatile & Adejobi (2012).
37 NASPA-CCN, 20.
38 Ibid.
39 Ibid.
40 Nigeria's (Intended) Nationally Determined Contribution.
41 The GHGs targeted are CO_2, N_2O, and CH_4.

The key measures of achieving Nigeria's emission reduction commitment include ending gas flaring by 2030; generating off-grid solar PV of 13 GW (13,000 MW);[42] efficient gas generation; increasing energy efficiency annually by 2% that will result in 30% efficiency by 2030; increasing the use of public transportation such as buses, trains, and light rail; increasing the capacity and efficiency of the electricity grid; and promoting the use of climate-smart agriculture and reforestation. Thus, the NDCs target key carbon-intensive sectors of the economy such as the oil and gas, energy, transport, agriculture and land use and transport sectors.

Notably, Nigeria aims to reduce emissions per real GDP from the base year from 0.873 kg CO_2e to 0.491 kg CO_2e in 2030, which will result in 43.8% CO_2e reduction in GHGs from the 2010-2014 BAU scenarios. Likewise, in monetary terms, it aims to increase its GDP per capita from US$2,950 as at 2014 base year to US$3,964 by 2030, resulting in 34.4% GDP per capita by 2030.[43] However, this reduction is attributed to both 20% unconditional and 45% conditional mitigation objectives respectively. Thus, Nigeria states that it will achieve 20% target GHG reduction without external support for implementation. In addition, the NDC set a conditional 40% reduction in GHGs contingent on international support in the form of climate finance, smart technology development and transfer, and capacity building. Therefore, climate finance is a condition for undertaking ambitious mitigation and adaptation for further incremental reduction of GHG emissions.

The estimated cost for implementing the mitigation and adaptation measures stated in its NDC is $142b, while the national benefit for implementing these measures is calculated to be about $304b. This implies that GHG emissions per capita will reduce by 0.68 tonnes with unconditional activities but with additional support and climate finance Nigeria can reduce her per capita emission by 1.53 tonnes GHG. The NDC cautions that some of the policies and mitigation measures contained therein can only be implemented with significant international support. Therefore, mitigation measures that require substantial investment, even if cost-effective over the life of the investment will be carefully reviewed before being implemented. Nigeria's NDCs represent an integrated and comprehensive strategic approach towards promoting a low carbon, high growth, climate-resilient path for national sustainable development. However, the key question to consider is if the existing legal and regulatory framework supports this strategic approach – a low carbon economy and towards sustainable development.

42 Note that the NDC does not specify a time frame within which this will be achieved.

43 Nigeria's (Intended) Nationally Determined Contribution.

4 Nigeria's NDC commitments: existing legislative and regulatory framework

A regulatory and institutional framework is required for a coherent response to climate change. Unless this is in place, sectoral climate change actions will struggle to be implemented, and existing policies, legislation and regulations will work at cross purposes. Creating and managing an effective climate change response takes place through institutional arrangements. Cortner et al.[44] define institutions as the expression of the terms of collective human experience; institutions express how people interact with each other and their environment and they represent a means through which social problems are resolved.

Against the backdrop of the adverse impact of climate change on environmental, economic and social sectors and Nigeria's commitments under its NDCs, what are the existing legal and regulatory frameworks to assist in the effective implementation of Nigeria's commitments and what legislative and regulatory gaps exist? Currently, Nigeria does not have a climate change legislation, although legislation on climate change is gradually becoming an international global standard for countries keen on integrating climate change response into their development plans to ensure sustainable development. In addition to the fact that Nigeria does not have a climate change law, there are certain pieces of legislation that act as a drawback on the existing regulatory and institutional framework.[45] There are also certain laws working at cross purposes with Nigeria's NDC commitment. The existing regulatory and institutional framework for implementing Nigeria's NDC commitments include the 1999 Constitution of Nigeria; the 2011 National Adaptation Strategy and Plan of Action on Climate Change for Nigeria (NASPA-CCN); the 2007 National Environmental Standards and Regulations Enforcement Agency (Establishment) Act (NESREA); the Environmental Impact Assessment Act; the 1988 National Policy on Environment (revised in 2016); the 2006 National Forestry Policy; and on the institutional side the Department of Climate Change and the Ministry of Environment.

4.1 The 1999 Constitution of Nigeria

The 1999 Constitution of Nigeria is the first of the three previous constitutions to include a specific provision on the environment.[46] This provision is contained in

44 Cortner (1988: 160).

45 Associated Gas Re-injection Act, Cap A25, LFN 2004 and The Associated Gas Re-injection (Continued Flaring of Gas) Regulation, LFN, 2004.

46 It is important to note however that earlier Constitutions like the 1979 Constitution had considerable provisions which had great significance for environmental management. For example, in the way the Constitution contemplated the conservation and rational use of the environment.

Section 20 of the Constitution which states that "the State shall protect and improve the environment and safeguard the water, air and land, forest and wildlife of Nigeria".[47] The wording of Section 20 is quite broad to promote a broad framework for environmental protection and management. However, this provision is hampered because it is included under Chapter II of the Constitution and therefore forms part of the non-justiciable "Fundamental Objectives and Directives Principles of State Policy (FODPSP)".[48] Chapter IV, unlike Chapter II, the FODPSP, guarantees certain rights classified as fundamental human rights including the right to life which are justiciable and adequately protected by implementation mechanisms.[49]

Section 20 is further hampered by Section 6(6)(c) of the Constitution which provides that:

> The judicial power vested in the judiciary shall not extend to any issue or question as to whether any act of omission by any authority or person or as to whether any law or any judicial decision is in conformity with the Fundamental Objectives and Directive Principles of State Policy.

This imperative effectively limits the powers of the courts to consider issues bordering on environmental rights and disables the citizens from seeking to claim or the courts to enforce environmental rights. This is despite the fact that Section 20 of the 1999 Constitution forms part of the rights guaranteed by the African Charter on Human and Peoples' Rights (the African Charter), which Nigeria is a signatory to. The African Charter was domesticated in Nigeria in 1983 under the African Charter on Human and Peoples' Rights (ratification and enforcement) Act Cap A9 LFN 2004. The African Charter is a regional treaty that affirms both civil and political rights such as those guaranteed by Chapter IV of the 1999 Constitution as well as economic, social and cultural rights such as those provided for under Chapter II of the 1999 Constitution and it makes no distinction between them. However, the Nigerian Supreme Court has severally held that where there is a conflict between Treaties and the Constitution, the provisions of the Constitution shall prevail in the event of a conflict.[50]

For a detailed appraisal of provisions of the Nigerian Constitution with respect to environmental management, see Fagbohun (2002: 24).

47 Constitution of the Federal Republic of Nigeria, 1999.

48 For further reading on this see Okere (1983).

49 For instance the Fundamental Human Rights Enforcement Procedure Rules of 2000 provides the implementation mechanism for protecting the fundamental rights enshrined in the 1999 Constitution.

50 In the case of *Sani Abacha v. Gani Fawehinmi* (2000) 6 Nigerian Weekly Law Report (NWLR) (Part 660) at 228 the Supreme Court held that although the African Charter is superior to other laws, it is subordinate to the Constitution of Nigeria. It is interesting to note that the African Charter has been accorded superior status in some African countries. Also see *Onooha Kalu v. The State* (1998) 13 NWLR (Part 583). Compare the position of the Nigerian Supreme Court with the Indian Supreme Court. Just like Nigeria, economic social and cultural rights are not enforceable in India because those rights are contained in the part of the Constitution dealing with fundamental objectives and directive principles of state policy. However, the courts in India have through an expansive interpretation of the civil and political rights guaranteed under

Constitutional provisions can play an empowering role in engendering effective protection of the environment and strengthening of environmental institutions.[51] Constitutions can guarantee environmental rights, which are increasingly recognised as a fundamental human right to "adequate conditions of life".[52] However, as mentioned earlier, the realities of Nigeria being an oil-producing nation makes it imperative to make Section 20 justiciable or like in India, although there is no specific provision in their fundamental human rights chapter bestowing a right to clean environment, this right has been made incidental to fundamental rights, such as the right to life, through judicial activism.[53]

4.2 The National Adaptation Strategy and Plan of Action on Climate Change for Nigeria

In November 2011, Nigeria launched its National Adaptation Strategy and Plan of Action on Climate Change for Nigeria (NASPA-CCN).[54] The Strategy aims to ensure that climate change adaptation is an integral component of sustainable development.[55] The objectives of Nigeria's Climate Change Policy document are to reduce the impacts of climate change through adaptation measures that can be undertaken by the federal, state and local governments, civil society, the private sector, communities and individuals.

The climate change policy document recommended strategies for the following 13 priority sectors: agriculture, freshwater resources, coastal water resources and fisheries, forests, biodiversity, health and sanitation, human settlements and housing, energy, transportation and communications, industry and commerce, disaster, migration and security, livelihoods, vulnerable groups, and education. For instance, the strategy for agriculture includes to adopt better soil management practices and provide early warning/meteorological forecasts and to implement strategies for improved resource

---

its constitution, enforced and promoted economic social and political rights. See the case of *Olga Tellis v. Bombay Municipal Corporation* (1985) 3 SCC 545. See also Okenwa (2015).

51 Bruch et al. (2011).

52 There is a new trend of constitutions that guarantee environmental rights. These constitutions not only provide for environmental rights but also stipulate both environmental rights and duties, including the State's duties. For a review of environmental mental rights and duties in African constitutions, see C Bruch "Breathing Life into Fundamental Principles: Implementing Constitutional Environmental Protections in Africa. Environmental Governance in Africa" (2011) Working Papers Series World Resources Institute.

53 South Africa and India: *Minister of Health v. Treatment Action Campaign* 2002 (5) SA 721 (CC); and *Olga Tellis v. Bombay Municipal Corporation* (1985) 3 SCC 545.

54 See <http://nigeriaclimatechange.org/naspa.pdf> (accessed 10-12-2017).

55 The other strategies include: reduce the vulnerability and enhance the resilience and adaptive capacity of all economic sectors and of all people, particularly women, children, and resource-poor men; and capture the opportunities that arise as a result of climate change.

management, as in, increase use of irrigation systems that use low amounts of water; increase rainwater and sustainable groundwater harvesting for use in agriculture.

4.3 The 2007 National Environmental Standards and Regulations Enforcement Agency (Establishment) Act

The 2007 National Environmental Standards and Regulations Enforcement Agency (Establishment) Act (NESREA) established a National Environmental Standards and Regulations Enforcement Agency as the regulator charged with responsibility for the protection and development of the environment in Nigeria.[56] NESREA among other things is empowered to enforce all environmental laws, guidelines, policies, standards and regulations in Nigeria, as well as enforcing compliance with the provisions of all international agreements, protocols, conventions and treaties on the environment to which Nigeria is a signatory.[57] Within the context of climate change, the following regulations and standards have been set by NESREA: National Environmental (Ozone Layer Protection) Regulations, 2009; National Effluent Limitation Regulations, Special Instrument No. 8, 1991; National Environmental Protection (Effluent Limitation) Regulations, 1991; National Environmental (Control of Bush, Forest Fire and Open Burning) Regulations, 2011; and National Environmental (Control of Vehicular Emissions from Petrol and Diesel Engines) Regulations, 2011.

In furtherance of its overseeing role and in order to achieve an integrated climate change response, it is expected that NESREA will coordinate, supervise and monitor the implementation of these standards and regulations in a holistic manner. However, this will be nearly impossible without a comprehensive and coherent regulatory framework that ties everything together.

4.4 The National Policy on the Environment

The National Policy on Environment 1991, revised in 1999 and 2016 defines a new holistic framework to guide the management of the environment and natural resources and to ensure environmental protection and the conservation of natural resources for

56 NESREA website <http://www.nesrea.gov.ng/> (accessed 10-12-2017). The vision and mission of NESREA are "to ensure a cleaner and healthier environment for Nigerians" and "to inspire personal and collective responsibility in building an environmentally conscious society for the achievement of sustainable development in Nigeria".

57 Section 7 NESREA Act.

sustainable development.[58] The policy prescribes sectoral and cross-sectoral strategic policy statements and actions for the management of the different sector of the country's environment. The policy is guided by sound environmental principles such as the public trust doctrine,[59] the polluter pays principle, the precautionary principle, intra and inter-generational equity and an environmental right. The policy recognises emerging environmental challenges such as climate change, transboundary water resources, disasters, conflicts, genetically modified organisms and biosafety.

4.5 The 2006 National Forestry Policy

Nigeria's Forestry Policy[60] aims to encourage and support an aggressive establishment of plantations of economic trees and foster the redirection of development resources. The guiding principles of the policy are based on reducing the decline of forest resources and streamlining the contribution of forests to economic development and growth, particularly the National Economic Empowerment and Development Strategy (NEEDS).[61] The management strategy includes: (i) maintaining a sustainable supply of forest produce for internal consumption and exports; and (ii) increasing revenue to government. An examination of the strategy indicates that the policy is more concerned with the economic benefits of the forestry resources of Nigeria. There is little or no focus on its environmental management and conservation, its role in combating climate change[62] and achieving sustainable development. The shortcomings identified in this policy could be a result of the fact that the document was formulated in 2006 and it is due for an update to bring it up to speed with global best practices for forest management and governance.[63]

4.6 Proposed Bill to establish a National Climate Change Commission

There is a Climate Change Commission Bill pending before the Senate and the House of Representatives. The proposed Bill establishes a National Climate Change

58 National Policy on the Environment (revised 2016), at <http://environment.gov.ng/media/attachments/2017/09/22/revised-national-policy-on-the-environment-final-draft.pdf> (accessed 25-11-2017).

59 On John Sax's theory of Public Trust Doctrine, see Rose (1998).

60 See <www.fao.org/forestry/15148-0c4acebeb8e7e45af360ec63fcc4c1678.pdf> (accessed 12-12-2017).

61 The four key strategies of NEEDS are: reorienting values, reducing poverty, creating wealth and generating employment.

62 Forest is a veritable source for carbon sequestration and GHG mitigation.

63 For further reading on the National Forest Policy see Faleyimu & Agbeja (2012) and Aruofor (2003).

Commission as a statutory body with a mandate to manage and control climate change and other related environmental matters.[64] When passed into law, the Bill will provide appropriate policies, institutions and the required planning and coordination for climate change response and governance in Nigeria. Furthermore, the proposed Climate Change Commission, when it is eventually established, will take over and expand the current role and functions of the Department of Climate Change, which is currently subsumed under the Federal Ministry of Environment.

4.7 The Department of Climate Change

The Department of Climate Change is a parastatal under the Federal Ministry of Environment and is the national focal point for climate change in Nigeria.[65] The Department coordinates activities towards national implementation of the UNFCCC and the Kyoto Protocol. The Department collaborates with other relevant government organisations, non-governmental organisations, academia and private sector under a Committee known as Inter-ministerial Committee on Climate Change (ICCC).[66] The ICCC is a policy advisory organ under the Chairmanship of the Federal Ministry of Environment. The Committee meets regularly on a quarterly basis and on ad-hoc basis to review policies on climate change, to advise government on appropriate actions, and to present Nigeria's position at meetings where climate change issues are being discussed or negotiated. The Department serves as the Designated National Authority (DNA) for the implementation of Clean Development Mechanism (CDM) projects in Nigeria.

5 Nigeria's NDC commitment: gaps, contradictions and imperatives for sustainable development

Globe International,[67] a non-governmental organisation committed to developing and overseeing the implementation of local or national laws in pursuit of sustainable development and climate change, recently carried out an audit of climate change-related legislation across the globe. According to the study, countries in sub-Saharan Africa achieved major developments in formulating national plans and strategies on climate change.[68] Kenya adopted the 2013-2017 Climate Change Action Plan, Mozambique adopted the 2013-2025 National Strategy for Climate Change with the aim of reducing

64 Section 1 of the Bill <www.nassnig.org/nass2/legislation.php?id=1423> (accessed 12-12-2017).
65 See <http://www.climatechange.gov.ng/> (accessed 11-12-2017).
66 See <http://climatechange.gov.ng/what-we-do/> (accessed 10-7-2018).
67 See <http://globelegislators.org/about-globe> (accessed 11-12-2017).
68 See <http://www.globeinternational.org/pdfviewer> (accessed 11-12-17).

vulnerability to climate change and improving living conditions. Tanzania passed its National Strategy on REDD+ in March 2013. Rwanda approved its Second Economic Development and Poverty Reduction Strategy (2013-2018). However, it is important to note that national strategies, policies and plans such as Nigeria's NASPA-CCN only form the basis for future legislation and that they do not replace the need for national legislation on climate change.

There are several requirements for the NDCs. Generally, a country's NDC should: be ambitious in terms of its set goals; result in transformation of GHG intensive industries; be transparent, such that stakeholders can monitor effective implementation of stated goals; be equitable with regards to country's fair share of emission reduction burden; and ensure that climate change considerations are infused into relevant national policies and programmes such as those on sustainable development, environmental protection, poverty alleviation. However, and more importantly, individual country's NDC must establish linkages with the sustainable development goals (SDGs).

In a bid to achieve the NDCs, the Department of Climate Change of the Federal Ministry of Environment has developed action plans, policy and strategic documents such as the National Climate Change Strategy and Action Plan (2018-2022); the High-Level Road Map on Implementation of the Intended Nationally Determined Contributions (August 2016); and sectoral action plans of the agriculture, the forest, the industry, the oil and gas and the power and transport sectors. It has also launched Nigeria's Sovereign Green Bond in 2017; it is pursuing the passing of the Climate Change Bill at the National Assembly and is engaged in capacity building projects, advocacy, and tree planting and renewable energy/energy efficiency initiatives.[69]

However, despite these laudable strategies, there are existing (old) and relatively new national policies and action plans that threaten to jeopardise the achievement of Nigeria's NDC commitments, such as the Associated Gas Re-injection Act and its Associated Gas Re-injection (Continued Flaring of Gas) Regulations,[70] fuel subsidy, and Nigeria's Coal Power Project.

5.1 Oil and gas sector and flare out date

Gas flaring is the highest contributor to GHG emissions in Nigeria. The country is rated one of the highest gas flaring nations globally.[71] Developing countries are responsible for about 85% of the global emissions caused by flaring, and yet it is in these

69 Odogwu (2017).

70 Cap. A25 laws of the Federation of Nigeria, 2004. Note that there is a proposed amendment to this Act, namely the Associated Gas Re-injection (Amendment) Bill 2010.

71 World Bank (2016).

countries that the associated gas could, for example, be used to provide access to affordable and clean energy for industries and households use.

It is estimated that Nigeria has the ninth largest gas reserves in the world, with 192 tcf of gas reserves. Presently, large quantities of associated gas are produced with crude oil, and a significant quantity is unutilised and flared. Approximately 330Bscf (or 19%) is flared annually. Despite the abundant reserve, Nigeria suffers from an acute energy crisis (electricity) due to several factors, including the inability of the gas sector to meet domestic demand for power generation.

Nigeria's NDCs aim to achieve a flare out date by 2030. The mitigation measures identified in the oil and gas sector are the enforcement of gas flaring restrictions, the development of gas-to-power plants at sites where associated gas is being flared, the blending of 10% by volume of fuel-ethanol with gasoline (E10) and of 20% by volume of biodiesel with petroleum diesel (B20) for use in the transportation fuels sectors. Achieving the flare out date is important for climate change mitigation and equally important for the achievement of the SDGs. However, for Nigeria to achieve its flare out date of 2030, there are some hurdles to consider. Achieving the flare out date requires enabling laws and the effective implementation of such laws and regulations. The provision of infrastructures such as gas gathering infrastructure, the buy-in of oil and gas companies involved in gas flaring and the respective political will are required to achieve the flare out date. Further prerequisites include to remove barriers to the diffusion of clean fuel such as natural gas and subsidies for non-sustainable fuels such as kerosene, to discourage the use of 'dirty fuels' such as firewood and charcoal at the household level, and to enhance access to clean energy.

Gas flaring is the main environmental challenge in Niger Delta of Nigeria, and it contributes more to greenhouse gases than all other oil producing nation in sub-Saharan Africa combined.[72] The Nigeria National Gas Policy (2017) also acknowledges the fact that the flaring of natural gas that is produced in association with oil is one of the most egregious environmental and energy waste practices in the Nigerian petroleum industry.[73] The practice of gas flaring continues in Nigeria, although, it has reduced. Although Nigeria still flares a significant portion of its gross natural gas production (19% of AG, 331 sbcf in 2015), the amount of gas flared has significantly reduced in recent years.[74] According to the ranking of top 30 flaring countries, Nigeria is ranked 6th highest flaring nation between the period 2013 to 2017.[75]

72 Aghalino (2009); Eregha & Irughe (2009); Emoyan et al. (2008); and Kachikwu (2017: 9).

73 National Gas Policy: Nigerian Government Policy and Action 2017, at <http://www.petroleumindustrybill.com/wp-content/uploads/2017/06/National-Gas-Policy-Approved-By-FEC-in-June-2017.pdf> (accessed 10-7-2018).

74 See <http://businessnews.com.ng/2016/11/18/fg-to-introduce-new-penalty-for-gas-flaring/> (accessed 10-7-2018).

75 See <http://www.worldbank.org/en/programs/gasflaringreduction#7> (accessed 15-11-2018).

The Associated Gas Reinjection Act 1979 and its Associated Gas Re-injection (Continued Flaring of Gas) Regulations[76] were the main regulatory framework for gas flaring in Nigeria until 2018 when the Flare Gas (Prevention of Waste and Pollution Regulations) 2018[77] was signed into law by the President of Nigeria. The Regulation is made pursuant to Section 9 of the Petroleum Act and Section 5 of the Associated Gas Re-Injection Act. The Regulation introduces a new and stiffer payment of penalties for gas flaring,[78] it adopts the polluters pay principle and it mimics a carbon tax regime. The Regulation further imposes reporting obligations on producers and flare out projects for the purpose of data reporting for gas flaring activities at project site. The Regulation has increased the payment of penalties from the meagre N10 (Naira) per thousand standard cubic feet to $2 per thousand standard cubic feet of gas. Nigeria having ratified the Paris Agreement, and being a signatory to the Global Gas Flaring Partnership (GGFR) principles for global flare-out by 2030 whilst committing to a national flare-out target by year 2020. Furthermore, the Nigerian Gas Flare Commercialisation Programme ("NGFCP") was established to harness gas that was hitherto flared in order to, amongst other objectives, stimulate economic growth, drive investments, provide jobs and protect the environment from the menace of gas flaring.[79] The objective of the NGFCP is to eliminate gas flaring through sustainable gas utilisation projects developed by third party investors who will participate in a competitive and transparent bid process. The Programme also aims to implement the National Gas Policy commitments for stricter regulation on flaring and to provide a pathway to ultimate flare-out.[80]

5.2 Nigeria's coal-to-power generation project

The Federal Government in 2017 partnered with the African Development Bank (AfDB) to fund coal projects in Nigeria. The Ministry of Mines and Steel Development and the Ministry of Power are collaborating on the coal projects which is expected to account for about 30% of the country's power mix.[81] The project plans to generate

76 Cap. A25 laws of the Federation of Nigeria, 2004. The Act and the regulation made pursuant to it failed woefully in addressing the perennial problem of gas flaring and energy resource waste in Nigeria.

77 See S.I. No. 9 of 2018.

78 The former penalty was gas flare penalty of N10/Mscf (equivalent US$0.03) of associated gas flared.

79 See <http://www.ngfcp.gov.ng/about-us/welcome-by-the-steering-committee-chairman/> (accessed 15-11-2018).

80 National Gas Policy: Nigerian Government Policy and Action 2017, at <http://www.petroleumindustrybill.com/wp-content/uploads/2017/06/National-Gas-Policy-Approved-By-FEC-in-June-2017.pdf.> (accessed 10-7-2018).

81 Adoyi (2017).

about 30% of electricity through coal. This definitely negates the commitments under the NDCs and Nigeria's gas policy because coal mining is the highest source of GHG emissions. Furthermore, this project would impact on water management strategies, huge freshwater demand, ocean acidification, and air, water and land pollution, which negates Nigeria's climate change and sustainable development strategy.

5.3 The energy sector

In the energy sector, the NDCs aim to increase the use of renewable energy in Nigeria's energy mix, build multi-cycle power stations, increase the capacity of existing power stations by 20-50 MW, enhance energy efficiency by attaining 2% per year energy efficiency culminating in 30% efficiency by 2030, and encourage use of natural gas rather than liquid fuels. Prior to the privatisation of the electricity sector in Nigeria, the sector performed below expectations, and some would argue that in spite of privatisation, the sector is still performing below expectations.[82]

A state enterprise known as the National Electric Power Authority (NEPA) was established as an integrated monopoly services provider responsible for generation, transmission, distribution and sales of electricity faced overwhelming challenges in terms of its three core areas of power generation, transmission and distribution.[83] Some of the challenges that plagued the now defunct NEPA included: a lack of infrastructural development to match Nigeria burgeoning population and commercial activities; funding, irregular maintenance and obsolete power plants; inefficient and grossly inadequate transmission capabilities; vandalisation of transmission infrastructures and distribution facilities; inadequate power distribution facilities; poor revenue collection system; fragile and overloaded distribution networks; an inaccurate and unreliable billing system; and corruption and mismanagement of funds.[84] Liberalisation and commercialisation of the sector led to the Electricity Act of 1990 and its Amendment Act of 1988, the dissolution of NEPA and its replacement with the Power Holding Company of Nigeria (PHCN).[85] The current governance structure and legal framework for the electricity sector in Nigeria is the Electric Power Sector Reform (EPSR) Act, 2005.

---

82 Adeyemo & Salami (2008: 408).

83 Sections 1 and 7 of the National Electric Power Authority Act 1972, LFN. For example, the current electricity grid is unable to reliably serve the teeming population and the industrial sector, most rural communities remain off the grid and about 60% of the population lack access to electricity. As a result of this shortfall in generation capacity, generators are widely used to meet household and industry energy needs. These generators are inefficient and polluting. See also Amokaye (2015: 737).

84 Omoluabi (2012).

85 For a historical overview of the electricity reform in Nigeria, see Oke (2013).

This Act unbundled the State's stake in the power sector,[86] especially the generation and marketing elements, and it made electricity generation, sales and marketing open to independent power providers.

The current grid generation capacity is unable to meet the energy needs of industrial and urban consumers. As a result of this shortfall, industrial and other consumers have resorted to the use of inefficient and polluting generators for electricity. In addition, most rural communities remain off the grid, and it is estimated that at the current rate of grid expansion, these communities will remain largely under-served, and about 60% of the population lack access to electricity.[87] Of particular importance to Nigeria's NDC commitments is the infrastructural deficiency with regards to the distribution of electricity and the diversification of the national grid and diversification of energy mix to include renewables such as wind, solar and energy. The EPSR Act is silent on the issue of diversifying Nigeria's energy mix. However, the National Energy Master Plan (NEMP) and National Renewable Energy & Energy Efficiency Policy (NREEEP),[88] 2014 are policy documents that seek to address this gap. The NEMP provides the roadmap for achieving Nigeria's energy objectives in relevant sectors of the economy. In that regard, the NEPM focuses on all energy sources including renewable energy and efficiency and other crosscutting issues such as energy financing, capacity development. For instance, to achieve Nigeria's renewable energy objective and to encourage the diffusion of renewables, the NEMP recommends that an enabling regulatory and financial environment should be created in order to attract foreign direct investment and indigenous participation in renewable energy.[89]

However, more is required to ensure availability of affordable energy options, incentives to encourage diversification of the energy mix, and devolution of governance to local communities' governmental structure, in order to maximise the benefit of the reformed electricity sector in Nigeria. Furthermore, the proposed policy documents will ensure a robust and sustainable energy mix and the development of varied renewable energy sources in Nigeria.

86 Note, however, that states usually retain control of electricity transmission and distribution, which are natural monopolies for national security reasons.

87 Nigeria's Intended Nationally Determined Contribution, at <http://www4.unfccc.int/submissions/INDC/Published%20Documents/Nigeria/1/Approved%20Nigeria's%20INDC_271115.pdf> (accessed 30-11-2017).

88 See <http://www.energy.gov.ng/> (accessed 30-11-2017). Note that these documents are currently open for review and comments.

89 See <www.energy.gov.ng.> (accessed 10-7-2018).

6 Nigeria's NDC commitments: imperatives towards harnessing the sustainable development benefits of the Paris Agreement

Response to climate change and emission reductions are undertaken on the basis of equity, sustainable development and efforts to eradicate poverty, which are critical development priorities for many developing countries. Although climate change will inevitably cause challenges to Nigeria's growth, it also provides an opportunity for the country to grow faster and cleaner and for Nigeria to develop her own capacity for industrialisation. Furthermore, the Paris Agreement provides a strong basis for response to climate change, and to achieve sustainable development through effective implementation of national NDCs. However, for Nigeria to seize the opportunities inherent in the Paris Agreement for mitigation and adaptation to climate change and to fulfil its commitments under the Paris Agreement, it has to address some of the legislative and regulatory challenges highlighted above.

It is imperative, therefore, that the NDC strategies and goals are mainstreamed into all national development strategies and the SDGs currently being implemented. To that end, this chapter proffers the following recommendations:

- A legislative audit of existing laws and regulations, which will help to eradicate the current overlaps and inconsistencies in the various legislations that will invariably affect NDC implementation. A comprehensive regulatory and institutional framework will ensure that climate change mitigation and adaptation strategies and policies are integrated with long-term national development plans and policies. Coherence is necessary between the regulatory and institutional frameworks on the ground in order to ensure that they work in synergy in order to achieve sustainable development – a panacea to the adverse effects of climate change.
- Establish links between NDCs and domestic strategy and policy agenda. An NDC that is strongly linked with the domestic strategy and policy agenda has a greater chance of promoting sustainable development and meeting national targets. This can be achieved by unpacking the NDC at sectoral levels such that high-level policies and goals translate into actionable roadmaps among the relevant sectors of the economy.
- Establish a strong and adequate institutional and regulatory framework that will enhance development, coordination and implementation of climate policies and programmes nationally. Strong and independent government agencies should have a key role such that they can coordinate and drive the NDC implementation process amongst the relevant sectors of the economy. To achieve this, Nigeria should eradicate institutional barriers and rivalry amongst national agencies and improve coordination at the national level. The institutional framework must ensure that key agencies or ministries work together.

- Assess capacity building needs across government agencies and coordinate capacity building amongst relevant ministries and agencies. Relevant ministries and agencies should identify potential capacity needs. This will increase Nigeria's capacity to initiate and implement climate change policies and programmes and also to attract climate finance and investments. Furthermore, the relevant ministries and agencies should raise awareness among stakeholders about the benefits of the implementation of the NDCs.
- Identify mitigation potentials in key sectors of the economy. Nigeria should invest in research and data collation on issues such as in-country analysis of GHGs and the development of GHG inventories, an understanding of mitigation potentials in key sectors of the economy, and baseline study in order to determine GHG projections and implement mitigation strategies.
- Establish clear links to the 2015 SDGs. This creates an unprecedented opportunity to set a clear path for development for the next generation. Action on climate change is essential in meeting development aims, including poverty eradication, health, education, food and energy security. The various agreements on climate change, including the Paris Agreement, and the SDGs should be seen as complementary, with opportunities for mutual benefit in areas such as low carbon development, climate adaptation and resilience.

7 Conclusion

The NDCs are only one of many steps on a long road to the ultimate objective of a comprehensive climate change regime. They provide the mandate and framework for concerted action. The challenge now is to implement the NDCs at national levels towards a low carbon and climate resilient future at all levels. Good NDCs should be ambitious; result in a transformation in carbon-intensive sectors and industries; be transparent, so that stakeholders can track progress and ensure countries meet their stated goals; and be equitable in order that each country does its fair share to address climate change. For many developing countries, apart from domestic efforts discussed in the recommendations, the successful implementation of NDCs requires continued financial and other support from developed countries to enhance national capacity and a successful transition to a low carbon economy.

References

Abaje, I, C Ndabula & AH Garba (2014) "Is the changing rainfall patterns of Kano State and its adverse impact an indication of climate change?" 10(2) *European Scientific Journal* 192-206.

Adeyemo, D & A Salami (2008) "A review of privatization and public enterprises reform in Nigeria" 4(4) *Contemporary Management Research* 401.

Adoyi, A (2017) "FG partners ADB on coal power generation" *Daily Post* (25-4-2017), at <http://dailypost.ng/2017/04/25/fg-partners-adb-coal-power-generation/.> (accessed 10-7-2018).

African Climate Policy Centre (2011) *Climate change and health across Africa: issues and options* Working Paper 20, at <https://www.uncclearn.org/sites/default/files/inventory/uneca15.pdf> (accessed 20-7-18).

Aghalino, SO (2009) "Gas flaring, environmental pollution and abatement measures in Nigeria 1969-2001" 11(4) *Journal of Sustainable Development in Africa* 219-238.

Amokaye, O (2015) *Environmental law and practice in Nigeria* 2nd edition.

Aruofor, R (2003) *Forestry outlook studies in Africa: Nigeria*, at <http://www.fao.org/tempref/docrep/fao/005/y8732e/y8732e00.pdf> (accessed 20-7-2018).

Bob, U & S Bronkhorst (2010) "Environmental conflicts: key issues and management implications" 10(2) *African Journal on Conflict Resolution* 9-30, at <https://www.ajol.info/index.php/ajcr/article/view/63307/51191> (accessed 20-7-2018).

Bruch, C, W Coker & C Van Arsdale (2001) *Breathing life into fundamental principles: implementing constitutional environmental protections in Africa. Environmental governance in Africa* Working Papers Series World Resources Institute, at <http://www.wri.org/sites/default/files/eaa_bruch.pdf> (accessed 20-7-2018).

Conway, G (2009) *The science of climate change in Africa: impacts and adaptation* Grantham Institute for Climate Change Discussion Paper No. 1, at <https://ag4impact.org/wp-content/uploads/2010/05/Grantham_Institue_-_The_science_of_climate_change_in_Africa.pdf> (accessed 11-10-2017).

Cortner, HJ, MG Wallace, S Burke & MA Moote (1988) "Institutions matter: the need to address the institutional challenges of ecosystem management" 40 *Journal of Landscape and Urban Planning* 159-166.

Emoyan, OO, IA Akpoborie & EE Akpohonor (2008) "The oil and gas industry and the Niger Delta implication for the environment" 12(3) *Journal of Applied Science Environmental Management* 29-37.

Eregha, PB & IR Irughe (2009) "Oil induced environmental degradation in Nigeria's Niger-Delta: the multiplier effects" 11(4) *Journal of Sustainable Development in Africa* 160-175.

Fagbohun, O (2002) "Reappraising the Nigerian Constitution for environmental management" 1(1) *Ambrose Alli University Law Journal* 24-47.

Faleyimu, O & B Agbeja (2012) "Constraints to forest policy implementation in the Southwest Nigeria: causes, consequences and cure" 2(2) *Journal of Resources and Environment* 37-44.

Fatile, J & S Adejobi (2012) "Climate change, environment and conflicts in Nigeria" 6(1) *British Journal of Arts and Social Sciences* 11-20.

Fatile, J, OS Adejobi & RO Olorunnimbe (2012) "Vulnerability to climate change and conflict in Nigeria" 4 *Journal of Social Science and Public Policy* 42-83.

FAO / Food and Agriculture Organisation of the United Nations (2008) *Climate change and food security: a framework document*, at <http://www.fao.org/docrep/010/k2595e/k2595e00.htm> (accessed 31-12-2017).

Hare, W, C Stockwell, C Flachsland & S Oberthür (2010) "The architecture of the global climate regime: a top-down perspective" 10(6) *Climate Policy* 600-614.

Ibeabuchi, U, AU Egbu & OA Kalu (2018) "Coastal megacities: the case of Lagos" 2(4) *International Journal of Research and Innovation in Social Science* 47-58, at <http://www.rsisinternational.org/journals/ijriss/Digital-Library/volume-2-issue-4/47-58.pdf> (accessed 10-07-2018)

IPCC / Intergovernmental Panel on Climate Change (2014) *Climate change 2014: Synthesis Report* Contribution of Working Groups I, II and III to the Fifth Assessment Report of the Intergovernmental Panel on Climate Change [Core Writing Team, R.K. Pachauri and L.A. Meyer (eds)].

Kachikwu, EI (2017) *Environmental law and the Niger Delta imperatives.*

Mansbach, R & K Taylor (2012) *Introduction to global politics.*

Nachmany, M, S Fankhauser, J Davidová, N Kingsmill, T Landesman, H Roppongi, P Schleifer, J Setzer, A Sharman, C Stolle Singleton, J Sundaresan & T Townshend (2015) *The 2015 global climate legislation study: a review of climate change legislation in 99 countries*, at <http://www.lse.ac.uk/GranthamInstitute/wp-content/uploads/2015/05/Global_climate_legislation_study_20151.pdf> (accessed 31-12-2017).

Odogwu, G (2017) "Contradictions in Nigeria's Nationally Determined Contributions" *Punch* (2-11-2017), at <http://punchng.com/contradictions-in-nigerias-nationally-determined-contributions/> (accessed 27-11-2017).

Oke, Y (2013) *Nigerian electricity law and regulation.*

Okenwa, CA (2015) "Has the controversy between the superiority of international law and municipal law been resolved in theory and practice?" 35 *Journal of Law, Policy and Globalization* 116-124.

Okere BO (1983) "Fundamental objectives and directive principles of state policy under the Nigerian Constitution" 32 *International and Comparative Law Quarterly* 214-228.

Omoluabi, VS (2012) *An appraisal of the legal framework for the privatization and reform programme for the energy sector in Nigeria*, at <http://kubanni.abu.edu.ng/jspui/bitstream/123456789/731/1/AN%20APPRAISAL%20OF%20THE%20LEGAL%20FRAMEWORK%20FOR%20THE%20PRIVATIZATION%20AND%20REFORM%20PROGRAMME%20FOR%20THE%20ENERGY%20SECTOR%20IN%20NIGERIA.pdf> (accessed 20-7-2018).

Parry, ML, OF Canziani, JP Palutikof, PJ van der Linden & CE Hanson (eds) (2007) *Climate change 2007: impacts, adaptation and vulnerability.* Contribution of Working Group II to the Fourth Assessment Report of the Intergovernmental Panel on Climate Change.

Raleigh, C, L Jordan & I Salehyan (2008) *Assessing the impact of climate change on migration and conflict*, Working Paper at <http://siteresources.worldbank.org/EXTSOCIALDEVELOPMENT/Resources/SDCCWorkingPaper_MigrationandConflict.pdf> (accessed 20-7-2018).

Rose, CM (1998) *Joseph Sax and the idea of the public trust* Faculty Scholarship Series Paper 1805, at <http://digitalcommons.law.yale.edu/fsspapers/1805> (accessed 20-7-2018).

Salkida, A (2012) "Africa's vanishing Lake Chad: Action needed to counter an "ecological catastrophe" *Africa Renewal Magazine*, at <http://www.un.org/africarenewal/magazine/april-2012/africa%E2%80%99s-vanishing-lake-chad> (31-12-2017).

Stern, N (2006) *Stern review: the economics of climate change.*

Tadesse, D (2010) *The impact of climate change in Africa.*

Tunde, A (2011) "Perception of climate variability on agriculture and food security by men and women farmers in Idanre L.G.A, Ondo State Nigeria" 4(2) *Ethiopian Journal of Environmental Studies and Management* 19-32.

van Asselt, H & F Zelli (2018) "International governance" in Jordan, A, D Huitema, H van Asselt & J Forster *Governing climate change – polycentricity in action?* 29-46.

World Bank (2016) "Top 30 gas flaring nations" at <http://www.worldbank.org/content/dam/photos/780x439/2016/dec/Slide2.JPG> (accessed 20-7-2018).

Chapter 4:
Bridging the gap between climate change and energy policy options: what next for Nigeria?

Morakinyo Adedayo Ayoade

1 Introduction

The disruption of the global climatic system as a result of human developmental activities is responsible for climate change concerns constituting a definitive issue for the 21st century. Stakeholders as varied as international organisations, governments, business, non-governmental organisations (NGOs) and the world's population, are interested in this complex issue. Discussions on climate change are difficult due to the different interests of powerful stakeholders. This is particularly the case, where there is a direct clash in policy interests such as that between climate change and the energy sector. Policy makers are important in this context as the need to balance the interests of competing parties at the international and domestic arena, means there is a need to achieve a modicum of consensus say between developed country consumers and poor developing countries.

While climate change policy is primarily driven at international level due to the integrated nature of the global ecosystem, the centrality of nation states means that any meaningful analysis of the topic requires national perspectives. Climate change refers to the altered response of the climatic system to increased concentrations of greenhouse gases (GHGs) in the atmosphere.[1] Scientific convergence, despite some skeptics, indicates that a notable increase in the average temperature of the Earth's atmosphere, oceans and land mass will result in devastating weather pattern shifts causing loss of biodiversity, heat waves, drought, rising sea level, human migration, decreased agricultural yields, etc.[2]

Climate change policy concerns specific guidelines or strategies formulated at the international, national, or even local level to address climate change. This can be climate mitigation focused on minimising the extent of climate change; or climate adaptation that tries to minimise risks posed by the consequences of climate change. Energy policy, on the other hand, is concerned with the way and manner energy development

1 Hunter et al. (1998: 609).
2 Zaelke & Cameron (1990: 253-260).

issues such as production, distribution and consumption are treated. It encompasses oil and gas exploration and development, refining, renewable energy, coal and electricity.

Climate change and energy are intrinsically linked, as energy is central to the development of modern society. Today, prosperity is based on the production and consumption of large amounts of energy, which is problematic as energy accounts for about 75% of total GHG emissions and 80% of carbon dioxide (CO_2).[3] The threat of climate change is addressed by an evolving and increasingly sophisticated legal architecture that is based on the UN Framework Convention on Climate Change (UNFCCC) 1992, the Kyoto Protocol 1997 and the Paris Agreement 2016. Also potentially relevant are regional and sub-regional pronouncements on climate change. Interestingly, anxiety about climate change and advocacy for action started as far back as the 1970s and continued into the 1980s until the UNFCCC came into play.[4] Parallel to this are some key energy documents such as the United Nations Sustainable Energy for All Initiative 2012 and International Energy Charter 2015.[5]

Climate change imperatives directly confront the interests of developing producer nations, particularly, those like Nigeria which is a mono-product economy that is dependent on foreign sales of crude oil and gas for economic growth. A member of the Organisation of Petroleum Exporting Countries (OPEC) since 1971, Nigeria is the largest oil and gas producer in Africa that also controls its largest natural gas reserves. Unfortunately, the country is experiencing problems with crude oil refining, as well as a huge deficit in electricity production that is urgently needed for its ever-expanding population. This is despite being richly endowed with coal and bitumen as well as renewable energy sources like solar, wind, biomass and hydro resources.

On the face of it, there is a direct conflict between Nigeria's economic and development interests and the demands for climate change action mostly emanating from the international sphere and mostly caused by industrialisation activities in developed countries. There is thus a tension between the short-term national interest and the need to transition to sustainable energy systems. That said, Nigeria has put in place an extensive network of energy policies potentially impacting climate change. This majorly includes the National Energy Policy 2003, Renewable Energy Action Program (REAP) 2006, Bio-Fuels Policy 2007 and the National Renewable Energy and Energy Efficiency Policy (NREEEP) 2015.

The chapter adopts an analytical methodology to critically evaluate Nigeria's response to its international climate change obligations in the context of energy policy.[6] Therefore, the chapter is arranged as follows: Part 2 provides the contextual

3 International Energy Agency (2018).

4 Ong (2010: 450-451).

5 Please note that the chapter will be limited to these documents and will not include all international energy documentation.

6 Note that the focus of the chapter is on climate change and energy and no attempt will be made to engage environmental policy or related issues.

background linking climate change and energy; Part 3 assesses international climate change and energy-related obligations accepted by Nigeria; while Part 4 deals with the relationship between Nigerian energy policy and climate change. Part 5 integrates climate change and national energy policy. It is argued that there is a need to integrate radically climate change and energy policy. It further observes that difficult decisions have to be taken if Nigeria is to eventually transit to a low carbon economy based on its policy choices.

2 Contextual background: linkages between climate change and energy

The issue of climate change is quite complex and controversial as there is some scientific disagreement on the criteria for climate change.[7] According to the Intergovernmental Panel on Climate Change (IPCC), climate change constitutes:[8]

> a change in the state of the climate that can be identified [e.g., by using statistical tests] by changes in the mean and/or the variability of its properties and that persists for an extended period, typically decades or longer.

Thus, climate change includes sporadic weather events as well as the slow rise in global mean surface temperature.[9] Essentially, the IPCC's definition refers to any change in climate over time, whether due to natural variability or human activity. Meanwhile, the UNFCCC defines climate change as attributes directly or indirectly linked to human activity that alters the composition of the global atmosphere – in addition to natural climate variability – observed over comparable periods of time.[10] According to Kerr[11], the main cause of climate change is attributable to "higher concentrations of greenhouse gases in the earth's atmosphere leading to increased trapping of infrared radiation". Climate change thus poses a threat to sustainable development, socio-economic development, human rights and efforts to protect the environment.[12] Major GHGs such as carbon dioxide, methane, nitrous dioxide and chlorofluorocarbons (CFCs) are emitted from energy generating fossil fuels. For this reason, industrialised countries are alarmed at the projected upward trend in fossil energy use in developing countries,[13] despite their free use of fossil fuels to climb up the development ladder.

---

7 Todorov (1986: 258-259); United Nations Framework Convention on Climate Change (1992); Smith (2017: 22).
8 IPCC (2007).
9 Ifeanyi-Obi (2012); Smith et al. (2017: 22).
10 IPCC (2007).
11 Kerr (2002).
12 Segger (2016: 202-203).
13 Sagar (2006: 71).

Climate change particularly engages the energy sector due to the centrality of energy as the source of problems as well as a solution.[14] Today, energy security and climate change concerns are challenging due to existing energy systems based on fossil fuels.[15] Energy security refers to the availability of adequate, reliable and affordable energy, which is a necessity for modern economies. Hence, the need for well-designed energy policies capable of addressing complex issues, as national energy policies stretch to include international treaties, legislation, regulation, guidelines etc. Furthermore, energy policies address climate change and seek to reconcile global policy objectives with domestic law and interests.[16]

Fossil fuels such as oil, natural gas and coal currently dominate the global energy mix and are responsible for about 80% of commercial energy supply.[17] This is driven by economics as fossil fuels are relatively low cost, energy dense, flexible and highly convenient when compared with nuclear power and renewable energy resources.[18] Energy services underpin human activity and civilisation by fueling needs as diverse as cooking, heating, lighting, industry, health, education, communication and transport.[19] Put simply, energy equals development as there is a correlation between GDP growth and per-capita energy consumption.

Nigeria is influential on the global energy sector due to its status as the world's sixth largest crude oil exporter. Its crude oil reserves are put at 37.2 billion barrels, and natural gas reserves are estimated at 187 trillion cubic feet.[20] Notwithstanding these energy advantages, the country contributes to climate change by flaring an estimated 2.5 million cubic feet of gas per day which is equivalent to the daily consumption of all African countries.[21] This means that over 400 million tons of carbon are vented into the atmosphere.[22] Also, its overdependence on crude oil exports has negatively impacted on industrial activities and agriculture; worsening its development trajectory. But importantly, climate change is already manifesting in the nation with intensifying soil erosion, landslides, seasonal droughts, and excessive flooding threatening its extensive coastline.[23] In parts of northern Nigeria, villages have been abandoned due to

---

14 Beecher & Kalmbach (2012: 4).

15 Hansen (2008).

16 Farah & Rossi (2011: 232). Elements of an energy policy include the level of energy sufficiency of the nation, the location of future energy sources, and how it will be consumed, as well as national security and foreign policy considerations. See Hamilton (2013).

17 MacGill (2008: 86).

18 Ibid.

19 World Energy Council (2007).

20 Nwaogaidu (2013: 163).

21 Ismail & Umukoro (2012: 292).

22 Ogbodo & Stewart (2014: 17-18).

23 Akinyemi (2014: 48); National Adaptation Strategy and Plan of Action on Climate Change for Nigeria (NASPA-CCN) (November 2011), iii-iv, at <http://csdevnet.org/wp-content/uploads/NATIONAL-ADAPTATION-STRATEGY-AND-PLAN-OF-ACTION.pdf> (accessed 27-12-2017).

encroaching desertification and migration of animal herders has caused violent clashes with farming communities throughout the country.

Interestingly, Nigeria is blessed with both conventional and non-conventional renewable energy sources scattered across the country. Renewable energy, in the form of energy produced from solar, wind, sustainably managed hydro, geothermal and biomass resources, is available as an alternative to fossil fuels. Hydropower generation is vulnerable to changing weather patterns due to its sensitivity to the amount, timing and geographical spread of rainfall.[24] Such is the complexity of the climate change debate and susceptibility to new scientific evidence that it is worthy to note that there is some dispute on hydro and biomass as legitimate sources of renewable energy.[25]

Table 1: Nigeria's energy reserves/potentials[26]

Resource	Reserves	Reserves Billion toe	% Fossil
Crude oil	33 billion bbl	4.488	31.1
Natural gas	4502.4 billion m^3 (159 trillion scf)	3.859	26.7
Coal & Lignite	2.7 billion tones	1.882	13.0
Tar Sands	31 billion bbl oil equiv.	4.216	29.2
Sub-Total (Fossil Fuels)		**14.445**	**100.0**
Hydropower, large scale	10,000MW		
Hydropower, small scale	734 MW	Provisional	
Fuelwood	13,071,464 has (forest land 1981)	Estimate	
Animal waste	61million tones/yr	" "	
Crop Residue	83million tones/yr	" "	
Solar Radiation	3.5-7.0kWh/m^2-day		
Wind	2-4 m/s (annual average)		

24 Ladan (2009: 7-8).
25 Daigneau (2013); Mckie (2017).
26 Source: Renewable Energy Master Plan.

3 International climate change and energy-related obligations

3.1 International instruments on climate change

The starting point on international action to combat climate change commenced at the Earth Summit in Rio de Janeiro in 1992 when 154 countries joined the United Nations Framework Convention on Climate Change (UNFCCC). This foundation treaty sets the ground rules for inter-state cooperation. To assist easy acceptance, it does not oblige countries to make quantitative reductions to GHG emissions, nor does it have an enforcement mechanism. Entering into force on 21 March 1994, the key provision of the UNFCCC is stated in Article 2 titled objectives:

> The ultimate objective of this Convention and any related legal instrument that the Conference of the Parties may adapt is to achieve, in accordance with the relevant provisions of the Convention, stabilization of greenhouse gas concentrations in the atmosphere at a level that would prevent dangerous anthropogenic interference with the climate system. Such a level should be achieved within a time frame sufficient to allow ecosystems to adapt naturally to climate change, to ensure that food production is not threatened and to enable economic development to proceed in a sustainable manner.

The provision evidences the need to stabilise GHGs to avoid dangerous disruption of the climatic system within time frames that would allow for natural adaptation. This is in line with the preamble of the UNFCCC which acknowledged that climate change and its adverse impact are a "common concern of mankind". Also important is the acknowledgement that climate change action can only be effective through an international response that integrates cooperation among all countries.

While cooperation on the part of all countries is required, there is some recognition that a 'one size fits all' approach will not work due to the development gap between developed and developing countries.[27] Noting that developed and developing states have common but differentiated responsibilities and respective capabilities is a realistic posture on past responsibility and actual ability to act. Thus, Annex I parties primarily comprises of developed countries, while non-Annex I parties are made up of developing nations like Nigeria. The only soft commitments in the UNFCCC are on Annex I parties who are obliged to adapt national policies to mitigate climate change in order to return emissions to 1990 levels. At the same time, the extent to which

27 Article 3(1) UNFCCC states that: "The parties should protect the climate system for the benefit of present and future generations of mankind, on the basis of equity and in accordance with their common but differentiated responsibilities and respective capabilities. Accordingly, the developed country Parties should take the lead in combating climate change and the adverse effects thereof". The principle is also replicated in the Kyoto Protocol. Perhaps an alternative approach is to consider climate change from the polluter pays principle prism which will demand that developed countries are responsible for climate change and thus should bear the costs of prevention and remediation. See Maguire (2012: 109-110).

developing countries can meet their commitments is dependent on developed countries financial and technical assistance.

International moves against climate change were taken further when the Kyoto Protocol was concluded on 11 December 1997. The Protocol is a global agreement concluded under the terms of the UNFCCC and was the result of over two years of intense negotiations. Unlike the UNFCCC, it establishes for the first time, binding emission limits for developed country parties. Such parties are required to reduce their collective GHG emissions by 5.2% compared to 1990 levels between 2008 and 2012. Nonetheless, the Protocol softens the impact of binding targets by allowing developed countries access to three flexible implementation mechanisms that recognise compliance costs in meeting emissions targets. These market-based instruments integrate private sector and developing country participation in reducing GHG emissions. The Kyoto mechanisms are: (i) emissions trading that allows a country that has higher emissions to purchase the right to emit more, whilst a country with fewer emissions can trade its right to emit to other developed countries; (ii) the Clean Development Mechanism (CDM) allows developed countries to reduce emissions by financing emission reduction projects, e.g., planting a forest in developing states like Nigeria; and (iii) joint implementation which allows a developed country to invest in an emission reduction project in another developed country as a means of reducing emissions.[28]

More recent efforts to strengthen climate action are contained in the Paris Agreement of 2015. 150 heads of state and government gathered at the Conference of the Parties (COP) 21 in Paris summoned the political will for unprecedented action. Article 2(1)(a) of the Agreement pushes state parties to toughen the global response to climate change by:

> Holding the increase in the global average temperature to well below 2°C above pre-industrial levels and pursuing efforts to limit the temperature increase to 1.5°C above pre-industrial levels, recognizing that this would significantly reduce the risks and impact of climate change.

This ambitious target saw over 1,300 non-state actors such as major companies and large cities participate in pledging to meet global emissions reductions. The Paris Agreement represents six years of complex negotiations under the UNFCCC, with the added pressure of trying to avoid the fate of the failed 2009 Copenhagen Conference. Moreover, the Agreement provides for a universal and nationally driven approach that differentiates nations on the basis of capacity and not developed or developing country.

Unlike the Kyoto Protocol, the Paris Agreement does not formulate country-specific targets. Instead, it relies on voluntary mitigation measures and progressively ambitious mitigation contributions. Furthermore, the Agreement puts in place an enhanced transparency and accountability framework for countries in which there is frequent reporting on internationally agreed emission standards; progress tracking every two years to

28 Thornton & Beckwith (2004: 60-61).

ensure countries are on course; as well as a robust expert review of progress and targets achievements to avoid corner cutting.[29]

Put simply, the Paris Agreement provides a common framework that allows countries to determine their nationally determined contributions taking into account their capacities as well as the overall goal of the agreement. This collaborative approach seems to provide the basis for concerted long-term cooperation over climate change, though the jury is still out.

3.1.1 United Nations Sustainable Energy for All Initiative 2012

The years 2014-2024 have been declared the Decade of Sustainable Energy for All (SE4ALL) by the UN General Assembly in Resolution 65/151 in 2012, which cements the importance of energy to sustainable development and climate change mitigation. Three objectives are to be achieved by 2030: universal access to modern energy services; doubling the improvement rate in energy efficiency, and doubling the renewable energy share in the global energy mix.[30] It recognises that mounting energy emissions are a contributor to climate change and that the provision of cleaner and more efficient sustainable energy is in the interest of all countries.

The SE4ALL is an initiative driven by the Office of the Secretary General of the United Nations. Perhaps influential at best, it does not have the solidity of a global instrument prescribing standards of behaviour to member states. Considered together with the International Renewable Energy Agency (IRENA), an intergovernmental organisation that supports countries transiting to sustainable energy, it provides strong policy directions that underscore the significance of sustainable development and the push towards low carbon economic growth and prosperity. All of these have influential overtones on 150 SE4ALL countries policymakers, including Nigeria.

3.1.2 International Energy Charter 2015

The International Energy Charter (IEC) in its preamble states that it is a political intention declaration merely aimed at strengthening energy cooperation between signatories and does not result in financially or legally binding obligations. This Charter, however, sets out a framework for long-term cooperation at the regional and global

---

29 OPEC (2016). The Organisation of Petroleum Exporting Countries (OPEC) welcomed the Paris Agreements in the following terms: "The world has reached a critical turning point with the Paris Agreement. Its ratification and orderly implementation will put the entire world community on a sustainable path that secures everyone's future and preserves the planet for coming generations".

30 Sustainable Energy for All (2012).

level for sustainable energy development, energy security and the use of energy in an environmentally sound manner.[31]

Nigeria is one of 90 signatories among other 10 African countries that seek to strengthen and integrate regional energy markets in order to enhance global market efficiency by providing, e.g., access to energy markets, liberalised trade under the World Trade Organisation, investment protection, diversification of energy sources, access to sustainable energy and energy efficiency.[32] The IEC is an update of the legally binding Energy Charter Treaty 1994 which promotes energy security through open and competitive energy markets.[33] Sadly, despite an admirable bent towards energy sustainability, there is no attempt to integrate climate change, though this is now an increasingly central part of the global policy agenda.

3.1.3 African Union climate change policy

African countries like Nigeria, through the African Union (AU), have addressed climate change in light of its transboundary nature and the vulnerability of member states. Driving the process is the role of the AU's Assembly of Heads of State and Government (the Assembly) which has rightly focused on developing a common negotiation position for its member countries. Thus, enhancing Africa's negotiating and bargaining power over the negligible power of its individual countries.

The principal strands of AU climate change policy are: (i) the Eighth AU Summit which endorsed climate change efforts in the Climate Information for Development Needs: An Action Plan for Africa Report 2007, which basically called on members to integrate climate change into national development plans; (ii) the Algiers Declaration on Climate Change 2009 that established a common African negotiation stance for the fifteenth Conference of the Parties to the UNFCCC (COP15) – developed countries should have mitigation commitments, while developing states mitigation actions should be voluntary and dependent on their access to technology, finance and capacity building; (iii) institutionalisation of climate change through the Conference of African Heads of State and Government on Climate Change (CAHOSCC); and (iv) the Draft AU Strategy on Climate Change 2014 that focused on the different obligations of developed and developing countries in line with the UNFCCC and Kyoto Protocol.[34]

The aim of the 2014 AU Strategy is to achieve climate-smart socio-economic development on a continent populated with some of the poorest countries in the world.

---

31 International Energy Charter (2015), at <http://www.energycharter.org/fileadmin/DocumentsMedia/Legal/IEC_EN.pdf> (accessed 24-12-2017).

32 Ibid.

33 Energy Charter Treaty (1994), at <https://energycharter.org/process/energy-charter-treaty-1994/energy-charter-treaty/> (accessed 27-12-2017).

34 Chinwuba & Ayoade (2013: 86-87). See also Jarso (2010-2011).

In relation to energy, the Strategy advocates that Africa must focus on increased energy access and security, whilst at the same time, reducing emissions. Other climate change governance activities are undertaken through the New Partnership for Africa's Development (NEPAD) and the African Ministerial Conference on the Environment.

3.1.4 Economic Community of West African States

The Economic Community of West African States (ECOWAS) was modelled on the basis of the European Union and established on 28 May 1975 to coordinate and promote trade, cooperation and development in the sub-region. Even the ECOWAS revised Treaty of 1993 focuses inter alia on energy cooperation as well as economic, social and cultural activities to alleviate poverty and raise the standard of living of its people. ECOWAS does not have a specific climate change policy, though there is a 2008 ECOWAS environmental policy. Be that as it may, the ECOWAS Lomé Declaration on Climate Change and Protection of Civilians in West Africa, 2009 recommends that a special fund be established to ameliorate climate change induced inputs. Also, member states are urged to establish and promote adaptation mechanisms taking into account regional cooperation and national expertise.[35]

The ECOWAS energy policy, on the other hand, can be found in diverse documents that have sought to inter alia mainstream renewable energy and energy efficiency at the regional level in order to harmonise the legal and regulatory architecture of its member states. First is the ECOWAS Energy Charter Protocol, 2003, which is majorly concerned with international cooperation for investment promotion and protection, since it is based on the Energy Charter Treaty which it simply copies. Article 19 of the 2003 Protocol on environmental aspects does not explicitly refer to climate change, though, it reflects the importance of environmentally compliant energy investments, improving energy efficiency, and utilising renewable energy.[36]

The ECOWAS Renewable Energy Policy 2015 tries to remove barriers to renewable energy and aims to increase the renewable energy share in the total energy mix (large hydro inclusive) to 35% in 2020 and 48% in 2030.[37] To achieve this ambitious target, member states, including Nigeria, are assisted in putting action plans in place to make the goals achievable. Simultaneously, the ECOWAS Energy Efficiency Policy provides a framework for energy efficiency investments to stimulate job creation and socio-economic development; also doubling energy efficiency by 2020, assists energy

35 See Paragraph 19 of the Lomé Declaration on Climate Change and the Protection of Civilians in West Africa (2009).

36 ECOWAS Energy Protocol A/P4/1/03 2003, at <http:///www.energy.gov.si/EcowasProtocol.pdf> (accessed 24-12-2017).

37 ECOWAS Renewable Energy Policy (2015), at <http://www.ecreee.org/sites/default/files/ documents/ecowas_renewable_energy_policy.pdf> (accessed 26-12-2017).

access, energy security, and climate mitigation and adaptation.[38] The document specifically mentions environmental protection and the need to reduce GHG emissions which is assisted by the operation of the ECOWAS Centre for Renewable Energy and Energy Efficiency (ECREEE).

4 Nigerian energy policy and climate action

Nigeria's energy policy is based on the National Energy Policy 2003, which encapsulates the entire energy landscape of the nation. The aim of the policy is to guarantee adequate, reliable and sustainable energy supply at appropriate costs and in an environmentally responsive manner in order to benefit the economy for national development. Five of its six chapters are structured into energy sources, energy utilisation, energy issues, energy financing and planning and policy implementation.[39] The goal is to optimally use energy resources for the sustainable development of the country.

The 2003 National Energy Policy (NEP) was the first governmental attempt to guide energy policy, and there is an explicit acknowledgement that energy is critical to national development goals. The role of government and the state is to take the lead in the energy sector in order to overcome challenges. Yet, there is a recognition that overdependence of oil can be overcome through aggressive research, diversification of energy resources, and human capacity development.[40] Energy policy objectives were summed up as follows and this is fully reproduced due to its importance:[41]

i. To ensure the development of the nation's energy resources, with diversified energy resources option, for the achievement of national energy security and an efficient energy delivery system with an optimal energy resource mix.

ii. To guarantee increased contribution of energy productive activities to national income.

iii. To guarantee adequate, reliable and sustainable supply of energy at appropriate costs and in an environmentally friendly manner to the various sectors of the economy for national development.

iv. To guarantee an efficient and cost effective consumption pattern of energy resources.

---

38 ECOWAS Energy Efficiency Policy (2012), at <http://www.ecreee.org/sites/default/files/ documents/basic_page/081012-ecowas-ee-policy-final-en.pdf> (accessed 24-12-2017).

39 National Energy Policy (2003). The ability of the federal government to make policy for the nation is derived from the Constitution of the Federal Republic of Nigeria 1999 (as amended). In particular, Section 16, Part II of the Constitution deals with the economic objectives of the nation and empowers the executive arm of government to make policy. Also Section 16(2)(b) of the Constitution directs that the state has harness and distribute the material resources of the nation for the common good. Furthermore, under the Second Schedule to the Constitution, mines and minerals including oil fields and natural gas are reserved to the exclusive legislative list which implies that only the National Assembly can legislate on this issue, and this also makes it an exclusive matter of the federal government.

40 National Energy Policy (2003).

41 Ibid.

v. To accelerate the process of acquisition and diffusion of technology and managerial expertise in the energy sector and indigenous participation in energy sector industries for stability and self-reliance.

vi. To promote increased investments and development of the energy sector industries with substantial private sector participation.

vii. To ensure a comprehensive, integrated and well informed energy sector plans and programs for effective development.

viii. To foster international cooperation in energy trade and projects development in both the African region and the world at large.

ix. To successfully use the nation's abundant energy resources to promote international cooperation.

This laudable set of objectives is of course reflective of the traditional approach to energy policy, which is to essentially focus on short-term development concerns, including the need to participate in the sector as the owner of the natural resource. Criticism of the NEP might include its failure to take account of the indigenous host communities that live with the consequences of oil production and development; and the failure to differentiate between onshore and offshore oil and gas resources. Of course, there is no mention of climate change as this was not yet a major international policy concern. It does, however, discern the importance of international cooperation in developing energy resources.

In relation to electricity, the NEP recognised the inadequacy of supply and the fact that the sector was then 98% owned by the Federal Government. Inadequate electricity meant that the commercial and industrial sectors relied on polluting generators which account for over half of consumed grid electricity. Hence, the policy advocates private sector involvement to ensure reliable power and the need to broaden energy options for generating power.[42] Its aim is to make electricity available to 75% of the populace. Interestingly, renewable energy resources were not considered, particularly mainstream, though there was a strategy to use renewable energy for the agricultural sector.[43]

Institutional support for energy policy can be found in the Energy Commission of Nigeria (ECN). Established by the Federal Government by Act No. 62 of 1979, as amended by Act No. 32 of 1988 and Act No. 19 of 1989, the ECN is charged with the strategic planning, monitoring and coordination of national energy policy. This includes policy implementation, promotion of diverse energy sources through guidelines, research, information dissemination, and periodic master plans. The ECN is responsible for advising the federal, state and local governments on the funding of energy research, production, etc. It also acts as the national energy data bank and liaises with all international organisations on energy-related matters.[44]

42 Ibid: 36.

43 Ibid: 72.

44 Energy Commission of Nigeria (2014).

Importantly, the NEP already outlines the key elements for the development and application of renewable energy. This includes the promotion and use of renewable energy to ensure decentralised energy supply, especially to rural areas; develop, promote and harness all viable renewable options into the national energy mix; discourage the use of wood as fuel; promote efficient use of biomass energy resources; and awareness to develop newly emergent sources of renewable energy by keeping abreast of international and technological trends. The NEP was first revised and updated in 2006, though, the latest draft revision was in 2013. The 2013 draft rightly includes an environmental and climate change policy, energy policy issues such as bilateral, regional, and international cooperation, local content, gender, human resources development and training. This is in addition to policies on energy financing, planning, and policy implementation.

Following on from the NEP, the Renewable Energy Master Plan for Nigeria (REMP) was produced in 2006 with support from the United Nations Development Programme (UNDP). It sought to assist Nigeria transition from a monolithic fossil-based economy to a less carbon-intensive economy utilising gas, and with a larger role for renewable energy. The overall objective was to provide a roadmap for national development through accelerated development and use of renewable energy resources.[45] In line with this, the Renewable Electricity Policy Guidelines were issued in December 2006 to further buttress the Federal Government's vision and policy to derive electric power from renewable energy. Moreover, the guidelines ensure that regulatory policy on renewable energy must be in line with Nigeria's international obligations on climate change. Thus, as Nigeria is a signatory to the Kyoto Protocol and eligible to participate in the Clean Development Mechanism (CDM), participation on such climate change mitigation activities is essential and has resulted in gas utilisation projects and even a hydropower rehabilitation project with countries like Norway, Italy, UK, France and Sweden.

Since socio-economic development is driven by energy, Nigerian policymakers have long realised that development goals such as the then Millennium Development Goals cannot be met without substantial improvement in energy supply and consumption. Also, the Vision 20:2020 (2008) blueprint to propel Nigeria into the rank of the top 20 largest economies by 2020 tacitly accepts this and seeks to increase energy supply from 4,000 MW in 2007 to 35,000 MW in 2020. At the same time, refining capacity should rise sharply from 445,000 bpd to 1,500,000 bpd in 2020.[46]

Vision 20:2020 envisages the usage of coal reserves estimated at 2.75 billion tones for energy production using clean coal technology.[47] This is in addition to electric power generation from tar sands or bitumen, hydropower, solar energy, wind power,

45 Sambo (2009: 6-8).
46 Energy Commission of Nigeria (2014: 6).
47 Ibid: 16.

biomass and uranium. It emphasises gas more than electricity as environmentally cleaner to oil and coal options. The added benefit would be to end gas flaring by 2008, an objective that has not been achieved.[48] Unfortunately, the vision essentially failed at conception, and much of its commendable aims were not accomplished. Promotion of renewable energy for environmental reasons, for instance, is in consonance with Nigeria's climate change obligations, though, the document does not mention climate change.

The Nigerian Bio-Fuel Policy and Incentives 2007 is yet another attractive policy recognition of the need to minimise fossil fuels and its related GHG emissions. The objective of this document is to provide a beneficial environment conducive to the development of a home-grown ethanol fuel industry, which will reduce dependence on imported gasoline and provide sustainable jobs. To ensure this, various financial incentives and tax waivers have been provided for this infant industry. Despite this, the policy has not recorded much success though biofuels can play an important role in mitigating climate change. Notable, however, is that there is no actual mention of climate change in this important document.

Perhaps more valuable is the National Renewable Energy and Energy Efficiency Policy (NREEEP) 2016. This policy document harmonises Nigeria's renewable energy and energy efficient policy with the ECOWAS Renewable Energy Policy (EREP) and ECOWAS Energy Efficiency Policies (EEEP). Its great advantage is to provide a system to implement the National Renewable Energy Action Plan (NREAP) and a National Energy Efficiency Action Plan (NEEAP) to carry out Nigeria's international obligations.

Linked to the NEP 2003, NREEP seeks to provide, for instance, Mandatory or Voluntary Renewable Portfolio Standards (RPS) which determine the amount of energy generated from renewables by a target year; Power Production Tax Credit (PPTC) to encourage electricity producers to generate from renewable sources; Feed-in-Tariff (FIT) offering a favorable pricing structure for renewable; Public Benefits Fund (PBF) that allows a tariff percentage to support on and off-grid renewable energy projects; and the provision of generous tax holidays, capital grants and other incentives.[49] Behind this is the desire that renewable energy constitutes about 20% of total energy supply in the long term, whilst there will be reliable electricity in the near term to meet the aims of Vision 20:2020.[50] Again, in this document, there is no mention of climate

48 Ibid: 19.

49 National Renewable Energy and Energy Efficiency Policy (2015). It is interesting that the Ministry of Power, and not the Energy Commission of Nigeria developed this policy. Other interesting aspects of the policy include that it allows for the active participation of states, local governments, and NGOs in renewable energy and energy efficiency matters. In addition, it provides for a monitoring and evaluation watchdog group under the control of the Minister of Power. The latter is supposed to tackle the notorious deficiency of government in implementing and enforcing its own rules.

50 National Renewable Energy and Energy Efficiency Policy (2015).

change implications of the policy, though its overall purpose does fit into a climate mitigation agenda.

This section is devoted to the latest policy documents governing the petroleum and natural gas sectors. The National Petroleum Policy (NPP), 2017 and Natural Gas Policy (NGP), 2017 are rather important as they represent the latest thinking of policy-makers and their being written at a period in which climate change is at the top of the regulatory agenda around the world. The central objective of the NPP is to maximise hydrocarbon production for national economic growth so that the sector is much more than a provider of foreign exchange. For the NGP, its purpose is to centralise the role of natural gas in the national industrial economy and at the same time capture international markets. Despite the attractive roadmap and action plans provided in both documents, there is still a significant failure to take climate change into account as there is barely any mention of this important issue. This is particularly regrettable bearing in mind the link between gas and electricity generation.

The Nigerian electricity sector is underpinned by the National Electric Power Policy (NEPP) 2001, which was developed by the Electric Power Reform Implementation Committee which provided for the privatisation of the electricity sector, establishment of an independent regulator, and wholesale market trading structures.[51] This was supported by the Electric Power Sector Reform Act (ESPRA) passed by the National Assembly in 2005. ESPRA is primarily concerned with licensing and regulation and does not particularly concern itself with the link between energy policy and climate change. For instance, the regulator, the Nigerian Electricity Regulatory Commission's (NERC) job is focused on general regulation, and there is neither mention of renewable energy nor climate change as areas of interest.[52]

Despite the number of policy options available to the Nigerian government, it is clear that much of the policies cannot be regarded as successful, particularly as regards climate change obligations. While some of the documents nod towards the need to take climate change into account, there is no instrument that gives policy priority or prominence to climate change; take for instance, the failure to end gas flaring and the moves towards coal use in the Vision 20:2020, which is perhaps indicative of the general lapses in extant policies from the climate change perspective.

From the above, it could be rightly surmised that the Nigerian state is publically committed to combating climate change. While the UNFCCC, the Kyoto Protocol and the Paris Agreement have been ratified, there has been no attempt to domesticate the agreements into national law for implementation and enforcement. Under Section 12 of the 1999 Constitution, an act of the National Assembly is essential to treaty implementation and application. However, the National Environmental Standards and Regulations Enforcement Agency (NESREA) does have the statutory responsibility of

51 Maduekwe (2011).

52 Section 32 of the Electric Power Sector Reform Act, 2005.

enforcing international agreements, protocols, treaties and conventions on the environment including climate change.

Furthermore, the Nigerian government has put in place a National Policy on Climate Change and Response Strategy (NCC-RC) and National Adaptation Strategy and Plan of Action on Climate Change for Nigeria (NASPA-CCN) 2011.[53] These documents are reactive to climate change, but neither focused on energy issues nor on sustainable energy. All the same, NASPA-CNN provides specific strategies for the energy sector, and this includes measures on higher specifications and construction of energy infrastructure; risk assessments to increase energy sector resilience; develop secure energy backup mechanisms; and expand sustainable energy sources.[54]

5 Integrating climate change and national energy policy options

The central role of energy to development is incontrovertible, as earlier discussed. In Nigeria, the Federal Government has the overall responsibility for formulating, enacting and also enforcing all climate change and energy policies. Turning to the issue of climate change, the inspiration is external and arrived in the form of climate change obligations freely entered into by the Nigerian state. This extends from the UNFCCC to the Kyoto Protocol and now the Paris Agreement.

As also noted, energy policy is rather fragmented, though the principal instrument is the National Energy Policy, 2003 which tries to encompass every component of the fossil and renewable energy options available to policymakers. Despite the huge importance of energy policy to Nigeria, an outdated instrument is in place, as even the most up-to-date revised draft of 2013 does not seem particularly reflective of climate change. Supporting instruments such as the Renewable Energy Master Plan for Nigeria, the Renewable Electricity Policy Guidelines 2006, Vision 20:2020, and most recently, the National Renewable Energy and Energy Efficiency Policy 2016 derived from ECOWAS, do unveil a rough strategy pointing towards sustainable energy.

In sum, Nigeria's energy policy consists of domestic and transnational elements that perhaps coexist uncomfortably. This is due to the central dilemma facing policymakers all over the world, though it is particularly sharp for energy-producing developing countries. Fossil fuels (oil, natural gas and coal) are the traditional tools for industrial, economic development and national prosperity. Not only can such countries not sell on such products, but indeed it cannot be freely utilised domestically. Evidently, there is a need for robust policy imperatives that will enable a sustainable energy transition.

53 National Adaptation Strategy and Plan of Action on Climate Change for Nigeria (2011), at <http://csdevnet.org/wp-content/uploads/NATIONAL-ADAPTATION-STRATEGY-AND-PLAN-OF-ACTION.pdf> (accessed 25-12-2017).

54 National Adaptation Strategy and Plan of Action on Climate Change for Nigeria (2011).

On the one hand, the international global agenda has instituted and promoted climate change mitigation and adaptation as a crucial policy goal to save the planet from serious global warming ramifications. Against this, economic self-interest and existing energy policies are directed towards carbon-intensive activities as shown in the Natural Gas and Petroleum Policies of 2017. Perhaps more serious is the argument that rich developed countries are yet to definitively prove that a low carbon economy is not only possible but that it is compatible with socio-economic prosperity.

Notwithstanding these difficulties, mainstreaming of climate change policy is slowly emerging with the 2012 Nigerian Federal Executive Council (FEC) adoption of the National Policy on Climate Change and Response Strategy (NASPA-CCN) as the key document for implementing climate action. The FEC which is the highest ranking executive body in the nation has provided backing for its key objective which is to promote low carbon, sustainable high economic growth to build climate change resilience. Interestingly, the document was developed by the Nigerian government and civil society organisations. Of course, stakeholders' participation increases policy credibility and adds to potential regulatory success.

Undoubtedly, there is clearly a sufficient number of policies governing climate change and energy in Nigeria. Yet there remains a gap between the two concepts which undermines their viability and effectiveness. One would, thus, posit that there is an urgent need to integrate climate change and energy policy into one integrated policy. The existing approach where they are treated separately allows for policy contradiction and is not sustainable in the long term. This would mean a substantial overhaul of extant climate change and energy policies through a stakeholders meeting that will incorporate government, sectoral experts, NGOs and civil society. However, transparent and accountable the process to develop an integrated climate change and energy policy may be, there might not be much actual change unless the policy is reinforced through legislation. Policy provides guidance, while implementation, compliance and enforcement benefit from the imperatives of statutory enactment. With regard to climate change in Nigeria, for instance, there is no climate change law in place, though, the federal legislative arm, the National Assembly, has over the years introduced bills on climate change that would, if signed into law, begin the process of mainstreaming climate change adaptation and mitigation action.

In relation to renewable energy policy which is scattered into diverse documents such as the 2001 National Electric Power Policy and the National Renewable Energy and Energy Efficiency Policy 2016, there is a need for policy integration with climate change and legislative enactment. At present, countries like China and India have sought to provide legislative backing for renewable energy through China's Renewable Energy Law of 2005 and India's draft National Renewable Energy Act, 2015.[55] However, we argue beyond the narrow confines of renewable energy law, for the need

55 Ogbodo & Stewart (2014: 17-18).

to put in place a Nigerian Climate Change and Energy Policy as well as National Climate Change and Energy Act. The proposed integrated policy and statute will bridge the policy gap between climate change and the energy sector, and provide the legislative architecture for the transit to a low carbon economy. Both policy and law should make it clear that the dangers emanating from climate change shifts and Nigeria's international commitments to tackle climate change are the basis for the new approach. The new instruments will encompass, among others: fossil fuel developments and target dates for leaving resources in the ground; financial incentives driven investments in renewable energy and low carbon sources; significant reduction in GHG emissions; and increased improvements in energy efficiency.

Furthermore, there is the need for a robust institutional governance infrastructure to ensure proper implementation and compliance. Nigeria's experience in the energy sector, and indeed other sectors of the economy, unveils myriad laws but rather poor compliance and enforcement. Such lacunae cannot be permitted in this sensitive arena as the proposed changes have fundamental and profound implications for the national economy and well-being of Nigerians. Although institutions such as the National Climate Change Trust Fund, the Department of Climate Change in the Federal Ministry of the Environment and the Energy Commission of Nigeria already have specific mandates, there is a need to merge all the relevant extant bodies to create a Climate Change and Energy Agency or government department to ensure a smooth transit to a low carbon future.

6 Conclusion

The global agenda on climate change is increasingly cohesive and dominant as every nation now has to take cognisance of the transformation of international commitments into targets and goals within domestic legal frameworks. Starting from the 'soft' approach of the UNFCCC, there is a gradual hardening of climate change policy as it transits from the Kyoto Protocol to the much more rigorous Paris Agreement which requires state parties including Nigeria to limit surface temperature rise to less than 2°C. On the face of it, international consensus even when the AU and ECOWAS are included, is seemingly gathering momentum.

The transnational approach to energy policy may be regarded as more nebulous to some extent. This is the case where one considers the UN driven SE4ALL and International Energy Charter, which are soft law and with debatable prospects of becoming hard law. Perhaps this criticism is not justified as the history of energy operations is soaked in state sovereignty and nationalism. Also, the difficulty of reaching consensus among a wide range of countries with diverse development and aspirations means that an initial soft law approach is inevitable for a developing international energy policy.

One reasonably common thread is the need for international cooperation and investment. This view is similarly replicated in the ECOWAS Energy Charter Protocol.

At the national level, substantial government policies already exist in the National Policy on Climate Change and Response Strategy, 2012 and the National Energy Policy, 2003. These principal instruments are supported by policies as diverse as the Renewable Energy Master Plan, Renewable Electricity Policy Guidelines, and the National Renewable Energy and Energy Efficiency Policy. Also commendable is the concrete support of ECOWAS instruments and institutions which is recognition that there is a global approach to solutions.

The main problem with this large network of policies and even the few laws is that they are essentially parallel to each other. While there is minor recognition of climate change in some energy policy instruments, there is no strategy to centralise climate change as a fundamental aspect of energy governance. The suggestion in this chapter is the need to bridge the gap by integrating climate change and energy into a holistic document. The view is that only a tripartite Nigeria Climate Change and Energy Policy, a National Climate Change and Energy Act and a Climate Change and Energy Agency will provide the building blocks for sustainable clean energy. This radical integration of climate change and energy policy and law is not without substantial challenges. Undoubtedly, there will have to be substantial political will on the part of the Nigerian government, which must be accompanied by the backing of stakeholders, especially, the business and industrial sector, civil society and the general public. Whatever the case, the writing is now on the wall as the transformation of climate change and energy at the international, regional and national level becomes a reality. This informs the need for Nigerian policymakers to be proactive in planning the county's transition to a sustainable low carbon future.

References

Akinyemi, O, A Ogundipe & P Alege (2014) "Energy supply and climate change in Nigeria" (2014) 4(14) *Journal of Environmental and Earth Science* 47-61.

Beecher, JA & JA Kalmbach (2012) "Climate change and energy" in J Winkler, J Andresen, J Hatfield, D Bidwell & D Brown *U.S. national climate assessment Midwest Technical Input Report*, at <http://glisa.msu.edu/docs/NCA/MTIT_Energy.pdf.> (accessed 25-12-2017).

Chinwuba, NN & MA Ayoade (2013) "Nigeria: adequacy and effectiveness of legal and institutional framework in mitigating and adapting to climate change" 1(3) *Olabisi Onabanjo University Journal of Public Law* 86.

Daigneau, E (2013) "Is hydropower a renewable energy or not?", *Governing the States and Localities* (at <http://www.governing.com/topics/transportation-infrastructure/gov-hydropower-renewable-energy.html> (accessed 29-12-2017).

Energy Commission of Nigeria (2014) *Energy implications of Vision 20:2020 and beyond.*

Farah, PD & P Rossi (2011) "National energy policies and energy security in the context of climate change and global environmental risks: a theoretical framework for reconciling domestic and international law through a multiscalar and multilevel approach" 2(6) *European Energy and Environmental Law Review* 232.

Hamilton, MS (2013) *Energy policy analysis: a conceptual framework.*

Hansen, J (2008) "Climate tipping points: the threat to the planet" Presentation given 19 February 2008 at Illinois Wesleyan University, at <http://www.columbia.edu/~jehil/> (accessed 24-12-2017).

Hunter, D, J Salzman & D Zaelke (eds) (1998*) International Environmental Law and Policy.*

Ifeanyi-Obi, CC (2012) "Climate change, effects and adaptation strategies: implication for agricultural extension system in Nigeria" 2(2) *Greener Journal of Agricultural Sciences* 53-60.

International Energy Agency (2018) "Climate change", at <https://www.iea.org/topics/climatechange/> (accessed 20-12-2017).

IPCC / Intergovernmental Panel on Climate Change (2007) *Climate change 2007: Synthesis Report*, at <http://www.ipcc.ch /publications and data/ar4/syr/en/main.html> (accessed 23-12-2017).

Ismail, OS & GE Umukoro (2012) "Global impact of gas flaring" 4 *Energy and Power Engineering* 290-302.

Jarso, JF (2011) "Africa and the climate change agenda: hurdles and prospects in sustaining the outcomes of the Seventh African Forum" 11(2) *Sustainable Development Law & Policy* 38-89.

Kerr, M (2002) *Tort based climate change litigation in Australia* Discussion Paper, at <http://www.acfonline.org.au uploads/res climate changejlitigation.pdf> (accessed 24-12-2017).

Ladan, MT (2009) "Promoting efficient and renewable energy for sustainable development and climate change mitigation in Nigeria: policy, legislative and regulatory challenges" Paper delivered at the 3rd Symposium and 2nd Scientific Conference of ASSELLAU, University of Nairobi, Kenya, 23-25 March 2009.

MacGill, I (2008) "Assessing Australia's sustainable energy technology options: key issues, uncertainties, priorities and potential choices" 11 *Asia Pacific Journal of Environmental Law* 85.

Maduekwe, NC (2011) "Unbundling and privatisation of the Nigerian electricity sector: reality or myth?" Centre for Energy, Petroleum and Mineral Law Policy", at http://www.dundee.ac.uk/cepmlp/gateway/files.php? (accessed 25-12-2017).

Maguire, R (2012) "Incorporating international environmental legal principles into future climate change instruments" 2 *Carbon and Climate Change Law Review* 109-110.

Mckie, R (2018) "Burning wood for power is 'misguided' say climate experts" *The Observer* (31-12-2017) <https://www.theguardian.com/environment/2017/dec31/biomasss-burning-misguided-say-climate-experts#img-1> (accessed 31-12-2017).

Nwaogaidu, JC (2013) *Globalisation and social inequality: an empirical study of Nigerian society.*

Ogbodo, SG & N Stewart (2014) "Climate change and Nigeria's sustainable development of Vision 20-2020" 20(1) *Annual Survey of International & Comparative Law* 17-34.

Ong DM (2010), "International legal efforts to address human-induced global climate change" in M Fitzmaurice, DM Ong & P Merkouris (eds) *Research handbook on international environmental law.*

OPEC (2016) "OPEC embraces adoption of historic Paris Agreement on Climate Change" *OPEC Bulletin Commentary* (January-February 2016), at <http://www.opec.org/opec_web/en/press_room/3432.htm> (accessed 26-12-2017).

Sagar, AD, HH Oliver & AP Chikkatur (2006) "Climate Change, Energy and Developing Countries" 7 *Vermont Journal of Environmental Law* 71-94.

Sambo, AS (2009) "The place of renewable energy in the Nigerian energy sector" Presented at the World Future Council Workshop on Renewable Energy Policies, Addis Ababa, Ethiopia UNGA resolutions and other resolutions or decisions or policy.

Segger, M (2006) "Advancing the Paris Agreement on Climate Change for sustainable development" 5(2) *Cambridge Journal of International and Comparative Law* 202-237.

Smith, JA, J Vargo & S Pollock Hoverter (2017) "Climate change and public health policy" 45(1) *Journal of Law Medicine and Ethics* 82-85.

Sustainable Energy For All (2012) "Sustainable energy for all: an overview", at <http://www.un.org/millenniumgoals/pdf/SEFA.pdf> (accessed 24-12-2017).

Thornton, J & S Beckwith (2004) *Environmental law.*

Todorov, AV (1986) "Reply" 25 *Journal of Applied Climate and Meteorology* 258-259.

World Energy Council (2007) *Energy and climate change.*

Zaelke, D & J Cameron (1990) "Global warming and climate change – an overview of the international legal process" 5(2) *American University International Law Review* 249-290.

Chapter 5: Climate change, human security and the humanitarian crisis in the Lake Chad Basin region: selected legal and developmental aspects with a special focus on water governance

Oliver C. Ruppel & Mark B. Funteh

1 Introduction

Since independence from either the French or the English in the early 1960s, the countries of the Lake Chad Basin (LCB) region, with a longstanding history of violent conflict, have been plagued by serious humanitarian crises. This is inter alia due to complex political instability, weak economic and social policies, which have prolonged the national and international conflicts. Low levels of economic development vary between riparian nation states, poor education systems, widespread illiteracy, sharp gender disparities, high health risks, water and food insecurity are marks of the crisis-stricken region. The LCB area represents the poorest, most marginalised and neglected part of each respective country, with poor provision of basic infrastructure and social services; a situation that disfavours various aspects of human security. Nigeria has been hit by successive incidents of unrest, including *coup d'états*, civil wars and the recent rise of the Islamist extremist group Boko Haram, founded in 2002, that has terrorised the entire region. Chad has for a long time experienced a seemingly endless crisis of civil war since 1963. As an enclave country, it has often been exposed to threats of attacks, human trafficking and armed conflict from Libya, Darfur (South Sudan) and the Central African Republic. Being part of the route that migrants take to reach Europe, the Chadian desert supports the migrations of young people fleeing the unbearable situations of their origins. Niger, ranking second lowest in the world on the Human Development Index[1], suffers from continual structural calamities, weak sectoral policies and low levels of investment and development aid, as well as an influx of refugees from Mali and Nigeria. Meanwhile, Cameroon – despite its development deficits – has since 1967 borne the burden of huge refugee inflows from many neighbouring states. Following huge crop damage by locust swarms; the stagnation or decline of crop production, fishing and animal husbandry activities; the constant mobility of people; a sustained crime wave; and health, food and price insecurity despite

1 UNDP (2016). The Central African Republic ranks lowest in the world.

international and national efforts, research worldwide seeks a new understanding of the persistence of the humanitarian crises in the region.

Lake Chad is an international shallow fresh-water lake, which has receded significantly over the past decades due to overuse, poor management practices and expanding desertification. The LCB is located between Latitude 6° and 24° N and Longitude 7° and 24 E°. Covering 2,434,000 km^2, which is an estimated 8% of the total African surface area, the Basin is shared by the riparian countries of Chad (45%), Niger (28%), the Central African Republic (CAR) (9%), Nigeria (7%), Algeria (4%), Sudan (4%), Cameroon (2%) and Libya (0.5%).[2] However, only four of these are in direct contact with the lake, namely Cameroon, Chad, Niger and Nigeria.

Chad and Niger are the countries with the largest shared territory, but three-quarters of the lake water come from the CAR and Cameroon. More than 70 ethnic groups and a total population of about 38 million form the predominantly rural population around Lake Chad, most of which depend on the region's natural resources for their livelihoods.[3] The Human Development Indices (HDI) – a summary measure of average achievement in key dimensions of human development: a long and healthy life, being knowledgeable and have a decent standard of living – in the region are among the lowest in the world.[4]

According to the United Nations, the long-running violence and military counter-offensives have affected 21 million people across the LCB and left nearly half of the region's population – 9.2 million people – in critical need of aid.[5] Chad, Niger and Nigeria have experienced periods of military rule. Chad and Nigerian politics are shaped by oil exploration. Transitions from military rule to democracy have occurred in Niger and Nigeria.[6] The LCB is conflict dense. Attacks have taken place in northern Cameroon since March 2014 and in southern Niger and western Chad since early 2015. Fighters move freely across national borders. They have some level of support from certain local populations in all four countries although there is also much anger directed against them due to continuing tactics of committing attacks against civilians.[7] Cameroon has seen a recent escalation of conflict and violence in its northeast and southwest regions, marked by violence against Anglophone activists by security forces,[8] bomb blasts and the proclamation of the independence of Ambazonia by secessionist groups.[9]

2 Odada et al. (2006: 1).
3 With further references see Nagarajan et al. (2018).
4 UNDP (2016); and Nett & Rüttinger (2016).
5 UNOCHA (2016).
6 Nagarajan et al. (2018: 9).
7 Ibid: 13.
8 Ruppel & Stell (2017).
9 ICG (2017).

In Chad, already hosting hundreds of thousands of refugees from conflicts in neighbouring Sudan and the CAR, clashes between settled farmers and nomads over land use rights and access to water occur frequently in the north. Niger, with a history of conflict between the state and some of its Tuareg communities, has also, due to its geographical location, felt the spill-over of conflict from neighbours Mali and Libya as well as Nigeria. New sites of conflict have manifested in Nigeria since its 2015 elections around the pro-secessionist mobilisation by and state reaction to the Indigenous Peoples of Biafra (IPOB) in the southeast and tensions around the killing of over 300 unarmed members of the Islamic Movement of Nigeria (IMN), a Shiite group, by the military, detention of their leader and protests ending in violence which add to preexisting conflict around oil extraction in the Niger Delta, rural banditry and inter-communal violence.[10]

While the peoples of Niger and Chad are predominantly Muslim, Cameroon has a Christian majority with a significant Muslim minority and Nigeria roughly equal numbers of Christians and Muslims.[11] The role played by ethnic heterogeneity in local resource conflicts in the LCB region contributes to its population dynamics. The ethnic composition remains a crucial factor for mobilisation, turning the protest into collective violence triggered by language and religious loyalties. In trying to make a living through the exploitation of scarce water and land resources, the multi-ethnic groups have often engaged in interethnic and sectoral conflicts.[12] One particular instance is the recurrent deadly clashes between the Shuwa Arabs from the east of Lake Chad and the Fulani pastoralists from the south-west, over the limited fishing and animal husbandry opportunities at the southern pool of the Basin.[13]

As of 2016, over 30 million people inhabited the LCB.[14] This rapidly growing population – with an average growth rate of 2.6% – is ethnically highly heterogeneous, with over 70 groups who are Christian, Muslim and Animist by faith. The main groups are Kanuri, Maba, Buduma, Hausa, Kanembu, Kotoko, Bagger, Haddad, Kuri, Fulani, Massa, Mundang and Manga, and they often straddle the region's international borders, with the largest cities being Kano and Maiduguri in Nigeria, Maroua in Cameroon, N'Djamena in Chad and Diffa in Niger.[15]

10 Nagarajan et al. (2018: 17).
11 Ibid: 12.
12 Le Barbe & Lebel (1997).
13 Odada et al. (2006).
14 Cf. <https://www.gwp.org/en/WACDEP/IMPLEMENTATION/Where/Lake-Chad/> (accessed 18-5-2018).
15 Okpara et al. (2015: 2).

2 Diverse climate

The LCB region is located in the Sahel at the southernmost edge of the Sahara, but the lake itself is largely fed by precipitation further south in the humid tropics. This unique geography has created an oasis in an otherwise largely arid region. The LCB features strong diversity in climate, from the desert in the north to humid tropics in the south.[16] According to the Intergovernmental Panel on Climate Change (IPCC), the Sahel is the world's region with the most substantial and sustained decline in rainfall recorded, and climatic conditions are expected to deteriorate further.[17] Temperatures are projected to increase, and if the shrinking of Lake Chad continues at the current pace, the lake could completely disappear within the next 20 years.[18]

While the LCB region is generally and historically subjected to intense drought events, water scarcity is increasingly associated with the myriad of socio-economic and livelihood shifts around the lake, for which climate variability acts as an amplifier. Both overexploitation and climate change have the potential to contribute to increased conflicts over the distribution of natural resources.[19]

Depending on precipitation rates, which vary from an average of 1,400 mm/year in the south to 10 mm/year in the north, four climatic zones may be identified in the LCB, namely: the humid zone in the Basin's southern part (the territory of Cameroon and CAR); the dry sub-humid zone (the territory of CAR and Chad); the semi-arid zone in the central part of the Basin (the territory of Nigeria, Chad and Niger); and the northern arid and hyper-arid zone (territory of Niger and Chad). The northern half of the Basin is desert, containing the Tenere desert. Erg of Bilma and Djurab lying south of that comprises the Sahel zone, which is dry savanna and thorny shrub savanna. The main rivers are skirted by riparian forests, flooding savannas and wetland areas. In the far south, there are dry forests.[20]

Lake Chad constantly changes in response to variations in temperature and rainfall. A variety of ecological zones surround the lake, including deserts, forests, wetlands, savannas and mountains.[21] Three main drainage systems supply its water, namely the Chari-Logone River (in the CAR), the Komadugu-Yobe River (in Nigeria) and the Yedsaram/Ngadda River (in Cameroon). Lake Chad is, in fact, a tropical lake with associated wetlands. It has a northern and a southern basin of roughly the same size, which are separated by a sand barrier, referred to as the Great Barrier. It is very shallow with a general depth of less than four metres. The main rivers feeding the lake flow

---

16 Nagarajan et al. (2018).
17 Niang & Ruppel (2014: 1209).
18 See Nett & Rüttinger (2016: 13) with further references.
19 Niang & Ruppel (2014).
20 FAO (2009: 2).
21 Ovie & Emma (2011); Sullivan & Rohde (2002).

into its southern basin. When the water level is too low, the Great Barrier prevents water from flowing to the northern basin, causing that segment of the lake to dry up.[22]

3 Livelihood and sustainability

The LCB supports the human population, as well as millions of wildlife that include birds, mammals, reptiles and amphibians. There are populations of elephants, giraffes and lions. The local economy in the upper part of the catchment area is based on fishing, agriculture and pastoralism. Agriculture is primarily undertaken in rain-fed areas in the south and flooded areas. Hydrological and biophysical changes resulting from natural climatic variability and various human activities threaten the entire LCB, but the lake itself and the natural resources and ecosystem services are used by communities to pursue their livelihoods.[23]

Livelihoods are sustained by activities dear to the peoples' hearts. The main activities in the LCB are economic and include farming, herding and fishing, as mentioned earlier. At least 40% of the rural population of the Basin lives in poverty and routinely faces chronic food shortages.[24] Crop production based on rain is possible only in the southern belt, as highlighted earlier. Flood recession agriculture is practised around the LCB and in the riverine wetlands. Nomadic herders migrate with their animals into the grasslands of the northern part of the Basin for a few weeks during each short rainy season, where their livestock intensively graze the highly nutritious grasses. When the dry season starts, the herders move back south, either to grazing lands around the lakes and floodplains or the savannas further to the south. Livestock rearing is, in fact, most well developed in the northern section of the Basin,[25] while farming activities can be traced mostly on the edges of Lake Chad and in the south of the Basin.

All the LCB countries have alarming levels of hunger, with some witnessing extreme levels. The Global Hunger Index (GHI) is a multidimensional statistical tool that describes the state of hunger in different countries. The GHI value for Chad is over 30 and is between 20 and 29.9 for the other basin countries.[26] With poverty conspicuous throughout the Basin, many young people seek to flee the region or join armed groups leading to increased social unrest. It is expected that this will worsen in the coming years, as the security and economic situations have reached a critical point, demographic growth is large, and climate change is negatively affecting agriculture. Furthermore, with increasing environmental challenges, multi-activity has become common as individuals engage in several livelihood activities from fishing, livestock

22 McMichael et al. (2003).
23 UNEP (2004).
24 FAO (2017).
25 FAO (1983).
26 Cf. <http://www.globalhungerindex.org/pdf/en/2017.pdf> (accessed 18-5-2018).

rearing, agricultural, trading and handicraft making to secure revenue to sustain their livelihoods.[27]

4 Hydrological and biophysical changes

The LCB area has experienced serious hydrological and biophysical changes caused by climatic variability and various human activities. These threaten the entire LCB, the lake itself and the ecosystem and natural resources used by communities to pursue their livelihoods.[28] The depletion of soil fertility and freshwater supplies and the mismanagement of water catchment basins as a consequence of excessive deforestation have also contributed to encroachment by the Sahara Desert. The climatic changes have imposed on the region high temperatures, strong winds, high evapotranspiration (estimated at 2,200 mm/annum) and fluctuating rainfall patterns.[29] Annual rainfall varies spatially from nearly 1,400 mm along the southern pools to less than 150 mm near the northern end.[30] In fact, a short rainy season (June, July, August and September) and a longer dry spell are pronounced characteristics of spatial-temporal distribution of rainfall in the LCB.[31]

Because of the strategic location of the Basin, in a climatic transition zone, regions at the south of the lake tend to experience more rainfall than those at the north of the lake. The mean monthly rainfall for eight stations within the LCB area that are located in the southern parts of the Basin shows that distribution is common in tropical rainfall regions. Here, rainfall occurs from April to early November. The northern portion, however, only experiences (often very light) rainfall for a shorter period in July, August and September. What this means is that the level and size of Lake Chad depend on precipitation in the southern parts and how much of the run-off is transferred through the floodplains of the Basin to the lake.[32]

The distribution of surface water bodies has a high correlation with rainfall distribution. The southern parts have a few perennial rivers that act as lifelines to agricultural activities and human needs, while the north-east and north-west regions are characterised by intermittent water bodies that have low seasonal flow and dry up quickly at the onset of drought.[33]

Studies concerning mild and prolonged drought years in northern Cameroon show that the riverbeds of these intermittent streams are desiccated, primarily as a result of substantial water abstraction for irrigation and nomadic pasturing.[34]

---

27 Mekonnen (2016).
28 Niang & Ruppel (2014); and UNEP (2004).
29 FAO (2009: 33).
30 Odada et al. (2006).
31 Coe & Foley (2001); Nicholson, Yin & Ba (2000); and Caminade & Terray (2010).
32 Charney (1975: 193-202).
33 Okonkwo & Demoz (2013).
34 Lienou et al. (2005).

The distribution of decadal monthly rainfall and temperatures suggests that there is a relationship between high temperature and low rainfall. Increased temperature leading to increased evapotranspiration is associated with increased drought.[35] Peak rainfall in August corresponds to the northward movement of the intertropical convergence zone (ITCZ).[36] Consequently, the history of drought in the Basin is defined by its changing rainfall patterns.[37]

From the middle of the 1960s, rainfall started to drop intermittently until the droughts of 1972-1975, which coincided with the shrinking of the Basin surface water level to 10,700 km^2 from its initial level of 25,000 km^2 in 1963.[38] Another drought, which occurred in 1982-1985, resulted in a drop in water levels in the LCB to 1,410 km^2,[39] the lowest basin surface level recorded over the past 100 years. This is evident in many river beds. Lake Chad was identified as one of the lakes at greatest risk of socio-political stress.[40] Over 13 years since this observation, the state of the lake's Basin has worsened in as much as it has shrunk by over 90% compared with its size (25,000 km^2) in the 1960s.[41] Lake Chad was vastly bigger (up to 400,000 km^2) several thousands of years ago than it was in the 1960s when it was known as Lake Megachad.[42] For the entire 20th century, the lake was at its highest level between 1960 and 1963.[43]

Furthermore, stream flow modification and water diversion, associated with the construction of large irrigation and water development projects along the Chari-Logone River and Kamadugu-Yobe River, are also identified as contributing to the shrinkage of the Basin over the period 1970-2013.[44] The construction (between 1979 and 1990) of the Yaguou-Tekele Dyke and Maga Dam beside the Chari-Logone River in Chad, and a series of other dams, such as the Alau Dam, Tiga Dam, and the Yeders Dam at the Nigerian end of the Kamadugu-Yobe River, has had a great impact on the lake's waters.[45] Between 1970 and 1990, the average water discharge from the Chari-Logone River to the Basin was 55% of the average of the period 1950 to 1970.[46]

It is estimated that about one-third of the water flow (since the 1980s) is diverted from the Chari-Logone River in the CAR before it reaches the LCB.[47] Water diversion

35 Dai et al. (2004).
36 Lélé & Lamb (2010).
37 Malo & Nicholson (1990).
38 Okpara et al. (2015: 7).
39 GIWA (2004).
40 Wolf et al. (2003).
41 Gao et al. (2011).
42 Drake & Bristow (2006).
43 USGS (2014).
44 Ibid.
45 Onuoha (2008).
46 Olivry et al. (1996).
47 Glantz (2004).

for irrigation and hydropower generation increased greatly between 1981 and 1990.[48] About 50% of the depletion in the lake's size since the late 1970s to 2000 was attributed to unsustainable water diversion and use for human activities, but recently arguments attributing water shortage to evaporation due to global warming are growing more popular.[49]

Consequently, the current state of the lake is one of acute water shortage. In 2000, the water supply was less than 500 m^3 per person per year.[50] This has not changed to date though the population has continued to increase. A change from cultivation of low water intensity food crops (such as wheat) to high water intensity food crops (such as rice) has added to water scarcity.[51]

Reduced water levels have caused increased alkalinity, increased anoxic conditions and worsened the effects of eutrophication.[52] Because the lake region is generally and historically subjected to intense drought events, water scarcity is increasingly associated with the myriad of socio-economic and livelihood shifts around the lake, for which climate variability acts as an amplifier. This has had a direct effect on food yields and famine in the area.

Relying on ecosystem health, subsistence farmers, fisherfolk and pastoralists suffer from accentuated unpredictability and relative decline in rainfall levels. In this dry region, even a one-degree global temperature rise contributes significantly to the decline of the lake, which equates to the destruction of people's vital resources and livelihoods. Accordingly, drastic consequences of global climate change fall on those whose activities have contributed the least emissions. With desertification erasing some fishing areas over time, shrinking the lake to reveal more land for cultivation, combined with the reduction of fish stocks from overfishing and as a consequence of the lake's recession, many fishermen have given up fishing to begin farming.

Household groups have switched livelihood strategies as the demand for water and water scarcity have simultaneously increased. These chain reactions have often heightened competition between farmers and other livelihoods. Impacts on income, food and nutrition security, labour generation and poverty alleviation are clear as climate-related water stress, and shortages exacerbate community vulnerabilities. Relying on increasingly exhaustive coping strategies and social networks to meet food security needs, people have moved around the Basin and diversified livelihood activities and adopted more drastic behaviours. As a result, the resilience of the socio-ecological system of the region is threatened as resources become more intensely used and depleted.

Reduced rainfall and streamflow modification reduce fishing grounds and modify habitats, which translate to declining fish catch and trade, lowered income,

---

48 GIWA (2004).
49 Coe & Foley (2001).
50 Henninger et al. (2000).
51 Odada et al. (2006).
52 Ovie & Emma (2011).

unemployment and increased poverty, and, ultimately, food and nutrition insecurity. For 40 years the only water in the lake has been found at its deepest point, namely the southern pool and to a certain extent in the marshes, in spite of high flow rates occurring elsewhere. The relative flatness of the terrain means that variations of a few centimetres flood the islands, as happened in 2012, or result in the lake shoreline receding by several kilometres. Such variations have not, however, been beneficial to fish reproduction, forcing fishermen to diversify their activities and move into farming, owing to the uncertainty and insecurity caused by the varying water levels of the lake.[53] The species of fish currently caught by fishermen, although once plentiful and varied, are struggling to survive the onslaught of overfishing and the drop in water levels caused by the variable climate. The reduced water levels have not only led to decreased fish catches but have also increased the productive capital expenditure of fishers, especially for hitherto near-shore fishers. Changes in fish distributions and productivity not only increase productive capital considerably but also inflate the cost of fish.

In the same vein, the lake's fishing communities have had to move in response to declining fishing grounds caused by a gradual but steady decline in water area.[54] Furthermore, the siltation of water bodies and watercourses, the proliferation of invasive aquatic plants, premature dewatering, the reduced biodiversity, increasing water pollution, and harmful fishing practices have not helped the fishing environment, as there has been a serious decline in fish production over several decades and the disappearance of once-common species. This has also affected the livestock herders and pastoralists. Livelihood patterns have shifted in large part owing to growing water shortages in the Basin. For example, decreased grazing land for animals has led herders to shift from rearing grazing animals (cattle and camels) to browsing animals (sheep and goats),[55] which has led to an increased removal of vegetation cover.[56] Moreover, water shortage has initiated shifts in livelihood patterns.[57] This, in turn, has led to increased removal of vegetation cover.[58] A declining annual fish catch (for example, the annual fish catch from the lake's fisheries decreased from 141,000 tonnes in the early 1970s to 70,000 tonnes in 2002) explains that fishers engaged in small-scale open water fisheries have had to switch to swamp and floodplain fisheries.[59] This required a change in fishing gear, from open water gear to specialised passive gears such as gill nets, cane traps and hooks. Because of reduced fishing areas, large-scale fishers have had to invest in bigger and safer boats to enable them to travel longer distances to access the

53 Cf. <http://www.cblt.org/sites/default/files/download_documents/report_on_the_state_of_the_lake_chad_basin_ecosystem.pdf> (accessed 18-5-2018).

54 Ovie & Emma (2011).

55 Onuoha (2008).

56 USGS (2014); and Herrmann et al. (2005: 394).

57 Living Waters (2003).

58 USGS (2014).

59 Cf. <http://www.cblt.org/sites/default/files/download_documents/report_on_the_state_of_the_lake_chad_basin_ecosystem.pdf> (accessed 18-5-2018).

open waters of the lake to catch species of higher value, as indicated earlier. Only the wealthy fishing households can make these adjustments, while the poor become poorer and remain more exposed to the exploits of terrorists in the region.[60]

5 Human security, conflict and migration

Adverse climatic events not only deepen poverty vulnerability but also have an impact on all aspects of human security, either directly or indirectly. Issues that potentially interrelate between climate change and human security include water stress, land use, food security, health security, environmentally induced migration and violent conflict.[61] Both overexploitation and climate change will continue to contribute to increased conflicts over the distribution of natural resources.[62]

Although violent conflict and migration are caused by different interacting factors, including social, demographic and economic drivers, it may be observed that migration and violent conflict in the LCB are also sensitive to the impacts of climate change. In fact, climate change has the potential to act as a risk multiplier threatening the stability of states and societies.[63] Examples of climate change impacts closely related to migration are floods and droughts exacerbated by climate change, which have resulted in an increased rural-urban migration. The nexus between climate change and violent conflict on the African continent has become the focus of a growing body of research in recent years. Mechanisms linking climate change to violent conflict include worsening livelihood conditions; migration and changing pastoral mobility patterns; tactical considerations of armed groups; and exploitation of local grievances by the elite.[64]

Extreme weather events can be a cause of violent conflict as they have the potential to intensify competition over scarce resources, especially in regions that lack efficient conflict management institutions. As droughts and expansion of the Sahel continues, southward migration has increased since people move south to seek basic resources for their survival and that of their livestock. This southward migratory trend, however, has not curbed natural resource degradation due to overexploitation.[65]

One major concern regarding human security is the issue of forced migration in fragile contexts. In recent years the number of forcefully displaced persons has increased significantly and caused a number of short-term human security needs, as well

60 Ovie & Emma (2011).
61 Ruppel (2013).
62 Niang & Ruppel (2014).
63 Rüttinger et al. (2015).
64 SIPRI (2017).
65 GIWA (2004).

as long-term challenges, including dealing with the legal status of displaced persons in a host country.[66]

Most forcefully displaced persons are internally displaced, namely displaced within the borders of their home country; and forced displacements are closely associated with violent conflicts. Official data differs in tracking ongoing migrations and displacements, as such numbers are mostly approximations of forced migration, unable to qualify the chaos of daily life within the Basin, which has lost many types of security. Capturing the threats within LCB, the United Nations Office for the Coordination of Humanitarian Affairs (OCHA) reported that as of 30 March 2016, beyond those taking refuge outside their home countries, the number of internally displaced people had surged. According to the International Organization for Migration (IOM) in 2017, displaced people were recorded in the following countries: Nigeria (3 million), Niger (252,000), Cameroon (396,000) and Chad (176,000). In total, 17,300,000 people are living in the affected area of which 2,200,000 are internally displaced people and 1,400,000 returnees.[67]

Added to this, are the death tolls, destruction of schools and hospitals, and the blocking of food supplies, market holdings, trans-border transactions and so on, in the region. Moreover, the relationship between climate change and armed conflict has an amplifying effect on the subsequent humanitarian and hunger crises in the region.

Community assets and food reserves are destroyed as Boko Haram strikes, which worsens already severe problems of food security and increases the prevalence of acute malnutrition in the region. Within a previously poor nutritional situation, due largely to food shortages resulting from environmental challenges, the incidence of conflict and regional insecurity (beyond pre-existing drought and desertification disasters, which steadily damage natural capital) appear as overlaying causes and effects of the regional crisis. Hence, the protracted conflict-induced humanitarian situation appears as a prolonged shock to a regional system already dealing with local food and nutrition insecurity for decades. Therefore, interruptions to daily life and routine coping strategies employed within areas of poor economic and low human development have compounded impacts, drastically affecting people throughout the region in one way or another and reducing their already constricted strategies for coping in a harsh environment. In many cases people have been uprooted from their homes, thereby losing social and physical capital, and, in other cases, have been compelled to drastically alter their networks, activities and previous sources of income.

According to recent reports from the Nigerian military, Boko Haram has resorted to using natural resources as a weapon and part of their strategy of violence. They have poisoned water sources such as wells and streams in areas where they were dislodged by state troops, making water use dangerous for both humans and livestock. While it

66 SIPRI (2017).
67 IOM (2017).

remains unclear whether this strategy is being systematically used as a weapon against civilians, it underlines the strategic importance of natural resources in the conflict.[68]

Ultimately, the causes for displacement and migration are manifold; however, climate change in the LCB region is definitely one of the interlinking issues. Other potential drivers of migration are push and pull factors related to the overall situation in the LCB region, and intervening factors that facilitate or restrict migration, all of which interact in different ways.[69] However, human mobility is a strategy (not only a reaction) to climatic changes that is characteristic of the LCB region, and the nature of the response is determined by the economic context of the specific communities.[70] For instance, family and kinship groups straddle national borders, and historically, people have migrated and traded freely across the region. There was always thriving cross-border trade in agricultural produce, fish as well as other goods and commodities. Lake Chad acted as a trading hub offering economic opportunities and resources of which people living around the lake took advantage despite the lack of national government policies to support this.[71]

6 Water scarcity and regional security

The importance of Lake Chad's transboundary waters creates a situation where conditions in one country can create adverse repercussions in another. A river basin is a source of ecological interdependence under which water stress and conflicts in one country can be transmitted to another.[72] This has regional security implications.

Research shows that when there were increased water crises in the region during the droughts of the 1980s and 1990s, people struggled for the scarce fertile areas and wetlands.[73] This crisis phenomenon has become the order of the day in the region since then. For instance, several militarised conflicts occurred over competing river claims, especially as resource users migrated in response to the shrinking lake. For example, between 1980 and 1994, almost 60,000 Nigerians followed the receding lake waters, fishing, cultivating crops and rearing animals within Cameroon's border of the LCB.[74]

By triggering hostilities with neighbours and damaging relationships between nations sharing the lake's common pool resources, the shrinking lake threatens regional security. In 1982 local people from Cameroon and Nigeria clashed over access to the

68 See Nett & Rüttinger (2016: 14-18) with further references.
69 Black et al. (2011).
70 Niang & Ruppel (2014).
71 Nagarajan et al. (2018: 10).
72 Tir & Stinnett (2012).
73 Hall (2009).
74 Ibid.

water resources around the southern end of the LCB.[75] In 1983, Chad engaged in a violent interstate conflict with Nigeria over the status of the islands in the lake with which both countries have borders.[76] This violence resulted in over 100 casualties.[77]

In the late 1980s, Nigeria and the Niger Republic clashed over water diversion and access to the Komadugu-Yobe River flow within the LCB. In 1992, there were clashes between upstream (Nigeria) and downstream (Niger) communities over access to the waters from the Tiga and Challawa Gorge Dams at the south-western end of Lake Chad.[78] All of these conflicts also increased the number of displaced people in the region.

With climate change causing reduced rainfall, reduced river runoff and more frequent droughts, the extent and impacts of water scarcity are far-reaching, particularly in the context of livelihood security. Thus, a collaborative stand exists between climate change, water scarcity, conflict and migration. Since 2005, competition and conflict over the use of water resources within the lake have continued to create security concerns at the lake's southern pool where the largest population of resource users live.[79] Water shortages and loss of livelihood options have driven vulnerable people into risky behaviours such as drug trafficking and the trading of arms. Large cohorts of young people deprived of their sources of livelihood constitute the major portion of terrorist groups and rebels in third world militias.[80] The rise of violent jihadist militants, who have killed over 10,000 people in the southern part of the lake, has been linked to loss of livelihoods and joblessness created by environmental degradation around the lake.[81] As water scarcity and poverty become more amplified and intense, the economic and political value that communities and nations place on the lake's resources are expected to increase.[82]

Growth in unilateral consumption and unregulated allocation and use of water (for instance through damming, diverting, dumping and draining activities) by one nation decreases the amount available to another state. In the wake of the droughts and water shortages of the 1980s, each riparian country unilaterally took decisions to construct dams and divert water away from the lake without recourse to existing water agreements and consultations with the Lake Chad Basin Commission (LCBC). This implied that previously agreed-upon river diversion arrangements (e.g. for agriculture, human consumption and industrial use) became politically problematic as the water levels of

---

75 Odada et al. (2006).
76 UCDP (2008).
77 Wallensteen & Margareta (1999).
78 Odada et al. (2006).
79 GIWA (2004).
80 Ohlsson (2003).
81 Ifabiyi (2013).
82 Onuoha (2008).

rivers flowing into the Basin continued to drop and as the resulting externalities became a burden for downstream countries.[83]

Water resources comprise less than 1,000 m^3/person/annum, and, as in the case of the LCB, water scarcity creates discontent and desperation, especially when it constrains socio-economic development.[84] Since the droughts of the 1970s and 1980s, agricultural production has continued to decline. For example, annual sorghum yield was less than 250,000 tonnes during the 1972 to 1975 droughts and 180,000 tonnes during the 1982-1985 droughts.[85] These yields have further declined to date.[86] The retreat of the lake resulting from a series of relatively dry years has created new areas of cultivable land, which has proven beneficial to local farmers. However, these farmers are particularly affected by seasonal variability, as the receding water levels affect their harvests and the quality of their products with related effects, like food shortages, malnutrition, high market prices and high levels of poverty and hunger.

It is also noticeable that, owing to diminishing rainfall, resources have been depleted and desertification has advanced in the region. Productive activities, including agriculture, fishing, livestock rearing and the trade of the respective products, have also been interrupted by Boko Haram's insurgency and systemic violence via methods such as poisoning of water resources, and also "pillaging of villages, destruction of public buildings, systematic abduction, imprisonment, rape and forced marriages of girls and women, and forced recruitment or execution of boys and men".[87] Where the locals can no longer sustain a living from their environment, looking elsewhere for survival becomes a better option. That better option was found with Boko Haram who offered the poverty-stricken population opportunities for a livelihood. When the youths' livelihood activities or bread-winning actions are cut off or reduced in the region, the only means of surviving hardship was to acquiesce to the attractive offers.[88]

7 Water governance

Effective water governance is essential for human security. This – in the context of climate change – also needs to take adaptation opportunities into account.[89] Water action, peace action and climate action need to move closer together to engender social stability in the transboundary lake region.[90] Conflicts about water in the LCB are

83 Odada et al. (2006).
84 Gleick (2000).
85 GIWA (2004).
86 USGS (2016).
87 Nett & Rüttinger (2016).
88 BIR (2015); Funteh (2015); and Mercy Corps (2016).
89 Babcicky (2013).
90 Gustafsson (2016).

interlinked issues regarding their environmental, vulnerability and security implications. In fact, the need to harmonise and drive actions on resource management and governance was already recognised in the mid-1960s following the adoption of the Fort Lamy Convention, which led to the establishment of the LCBC.[91]

7.1 The Fort Lamy Convention

The political basis for international boundary settlement between the LCB countries was provided by a formal declaration at the Fort Lamy Conference of heads of government in December 1962, where all riparian states agreed to recognise the existing national boundaries of the lake and by the subsequent solemn resolution of the Organisation of African Unity in July 1964 that its member states undertake to respect the frontiers existing at the time when they became independent.[92]

From the *uti possidetis* rule follows a need for careful documentary research to determine the historical origins and current validity of the water boundaries agreed upon between the then colonial powers in the LCB, namely, Great Britain, France, and (until 1919) Germany.[93] After the First World War and the defeat of Germany, former German territories fell to the League of Nations in 1919.[94] According to Article 118 of the Treaty of Versailles, Germany had to renounce its rights over its former colonial territories:

> In territory outside her European frontiers as fixed by the present Treaty, Germany renounces all rights, titles and privileges whatever in or over territory which belonged to her or to her allies, and all rights, titles and privileges whatever their origin which she held as against the Allied and Associated Powers. Germany hereby undertakes to recognise and to conform to the measures which may be taken now or in the future by the Principal Allied and Associated Powers, in agreement where necessary with third Powers, in order to carry the above stipulation into effect.

After the liberalisation of Africa from colonialism, African leaders chose to keep colonial boundaries for the interest of stability and certainty by utilising the *uti possidetis* principle. Since 1964, the water resources of Lake Chad have largely been regulated by the Lake Chad Basin Commission Convention and Statute signed on 22 May 1964 in Fort Lamy (today named N'Djamena).[95]

The Fort Lamy Convention, an instrument of public international law, attempts to balance the conflicting interests of member states. On the one hand, it prohibits any unilateral exploitation of Lake Chad's water by its member states, whereas, on the other hand, it recognises their sovereign rights over the water resources in the basin.

---

91 Sand (1974: 68).
92 Ibid.
93 For further references to the relevant colonial treaties see Sand (1974: 68).
94 Regarding former Namibian and Cameroonian German territories, see for further information Ruppel & Ruppel-Schlichting (2016 and 2018).
95 Jacobs & Mostert (2007: 15).

These opposite aims are difficult to reconcile and contribute to disputes as history has shown.[96]

Generally, the Fort Lamy Convention permits its member states to exploit the resources of the LCB and to utilise the surface and underground waters. The Convention acknowledges the right of member states to plan water-related projects if they consult the LCBC beforehand. While the Convention mainly deals with matters of diplomatic form and procedure, the Statute details the functions of the LCBC,[97] and certain principles of substance, including the basic compromise formula of Article 5 which requires member states to consult with the LCBC before undertaking new projects likely to have an appreciable effect on the overall water balance or water quality of the basin.[98]

Article 5 is the cornerstone provision of the Fort Lamy Convention, which establishes the principle of prior consultation between member states before they initiate measures likely to have marked influence on water quantity or quality, including groundwater reserves. It provides as follows:

> The Member States undertake a refrain from adopting, without referring to the Commission beforehand, any measures likely to exert a marked influence either upon the extent of water losses, or upon the form of the annual hydro graph and limnograph and certain other characteristics of the Lake, upon the conditions of their exploitation by other bordering States, upon the sanitary condition of the water resources or upon the biological characteristics of the fauna and the flora of the Basin.
>
> In particular, the Member States agree not to undertake in that part of the Basin falling within their jurisdiction any work in connection with the development of water resources or the soil likely to have a marked influence upon the system of the water courses and levels of the Basin without adequate notice and prior consultations with the Commission, provided always that the Member States shall retain the liberty of completing any plans and schemes in the course of execution or such plans and schemes as may be initiated over a period of 3 years to run from the signature of the present Convention.

Article 5(2) can be seen as the environmental regulatory arm of the Fort Lamy Convention. It uses, but does not define, the term 'marked influence'. In accordance with the object and purpose of the Fort Lamy Convention, the term should be understood as meaning a measurable and not totally negligible impact on the ecosystem of the basin and the interest of other riparian States.[99]

Regarding navigation on Lake Chad and its tributaries, Article 7 of the Fort Lamy Convention provides that the member states "shall draw up common rules to facilitate as far as possible navigation…on the lake and its surrounding navigable waterways", whereas Article 3 provides that the basin is to be open to use of all member states, without prejudice to the sovereign rights of each, and subject to the establishment of

---

96 Lorenzmeier (2013).

97 The legal texts are available online at <http://www.fao.org/docrep/w7414b/w7414b05.htm> (accessed 6-6-2018).

98 Sand (1974).

99 Ibid.

common rules for the purpose of facilitating navigation on the lake and navigable waters in the basin. Read in conjunction, the provisions prescribe that navigation on Lake Chad still falls under the control of riparian states, which is only regulated by international norms. Article 7 of the Fort Lamy Convention treats the LCB as being of common interest to the riparian states and not as common property.[100]

As the shrinking of the water reserves of the LCB shows, the approaches to resource management in the Lake Chad region have been inadequate. Additionally, droughts, population increase and movement, as well as civil strife are common in the region and have placed constraints on the effective management of transboundary water resources in the area. In order to achieve the aim of sound biodiversity conservation and development in the region, an improvement and strengthening of the rules on environmental protection and their implementation is necessary.[101] Altogether, the "loopholes in the Fort Lamy Convention have long been recognised", and the implementation of the Fort Lamy Convention has had limited success when it comes to the shrinking of the water reserves of Lake Chad.[102]

7.2 The Lake Chad Basin Commission (LCBC)

The LCBC was established on 22 May 1964 by the four countries that border Lake Chad: Cameroon, Niger, Nigeria and Chad. The CAR joined the organisation in 1996 and Libya was admitted in 2008. Observer status is held by Sudan, Egypt, the Republic of Congo and the Democratic Republic of Congo. N'Djamena, the capital of Chad, hosts the Headquarters of the Commission.[103]

Chapter IV of the Statutes of the Fort Lamy Convention regulates the LCBC, which in terms of Article 17 shall, in all respects, enjoy the status of an international body. According to Article 9, the LCBC has the following terms of reference:

> (a) Preparing joint rules, permitting the complete application of the principles affirmed under the present Statutes and the Convention to which it is appended, and ensuring an effective implementation of such rules;
>
> (b) Assembling, examining and diffusing information on the projects prepared by Member States and recommending the planning of joint works and research programmes within the Chad Basin;
>
> (c) Maintaining liaison between the Member States with a view to the most efficient utilisation of the waters of the Basin;
>
> (d) Following up the execution of works and studies in the Chad Basin falling within the present Convention and keeping Member States informed at least once a year through the exploitation of systematic periodic reports which each State undertakes to address to it;

100 Lorenzmeier (2013: 3).
101 Ibid.
102 Aginam (2008: 206).
103 See <http://www.cblt.org/en/lake-chad-basin-commission> (accessed 18-5-2018).

(e) Formulating common rules concerning navigation;
(f) Establishing regulations governing its personnel and ensuring their application;
(g) Examining complaints and assisting in settling disputes;
(h) Supervising the implementation of the provisions of the present Statutes and the Convention to which it is appended.

Article 11 stipulates that the joint regulations and recommendations of the LCBC shall be transmitted to the governments of the member states for their decision. The mandate of the LCBC is to sustainably and equitably manage Lake Chad and other shared water resources of the LCB, to preserve the ecosystems of the LCB, and to promote regional integration, peace and security across the Basin. Promoting international cooperation between the riparian countries in the LCB is the main task of the LCBC. Moreover, the LCBC has a mandate for examining complaints and promoting the settlement of disputes between the parties. It also serves as a general forum for the riparian states on other issues like environmental protection. The work of the LCBC has to be seen in the light of the difficulties the region is facing, its weak powers, and its serious lack of financing. On the positive side, the work of the LCBC contributes to the peaceful settlement of disputes in the region, and as an international body, it is a perfect tool for the harmonisation of conflicting national objectives.[104]

Most importantly, the LCBC is in charge of managing all surface and groundwater resources in the LCB, including aquifers. It is the role of the LCBC to ensure the most efficient use of the Basin's waters. This requires regional (as opposed to national) development, coordination and implementation of measures that provide integrated management mechanisms. Such orchestration of both national and regional activities in the LCB water governance system would ideally also be prepared to mitigate the causes and adapt to the effects of climate change at regional, national and local levels. More recent approaches to water governance and resource management in the LCB region have led to the adoption of the Water Charter for the LCB[105] in 2012 with the aim of facilitating the implementation of the Lake Chad Vision 2025[106] and the Strategic Action Programme for the LCB of 2008.[107]

104 Lorenzmeier (2013).
105 See <https://www.africanwaterfacility.org/fileadmin/uploads/awf/Projects/MULTIN-LAKE CHAD-Water-Charter.pdf> (accessed 12-7-2018).
106 See <https://www.cblt.org/sites/default/files/vision_2025_en.pdf> (accessed 5-6-2018).
107 Cf. <https://iwlearn.net/resolveuid/2cc8f6b24b896184e77164ab75cbf7b1> (accessed 5-6-2018).

7.3 The Water Charter for the Lake Chad Basin

The creation of the Water Charter for the LCB[108] is a response to the fact that precipitation and hydraulic flow conditions in the tributaries of Lake Chad are extremely variable and are likely to be affected by climate change; and that an uncontrolled increase in abstractions could cause significant effects and critically reduce the volume and surface area of the lake as groundwater resources are inadequately managed, and the basin's ecosystems are very sensitive to variations in inflows and pollutant discharge. The risk of the lake drying up, the unavailability of sufficient good quality water resources, the disappearance of animal and plant species, widespread poverty, and risks of inter-community and interstate conflict within the Basin prompt the need for more effective measures to strengthen the legal and institutional framework for the sustainable management of the Basin's environment.

The parties to the Water Charter (Cameroon, CAR, Libya, Niger, Nigeria and Chad) commit themselves toward the following international instruments:

- the United Nations Organisation of 26 June 1945;
- the Constitutive Act of the African Union of 11 July 2000;
- the Revised Treaty of the Community of West African States (ECOWAS) signed on 24 July 1993;
- the Treaty Establishing the Economic Community of Central African States (ECCAS) signed on 18 October 1983;
- the Treaty Establishing the Arab Maghreb Union (AMU) signed on 17 February 1989; and
- the Lake Chad Basin Commission Convention and Statute signed on 22 May 1964 in Fort Lamy.

Moreover, the parties recognise the importance of the provisions made by non-binding international instruments and fundamental principles on international watercourses and lakes, in particular:

- the 1966 Helsinki Rules on the Use of International Watercourses, adopted in Helsinki in 1966;
- the United Nations Resolution 34/186 of 1979 establishing principles for conduct to ensure the conservation and harmonious use of shared natural resources, adopted in New York in 1979;
- the Declaration of the International Conference of Water and the Environment on sustainable development, adopted in Dublin in 1992;
- the 1992 Declaration of the United Nations Conference on the Environment and Development and the Action Plan of the United Nations Conference on the Environment and Development, in particular, Chapter 18 on the protection

108 Document available at <https://www.africanwaterfacility.org/fileadmin/uploads/awf/Projects/MULTIN-LAKECHAD-Water-Charter.pdf> (accessed 5-6-2018).

of freshwater resources and their quality, adopted in Rio de Janeiro in 1992;
- the Declaration of the International Conference of Water and Sustainable Development held in Paris in 1998;
- the Millennium Declaration including the Millennium Development Goals adopted in New York in 2000; and the
- the Ministerial Declaration of the International Conference on Fresh Water held in Bonn in December 2001.

The Water Charter also refers to binding international agreements to codified law on international watercourses and waterbodies and its gradual development, inter alia:
- the African Convention on the Conservation of Nature and Natural Resources dated 16 September 1968, amended on 11 July 2003 in Maputo;
- the Convention on Wetlands of International Importance especially as Waterfowl Habitat, dated 2 February 1971;
- the Convention on the Protection and Use of Transboundary Watercourses and International Lakes, adopted on 17 March 1992; and
- the Convention on the Law of Non-Navigational Uses of International Watercourses, adopted on 21 May 1997.

The major aims of the Water Charter are to regulate the following issues:
- quantitative management of surface and groundwater resources;
- protection and preservation of water quality in the basin's aquatic ecosystems;
- emergency planning and preparedness to ensure the protection of people, the environment and water resources;
- ban on significant harm to others;
- water-borne disease;
- navigation;
- prior notification of planned measures;
- enforcement of environment, water, fishing and navigation rights and regulations;
- collection and exchange of data and information;
- common facilities, facilities of common interest and infrastructure asset management and ownership;
- rights of the basin populations;
- promotional actions;
- implementation of the charter;
- settlement of disputes;
- partnership; and
- financing.

According of Article 1 of the Water Charter, Lake Chad and the watercourses, aquifers and aquatic ecosystems contained in its hydrographic basin, are declared international waters. They are common heritage belonging to the member states of the LCBC. It further provides that member states shall cooperate to achieve the sustainable management and development of Lake Chad in compliance with the rules and principles governing international lakes and watercourses.

In Article 3, the Water Charter stipulates that it constitutes a binding framework the global purpose of which is the sustainable development of the LCB through integrated, equitable, coordinated management of the Basin's shared water resources and environment. It also promotes good governance, sub-regional cooperation and solidarity based on the common interests of member states as key ideals. The Water Charter falls under the framework set by the Fort Lamy Convention for the creation of the LCBC, and the Statute of the Commission signed on 22 May 1964 at Fort Lamy, which it refines and supplements.[109] This is important to note when it comes to the conflict of laws, as the Fort Lamy Convention can be regarded as *lex generalis* and the Water Charter is *lex specialis* to the Convention.

The Water Charter urges member states to use the LCB's surface water and aquifers in their respective national jurisdictions equitably and reasonably to obtain optimal, sustainable benefits that are compatible with the legitimate interests of all the countries in the Basin and with the protection of Lake Chad and the watercourses, aquifers and aquatic ecosystems contained in its hydrographic basin.[110] In the event of natural disasters or disasters caused by human activities affecting Lake Chad or these watercourses, aquifers and aquatic ecosystems, member states are obliged to immediately notify all other Basin countries and the LCBC, thereby allowing them to proceed as necessary to prevent or reduce the effects of the emergency situation on their national territories.[111]

Interestingly, the Water Charter acknowledges that citizens of member states have a right to water and sanitation, which is a fundamental human right and is necessary for human dignity.[112] Member states are obliged to take all normative, institutional and operational measures necessary to guarantee that this right is effectively implemented.[113] Moreover, member states are required to make all necessary internal arrangements, in particular judicial, institutional, operational and financial arrangements, to ensure effective enforcement of the Water Charter.[114]

Where disputes arise from the application or interpretation of the present Water Charter, member states are urged to settle these in a peaceful manner and in accordance with the United Nations Charter, the Constitutive Act of the African Union and the Declaration on Principles of International Law concerning Friendly Relations and

109 Article 6.
110 Article 10.
111 Article 37.
112 Article 72.
113 Ibid.
114 Article 83.

Cooperation among States.[115] Member states are required to seek solutions to their dispute employing direct negotiation,[116] and only if they fail to come to an agreement after negotiation, bring the dispute to the Commission for attempted settlement by way of mediation.[117] If the Commission is unable to settle the dispute, any party to the dispute may bring the matter before the competent regional and sub-regional authorities, which shall, in turn, seek to mediate the dispute.[118] If all the aforementioned dispute resolution mechanisms fail, the disputing parties must bring the case for arbitration or judicial dispute resolution before the International Court of Justice.[119]

7.4 Other relevant international and regional instruments

There are several other important international and regional instruments of key relevance to water governance in the LCB. These are briefly outlined below.

On 25 September 2015, the United Nations General Assembly adopted Resolution 70/1 (Transforming Our World: The 2030 Agenda for Sustainable Development)[120] containing 17 sustainable development goals (SDGs) and targets aimed at ending poverty, protecting the planet and ensuring prosperity for all. Each goal has specific targets to be achieved over the next 15 years. For the goals to be reached, everyone needs to do their part including governments, the private sector and civil society. The 2030 Agenda for Sustainable Development is guided by the purposes and principles of the Charter of the United Nations, including full respect for international law. It is also relevant in the context of the implementation of the LCB Water Charter, and the following goals are particularly relevant for the LCB:

- Goal 1: End poverty in all its forms everywhere;
- Goal 2: End hunger, achieve food security and improved nutrition and promote sustainable agriculture;
- Goal 3: Ensure healthy lives and promote well-being for all at all ages;
- Goal 6: Ensure availability and sustainable management of water and sanitation for all;
- Goal 7: Ensure access to affordable, reliable, sustainable and modern energy for all;
- Goal 8: Promote sustained, inclusive and sustainable economic growth, full and productive employment and decent work for all;

115 Article 85.
116 Article 86.
117 Article 87.
118 Article 88.
119 Article 89.
120 UNGA Res 70/1 'Transforming our World: The 2030 Agenda for Sustainable Development' (21 October 2015 UN Doc A/RES/70/1).

- Goal 9: Build resilient infrastructure, promote inclusive and sustainable industrialisation and foster innovation;
- Goal 10: Reduce inequality within and among countries;
- Goal 11: Make cities and human settlements inclusive, safe, resilient and sustainable;
- Goal 12: Ensure sustainable consumption and production patterns;
- Goal 13: Take urgent action to combat climate change and its impacts;
- Goal 15: Protect, restore and promote sustainable use of terrestrial ecosystems, sustainably manage forests, combat desertification, and halt and reverse land degradation and halt biodiversity loss;
- Goal 16: Promote peaceful and inclusive societies for sustainable development, provide access to justice for all and build effective, accountable and inclusive institutions at all levels; and
- Goal 17: Strengthen the means of implementation and revitalise the Global Partnership for Sustainable Development.

People residing in and around the LCB also need to be protected in terms Article 22 of the African Charter on Human and Peoples' Rights (1986), especially when it comes to the alleviation of poverty. Article 1 of the African Charter compels states to "adopt legislative or other measures to give effect" to the rights protected under the African Charter. Article 22 further stipulates that all people "have the right to their economic, social and cultural development with due regard to their freedom and identity and in the equal enjoyment of the common heritage of mankind" and that states have a duty, individually or collectively, "to ensure the exercise of the right to development". Finally, Article 24 of the African Charter prescribes that all people "shall have the right to a general satisfactory environment favourable to their development".

Similarly, the LCB Water Charter is also subject to various Regional Economic Communities' (RECs) regulatory regimes, such as the Central African Economic and Monetary Community (CEMAC) and the Economic Community of Central African States (ECCAS). CEMAC is composed of six central African states, namely: Cameroon, Republic of the Congo, Gabon, Equatorial Guinea, CAR and Chad. Its main mission is to promote peace and the harmonious development of its member states by establishing an economic union and a monetary union. The CEMAC countries are founder members of the African Union (AU), successor to the Organization of African Unity (OAU). However, all the CEMAC countries also belong to the ECCAS. In addition to the CEMAC countries, ECCAS includes Burundi and the Democratic Republic of the Congo (members of the Economic Community of the Great Lakes Countries), as well as Angola and Sao Tomé and Principe. ECCAS is one of the eight Regional Economic Communities (RECs) designated by the African Union as pillars for the implementation of the African Economic Community. At the ECCAS level, the organisation of a Conference of Ministers responsible for the forests of Central Africa in 2000 provided a framework for harmonisation initiatives. This followed the

Declaration of Yaoundé, in which the ECCAS heads of state proclaimed, among other things, their support for the preservation of biodiversity and the sustainable management of tropical forests. These commitments were institutionalised in the Treaty on the Conservation and Sustainable Management of Forest Ecosystems in Central Africa and to Establish the Central African Forests Commission (COMIFAC) (2005). COMIFAC is the body responsible for formulating, harmonising and monitoring forestry and environmental policies in Central Africa.[121] Unfortunately, COMIFAC so far has not fulfilled the necessary regional legislative harmonisation imperatives.

8 Conclusion

The reflection on selected developmental and legal aspects shows the interdependent complexity of climate change, human security, water governance and the humanitarian crisis in the LCB region. Millions of people depend on Lake Chad. However, the lake's volume has decreased by 90% in area in the last 40 years due to increased drought, as well as human-related causes such as increased irrigation withdrawals. Existing regulatory regimes seem inadequate in preventing the above.

Research has also highlighted the interconnections between the impacts of climate change on natural resources, dependent livelihoods and food insecurity on the one hand; and tension, conflict and mobility on the other.[122] The ongoing crisis is affecting more than 17 million people across northeastern Nigeria, Cameroon's far north, western Chad and south-eastern Niger. Caused by the ravages of violent conflict, extreme poverty, underdevelopment and climate change, more than 10.8 million people are in need of humanitarian assistance.[123] To give more attention to the vulnerability aspect, attempts to link environmental issues to humanitarian security should influence the understanding of the interactions between water scarcity and socio-economic predicaments, which are exacerbated by climate change.

Conflict and fragility are decreasing the resilience of communities making them more vulnerable to climate change which at the same time is further undermining livelihoods and exacerbating the competition around increasingly scarce natural resources. If not broken, this vicious circle threatens to perpetuate the current crisis and take the region further down the path of conflict and fragility.[124] The scarcer resources become, the more power vests in those who control them. Moreover, where state or customary institutions are unable to equitably manage natural resources, competition for scarce resources is more likely to result in violence and situations of fragility.[125] The nexus

121 Article 5 of the abovementioned Treaty.
122 See with further references IOM (2018: 52).
123 CARE (2018).
124 Nagarajan et al. (2018: 25-26).
125 Nett & Rüttinger (2016: 19).

between climate change, vulnerability and humanitarian crises can only be unpacked holistically. In response to this, foreign policymakers have attempted to identify entry points for intervention in the region and effective modes of engagement.[126] The role of humanitarian aid and development cooperation play an increasing role in addressing the root causes of the LCB crisis.[127] This justifies why the integration of climate adaptation, water governance and conflict management in conflict-prone settings is now incorporated within progressive discourses of international environment and development agendas.[128]

Drawing upon evidence in the region, the explanation for conflicts over scarce resources, land, water, and so on, lies in the vulnerable status of the people, and is reinforced by environmental change. Trying to understand the link between conflict and environmental change is not so much a matter of challenging issues intellectually as attempting to bring solutions to the issues. Therefore, science, politics and law need to be brought together to make a significant and timely difference to humanity and especially to those most severely affected.[129]

Climate change permeates the law in many ways creating intersections of law in its diverse fields. Climate change law, an emerging legal discipline, is both international and domestic in nature.[130] Climate law (national, regional and international) should also form part of a social protection system for the LCB region, which has been facing a longstanding history of violent conflict and crisis. This is partly due to complex political instability and weak regulatory, economic and social policies. Regarding the legal dispensation, it will still have to be seen how the implementation and domestication of the LCB Water Charter will help to improve the situation on the ground. It is further hoped that the substantive financial commitments made by the international community can propel its implementation, also in light of other African Union and regional regulatory obligations.

One key challenge according to the Lake Chad Development and Climate Resilience Action Plan (2015) is to improve water and natural resources governance of the LCB, especially when it comes to more effective decision making, control and participation in public policy.[131] This has also been acknowledged by Resolution 2349/2017 of the United Nations Security Council, which recognises the complex challenges faced by the LCB region and welcomes the development of programmes by the respective governments to help build and sustain peace by addressing the root causes of

126 Nagarajan et al. (2018: 27).
127 Ibid.
128 Ludwig et al. (2011).
129 Ruppel (2012 and 2013); Ruppel & Ruppel-Schlichting (2012); and Ruppel & Wulff (2016).
130 Ruppel (2013: 37).
131 See <http://documents.worldbank.org/curated/en/489801468186879029/pdf/102851-v2-WP-P149275-Box394847B-PUBLIC-v2-main-report-Lake-Chad-Development-and-Action-Plan-English.pdf> (accessed 28-5-2018).

the crisis. In the same resolution, the Security Council calls upon respective governments to strengthen their coordination and prioritisation within these programmes to enable more effective implementation.[132]

Whether climate change is gradually moving from mere politicisation towards a state of securitisation remains to be seen.[133] Once an issue is successfully securitised it moves out of the sphere of normal politics to be dealt with as an emergency issue without the normal democratic processes being brought to bear, and the securitising actor can, through this process, infuse the concept of 'security' with any meaning desired.[134] Although such development would have some merits, in the context of the post-2015 Development Agenda, human security has already become a critical reference point.[135] The Declaration on the SDGs emphasises a world free of poverty, hunger, disease, want, fear and violence; with equitable and universal access to quality education, health care, social protection, safe drinking water and sanitation; where food is sufficient, safe, affordable and nutritious; where habitats are safe, resilient and sustainable; and where there is universal access to affordable, reliable and sustainable energy.[136] Although the term human security itself is not mentioned in the declaration, it stresses that sustainable development cannot be realised without peace and security and that peace and security will be at risk without sustainable development.[137] This is particularly true in the LCB, where water poverty affects large sectors of the population with no access to safe drinking water or which experience droughts impeding agricultural production.[138]

There are also growing suggestions that the 2015 Paris Agreement on climate change and the SDGs should provide vital entry points to spearhead opportunities for cross-thematic integration of vital issues confronting less developed nations. At a minimum, the template provided by these international processes can facilitate ways in which institutional, financial, technical and political dimensions of policy integration can be understood, reconciled and/or negotiated.[139] After all, the Paris Agreement is an agreement under international law. Its central objective is the determination of binding quality goals for the protection of the climate for nearly the entire international community. For the first time in human history, the international community has agreed to a quantified climate protection goal. If this goal is to be reached it will be through Nationally Determined Contributions (NDCs). All countries in the LCB

---

132 Resolution 2349 (2017) S/RES/2349 (2017), adopted by the Security Council at its 7911th meeting on 31 March 2017.

133 Ruppel (2013: 23).

134 Taureck (2006: 55).

135 Wählisch (2016: 5).

136 UNGA Res 70/1 'Transforming our World: The 2030 Agenda for Sustainable Development' (21 October 2015 UN Doc A/RES/70/1).

137 Wählisch (2016: 6).

138 See also wording on water scarcity in Africa in Pope Francis' *Laudato Si* (2015: 28).

139 Okpara et al. (2018: 40).

region submitted their NDCs prior to COP21 in Paris. Although the failure to reach the announced NDCs is not sanctionable according to the Paris Agreement, the LCB countries are expected to make national provisions to guarantee enforcement of their commitments.[140] Thus, the next step will be to begin implementing measures to achieve the NDCs. In the LCB, as in other regions of the world, this requires a firm political will to act, to develop and implement policy means that will contribute to reaching these national goals.[141]

References

Aginam, O (2008) "International law and shared watercourses: the River Niger, Lake Chad and their West African riparian states" in M Kitissou, M Ndulo, M Nagel & M Grieco (eds) *The hydropolitics of Africa: a contemporary challenge* 197-218.

Babcicky, P (2013) "A conflict sensitive approach to climate change adaptation" 25(4) *Peace Review* 480.

BIR / Bataillon d'Intervention Rapide (2015) *Intelligence Report*.

Black, R, N Adger, NW Arnell, S Dercon, A Geddes & D Thomas (2011) "The effect of environmental change on human migration" 21(1) *Global Environmental Change* S3-S11.

Caminade, C & L Terray (2010) "Twentieth Century Sahel rainfall variability as simulated by the ARPEGE AGCM, and future changes" 35(1) *Climate Dynamics* 75-94.

CARE (2018) *Humanitarian crisis in Nigeria and the Lake Chad Basin*, at <https://www.care.org/emergencies/global-hunger-crisis/humanitarian-crisis-nigeria-and-lake-chad-basin> (accessed 22-5-2018).

Charney, JG (1975) "Dynamics of deserts and drought in Sahel" 101 *Quarterly Journal of Royal Meteorological Society* 193-202.

Coe, MT & JA Foley (2001) "Human and natural impacts on the water resources of the Lake Chad Basin" 106 *Journal of Geophysical Research* 3349-3356.

Dai, A, KE Trenberth & T Qian (2004) "A global data set of Palmer Drought Severity Index for 1870-2002: relationship with soil moisture and effects of surface warming" 5 *Journal of Hydrometeorology* 1117-1130.

Drake, N & C Bristow (2006) "Shorelines in the Sahara: Geomorphological evidence for an enhanced monsoon from palaeolake Megachad" 16 *The Holocene* 901-911.

FAO / Food and Agricultural Organization, UNDP / United Nations Development Programme and Lake Chad Basin Commission (1983) *Well-drilling for groundwater exploitation purposes in the conventional Lake Chad Basin*.

FAO / Food and Agricultural Organization (2009) *Adaptive water management in the Lake Chad Basin: addressing current challenges and adapting to future needs*. Food and Agriculture Organization (FAO) Water Seminar Proceedings of the World Water Week, Stockholm, 16-22 August, at <http://www.fao.org/fileadmin/user_upload/faowater/docs/ChadWWW09.pdf> (accessed 3-6-2018).

140 Ruppel & Wulff (2016).
141 See also KAS (2018).

FAO / Food and Agricultural Organization (2017) Lake Chad Basin crisis. Response strategy (2017-2019), <at http://www.fao.org/3/a-bs126e.pdfhttp://www.fao.org/3/a-bs126e.pdf> (accessed 12-7-2018).

Funteh, MB (2015) "The paradox of Cameroon-Nigeria interactions: connecting between the edges of opportunity/benefit and quandary" 6(3) *International Journal of Peace and Development Studies* 30-48.

Gao, H, T Bohn, E Podest & K McDonald (2011) "On the causes of the shrinking of Lake Chad" 6034021 *Environmental Research Letters* 1-7.

GIWA / Global International Waters Assessment (2004) *Africa water atlas, Volume 1.*

Glantz, MH (2004) *Lake Chad and the Aral Sea: a sad tale of two lakes*, at <http://www.fragilecologies.com/sep09_04.html> (accessed 10-6-2018).

Gleick, PH (2000) "The world's water 2000-2001" *The Biennial Report on Freshwater Resources* 19.

Gustafsson, M (2016) *How do development organisations integrate climate and conflict risks? Experiences and lessons learnt from the UK, Germany and the Netherlands*, at <http://www.statsvet.su.se/polopoly_fs/1.282384.1463143383 1/menu/standard/file/How%20do%20Development%20 Organisations%20Integrate%20Climate%20and%20Conflict%20Risks.pdf> (accessed 10-5-2018).

Hall, EL (2009) *Conflict for resources: water in the Lake Chad Basin* Research Monograph, School of Advanced Military Studies, United States Army Command and General Staff College.

Henninger, N, C Revenga, J Brunner, K Kassem & R Payne (2000) *Pilot analysis of global ecosystems: freshwater systems*, at <http://www.wri.org/publication/pilot-analysis-global-ecosystems-2> (accessed 3-4-2018).

Ifabiyi, IP (2013) "Recharging the Lake Chad: the hydro-politics of national security and regional integration in Africa" 7 *African Research Review* 196-216.

ICG / International Crisis Group (2017) *Cameroon: a worsening Anglophone crisis calls for strong measures*, at <https://d2071andvip0wj.cloudfront.net/b130-cameroon-a-worsening-anglophone-crisis-calls-for-strong-measures.pdf> (accessed 12-6-2018).

IOM / International Organization for Migration (2017) *Lake Chad Basin crisis. Snapshot*, at <https://displacement.iom.int/reports/lake-chad-basin-crisis-iom-response-snapshot-december-2017> (accessed 12-6-2018).

IOM / International Organization for Migration (2018) *World migration report 2018.*

Jacobs, J & H Mostert (2007) "Boundary disputes in Africa" in *Max Planck Encyclopaedia of Public International Law.*

KAS / Konrad-Adenauer-Stiftung (2018) *Science, economics and politics of climate change: a guide for policymakers in Cameroon.*

Le Barbe, L & T Lebel (1997) "Rainfall climatology of the HAPEX-Sahel region during the years 1950-1990" 188 *Journal of Hydrology* 43-73.

Lélé, MI & PJ Lamb (2010) "Variability of the Inter-Tropical Front (ITF) and rainfall over the West African Sudan-Sahel zone" 23 *Journal of Climate* 3984-4004.

Lienou, GG, JC Mahe Olivry, E Naah, L Servat, D Sigha-Nkamdkou, JN Sighomnou, E Ngoupayou, E Ekodeck & JE Paturel (2005) "Flow regimes of suspended solids in Cameroon: review and synthesis at the level of principal ecosystems; diverse climate and human actions" 50(1) *Hydrological Science Journal* 111-123.

Living Waters (2003) *Managing rivers wisely: Lake Chad*, at <assets.panda.org/downloads/mrwlakechadcasestudy.pdf> (accessed 10-3-2018).

Lorenzmeier, S (2013) "Lake Chad" in *Max Planck Encyclopaedia of Public International Law.*

Ludwig, R, R Roson, C Zografos & G Kallis (2011) "Towards an inter-disciplinary research agenda on climate change, water and security in southern Europe and neighbouring countries" 14(7) *Environmental Science and Policy* 794-803.

Malo, AR & SE Nicholson (1990) "A Study of rainfall and vegetation dynamics in the African Sahel using normalized difference vegetation index" 19(1) *Journal of Arid Environments* 1-24.

Mekonnen, DT (2016) *The Lake Chad development and climate resilience action plan: summary.*

McMichael, AJ, CF Corvalán, KL Ebi & JD Scheraga (eds) (2003) *Climate change and human health risks and responses.*

Mercy Corps (2016) *Motivations and empty promises: voices of former Boko Haram combatants and Nigerian youth,* at <https://www.mercycorps.org.uk/research-resources/motivations-and-empty-promises-voices-former-boko-haram-combatants-and-nigerian> (accessed 26-5-2018).

Nagarajan, C, B Pohl, L Rüttinger, F Sylvestre, J Vivekananda, M Wall & S Wolfmaier (2018) *Climate-fragility profile: Lake Chad Basin.*

Nett, K & L Rüttinger (2016) *Insurgency, terrorism and organised crime in a warming climate; analysing the links between climate change and non-state armed groups.*

Niang, I, & OC Ruppel (2014) "Africa" in VR Barros, CB Field, DJ Dokken, MD Mastandrea, KJ Mach, TE Bilir, M Chatterjee, KL Ebi, YO Estrada, RC Genova, B Girma, ES Kissel, AN Levy, S MacCracken, PR Mastrandrea & LL White (eds) *Climate change 2014: impact, adaptation, and vulnerability: contribution of Working Group II to the Fifth Assessment Report of the Intergovernmental Panel on Climate Change* 1199-1265.

Nicholson, SE, X Yin & MB Ba (2000) "On the feasibility of using a lake water balance model to infer rainfall: an example from Lake Victoria" 45(1) *Hydrological Science Journal* 75-95.

Odada, E, L Oyebande & J Oguntola (2006) *Lake Chad: experience and lessons learned,* at <http://www.ilec.or.jp/eg/lbmi/pdf/06_Lake_Chad_27February2006.pdf> (accessed 12-5-2018).

Ohlsson, L (2003) "The risk of livelihood conflicts and the nature of policy measures required" in N Nicholas & L Kittrie (eds) *Seeds of true peace: responding to the discontents of a global community* 49.

Okonkwo, C & B Demoz (2013) "Characteristics of drought indices and rainfall in the Lake Chad Basin" 34(22) *International Journal of Remote Sensing* 7945-7961.

Okpara, UT, LC Stringer, A Dongill & D Mohammed (2015) "Conflict and water in Lake Chad" 15(4) *Progress in Development Studies* 308-325.

Olivry, J, G Chouret, G Vuillaume, J Lemoalle & J Bricquet (1996) "Hydrology of the Lake Chad Basin" 12 *Monographs of Hydrology* 266.

Onuoha, FC (2008) "Environmental degradation, livelihood and conflict: A focus on the implications of the diminishing Lake Chad Basin for North-Eastern Nigeria" 8(2) *African Journal on Conflict Resolution* 35-61.

Ovie, IS & B Emma (2011) "Identification and reduction of climate change vulnerability in the fisheries of the Lake Chad basin" in C De Young, S Sheridan, S Davies & A Hjort (eds) *Climate change implications for fishing communities in the Lake Chad Basin* 23.

Pope Francis (2015) *Laudato Si': on care for our common home* (Encyclical), at <http://w2.vatican.va/content/francesco/en/encyclicals/documents/papa-francesco_20150524_enciclica-laudato-si.html> (accessed 10-3-2018).

Rüttinger, L, G Stang, D Smith, D, Tänzler & J Vivekanada (2015) *A new climate for peace – taking action on climate and fragility risks.*

Ruppel, OC (2012) "Wasser und Land – Brennpunkte innerhalb der Entwicklungsgemeinschaft des südlichen Afrika (SADC)" in M Reder & H Pfeifer (eds) *Kampf um Ressourcen. Weltordnung zwischen Konkurrenz und Kooperation – Globale Solidarität, Schritte zu einer neuen Weltkultur* 59.

Ruppel, OC (2013) "Intersections of law and cooperative global climate governance – challenges in the Anthropocene" in OC Ruppel, C Roschmann & K Ruppel-Schlichting (eds) *Climate change: international law and global governance. Volume I: Legal responses and global responsibility* 29.

Ruppel, OC & K Ruppel-Schlichting (2012) "Climate change and human security: relevant for regional integration in SADC?" in T Hartzenberg, G Erasmus & A Du Pisani (eds), *Monitoring regional integration in southern Africa – 2011 Yearbook for Regional Integration* 32.

Ruppel, OC & Ruppel-Schlichting, K (2016) "Namibia and its legal setup" in OC Ruppel & K Ruppel-Schlichting (eds) *Environmental law and policy in Namibia: towards making Africa the tree of life* 3 ed. 1.

Ruppel, OC & K Ruppel-Schlichting (2018) "Cameroon in a nutshell – human and natural environment, historical overview and legal setup" in OC Ruppel & ED Kam Yogo (eds) *Environmental law and policy in Cameroon: towards making Africa the tree of life*.

Ruppel, OC & M Stell (unpublished 2017, on file with the author) *Länderbericht: Kamerun, die ehemalig deutsche Kolonie: Stabilitätsanker Zentralafrikas in politisch unruhigen Gewässern*?.

Ruppel, OC & A Wulff (2016) "Climate change and energy security in the Anthropocene: Africa in the light of the Paris Climate Protection Agreement" 2 *International Reports, Climate-Energy-Security, Konrad Adenauer Stiftung* 46.

Sand, PH (1974) "Development of international water law in the Lake Chad Basin" 34(1) *Zeitschrift für Ausländisches Öffentliches Recht und Völkerrecht* 52-82.

SIPRI / Stockholm International Peace Research Institute (2017) *Yearbook (2017) armaments, disarmament and international security*.

Sullivan, S & R Rohde (2002) "On non-equilibrium in arid and semiarid grazing systems" 29(12) *Journal of Biogeography* 1595-1618.

Taureck, R (2006) "Securitization theory and securitization studies" 9(1) *Journal of International Relations and Development* 53-61.

Tir, J & D Stinnett (2012) "Weathering climate change: Can institutions mitigate international water conflict?" 49(1) *Journal of Peace Research* 211-225.

UCDP / Uppsala Conflict Dataset Project (2008) *Armed conflict data 1946-2007*, at <http://www.pcr.uu.se/research/ucdp/datasets/ucdp_prio_armed_conflict_dataset/> (accessed 20-2-2018).

UNDP / United Nations Development Programme (2016) *Human Development Report 2016*, at <http://hdr.undp.org/sites/default/files/2016_human_development_report.pdf> (accessed 7-7-2018).

UNEP / United Nations Environment Programme (2004) *Lake Chad Basin* (GIWA / Global International Waters Assessment Regional Assessment 43).

UNOCHA / United Nations Office for the Coordination of Humanitarian Affairs (2016) *Lake Chad Basin emergency: revised requirement and response priorities*.

USGS / United States Geological Survey (2014) *Earth-shots: Satellite images of the environmental changes in Lake Chad, West Africa*, at <http://earthshots.usgs.gov/earthshots/Lake-Chad-WestAfrica> (accessed 2-3-2018).

USGS / United States Geological Survey (2016) *Mineral commodity summaries 2016*, at <https://minerals.usgs.gov/minerals/pubs/mcs/2016/mcs2016.pdf> (accessed 3-4-2018).

Wählisch, M (2016) "Human security" in *Max Planck Encyclopaedia of Public International Law*.

Wallensteen, P, & S Margareta (1999) "Armed conflict 1980-1998" 18 *Journal of Peace Research* 593.

Wolf, AT, SB Yoffe & M Giordano (2003) "International waters: identifying basins at risk" 5(1) *Water Policy* 29-60.

Chapter 6:
Forests, forest rights, benefit-sharing and climate change implications under Cameroonian law

Christopher F. Tamasang

1 Introduction

In addition to the vital functions of forests, international climate change negotiations have given an additional dimension to the value of forests regarding their climate change mitigation (CCM) relevance. Cameroon's forestry legal framework classifies forests into various types, and a corresponding bundle of rights is attached to each forest type in addition to a mechanism for the allocation and sharing of benefits. The implementation of this legal framework has CCM implications. This chapter identifies the various forest types, the bundle of rights attached thereto and the formula for allocating and sharing benefits under the forestry laws, analysing their implications for CCM. The chapter argues that although Cameroon's forestry legislation puts in place a bundle of rights attached to each forest type and a mechanism for benefit-sharing (BS), the forest rights are not adequate for some relevant stakeholders involved in forest management, and the BS mechanism is plagued with inherent flaws. By extension, it does not enhance the role of forests in contributing to CCM in Cameroon. The principal objective of this chapter is to demonstrate that the role of forests in contributing to CCM in Cameroon, which can only be enhanced by the establishment of adequate forest rights for relevant stakeholders involved in forests management, and the effective implementation of a fair and equitable BS paradigm aimed at incentivising sustainable forest management (SFM) and forest conservation. The chapter analyses Cameroon's legislation, focusing specifically on how it provides for the protection of the various types of forests, forest rights, mechanisms for BS, assessing their CCM implications in Cameroon. The chapter concludes that the role of the country's forests in contributing to CCM is greatly hindered due to aninadequate and inappropriate recognition of forest rights reserved for some relevant stakeholders involved in forest management and a corresponding inadequate and inappropriate BS formula, underscoring the need for urgent legal reforms. The chapter ends with some recommendations.

1.1 Contextualising the study

Global climatic change primarily driven by the quest for economic development across countries is accelerating. Humankind has altered the natural global environment to the extent that the earth is becoming warmer, causing climate change that has suddenly vaulted to the top of global agenda, traceable to global initiatives intended to address the phenomenon, its causes and adverse effects on common concerns of humankind.[1] One such leading global initiative is the United Nations Framework Convention on Climate Change (UNFCCC) signed in 1992 as one of the outcomes of the Rio Conference on Environment and Development according to which, climate change is attributed directly or indirectly to human activity that alters the composition of the global atmosphere and which is in addition to natural climate variability observed over comparable time periods.[2] The UNFCCC identifies two policy responses to address climate change; to wit: climate change mitigation (CCM) by reducing greenhouse gases (GHGs) in the atmosphere and enhancing carbon sinks, and adaptation to the impacts of climate change.[3] CCM is thus any intervention strategy or action taken to reduce GHG concentrations in the atmosphere by avoiding further emissions from sources or by enhancing sinks of GHGs (principally atmospheric carbon dioxide (CO_2)). The UNFCCC has as an ultimate objective, the stabilisation of GHG concentrations in the atmosphere at a level that would prevent dangerous anthropogenic interference with the climate system and such a level should be achieved within a period sufficient to allow ecosystems to adapt naturally to climate change, to ensure that food production is not threatened and to enable economic development to proceed in a sustainable manner.[4]

To minimise potentially severe climate change impacts, the UNFCCC negotiations have set a goal of limiting global warming to 2°C above pre-industrial levels.[5] Likewise, the 2015 Paris Agreement has as a primary goal, to keep a global temperature rise this century below 2°C and to drive efforts to limit temperature increase even further to 1.5°C above pre-industrial levels.[6] Just like the UNFCCC, the Paris Agreement identifies forests as one of the significant sinks and reservoirs of GHGs and directs parties to take action to implement activities relating to reducing emissions from deforestation and forest degradation. It emphasises the role of conservation, sustainable management of forests and enhancement of forest carbon stocks under its Article 5. Since Cameroon is not an industrialised country, its various forest types will play a critical role in helping the government in achieving its 32% emissions reduction

1 Tamasang (2009: 172).
2 Article 1(2) of the UNFCCC.
3 Article 2 of the UNFCCC.
4 Article 2 of the UNFCCC.
5 Article 17 of Kyoto Protocol to the UNFCCC.
6 See Article 17 of the Paris Climate Change Agreement adopted on 15 December 2015, signed in New York on 22 April 2016 and entered into force on 4 November 2016.

pledged under its Nationally Determined Contributions (NDCs). Originally submitted as Intended Nationally Determined Contributions (INDCs), these become binding NDCs when a country ratifies the Paris Agreement.[7] For the country's forest to ait in achieving the above emission reduction, the various types of forests must be managed sustainably. This would, however, depend on the extent to which the various forests types classified, rights thereto attached and the benefit-sharing entitlements are implemented.

Forests play some vital economic, socio-cultural, ecological and environmental functions[8] and when sustainably managed, can play a central role in mitigating climate change. The intrinsic relationship between climate change and forests has brought renewed attention to forests and land use. The international climate change negotiations have provided an additional dimension to the value of forests in terms of their carbon sequestration[9] and carbon-storing potential, which have CCM relevance. This crucial role of forests in contributing to CCM has been broadly acknowledged and has become the central issue in the global forest-related dialogue and policy processes and their role in CCM is receiving increasing attention.[10] Forests play an important role in stabilising GHG concentrations in the atmosphere,[11] and as the most significant terrestrial carbon reservoir covering nearly one-third of the earth's land surface, they account for almost half of the earth's terrestrial carbon pool.[12] In their growth process, forests transform the gas to the solid carbon that makes up their bark, wood, leaves and roots. Globally, forests potentially provide abatement equivalent to about 25% of current

7 Under the Paris Agreement, the INDC become the first NDCs when a country ratifies the Agreement, unless they decide to submit a new NDC at the same time. Thus, the NDC became the first greenhouse gas targets under the UNFCCC that applied equally to both developed and developing countries upon ratification of the Agreement. On 28 September 2015, Cameroon submitted its INDCs to the Secretariat of the UNFCCC. In its INDCs, Cameroon pledged a 32% reduction in emissions by 2035 compared to business-as-usual levels, taking 2010 as the reference year and conditional upon international support in the form of financing, capacity building and transfer of technology.

8 Forests have important functions including: in economic development; provide revenue for the state, basic needs for rural population; ecologically, socially and culturally; protection of the soil and watersheds or catchments, enhance agricultural activities especially agroforestry, provide opportunities for public education, research and recreation, a source of medicinal plants, provide habitats/home to the majority of terrestrial species, protect biodiversity. For more on such functions, see Tamasang (2007); IUCN (2017); COICA (2013); Desclée et al. (2013); FAO (2005); and Rautner et al. (2013).

9 In this context, carbon sequestration refers to the uptake and storage of carbon by forests. It is the process of removing carbon from the atmosphere and depositing it in a reservoir. Carbon sequestration is an ecosystem service that provides a vital contribution to CCM and this service can be enhanced by maintaining ecosystem resilience in space and time.

10 The Bali Action Plan (2008) under the auspices of the UNFCCC, sought to mobilise positive incentives for countries to reduce their forest-based GHG emissions. See Weaver (2011); Kadar (2011: 185); and UNEP (2014: vi).

11 Article 2 of the Kyoto Protocol to the UNFCCC.

12 CPF *Strategic framework for forests and climate change* (2008: iii).

CO_2 emissions from fossil fuels by 2030, through a combination of national strategies.[13] The total volume of carbon locked up in forests is currently greater than that held in the atmosphere according to the 2006 Stern Report.[14] Forests have a tremendous capacity to cause as well as avoid and remove carbon emissions. Preserving forests means that carbon is stored in them rather than emitted into the atmosphere, where it accelerates climate change.[15] When forests are cleared or degraded, their stored carbon is released into the atmosphere as CO_2. Forests thus play an important role in the global carbon cycle as both a sink (absorbing CO_2) and a source (emitting CO_2). What happens to forests, therefore, has crucial implications in the climate change saga. Although the largest share of GHG emissions is as a result of the combustion of fossil fuels; in 2005 about 18% of annual global GHG emissions were attributable to deforestation and other land use change.[16] In 2011, the FAO stated that an estimated 17.4% of GHG emissions are derived from the forest sector, in large part due to deforestation and that forests have considerable potential for carbon sequestration.[17] Other estimates indicate that tropical deforestation and forest degradation account for between 12 to 25% of global anthropogenic emissions resulting from land use change, depending on the year and the measurement methodology used.[18] Accordingly, forest-based CCM efforts must be balanced with other forest objectives. Forests can and must be part of the solution to keeping the climate within the globally accepted two-degree temperature increase limit.

Forest management usually involves the reconciliation of multiple and sometimes conflicting rights and the allocation and sharing of benefits derived from the same. That said, there is a nexus between forests, forest rights, BS and CCM. Climate Smart Forestry or Climate Friendly Forestry (forest management that does not cause climate change, but contributes to CCM) strongly depends on the nature of forest rights and BS scheme, which can act as an incentive or disincentive to sustainable forest management (SFM) and forest conservation with implications for CCM. In fact, the legal guarantee of adequate forest rights for all relevant stakeholders in forest management and a fair and equitable BS paradigm are incentives for forest protection that can greatly enhance their CCM role. Thus, strengthening forest rights and the BS scheme can serve as an incentive for forestry actions that contribute to CCM. However, ensuring adequate forest rights and a fair and equitable BS mechanism seem to be an undervalued and often-overlooked strategy for enhancing forests' CCM role in Cameroon.

---

13 Reinhard (2011: 4).

14 Ibid.

15 OECD (2015).

16 Secretariat of the Convention on Biological Diversity (2009: 52); Boyd (2014: 470); Pittock (2009: 1570); and Costenbader (2011: 3).

17 FAO (2011).

18 See Van Asselt (2012: 1214); Norman & Smita (2014: 3); Alix-Garcia & Wolff (2014: 361-363); Brack (2012: 4); Emily & Hisham (2014: 13); and Corbera & Schroeder (2010: 1).

The legal guarantee of forest rights for relevant stakeholders in forest management especially communities tends to lower deforestation and forest carbon emissions as stakeholders with secured forest rights will be motivated to maintain or enhance their forests' carbon stocks.

The 1994 Cameroonian Forestry Law[19] and its enabling instruments (implementation Decree[20], the joint MINADT/MINFI/MINFOF Order on the annual forestry fees[21]) constitute the main legal instruments implementing the counties' forestry policy. The law and related enabling instruments lay down the forestry, wildlife and fisheries regulations within a framework of integrated management, sustainable conservation and usage.[22] The implementation of the aforementioned is thus also relevant to forest rights, BS and CCM in Cameroon.

1.2 Theoretical and conceptual frameworks

In recent years, the management of natural resources such as forests, the rights attached thereto and corresponding benefit entitlements have become a significant concern of legal theorists. Going by the public trust theory of natural resource management, it provides that the state has the duty to hold natural or environmental resources in trust for the benefit of the public and not to make them subject to private ownership.[23] In addition, the theory of decentralisation and participation in environmental and natural resource governance requires the state to achieve sustainability objectives through collective action by ensuring broader and inclusive stakeholder participation. In the same vein, any meaningful discussion on rights in any field of study and on forest rights and benefit entitlements as articulated in this chapter cannot proceed without invoking Hohfeld's theoretical considerations and analysis of 'legal rights'[24] which has often been extolled as a paradigm of conceptual clarity of legal rights. Hohfeld's theory of legal rights, in a nutshell, seeks to clarify juridical relationships between the relevant parties.

The concept of forest rights is used in this chapter to depict the property rights tied to the various types of forests and their resources. In other words, forest rights are utilised here to represent ownership, access, use and management rights associated with the different types of forests and their resources. In addition, the concept of BS is

19 Law No. 94/01 of 20 January 1994 to lay down forestry, wildlife and fisheries regulations.
20 Decree No. 95/531/PM of 23 August 1995 setting the terms and conditions of application of the forest regime.
21 Joint Order No. 122/MINADT/MINFI/MINFOF of 29 April 1998 issued to lay down conditions for the use of revenue derived from forestry fees.
22 Section 1 of the 1994 Forestry Law.
23 For more on this theory, cf. Tamasang (2007: 4).
24 Hohfeld (1919).

employed in this chapter to connote the allocation and sharing of benefits derived from forest management.

Studies conducted on the classification of forests, forest rights and BS in Cameroon are instructive but not focused on the assessment of their implication for CCM. The research question guiding this chapter is whether the law on the classification of forests, the rights attached thereto and the BS paradigm favour Sustainable Forest Management (SFM) and forest conservation enhancing the role of forests in contributing to CCM in Cameroon? Thus, the thrust of the chapter is to demonstrate the role of forests in contributing to CCM in Cameroon can only be enhanced with the establishment of a system of adequate forest rights for all relevant stakeholders in forest management and a fair and equitable benefit allocation and sharing scheme, whose effective implementation can incentivise SFM and forest conservation. This is more so because the UNFCCC's REDD+[25] mechanism designed to mitigate climate change has added financial value to carbon stored in forests which is still considered to be a relatively new forest commodity.

1.3 Methodology

This chapter makes a content analysis of the forestry legal framework, including recent policy and legal developments on climate change and forest governance such as REDD+, the UNFCCC, its Kyoto Protocol, the Paris Agreement, and the NDCs. The author also makes use of desk research consisting of the reading and reviewing of records, with the aim of identifying policy and legislative changes that can be recommended with respect to forests, forest rights, BS and how they can enhance the role of forests in contributing to CCM in Cameroon.

2 Forest types, forest rights and their implications for climate change mitigation in Cameroon

Forest rights can be described as a bundle of rights that may include various combinations of ownership, access and use, management and alienation rights. In some cases, a single user may command all of the aforementioned rights, while in other cases, different users may claim some subset of these rights associated with the same area of forest.[26] For instance, it is possible for the state to claim ownership of forest lands

25 Reducing Emissions from Deforestation and Degradation, conservation of forest carbon stocks, enhancement of forest carbon stocks and sustainable forest management in developing countries.

26 UNEP (2015: 45); Springer & Larsen (2012: 4); and Climate Focus (2015).

giving a permit to a private entity to carry out other activities, while at the same time a community may have the right to live in and use the same forest. In Cameroon, these rights are poorly defined, weakly enforced, overlapping and - at times - generate tenure conflicts over these areas.[27] Of particular relevance to CCM, are ownership rights which are often exclusive; use or *usufruct* rights, which are more limited than ownership rights, and which can belong to other actors than the owner. They comprise individual and collective rights, tangible rights pertaining to physical land and resources such as trees and intangible rights, which cannot be physically acquired. That for instance applies to carbon credits derived from carbon stored in trees and biomass, which today constitute a new but controversial forest commodity. This is especially true when it comes to ownership and benefit due to a lack of existing legislation in Cameroon.

2.1 Types of forests and related rights under Cameroonian law

The 1994 Forestry Law classifies national forest into permanent forest estates (PFE) and non-permanent forest estates (NPFE).[28] PFE comprise lands that are used solely for forestry and/or as wildlife habitat[29] and consists of state and council forests[30], covering at least 30% of the total area of the national territory, reflecting the country's ecological diversity.[31] NPFE or unclassified forests comprise forest lands that may be used for other purposes than forestry[32] and consist of communal forests, community forests and forests belonging to private individuals.[33] In classifying forests, the 1994 Forestry legislator established different rights attached to the different types of forests. The nature and exercise of such rights may also have implications for CCM in Cameroon.

2.1.1 State forests, rights attached thereto and climate change mitigation implications

Under Section 24(1) of the 1994 Forestry Law, state forests include (a) areas protected for wildlife, such as national parks, game reserves, hunting areas, game ranches belonging to the state, wildlife sanctuaries, buffer zones and zoological gardens belonging to the state. Section 24(1)(b) provides for forest reserves consisting of production

27 See Korwin (2016); Blomley (2013: 11); and Mboh et al. (2012: 25).
28 Section 20(1).
29 Section 20(2).
30 Section 21(2)(a) and (b).
31 Section 22 (1).
32 Section 20(3).
33 See Section 34(a), (b) and (c) respectively.

forests, protection forests, integral ecological reserves, recreation forests, teaching and research forests, plant life sanctuaries, botanical gardens and forest plantations.

Under Section 26(1), the instrument classifying a state forest is expected to take into account the social environment of the local population, who are entitled to maintain their logging rights in such forests. However, under Section 26(2), such rights may be limited if they are contrary to the purpose of the forest. In such a case, the local population is entitled to compensation. Article 26(1) of the Decree implementing the 1994 Forestry Law further provides that the population living around state forests is entitled to maintain their *usufruct* rights consisting in carrying out within these forests their traditional activities, such as collecting secondary forest products, notably raffia, palms, bamboo, cane or foodstuff and firewood.

Article 26(2) of the Decree further provides that in order to meet the domestic needs for poles and firewood, the neighbouring populations concerned can cut down a number of trees commensurate to such needs. They are, however, strictly forbidden to sell or exchange wood from such trees. The respect and effective implementation of these rights of the local population could constitute an incentive for improved SFM and conservation of state forests, both relevant for CCM. This can motivate local populations to adopt more sustainable exploitation methods that do not contribute to deforestation and forest degradation, thereby maintaining the carbon stocks of such forests. However, the forest rights recognised by the aforementioned legal provisions are inadequate for the local population since their implementation has not been effective. This inadequacy is captured in the discussion that follows.

2.1.2 Council forests, rights derived therefrom and climate change mitigation implications

Under Section 30(1) of the 1994 Forestry Law, a council forest is a forest that has been classified on behalf of a local council or has been planted by the local council. Section 32(3) provides that forest products stemming from the exploitation of council forests are the sole property of the council concerned. Under Section 67(2) councils, for the exploitation of their forests, receive the selling price of forest products and the annual royalty for the forest area. Section 30(2) determines the management objectives of council forests, as well as logging rights by the respective local population. These entitlements can motivate more SFM of council forests, contributing to CCM. Section 32(3) can also enfold positive implications for CCM then belonging to the council in question. In the same vein, Section 67(2), which gives the council the right to the entitlement of the selling price of forest products and the annual royalty is another incentive for SFM with potential CCM effects. Notwithstanding these promising legal provisions on council forests and rights attached thereto, the law remains inadequate with respect to the rights of the local population as critically examined below.

2.1.3 Community forest, rights related thereto and climate change mitigation implications

Cameroon's forestry legislation encourages the participation of local populations in the management of forests and their resources in order to contribute in improving their livelihoods, notably through community forests (CFs). CFs are defined by the Decree implementing the 1994 Forestry Law as a forest of the non-permanent forest estate, object of a management agreement between a village community and the service in charge of forestry. The management of such forest is the responsibility of the village community concerned, with the technical assistance of the service in charge of forestry.[34]

Under Cameroonian law, CFs comprise forest lands that may be used for other purposes than forestry[35] and under Section 37(1) of the 1994 Forestry Law. Village communities have the right to participate in the management of forest resources. Forests which may be subject to a CF management agreement are those situated in the outskirts of, or close to one or more communities in which the inhabitants carry out their activities.[36] The populations concerned are those that are authorised to carry out their activities therein not only as custodians of the forest, and within the framework of *usufruct* rights, but also as entities recognised under existing legislation.[37] Forest products of all kinds resulting from the management of CFs belong solely to the village communities concerned.[38] Like in the above forest types, CF and the rights flowing from its management under Cameroonian law are inadequate in enhancing such forests' CCM role. This inadequacy is given a critical assessment below.

2.1.4 Communal forests, rights emanating therefrom and climate change mitigation implications

According to Section 34(a) of the 1994 Forestry Law, communal forests comprise forest lands that may be used for other purposes than forestry. Under Section 35, communal forests include orchards, agricultural plantations, fallow land, wooded land adjoining an agricultural farm, pastoral and agro-forestry facilities. Citizens living around communal forests are granted logging rights. However, for purposes of conservation or protection, the minister in charge of forests may restrict such rights, particularly in

34 Article 3(11) of the Decree.
35 Section 34(b) of the 1994 Forestry Law.
36 Article 27(2) of the Decree.
37 For more on this, cf. Tamasang (2007: 159).
38 Section 37(5) of the 1994 Forestry Law. See also the proviso to Section 67 of the 1994 Forestry Law which provides that village communities and individuals are only entitled to payment of the selling price of the products extracted from their forests.

relation to grazing, pasturing, felling, logging and mutilation of protected species.[39] Notwithstanding the aforementioned, for the development of neighbouring village communities of certain communal forests under exploitation, part of the proceeds from the sale of forest products are reserved for these communities.[40] The effective implementation of the rights attached to communal forests can produce positive CCM outcomes. For instance, their right to a share the proceeds from the sale of forest products can incentivise them to avoid unsustainable activities that lead to forest destruction which in turn contributes to climate change.

2.1.5 Private forests, rights thereto attached and climate change mitigation implications

According to Section 34(c) of the 1994 Forestry Law, private forest comprises forest lands that may be used for other purposes than forestry. Under Section 39(1) individual natural persons or corporate bodies may plant forests on land they acquire in accordance with the laws and regulations in force referred to as private forests. However, the ownership over natural resources in private forests is limited by Section 39(4) according to which forest products under Section 9(2) (which classifies various products or resources as special[41]) belong to the state. The state's monopoly over such special products may stifle incentives to support SFM and forest conservation efforts with negative CCM outcomes. Within the framework of REDD+ implementation, such special products may be extended to include carbon stored in trees and under this legal construct, most carbon credits realised from REDD+ within private forests belongs to the state. This bears the significant risk of private forest owners being exempted from adequate financial rewards, thus de-incentivising SFM and conservation efforts as well as hindering positive CCM results. This insufficiency of the law will be elaborated further in the sub-section below.

2.2 Discussion on forest types, rights thereto attached and climate change mitigation implications under Cameroonian law

Cameroonian forestry legislation provides different stakeholders in forest management with a bundle of rights attached to the various forest types. The adequate implementation of such rights may be favourable or disfavourable to CCM. The law makes it

39 Section 36(1) of the 1994 Forestry Law.

40 Section 68(2) of the 1994 Forestry Law.

41 Section 9(2) of the 1994 Forestry Law classifies various products as special and belonging to the state: namely, ebony, ivory, wild animal horns, certain plants and medicinal species or those which are of particular interest.

obligatory to consider these rights especially in light of the social interests of local populations. In this respect, the right to benefit belongs to the various forest owners, managers and users, with an additional use right (rights to harvest and use forest products) accorded to the local population under basically all forest types in Cameroon. In the same spirit, the UN-REDD Programme standards under Criterion 7 requires national REDD+ programmes to respect and promote the recognition and exercise of the rights of indigenous peoples (IPs), local communities and other vulnerable and marginalised groups to land, territories and resources, including carbon.[42] Despite the promising legal provisions guaranteeing the enjoyment of forest rights by relevant stakeholders in forest management under Cameroonian law, especially the rights of local populations are considered inadequate as their implementation has not been effective. This reality is stifling incentives to support SFM, forest conservation efforts and CCM.

Although Section 8(1) of the 1994 Forestry Law recognises the rights of the local population to harvest all forest products freely for their personal use, except the protected species, it precludes any sale of such products. In the same manner, Article 26(2) of the Decree implementing the 1994 Forestry Law strictly forbid neighbouring populations from selling or exchanging wood from trees harvested in order to meet the domestic needs for poles and firewood. Also, under Section 26(2) of the 1994 Forestry Law, logging rights of the local population guaranteed under Section 26(1) may be limited if they are contrary to the purpose of the forest. Such legal restrictions are harsh on communities living in close proximity to such forest resources as their subsistence entirely depends on them. Furthermore, forests are subject to multiple and conflicting usages. Stakeholders in forest management have different and often opposing rights and mandates over forest areas. Often numerous plans exist in the same forests targeting different priorities. Such priorities deal for instance with timber harvesting, biodiversity conservation, the collection of non-timber forest products, agriculture etc. Conflicting natural resource policies do not create a sound forestry policy and legislative base to promote CCM. The fact that Cameroon does not have a comprehensive land use plan leads to problems of overlapping usage titles. Conflicts have been noted between and among conservation priorities, mining and logging concessions and the livelihoods of local populations.[43] These conflicts also carry the potential for large-scale forest destruction lacking a favourable legal environment for CCM.

Moreover, a critical assessment of relevant laws reveals that the bundle of rights available for local communities tend to be more limited to use and management rights (and often) for a limited period of time (e.g. 25 years for CF[44]) despite the long-term

---

42 See UN-REDD Programme (2011: criterion 7).

43 See Megevand et al. (2013: 127).

44 See Articles 37, 38 & 39 of the 1994 Forestry Law.

investment needed in many forest areas for sustainable management. The forestry law also limits forest tenure and management rights of local communities by for instance:

- providing maximum limits for CF areas (5,000 hectares);
- non-recognition of existing customary forest tenure claims; and
- restricting CF to selected forest areas on the outskirt.

The forestry law further contains legal clauses that allow the state to repossess forests if management is not deemed acceptable, leaving communities vulnerable. The CF model is seen as a weak response to customary claims, providing only temporary and easily revoked use and management rights to small and degraded forest areas.[45] This creates insecurity which is a potential driver for unsustainable activities which do not favour CCM.

Moreover, the acquisition and management of CF are slow due to stringent legal requirements, cumbersome and costly procedures.[46] Some CFs in Cameroon have also resulted in negative experiences such as confiscation by elites in complicity with business interests with the low involvement of communities, resulting in mismanagement and embezzlement of revenues.[47] In fact, CF is perceived negatively because of the failure to deliver broad-based positive community benefits compounded by corruption and administrative inconveniences that decrease the motivation of communities to acquire and manage CF.

In addition, forest tenure rights take a weaker form with implications for effective forest stewardship as vulnerable forest-dependent people are granted limited *usufruct* rights while economically valuable resources are claimed by the state and its business allies. In fact, customary ownership of forests and its valuable resources are at times "hijacked" from local populations, making them tenants of the state and subject to state regulation. Forest-dependent people consider forest resource management under state control as unfair and merely beneficial to industrial forestry companies.[48]

Cameroon's land and forest tenure laws create a degree of uncertainty regarding tenure rights. In particular, customary tenure is generally not recognised under the Land Tenure Ordinance as all land without a registered land title is treated as state land[49] implying that customary landholdings are also treated as state-owned land

45 Carodenuto et al. (2014: 121).

46 The 1994 Forestry Law allows local communities to apply for and obtain CF under stringent conditions such as the need to create a legal management entity which is not necessary, developing management plan, annual report writing, and recording inventories; which are cumbersome and hard for local communities to comply.

47 Fobissie et al. (2012: 15).

48 Chia et al. (2013: 499). See also Awung & Marchant (2016: 20).

49 Cameroon land tenure is governed by Ordinance No. 74/1 of 6 July 1974 to establish rules governing land tenure, the 1995 Indicative Land Use Framework, and other pieces of legislation including the local cultural and traditional land tenure systems and according to the 1974 Land Ordinance, all uninhabited forestland without land title is owned by the state which abolishes ancestral rights that were recognised in the pre-independence period, making registration the only way to claim ownership and places all unregistered lands under state control. Land

including their forests. Most forests in Cameroon are classified as national and state-owned despite century-old claims by forest-dependent communities and their contributions to SFM and limited contributions of state-controlled forests to local livelihoods and development. Indeed, there is a general conception that IPs' forest tenure rights were established even before the state came into existence. It is thus critical that forest-dependent communities be given more forest ownership and management rights. Otherwise, they may resist such forest management projects as for example in the case of the local population against the Kilum-Ijum Mountain Biodiversity Conservation project.[50] If the state continues with the exclusionary policy and if the rights of vulnerable communities are not strengthened, they have little incentive to protect forests. In fact, it has been suggested that effective decentralisation of forest management rights and responsibilities, especially with the involvement of local communities, can provide for more effective management of forest resources compared to state-managed forests.[51]

Without secure tenure, local forest users have few incentives and lack the legal mandate to invest in protecting forests.[52] The importance of strengthening forest tenure rights, especially for IPs and local communities is well recognised under the REDD+ initiative. At the 16th Conference of Parties to the UNFCCC in Cancun in 2010, social and environmental safeguards were developed to avoid the negative impacts of REDD+ actions[53] including "respect for the knowledge and rights of indigenous peoples and members of local communities",[54] and "the full and effective participation of relevant stakeholders, in particular, indigenous peoples and local communities".[55] Legal certainty of forest tenure rights is a prerequisite for reducing environmental and social risks.[56] In the absence of a comprehensive policy to address the rights of forest-dependent communities in Cameroon, certain ad hoc policies have been established for individual programmes in response to pressure from international organisations. For instance, to meet the World Bank Operational Policies on IPs, the Pygmy Peoples Development Plan was established as part of the Forest and Environment Sector Programme to facilitate access to CF by the Pygmies such as the Baka people and to ensure fair distribution of the annual forestry fees (referred to herein by its French acronym

certificate is the official certificate of real property rights according to Article 1 of Decree No. 6/165 of 27 April 1976 to establish the conditions for obtaining land certificates as amended and supplemented by Decree No. 2005/481 of 16 December 2005.

50 The government of Cameroon, in its effort to maintain the natural biodiversity of the Kilum-Ijim mountain forest, entered into a contract with the NGO BirdLife International to conserve the mountain's forest. This decision was taken without involving the inhabitants who were all asked to quit the forest. As a result, the decision was never implemented due to resistance from the local population.

51 Viana et al. (2012: 12); Tassa et al. (2010); and Lastarria-Cornhiel et al. (2012: 102).

52 Sam & Shepherd (2011).

53 UNFCCC Decision 1/CP.16 ("Cancun Agreement"), Appendix I.

54 Paragraph 2(c).

55 Paragraph 2(d).

56 Day & Naughton-Treves (2012: 1); and Moore et al. (2012: 83).

as RFA[57]) and the Wildlife Tax. The Voluntary Guidelines on Responsible Governance of Tenure further stresses the need for national laws and processes to protect communities with customary tenure systems from encroachment or displacement, helping communities document and publicly make available information about the forests and lands they control and to register documented customary systems in order to secure customary rights.[58] Be that as it may, a complete bundle of rights under CF could also promote better protection of standing forest and restoration of degraded forest.[59] There is a growing body of literature linking community forest rights with healthier forests and lower CO_2 emissions. Legal recognition and government support of community forest rights can thus help maintain and protect healthy forests, ensuring their role as carbon sinks.[60]

Forest communities already have a genuine interest in protecting forests, as they depend on them for their livelihoods and culture. In line with this opportunity to sustainably manage forests, Cameroon under the REDD+ readiness process has engaged forest-dependent communities as a key stakeholder though with very limited representation of only one member out of the 19 members constituting the National REDD+ Steering Committee.[61] It has been suggested that the government can meet its climate goals while also improving citizens' livelihoods by protecting and expanding the amount of officially recognised CFs.[62] These can sequester considerable amounts of carbon. Important carbon stocks in many forests around the world have been maintained and enhanced thanks to the management practices of local communities, which range from conservation to reforestation to community fire management.[63] Hence, enhancing forest rights of forest communities presents an enormous opportunity to fight climate change. This would, of course, require the need to simplify the conditions and procedures for the acquisition and management of CFs. Strengthening community forest rights is not just question pertaining to land and resources. It is also a cost-effective CCM solution. In fact, community forest rights should be part of the national CCM Policy. However, it's not sufficient to legally recognise their forest rights. The government must also protect these rights by supporting communities in the sustainable management of their forests.

Customary rules should prescribe clear and acceptable claims to lands for forest-dependent communities while such claims should not be contradicted or nullified by

57 *Redevance forestière annuelle.*

58 See UNEP (2015: 49).

59 Bond (2009: 99).

60 See <http://www.wri.org/blog/2014/12/why-community-forest-rights-should-be-part-national-climate-change-policies> (accessed 22-3-2018).

61 See Order No. 103/CAB/PM of 13 June 2012 pertaining to the creation, the organisation, and the operation of the REDD+ Steering Committee.

62 See <http://www.wri.org/blog/2014/07/community-forests-undervalued-approach-climate-change-mitigation> (accessed 22-3-2018).

63 FAO (2010: 4).

state regulation. This insufficiency of the law in recognising such claim rights leaves communities vulnerable to losing their land, making forests vulnerable to being cut down. Thus, strengthening customary tenure rights over forest lands can guarantee legitimacy and local support for SFM and forest conservation which are good for CCM. Strengthening customary tenure rights has to be understood as the process by which the government legally and unequivocally cedes claims of forest ownership and management rights to local communities that have historically used and occupied such forests. However, the strengthening of such rights for forest-dependent communities should go in tandem with the enforcement and monitoring of related legal reforms.

2.2.1 Clarification of carbon rights as a new forest resource under Cameroonian law

International legal instruments[64] envisage a new forest product known as carbon, which could emerge as a tradable commodity in the process of mitigating climate change. While this has been commended as a laudable initiative, the instruments, unfortunately, do not clearly define the rights relating to this transaction. This probably explains why such initiative had never really been successful within the SFM conversation. REDD+ negotiations which are an upshot of the UNFCCC and its numerous Conference of Parties' decisions have not made the situation any better in terms of clarifying carbon BS under this new forest management paradigm. The majority of the countries, including Cameroon, are therefore at odds as to crafting domestic legislation relating to the subject. Another explanation for the silence is that it is a relatively new development in the forest management paradigm requiring ample time to monitor its operation in national settings. The legal clarification of carbon rights could be challenging, as multiple stakeholders may claim rights over forest carbon, including communities, governments and carbon project implementers. Ownership of carbon rights is a contentious issue[65] as most of the REDD+ participating countries, including Cameroon, do not have explicit laws regarding the carbon rights. In addition to forest tenure clarification, the question as to who should own the carbon embodied in both old and new forests requires legal clarity in Cameroon. This would create an incentive for engagement in forest carbon sequestration projects which could become favourable for CCM.

Following the classification of forests under Cameroonian law, rights over carbon may belong to the state, councils, a group such as a community or an individual. On the strength of forest classification, the right to carbon would belong to the state where it is a state forest while the right to carbon on community and private forests would

64 Cf. Kyoto Protocol to the UNFCCC.
65 Sherpa & Brower (2015: 27); and Loft et al. (2015: 1036).

belong to the owners of these forests,[66] and the carbon on council forests and national land would respectively belong to councils[67] and to the nation managed by the state. Thus, carbon can be made a publicly owned resource, a communal resource or a private resource. However, certain forest products are classified as special, and the list of special products is fixed when necessary, by the competent ministry.[68] The discretionary power of the minister may also allow the inclusion of carbon into the special products list. Under this legal construct, most carbon credits realised will go to the state with significant risk that communities will not reap adequate financial rewards, stifling incentives to support forest conservation efforts. In fact, in Cameroon, most forests storing carbon are mostly owned by the state who will by implication be the main beneficiary of any carbon benefit. Options for the clarification of carbon rights have been suggested by Costenbader as follows:[69]

- The carbon is privately owned expressed in a contract or a covenant that runs with the land, binding anyone who owns the property in the future; or the carbon is the object of a separate, alienable property right, such as a *usufruct right*[70] or *profit à prendre*[71], which the owner can sell without conveying land ownership.
- The carbon is a publicly owned asset where the government holds it as trustee for the benefit of forest owners or of the public, with the power to sell it.

Where carbon projects are planned and implemented in a centralised manner, payment for carbon benefits can be allocated and distributed through the existing RFA BS mechanisms. From the foregoing, one may conclude that carbon rights are rights over an 'intangible asset' referred to as carbon, a new form of resource which may or may not be separate from trees / biomass in which it resides, and which may be transferred or commercialised separately.

Generally, one of the major factors driving forest destruction in Cameroon is due to inadequate and insecure rights over forests and its resources. Consequently, enhancing and securing such rights is fundamental when ensuring the long-term permanence of the CCM role of forests. The participatory approach adopted under the REDD+

---

66 Natural resources found within a private forest are owned by the individual as defined by Section 39(1) of the 1994 Forestry Law.

67 Article 32(3) of the 1994 Forestry Law which states that forest products of all kinds resulting from the exploitation of council forest shall be the sole property of the council concerned.

68 Section 9(2) of the 1994 Forestry Law classifies various products or resources as special and thus as belonging to the state: namely, ebony, ivory, wild animal horns, certain plants and medicinal species or those which are of particular interest.

69 Costenbader (2011: 27).

70 *Usufruct* is "the right of enjoying a thing, the property of which is vested in another, and to draw from the same all the profit, utility and advantage which it may produce, without altering the substance of the thing".

71 *Profit à prendre* is "the right to share in the land owned by another. In particular, *profit à prendre* enables a person to take part of the soil or produce of land that someone else owns".

readiness process could build genuine support, especially from forest-dependent communities if there is strong political will to initiate reforms that enhance and protect their rights thereby making these communities active stakeholders in forest management - especially in the context of CCM.

3 Benefit-sharing in the context of forest management and implications for climate change mitigation under Cameroonian law

BS may be defined as the distribution of monetary and non-monetary benefits derived from forest management to relevant stakeholders within a country's legal architecture. With the advent of carbon as a forest commodity, it is important to highlight carbon in the context of BS, which has been defined as an –[72]

> agreement between stakeholders, such as private sector, local communities, government and non-profit organisations, about the equitable distribution of benefits related to the commercialisation of forest carbon.

Carbon BS may therefore be understood as the distribution of benefits derived from the sale of carbon credits. BS considerations are important determinants of forest-based efforts to mitigate climate change. Yet, an appropriate mechanism for fair and equitable BS is challenging. A well-functioning BS scheme provides incentives for actions that protect forests, which is essential for CCM. There are existing BS mechanisms under Cameroonian law, but just like carbon rights, there is a limited appetite to establish a legislative carbon BS scheme in Cameroon to date. However, there are existing formulae for BS on which carbon BS may hinge.

3.1 Current benefit-sharing schemes under Cameroonian law and implications for climate change mitigation

BS constitutes a key aspect of CCM because it helps to create necessary incentives to engage in SFM, forest conservation and carbon projects. When designed and implemented appropriately, a BS mechanism can encourage climate-smart forestry. An effective, fair and equitable paradigm for BS can secure the positive outcome of SFM, forest conservation and carbon projects while unfair and inequitable distribution is a threat to participation in such efforts. In fact, a fair and equitable BS mechanism that is well implemented can incentivise SFM and forest conservation by forest rights holders and can lead to decreased pressure on forest ecosystems, and by extension enhance the role of the forest in contributing to CCM while, unfair and inequitable BS mechanism is a disincentive to SFM and forest conservation and can lead to increased

72 Lindhjem et al. (2010: 25).

pressure on forest ecosystems, and by extension limit forests' CCM role. In the case of carbon BS, one of the challenges is the task of receiving funds from international sources and distributing them fairly and equitably to relevant national actors. National and foreign investors and other supporting actors most relevant to national forest governance will require fair and equitable BS arrangements to compensate them for their participation in SFM, forest conservation and carbon projects. Thus, a BS scheme needs to target different actors across various levels. A BS formula is complex to establish, due to the range of stakeholders involved, their interests and scales at which they intervene in SFM, forest conservation and carbon projects. The establishment of a BS mechanism across levels that is accepted by relevant stakeholders is challenging but critical. Such a mechanism should not only look at rules and modalities for distribution, but also at how conflicts arising in the process can be resolved so that incentives do not generate countervailing reactions.[73] A generic approach to BS is not appropriate because every country is likely to have unique circumstances, preferences and needs that inevitably influence BS arrangements.

In the case of carbon, there are no specific legal provisions in Cameroon on how carbon benefits will be shared among relevant actors. In the absence of such legal specificity, Cameroon's approach to national carbon BS can be derived from Cameroon's REDD+ Readiness Preparation Proposal (R-PP). This approach is based on the experience of other revenue sharing mechanisms currently in place, such as the redistribution mechanism of annual forestry fees (RFA).[74] Under relevant legislations, royalties or revenues from the exploitation of forest resources are paid to the state.[75] In fact, any economic and financial benefits resulting from the exploitation of forest resources are subject to the payment of royalties (RFA) to the state.[76] In turn, the state distributes royalties collected in the following proportions: 50% to the state, 20% to municipalities adjacent to the forest concessions, 20% to FEICOM (Special Equipment and Inter-municipality Intervention Fund) and 10% to the local population affected by the project.[77] In addition to this scheme, the 1994 Forestry Law requires the project owner to undertake to carry out industrial installations, developmental works and to

73 Minang et al. (2014).

74 Forest Carbon Partnership Facility Cameroon (2013: 72).

75 Cf. Sections 66, 67 and 68 of the 1994 Forestry Law. These provisions are supplemented by those of Section 14(2) of Law No. 98/9 of 1 July 1998 Finance Law of the Republic of Cameroon, which fixed the annual forestry fee at CFAF 1,500/ha for forest concessions and CFAF 2,500/ha for the exploitation of sales of standing volume. The same provisions provide for the distribution of the said annual forestry fee as follows: 50% for the state, 40% for local councils and 10% for bordering villages. See also Decree No. 96/642/PM of 17 September 1996, fixing the amount and the modalities of tax recovery and the rights of royalties relating to forestry activities.

76 Decree No. 96/642/PM of 17 September 1996, fixing the amount and the modalities of tax recovery and the rights of royalties and tax relative to forestry activities.

77 Decree No. 96/237/PM of 10 April 1996 defining the conditions for the functioning of special funds provided in the 1994 Forestry Law.

provide social amenities for the benefit of the local population.[78] Joint Order No. 122/MINADT/MINFI/MINFOF of 29 April 1998 issued to lay down conditions for the use of revenue derived from forestry fees was found to be ineffective and was replaced by another joint order issued on 3 June 2010, which because of implementation difficulties, was subsequently repealed by joint Order No. 76/MINADT/MINFI/MINFOF of 26 June 2012 to lay down conditions for the planning, use and monitoring of the management of forest and wildlife revenue allocated to councils and local communities.[79]

BS revolves around different kinds of benefits to be shared, how stakeholders are entitled to receive the benefits and the rules governing the allocation and sharing of those benefits. With respect to the different kinds of benefits, they can be grouped as either being monetary or non-monetary in nature. This is in line with the prescription of Article 5(4) of the Nagoya Protocol on Access to Genetic Resources and the Fair and Equitable Sharing of Benefits Arising from their Utilization.[80] From a monetary point of view, benefits are allocated and shared under the RFA system in Cameroon as seen above. Apart from direct cash flows, non-monetary benefits could also be made by building social infrastructures promoting community development and poverty reduction activities. In this respect, Sections 50 and 61(3) & (4) of the 1994 Forestry Law require the project participant to undertake to carry out industrial installations, developmental works and to provide social amenities for the benefit of the local population. From another perspective, there are three main types of benefits:

The first type comprises the (net) benefits from the implementation of a carbon project under which those implementing it may derive gains from the sale of carbon credits with the direct costs consisting of transaction and implementation costs, such as for guarding forests against illegal logging and forest clearing. The second type consists of (net) benefits from changes in forest use such as the foregone agricultural and timber rent (profit), or the opportunity costs of forest conservation. That is, lost opportunities because some uses are stopped or downscaled. The third type of benefits consists of indirect (net) benefits from the implementation of carbon projects, including improved governance, such as strengthening of tenure rights and law enforcement, technology transfer, enhanced participation in decision-making, preservation of biodiversity and/or other ecosystem services and infrastructure provisions.[81]

78 This includes construction of roads, bridges, schools, hospitals, and recreational facilities. See Sections 50(3) and 61(3) and (4) of the 1994 Forestry Law.

79 Assembe-Mvondo et al. (2015: 1).

80 See the Nagoya Protocol on Access to Genetic Resources and the Fair and Equitable Sharing of Benefits Arising from their Utilization to the Convention on Biological Diversity which aims at sharing the benefits arising from the utilisation of genetic resources in a fair and equitable way. It entered into force on 12 October 2014, 90 days after the date of deposit of the fiftieth instrument of ratification.

81 See generally Luttrell et al. (2013); Denier et al. (2014); Lindhjem et al. (2010); and Loft et al. (2014).

With respect to the stakeholders entitled to receive the benefits, the RFA has clearly identified the various stakeholders to include the state, councils in case of council forests and the municipalities adjacent to the forest concessions. Individuals are eligible in the case of private forests, FEICOM, the local population affected by the project and local communities in the case of CFs. However, the beneficiaries of benefits increase with the multiplicity of stakeholders with divergent interests involved in carbon projects implementation such as project developers and implementers, wider communities, intermediaries and relevant government departments. If a programme is too narrowly targeted and focuses on just a few key actors, it risks not being sufficiently broad enough to align incentives, cultivate support, build legitimacy and prevent leakage.[82]

The rules governing the allocation and sharing of benefits are those found under the existing RFA in Cameroon, which are held not be fair and equitable with respect to the meagre percentage allocated to the local population and the unfair procedures for the transmission of the revenue to the local communities, which must pass through unaccountable local councils and under the management of corrupt elites.

3.2 Discussion on benefit-sharing under Cameroonian law and implications for climate change mitigation

The long-term success of forest-based CCM efforts depends upon ensuring that BS under any scheme is perceived as fair and equitable by relevant stakeholders especially forest-dependent communities. The BS mechanism as provided by the RFA in Cameroon leaves much to be desired in terms of value, fairness, equality and transparency. In fact, the scheme is plagued with a number of flaws. The materialisation of BS has been weak. The Ministries of Forestry and Finance negotiate the terms of BS with no consultation process with the local community before fixing the amount to be paid contrary to the requirement to hold a briefing meeting during which the community through the traditional authorities is notified of the envisaged amount.[83] The 10% share seems insignificant compared to what companies extract from the forest and compared to what they pay into the Public Treasury. The BS scheme allocating only 10% of revenue to local communities is likely to trigger negative responses from community members. This is so because they may contend that this proportion is inadequate and cannot provide the infrastructure required for sustainable societal development.[84] The meagre 10% share allocated to local communities is managed by local governments with a widespread report by communities on the insufficient investment of the revenue

82 Kelley et al. (2012: 4).

83 See Decree No. 96/237/PM of 10 April 1996, fixing the modalities of the functioning of the special fund for Forestry, Wildlife and Fisheries.

84 Alemagi (2011: 70).

in concerned villages. The 10% often end up in private pockets of elites as a result of the top-down preferences of central and local governments on communities. The management of the RFA at the community level has been very controversial because of large-scale misappropriation. BS, which is often thought to be pro-poor is not necessarily pro-poor in nature as in some forest communities, more powerful actors tend to be given priority in benefits sharing.[85]Elite capture and diversion of benefits can lead to perverse incentives with a tendency to degrade forests or to result in the exclusion of vulnerable right holders from benefits, compromising forests' CCM role.

The RFA BS mechanism, which is also proposed in the R-PP for the sharing of carbon benefits is inappropriate as it has been plagued by problems since its inception, evident by insufficient transparency over the use of funds, which is prone to misappropriation, both within MINFI and at the municipal and village levels with limited mechanism for independent actors to hold them accountable. In this respect, benefits could be captured at higher levels, without reaching those who matter most and who have less power to influence such processes. This could undermine local populations' participation and support for SFM, forest conservation and carbon projects and potentially endanger the permanence of any carbon being sequestered over the long term. The weaknesses in Cameroon's BS system require numerous adjustments in terms of necessary legal reforms.

Indonesia's July 2009 REDD Revenue-Sharing Regulation was the first of its kind in providing that national, municipal, and provincial governments would receive 10-50% of carbon credit funds from forest projects, while local forest communities would receive 20-70%, depending on the type of forest. For instance, in 'customary' forests, government would receive 10%, communities 70% and developers 20%.[86]

A key concern is that of giving large sums of money to governments with poor track records, low institutional and governance capacities and weak commitments to transparency, accountability and participation, a weak rule of law and inadequate public financial management capacity.[87] In the case of carbon benefits, there is genuine concern that governments or brokers will appropriate carbon revenue.[88] The RFA BS mechanism in Cameroon suggests that IPs and local communities may be at risk of not receiving adequate shares of carbon benefits, especially in light of the high potential for corruption. In fact, IPs in Cameroon continue to be concerned about accountability and embezzlement by local and national elites at the expense of local economic development and welfare. Not only will they receive little or no payment under the RFA BS scheme. They are deemed to even lose their traditional rights to forests and associated resources. Poverty remains endemic in most forest communities that accommodate

85 Sam & Shepherd (2011).
86 Costenbader (2009: 78).
87 Ibid: 57.
88 Katerere et al. (2009: 19).

logging concessions with the two main beneficiaries of revenues being the government and the forest products firms. Carbon benefits may not go beyond these categories of stakeholders, which may cause local communities to embark on more unsustainable forest activities out of frustration. Explicit controls are therefore required to prevent the capture of benefits. This requires the establishment of a system that is fair, equitable and transparent, which instils confidence and must be given a legal base through legislation. If stakeholders do not perceive the BS scheme as fair and equitable, the legitimacy of SFM, forest conservation, carbon projects and buy-ins from dissatisfied stakeholders will be weakened.

In general, such a system must strive to ensure that payments are allocated and shared in a manner that is both fair and equitable (adequately compensate relevant stakeholders especially forest-dependent communities) as well as effective (leading to forest-based carbon emissions reductions and carbon stocks enhancement). The BS paradigm established by the Nagoya Protocol on Access to Genetic Resources and the Fair and Equitable Sharing of Benefits is worth mentioning here. In accordance with Article 15(3) and (7) of the Convention on Biological Diversity, benefits should be shared in a fair and equitable way and that such sharing shall be upon mutually agreed terms.[89] Article 5(2) and (3) of the Protocol directs that each Party takes legislative, administrative or policy measures, as appropriate, with the aim of ensuring that benefits arising from the utilisation of genetic resources that are held by indigenous and local communities, in accordance with domestic legislation regarding the established rights of these indigenous and local communities over these genetic resources are shared in a fair and equitable way with the communities concerned and based on mutually agreed terms. Although not designed for forest and carbon BS, the Nagoya Protocol's BS mechanism can be adopted by the government in designing an appropriate BS mechanism.

Fundamental issues in the design of a BS mechanism include criteria for allocating benefits, eligibility to benefit, transparency in the process, the timing of payment and the responsibilities of actors in the BS process at all levels. In designing such a scheme, special attention must be given to the marginalised and vulnerable forest-dependent communities, who have limited voices and influence. Their special involvement in the design of a BS mechanism in Cameroon will provide incentives for actions that are relevant for forest protection, as well as building trust and legitimacy, strengthen local governance and aligning BS with pro-poor and local development strategies, which are all essential for CCM. In the light of this reasoning, the UN-REDD Programme standards under Criterion 12 requires that the design, planning and implementation of national REDD+ programmes among others, should ensure equitable, non-

89 See Article 5(1) of the Nagoya Protocol on Access to Genetic Resources and the Fair and Equitable Sharing of Benefits Arising from their Utilization to the Convention on Biological Diversity.

discriminatory and transparent BS among relevant stakeholders, with special attention to the most vulnerable and marginalised groups.[90] It is therefore imperative to consider paying benefits to communities' accounts without going through local governments. One option being tested in Brazil under the REDD+ initiative is to use commercial banks to transfer payments from the voluntary carbon market to farmers and community organisations.[91] Appropriate BS arrangement can induce cooperation,[92] SFM and forest conservation that enhance the role of the forest in contributing to CCM.

If the proposed BS framework is not considered by policymakers, revenue will continue to be distributed based on the existing flawed RFA BS mechanism, where revenue accrues to the state, local councils and elites at the detriment of local communities, undermining SFM which is not healthy for CCM. An appropriate BS mechanism also requires that a conducive institutional set-up is established to deliver and manage such benefits.

4 Conclusions and recommendations

4.1 Conclusions

This chapter has established that Cameroonian law has classified forests into various types, giving different categories of stakeholders including the state, councils, local communities and private individuals or corporate entities the enjoyment of a bundle of rights attached to the various forest types. These categories of forest right holders are also entitled to benefits derived from forest management. The development of the carbon concept has also increased the number of stakeholders in forest management, who enjoy some rights with corresponding carbon benefits entitlements. However, some stakeholders involved in forest management such as forest-dependent communities enjoy limited and weaker rights with inadequate benefits compared to the councils, the state, its well-positioned elites and its economic business allies under the RFA on which carbon BS will hinge. The forest rights and the RFA BS mechanism have not been effectively implemented. More often, vulnerable groups face implementation challenges, mostly related to poor governance, posing as a major constraint to forest's contribution to CCM. Thus, although the forestry legal framework classifies forests and puts in place a bundle of forest rights enjoyed by different categories of stakeholders with corresponding BS scheme, inherent weaknesses exist in the law. The prevailing forest rights arrangements and BS frameworks in Cameroon are inadequate to incentivise forest-dependent communities to practice SFM, forest conservation and

90 See UN-REDD Programme (2011: criterion 12).
91 Bond (2009: 103).
92 See IUCN (2009: 5).

engage in carbon projects which is not healthy for CCM. Government actions that weaken the exercise of limited and weak forest rights and the unfair and inequitable BS mechanism could contribute to forest destruction and carbon emissions that can compromise forest-based CCM efforts. Despite a theoretical decentralisation and transfer of powers and rights with corresponding benefits to different forest stakeholders, the practical forestry management reinforces a central stakeholders' power with strong political and economic incentives for elites and central bureaucracies to consolidate their control over forests. In fact, the poor enforcement of the forestry legislation with respect to forest rights and BS owing to weak governance, an absence of the rule of law, vested interests and insufficient political will, has led to a wide gap between policy rhetoric and on-the-ground practice. Under the existing legal and governance reality, the role of the forest in contributing to CCM is greatly hindered, underscoring the urgent need for legislative reforms, which seem critical if the government of Cameroon wishes to deliver its promise under the NDCs in achieving the goals of the Paris Agreement.[93]

4.2 Recommendations

A key recommendation calls for an enhancement of the role of forests in contributing to CCM under Cameroonian law. Relevant laws need to be revised to effectively decentralise and promote participatory forest management that gives adequate forest rights to the relevant stakeholders. An appropriate forest management and a corresponding fair and equitable BS paradigm need to be supported by a genuine political commitment that allows and fosters on-the-ground implementation. This is premised on the reasoning that adequate rights over forest management with an associated fair and equitable BS paradigm encourage more SFM, forest conservation and carbon projects for a better forest-based CCM outcome. In order to enhance forests' contribution to CCM in Cameroon, there is a need for forest management to operate in a legal context of adequate and secure forest rights for relevant stakeholders. Moreover, the BS formula needs to be harnessed to overcome the inherent flaws plaguing the RFA BS scheme.

References

93 Under 17, the Paris Agreement has as primary goal, to keep a global temperature rise this century below 2°C and to drive efforts to limit temperature increase even further to 1.52°C above pre-industrial levels.

Agyei, K (2012) *The implications of land tenure and benefit sharing approaches on the REDD+ scheme for forest fringe communities in Ghana* Master of Climate Change Thesis, The Australian National University Crawford School of Public Policy.

Alemagi, D (2011) "Sustainable development in Cameroon's forestry sector: progress, challenges, and strategies for improvement" 5(2) *African Journal of Environmental Science and Technology* 65-72.

Alix-Garcia, J & H Wolff (2014) "Payment for ecosystem services from forests" 6 *Annual Review of Resource Economics* 361-380.

Angu Angu, K, PR Oyono, G Lescuyer, L Feintrenie, RA Samndong, D Endamana, S Assembe-Mvondo, AJ Eyebé, G Walters, S Le Bel, C Fargeot, R Tsanga & J Kiyulu (2013) "Rural societies and multiple land use practices: perceptions of conservation and development projects within the framework of multiple land use systems in Central Africa" in de C Wasseige, J Flynn, D Louppe, F Hiol Hiol & P Mayaux (eds) *The Forests of the Congo Basin – State of the Forest* 241-266.

Assembe-Mvondo, S, G Wong, L Loft & JS Tjajadi (2015) *Comparative assessment of forest revenue redistribution mechanisms in Cameroon: Lessons for REDD+ benefit sharing* CIFOR Working Paper No. 190.

Awung, NS & R Marchant (2016) "Investigating the role of the local community as co-managers of the Mount Cameroon National Park Conservation Project" 36(3) *Environments* 1-22, at <www.mdpi.com/journal/environments> (accessed 12-10-2017).

Blomley, T (2013) *Lessons learned from community forestry in Africa and their relevance for REDD+*.

Bond, I (2009) "CBNRM as a mechanism for addressing global environmental challenges" in D Roe, F Nelson & C Sandbrook (eds) *Community management of natural resources in Africa: impacts, experiences and future directions* 95-104.

Boyd, W (2014) "Climate change, fragmentation, and the challenges of global environmental law: elements of a post-copenhagen, assemblage" 32(2) *Journal of International Law* 457-550.

Brack, D (2012) "Climate funding opportunities: REDD+ funds, funding activities related to reducing emissions from deforestation and forest degradation (REDD+)" Briefing Sessions on Climate Funding Opportunities Organised by the ACP Secretariat/Intra-ACP Global Climate Change Alliance (GCCA) Programme under the 10th EDF Intra-ACP Financial Framework Brussels ACP Secretariat.

Bradley, A (2012) "Does community forestry provide a suitable platform for REDD? A case study from Oddar Meanchey, Cambodia" in L Naughton-Treves & C Day (eds) *Lessons about land tenure, forest governance and REDD+: case studies from Africa, Asia and Latin America* 61-72, at <www.rmportal.net/landtenureforestsworkshop> (accessed 17-10-2017).

Carodenuto, S, J Statz, D Hubert & Y Decleire (2014) "Local participation from VPA to REDD+ in Cameroon" 55 *ETFRN News* 118-124.

Chapman, S & M Wilder (2014) *Defining the legal elements of benefit-sharing in the context of REDD+* REDD+ Law Project Working Paper, at <http://www.4cmr.group.cam.ac.uk> (accessed 09-09-2015).

Chia, EL, OA Somorin, DJ Sonwa & AM Tiani (2013) "Local vulnerability, forest communities and forest-carbon conservation: case of southern Cameroon" 5(8) *International Journal of Biodiversity and Conservation* 498-507, at <http://www.academicjournals.org/IJBC> (accessed 12-10-2017).

Climate Focus (2015) *Progress on the New York Declaration on Forests – an assessment framework and initial report: technical annexes. Goal 10: strengthen forest governance, transparency and the rule of law, while also empowering communities and recognizing the rights of indigenous peoples, especially those pertaining to their lands and resources*, at <www.forestdeclaration.org> (accessed 17-10-2017).

COICA (2013) *Indigenous REDD+ alternative: indigenous territories of harmonious life to cool the planet.*

Corbera, E & H Schroeder (2010) "Governing and implementing REDD+" *Environmental Science and Policy* 1-11.

Costenbader, J (ed.) (2009) *Legal frameworks for REDD: design and implementation at the national level*, at <http://cmsdata.iucn.org/downloads/eplp_77.pdf> (accessed 20-7-2018).

CPF / Collaborative Partnership on Forests (2008) *Strategic framework for forests and climate change* A proposal by the Collaborative Partnership on Forests for a coordinated forest-sector response to climate change, at <http://www.cpfweb.org/32826-07a76ac1e5c8e0b0172dcb023cf375303.pdf> (accessed 05-01-2015).

Day, C & L Naughton-Treves (2012) "Lessons from early efforts to secure land tenure within forest carbon management projects" in L Naughton-Treves & C Day (eds) *Lessons about land tenure, forest governance and REDD+: case studies from Africa, Asia and Latin America* 1-10, at <www.rmportal.net/landtenureforestsworkshop> (accessed 17-10-2017).

Denier, L, S Korwin, M Leggett & C MacFarquhar (2014) *The little book of legal frameworks for REDD.*

Desclée, B, P Mayaux, M Hansen, PL Amani, C Sannier, B Mertens, T Häusler, RN Siwe, H Poilvé, V Gond, M Rahm, J Haarpainter & JPK Lubamba (2013) "Evolution of forest cover at a national and regional scale and drivers of change" in C de Wasseige, J Flynn, D Louppe, F Hiol Hiol, P Mayaux (eds) *The forests of the Congo Basin – state of the forest* 21-46.

Dkamela, GP (2010) *The context of REDD+ in Cameroon: drivers, agents and institutions* CIFOR Occasional Paper No. 57.

Emily, AE & Z Hisham (2014) *The effects of REDD+ on forest people in Africa: access, distribution, and participation in governance* Responsive Forest Governance Initiative (RFGI) Working Paper No. 1.

FAO / Food and Agriculture Oranization of the United Nations (2005) *Global forest resources assessment 2005* FAO Forestry Paper No. 147.

FAO / Food and Agriculture Oranization of the United Nations (2010) *Managing forests for climate change*, at <http://www.fao.org/docrep/013/i1960e/i1960e00.pdf> (accessed 30-3-2018).

FAO / Food and Agriculture Oranization of the United Nations (2011) *Climate change for forest policy-makers: an approach for integrating climate change into national forest programmes in support of sustainable forest management* Version 1.0.

Fobissie, BK, EP Essomba, N Sonne, SN Ndobé & V Retana (2012) *Social safeguards and the rights of indigenous peoples in the REDD+ process of Cameroon: lessons from experiences in natural resources management.*

Forest Carbon Partnership Facility Cameroon (2013) *Readiness Preparation Proposal (R-PP).*

Hohfeld, WN (1919) "Fundamental legal conceptions as applied in judicial reasoning" 26(8) *The Yale Law Journal* 710-770.

IUCN / International Union for Conservation of Nature (2009) *REDD-plus and benefit sharing: experiences in forest conservation and other resource management sectors.*

IUCN / International Union for Conservation of Nature (2017) "Issues briefs" November 2017, at <iucn.org/issues-briefs.pdf> (accessed 30-3-2018).

Kadar, P (2011) "The climate change and the power industry" in J Blanco & H Kheradmand *Climate change – research and technology for adaptation and mitigation.*

Katerere, Y, PA Minang & H Vanhanen (2009) *Making sub-Saharan African forests work for people and nature: policy approaches in a changing global environment.*

Kelley, L, EM Madeira, J Blockhus & D Ganz (2012) *Synthesis of benefit-sharing mechanisms from the natural resource sector: lessons for REDD+*.

Korwin, S (2016) *REDD+ and corruption risks for Africa's forests: case studies from Cameroon, Ghana, Zambia and Zimbabwe*.

Lastarria-Cornhiel, S, MM Feijóo, L Naughton-Treves & L Suárez (2012) "Efforts to secure indigenous communal land rights in northwest Ecuador – a vital foundation for direct incentive forest conservation programs" in L Naughton-Treves & C Day (eds) *Lessons about land tenure, forest governance and REDD+: case studies from Africa, Asia and Latin America* 101-112, at <www.rmportal.net/landtenureforestsworkshop> (accessed 17-10-2017).

Lindhjem, H, I Aronsen, KG Bråten & A Gleinsvik (2010) *Experiences with benefit sharing: issues and options for REDD-Plus* Economic Report No. R-2010-018.

Loft, L, P Thu Thuy & C Luttrell (2014) *Lessons from payments for ecosystem services for REDD+ benefit-sharing mechanisms* CIFOR Infobriefs No. 68.

Loft, L, R Ashwin, FG Maria, TP Thu, APR Ida, A Samuel, GT Jazmín, M Esther & A Krister (2015), "Taking stock of carbon rights in REDD+ candidate countries: concept meets reality", 6 *Forests* 1031-1060, at <www.mdpi.com/journal/forests> (accessed 11-10-2017).

Luttrell, C, L Loft, MF Gebara, D Kweka, M Brockhaus, A Angelsen, & WD Sunderlin (2013) "Who should benefit from REDD+? Rationales and realities" 18(4) *Ecology and Society* 52-70.

Megevand, C, A Mosnier, J Hourticq, K Sanders, N Doetinchem & C Streck (2013) *Deforestation trends in the Congo Basin: reconciling economic growth and forest protection*, at <http://documents.worldbank.org/curated/en/175211468257358269/Deforestation-trends-in-the-Congo-Basin-reconciling-economic-growth-and-forest-protection> (accessed 20-03-2018).

Mboh, C, D Skole, M Dieng, C Justice, D Kwesha, L Mane, M El Gamri, V Von Vordzogbe & H Virji (2012) *Challenges and prospects for REDD+ in Africa: desk review of REDD+ implementation in Africa* GLP Report No. 3, at <http://www.worldagroforestry.org/downloads/Publications/PDFS/B17421.pdf> (accessed 2-8.2018).

Minang, PA, M Van Noordwijk, LA Dugumaa, D Alemagi, TH Dod, F Bernarda, P Agung, V Robiglioe, D Catacutand, S Suyantob, A Armas, C Silva Aguade, M Feudjioc, G Galudrab, R Maryani, D Whitef, A Widayati, E Kahurani, S Namirembea & B Leimona (2014) *REDD+ readiness progress across countries: time for reconsideration*.

Moore, C, T Hansel & A Johnson (2012) "REDD+ in Lao PDR: is it also a "plus" for forest-dependent communities? a case study from the Nam Et Phou Louey National Protected Area; Lao, PDR" in L Naughton-Treves & C Day (eds) *Lessons about land tenure, forest governance and REDD+: case studies from Africa, Asia and Latin America* 83-92, at <www.rmportal.net/landtenureforestsworkshop> (accessed 17-10-2017).

Murphree, M & R Taylor (2009) "CBNRM in Africa: current constraints and opportunities" in D Roe, F Nelson & C Sandbrook (eds) *Community management of natural resources in Africa: impacts, experiences and future directions* 105-120.

Naughton-Treves, L & C Day (eds) (2012) *Lessons about land tenure, forest governance and REDD+: case studies from Africa, Asia and Latin America* 61-72, at <www.rmportal.net/landtenureforestsworkshop> (accessed 17-10-2017).

Norman, M & N Smita (2014) *The state of REDD+ finance* CGD Working Paper No. 378.

OECD / Organisation for Economic Co-operation and Development (2015) "Reducing emissions from deforestation and forest degradation" in *Development co-operation report 2015: making partnerships effective coalitions for action*.

Pittock, AB (2009) *Climate change: the science, impacts and solutions* 2nd ed.

Rautner, M, M Leggett & F Davis (2013) *The little book of big deforestation drivers*.

Reinhard, W (2011) *Making REDD work: a practitioner's guide for successful implementation of REDD.*

Sam, T & G Shepherd (2011) *Community forest management* Background Paper for The United Nations Forum on Forests Secretariat UNFF: Forests for People, Livelihoods and Poverty Eradication, held at the United Nations headquarters in New York City, from 24 January to 4 February 2011.

Secretariat of the Convention on Biological Diversity (2009) *Connecting biodiversity and climate change mitigation and adaptation: report of the second ad hoc technical expert group on biodiversity and climate change* Montreal Technical Series No. 41.

Sherpa, DT & A Brower (2015) "Equity in sharing the potential benefits of REDD+ in Nepal" 13(1) *Journal of Forest and Livelihood* 20-29.

Springer, J & PB Larsen (2012) *Community tenure and REDD+* WWF Report.

Suzuki, R (2011) "Drivers of deforestation and REDD+: can REDD+ compete?" 5 *REDD-Net Bulletin Asia-Pacific.*

Tamasang, CF (2007) *Community forest management entities as effective tools for local level participation under Cameroonian law: a case study of Kilium/Tjim mountain forest* PhD Thesis Faculty of Law and Political Science University of Yaounde II SOA.

Tamasang, CF (2009) "The clean development mechanism and forestry projects in Africa: the case of forestry projects in Cameroon" in R Mwebaza & LJ Kotzé (eds) *Environmental governance and climate change in Africa: legal perspectives* 171-195.

Tassa, DT, R Da Re & L Secco (2010) "Benefit sharing mechanisms and governance issues in participatory forest management-REDD related projects: a community forest case-study in Tanzania" Berlin Conference on the Human Dimensions of Global Environmental Change Berlin 8-9 October 2010.

UNEP / Unites Nations Environment Programme (2014) *Forests in a changing climate: a sourcebook for integrating REDD+ into academic programmes.*

UNEP / Unites Nations Environment Programme (2015) *REDD+ implementation: a manual for national legal practitioners.*

UN-REDD Programme (2011) *UN-REDD Programme social and environmental principles and criteria* Version 3 Draft for Consultation.

Viana, VM, AR Aquino, TM Pinto, LMT Lima, A Martinet, F Busson & JM Samye (2012) *REDD+ and community forestry: lessons learned from an exchange between Brazil and Africa.*

Van Asselt, H (2012) "Managing the fragmentation of international environmental law: forests at the intersection of the climate and biodiversity regimes"44 *International Law and Politics* 1205-1278.

Weaver, S (2011) *Climate protection through forest conservation in pacific island countries: approach, issues, and options for a pacific regional REDD+ policy framework roadmap.*

WWF / World Wide Fund For Nature (2013) *WWF guide to building REDD+ strategies: a toolkit for REDD+ practitioners around the globe.*

Chapter 7: Indigenous peoples and climate change in Cameroon

Daniel Armel Owona Mbarga

1 Introduction

Climate change is defined as modifications of the climate attributed directly or indirectly to human activity that alters the global atmosphere, contributing to natural climate variability over comparable time periods.[1] These changes are a reality. Indeed, the recurrence of extreme weather events[2] around the world is evidence of the fact that a gradual alteration of the climate system is happening. Proven or potential impacts are increasingly evident as a result of global warming, which are both harmful to humans and global ecosystems.[3]

Cameroon has also been affected by these climatic changes as evidenced in the various agro-ecological zones.[4] There have been floods, recurrent droughts, strong winds, heavy rainfall and significant annual water variations.[5] In addition, rising temperatures have increased evapotranspiration, leading to more frequent storms.[6] The most devastating cases occurred in 2000, 2003 and 2007 in the coastal highlands of the south west of the country, causing US$ 450,000 worth of damage.[7]

1 Article 1, United Nations Framework Convention on Climate Change of 9 May 1992.

2 Among the extreme events caused by climate change we have heat waves, droughts, floods, cyclones and forest fires. See IPCC (2014: 8).

3 Ibid: 4.

4 These are zones defined according to their ecological, climatic and edaphic characteristics. There are five in Cameroon, namely the Sudano-Sahelian zone, the high Guinean savannah zone, the highlands zone, the forest zone with bimodal rainfall, the coastal area with mono-modal rainfall. The first is characterised by savannahs, steppes and an arid climate. The North and Far North Regions are part of this zone. The high Guinean savannah zone, on the other hand is considered as the country's first watershed because a good number of major rivers take their rise from here. The Centre Region, the Sudano-Guinean savannah and the Adamawa plateau are part of this zone. The Upper plateau zone for its part includes the West and North West Regions. It is also considered as the country's second watershed. The forest zone with a bimodal rainfall includes the East and South Regions. In addition, it is a tropical forest particularly characterised by a dense hydrographical network. Finally, the coastal area with a mono-modal rainfall includes the coastal and mountainous zone with a humid equatorial climate. See Ministry of the Environment, Nature Protection and Sustainable Development (2015).

5 Ministry of Environment, Nature Protection and Sustainable Development (2015: 2; 23-24).

6 Ibid: 38.

7 Ibid.

Such phenomena are obviously not without consequences for Cameroon's population. Over the last 20 years, floods have affected more than 90,000 people and killed more than 100 throughout the country.[8] In the Sudano-Sahelian agro-ecological zone, in particular,[9] floods killed 153 people in 2011 and 2012.[10] Heat waves in this zone greatly increase the risk of mortality, food insecurity and famine as well as skin and other diseases such as malaria and others.[11] In the coastal zone with mono-modal rainfall, the amount and variability of rainfall greatly increased the risk of death from water-borne diseases.[12]

Future predictions concerning the effects of climate change in Cameroon are equally disturbing. According to the National Plan for Adaptation to Climate Change (PNACC), it is predicted that an average of five droughts per decade may cause at least 500 deaths in the Sudano-Sahelian zone.[13] This serves as an example for the growing gravity of the consequences of climate change on human beings.

Climate related impacts are particularly alarming for vulnerable groups such as indigenous peoples.[14] Indigenous peoples are expected to be more and more affected by climate change because their livelihoods largely depend on land use and natural resources.[15] At the same time, they are among those who have least contributed to carbon emissions.[16]

To date, there is no internationally accepted definition of the term 'indigenous peoples'. As proof, the United Nations Declaration on the Rights of Indigenous Peoples adopted by the General Assembly on 13 September 2007 does not define the term. This is because there is no comprehensive definition that embodies the current diversity of cultures, history and circumstances of indigenous peoples.[17] It is for this reason that the organisations that represented indigenous people during the development of the above-mentioned United Nations declaration explicitly rejected any definition of who they were.[18] As Kobila stated, we "notice the inappropriateness to define the concept of indigenous peoples".[19] Thus, in order to identify indigenous peoples, it is

---

8 Ibid.

9 With its mono-modal rainfall the coastal zone is one of the areas most vulnerable to climate change. See Ministry of the Environment, Nature Protection and Sustainable Development (2015: 49).

10 Ministry of the Environment, Nature Protection and Sustainable Development (2015: 39).

11 Ibid: 48.

12 Ibid: 44.

13 Ibid: 41.

14 The Cameroonian Government acknowledges the existence of vulnerable indigenous peoples in the country. See <http://www.minas.cm/index.php?option=com_content&view=article&id=157&Itemid=183&lang=fr> (accessed 4-3-2018).

15 IUCN (2010: 2).

16 Ibid.

17 *Centre for Minority Rights Development (Kenya) and Minority Rights Group (on behalf of Endorois Welfare Council) v. Kenya* 276/03 (2009: 18).

18 Geslin (2010: 7).

19 See Kobila (2009: 28).

necessary to refer to various criteria established at the universal, regional and national levels.

At the universal level, Martinez Cobo's study of "the Problem of Discrimination against Indigenous Peoples", prepared under the auspices of the United Nations, identifies precedence over a given territory before colonisation, non-dominance and marginalisation from an economic, political and socio-cultural point of view, as well as the claim of one's own identity, as distinct criteria.[20]

At the regional level, through its Working Group on Indigenous Populations/Communities, the African Commission on Human and Peoples' Rights notes that certain criteria such as precedence set out in Cobo's study are unworkable in the African context.[21] Indeed, except in specific cases such as the San people in southern Africa and the Pygmies in central Africa, all Africans are indigenous because they have always lived in this territory.[22] Therefore, the African Commission advocates that the identification of indigenous peoples should be based on selected criteria taking the African context into consideration. These include:[23]

- self-definition as indigenous peoples distinct from other groups within a State;
- special attachment to and use of their traditional heritage by which their ancestral lands and territories are of crucial importance to their physical and cultural survival; and
- experience of subjugation and marginalisation because of their culture, lifestyle or ways of production, which differ from the hegemonic and dominant model of the national majority.

Based on these criteria, the African Court on Human and Peoples' Rights also established criteria, which it considers important for identifying indigenous peoples:[24]

> The presence of priority in time with respect to the occupation and use of a specific territory; a voluntary perpetuation of cultural distinctiveness, which may include aspects of language, social organisation, religion and spiritual values, modes of production, laws and institutions; self-identification as well as recognition by other groups, or by State authorities that they are a distinct collectivity; and an experience of subjugation, marginalisation, dispossession, exclusion or discrimination, whether or not these conditions persist.

Finally, at the national level, even though Cameroon recognises subjective rights of indigenous peoples in the Preamble of its Constitution, its conception seems different from the one advocated at the universal level. It is the underlying conception used in this chapter hereinafter. It draws from the spirit and letter of Article 57(3) of the

---

20 Cameroon's Ministry of Forestry and Wildlife (2011:14).

21 African Commission on Human and Peoples' Rights Experts Working Group on Indigenous Populations / Communities (2005: 103).

22 Ibid.

23 Ibid: 103-104.

24 *African Commission on Human and People's Rights v. Republic of Kenya* Application No. 006/2012 (2017: 31).

Constitution. According to this Article, the Regional Council is headed by an indigene elected from among its members for the life of the Council. The Constitution recognises the existence of indigenous peoples in each of the ten regions of the country.[25] It holds that all people are indigenous to their land.[26] As such, Cameroon gives this concept a meaning similar to that of the African Commission on Human and Peoples' Rights. However, only those indigenous peoples whose vulnerability has been established on account of their socio-economic status, as a result of historical injustices, are eligible to the special constitutional and international protection of indigenous peoples.[27] This autochthony is in the same vein as that of the colonisers before independence. Indeed, since the time East Cameroon was a French-mandated territory under the League of Nations, the entire so-called native population was considered indigenous. Evidence of this can be found in an annual report submitted to the Council of the League of Nations at its sixth session between June and July 1925, in which the expression 'indigenous population' refers to people as listed below:[28]

> In the three constituencies of Garoua, Maroua and Ngaoundere, we are dealing with a society where conquerors, whose organisation reminds of feudalism, are placed at the head of the indigenous population.

Some indigenous people considered as vulnerable include[29] the Mbororo and Pygmies because their vulnerability to climate change is often raised.[30] The Mbororo are nomadic Fulani known for their engagement in pastoral activity,[31] who roam the bush in search of pastures.[32] Estimated at more than 60,000 people, they are subdivided into three main groups, namely the Jafun, Woodabe and Aku.[33] They are found throughout Cameroon but mainly in the north west, west, north, Adamawa and east regions.[34] The Pygmies are considered as the first inhabitants of the African tropical forests and their lifestyle is based on hunting and gathering.[35] They are mainly found in the east, south and central regions and in the southern part of the coastal zone.[36] The Pygmies consist of three major groups: the Bakas, the Bagyelis and Bedzans.[37]

---

25 Kobila (2009: 100).
26 Ibid: 99.
27 Ibid: 100.
28 France (1925: 54).
29 The author agrees with Kobila (2009: 102) that establishing a limited list of vulnerable indigenous populations does not coincide with the understanding of the Cameroonian Constitution in its Article 57(3).
30 See Nguegang Tayou (2017) and the Project: Population Resilience to Climate Change, funded by the United Nations Development Programme.
31 Mouiche (2012: 152).
32 Ibid: 153.
33 Nguiffo & Mballa (2009: 1).
34 Mouiche (2012: 153).
35 Ibid.
36 Nguiffo & Mballa (2009: 1-2).
37 Ibid.

Indigenous marginalisation has been evidenced by historical exclusion from decision-making processes and by the fact that they are often pushed into resource-poor and climate-sensitive regions because of development activities.[38] When combined with the effects of climate change, their vulnerability is exacerbated.

Cameroonian climate policy must, therefore, take indigenous peoples into account in order to protect them against the impacts of climate change. The State of Cameroon is also obliged to do so in light of its legal obligation as a signatory to the Paris Agreement.[39] Article 7 of this Agreement stipulates that parties should take into account and draw on the best available scientific knowledge and, as appropriate, traditional knowledge, indigenous know-how and knowledge and local knowledge systems, to adapt relevant socio-economic and environmental policies and measures. Hence, it is necessary to examine the level of protection of indigenous populations in Cameroon's climate policy.

Despite the existence of several articles focusing on indigenous populations in Cameroon,[40] these writings do not address the issue of climate change. Thus, this chapter attempts to progress research on this particular topic by evaluating the level protection of indigenous populations in light of the growing impacts of climate change.

2 Little initial consideration of the indigenous populations

Cameroon signed and ratified the United Nations Framework Convention on Climate Change (UNFCCC),[41] which represents the instrument that formalises the international legal system on climate change. Cameroon's climate policy reveals that indigenous people have been accorded a far more central role in recent times. Between 1996 and 2005, Cameroon has developed several planning documents pertinent to climate change including the National Environmental Management Plan (NEMP) of February 1996 and Cameroon's First Initial National Communication to the UNFCCC in 2005. These documents reveal an undifferentiated participation of indigenous peoples not only in the preparation phase but also regarding the proposed response strategies.

38 IUCN (2010: 2).

39 Cameroon ratified the Paris Agreement on 29 July 2016. See <https://www.ecolex.org/> (accessed 10-12-2017).

40 See for example Abega (1996-1997); Abega & Bigombe Logo (2006); Atsiga Essala (1999); Bigombe Logo (2000).

41 Signature in 1992 and retification in 1994; the Convention entered into force in Cameroon on 17 January 1995. See <https://www.ecolex.org/details/treaty/united-nations-framework-convention-on-climate-change-tre-001147/?q=Convention+cadre+des+Nations+Unies+sur+les+changements+climatiques> (accessed 10-12-2017).

2.1 Undifferentiated participation of indigenous peoples in the development of strategy papers on climate change

Strategy or planning papers are usually developed after consultation with various stakeholders, including experts, members of government, donors and private persons, who can intervene at various stages of the process. With the aim of developing policies, strategies and actions for the protection of the environment and the rational management of natural resources for sustainable development,[42] the NEMP reflects Cameroon's climate-related aspirations. The strategy was developed in line with the expectations under the UNFCCC.[43] It was also developed with the participation of the populations concerned, such as rural and urban communities, the government and the public service, specialised non-governmental organisations, professional associations, and all users of natural resources, including forests and pastures as well as donors and international cooperation agencies.[44] Although indigenous peoples have not been mentioned explicitly, it can be deduced that they had been included in the general reference 'users of natural resources' since Pygmies use forests and Mbororos rely on pastures, which are both natural resources.

2.2 Lack of differentiation of the indigenous peoples in the response strategies developed

The state of vulnerability of the population should be assessed also taking into account the potential variability of the impacts of climate change on urban dwellers and indigenous populations, particularly as regards to the way they can cope or adapt to these changes. Cameroonian responses developed to address the effects of climate change envisage mitigation and adaptation. The former refers to measures that contribute to the reduction of the negative impacts of climate change, while the latter refers to measures that contribute to the modifications of lifestyles in a bid to cope with the consequences of climate change. Various measures proposed in the initial national communication shall mitigate the growth of greenhouse gases in the forestry sector. These include the reduction of emissions from biomass use, the expansion of sequestration sinks of forest emissions and the change in land use.[45]

As concerns adaptation to the adverse effects of climate change, the initial national communication takes into account the strategies used by farmers in the Benue Valley, particularly the change in cultivation practices, the constitution of safety stocks, the

---

42 Ministry of the Environment and Forests (1996: 6).

43 For the analysis of incentives particularly financial, that moved Cameroon to include climate change in its political agenda, see Kede (2017).

44 Ibid: 6. See also Ministry of the Environment and Forests (1996: 6).

45 Ministry of the Environment and Forests (2005: 71).

change of date for certain operations and the use of new plots.[46] Upon observation, it is noticeable that the response strategies proposed in the initial national communication do not include indigenous peoples. Yet, these strategies should take into account traditional knowledge of indigenous peoples as they possess knowledge capable of facilitating adaption to climate risks.[47] This is, for instance, the case for mixed cropping or higher crop diversification on the same plot. The objective of this strategy is not only to reduce crop vulnerability but to multiply the quality of plants in the field. Thus, if some of the plants are not resistant to variations due to climate change, the others may be.[48] This allows Pygmies to adapt to climate disruptions.[49] In addition, the traditional system of forecasting the beginning and the end of the rainy season can be seen as another asset of traditional knowledge. The Baka, for instance, determine the beginning of the rainy season based on the first appearance of edible black head caterpillars.[50] Rains usually start exactly two weeks after the appearance of these caterpillars.[51] This makes it possible to adapt to irregular rainy seasons due to climate change.

Thus, between 1996 and 2005, the potential participation of indigenous people in the fight against climate change was not taken into account. Yet, they could make a significant contribution in this area. It is undoubtedly for this reason that Cameroon's climate policy has recently given greater importance to these populations.

3 Recent expansion of the inclusion of indigenous peoples

As from 2012, it is noticeable that indigenous people have been more and more integrated into Cameroon's climate policy consultation processes. In fact, a careful observation of documents such as the National Adaptation Plan (PNACC)[52] of 24 June 2015, the 2015 planned determined contribution at the national level and the 2012 proposed measures for the state of preparedness (R-PP), show governmental recognition of the contribution of indigenous peoples in the development of climate strategy papers, as well as the consideration of their vulnerability in proposed responses.

46 Ibid: 94-95.
47 World Bank (2010: 108).
48 Fosso (2014).
49 Ibid.
50 Ibid.
51 Ibid.
52 The national plan on Adaptation to Climate Change is a national strategy paper, which is aimed at guiding the government and stakeholders in approaching adaptation to climate change. See Ministry of Environment, Nature Protection and Sustainable Development (2015: 27).

3.1 Government recognition of the contribution of indigenous peoples in the development of climate strategy papers

The recognition of the contribution of indigenous peoples in the preparation of strategy papers in the fight against climate change is the result of the internalisation of international commitments to which Cameroon has subscribed. In developing its PNACC, for example, Cameroon has followed the UNFCCC recommendations as well as those of the Cancun Framework for Adaptation,[53] taking into account and drawing on traditional and indigenous approaches.

Furthermore, the proposal for the state of preparedness measures (R-PP) within the framework of the mechanism on reducing emissions from deforestation and forest degradation (REDD+) states that indigenous peoples are among the 21 members of the REDD+ Steering Committee.[54] This Committee is responsible for planning policy and strategy proposals for the REDD+ initiative, developing selection criteria for the projects that shall be submitted to the Minister in charge of the environment, and validating the work and approving the action plan of the Technical Secretariat.[55] They, therefore, play a major role in the decision-making process on climate. In addition, the participation of indigenous peoples is evaluated at 7% in the regional and national consultation workshops for the finalisation of the R-PP.[56] This involvement is explained by the relevance of indigenous peoples in the REDD+ framework and the choice Cameroon has made to develop a REDD+ mechanism that particularly targets the development of vulnerable groups. [57]

3.2 Taking into account the vulnerability of indigenous peoples in proposed response strategies

As part of recommendations for the sectoral policy, the PNACC takes into account the vulnerability of the indigenous populations in terms of gender, vulnerability, social protection and national solidarity sectors. The objective here is to reduce the vulnerability of marginalised populations and to build their capacities, autonomy and independence.[58] The PNACC also recommends the development of a specific plan to support indigenous peoples in the event of disaster.[59]

53 Ministry of Environment, Nature Protection and Sustainable Development (2015: 27).
54 Republic of Cameroon (2012: 11).
55 Ibid.
56 Ibid: 18.
57 Ibid.
58 Ministry of Environment, Nature Protection and Sustainable Development (2015: 80).
59 Ibid: 81.

In addition, the PNACC also takes into account the vulnerability of indigenous peoples within the framework of its proposed projects. An example is a project focusing on the improvement of local governance structures in response to climate change, to strengthen local mechanisms for securing the rights of use and access to land ownership for the main stakeholders, particularly indigenous peoples.[60] The nationally determined contribution (NDC) of Cameroon projects to build capacities of indigenous peoples, within the framework of adaptation measures.[61] This shows the growing role that indigenous peoples are playing in contemporary Cameroonian climate policy.

4 Conclusion

While in the past, the capacity of indigenous peoples in Cameroon's climate policy was underutilised and underrepresented, in recent years, they have been more and more integrated into the Cameroonian climate policy and strategy. This happened for good reasons: First, the influence of Cameroon's international commitments towards a greater inclusion of indigenous peoples in climate change planning. Secondly and perhaps even more important, the realisation of the value that indigenous and traditional knowledge can play in overcoming their vulnerability in the implementation of concrete projects.

References

Abega, SC (1996-1997) *La communication avec les Pygmées Baka.*

Abega, SC & P Bigombe Logo (eds) (2006) *La marginalisation des Pygmées d'Afrique centrale.*

African Commission's Working Group of Experts on Indigenous Populations/Communities (2005) *Rapport du Groupe de travail d'experts de la Commission africaine des droits de l'homme et des peuples sur les populations/communautés* autochtones, at <https://www.iwgia.org/images/publications//African_Commission_book_French.pdf> (accessed 20-7-2018).

Atsiga Essala, L (1999) "L'exploitation des populations marginales : le cas des Pygmées du Cameroun" 2 *Les formes contemporaines d'esclavage, Cahier africain des droits de l'homme* 155-177.

Bigombe Logo, P (2000) "Droits des peuples autochtones au Cameroun: le dilemme de la reconnaissance et de la banalisation" 37 *Bulletin IKEWAN* 9-11.

Fosso, LC (2014) *Stratégies indigènes d'adaptation aux changements climatiques: cas des populations autochtones et communautés locales autour du parc national de Boumba Bek, Est Cameroun* Dissertation University of Dschang.

France (1925) *Rapport annuel du Gouvernement français sur l'administration sous mandat des territoires du Cameroun pour l'année 1924.*

60 Ibid: 110.
61 Republic of Cameroon (2015: 15).

Geslin, A (2010) *La protection internationale des peuples autochtones : de la reconnaissance d'une identité transnationale autochtone à l'interculturalité normative* Annuaire français de droit international.

IPCC / Intergovernmental Panel on Climate Change (2014) *Changements climatiques 2014. Rapports de synthèse. Résumé à l'intention des décideurs*, at <http://www.ipcc.ch/pdf/assessment-report/ar5/syr/AR5_SYR_FINAL_SPM_fr.pdf> (accessed 20-7-2018).

IUCN / International Union for Nature Conservation (2010) *Indigenous peoples and REDD-plus. Challenges and opportunities for the engagement of indigenous peoples and local communities in REDD-plus*, at <https://www.iucn.org/downloads/a4_iucn_indigenous_peoples_and_redd_.pdf> (accessed 20-7-2018).

Kede EY (2017) *La gouvernance climatique au Cameroun. Sociologie d'une action publique internationale en contexte africain.*

Kobila JM (2009) *La protection des minorités et des peuples autochtones au Cameroun. Entre reconnaissance interne consacrée et consécration universelle réaffirmée.*

Ministry of Environment and Forests (1996) *Plan national de gestion de l'environnement*, at <http://api.commissiemer.nl/docs/cms/O83_032_detb_PNGEVOL1.pdf> (accessed 20-7-2018).

Ministry of Environment and Forests (2005) *Communication nationale initiale*, at <http://unfccc.int/resource/docs/natc/cmrnc1f.pdf> (accessed 20-7-2018).

Ministry of Environment, Nature Protection and Sustainable Development (2015) *Plan national d'adaptation aux changements climatiques du Cameroun*, at <http://www4.unfccc.int/nap/Documents/Parties/PNACC_Cameroun_VF_Valid%C3%A9e_24062015%20-%20FINAL.pdf> (accessed 20-7-2018).

Ministry of Forests and Wildlife (2011) *Projet de conservation et d'utilisation durable de la forêt de Ngoyla-Mintom. Plan pour les peuples autochtones et vulnérables (PPAV)*, at <http://www.minfof.cm/documentation/Ngoyla-Mintom-PPAV%20-%20Final.pdf> (accessed 20-7-2018).

Mouiche, I (2012) *Démocratisation et intégration sociopolitique des minorités ethniques au Cameroun: Entre dogmatisme du principe majoritaire et centralité des partis politiques.*

Nguegang Tayou, SA (2017) *Genre et vulnérabilité des peuples autochtones au changement climatique : cas des Mbororo du Cameroun* Dissertation Catholic University of Louvain.

Nguiffo, S & N Mballa (2009) *Les dispositions constitutionnelles, législatives et administratives relatives aux populations autochtones au Cameroun*, at <http://docplayer.fr/68592794-Les-dispositions-constitutionnelles-legislatives-et-administratives-relatives-aux-populations-autochtones-au-cameroun-samuel-nguiffo-et-nadine-mballa.html> (accessed 20-7-2018).

Republic of Cameroon (2012) *Readiness preparation proposal (R-PP)*, at <https://www.forestcarbonpartnership.org/sites/fcp/files/Documents/PDF/Oct2012/Cameroon%20final%20R-PP-English-October%2C%202012.pdf> (accessed 20-7-2018).

Republic of Cameroon (2015) *Contribution prévue déterminée au niveau national*, at <http://www4.unfccc.int/ndcregistry/PublishedDocuments/Cameroon%20First/CPDN%20CMR%20Final.pdf> (accessed 20-7-2018).

United Nations Permanent Forum on Indigenous Issues (2008) *Climate change and indigenous peoples*, at <http://www.un.org/en/events/indigenousday/pdf/Backgrounder_ClimateChange_FINAL.pdf> (accessed 20-7-2018).

World Bank (2010) *Nouveaux horizons. Développement et changement climatique.*

Chapter 8: REDD+ and benefit sharing: an examination of the legal framework in Uganda

Hadijah Yahyah

1 Introduction

Reducing Emissions from Deforestation and Forest Degradation, as well as Conservation, Sustainable Management of Forests and Enhancement of Forest Carbon Stocks (REDD+) is a voluntary initiative established under the United Nations Framework Convention on Climate Change (UNFCCC) to create financial incentives for developing countries to reduce forest-related greenhouse gas emissions.[1] REDD+ activities have the potential to deliver a wide range of benefits to the climate, to biodiversity and to communities that depend on forests. By the same token, REDD+ poses risks of negative impacts, particularly if the rights of local communities are not respected, if a gender-sensitive approach is not taken and if REDD+ activities are not embedded in the overall framework of the environment.[2]

Uganda's REDD+ Programme, which is implemented as a National REDD+ Process, is a national effort to contribute to the mitigation of climate change, and improve the livelihoods of local, indigenous as well as forest-dependent communities. Uganda's REDD+ Readiness process aims to design a socially and environmentally viable national strategy for reducing emissions from deforestation and forest degradation, and a national reference scenario of emissions from deforestation and forest degradation. This takes into account the national circumstances and the emerging guidance from the global climate change convention.

Benefit sharing refers to a commitment to channel some returns, whether monetary or non-monetary, back to the range of designated participants or affected communities.[3] A proportion of revenue earned by the State is returned to local communities through indirect and direct benefit-sharing arrangements. Direct benefit sharing refers to cash payments to individuals or communities, and indirect benefit sharing includes other non-cash benefits, including infrastructure or community facilities, and grassroots development activities.

---

1 Decision 2/COP13.
2 UNEP (2015).
3 IUCN (2012: 6); also see Lindhjem et al. (2010).

Benefit sharing is attracting increasing attention worldwide as a uniquely powerful, practical and adaptable conservation tool in natural resource management. It serves to underpin the sort of partnerships needed to involve people in development decisions that affect them genuinely and is a practical way for REDD+ and sustainable forest management to contribute to sustainable development.

REDD+, which includes the conservation of forest carbon stocks, conservation and sustainable management of forests, and enhancement of forest carbon stocks, is one of the most important climate initiatives of the 21st century and is being developed into an incentive-based conservation programme. It has the potential to contribute to low-carbon sustainable development and poverty reduction while reducing emissions and sequestering carbon.[4] For REDD+ to result in lasting emission reductions and realise sustainable benefits for forest management communities and avoid making vulnerable people worse off, a system of equitable, effective and efficient benefit sharing is imperative through policy, and legal and institutional arrangements.

REDD+ initiatives are increasingly taking forest governance issues into account, which helps to make it an effective instrument to slow, halt and reverse forest cover and carbon loss. Uganda is both a party to the UNFCCC, and a signatory to the Kyoto Protocol and the Paris Agreement that resulted out of the COP21 decisions in Paris, France.

2 The conceptual and theoretical basis of this chapter

It is widely recognised that the conservation of tropical forests largely depends on incentivising and supporting the countries that host these forests and the people who live and work in them.[5] It is also recognised that incentive mechanisms such as REDD+ can quite substantially increase benefit flows to forest managers.[6]

The central principle underlying REDD+ is the transfer of financial incentives from developed to developing countries to reduce deforestation and forest degradation. The scale of the benefits is usually linked to the rates of 'forest manager' defined here as any group or individual that depends upon the forest to generate income or to subsist, including private landholders. In this regard, REDD+ can provide substantial financial benefits to developing tropical countries. The way in which these benefits are to be distributed has become a persistent problem in REDD+. Particular concerns are that the benefits may not be equitably shared between stakeholders and that people with less power in the benefit-sharing decision-making processes could lose out.[7]

---

4 Ibid.
5 Wollenberg & Springate-Baginski (2009).
6 Agrawal & Angelsen (2009).
7 Griffiths (2008); Costenbader (2011).

Peskett et al.[8] and Griffiths[9] argue that equity in benefit-sharing mechanisms is a fundamental condition if REDD+ is to be effective and that this, in turn, depends on the degree of local participation in the process of developing and implementing benefits. However, despite concerns raised in the literature about the impact of benefit-sharing mechanisms on the effectiveness of REDD+, as reflected in overall reductions in deforestation,[10] scholars have been unable to agree on how to make benefit-sharing mechanisms more equitable.[11] Indeed, still lacking is a clear understanding of what benefit-sharing mechanisms entail; the types of benefits REDD+ will deliver and the processes by which the organisation will deliver them.

The term 'benefit sharing' relates to many different instances (e.g. governance structures and institutions set up to collect compensation and rents from the provision of the ecosystem services of carbon sequestration and storage; and distribution of the direct and indirect benefits among affected stakeholders), which hampers efforts to identify the main issues and the optimum approach.[12] In particular, it is not always clear what types of benefits need to be shared; how 'legitimate' beneficiaries should be identified, particularly in cases where deforestation is the result of illegal activities; or how benefit-sharing systems can be managed at the various levels of government (i.e. national, sub-national, local).

According to the Bali Action Plan, benefit-sharing mechanisms and the related benefits will be created as part of the policy approaches and measures for REDD+. Two types of policies and standards related to benefit-sharing mechanisms have been identified: those that aim to generate compensation (benefits designed to cover the foregone opportunity costs of deforestation) and those that generate incentives (benefits designed to encourage positive behaviours).[13] Both incentives and compensation can be delivered up front, to enable REDD+ to commence, or, dispensed over time, to ensure that REDD+ actions continue according to performance.

In this chapter, compensation is considered as a type of incentive, because it serves to encourage conservation behaviours. Another category of policies and measures related to benefit-sharing mechanisms consists of those that aim to generate interventions.[14] In this context, interventions are actions designed to create legal, administrative and technical benefits and include the regularisation of land tenure, institutional arrangements, monitoring systems and other activities that are necessary to facilitate and guarantee positive outcomes from REDD+.

---

8 Peskett et al. (2008).
9 Griffiths (2008).
10 Luttrell et al. (2007).
11 Agrawal & Angelsen (2009); Johns & Schlamadinger (2009).
12 Costenbader (2011).
13 Brown (2008); and Peskett et al. (2008).
14 Ibid.

Another critical consideration is the process by which the mechanisms distribute the benefits: directly or indirectly.[15] Direct benefit sharing involves giving benefits directly to forest managers (e.g. payment for environmental services or PES; and technical materials); whereas indirect benefit sharing encompasses benefits that aim to foster broader development and adaptation actions that enhance co-benefits (e.g. access to education and health services).

Mechanisms would involve the delivery of benefits at both national and local levels. The choice of policies and measures to establish benefit-sharing mechanisms will affect the whole structure of a REDD+ scheme by determining who is to be given incentives to do what, and the kinds of interventions that are needed to facilitate the successful implementation of the process.

2.1 Local participation

It has been argued by some scholars that active local involvement is necessary to identify beneficiaries, appropriate benefits, the timeframe for implementation and how benefits will be received, as part of the design and implementation of benefit-sharing mechanisms for REDD+ schemes.[16] For this chapter, it is important to define 'local participation'. The Food and Agriculture Organisation (FAO) of the United Nations describes participatory forestry as those processes and mechanisms that enable people with a direct stake in forest resources (i.e. local people) to take part in decision-making in all aspects of forest management, from managing resources to formulating and implementing institutional frameworks.[17] More specifically, community forestry refers to a component of participatory forestry that focuses on local communities as key stakeholders for sustainability.

However, the meaning of 'local' itself is controversial.[18] Definitions of local people and forest-dependent communities, for example, are usually specific to their geographical area, and various terms are used for people who live in or near forest areas or who are from such areas.[19] In this chapter, 'local' is defined as any group that depends on the forest to generate income or to subsist, including private landholders. These people, referred to in this chapter as 'forest managers,' derive substantial benefits from the forest and therefore are more inclined to manage and take care of it. They will be the first to feel the impact of any changes in the forest cover or the quality of the forest and the services it provides.

---

15 Peskett et al. (2008); and Luttrell et al. (2012).
16 Santilli et al. (2005); Nepstad et al. (2007); Griffiths (2008); and Peskett et al. (2008).
17 See <http://www.fao.org/forestry/participatory/en/> (accessed 1-8-2018).
18 Raffles (1999).
19 Gebara (2013).

'Participation' too can have different meanings depending on the context. Whatever the definition, participation is highly context-specific, and its effects range from coercion to full local control. There are two distinct perspectives for participatory approaches: participation as a means, i.e. to improve the effectiveness of specific interventions; and participation as an end, i.e. as a necessary tool for equity and the empowerment of marginalised groups.[20] Furthermore, according to Pimbert and Pretty,[21] there are different levels of participation, from simple sharing of information to transfer of power.

The crucial role of local participation in the design of benefit-sharing mechanisms is to develop approaches that are flexible, suitable and able to ensure the effectiveness of forest managers' efforts to reduce deforestation and forest degradation.[22] Such methods are most likely to result from interactive and self-mobilisation participation because these types of engagements involve forest managers taking control of local decisions and resources. There is a risk, however, that benefit-sharing mechanisms will end up reinforcing the status quo and that the power of the benefits will remain in the hands of project developers or central governments, to be distributed according to their criteria,[23] producing unfair outcomes.

Local participation has also been found to have significant implications for related aspects of REDD+, such as monitoring activities.[24] Fry, for example, argues that national systems should be built, at least partly, on community-based monitoring, reporting and verification (MRV) protocols that maximise local people's involvement in forest monitoring and the assessment of social impacts.[25]

Hajek et al.[26] demonstrate the potential for technological and organisational innovation when a diverse group of local and international for-profit and not-for-profit actors come together to design and implement a project.[27]

The literature contains a range of findings indicating the necessity of local knowledge and engagement when creating and enforcing rules for forest management.[28] Overall, the results show that the design of national policies and measures should include flexible approaches for benefit-sharing mechanisms, which can be adapted to the needs of forest managers and to the area in which the REDD+ scheme is to be developed. Moreover, if changes in forest management and forest conditions are to be achieved, social change at all levels will first be necessary. Policies and measures should, therefore, include tools and subsidies to achieve such social change.

---

20 Cleaver (1999); Diamond (2002).
21 Pimbert & Pretty (1995).
22 Ibid: 22.
23 Griffiths (2008).
24 Corbera & Schroeder (2011).
25 Ibid.
26 Hajek et al. (2011)
27 Corbera & Schroeder (2011).
28 Gibson et al. (2005).

2.2 Equity

Equity is a critical element in the design and implementation of benefit-sharing mechanisms for schemes such as REDD+.[29] The literature contains a range of equity discourses on REDD+ benefit sharing,[30] and these discourses, along with ideologies and definitions associated with benefit sharing, concern a variety of objectives, ranging from the need to provide compensation for costs incurred, the need to ensure co-benefits (e.g. biodiversity) and the need to recognise legal rights and ensure fair outcomes.

A significant concern when incorporating equity into REDD+ schemes is that, in order to meet the inclusion criteria (as defined in the Clean Development Mechanism), REDD+ must provide benefits to the vast majority of landowners that are likely to be responsible for the bulk of emissions from deforestation and forest degradation and this would be unfair to those who have been conserving the forests for a long time, such as indigenous communities.[31]

Most of the various definitions of equity are based on ideas of distributive and procedural justice,[32] which are as varied as the cultures from which they originate.[33] Therefore, the definition of equity will always vary from one REDD+ country to another and may change with time. Another important consideration is the way in which equity is analysed, both in the outcomes of a distributional scheme and in the process of agreeing on such a scheme.[34] This distinction is described by Brown and Corbera[35] as, respectively, equity in outcomes and equity in decision making,where the first refers to the distribution of project outcomes among project participants,[36] and the latter concerns procedural fairness within the project framework and considers the issues of recognition and inclusion in strategic management decisions.[37]

Another form of representing these concepts is found in the definition of McDermott et al.[38], who describe local equity as a global value of ecosystem services. They identify three interrelated dimensions of distributive equity, procedural equity and contextual equity.

29 Pagiola & Platais (2007); Grieg-Gran (2008); Peskett et al. (2008); Pascual et al. (2010); and McDermott et al. (2012).
30 Luttrell et al. (2013).
31 Griffiths (2008); and Bond et al. (2009).
32 Rawls (1971); Dobson (1998); and McDermott et al. (2012).
33 Sachs & Santarius (2007).
34 Lind & Taylor (1988).
35 Brown & Corberal (2003).
36 Corbera et al. (2007).
37 Fraser (1997); and Corbera et al. (2007).
38 McDermott et al. (2012).

For McDermott et al.[39], distributive equity is concerned with outcomes in the allocation among stakeholders of the costs, risks and benefits resulting from environmental policy or resource management decisions and hence primarily represents the economic dimension of equity. In this context, the equitable distribution of benefits can be justified by one of the various principles: equality, social welfare, merit and need.

Procedural equity, according to McDermott et al.[40], refers to fairness in the political processes that allocate resources and resolve disputes. It involves representation, recognition/inclusion, and voice and participation in decision-making.

Contextual equity links the other two dimensions, state McDermott et al.,[41] by taking into account the pre-existing conditions under which people engage in procedures and benefit distributions and which limit or enable their capacity to do both. This concept builds on Brown and Corbera's idea of 'equity in access' by incorporating context, capabilities and power.

In terms of distributive equity, Pascual et al.[42] summarise different economic fairness criteria that could be applied in PES schemes, including: (i) 'compensation', where payments compensate landholders for the foregone benefits related to the provision of environmental services; (ii) 'common goods', where payments are invested in common goods, so all providers benefit indirectly; (iii) 'egalitarian', where funds are distributed equally among all providers; (iv) 'maxi-min', where the aim of payments is to maximise the net benefit to the poorest landholders; (v) 'actual provision', where payments to landowners correspond with the actual outcome level of provision of environmental services; (vi) 'expected provision', where payments to landholders depend on the expected level of provision of services for a given land use; and (vii) status quo, where payments maintain previous standards of relative distribution of income among providers.

This chapter adopts the view that equity in decision making will directly influence equity in outcomes, as argued by Corbera et al.,[43] and employs this distinction to analyse the way in which benefit-sharing mechanisms were designed and implemented in several projects.

To analyse equity in the decision-making process, the author uses Pimbert and Pretty's[44] typologies of participation to examine how local forest managers were engaged in the design and implementation of benefit-sharing mechanisms. To analyse equity in the outcomes, the author looks at the fairness of the benefits distributed.[45]

---

39 Ibid.
40 Ibid.
41 Ibid.
42 Pascual et al. (2010).
43 Corbera et al. (2007).
44 Pimbert & Pretty (1995).
45 Muller (2001).

This permits the inclusion of a range of economic fairness criteria,[46] without the need to choose just one specific approach. Therefore, a contextualised assessment of forest managers' needs and of the interventions that are necessary in each case appears to be a critical step in determining equity parameters when identifying the benefits and optimum benefit-sharing mechanisms for REDD+ schemes at the local level. Furthermore, as shown by Corbera et al.[47], a more contextually informed definition of the benefits is critical for achieving equity in benefit sharing.

3 The forestry sector and REDD+ benefit-sharing governance in Uganda

Uganda's forests may be categorised into four broad types: well-stocked Tropical High Forests (THF) (430,888 ha); degraded THF (136,280 ha); woodland (including montane) (1,161,610 ha); and plantation forest (107,608 ha). Together they cover 1.84 million ha, approximately 10% of the country's land area.[48] Well-stocked THF are found mainly in central forest reserves (CFRs) in the west (Bugoma, Budongo, Kalinzu-Maramagambo, Katsyoha-Kitomi) and national parks (Bwindi Impenetrable, Mgahinga, Mount Rwenzori, Mount Elgon, Kibale and Semuliki). Low-stocked THF are found around the shores and islands of Lake Victoria, while woodland is found mainly in the northern, central and western regions. The eastern part of the country is largely forest-poor, except for Mount Elgon.

The forestry sector in Uganda faces many challenges due to continued destruction and degradation of forests; loss of forest cover; increased pressure on forests in protected areas due to rapid degradation of forests on private lands; inadequate enforcement of forest laws; uncontrolled encroachment on forests in protected areas, especially in the central forest reserves; unclear land rights that result in issuance of land titles for land in the protected areas and disputes over land use; growing population pressures on the remaining forests; weak sector governance; political interference in the management of protected forest estate; and a resultant failure to contribute to improving livelihoods and forest-based development to the levels expected in the Forestry Policy and the National Forest Plan.

According to UNEP World Conservation Monitoring Centre Uganda is among the few countries with the highest deforestation rate globally. The natural forest cover has experienced a steady decline in the area in the past decades. In 1990, forest cover was estimated at 24% of the total land area. In 2000, forests were expected to have covered

46 Pascual et al. (2010).
47 Corbera et al. (2007).
48 FIPU (2017: xii).

3.12 million hectares but had declined to 2.42 million hectares in 2015, about 11.8% of the total land area.[49]

According to Uganda's (Intended) Nationally Determined Contributions (INDC),[50] forestry sector priorities include enhancing forest ecosystems resilience through promoting intensified and sustained restoration efforts (afforestation and reforestation programmes); biodiversity and watershed conservation (including re-establishment of wildlife corridors) and encouraging agro-forestry; and supporting and encouraging efficient biomass energy production and utilisation technologies. The Government of Uganda is in an advanced stage of developing a national REDD+ strategy as a long-term measure for tackling deforestation and forest degradation, ensuring sustainable forest management, and enhancing carbon stocks and forest biodiversity conservation,[51] while meeting the demands for energy and other forest products. The intended REDD+ strategy options have to be developed for enhancing positive impacts of strategy options, and reducing any likely adverse social and environmental effects on forest-dependent communities and the communities overall.

Uganda has participated in REDD+ preparatory activities, e.g. institutional setup, strategy preparation, capacity building and awareness since 2008 in partnership with the Forest Carbon Partnership Facility (FCPF) of the World Bank. As a REDD+ participating country, Uganda submitted its Nationally Determined Contributions (NDCs) to the UNFCCC way before the COP21 and efforts are underway to have these implemented. The Uganda REDD+ national focal point and team are in an advanced stage of drafting the country's national REDD+ strategy.

REDD+ is part of the National Climate Change Policy (NCCP) that aims for a harmonised and coordinated approach towards a climate-resilient and low-carbon development path for sustainable development in Uganda. It is both a mitigation and adaptation action under Uganda's Climate Change Policy (2015). The REDD+ process recognises and seeks to collaborate with a variety of climate change initiatives and programmes of government, non-governmental organisations (NGOs), civil society organisations (CSOs), private sector, forest-dependent communities and the general public to ensure that appropriate strategies for reducing emissions from deforestation and forest degradation are developed and effectively implemented. The REDD+ Readiness process also interacts with and utilises areas of synergy and complementarities with ongoing climate change initiatives at national and local levels.

Since July 2013, Uganda has been implementing the REDD+ Readiness phase under the National Climate Change Advisory Committee (policy level coordination) and Ministry of Water and Environment (technical and management). The Forestry Sector

49 GoU (2017: 5).

50 Uganda made the first submission to the UNFCCC Secretariat in January 2017.

51 See <https://www.forestcarbonpartnership.org/sites/fcp/files/2014/June/Uganda%20FCPF%> (accessed 30-3-2018).

Support Department of the Ministry of Water and Environment serves as the REDD+ Secretariat. The REDD+ Readiness activities are derived from the Readiness-Preparedness Proposals (R-PP). By the end of 2017, Uganda had made important progress in elaborating on its nationally agreed strategies and actions for reducing deforestation and forest degradation, sustainable forest management, enhancing the role of conservation of biodiversity, and enhancing carbon stocks. These strategies will be packaged into Uganda's REDD+ Strategy and Action Plan document. Additionally, the following baselines and measures will have been developed: the National Reference Emission Level/Forest Reference Level, National Forest Monitoring System, National Forest and Safeguards Information System, Benefit Sharing Arrangements, Environmental and Social Management Framework, Forest Grievances and Redress Mechanism, and Standards for REDD+ Field activities in Uganda. In addition to the list above, Uganda's capacity to implement the National REDD+ Strategy will have been strengthened at various scales and across different sector and players.

Examples of REDD+-related projects in Uganda include: Uganda Carbon Bureau, Katoomba Group Incubator, Katoomba Group REDD+ Opportunities Scoping Exercise, the International Small Groups Tree Planting Project, and the Nile Basin Reforestation Project, among others.

Benefit sharing has been highlighted as a critical aspect of all the REDD+ processes such as the Readiness-Preparedness Proposals (R-PPs). For example, most of the R-PPs and National Program Documents refer to the importance of developing benefit-sharing systems and some also make commitments to transparent and equitable benefit sharing.

Benefit- or revenue-sharing mechanisms in the context of REDD+ are defined as agreements between stakeholders, such as private sector, local communities, government and non-profit organisations, about the equitable distribution of benefits related to the commercialisation of forest carbon. Schroeder[52] suggests the following definition for non-human genetic resources: "Benefit sharing is the action of giving a portion of advantages or profits derived from the use of non-human genetic or traditional knowledge to the resource providers to achieve justice in exchange". In other words, benefit sharing is not an act of charitable giving – if we use resources we do not own, justice demands some form of compensation in return.

Uganda's NDC prioritises adaptation. The country continues to work on reducing its vulnerabilities and addressing adaptation in agriculture and livestock, forestry, infrastructure (with an emphasis on human settlements, social infrastructure and transport), water, energy, health and disaster risk management sectors. Sustainable Land Management (SLM) and Climate Smart Agriculture (CSA) will be scaled up to increase resilience at the grassroots level while fostering gender and social equity.

52 Schroeder (2007).

At the sectoral level, efforts are still underway to ensure climate change is mainstreamed into governmental policies and institutional frameworks through sectoral policies. Some of these sectoral policies were developed before climate change became the subject of a high-level policy and development priority, and although they align with the NDP II, they have not been systematically aligned with the country's NDC and climate change objectives. Local level policies also include District Development Plans (DDPs) that are aligned with NDP II and reflect the priorities of each of the 135 districts and local governments in Uganda. The DDPs provide the main entry point for climate change priorities, particularly the integration of the NDC into local government decision-making systems.

As the country moves towards activating these policies, it is in the process of: (i) establishing institutional frameworks that will disseminate action across levels of government; (ii) coordinating relevant actors (including those outside the government, such as the private sector, multilateral and bilateral partners, and civil society organisations) to rally behind the country's climate ambitions; (iii) identifying and articulating roles and responsibilities for each actor; and (iv) establishing monitoring and evaluation (M&E) frameworks for increased accountability and transparent reporting of progress towards future goals.

Already significant work is being done to articulate national objectives on climate change mitigation and adaptation. To respond to climate change impacts, the Government of Uganda has successfully leveraged international support to better understand its risks and vulnerabilities to projected climate change impacts.[53] While more attention has been given to adaptation efforts, work is also being done to limit increases in greenhouse gas (GHG) emissions as the country prioritises economic development strategies. This is reflected in the country's NDC commitment to reduce emissions by 22% (including land use, land use change and forestry (LULUCF)) by 2030, and potentially by 30% with assistance from the international community.

In addition to policy frameworks, strategic plans and budgeting processes focused on priority sectors, there are other longer-term ideas being explored for future implementation. Over time, Uganda is pursuing several ambitious projects for climate action implementation. It is very close to finalising both a Green Growth Development Strategy (GGDS) and a Climate Change Bill (still in draft form). Beyond these items, there are other aims being considered and analysed to consider feasibility, general structure, delegates and partnerships to champion these items. Another initiative currently under consideration is a national budget tagging and tracking system that will allow national budget planners to identify and track expenditure on climate-related projects and

53 These policies include the National Environmental Management Policy, the National Policy for the Conservation and Management of Wetland Resources, the National Water Policy, the National Forest Policy, the National Agricultural Policy, the Energy Policy for Uganda, the Renewable Energy Policy, the Oil and Gas Policy and Transport Policy, and the Disaster Preparedness and Management Policy, among others.

identify gaps in funding. Through coordinated efforts with development partners and international communities, the country will be better able to fill funding gaps quickly with a better understanding of project needs and potential sources.

At the local government level, the district natural resources officer (the district focal point on climate change) supports the integration of climate change policies into District Development Plans and budgets. These officers sit on the district technical planning committee, as well as on the district risk reduction and management committees and the environment committees. These committees are critical for planning local government participation in NDC implementation.

Uganda has gained experience with benefit-sharing mechanisms in the environment sector,[54] and in joint forest management, and the country has forest legislation that provides for community forestry. Despite the apparent rationale for benefit sharing, there is still very little clarity on what benefit sharing means in the context of REDD+.

3.1 The international regulatory framework for REDD+ and benefit sharing

At the international level, Uganda ratified the United Nations Framework Convention on Climate Change (UNFCCC) on 8 September 1993 and the Convention on Biological Diversity (CBD), the Kyoto Protocol, Nagoya Protocol on Access and Benefit Sharing,[55] and the Paris Agreement of the COP21 in which Article 5 legitimises REDD+. The UNFCCC obliges all parties explicitly to cooperate in preparing for adaptation to the impacts of climate change and to develop an elaborate, appropriate and integrated plan for water resources and agriculture.[56] The UNFCCC also obliges all parties to take climate change considerations into account in their relevant social, economic and environmental policies and actions.

The Paris Agreement allows parties to make unconditional and conditional pledges to reduce emissions. Clarity will be needed regarding whether REDD+ actions included in an NDC are considered conditional emissions reductions.

Uganda is effectively engaged with the international community to carry forward NDC implementation and climate change work collaboratively. Uganda joined the NDC Partnership during the United Nations Climate Change Conference in 2016 (COP22). Since then, the country has actively engaged with the NDC Partnership to identify areas of intervention, such as challenges and opportunities, available for NDC implementation. In June 2017, the NDC Partnership and implementing partners facilitated the Strategic Dialogue on Achieving Uganda's Climate Goals, to identify ways forward for NDC implementation and corresponding Sector Strategic Investment

54 IUCN (2015).
55 Party since 12 October, 2014.
56 Article 2 of the UNFCCC.

Plans that connect financing with action plans to get projects off the ground. In August 2017, a follow-up mission was organised to build on previous conversations and prioritise initial support activities from the NDC Partnership to Uganda on NDC implementation.

Some work between development partners is already organised by sector. The World Resources Institute (WRI) has done extensive research to uncover linkages between sustainable development goals (SDGs) and NDCs. As members of the NDC Partnership, they have the opportunity to provide assistance in ensuring that these international sustainable development and climate targets are reflected in national and sub-national performance indicators.

Other members within the NDC Partnership also have a strong local presence in Uganda on climate planning activities. Since the Climate Change Department (CCD) was established, the United Nations Development Programme (UNDP), through the Low Emissions Capacity Building (LECB) Project, has built institutional and technical capacity in key sectors; supported the development of the GHG inventory unit and the national GHG inventory system; supported the development of the GGDS; and designed several Nationally Appropriate Mitigation Actions (NAMAs) through highly consultative stakeholder engagement processes. Finance has been accessed to implement two NAMAs, namely a project on wastewater treatment with funding from the Global Environment Facility (GEF) and a project to support greening public schools with funding from the NAMA Facility.

In its planned support to Uganda on NDC-related activity, UNDP will focus on implementing mitigation actions, strengthening the national GHG inventory system and creating systems for gender-responsive NDC implementation.

Finally, to build information systems on climate change impacts and monitoring systems, Uganda secured USD4 million from the Least Developed Country Fund, with support from UNDP, to implement the Strengthen Climate Information and Early Warning Systems in Uganda to Support Climate Resilient Development Project. Aligned with Uganda's National Adaptation Programme of Action (NAPA), this project will allow Uganda to monitor long-range climate impacts, detect extreme events, and more quickly deliver response mechanisms that protect local people and economies.[57]

Building on the momentum of these existing efforts, there are several ambitious climate projects that the Government of Uganda is seeking to move forward now, including:[58] the passage of a climate change bill; the establishment of a climate levy with revenues to be earmarked for financing climate action or the creation of an

57 See <http://www.greenclimate.fund/-/building-resilient-communities-wetlands-ecosystems-and-associated-catchments-in-uganda> (accessed 1-8-2018).

58 See <http://adaptation-undp.org/projects/ldcf-ews-uganda NOVEMBER 2017> (accessed 1-8-2018).

(autonomous) climate fund, which could receive funds from development partners, the private sector, and the government; the development of robust green sectoral investment plans; and development of an expenditure tracking system to monitor resource allocation and use for climate action and NDC measures.

Some groundwork has already been laid for these projects and some are at an advanced stage (including the Climate Change Bill). Ongoing support, which can be provided through the NDC Partnership, will be needed to ensure that each project is funded, implemented and monitored en route to achieving its intended objective.

At the regional level, Uganda is party to the East African Community (EAC) Treaty,[59] EAC Protocol on Environment and Natural Resources Management and the East African Community Climate Change Policy (EACCCP). EAC Protocol on Environment and Natural Resources Management provides that states shall develop and harmonise their laws, policies and strategies for mitigating the effects of greenhouse gas emissions and the manner and procedures for benefiting from climate change adaptation and mitigation activities and strategy. The EAC Secretariat is currently developing the East African Climate Change Strategy and Master Plan (EACCCMP) which attempts to define the region's priority actions to address climate change.

Uganda is also a party to regional treaties that could add value to the implementation of REDD+, including the New Partnerships for African Development (NEPAD), 2001; Common Market for Eastern and Southern Africa (COMESA) Treaty, 1993; and the Inter-Governmental Authority for Development (IGAD), 1986. Others include the 2001 Constitutive Act of the African Union (AU), Pan African Parliament and Africa Court of Justice, 1981; African Charter on Human and Peoples' Rights, 2003; Maputo Convention-African Convention on conservation of nature and natural resources, and 1991 Bamako Convention on control of transboundary movement and management of hazardous wastes in Africa. Implementation of the REDD+ will benefit from experiences and lessons learned from implementation of these regional treaties.

3.2 The national regulatory framework for REDD+ and benefit sharing in Uganda

The legal framework for the environmental sector is based on the Constitution of the Republic of Uganda (1995).[60] For example, the Constitution obliges the State to protect critical natural resources including land, water, wetlands, minerals, oil, fauna and flora on behalf of the people of Uganda. The government of Uganda has a constitutional duty to protect forests in their natural sites from destruction by all, including private investors. The Constitution mandates Parliament to enact legislation: to preserve and

59 Articles 111, 112, and 114 of the EAC Treaty provide for the cooperation in environment and natural resources.

60 Part XIII of the Constitution of Uganda of 1995.

protect the environment from abuse, pollution and degradation; to manage the environment for sustainable development; and to promote environmental awareness.[61]

Uganda's parliament has enacted several laws to further these constitutional objectives. They include the National Environment Act, Cap 153 (1995),[62] National Forestry Policy (2002), and National Forestry and Tree Planting Act (2003). The law classifies forests into central, local, community and private forest reserves.[63] Central and local forest reserves are held in trust by the national and local governments respectively. The governments are legally mandated to protect the forests for ecological, forestry and tourism purposes, for the benefit of the people of Uganda.[64] However, collaborative forest management arrangements can be entered into between a respective government and a local community for the management of central and local forests.

Though community forests are designated as such by the Minister in consultation with a District land board and a local community,[65] the law still gives immense powers to the Minister. The powers include: to appoint a responsible body to manage a community forest and to consent to the use of community forests for any purpose other than forest conservation. It is through such provisions that those local communities lack tenure to the forests in their territories.

The Uganda Forest Policy (UFP), the National Forestry and Tree Planting Act (NFTPA) and the 2016 regulations made thereunder, provide an enabling legal framework for a variety of community groups to participate in forestry and forestry management, including community forests and ownership of trees on private land. The Policy provides for improved management of forestry on land outside state control through raising awareness on land and tree ownership. The NFTPA and regulations provide for the declaration, management and use of community forests (CFs) and private forests (PFs). The forestry regulations do promote collaborative arrangements with private sector and communities including carbon sequestration credits.

Other policies include the National Adaptation Plan (NAP), National Adaptation Programme of Action for Climate Change (NAPA), Second National Development Plan (NDPII) and National Climate Change Policy (NCCP) (2015).

The Uganda Wildlife Act provides for the promotion of community conservation of wildlife resources which are essential for the management of wildlife in CFs.

The Land Act (1998) provides a framework for recognition of community land rights as it recognises customary land tenure[66] applicable to a specific area of land and

61 Article 245 of the Constitution of Uganda of 1995.
62 Section 18(1) of the National Environment Act, Cap 153 of 1995.
63 Section 1 of the National Forestry and Tree Planting Act of 2003.
64 Section 5(1) of the National Forestry and Tree Planting Act of 2003.
65 Section 17(1) of the National Forestry and Tree Planting Act of 2003.
66 Section 2 of the Land Act of 1998.

particular description or class of persons.[67] Under the Act, the customary land is managed according to conventional regulations.

The Land Act and its regulations regulate the establishment of Communal Land Associations (CLAs) and communal ownership and management of land-based resources therein by the other laws. The National Environment Act (NEA) provides for the protection of traditional uses of forests which are indispensable to the local communities.[68] However, to make these effective, there are still several provisions for the government to operationalise.

Other environmental related laws include: the Local Governments Act (1997); the Uganda Wildlife Act Cap 200 (of 1996);[69] the Agricultural Seeds and Plant Act (1994); and the Regulations on Access to Genetic Resources and Benefit Sharing 2005. The policies include: the National Energy Policy (2002); the National Environment Policy (1995); the National Wetlands Policy (1994); the Climate Change Policy (2012); the Renewable Energy Policy for Uganda (2007); and the Uganda Wildlife Policy (2003). The policy and law are reflected in the National Forest Plan (2011).[70]

Also, Uganda's National Development Plan (2010/11-2014/15) categorises forestry as a primary growth sector with prospects for investment both from the national budget and the private sector. The National Development Plan emphasises "sustainable development through preservation of natural resources such as forests".[71] The National Development Plan (NDP) also aims to increase forest cover from 3,604,176 ha to 4,933,746 ha by 2015 and has committed itself to enhance capacity for: (i) enforcing forestry law; (ii) private tree planting; and (iii) farm forestry.[72] Likewise, the objectives of Uganda's Second National Development Plan (2015/16-2019/20)[73] include to increase afforestation and reforestation for sustainable forestry.

Uganda's Vision 2040 is explicit on carbon trading as a means of conserving forests for climate change mitigation. It provides that Uganda will promote carbon trade that will increase forest cover, as well as incomes of the rural communities. It further provides for the promotion of conservation programmes that will not only restore but also sustain an optimum level of forest cover in the country.[74]

67 Section 3(1) of the Land Act of 1998.

68 Section 17(4) of the National Environment Act, Cap 153 of 1995.

69 Provides for revenue sharing where 20% of the park entry fees collected from a Protected Area (PA) is given to the local government(s) of the areas surrounding such Protected Areas.

70 See <https://www.forestcarbonpartnership.org/sites/fcp/files/2017/Sep/Uganda% 20FCPF%2> (accessed 30-3-2018).

71 GoU (2010: 41).

72 Ibid: 95.

73 GoU (2015: 170).

74 GoU (2013: 99).

3.3 Institutional arrangements for REDD+ benefit-sharing governance in Uganda

Governance can be described as being about the use of power to make and enforce decisions. Decisions regarding how forests are managed and used involve a wide range of stakeholders. In Uganda, the government is responsible for management of forests in protected areas and therefore it is a government which decides on how the forests are managed and how the local communities are engaged in the decision-making process. Nevertheless, the communities use the forests for their livelihoods, and thus there are often running conflicts on access. In areas where Collaborative Forest Management (CFM) or Collaborative Resource Management (CRM) is being practised, both sides have moved closer in reconciling their perceptions on resource use.

The critical forestry sector institutions include the Community Forest Management Unit under the National Forestry Authority (NFA) which is in charge of managing the 506 CFRs and providing specific technical services; the Community Conservation Division under Uganda Wildlife Authority (UWA) which manages the forests in the National Parks and Wildlife Reserves; the Climate Change Unit and the Forest Sector Support Department under the Ministry of Water and Environment which is in charge of policy, sector coordination and support to districts; and the District Forest Services which provide decentralised forestry services in all districts and manage local forest reserves.

Other key actors in forest management include the National Environment Management Authority which coordinates and supervises all environmental issues in the country. The Ministry of Finance, Planning and Economic Development is responsible for directing national development and allocating the necessary financial resources.

Donors, NGOs and the private sector (landowners and forest owners) contribute actively to forest management especially by implementing those activities constrained by funding or whose management is not suitable for government service institutions. One of the challenges is the short-term cycle of their projects and duplication of activities due to poor coordination. Also, there is tenure insecurity among land and forest owners that can provide a disincentive to forestry investment.

3.4 Case examples of benefit sharing mechanisms in Uganda

The Uganda Wildlife Authority (UWA) is obliged to share 20% of its park entry fees with the local governments adjacent to the forest reserves. This obligation is based on the acknowledgement that communities on the frontline of protected areas endure a disproportionate burden of the costs associated with the conservation of protected areas.[75] The Uganda Wildlife Act is operationalised by the Uganda Wildlife Authority

75 Katoomba Group (2009); REDD-net (2010).

Revenue Sharing Guidelines (2012). These guidelines identify the tripartite aims of benefit sharing as:

- providing an enabling environment for establishing good relations between the protected areas and their neighbouring local communities;
- demonstrating the economic value of protected areas and conservation in general to communities neighbouring protected areas; and
- strengthening the support and acceptance for protected areas (PAs) and conservation activities from communities living adjacent to these areas.

The guidelines also provide the criteria for the selection of community projects to fund, using the money received. The requirements comprise two parts: i) contribution to the reduction of human–wildlife conflict; and ii) contribution to the improvement of livelihoods of households in frontline local council.

The Mount Elgon Regional Conservation Programme (MERECP) uses the concept of community revolving funds (CRFs) to distribute benefits to communities based on performance, measured by their contribution towards the enhancement of planted forests. CRFs are extended to community groups, non-government organisations (NGOs) and community-based organisations.[76]

CSOs like the Environmental Conservation Trust of Uganda (ECOTRUST) are implementing payments for ecosystem service (PES) schemes that have benefit-sharing arrangements that could provide lessons for future REDD+ community projects.

4 Key issues arising

Poor law enforcement – despite the existence of sound policies, laws and regulations – has resulted in an illegal cross-border timber trade in contravention of Uganda's international commitments on trade in wild fauna and flora, in deforestation for charcoal and firewood and in unsustainable harvesting of timber.

Poor standards of governance in Uganda's public administration are recognised as a significant concern by the Government of Uganda across all sectors, including forestry.[77] Poor governance lowers compliance with environmental and other regulations and is compounded by the lack of coordination between key actors in related sectors like forestry, agriculture and wetlands, trade and investment. Conflicting decisions are often made, for example with those seeking development investments nearby or within forest and wetlands areas which are incompatible with conservation objectives.

Gaps remain in Uganda's policy and legal frameworks about REDD+. For example, inadequate licensing of the carbon trade and definitions of carbon rights could potentially affect implementation of the REDD+ strategy. Unclear laws may allow

76 Mwayafu & Kimbowa (2011).
77 GoU (2010).

landowners to make land use choices (for instance a return to commercial agriculture) based on market opportunities rather than on REDD+ contractual obligations that may emphasise forest conservation.

There is no standard benefit-sharing mechanism in Uganda. Some benefit-sharing mechanisms are currently being used in natural resource management (NRM), but until the benefit-sharing mechanism is harmonised at the national level, implementation of REDD+ projects and programmes will remain problematic owing to lack of guiding principles to address sociocultural, economic and ecological concerns, high coordination costs owing to a lack of established mechanisms for government institutions to collaborate, the existence of bureaucratic red-tape, differing approaches and conception of issues due to different professions and conflicting roles. This results in separate ministries with well-protected territories buttressed and prioritised by development partners.

There is concern that many of the proposals to tackle the drivers of deforestation and forest degradation do not take into account or seek to address the economic aspects of the trade in illegal charcoal, firewood and timber; including the provision of economic alternatives for those engaged in these activities. These proposals could be more useful if they incorporate more technology transfer options (like improved charcoal kilns and selection of suitable tree species) and skills and entrepreneurship development for nature-based activities that are compatible with forest conservation.

There is little understanding among citizens of what implications REDD+ might have at the national and local levels. While the process of developing the R-PP involved stakeholder consultations, many people remain unaware of the REDD+ mechanism. For example, the R-PP consultations turned out to be mostly REDD+ awareness sessions. Therefore, there is a need to ensure that the next steps – like the development of the REDD+ strategy – build in robust awareness creation alongside the consultation processes to secure meaningful participation and the views of forest stakeholders.

There are several challenges cited in the implementation of the CFM arrangements, which should serve as learning points for REDD+ architecture. The most significant challenge is that the law does not provide for benefit-sharing mechanisms for the communities participating in CFM arrangements. That is, for the higher-ranked resources like poles and timber, without apparent benefit guidelines, NFA cannot provide proportionate returns to the communities from the different concessions. Till the present, NFA has used an unstructured case-by-case method to offer returns to participating communities. As a result, some of the communities reported some levels of dissatisfaction with the way NFA has implemented the signed agreements. It may serve as a disincentive for the currently enrolled Community Best Organisations (CBOs) to meet their obligations, but also a deterrent for any new CBOs to engage in CFM arrangements. NFA, on the other hand, reported that CFM arrangements carry high transaction costs for negotiating and enforcement.

Further, the CBOs reported that the groups had not been supported to start up alternative livelihood activities and this makes them still dependent on forest resources. Also, they stated that the CFM/NFA agreements had never been reviewed (since 2002) and yet some essential elements were missed out in the first document. But also several socioeconomic changes warrant revisions of some sections in the documents.

Although CFM and CRM as known under the Uganda Wildlife Act for central management of forests and wildlife protected areas (national parks and reserves) in Uganda are well-embedded in policy and practice, CFM has no adequate provision for benefit sharing. Also, there is no role of local governments in the management of Central Forest Reserves (CFRs). The Forestry Act recognises community forests (CFs), but there has not been an active registration of CFs. There are guidelines for registration, declaration and management of community forests which regulate access to the CFs through setting up community institutions for equitable governance, registration and planning for sustainable management of the CFs. The guidelines provide that CFs should develop a management plan that reflects the needs of all stakeholders in the CFs, including non-members.

There are also guidelines for registration and management of private natural forests which help private forest owners (PFOs) to bring their natural forests under responsible forest management. The instructions enable PFOs to advocate for incentives for improved management of natural forests and the accompanying flow of benefits to the stakeholders. However, the procedure and requirement for developing Forest Management Plans (FMPs) are deemed complicated and too technical for community or private forest owners. The Forest Management Plans are linear on paper but cyclical in practice, hence the need to better translate and explain how regulations work in practice.

The NFTPA allows domestic use of forest produce by local communities but still does not define tenure rights. The rights and benefits are left to be established in individual CFM agreements merely as interests to recognise in the FMP. The NFA developed guidelines for CFM that provide for public participation in forest management. However, these policy frameworks do not provide guidance on the publicity of information on access to land for forest plantation establishment. The Uganda Wildlife Act provides clear terms for historical rights of individuals in Wildlife Conservation Areas (WCAs), but there are no guidelines for recognition and formalisation of these rights.

The Forestry law provides for a national tree fund meant to provide a financing mechanism to promote tree planting and growing efforts of a non-commercial nature, among others; however, the fund is yet to be established.

While the procedures for responsible forest management, including partnerships with the local communities, are provided for in the policies and laws of Uganda, the practice on the ground often falls short of these policy ideas. In a study titled "The Effectiveness of Collaborative Forest Management as a Means of Engaging Local Communities in Forest Conservation", 30% of the respondents expressed little or no satisfaction with the CFM arrangements.[78] At the top of the list is corruption, which is intimately connected with the appropriation of benefits intended for the local communities by the wealthy. For example, in Budongo Central Forest Reserve (CFR), CFM communities had been promised that they would be allowed to convert into charcoal the branch wood left by timber harvesters. However, the top leadership of the National Forestry Authority (NFA) did an about-turn and sold the branch wood to the same timber cutters without the knowledge of the local community partners. In another incident in Bugoma CFR, CFM groups reported a local wealthy timber businessman who had been licensed to grow trees in the grassland within the CFM area. The CFM agreement had provided that land for tree growing in the CFR would be one of the benefits accruing to the local community partners, but the NFA went against this provision in the agreement.[79]

Therefore governance in the forestry sector is an essential consideration for the design of REDD+ benefit-sharing mechanisms. This is especially important regarding benefits intended for local people, because they may not be able to marshal sufficient power to fight for their contractual rights unless their capacity to this effect is built.

5 Conclusions and recommendations

5.1 Conclusions

Although there are some provisions on benefit sharing in the different instruments, specifically in Uganda's forest legal and policy frameworks, they are weak in respect of benefit-sharing issues. The institutional gaps and implementation challenges make this situation worse. The major policy, legislative and institutional gaps and implementation challenges include: a lack of a comprehensive policy on costs and benefit sharing with clear mechanisms and approaches for benefit sharing; a lack of benefit-sharing guidelines to guide the effective implementation of existing legal and policy provisions; a lack of full information on the benefits available for sharing; weak community institutions that cannot negotiate for adequate benefits and enforce rights; weak linkages of government institutional frameworks with other stakeholders; limited participation of communities in benefit-sharing decision-making processes; and unwillingness by the forest authorities to give real power or authority for forest management to the local communities. Furthermore, in the context of collaborative forest management arrangements, governments transfer their role and responsibilities to communities adjacent to forests without enough support and corresponding benefits.

78 Nsita (2012).
79 IUCN (2012).

The benefit sharing that takes place in Uganda has not had any significant impact on either the livelihoods of people or the forests. The arrangements and processes in their current form are ineffective in ensuring sustainable forest management and improved community livelihoods. There is a need for serious adjustment. Although the communities living adjacent to forests receive some benefits, they do not feel they are adequate. The poor people, who constitute the majority of those who live near the forests, are getting mainly firewood, herbal medicines, crafts materials, etc. for domestic consumption as benefits. These do not provide sufficient incentive to communities to focus on conservation. The communities know that valuable forest products like timber and land for tree planting are often enjoyed by those who are relatively better off, usually well connected politically and socially, and often staying far away from the forest and thus removed from the threats to livelihoods that originate from the forest, such as crop raiding, human injury and insecurity. The impact of benefit sharing on livelihoods is perceived as insufficient, because the anticipated increased incomes are unrealised and do not reflect any investment in changing lifestyles, e.g. investments in economic activities, such as local transport and small to medium enterprises. Only a few local forest people feel the impacts tied to food security and change in nutrition habits, which help to maintain healthy households.

Regarding institutions, the Government of Uganda has made efforts to escalate climate change as one of its priority areas on the development agenda.[80] This is demonstrated by its commitment to creating an institutional-enabling set up to manage and monitor climate change issues – which, in turn, serves as an excellent opportunity for implementation of the REDD+ projects. For example, in 2008, the Government of Uganda with financial support from the Royal Danish Embassy created the Climate Change Unit (CCU) in the Ministry of Water and Environment, to coordinate all issues concerned with climate change in Uganda. However, the CCU is understaffed, and this presents a challenge at grassroots level. The staffing gap is expected to be filled by employing other teams in the local governments, and by integrating climate change adaptation and mitigation in their sector plans. There is a willingness to incorporate a climate change unit within government structures. It is necessary that the local government and central government teams have their capacities developed to handle deforestation and forest degradation issues.

Where broad jurisdiction mechanisms are involved, distribution of REDD+ benefits through regular government (central and local) budget processes could be used, because the policies and procedures are well established. However, reflection on challenges that affected the implementation of the policies and procedures makes this a problem. Widespread corruption, lack of transparency, misappropriation of public funds, inherent bureaucracies and inflexible systems of procurement and financial management – which are characteristic of otherwise well-intentioned programmes –

80 GoU (2016).

will impact negatively on REDD+ benefit sharing. It will be quite a task to design REDD+ benefit-sharing arrangements that will be free from these vices if the methods are based on standard budgeting processes.

5.2 Recommendations

There is a need to set up a statutory national REDD+ institution. It should either be constituted as a separate law, or the institution could be placed, distinctly, within the Tree Fund which is already provided for in the NFTP Act and the accompanying Forestry Regulations. A semi-autonomous institution could be designed to overcome most of the drawbacks that characterise implementation of the normal government budgets.

The development of an enabling environment for forestry management could include: community forest management groups, forest law enforcement and governance, and strengthening forest institutions responsible for forest management and development.

Experiences of the current benefit-sharing initiatives in the forestry sector make it clear that REDD+ payments alone will not be enough to give sufficient motivation to all parties involved in working efficiently towards responsible forest management (RFM). Unless a clear rationale for distributing the benefits is developed, conflicts among eligible beneficiaries will arise around how benefits and interest are distributed.

To ensure equitable sharing of benefits and participation through mechanisms designed for payments to be made in such a way that the best performers get more, and the nation-performers get nothing, the REDD+ implementation programmes should be designed to build the capacity of the local people, so that all eligible stakeholders can play their roles efficiently, and thus equitably share the benefits that accrue. This will minimise the frustration among the poor people who may have capacity inadequacies and thus be unable to attain what REDD+ considers best performers compared to the benefit-sharing arrangements prescribed by law. CFM and CRM are legally recognised but not overly prescriptive about what to do or not to do. This provides a flexible mechanism in which to deal with matters of equity.

There should be sharing arrangements specifying in broad terms as to the benefit-sharing principles and a framework within which benefit-sharing agreements can be negotiated. To the extent that the policies and agreement framework should be included in the Forestry Regulations, the passing of the Climate Change Bill into law is long overdue.

The decision-making bodies should be intimately involved in the channelling of REDD+ cash payments to eligible beneficiaries. Also, the capacities of the communities involved should be built to enable them to spearhead community-based advocacy when their rights are threatened. Frameworks that provide space for communities' voices and participation in the process need to be made very clear and enhanced.

Land/forest tenure lies at the heart of legitimate and equitable benefit-sharing arrangements. Tenure systems are recognised legally or by custom in Uganda, but the holders of the ownership/use rights are not as vigilant as it seems at first sight because they are multi-layered. This will therefore affect how REDD+ programmes are implemented, and thus how the benefits are shared. The land and forestry policies and laws provide general guidance on ownership and user rights/privileges. The forestry rules and statutory guidelines should specify what accrues to whom, especially in tenure types where ownership/use is multilayered. The poor people and local communities should be assisted with forming legal entities with titled/registered owner of land and forest holdings. However, it should be kept in mind that the carbon benefits may trigger a scramble for land grabbing by those who can secretly process land titles. Sufficient safeguards should be included in the registration process to ensure transparency.

The deliberate and demonstrable commitment of politicians at local and national levels should be generated before REDD+ programmes can be rationally effective. This also calls for an early start on concretising the conflict and grievous mechanism included in the REDD+ National Strategy.

What is required is an analysis of the NDC to establish baselines and cost implementation strategies (mirroring the NCCP Cost Implementation Strategy), the establishment of an improved data collection system linked with the National Statistics Office and the establishment of a robust MRV system that can be equally applied to goals and targets within the SDGs, NAP, NDCs, GGDS, NCCP and NDP II, as well as across sub-levels of government.

There is also a need to ensure that the various policies are aligned with each other so that efforts to implement any one of them are not redundant. This is especially true of the SDGs, NAP, NDCs and GGDS where effects are economy-wide and have large implications across sectors and ministries. As this work gets underway, the NDC Partnership members are already planning and implementing several projects that are working towards the country's NDC goals.

References

Agrawal, A & A Angelsen (2009) *Using community forest management to achieve REDD+ goals.*

Bond, I, M Grieg-Gran, S Wertz-Kanounnikoff, P Hazlewood, S Wunder & A Angelsen (2009) *Incentives to sustain forest ecosystem services* International Institute for Environment and Development Natural Resource Issues No. 16.

Brown, J (2008) *Reducing emissions from deforestation and degradation: understanding social implications of projects vs. national approaches* MSc Thesis Development.

Brown, K & E Corbera (2003) "Exploring equity and sustainable development in the new carbon economy" 3(1) *Climate Policy* S41-S46.

Cleaver, F (1999) "Paradoxes of participation: questioning participatory approaches to development" 11 *Journal of International Development* 597-612.

Corbera, E & H Schroeder (2011) *Governing and implementing REDD+.*

Corbera, E, K Brown & WN Adger (2007) "The equity and legitimacy of markets for ecosystem services" 28(4) *Development and Change* 517-613.

Costenbader, J (2011) *REDD+ Benefit sharing: a comparative assessment of three national policy approaches.*

Diamond, N (2002) *Participatory conservation for protected areas, an annotated bibliography of selected sources (1996-2001).*

Dobson, A (1998) *Justice and the environment: conceptions of environmental sustainability and theories of distributive justice.*

Fraser, N (1997) *Justice interruptus: critical reflections on the 'postsocialist' condition.*

Gebara, MF (2013) "Importance of local participation in achieving equity in benefit-sharing mechanisms for REDD+: a case study from the Juma Sustainable Development Reserve" 7(2) *International Journal of the Commons* 473-497.

Gibson, CC, JT Williams & E Ostrom (2005) "Local enforcement and better forests" 33 *World Development* 273-284.

GoU / Government of Uganda (2010) *National development plan 2010/11-2014/15*, at <http://npa.ug/wp-content/themes/npatheme/documents/NDP2.pdf> (accessed 1-8-2018).

GoU / Government of Uganda (2013) *Uganda's Vision 2040*, at <http://npa.ug/wp-content/themes/npatheme/documents/vision2040.pdf> (accessed 1-8-2018).

GoU / Government of Uganda (2015) *Second national development plan 2014/15-2019/20*, at <http://npa.ug/wp-content/uploads/NDPII-Final.pdf> (accessed 1-8-2018).

GoU / Government of Uganda (2016) *REDD+ annual report to FCPF.*

GoU / Government of Uganda (2017) *Proposed forest reference level for Uganda* Preliminary Document, at <https://redd.unfccc.int/files/uganda_frel_final_version_16.01.pdf> (accessed 1-8-2018).

Grieg-Gran, M (2008) *Equity considerations and potential impacts on indigenous or poor forest-dependent communities* International Institute for Environment and Development Draft Background Paper No. 9.

Griffiths, T (2008) *Seeing 'REDD' forests, climate change mitigation and the rights of indigenous peoples and local communities.*

Hajek, F, J Scriven, A Castro & MJ Ventresca (2011) "Regime building for REDD+: evidence on anatomy and proximate outcomes from a cluster of local initiatives in south-eastern Peru" 14 *Environmental Science and Policy* 201-215.

IUCN / International Union for Conservation of Nature (2012) *Benefit sharing in Uganda's forestry sector; issues and options for REDD implementation in Uganda*, at <https://cmsdata.iucn.org/downloads/redd__benefit_sharing_in_uganda___full_study.pdf> (accessed 1-8-2018).

IUCN / International Union for Conservation of Nature (2015) *Can REDD+ social safeguards reach the 'right' people? Lessons from Madagascar.*

Johns, T & B Schlamadinger (2009) "International policy and institutional barriers to reducing emissions from deforestation and degradation in developing countries" in C Palmer & S Engel (eds) *Avoided deforestation: prospects for mitigating climate change* 71-89.

Katoomba Group (2009) *REDD+ Opportunities Scoping Exercise (ROSE): a tool for prioritizing subnational REDD opportunities and constraints experiences in Ghana, Tanzania and Uganda*, at <http://www.katoombagroup.org/events/ROSE.pdf> (accessed 2-8-2018).

Lind, E & T Taylor (1988) *The social psychology of procedural justice.*

Luttrell, C, K Schreckenberg & L Peskett (2007) *The implications of carbon financing for pro-poor community forestry* Overseas Development Institute Forestry Briefing No. 14.

Luttrell, C, L Loft, MF Gebara, D Kweka, M Brockhaus, A Angelsen & WD Sunderlin (2013) "Who should benefit from REDD+? Rationales and realities" 18(4) *Ecology and Society* 52.

McDermott, M, S Mahanty & K Schreckenberg (2012) "Examining equity: a multidimensional framework for assessing equity in payments for ecosystem services" 33 *Environmental Science and Policy* 416-427.

Muller, B (2001) "Varieties of distributive justice in climate change: an editorial comment" 48 *Climatic Change* 273-288.

Mwayafu, D & R Kimbowa (2011) *Issues and options for benefit sharing in REDD+ in East Africa: a case study of Mount Elgon Regional Conservation Programme*, at <https://theredddesk.org/sites/default/files/mount_elgon_redd_project_1.pdf> (accessed 1-8-2018).

Nepstad, D, B Soares-Filho, F Merry, P Moutinho, H Rodrigues, M Bowman & S Schwartzman (2007) *The costs and benefits of reducing emissions from deforestation and degradation in the Brazilian Amazon.*

Nsita, SA (2012) *Sustainable management of mineral resources project: report on the survey of the beneficiaries of the small grants program* unpublished report submitted to the World Bank.

Pagiola, S & G Platais (2007) *Payments for environmental services: from theory to practice.*

Pascual, U, R Muradian, LC Rodriguez & A Duraiappah (2010) "Exploring the links between equity and efficiency in payments for environmental services: a conceptual approach" 69 *Ecological Economics* 1237-1244.

Peskett, L, D Huberman, E Bowen-Jones, G Edwards & J Brown (2008) *Making REDD Work for the Poor.*

Pimbert, MP & JN Pretty (1995) *Parks, people and professionals: putting "participation" into protected area management* Discussion Paper United Nations Research Institute for Social Development.

Raffles, H (1999) "Local theory: nature and the making of an Amazonian place" 14 *Cultural Anthropology* 323-360.

Rawls, J (1971) *A theory of justice.*

REDD-net (2010) *REDD+ and adaptation: will REDD+ contribute to adaptive capacity at the local level?*

Sachs, W & T Santarius (2007) *Fair future: resource conflicts, security, and global justice.*

Santilli, M, P Moutinho, S Schwartzman, D Nepstad, L Curran & C Mwayafu (2011) *Water resources management and REDD+ in East Africa.*

Schroeder, D (2007) "Benefit-sharing: it's time for a definition" 33 *Journal for Medical Ethics* 205-209.

UNEP / United Nations Environment Programme (2015) *REDD+ Implementation: a manual for national legal practitioners*, at <https://wedocs.unep.org/bitstream/handle/20.500.11822/9529/-REDD+_Implementation_A_Manual_for_National_Legal_Practitioners-2015redd-plus-manual.pdf.pdf?sequence=5&isAllowed=y> (accessed 1-8-2018).

Wollenberg, E & O Springate-Baginski (2009) Incentives +: how can REDD improve well-being in forest communities? CIFOR Info brief No. 21.

Chapter 9: Regulatory preparedness for non-motorised transport in Nairobi

Edna Odhiambo

1 Introduction

1.1 Global climate change and transport

There is scientific consensus that human activities are inducing dangerous warming[1] and the consequences will be severe and widespread. Droughts, floods, wildfires, heat waves, ocean acidification, sea level rise, among others, continue to threaten ecosystems and ultimately endanger human livability on earth.[2] Consequently, urgent and concerted climate action is needed to avert a looming catastrophe.

The Paris Agreement is a universal legally binding treaty adopted in 2015 and came into force in November 2016 as the successor to the Kyoto Protocol in an attempt to curb climate change. In stark contrast to Kyoto's top-down model of internationally set binding emission reduction targets, the Paris Agreement has adopted a bottom-up approach to addressing emissions through the Nationally Determined Contributions (NDCs). Each party drafts their own NDCs, which represent the nation's climate action plans taking into account local priorities and unique circumstances.

Transport contributes towards 23% of global greenhouse gas (GHG) emissions and is the second largest source of CO_2 from fossil fuel combustion after the power sector.[3] This figure is set to rise particularly with the growth of emissions from road transport.[4] An analysis of 133 NDCs reveals that 76% of the parties intend to mitigate emissions from the transport sector with a focus on urban transport.[5] Urban transport constitutes 40% of total transport energy consumption[6] and projections indicate that it will double by 2050.[7] This chapter postulates that the NDCs under the Paris Agreement present an opportune moment to advance low-carbon mobility options such as non-motorised transport (NMT) into city transport planning.

---

1 IPCC (2014: 4).
2 Ibid: 2, 5 and 8.
3 Ibid.
4 Partnership on Sustainable Low Carbon Transport (2015).
5 Ibid.
6 Sims et al. (2014).
7 International Energy Agency (2013).

1.2 Benefits of NMT

1.2.1 Emissions abatement

NMT substantially reduces GHGs from the transport sector because it is a viable alternative to motorised options, particularly for short trips and last mile connectivity. According to a study conducted in Mumbai, converting 10% of roads into NMT-friendly infrastructure will result in a reduction of carbon dioxide emissions by 7.63 million tons over the next five years.[8] This is a good indication of NMT's potential to address climate emissions from the transport sector. In many cities, including Nairobi, the lack of sufficient baseline data on NMT is a barrier to calculating the actual emission abatements achieved from NMT options such as walking and cycling. The importance of data will be canvassed below in subsequent parts of this chapter.

1.2.2 Increased economic opportunities

Studies conducted indicate that improved NMT infrastructure can increase economic productivity and development.[9] Such infrastructure increases local retail sales and property values because people walking and cycling are more likely to purchase goods and services as they pass by shops.[10] NMT facilities attract residents and industries that value environmental quality, physical fitness and outdoor recreation.[11] A study that evaluated the effects of walkability on the housing process concluded that walkability had a statistically significant positive impact on housing values.[12] In a typical metropolitan area, each walk score point[13] increase was associated with a $700 to $3,000 increase in home values.[14]

1.2.3 Health

NMT, also known as active transport, can substantially improve the health of citizens. According to the World Health Organization, approximately three million deaths are

---

8 Yelda (2015).
9 Victoria Transport Policy Institute (2004).
10 Local Government Commission (2001).
11 NBPC (1995); NAR & NAHB (2002); According to a survey of 2,000 representative home-buying U.S. households, 27% would like to be able to walk to more places from their home, and the following community amenities rated important or very important: jogging/bike trails (36%), sidewalks (28%), and shops within walking area (19%).
12 Litman (2010: 22).
13 Carr et al. (2010: 460).
14 Litman (2010: 23).

recorded annually as a result of outdoor air pollution.[15] Heavy motorisation is a major cause of air pollution, which can be mitigated by increased investment in NMT, which reduces congestion and in turn promotes better air quality. Additionally, walking and cycling encourage healthy lifestyles because of regular activity. This has a direct impact on reducing risks of lifestyle disease such as diabetes, cardiovascular diseases, high blood pressure and obesity.

1.2.4 Safety

According to the Nairobi NMT Policy, pedestrians constitute the highest number of road fatalities.[16] 47% of the population in Nairobi make their journeys on foot, implying that the majority of the population is most at risk due to inadequate investment in NMT facilities.[17] If NMT infrastructure is prioritised, a safer city for the majority of the citizenry will be achieved.

1.2.5 Accessibility

Non-motorised transport, particularly walking and cycling facilities, can improve the lives of many citizens through better access to economic opportunities, health care services and social engagements. It can also reduce the amount of money spent by families on transport, particularly in the low-income bracket. One study indicates that approximately 8-16% of household income, and in some cases even 25% of it, is spent on transport.[18] With options such as walking and cycling, many can have an option of low-cost transport, and this greatly reduces inequities in cities.

1.3 Kenya's transport sector emissions

Kenya's NDCs seek to reduce emissions by 30% by 2030 relative to the business as usual scenario of 143 $MtCO_2eq$.[19] Low carbon and efficient transport systems have been listed as one of the intended mitigation measures.[20] The transport sector contributed 11% (9.1 $MtCO_2e$) of total emissions in Kenya.[21] This figure is projected to

15 See <http://www.who.int/airpollution/ambient/health-impacts/en/> (accessed 16-2-2018).
16 Nairobi City County Government (2015: 5).
17 Ibid: 3.
18 See <www.fiafoundation.org> (accessed 5-3-2018).
19 Ministry of Environment and Natural Resources (2015: 1).
20 Ibid: 73.
21 Ibid.

increase to 15% (21.0 $MtCO_2e$) by 2030 due to an increase in the number of passenger and freight vehicles.[22]

According to the National Transport and Safety Authority (NTSA), Kenya is projected to have 4,141,189 vehicles in 2020 of which approximately 46% will be privately owned cars. Vehicle increase is set to rise annually at an average rate of 10%.[23] These statistics justify the need to invest in sustainable mobility such as NMT in the country's cities if Kenya is to decrease emissions from the transport sector.

1.4 Status of NMT in Nairobi

NMT caters for an average of 47% percent of daily trips in Nairobi with the rest being provided by public transit and private cars respectively.[24]

Despite this being the most used means of transport, there has been little improvement of NMT infrastructure over the past fifteen years.[25] NMT is marred with poor infrastructure mainly due to the lack of implementation of an integrated transport regulatory framework that supports multi-modal transport. The popularity of NMT is not attributed to choice or convenience, but rather, it is the only alternative for many citizens who are not catered for by an inefficient public transport system and high costs of motorised transport.[26]

Much focus has been placed on road expansion and increased motorisation in a manner that does not cater for multi-modal transport. Secondly, the privatisation of public passenger transport has led to stiff competition and an over-supply of vehicles. This, in turn, is causing congestion in the city, encroachment of the few NMT spaces as well as aggressive and unsafe driving adversely affecting NMT users.[27]

NMT users are most at risk of road fatalities, making it the most unsafe means of transport. According to road accidents data for 2010-2016 illustrated in Figure 1 below, pedestrians account for the highest number of road fatalities, and in 2016, 65% of traffic fatalities were pedestrians.[28]

22 Ibid.
23 National Transport and Safety Authority (2016).
24 Nairobi City County Government (2015: 3).
25 Ministry of Environment and Natural Resources (2015: 75).
26 Ibid: 73.
27 Ibid: 81.
28 Cummings & Obwocha (2018).

Figure 1: Traffic fatalities in Nairobi by road user, 2010-2016[29]

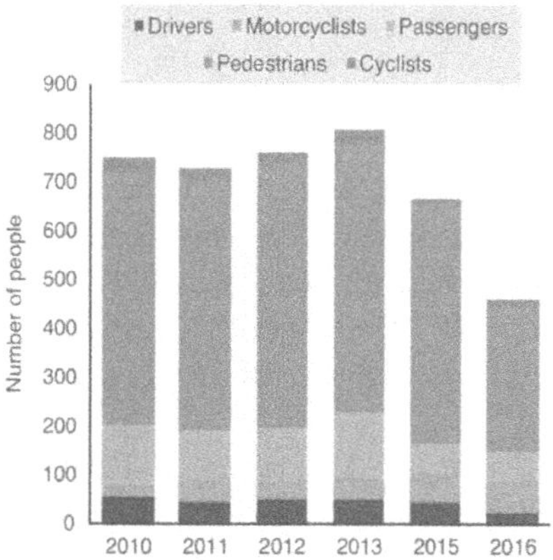

Statistics from NTSA indicate that 1,097 people died in road accidents by 11 May 2017, of which 416 were pedestrians.[30] By September 2017, the figure had risen to 714 pedestrians and 36 cyclists.[31] These figures are set to rise if updated to include fatalities from September to December. On 31 December 2017, 36 people died in a road carnage after a road accident along the Nakuru-Eldoret highway.[32] These figures reiterate the need to share the road and make it more conducive for other users besides vehicles.

2 Legislative framework for NMT in Nairobi

2.1 Constitution of Kenya, 2010

The Bill of Rights provides that all Kenyans have a right to a clean and healthy environment.[33] NMT plays a crucial role in mitigating air pollution from the transport sector and promoting a cleaner and healthier environment. Generally, the transport sector has a role to play in realising other rights such as equality, dignity, security, health, movement and reasonable access.

The Constitution further provides for county government functions regarding transport.[34] These include county roads, street lighting, traffic and parking, and public road transport. Therefore, counties have an essential role in promoting NMT infrastructure and other sustainable modes of transport.

29 Data from NTSA (2017).
30 Anjali (2017).
31 Wanambisi (2017).
32 Openda (2017).
33 The Constitution of Kenya (2010), Article 42.
34 The Constitution of Kenya (2010), Fourth Schedule.

2.2 NMT in transport legislative framework

2.2.1 The Kenya Roads Act, 2007

The Act was enacted to provide for the management and provision of road infrastructure including NMT in all classes of roads. Under part two, Section 3(1), the Act establishes the Kenya National Highways Authority (KeNHA) which is responsible for the management, development, rehabilitation and maintenance of national roads. Similarly, it establishes the Kenya Urban Roads Authority (KURA),[35] which is responsible for the management, development, rehabilitation and maintenance of all public roads in the cities and municipalities.

In this context, KURA has a role to play in addressing NMT challenges in Nairobi county's roads such as encroachment of pedestrian pathways, provision of walking and biking paths on roads, maintenance of NMT infrastructure and securing safety of NMT users.

2.2.2 National Transport and Safety Authority Act (NTSA), 2012

NTSA has the mandate to provide safe, reliable, efficient road transport and to implement policies relating to these issues. NTSA deals with registration, licensing and inspection of motor vehicles, educating the public on road safety, safety audits, compilation of road accident statistics, and overseeing testing and licensing of drivers.[36]

Bearing in mind that pedestrians account for approximately 50-60% of road accident fatalities, these functions of NTSA play a crucial role in ensuring the safety of NMT users. Further, the functions of safety and efficiency have implications for NTSA to ensure that transport policies adequately factor in low carbon mobility options such as NMT.

2.2.3 Traffic Act, 2015

This Act establishes the law relating to traffic on all public roads. Provisions on licencing of vehicles, speed limits, signage, and traffic offences go a long way in safeguarding NMT users and infrastructure. In particular, the Act criminalises offences that have been the leading causes of pedestrian deaths in Nairobi, such as: driving under the

35 The Kenya Road Act, Section 9(1).
36 National Transport and Safety Authority Act (NTSA) (2012), Section 4(2).

influence of drink;[37] driving on pavement;[38] pedestrian walkway, reckless driving and causing death by driving or obstruction;[39] reckless driving;[40] and driving without due care or attention.[41]

Drunken driving is a leading cause of pedestrian deaths. The Traffic (Breathalyser) Rules (2011) operationalise NTSA's mandate to ensure safety on roads by curbing drunk driving, an offence under the Traffic Act. NTSA used breathalysers to arrest and charge drunk drivers. Rule 3 of the Breathalyser Rules states as follows:

> Alcohol prohibition:
>
> (1) No person shall drive, attempt to drive or be in charge of a motor vehicle on a road or other public place if the person has consumed alcohol in such quantity that the blood alcohol concentration in his body is beyond the prescribed limit.
>
> (2) A person who contravenes sub-rule (1) commits an offence under section 44(1) and 45 of the Act.

However, this was challenged in court,[42] and it was held that drunk-driving should be charged under traffic laws, not breathalyser rules. The court noted that the breathalyser rules did not introduce any new offences other than those in the Traffic Act, adding that there is need to amend the Traffic Act to align it with the breathalyser rules.

Subsequently, NTSA stated that it would apply Section 44 (1) of the Traffic Act, which outlaws driving under the influence of alcohol or substances. Whichever section of the law is invoked, it is necessary to ensure that NTSA's mandate to protect road users is facilitated and not derailed by technicalities. Parliament should harmonise the provisions of the law to create an enabling environment for institutions to carry out their responsibilities. Additionally, coordination of the roles of the Kenya Roads Board (KRB), KeNHA, KURA, and NTSA is vital to avoid overlaps and conflicts as well as allow for efficient use of resources.

2.2.4 Kenya Roads Board Act, 1999

KRB is charged with coordination and implementation of all policies relating to the maintenance, rehabilitation and development of the road network with a view to achieving efficiency, cost-effectiveness and safety. Rehabilitation and safety of roads have direct implications for NMT. As part of increasing NMT infrastructure, several roads in Nairobi will have to be rehabilitated to include NMT options.

---

37 Traffic Act (2015), Section 44.

38 Traffic Act (2015), Section 45A.

39 Traffic Act (2015), Section 46.

40 Traffic Act (2015), Section 47.

41 Traffic Act (2015), Section 49.

42 *Reminisce Sports Bar Limited t/a Reminisce Bar & Grill & 3 others v. Cabinet Secretary Ministry of Transport & 7 others* (2017) eKLR.

2.3 NMT in the climate change legislative framework

2.3.1 Kenya Climate Change Act, 2016

The Act states that the National Climate Change Plan shall prescribe measures to enhance energy conservation, efficiency and use of renewable energy in industrial, commercial, transport, domestic and other uses.[43] Unfortunately, the National Climate Change Action Plan (2013-2017) makes no mention of investing in NMT as a climate mitigation strategy. It prioritises development of mass transit options such as bus rapid transit (BRT) and light rail transit (LRT) to the exclusion of NMT.[44] The Plan has not fully embraced the features of multi-modal transport and fails to cater for other forms of low carbon mobility.

According to a 2016 meeting on the Transport Sector NDC Analysis, an NMT study by the University of Cape Town on behalf of United Nations Environment Program is underway to document GHG abatement emissions, and some models for Nairobi may be available.[45] The report notes that:[46]

> The challenge remains in realising significant emission reductions from NMT given that the trend (at least in the short to medium term) is that bulk of commuters who cannot afford to travel by vehicles today will do so when they can and finally shift from using PSVs to purchasing personal cars.

This statement demonstrates why integrating NMT as a preferred mode of travel for short trips and last mile connectivity will have a long-term impact on emission reductions. Additionally, the NDC sector analysis report states that:[47]

> [NMT] is not considered as a priority mitigation option. The justification provided is that NMT emission reductions are not significant on a national scale, and levels of NMT will decrease over the coming decades if the government meets its development targets. Further, there is a significant overlap with the options for mass rapid transit systems. If designed and priced well, the improved access to transport services and reduced transport inefficiencies resulting from improved transit systems will greatly reduce the number of journeys undertaken by foot.

This approach may be problematic in the long term. Firstly, the analysis concludes that NMT's emission reductions are not significant on a national scale. Such assertions are not backed by baseline studies and projections. There is no data from evidence showing the impact of NMT on emission reductions. In fact, as will later be highlighted in this chapter, NMT has been lumped together with intermediate transport in some policies making it impossible to have any disaggregated data and targeted policy interventions on NMT.

---

43 Kenya Climate Change Act (2016), Section 13(3)(j).

44 Ministry of Environment and Mineral Resources (2013).

45 Ministry of Transport, Infrastructure, Housing and Urban Development (2016: 5).

46 Ibid.

47 Ministry of Environment and Natural Resources (2015: 81).

Secondly, the analysis adopts a narrow approach to NMT as it focuses exclusively on walking. While walking is the most popular, other modes of NMT, particularly bicycling, may grow if investment in infrastructure is made and proper integration is done. Adopting a multi-modal approach cannot be overemphasised as citizens need to have a choice as to what is the most appropriate and convenient means of access to goods, services and each other.

Thirdly, inadequate prioritisation and investment in NMT will push more residents to purchase private vehicles once they can afford to do so because public transport cannot be the panacea for all transport challenges. This does not adequately address the emission challenge from the transport sector. The efficiency of public transport is a fallacy if it does not encompass multi-modal forms of mobility. NMT becomes particularly vital since it is the most convenient for short trips and last mile connectivity.

3 Policy framework for NMT in Nairobi

3.1 Nairobi County Government Non-Motorised Transport Policy, 2015

The County Government of Nairobi has adopted an NMT Policy, which aims to make NMT "the mode of choice as a safe and reliable means of transport".[48] It recognises NMT as an effective means of mobility particularly for short trips and for last mile connectivity compared to the proposed mass transportation systems. The County is cognisant of NMT's advantage as a low carbon emitter.

The Policy reiterates the following challenges facing NMT in Nairobi: lack of NMT provision, encroachment of NMT spaces; high accident rates; weak land use development and planning; traffic congestion; radial network system; and inefficient public transport.[49] Its geographical scope is rather limited as it provides an analysis of a survey conducted along two road corridors – Jogoo and Juja.[50]

Commendably, it lays out targeted strategies (represented in Table 2 below)[51], which go a long way in providing targets for monitoring and evaluating progress. Additionally, it pledges at least 20% of the County's transport sector budget for NMT and public transport services and infrastructure.[52]

48 Nairobi City County Government (2015).
49 Nairobi City County Government (2015: 4-5).
50 Ibid: 6-12.
51 Ibid: 20.
52 Ibid: 23.

Table 1: Outputs and outcomes of the policy

Objective	Output	Outcome
1. Increase mobility and accessibility;	Safe and cohesive pedestrian facilities (footpaths, etc) from 500. km to 1,500 km by 2020	Increased modal share of walking from 47. to 50for trips up to 5km by 2025;
	Cohesive cycle network of lanes, tracks and destination facilities from 50km to 1,000km by 2020.	Increased modal share of cyclists from 2% to 10% for trips up to 15km by 2025;
	NMT facilities along and at major PT routes and terminals from 500to 1,500By 2020.	Increased modal share of public transport from 32to 35for all trips by 2025;
	Nairobi Streets and Roads Design Manual (NSRDM) is developed by 2017.	All roads within the County shall fully comply with the specifications of the NSRDM by 2025.
2. Improve transport safety and security;	Safe NMT crossings: Pedestrian signals from 185to 500. Footbridges and underpasses from 27 to 50.	Reduced pedestrian fatalities from 500to 50 or lessby 2025.
	Marked and visible crossings from 150to 500 by 2020;	Reduced cyclist fatalities from 20to5by 2025.
	Working street lights from 30,000to 65,000by 2020.	
3. Improve amenities for NMT;	No of benches, No of repair shops; No of stores; etc	Level of Service[23] (LOS) rating of streets improves from D to Bby 2025.
4. Increase recognition and image of NMT in Nairobi	Percentage of road users considering NMT as a mode for the poor reduces by 40% by 2020.	Diverse income groups using NMT as a mode of choice.

Local NMT planning is a step in the right direction. A report by UNEP reveals a growing trend among African countries to localise the development of NMT policies.[53] Localisation allows for the development of tangible informed targets derived from broader policy statements agreed upon nationally. Secondly, this gives sub-national governments the mandate to allocate budgetary resources for the improvement of NMT and effectively participate in monitoring and evaluation of it. Nevertheless, national NMT policies are equally important in encouraging synergistic efforts between the central and local governments.

The Policy is lacking in adequate baseline data and even admits to presenting outdated information due to a lack of documentation on NMT.[54] However, this challenge is not unique to Nairobi. According to UNEP,[55] lack of available baseline data is a major issue in monitoring and implementing NMT policies. Collecting baseline data on NMT varies from data collection principles used in motorised transport. NMT has

53 UN Environment (2016: 19).
54 Nairobi City County Government (2015: 4).
55 UN Environment (2016: 19).

characteristics such as shorter trips, less confinement to fixed paths hence unpredictable movements, more affected by weather conditions, larger margins of error while counting and less developed technology for data collection.[56]

3.2 Integrated National Transport Policy (INTP), 2009

INTP's mission is to "link transport policy with other sectoral policies, in order to achieve national and international development objectives in a socially, economically and environmentally sustainable manner".[57] It makes provision for NMT and intermediate means of transport (IMT), which include low engine capacity vehicles (motorcycles and motor tricycles and sidecars or trailers attached to these).

It does not distinctively address NMT; rather it combines it with IMT.[58] This grouping has challenges when trying to obtain disaggregated data and make targeted policy interventions on NMT. This data is particularly imperative when one wants to calculate the emission abatement from NMT.

The Policy has several intervention areas including tackling climate change. It mentions various strategies, but none of them mention NMT as a means of tackling atmospheric pollution from the transport sector.[59] This is indicative that NMT is not considered as a key strategy for climate action in the transport sector.

It acknowledges that NMT has lagged behind over the years due to a focus on motorised transport at the expense of NMT infrastructure. According to the Policy, NMT is not fully recognised by law and does not enjoy government's financial and technical support. It is not clear what 'full recognition' entails.

However, one can deduce that the national government has not prioritised NMT as an important mode of transport more so as a climate mitigation strategy in the transport sector. Rather, it views it as a default option for those who cannot afford and access public transport and other forms of motorised transport. This bias at the national level negatively affects the improvement and increased uptake of NMT infrastructure at the county level.

Among the strategies laid out is to "encourage development of NMT as a means of enhancing mobility and accessibility in urban areas".[60] This is important because it elevates NMT to equal status with other motorised modes of transport bringing out the need for equitable financial and technical allocation while integrating multi-modal transport. The Policy aims to increase the socio-economic impact of motorised

56 Minnesota Department of Transportation Bicycle and Pedestrian Data Collection Manual (2015: 33).
57 Ministry of Transport and Infrastructure (2009: 6).
58 Ibid: 45.
59 Ibid: 95-96.
60 Ibid: 46.

transport through NMT. Conspicuously missing is the environmental impacts of motorised transport which should be addressed separately if one is to understand the full benefits of NMT as a sustainable means of transport.

A number of issues facing NMT have been laid out by the Policy including gender bias, infrastructure development and maintenance, regulatory frameworks, safety, incentives for NMT and enforcement. Lack of adequate NMT infrastructure development and maintenance is a key issue, which the policy proposes to address by requiring road agencies to cater for NMT infrastructure in their projects as well as factor in technical and financial support for it.

In the urban areas, it proposes that each local authority or agency provides and maintains adequate sidewalks and pavements for pedestrians, separate lanes, parking bays, bridges, footpaths, and other facilities for NMT and intermediate means of transport (NMIMTs).[61] This provision creates a central role for the county governments, which should take a leading role in the provision and maintenance of adequate NMT infrastructure.

3.3 National Land Use Policy, 2017

Land use and transport planning are intimately intertwined. Various land use factors such as mobility management, density, centeredness and site design have direct implications for the transport sector. The Policy seeks to encourage the efficient, productive and sustainable use of land.[62] It acknowledges that land use in Kenya has been haphazard due to a lack of coordinated legal and policy frameworks.

This is evident particularly in Nairobi and other major cities facing the consequences of poor physical planning such as congestion, urban sprawl, accessibility, air pollution and safety. The same is reiterated in the NMT policy, which asserts that:

> Land use planning and development control is weak and does not encourage compact land use that is supportive to better transport provisions, especially for NMT users. The current land use encourages increasing trip distances making the use of NMT and public transport less attractive.

The Land Use Policy makes a mention of transport and infrastructure stating the need to continuously develop and upgrade transport infrastructure. It does not go into any detail on how this should be done. The mere mention of transport does not solve the myriad of issues faced in the interactions between poor land use and transport infrastructure. Moreover, implementation, monitoring and evaluating progress is illusory in the absence of targeted outputs and outcomes.

The Policy states that a majority of the residents in urban areas are in the low-income bracket. These residents are currently the major users of NMT, and they do not

61 Ibid: 47.

62 Ministry of Lands and Physical Planning (2017: 2).

enjoy choice on mobility. This brings into play a crucial discussion on how unsustainable transport trends of increased private motorisation and road expansion continues to disenfranchise the urban poor.

NMT is a preserve of the low-income earners, and such infrastructure is inadequate and poorly maintained. It is the most unsafe means of transport as users are most at risk of road accident fatalities. Public transport infrastructure is equally inadequate and unaffordable making it out of reach for the urban poor. The current state of affairs suggests that unsustainable transport planning is a key factor in exacerbating the plight of the urban poor's access to basic services. Though this discussion is beyond the ambit of this study, it deserves passing mention.

Lastly, the Policy seeks to address environmental degradation and climate change, which includes air pollution, and NMT plays an important role in securing these goals.[63] Further, it proposes the adoption of compact sustainable urban forms[64], which may be interpreted to include mixed land use, centeredness and connectedness, which in turn make a good case for the increased uptake of NMT.

3.4 Integrated Land Use Guidelines, 2011

The Guidelines,[65] if adopted, have positive implications for NMT as they deal with: i) ensuring the provision of pedestrian paths and bicycle paths in road construction and planning; ii) provision of subways for interurban connections and improved mass transit systems within both the urban areas and connecting urban centres; iii) provide time-frames during which private vehicles are not allowed within the Central Business District (CBD); and iv) provide for the location and enforcement of designated pedestrian drop-off and pick-up points for public transport.[66] These Guidelines should complement the provisions of the NMT policy.

3.5 Draft National Urban Development Policy (NUDP), 2016

The NUDP seeks to create a framework for sustainable urban development. It mentions transport as one of its thematic areas laying emphasis on addressing challenges faced in the urban transport sector. NUDP proposes that all urban areas and cities prepare and implement an appropriate transportation strategy with emphasis on mass transport, pedestrian and cycling modes. The mention of city-led pedestrian and

63 Ibid: 21.
64 Ibid: 47.
65 National Environment Management Authority (2011: 36-37).
66 Ibid: 36-37.

cycling strategies creates an impetus for promoting a localised NMT agenda as a means of achieving sustainable cities [67]

It also seeks to encourage compact land use, which as previously discussed, encourages NMT as a mode of choice. Additionally, it seeks to address climate change and improve the environmental management of urban areas through city-wide environmental planning and management, including adherence to environmental legislation and the mainstreaming of climate change in planning and development processes.[68] This may encourage transport planners to lay emphasis on low carbon mobility modes such as NMT.

3.6 Nairobi Integrated Urban Development Master Plan (NIUPLAN), 2014

The NIUPLAN tackles urban transport. It lists the rapid increase of private vehicles and the lack of efficient public transport systems as some of the key issues that need to be addressed. Though it does not provide detail, it mentions the development of efficient and sustainable transport systems as one of the planning strategies.[69] This strategy must factor in NMT to be considered 'efficient and sustainable' and avoid pitfalls of ignoring NMT or giving it late consideration in the design phase.

3.7 Nairobi County Integrated Development Plan, 2018-2022 (NCIDP)

The Nairobi County is expected to increase NMT facilities to 1,500 km from a current 300 km through the implementation of the NCIDP.[70] The NCIDP seeks to improve the integration between NMT and public transport and proposes the development of an NMT master plan.[71] Some of the key performance indicators include the length and number of NMT infrastructure constructed, level of utilisation of NMT infrastructure,[72] a decrease in the number of private vehicles accessing the CBD, and improved accessibility to CBD by NMT.[73]

As part of the measures to harness impact, there will be strict enforcement to ensure NMT facilities are effectively used and this can address the issue of encroachment of NMT spaces by vendors and public vehicles.[74] Civic education to encourage the public

67 Opiyo & Mitullah (2016).
68 Nabutola (2012).
69 Nairobi Integrated Urban Development Master Plan (2014: 2).
70 Nairobi County (2017: 47).
71 Ibid: 76.
72 Ibid: 178.
73 Ibid: 181.
74 Ibid: 180.

to own NMT facilities has also been mentioned.[75] This strategy is critical in changing perceptions and attitudes that NMT is a preserve for low-income earners and that private vehicles are a status symbol.

Climate change[76] and the Sustainable Development Goals (SDGs)[77] have also been listed as thematic areas of the NCIDP. If the NMT vision is realised, it will significantly address the growing emissions in the transport sector, and the SDGs on sustainable cities, climate action, energy efficiency, health and equality.

4 Conclusion and recommendations

Having evaluated legislation, policies and plans, it is evident that there is a commendable effort at the county level to promote the NMT agenda. However, despite the projections in vehicle increase and the attendant emissions, NMT has not been prioritised as a climate mitigation strategy in the transport sector unlike BRT and LRT.

NMT does not enjoy a standalone policy at the national level unlike what is discernible at the county level. In the instances where NMT is mentioned in national policy documents, it has not been fully accepted as a stand-alone means of transport and is always viewed as a corollary for other forms of transport. Below are recommendations advocating for the inclusion and prioritisation of NMT as a GHG abatement measure along with attendant benefits it can bring to safety, health, and accessibility.

4.1 Making a business case for NMT

NMT should be viewed as a viable economic development opportunity. Reduced traffic congestion could see increase in the national gross domestic product (GDP). Currently, significant revenue is lost in traffic congestion as productive person-hours are spent on the road. The government can have increased cost savings from reduced road and parking infrastructure development. Reduction in air pollution registers savings in the provision of healthcare particularly for deadly respiratory diseases not to mention savings from energy conservation and reaping benefits from strategic land use utilisation.

75 Ibid.
76 Ibid: 35.
77 Ibid: 102.

4.2 Autonomy of city governments to drive sustainable transport infrastructure

Autonomy of local governments is important in the promotion of sustainable infrastructure. A review of 30 Sub-Saharan countries reveals that administrative and fiscal decentralisation remain weak, thus undermining the authority of local governments. In particular, local governments have "no real responsibility for land management and no power over public utilities and pricing".[78] Bernard and Madiès'[79] study of four African countries confirms low fiscal capacities of local authorities and notes that capacity building for local administration officials is imperative if decentralisation will be attained.

The idea behind localisation of transport infrastructure projects is to make a case for cities as best suited to address climate impacts from transport because of their contribution and vulnerability to climate impacts. It also proffers an approach that emphasises the need to contextualize unique realities of local governments, hence creating an opportunity for them to steer their own infrastructural development.

4.3 Prioritising data on non-motorised transport

There is a glaring absence of baseline data on walking and cycling particularly in African cities. One of the recommendations from the African Mobility week is that urban areas should invest in data gathering to allow for critical evaluation of the cost-benefit of NMT infrastructure, while taking into account road safety and public health, especially for vulnerable groups.[80]

Data plays an important role in monitoring and evaluation, which can only be effective in the presence of reliable quality data. It also allows for evidence-based decision making. Some of the potential challenges that cities may have to contend with are the informality that surrounds them. Informal settlements, informal transport associations and hawkers are an integral part of our city, and these have direct implications on transport infrastructure. Adequate resource allocation for NMT research and user privacy rights, which are becoming an area of concern in big data, should be contemplated as well in this regard.

78 Paulais (2012: 111).
79 Dafflon & Madiès (2013).
80 UN Environment (2018).

4.4 Unpacking 'development'

According to the NDC Analysis Report, NMT usage will decrease as the government meets its development targets.[81] This statement brings into question, what does the government consider to be 'development'? Kenya Vision 2030,[82] the country's development blueprint, aims at providing a high quality of life to all its citizens in a clean and secure environment and is anchored upon the economic, social and political pillars. It is interesting that even though it seeks to achieve a clean environment, it does not include the 'environment' as one of its pillars and places it under the 'social' pillar.

As regards infrastructure, the aim is to: i) develop a 50-year Integrated National Transport Master Plan which is linked to the National Spatial Plan; ii) establish the Nairobi metropolitan region BRT to cover three transport corridors; and iii) develop a light rail transportation system for Nairobi and its suburbs which is projected to serve at least 150,000 passengers daily.[83] Progress in the transport sector in the context of Vision 2030 seems to be confined to BRT and LRT. This contradicts the objective of establishing an integrated transport plan.

For a plan to be considered integrated, it should adequately cater for multi-modal transport. Further, isn't getting more people out of their cars and having them walk or bike equally a sign of development? NMT not only reduces GHG emissions but also positively affects citizens' health. It decreases air pollution and gives people a chance to enjoy the environment around them.

There is, therefore, a need to re-define the term 'development' in a manner that truly embraces the three components of sustainability. Such an approach will influence the policy interventions in the transport planning sector to be representative of these three components in a manner that achieves GHG emissions abatement. It will also promote adequate financial and technological investment in NMT infrastructure.

4.5 Optimisation of bus rapid transit and light rail transit

The Kenyan emission mitigation strategy in the transport sector focuses on investing in the BRT and LRT in Nairobi and its suburbs. These forms of mass transit have been successful in many parts of the world particularly in addressing decongestion in cities. However, BRT and LRT and compact, pedestrian-oriented land-use development are mutually supportive. In essence, therefore, one cannot purport to exclude NMT from the agenda of BRT and LRT.

---

81 Ministry of Environment and Natural Resources (2015: 81).

82 Government of the Republic of Kenya (2007: vii).

83 Ibid: 14.

One of the features of BRT is reducing and eliminating delays in connectivity. This brings the trade-offs between spacing and convenience into sharp focus. Therefore, BRTs tend to have fewer stops (in comparison to LRT), and this is where NMT infrastructure becomes crucial in facilitating the last mile connectivity.

Adequate NMT infrastructure is a vital component of successful BRT and LRT systems, which can be most effective when integrated within a broader planning framework encompassing land use policies, zoning regulations, and economic and community development.[84] Climate responsive transport planning in Nairobi should, therefore, prioritise NMT as a complementary mitigation strategy to other forms of mass transit.

4.6 Behavioural change and civic education

The Nairobi NMT Policy seeks to make NMT the transport mode of choice. This statement is indicative of perceptions associated with NMT. According to the survey conducted along Jogoo and Juja roads, walking seemed to decline sharply with increased income, and the majority of the pedestrians (58.8%) earned less than Ksh20,000 a month.[85] The general public perception of pedestrians was that they are poor (22.6%) and belonged to the low-income group (14.4%).[86] The same case applied to cyclists and handcart operators who are also viewed as poor accounting for 11.9 % and 21.9 % respectively.[87] In particular, motorists perceived pedestrians as low-income earners (11.8%), cyclists as poor (21.9%) and handcart operators as a nuisance (35.1%).[88] Additionally, it was noted that motorists do not respect NMT users.[89] This explains the rampant encroachment of NMT spaces and endangerment of NMT users.

For NMT to be an effective climate mitigation strategy and a transport mode of choice, Nairobi residents must recognise, appreciate and respect its use and users. The perception that NMT is the preserve for low-income earners must change. Similarly, the attitude that owning a private vehicle is a status symbol must shift if we are to achieve sustainable mobility in Nairobi. The county and line ministries should take a leading role in changing these mindsets and helping the public un-learn and embrace an environmentally-friendly approach towards transport with its attendant health, social and economic benefits.

That said, many will not embrace NMT until adequate investments are made to improve and maintain NMT infrastructure, the safety of pedestrians is guaranteed, and

84 Institute for Transportation & Development Policy (2007).
85 Nairobi City County Government (2015: 6).
86 Ibid.
87 Ibid: 7.
88 Ibid: 6.
89 Ibid.

massive improvement of public transport is recorded. Having invested in NMT, the national and county governments may consider adopting market approaches to encourage NMT such as carbon tax on fuel, toll charges, increased parking fees, increased duty on private vehicles, incentives for carpooling, and stringent regulations on the importation of used motor vehicles.

It is evident that a one size fits all strategy will not achieve sustainable mobility and effectively reduce the growing transport emissions in Nairobi. Integrated approaches that factor in multi-modal means of mobility based on sound land use and urban planning are needed to push the NMT agenda forward.

References

Carr, LJ, SI Dunsiger & BH Marcus (2010) "Walk score™ as a global estimate of neighborhood walkability" 39(5) *American Journal of Preventive Medicine* 460-463.

Cummings, C & B Obwocha (2018) *At the crossroads – the politics of road safety in Nairobi*, at <https://www.odi.org/sites/odi.org.uk/files/resource-documents/12128.pdf> (accessed 3-3-2018).

Dafflon, B & T Madiès (2013) *The political economy of decentralization in sub-Saharan Africa: a new implementation model in Burkina Faso, Ghana, Kenya, and Senegal.*

Institute for Transportation & Development Policy (2007) *Bus rapid transit planning guide*, at <https://www.itdp.org/wp-content/uploads/2014/07/52.-Bus-Rapid-Transit-Guide-PartIntro-2007-09.pdf> (accessed 20-7-2018).

International Energy Agency (2013) *Policy pathways: a tale of renewed cities.*

IPCC / Intergovernmental Panel on Climate Change (2014) *Climate change 2014: synthesis report. Contribution of Working Groups I, II and III to the Fifth Assessment Report of the Intergovernmental Panel on Climate Change.*

Litman, T (2010) *Quantifying the benefits of non-motorized transportation for achieving mobility management objectives.*

Local Government Commission (2001) *The economic benefits of walkable communities.*

Ministry of Environment and Mineral Resources (2013) *Kenya national climate change action plan* (2013-2017).

Ministry of Environment and Natural Resources (2015) *Nationally determined contributions sector analysis report.*

Ministry of Lands and Physical Planning (2017) *National land use policy.*

Ministry of Transport and Infrastructure (2009) *Integrated national transport policy.*

Ministry of Transport, Infrastructure, Housing and Urban Development (2016) *Kenya's intended nationally determined contribution (INDC) transport sector analysis.*

Minnesota Department of Transportation (2015) *Bicycle and pedestrian data collection manual*, at <http://www.dot.state.mn.us/research/TS/2015/201533.pdf > (accessed 2-3-2018).

Mitullah, WV, M Vanderschuren & M Khayesi (eds) (2017) *Non-motorized transport integration into urban transport planning in Africa.*

Nabutola, W (2012) *National urban development policy making process: the Kenyan way: big challenges and some opportunities*, at <https://www.fig.net/resources/proceedings/fig_proceedings/fig2012/papers/ts02j/TS02J_nabutola_5828.pdf> (accessed 10-3-2018).

Nairobi County (2017) *Integrated development plan.*

NAR / National Association of Realtors & NAHB / National Association of Home Builders (2002) *Joint survey: survey suggests market-based vision of smart growth,* at <ww.realtor.org/SG3.nsf/Pages/NARNHAB02Survey? OpenDocument> (accessed 10-03-2018).

National Bicycle and Pedestrian Clearinghouse (2015) *Economic and social benefits of off-road bicycle and pedestrian facilities.*

National Transport and Safety Authority (2016) *New motor vehicles statistics for the last 10 years.*

Openda, J (2017) "At least 36 dead, 18 hurt after bus collides with truck at Migaa" *Daily Nation* (31-12-2017), at <http://www.nation.co.ke/counties/nakuru/27-dead-Migaa-bus-crash/1183314-4246712-e2r2yiz/index.html > (accessed 10-03-2018).

Opiyo, R & W Mitullah (2016) *Enhancing mobility in Kenya Counties through strategic policies formulation.*

Partnership on Sustainable Low Carbon Transport (2015) *Intended nationally determined contributions (INDCs) offer opportunities for ambitious action on transport and climate change*, Preliminary Analysis.

Paulais, T (2012) *Facing Africa's cities. The imperative of local investment.*

Sims R, R Schaeffer, F Creutzig, X Cruz-Núñez, M D'Agosto, D Dimitriu, MJ Figueroa Meza, L Fulton, S Kobayashi, O Lah, A McKinnon, P Newman, M Ouyang, JJ Schauer, D Sperling & G Tiwari (2014) "Transport" in O Edenhofer, R Pichs-Madruga, Y Sokona, E Farahani, S Kadner, K Seyboth, A Adler, I Baum, S Brunner, P Eickemeier, B Kriemann, J Savolainen, S Schlömer, C von Stechow, T Zwickel & JC Minx (eds) *Climate change 2014: mitigation of climate change. Contribution of Working Group III to the Fifth Assessment Report of the Intergovernmental Panel on Climate Change.*

UN Environment (2016) *Global outlook on walking and cycling,* at <http://www.unep.org/Transport/SharetheRoad> (accessed 12-03-2018).

UN Environment (2018) *African mobility week,* at <https://www.unenvironment.org/events/conference/africa-clean-mobility-week> (accessed 16-3-2018).

Victoria Transport Policy Institute (2004) *TDM and Economic Development.*

Wanambisi, L (2017) "Over 1,900 die in road accidents since January" *Capital fm,* at <https://www.capitalfm.co.ke/news/2017/09/over-1900-die-in-road-accidents-since-january/> (accessed 31-12-2017).

Wanjala, E (2017) "Road fatalities fall by 6.7% – NTSA" *The Star* (13-5-2017), at <https://www.the-star.co.ke/news/2017/05/13/road-fatalities-fall-by-67 ntsa_c1560498> (accessed 31-12-2017).

Yelda, S (2015) *Urban transportation and the environment, issues, alternatives and policy analysis.*

PART II:

NATURAL RESOURCES GOVERNANCE

Chapter 10: Wildlife conservation and community property rights in Kenya

Patricia Kameri-Mbote

1 Introduction

Property rights are granted for a variety of purposes including providing incentives for proper management of land. A property owner has a bundle of entitlements that include using, excluding others and alienation.[1] Kenya's pre-2010 law provided for the protection of property rights as constitutional rights. This protection did not, however, extend to according communities rights to own land. The Carter Commission[2] dealt with the allocation of land to communities in the 1930s, while the Swynnerton Plan[3] introduced the Torrens registration system for native-occupied land in the 1950s. Interestingly, the Swynnerton Plan acknowledged that there were communities in Kenya for whom private/individual rights to land were not suitable on account of their land uses. It recommended the establishment of group ranches, a form of group tenure, which is discussed below.

Policy and law over the years have, however, explicitly favoured private rights and encouraged the parcelling of community lands into private holdings. Indeed, the expectation was that all community land rights would eventually be converted to private rights. Another factor that has greatly influenced land-rights holding in Kenya is the preference for cultivation agriculture. This is despite the fact that only a third of Kenya's land mass is suitable for cultivation, with the rest being arid and semi-arid. Approximately 75% of the country's population lives within the medium to high potential (20% of land area) and the rest in the vast arid and semi-arid lands.[4]

Before the promulgation of the Constitution of Kenya (2010) (2010 Constitution) and the subsequent enactment of the Community Land Act (2016)[5] (Community Land Act), group/community ownership in Kenya was dealt with under trust land and group ranches. Trust land comprised of areas that were occupied by the natives during the colonial period and which had not been consolidated, adjudicated and registered in individuals' or group names, and native land that had not been taken over by the

1 Honoré (1961).
2 The Kenya Land Commission Report (1934).
3 Swynnerton (1955).
4 Ministry of Lands and Physical Planning (2017: 13).
5 Act 27 of 2016.

government.[6] It was governed by the Trust Lands Act[7] and vested in local authorities designated as county councils.[8] County councils managed all the resources within the trust land under their jurisdiction and controlled the development of that land.

With regard to group ranches, the Report of the East Africa Royal Commission of 1953-1955, concluding the policy on land tenure in the East African Protectorate as Kenya then was, noted that individualisation of land ownership ought to be the main aim. It, however, noted that such ownership need not be confined to individuals but could also extend to groups such as companies, cooperatives and customary associations of Africans.[9] Group ranches are demarcated areas of rangeland to which a group of pastoralists, who graze their individually or owned herds on it, have official land rights. It was designed for groups of herders shown to have customary rights over the range or pastureland in question which were governed by the now repealed Land (Group Representatives) Act.[10] Most group ranches are in the areas occupied by pastoral communities in Kenya. The composition of group ranches was an attempt at formalising traditional community structures. Group ranches did not, however, work well for a variety of reasons. Firstly, the group representatives lacked the authority of traditional leaders. Secondly, government policy emphasised individual rights and there was a prevalent view that group rights would eventually morph into individual rights. Despite this neglect, community claims to land remained.[11]

The absence of clear and secure property rights for communities has been an impediment to full enjoyment by communities of the incidents of property holding, productive use of land and national development. This presented a perverse incentive for communities to move away from community rights leading to defensive titling of land into individual holdings to protect their land from encroachment by government or other entities both within the trust lands and the group ranches. The latest available statistics indicate that over 60% of the total land area in Kenya is held under customary arrangements.[12] Much of this land is, however, being converted to private tenure through the process of land adjudication and there are no up to date figures on how much land still remains under community tenure. Some group ranches had already designated areas for wildlife conservation before the 2010 Constitution, but the lack of secure tenure left such areas open to conversion to alternative tenure and land uses.[13]

---

6 Section 115 of the Constitution of Kenya (1983) (Repealed).

7 Chapter 288 of the Laws of Kenya.

8 Section 114 of the Constitution of Kenya (1983) (Repealed).

9 East Africa Royal Commission (1955).

10 Chapter 287 of the Laws of Kenya, introduced as an Act of Parliament to provide for the incorporation of representatives of groups who have been recorded as owners of land under the Land Adjudication Act Chapter 284 of the Laws of Kenya.

11 Akech (2001).

12 Republic of Kenya (2004).

13 Interviews with group ranch leaders at Kaulo in Samburu and Isiolo in 2011.

It is within this context that both the 2010 Constitution and the first ever National Land Policy in Kenya (Sessional Paper No. 3 of 2009) provided for the recognition of community rights to land. The 2010 Constitution and the National Land Policy presented the yearned for opportunity to craft new land laws for the protection of public, private and community land.[14] The 2010 Constitution vests community land in communities identified on the basis of ethnicity, culture or similar community of interest.[15] It also provides that unregistered community land shall be held in trust by county governments (entities established under the 2010 Constitution in a bid to devolve power) on behalf of communities.[16] It comprises of: group ranches; land lawfully transferred to a specific community by any process of law; land declared to be community land by an Act of Parliament; and land lawfully held, managed or used by specific communities as community forests, grazing areas or shrines; ancestral lands and lands traditionally occupied by hunter-gatherer communities; or lawfully held as trust land by county governments.[17] No disposition or use of community land is allowed if it does not conform to legislation specifying the nature and extent of the rights of members of each community individually and collectively. The 2010 Constitution required Parliament to enact this law and this was done in 2016.

The Community Land Act and Regulations to implement it are now in place. The question that this chapter seeks to answer is the extent to which this law facilitates wildlife conservation granted the close relationship between pastoral communities to whom it applies and wildlife. This is within a context of unabated conversion of community land to private tenure before the promulgation of the 2010 Constitution and after its promulgation before the enactment and implementation of the Community Land Act.[18]

In designing the wildlife law and policy in the 2000s, among the key issues identified as barriers to wildlife conservation in Kenya were: land tenure insecurity; a failure to provide for multiple and compatible land uses through zoning; the lack of a legal framework for involvement of local communities in sustainable wildlife management despite the fact that wildlife shares land with communities and that the bulk of wildlife is outside protected areas; that communities have no rights to wildlife resources and no legal basis for claiming part of the benefits accruing from wildlife conservation and management or appropriating any value of wildlife despite the fact that they are obliged to keep the wildlife on their land and bear the costs; and the absence of incentives for landholders to conserve wildlife on their land.

The 2010 Constitution dealt with the equality and security of tenure under all tenure types. The Community Land Act and the Wildlife Conservation and Management Act

---

14 Article 61 of Constitution of Kenya (2010).
15 Article 63 of Constitution of Kenya (2010).
16 Article 63 of Constitution of Kenya (2010).
17 Article 63(2) of Constitution of Kenya (2010).
18 Musembi & Kameri-Mbote (2013: 5).

(2013)[19] (WCMA) were enacted to both align the land law and wildlife law to the 2010 Constitution and to respond to the concerns raised above. Additionally, the National Land Use Policy[20] seeks to guide "Kenya towards an environmentally and socially responsible use of land and land-based resources for socio-economic transformation of the people of Kenya"[21] and "to promote best land use practices for optimal utilization of the land resource in a productive, efficient, equitable and sustainable manner".[22]

This chapter assesses the extent to which the Community Land Act and the WCMA support wildlife conservation on community lands. Part one is the introduction. Part two conceptualises issues of wildlife conservation and land rights. Part three lays out the legal and policy framework for wildlife conservation and land rights assessing the extent to which community land rights have factored in wildlife conservation and vice versa. Part four provides the conclusion.

2 Conceptual framework

2.1 Wildlife conservation as a land use

Kenya boasts a varied diversity of flora and fauna.[23] It has over 7,800 animal and plant species and various other species that constitute wildlife, counting as a key revenue earner for government.[24] It is important to note that wildlife conservation is predicated on the manner in which land is held and used. Of the total land acreage in Kenya, community land is the largest, constituting nearly 66% of the total land mass while public land is 12%, with the remaining 22% being private land.[25] Given that community land forms the bulk of the total land mass in Kenya, it then follows that it is a crucial resource in terms of providing a habitat and migratory routes for wildlife. In another sense, community land alongside private land, which constitutes more than 85% of the total land mass in Kenya,[26] must be used if proper wildlife management is to be achieved. Most community lands in Kenya are in the arid and semi-arid parts of the country and lag behind in terms of economic development. Many of these lands have in recent times been earmarked for large infrastructural projects, which are likely to affect both communities and wildlife.[27] Moreover, while Article 62 of the 2010 Constitution envisages a total forest cover of 10% of the total land mass in Kenya, only

19 Act 47 of 2013.
20 Ministry of Lands and Physical Planning (2017).
21 Ibid: 4.
22 Ibid.
23 Kiambi & Opole (1992: 53).
24 World Conservation Monitoring Centre Kenya (1998).
25 Kimeu & Kairu (2016).
26 Ibid.
27 See for instance the Isiolo Resort City and the Standard Gauge Railway projects.

6.3% of the land mass at present is forested.[28] This means that Kenya still lags behind in terms of meeting the constitutionally and internationally recognised standard on forest cover, with forests forming a key habitat for wildlife.

Wildlife situated on community land usually share the land with the communities and their livestock, while wildlife on public land resides in protected areas - national parks and game reserves. It is estimated that 70% of Kenya's wildlife resides outside protected areas[29] as national parks comprise only 8% of Kenya's total land acreage.[30] Particular problems arise with respect to the delineation of land rights' regimes in areas hosting wildlife owing to the special nature of wildlife. To begin, wildlife is a 'fugitive resource', which is not easily associated with a particular user as owner in its *in situ* condition.[31]

Land on its part, being a finite and scarce resource, has multiple competing and sometimes incompatible values and uses.[32] Wildlife conservation is one of the uses to which land can be put and is invariably at odds with cultivation, urban or infrastructural development.[33] These latter uses are more economically lucrative in the short term and have greater support in national development policies compared to wildlife conservation.[34] It is therefore not surprising that because of the emphasis on crop production in national policy, agro-pastoralism is more common than pure pastoralism in many pastoralist areas that can support agriculture.[35] This shift in land use is accompanied by conversion of land tenure from group to individual rights. Many group ranches have been subdivided to individual holdings, which are perceived to be more secure and beneficial to the owners than group holdings.[36] The absence of a secure legal framework for community land rights largely fuelled this conversion.[37] Conversion of tenure is accompanied by conversion of land use from pastoralism, which is compatible with wildlife conservation, and has grave implications for conservation. It is worth noting that the change in tenure has not been accompanied by a change in lifestyle for many pastoralists who still keep large herds of livestock for livelihood and security against the economic uncertainties of life. Most of them have large herds on

28 Ministry of Lands and Physical Planning (2017: para. 4.21).

29 See generally: Western (1994).

30 Ibid.

31 Kameri-Mbote (2002: 29).

32 Republic of Kenya (2009: para. 29).

33 Ministry of Lands and Physical Planning (2017: 16). See <http://www.ardhi.go.ke/wp-content/uploads/2016/06/Draft-National-Land-Use-Policy-May-2016.pdf> (accessed 28-6-2016).

34 See, for example, the recently completed Standard Gauge Railway Line passes through the Nairobi National Park, Olingo (2016). The southern bypass road is also set to pass through the park.

35 This is the case in Amboseli area and Narok, which are home to the Maasai community. See Campbell et al. (2000: 337). The authors note that the Maasai are becoming partially or fully sedentary and embracing crop production to supplement their livestock production and support their families.

36 See generally: IUCN (2011).

37 Seno et al. (2013: 75).

land that is not able to sustain them leading to overgrazing. Drought and overall changes in climate have pushed the carrying capacity of many pastoral lands to the brink. In the quest for survival, herders have in recent times invaded private lands belonging to smallholder farmers and ranchers in places like Laikipia.[38] These pressures on land have implications for wildlife conservation.

The greatest threats to wildlife are loss of habitat, human interventions in ecosystems, poaching and over-use of resources.[39] The quest to optimise the uses to which land is put places wildlife in a disadvantaged position as urbanisation and agriculture take centre stage. The contest between deontological[40] (moral/equity) approaches to land and efficiency/utilitarian[41] approaches lies at the core of promotion of property rights' systems in spaces that host wildlife. Where conservation of wildlife is concerned, the situation is complicated by anthropocentric approaches that place human needs ahead of nature conservation. The emphasis on economic returns leads to the neglect of social and ecological concerns. The development of mega projects without taking into account habitat needs of wildlife is justified on grounds of the economic benefits of such projects in improving the lives of people. Where landscapes that host wildlife are occupied by poor people who hold land collectively, tenure reform geared towards individual ownership of land leads to the fragmentation of habitats and fencing of wild lands which affect the movement of animals.

The drive towards individual land rights follows from the exposition by Hardin[42] who proposed the institution of private property rights as a way to stem the tragedy of the commons and deal with the problem of unsustainable resource use in commonly held lands. It has however become increasingly clear that the fragmentation of community land into individual holdings does not guarantee sustainable resource management and can, to the contrary, fuel unsustainable harvesting of resources.[43] More recently, tenure reform has been informed by the perceived need to unlock the economic potential of 'dead capital' that land held communally is perceived to have remained for a long time.[44] In computing the value of land, nature conservation has unfortunately not been factored in. The competition for resources between humans in communally held landscapes and the wildlife pits conservation against people's welfare, and conservation is perceived as compounding poverty by taking land that would otherwise be available for use.

---

38 Kubania (2017).

39 Steidl & Powell (2006: 50).

40 See <http://lsolum.typepad.com/legal_theory_lexicon/2003/11/legal_theory_le_2.html> (accessed 28-10-2016).

41 Solow & Polasky (1999: 17). A utilitarian/efficiency approach to wildlife conservation is one that evaluates conservation on the basis on costs and benefits deriving therefrom.

42 Hardin (1968: 1243).

43 Kameri-Mbote (2002).

44 De Soto (2000). For a contrarian view on the same particularly within the African and Kenyan context, see Nyamu-Musembi (2006); and Okoth-Ogendo (2006).

Land rights are vested in various entities – individuals, communities or states granting such entities varying levels of exclusivity as regards usage and occupation of land. The existence of wildlife on land in many instances requires owners of the land to desist from some uses, which are incompatible with wildlife conservation. For poor people sharing landscapes with wildlife, the lure of alternative land uses is real in the quest for survival.[45] This is fanned by policies that over-emphasise private land rights and fail to take into account the needs of fugitive resources such as wildlife for vast lands. The situation is exacerbated by population growth leading to competition for land and resources between humans and wildlife.

2.2 Land rights and wildlife law

As noted above, the rights that accrue to landowners are referred to as a 'bundle of sticks'[46] or entitlements and include the rights to use, dispose, exclude, possess, manage, right to security, right to capital and to transmit.[47] Entitlements flow from the grant of land rights, which are delineated according to the bundle encapsulated in the grant. This explains why holders of freehold[48] and leasehold[49] titles have different bundles of rights. Rights to wildlife would therefore naturally be an incident of property. However, wildlife remains public property despite the fact that it is also found on community and private land. This challenges William Blackstone's eighteenth-century full liberal ownership theory where a private owner was perceived as having total exclusionary rights over their property over every other person.[50] Blackstone described property as:[51]

> ...that sole and despotic dominion which one man claims and exercises over the external things of the world, in total exclusion of the right of any other individual in the universe.

---

45 It is, therefore, not surprising that a number of landowners in areas such as Kajiado County have opted to dispose of their land in a bid to secure a bigger return on their capital. See Muiruri (2015).

46 Bundle of sticks is a metaphor used within the context of property law to denote the complexities of ownership and more specifically to connote the full extent/entitlements of private property ownership. The metaphor is credited to Justice Benjamin Cardozo. See further Ellickson (2011: 215).

47 Honoré has titled these as incidents of entitlements in property under the full liberal ownership concept. See further Honoré (1961).

48 Freehold title refers to an interest in land which upon the death of the holder, can descend to heirs or continue in perpetuity.

49 Leasehold title is an interest in land for a defined period/duration of time, upon expiry of which the land reverts to the lessor/grantor of the lease.

50 We use the phrase 'appeared to suggest' since there are serious doubts as to whether he was unaware of the qualifications to the concept of exclusivity of property. See in particular Blackstone (1769).

51 Blackstone (1769: 2).

This physicalist conception of property as the exclusive right to use and abuse the 'res' (thing that was the object of property) was used in Johnson's view to justify private property as a means:[52]

> ...to secure freedom and autonomy for individuals; the only obligation was to do no harm to others in the exercise of one's rights. People viewed ownership of land as the path to wealth, autonomy, and status. Ownership provided a circular justification for property rights that were themselves seen to naturally flow from ownership.

The full liberal ownership is less applicable in modern day due to ecological concerns, issues of social justice[53] and the emergence of new forms of intangible property. Indeed, the entitlements one has over land have been qualified over time with concerns about aviation, planning and environmental conservation being allowed to fetter the rights of landowners.[54] Further new forms of intangible property such as intellectual property,[55] electromagnetic spectrum[56] and more recently data,[57] have raised a need to reconsider the physicalist notion of property.

Land rights entitling owners to use their property pits communities against wildlife conservation authorities, which is a major challenge in Kenya's conservation arena. This is compounded by human-wildlife conflicts occasioned by the encroachment of wildlife and humans into each other's terrain. Increasing urbanisation is also a major factor in these threats in Kenya as people move from the rural areas to urban areas in search of employment. For instance, between 2010 and 2015, Kenya's urban population grew by 4.4%.[58] In 2013, the total urban population comprised 25% of the total population in the country.[59] This figure is projected to have increased since 2013. Increased urbanisation has necessitated destruction of ecological zones to construct houses for settlement thus exacerbating human-wildlife conflicts. Increased urbanisation has also contributed to the fragmentation of land and conversion of what was formerly pastoral and agricultural land into residential and commercial uses, thus creating conflict of these land uses with wildlife conservation.[60]

52 Johnson (2007: 250).

53 For a view that the exclusivity concept with regard to property as stated by Blackstone was more mythical than real and that Blackstone was misunderstood, see Rose (1998: 602).

54 See, for instance, *Baron Bernstein of Leigh v. Skyviews and General Ltd* [1978] QB 479 where Justice Griffiths referred to the *cujus* maxim as a "colourful phrase upon the lips of lawyers..." that is not as applicable in modern day.

55 Ministry of Lands and Physical Planning (2017).

56 Ibid.

57 Ibid.

58 Ibid: 13.

59 Ibid.

60 Ibid: 21.

2.3 Broader policy issues

2.3.1 Devolution

The new governance architecture that was ushered in by the 2010 Constitution is also of importance. It features devolution and some sharing of functions between the national and 47 county governments. This is a fundamental shift from the centralised approach that informed wildlife management in Kenya for a long time under the Wildlife (Conservation and Management) Act (1976).[61] While protection of the environment and natural resources and specifically the protection of animals and wildlife is a function of the national government,[62] there are interfaces with county governments. The latter are expected to implement specific national government policies on natural resources and the environment.[63] Counties are also required to develop County Integrated Development and County Physical Plans, which can facilitate sustainable management of wildlife.[64] The interface is further buttressed by the values in Articles 10 and 60 of the 2010 Constitution, which include public participation and community involvement. Participation and involvement are best realised at the local levels, which are within counties and have implications for the devolution of wildlife management that has been a concern for many African countries since the 1980s.[65]

Devolution radically departs from the previous situation where centralised wildlife authorities alienated wildlife resources from local communities.[66] Indeed, devolution has the potential to enlist community support for conservation[67] as it enhances community participation and promotes wildlife conservation particularly outside protected areas.[68] The engagement of communities is critical to framing incentives in conservation, to facilitate communities availing land for conservation and to provide a framework for involving them in dealing with poaching. This is in line with the chief objects of devolution namely, the enhancement of good governance and public participation at the community level.[69] Communities are then empowered to monitor and check abuses of wildlife and to participate in land-use planning and zoning in a manner that is compatible with proper wildlife management.[70] The WCMA and the Community

61 Kameri-Mbote (2008: 291).
62 Fourth Schedule Part I (Paragraph 22) of Constitution of Kenya (2010).
63 Fourth Schedule Part II (Paragraph 10) of Constitution of Kenya (2010).
64 Article 220(2) of the Constitution of Kenya (2010).
65 Roe et al. (2000: 3).
66 Kameri-Mbote (2002: 171).
67 For a characterisation of the benefits of decentralising wildlife management, see: Cirelli (2002: 58).
68 For further insights on the consequences of devolution of wildlife management, see: Poole & Leakey (1996: 55 and 58).
69 Olowu & Wunsch (2004: 2). Also see, Article 174(c) and (d) of the Constitution of Kenya (2010).
70 Kameri-Mbote (2010: 184).

Land Act are steps forward in terms of enhancing devolution of wildlife management and giving effect to the constitutional principles.

2.3.2 Vision 2030

Conservation in Kenya has also to be seen within the context of the country's Vision 2030[71] – the economic blueprint that seeks to transform Kenya to a middle-income economy by 2030. Infrastructure development, which depends on the availability of land, is a key component of this Vision. Many infrastructure projects have pitted communities and wildlife conservation organisations against the government as the former resist compulsory acquisition of their lands.[72] For instance, Kenya began the construction of a Standard Gauge Railway in 2014 and it was completed in 2017.[73] The railway runs through Nairobi National Park dividing it from north to south, though it is being built on a viaduct to ensure that only pillars will touch the ground of the park.[74] Nonetheless, the disruption caused will have negative effects to wildlife inhabiting the national park. However, the construction of the railway line through the park has been justified on the basis that it would save half the cost that would otherwise be incurred were the railway line to pass around the park.[75] This park, however, is hemmed between the city, residential areas and community lands and has survived years of wanton public land conversion to private land.[76] Opening up the park for the railway will disrupt the lives of communities who share the southern border with the park as well as provide a window for future conversion of the land from conservation use to urban development. The value of land in Nairobi has risen exponentially[77] and this is likely to fuel the drive towards conversion for other uses. It is indeed worth noting that the cost of the Standard Gauge Railway rose considerably on account of payments for land compulsorily acquired for the construction of the railway.[78] There are plans to expand the railway to link it to western Kenya. Compulsory acquisition of 100 acres of the park and 40 acres of Oloolua forest is required for this in addition to 1,000 parcels of private land bordering the park.[79]

---

71 Government of Kenya (2007).

72 For instance, a conservation lobby group named Kenya Coalition for Wildlife Conservation and Management sued the government against the intended construction of the Standard Gauge Railway through Nairobi National Park. See further: Ochieng (2016).

73 Cuddihy (2016).

74 Ibid.

75 Ibid.

76 Republic of Kenya (2004), popularly referred to as the 'Ndung'u Report'.

77 Mutanu (2015).

78 Anon (2014) and Anyanzwa (2016).

79 Rajab (2017).

Another example is the proposed construction of the Isiolo resort city and an international airport to enhance tourism within the region.[80] Significantly, the Lewa Wildlife Conservancy to the south, Samburu Game Reserve and Ewaso Ng'iro River to the west, and Buffalo Springs and Shaba National Reserve to the north, borders the land on which this development is proposed to take place, which are all habitats for wildlife.[81] Without doubt, the construction of these amenities, while meant to promote wildlife tourism, is likely to have deleterious effects on wildlife conservation. The idea seems to be to maximise the benefits from wildlife tourism through improved infrastructure. This, however, does not seem to consider the fact that the development may lead to negative impacts on the livelihood of communities who have lived with wildlife for many years. The developments are also likely to lead to destruction of the very resource they are seeking to enhance access to, as habitat is destroyed and opened up for settlement. It is important to note that poaching continues to be one of the greatest threats to wildlife in Kenya[82] and will likely be further fueled by opening up of conservation areas to influxes of humans. It is within this context[83] that the WCMA enhanced the penalties for poaching.[84] Needless to say, this approach is likely to be unsustainable in the long term as economic factors justifying infrastructure projects are hoisted over ecological concerns.

3 The legal framework for land rights and wildlife conservation

3.1 Land rights

The 2010 Constitution radically altered the land law terrain by redefining land categories and classifying them into: private, public and community land. Article 61 of the 2010 Constitution provides that all land in Kenya belongs to the people of Kenya collectively as a nation, as communities and as individuals. Article 61(2) classifies all land in Kenya as public, community and private. Wildlife is found in all these land categories. Article 66 of the 2010 Constitution mandates the state "to regulate the use of any land or any interest in or right over any land" including land-use planning. Protected areas that constitute national parks, national reserves and gazetted forests are public land but as pointed out above, public land alone cannot sustain wildlife[85] and

80 KNA (2012).
81 Ibid.
82 Vaughan (2016).
83 Nellemann et al. (2014).
84 Some of the penalties under the statute include life imprisonment for poachers and fines of up to Ksh. 20 million (Section 92 of the WCMA).
85 Watson et al. (2010: 8).

most of the wildlife in Kenya lives outside these national protected areas.[86] This calls for innovative ways of managing land taking wildlife habitat needs and the needs of individual and community landowners into account. It is noteworthy that most community land that hosts wildlife is also situated in the country's poorest areas.[87] The respective land law regimes present unique problems as far as wildlife conservation is concerned; and these concerns need to be addressed if land rights are to be supportive of conservation.

One of the most problematic issues is ownership of wildlife. As pointed out above, wildlife as a fugitive resource is not amenable to private ownership.[88] A private owner's interest to maximise the use of his land for optimum gain pits wildlife conservation as a land use against other more beneficial uses. With market forces driving up land values, this can be a hard choice. There have, however, been innovations developed and applied to promote wildlife conservation on private land such as the use of environmental easements.[89] In this context, the easements are used to restrict the rights of a landowner to put land to uses that are inimical to wildlife management.[90] While easements were developed under common law,[91] they have been included in Kenya's land rights[92] and environmental[93] regimes. Environmental easements are particularly relevant within the context of private land regimes and can serve as a useful tool for conserving wildlife particularly outside protected areas.[94] This is the tool that has been used in the establishment of wildlife conservancies on private lands.[95] Additionally, the Land Act (2012) contains detailed mechanisms on conservation of natural resources and ecologically sensitive parts of public[96] and private land.[97] The National Land Commission (NLC) is required to take appropriate action to maintain public land that has endemic species of flora and fauna, critical habitats or protected areas.[98] The Commission is also required to identify ecologically sensitive areas that are within

86 See <http://www.kws.go.ke/content/overview-0> (accessed 30-10-2016).

87 It is little surprising that pastoralist communities such as Maasais in Kajiados have been selling away land. See Muiruri (2015).

88 Kameri-Mbote (2002: 13).

89 Watson et al. (2010: 8).

90 Ibid.

91 Ibid.

92 See part X of the Land Registration Act (2012).

93 See Section 6 of EMCA and Section 68 of Wildlife Management and Conservation Act 2013.

94 Watson et al. (2010: 9).

95 For instance, the Northern Rangelands Trust (NRT) is a community based organisation that enables communities run conservancies allowing pastoralist communities to graze on the land while allowing for wildlife conservation on the same land.

96 Public land as provided under Article 63 of the Constitution of Kenya (2010) is a tenure classification where land is vested in the state (national government/county government or state agencies).

97 Private land as provided under Article 64 of the Constitution of Kenya (2010) is a tenure classification whereby land vests in an individual/private person.

98 Ministry of Lands and Physical Planning (2017: para. 2.5.10).

public lands, demarcate or take any other justified action on those areas and act to prevent environmental degradation.[99] In doing so, the Commission should work in consultation with the relevant institutions like Kenya Wildlife Service or Kenya Forest Service.

Significantly, the 2010 Constitution requires the state to ensure sustainable exploitation, utilisation, management and conservation of the environment and natural resource and the equitable sharing of the accruing benefits.[100] Further, the state is compelled to protect the indigenous knowledge, biodiversity and genetic resources of communities.[101] These are enabling provisions for harnessing community knowledge of ecosystems and habitat that are shared with wildlife.

The National Land Use Policy[102] (2017) proposes that the government should:

1. Identify, map and gazette critical wildlife migration and dispersal areas and corridors in consultation with the local communities and individual land owners;
2. Encourage the development of wildlife sanctuaries and conservancies and involve local communities and individuals living contiguous to the parks and protected areas in the co-management of such areas; and
3. Review the gazettement of forests and protected areas to foster the realization of their multiple values and ensure that they are protected for their ecosystem values and not merely to physically exclude human activities.

These recommendations aim to stem conflicts that arise where communities live in ecologically sensitive lands that have been placed under public authority's curatorship through gazettement, but which communities claim rights over by virtue of having occupied them before the gazettement. Section 24 of the Community Land Act addresses this by enabling the NLC to convert public land to community land on a case by case basis in accordance with the Land Act (2012).

Communal land in Kenya has the greatest potential to conserve wildlife and there have been efforts geared towards enabling the communities, particularly those that live with wildlife and those that border protected areas, to recognise the benefits of wildlife conservation through community benefit-sharing schemes relating to revenues derived from wildlife tourism.[103] More sophisticated mechanisms have been proposed in the WCMA which include the formation of community wildlife conservancies where a community or a number of communities come together and decide to set aside land collectively for wildlife management with a set of governing rules.[104]

While the Community Land Act does not expressly provide for conservation of wildlife, a reading of it as a whole points to ways of conserving wildlife. The Act in its entirety seeks to protect and promote the right of communities to manage their

99 Section 11(2) of the Land Act (2012).
100 Article 69(1)(a) of the Constitution of Kenya (2010).
101 Article 69(1)(c) of the Constitution of Kenya (2010).
102 Ministry of Lands and Physical Planning (2017).
103 Section 80 of the WCMA.
104 Section 39 of the WCMA.

lands. This will have a positive effect on the conservation of the wildlife resources on community land as communities identify with wildlife conservation as a land use. Moreover, the security of tenure provided for under the Act provides a good context for incorporating wildlife as part and parcel of the community, with the assurance that the benefits of conservation will be shared with the community.

Part II of the Community Land Act provides for the recognition, protection and registration of community land.[105] Significantly, communities may hold land as freehold, leasehold or under customary tenure.[106] The Act requires the maintenance of a community land register for each registration unit, which register should contain: a cadastral map showing the extent of the community land and identified areas of common interest; the name of the registered community; a register of members of the registered community which shall be updated annually; the user of the land; and such other particulars of members of the registered community as the Registrar may determine.[107] Section 17 underscores the rights of a registered community as proprietor of land whether acquired on first registration or subsequently for valuable consideration or by an order of court. It is categorical that such rights "shall not be liable to be defeated except as provided in this Act or any other written law, and shall be held on behalf of the community, together with all privileges and appurtenances belonging thereto, free from all other interests and claims whatsoever", subject to leases, charges and other encumbrances and to the conditions and restrictions, shown in the register; and such overriding interests as may affect the land. It remains to be seen how titling of community land will impact on wildlife conservation. It is important to note that easements on community land facilitate the designation of wildlife migratory routes and hence co-existence between communities and wildlife.

Under Section 12, there are different classes of holding community land which include: communal; family or clan; and reserve land. The provision for reserve land opens a pathway for the use of community land for conservation. Indeed among the uses for which a community may reserve land is community conservation.[108] Related to this is the provision that enables a registered community to submit a plan for the development, management and use of their land for approval to the county government on its own volition or at the request of such government.[109] The community is required to consider any conservation, environmental or heritage issues relevant to the development, management or use of the land before submitting such a plan.[110]

105 Act 27 of 2016.
106 Section 4 of the Community Land Act.
107 Section 10 of the Community Land Act.
108 Other uses are farming, urban development; cultural and heritage sites (Section 13(3) of the Community Land Act).
109 Section 19 of the Community Land Act.
110 Section 19(2)(a) of the Community Land Act.

Inadequate organisation or lack of a formalised central source of management and control of land resources in community lands has been the greatest challenge in integrating and appreciating wildlife resources as a land use in community land. Section 15 of the Act provides for the establishment of both a community assembly (consisting of all adult members of the community) and a community land management committee. These institutions are responsible for the management and administration of community land; coordinating the development of community land use plans in collaboration with the relevant authorities; and prescribing rules and regulations. The community assembly ratifies the rules and regulations and governs the community operations. These two institutions are therefore responsible for the formulation of the wildlife conservation and management policy within the respective community land.

Section 20 is devoted to conservation of natural resources on community land. It provides that registered communities should abide by applicable laws, policies and standards on natural resources, and further that they should establish measures to protect critical ecosystems and habitats. Registered communities are also required to provide: incentives for communities and individuals to invest in income generating natural resource conservation programmes; measures to facilitate the access, use and co-management of forests, water and other resources by communities who have customary rights to these resources; procedures for the registration of natural resources in an appropriate register; and procedures for the involvement of communities and other stakeholders in the management and utilisation of land-based natural resources.

If implemented, these measures can bridge the divide between land rights holding and conservation. They can also stem the impoverishment of communities by conservation initiatives that exclude them.

Under Section 28 of the Community Land Act, pastoral communities are entitled to grazing rights within community land. This entitlement is, however, subject to conditions that may be imposed such as: the kind and number of livestock that may be grazed; the part of land the pastoralists may graze on; and a grazing plan. Despite Section 13 of the Act providing for exclusivity of special purposes, the provision has not been strictly observed leading to prevalence of cultural practices that lead to unsustainable land use and inappropriate ecosystem management.[111] This has led to severely degraded rangelands, reduced productivity levels and unsustainability due to overgrazing, poor land husbandry practices and conversion of rangeland to crop farming and ultimately to the reduction of land available for wildlife conservation.[112]

The National Land Use Policy (2017) proposes that the government should address the problem of rangelands' degradation to secure pastoralists' livelihoods and tenure to land by: planning and developing rangelands according to their potential in livestock production, tourism, mining and energy production; establishing mechanisms for

111 Ministry of Lands and Physical Planning (2017).

112 Ibid: 17.

enforcing adherence to the optimum stocking rates for each area; establishing a framework for livestock management in rangelands including provision of water, pasture and fodder development; discouraging open access to grazing land by and among pastoralists by developing communal grazing area plans; establishing suitable methods for defining and registering land rights in pastoral areas while allowing pastoralists to maintain their unique land systems and livelihoods; ensuring that the rights of women in pastoral areas are recognised and protected; providing for flexible and negotiated cross-boundary access to protected areas, water, pastures and salt licks among different stakeholders for mutual benefit; mainstreaming climate change adaptation and mitigation in rangeland management; and ensuring that all land uses and practices under pastoral tenure conform to the principles of sustainable resource management.[113]

Section 29 of the Community Land Act provides for setting aside some land within the community land for special purposes, which include community conservation areas. Such areas can only be used for those specific purposes. The community could set up wildlife conservation areas using this provision. Section 35 requires the resources found in the community land to be sustainably and productively used for the benefit of the whole community including future generations. Indisputably, the community assembly, the community land management committee and community members bear a burden of conserving the wildlife resources on community land and sharing the benefits that accrue from such use.

Secure tenure for communities, incentives for investments and benefit-sharing are most likely to attract investment in wildlife conservation on community land. Such investments could include wildlife conservation centres run by the communities or by outsiders with the approval of the community. The community must ensure that such investments do not impact on the environment negatively. Communities can also use alternative dispute resolution mechanisms, including traditional dispute resolution mechanisms and mediation, to resolve disputes that arise among land uses or even community members under part VII of the Act. Dispute resolution procedures can be provided for in by-laws developed by the community. Fast-tracked dispute resolution is vital for sustainable conservation of wildlife resources.

3.2 Wildlife conservation

The principal statute governing wildlife is the WCMA. While the final version of the policy is yet to be completed, the latest version of the Draft National Wildlife Management Conservation Policy (2017)[114] aims to –

113 Ibid: 45-46.
114 Ministry of Environment and Natural Resources (2017: 2).

> ... promote a positive cultural relationship between people and wildlife, through the incorporation of indigenous and local knowledge systems; and negotiate a social contract with communities living with wildlife to provide space for wildlife.

It also aims at providing fiscal incentives to community owners and "support landowners and communities to set aside wildlife conservation areas and sanctuaries within the framework of approved land use plan of the area".

Other laws that constitute the wildlife conservation legal regime are mainly sectoral laws that govern specific sectors that have an impact on wildlife. Such laws include the Forest Conservation and Management Act (2016), the Environment Management and Coordination Act (1999) (EMCA) and the various land-use planning laws. Article 69 of the 2010 Constitution provides for the protection of biodiversity and natural resources (which include wildlife) by the state. This constitutional provision gives legal and constitutional mandate to the state to put in place laws, measures and policies to ensure the sustainable exploitation, utilisation, management and conservation of the environment and natural resources. It is in this light that the WCMA should be viewed.

The EMCA is the framework law for environmental management. Being overarching and cross-sectoral in nature, it has provisions that impact on wildlife conservation in general. For instance, under the EMCA, there is a requirement to conduct an environmental impact assessment before any activity with potential negative consequences on the environment may be carried out.[115] Furthermore, before the establishment of a protected area such as a national park or a game reserve, an environmental audit and a licence issued by the relevant authority (National Environmental Management Authority) is required.[116] The law also designates Kenya Wildlife Service (KWS) as the lead agency for matters relating to wildlife.[117]

Land-use planning laws also have an impact on wildlife conservation as they direct the use of land in different parts of the country. Their potency lies in their ability to guide management of natural resource management and can lead to sustainable or unsustainable practices depending on how they are framed. Kenya's land use policy was only concluded in 2017.[118] This implies that land use has historically been haphazardly planned with no proper zoning according to ecological regions.

The WCMA establishes KWS as the competent body responsible for protecting, managing and acting as the custodian of the country's wildlife resources.[119] Its functions include liaising with communities and private landowners in management and consultation, and offering security for wildlife.[120] Notably, wildlife resources are found in forests, lakes and maritime zones. Cooperation mechanisms between KWS, the

115 Section 58 of the EMCA (1999), Cap 387.
116 Ibid.
117 Section 6 of the WCMA.
118 Ministry of Lands and Physical Planning (2017).
119 Section 6 of the WCMA.
120 Section 7 of the WCMA.

NLC, Community Land Management Committees, county governments and the Kenya Forest Service are therefore critical. The cooperation will reduce duplication of roles and blame games that lead to inefficient resource management.

Section 11 of the Land Act (2012) requires the NLC to take appropriate measures to maintain public land that has endangered or endemic species of flora and fauna situated on it. This obligation includes demarcating such ecologically sensitive areas in consultation with the relevant institutions. The WCMA mandates the Cabinet Secretary, in consultation with the NLC, to develop a list of endangered species warranting special protection measures.[121] This protection is only possible through cooperation between KWS and the NLC. The creation of migratory wildlife corridors is also possible because the Land Act (2012) provides for rights of way and easements, while the WCMA provides for easements and protection orders.

The WCMA lays out values that guide conservation of wildlife as follows: devolution of wildlife conservation and management; effective public participation; conservation and management shall be encouraged using an ecosystem approach wherever possible; encouragement and recognition of wildlife conservation as a form of land use on public, community or private land; sustainability; benefits of wildlife conservation be derived by the land user in order to offset costs and to ensure the value and management of wildlife does not decline; and equitable sharing of the benefits accruing from wildlife conservation.[122]

This Act further defines KWS functions as to: conserve and manage national parks, wildlife conservation areas and sanctuaries under its jurisdiction; set up a county wildlife conservation committee for each county; develop mechanisms for benefit sharing with communities living in wildlife areas; assist and advise in the preparation of management plans for community and private wildlife conservancies; undertake and conduct enforcement activities such as anti-poaching operations, wildlife protection, intelligence gathering, investigations and other enforcement mechanisms to effect the provisions of the Act; promote and undertake extension programs to enhance wildlife conservation, education and training; advise the NLC, the Cabinet Secretary and the Council on the establishment of national parks, wildlife conservancies and sanctuaries; and grant licenses and monitor the observation of conditions of grant of such licenses.[123]

The WCMA also provides that benefits for wildlife conservation shall accrue to the land user to offset the costs of conservation.[124] In addition, benefits accruing from the use of wildlife resources shall be equitably shared between the county and national government, private landowners and communities.[125] Essentially, the WCMA

121 Section 46 of the WCMA.
122 Section 4 of the WCMA.
123 Section 7 of the WCMA.
124 Section 4(e) of the WCMA.
125 Section 19 of the WCMA.

introduces incentives to encourage conservation of wildlife by all stakeholders and as a source of income.[126] It also provides for the establishment of a Wildlife Endowment Fund whose functions are to: develop wildlife conservation initiatives; manage and restore protected areas and conservancies; protect endangered species, habitats and ecosystems; and support wildlife initiatives.[127]

To conserve wildlife, the Cabinet Secretary, upon recommendation of the relevant county government and after consultation with the NLC, may declare by notice in the Gazette any land under the jurisdiction of the county government to be a national reserve where such land is rich in biodiversity and wildlife resources, contains endangered species or is an important wildlife buffer zone, migratory route or dispersal area.[128] In the same spirit, the Cabinet Secretary may: acquire by purchase any land suitable to be declared a national park, wildlife corridor, migratory route or dispersal area under the Act;[129] or by notice in the Gazette publish a national list of wildlife ecosystems and habitats that are endangered and threatened and are in need of protection on the advice of the KWS and in consultation with the NLC.[130]

The WCMA provides the framework for setting up community wildlife associations or conservancies in Kenya.[131] Once registered, the conservancy is mandated to prepare management plans for the conservation of wildlife; assist KWS in combating illegal activities such as poaching and bushmeat trade; assist in problem animal control; and keep regional wildlife conservation areas informed of any development changes in their area that may affect wildlife.[132] Landowners are encouraged to donate land to the national government, county government, community or educational institutions for wildlife conservation.[133] The Act provides that any person or community who owns land inhabited by wildlife may individually or collectively establish a wildlife conservancy or sanctuary in accordance with the Act and the Wildlife Conservation and Management (Conservancy and Sanctuary) Regulations (2015). A community under this regulation is defined as a group of individuals or families who share common heritage or interest in an identifiable piece of land or natural resources. The regulations provide a procedure for the establishment and registration of conservancies; to promote the development of conservancies on private and community land; and to harmonise the standards for maintaining the conservancies.

KWS is tasked with the duty of registering conservancies. To register a conservancy, the community is required to submit: a concept proposal in the format provided

126 Section 70 of the WCMA.
127 Section 23(3) of the WCMA.
128 Section 35(1) of the WCMA.
129 Section 38(2) of the WCMA.
130 Section 46(1) of the WCMA.
131 Section 40 of the WCMA.
132 Section 41 of the WCMA.
133 Section 42 of the WCMA.

in the 5th schedule in not more than 1,000 words; a benefit-sharing plan; minutes of conservancy members agreeing to the establishment of the conservancy; and a receipt signifying the payment of the requisite fee. Qualifications for registration are set out in Section 10 and include an indication of the following: the acreage of the land to be dedicated to conservation; a concept proposal by the applicant; a land tenure system; the socio-economic and ecological viability of the conservancy; the diversity of the wildlife resources; and contiguous land use patterns and their effect on the proposed conservancy. Upon successful registration as a conservancy, a certificate is issued to the applicant.

It is important to point out that many individuals and communities had already established conservancies before the enactment of the WCMA.[134] The Act is, however, important as it provides the framework for the management of all conservancies.

3.3 Wildlife conservation on community lands

The problems identified as plaguing conservation on community lands before the promulgation of the 2010 Constitution included: land tenure insecurity; a failure to provide for multiple and compatible land uses through zoning; the lack of a legal framework for involving local communities in sustainable wildlife management despite the fact that wildlife shared land with communities and that the bulk of wildlife is outside protected areas; the fact that communities had no rights to wildlife resources; the lack of a legal basis for claiming part of the benefits accruing from wildlife conservation and management or appropriating any value of wildlife despite the fact that they were obliged to keep the wildlife on their land and bear the cost thereof; and the absence of incentives for landholders to conserve wildlife on their land. Other problems included the degradation and overuse of community land, which impacted on the ecosystems shared with wildlife.

The 2010 Constitution, the WCMA, the Community Land Act and their accompanying regulations have addressed these issues. What now remains is the implementation of these legal and policy provisions. Once successfully implemented, communities should be able to contribute to wildlife conservation and benefit from their efforts.

134 The Northern Rangelands Trust had already established about 15 community conservancies in Northern Kenya and a number of community conservancies had been established in the Narok area. Private land owners had also established conservancies in areas like Laikipia and a Kenya Wildlife Conservation Association had been set up.

4 Conclusion

Wildlife conservation is now every citizen's responsibility regardless of the category of land on which wildlife resources may be situated. The enabling legal and policy framework is in place for everybody's participation with incentives provided for landowners to avail their land for conservation. The National Land Use Policy (2017) provides an opportunity to synergise land tenure and land use. It requires that the allocation of land and issuance of title deeds be done on the basis of approved physical development plans; approved survey plans; approved local area zoning regulations; and policy guidelines. It also provides that areas of public land that have been identified as having high public value (such as watershed protection, important botanic or wildlife habitat and/or landscape values, cultural significance, road reserves for potential future highways) should not be allocated except under leases with conditions that reflect the high value or period by which the land may be required for a reserved use. The crafting of community area conservation plans taking into account human, livestock and wildlife needs will contribute to sustainable management of community lands and resources on them.

References

Akech, JM (2001) *Rescuing indigenous tenure from the ghetto of neglect.*

Anon (2014) "Kenya to sink Sh 10 bn into land for new railway" *Daily Nation* (16-6-2014).

Anyanzwa, J (2016) "Changes to Kenya's land laws to tame cost of public projects and debt" *Daily Nation* (4-9-2016).

Blackstone, W (1769) *Commentaries on the laws of England.*

Campbell, DJ, H Gichohi, A Mwangi & L Chege (2000) "Land use conflict in Kajiado District, Kenya" (17)4 *Land Use Policy* 337-348.

Cirelli, MT (2002) *Legal trends in wildlife management.*

Cuddihy, M (2016) "Nairobi National Park: Chinese construction of East Africa railway line a problem for conservationists" *ABC News* (17-10-2016).

De Soto, H (2000) *The mystery of capital: why capitalism triumphs in the West and fails everywhere else.*

Ellickson, RC (2011) "Two cheers for the bundle-of-sticks metaphor, three cheers for Merrill and Smith" 8(3) *Econ Journal Watch* 215-222.

Government of Kenya (2007) *Kenya Vision 2030: A Globally Competitive and Prosperous Kenya.*

Hardin, G (1968) "The tragedy of the commons" 162 *Science* 1243-1248.

Honoré, AM (1961) "Ownership" in A Guest (ed.) *Oxford essays in jurisprudence* 107-147.

IUCN / International Union for Conservation of Nature (2011) *The land we graze: a synthesis of case studies about how pastoralists organizations defend their land rights.*

Johnson, DR (2007) "Reflections on the bundle of rights" 32 *Vermont Law Review* 247-272.

Kameri-Mbote, P (2002) *Property rights and biodiversity management in Kenya.*

Kameri-Mbote, P (2008) "Aligning sectoral wildlife law to the framework environmental law" in CO Okidi, P Kameri-Mbote & M Akech (eds) *Environmental governance in Kenya: implementing the framework law*.

Kameri-Mbote, P (2010) "Innovative approaches in using property rights for wildlife management in Kenya" 13 *Waseda Proceedings of Comparative Law* 158.

Kiambi, K & M Opole (1992) "Promoting traditional trees and food plants in Kenya" in D Cooper, R Vellve & H Hobbelink (eds) *Growing diversity: genetic resources and local food security practical action* 53.

Kimeu, S & F Kairu (2016) *Securing tenure for land belonging to public schools: experiences, lessons and insights from transparency international kenya's land and corruption in Africa* Project Paper Prepared for presentation at the World Bank Land Conference on Land and Poverty, March 2016.

KNA (2012) "Six thousand acres for Isiolo resort city" *Daily Nation* (5-1-2012).

Kubania, J (2017) "Laikipia: the anatomy of a land grab" *Daily Nation* (13-11-2017).

Ministry of Environment and Natural Resources (2017) *Draft revised national wildlife management conservation policy*.

Ministry of Lands and Physical Planning (2017) *National land use policy* Sessional Paper No. 1.

Muiruri, B (2015) "New policy to curb sale of Maasai community land" *Daily Nation* (13-3-2015).

Musembi, C & P Kameri-Mbote (2013) "Mobility, marginality and tenure transformation in Kenya: explorations of community property rights in law and practice" 17(1) *Nomadic Peoples Journal* 5-32.

Mutanu, B (2015) "Upper Hill most costly as Nairobi land prices rise 535pc" *Business Daily* (29-1-2015).

Nellemann, C, R Henriksen, P Raxter, N Ash & E Mrema (eds) (2014) *The environmental crime crisis – threats to sustainable development from illegal exploitation and trade in wildlife and forest resources*.

Nyamu-Musembi, C (2006) *Breathing life into dead theories about property rights: de Soto and land relations in rural Africa*.

Ochieng, A (2016) "Tribunal halts Nairobi-Naivasha SGR construction" *Daily Nation* (19-9-2016).

Okoth-Ogendo, HWO (2006) *Formalising "informal" property systems: the problem of land rights reform in Africa* Background Paper prepared for the Commission for the Legal Empowerment of the Poor, Nairobi.

Seno, O, K Simon & S Tome (2013) "Socio-economic and ecological viability of pastoralism in Loitoktok" 17(1) *Nomadic Peoples Journal* 66-86.

Olingo A, (2016) "Lobby group wants more consultations over new SGR route" *The East African* (18-9-2016).

Olowu, D & J Wunsch (eds) (2004) *Local governance in Africa: the challenges of democratic decentralization*.

Poole, JH & RE Leakey "Kenya" in E Lutz & J Caldecott (eds) (1996) *Decentralization and biodiversity conservation*.

Rajab, R (2017) "State to take 100 acres of park for SGR" *The Star Newspaper* (23-12-2017).

Republic of Kenya (2004) *Report of the Commission of Inquiry into the illegal/irregular allocations of land*.

Republic of Kenya (2007) *Statistical abstract*.

Republic of Kenya (2009) *The national land policy* Sessional Paper No. 3 of 2009.

Roe, D, J Mayers, M Grieg-Cran, A Kothari, C Fabricius & R Hughes (eds) (2000) *Evaluating Eden: exploring the myths and realities of community-based wildlife management.*

Rose, CM (1998) "Canons of property talk, or Blackstone's anxiety" 108 *Yale Law Journal* 601-632.

Solow, AR & S Polasky (1999) "The endangered species act as a tool to conserve biological diversity" *Choices Third Quarter* 17-21.

Steidl, RJ & BF Powell (2006) "Assessing the effects of human activities on wildlife" 23 (2) *Visitor Impact Monitoring* 50-58.

Swynnerton, RJM (1955) *The Swynnerton Report: A plan to intensify the development of African agriculture in Kenya.*

Vaughan, A (2006) "Kenya's new front in poaching battle: The future is in the hands of our communities" *The Guardian* (30-5-2016).

Watson, R, KH Fitzgerald & N Gitahi (2010) *Expanding options for habitat conservation outside protected areas in Kenya: the use of environmental easements*, at <https://www.awf.org/sites/default/files/media/Resources/Books%20and%20Papers/AWF_Env_Easement_Technical_Paper_2_March_2010.pdf> (accessed 23-7-2018).

Western, D (1994) "Ecosystem conservation and rural development: the case of Amboseli" in D Western & S Strum (eds) *Natural connections: perspectives in community-based conservation.*

World Conservation Monitoring Centre Kenya (1998) *Conservation of biological diversity and forest ecosystems.*

Chapter 11: Criminal law protection of wildlife reserves in Cameroon

Marie Ngo Nonga

1 Introduction

Given its privileged geographical situation, nearly 92% of Africa's ecosystems are represented in Cameroon. It is, therefore, a country that is very rich in biodiversity. However, these biological resources are abundantly exploited both by the state and by the local populations, which have many of their activities primarily focused on the exploitation of natural resources. In fact, despite the legal status of protected areas,[1] wildlife reserves maintain their nurturing and health functions for the local populations, and the resources they contain are sought after for food, commercial, medicinal and cultural purposes. They highly contribute to the annual revenue of the state of Cameroon.

There are six wildlife reserves situated in different regions of Cameroon: Dja in the south; Douala-Edea and Lake-Ossa in the Littoral; Kimbi and Mbi-crater in the northwest and Santchou in the west.[2] Wildlife reserves are an integral part of what are commonly called protected areas. They are geographically defined areas managed to achieve specific conservation and sustainable development objectives of a given resource or resources.[3] A wildlife reserve is, therefore, an area set apart for the conservation, development and propagation of wild animal life, as well as for the protection and development of its habitat. Within these reserves, hunting is prohibited unless authorised by administrative authorities, and/or where other human activities are regulated or prohibited.[4]

1 The story of the birth of protected areas around the world began in the American State of Wyoming with the creation of Yellowstone National Park in 1872. On the African continent, the very first area is the Sabie Game Reserve of South Africa which became the Krüger National Park in 1898. In Cameroon, the first protected areas were created on 12 June and 19 November 1932, Mozogo Gokoro and Benue. To date, Cameroon has nearly 20 protected areas, national parks, reserves and sanctuaries, the touristic and eco-touristic assets of which are undeniable.

2 Gonmadje et al. (2015: 48).

3 Article 2 of Decree No. 95/466/PM of 20 July 1995 to lay down the conditions for the implementation of wildlife regulations.

4 Article 2(7) of the same Decree.

According to the National Environmental Management Programme (NEMP), Cameroon's wildlife has an immense potential of specimens[5] and is home to nearly half of the protected animal species in Africa.[6] It also has a varied biological diversity. Despite the exceptional character and legal status conferred on wildlife reserves, their degradation has accelerated in recent years. Cameroon ranks second in the 2013 world ranking by the International Union for Conservation of Nature (IUCN) of countries in which a significant number of major species are threatened, with a total of 260 species at risk.

The causes of degradation of wildlife reserves and their biodiversity are multiple and intrinsically linked to the development of human activities. The first is commercial poaching, aggravated by the frustration and impoverishment of local populations that depend on these resources for their subsistence needs. Secondly, people hunt the rarest animal species and harvest plant species with high market value.[7] It is also necessary to mention the precarious conditions in which state agents in charge of monitoring wildlife reserves live and which make them particularly vulnerable to corruption and excessive complacency towards poachers.

Furthermore, the insufficient technical and financial capacity of the forest administration is another factor threatening wildlife reserves. They lack modern equipment and watchtowers, which are necessary for viewing and identifying species and especially essential to observing the dynamics of species in order to prevent possible attacks and incursions by hunters.

Finally, the lack of cohesion in the policies relevant to protected area management is another source of their decline. Authorities continue to encourage the harvesting of animals by issuing a high number of licences and hunting permits, notwithstanding the unprecedented extinction of protected species and the subsequent destruction of biodiversity. Most environmental problems observed in wildlife reserves do not stem from the natural vulnerability of the ecosystems, but from the irrational management of these resources. It is, therefore, important to strengthen the effectiveness of the legal framework relevant to protecting wildlife reserves. Cornu's legal vocabulary defines protection as follows:[8]

> the precaution which, in response to the need of the person or what it covers, and generally corresponding to a duty for the person ensuring it, consists in protecting a person or good against a risk, in guaranteeing their security and integrity by legal or material means; it designates both the action of protecting and the laid down system of protection (measure, system, arrangement...).

5 PNGE (1996: 87).

6 Tchindjang et al. (2006: 17).

7 In this regard, see Judgement No. 1718/COR of 12 July 2010 of the Douala Court of First Instance against Amiah Awudu, Yeboa Eric and Osei, all three of Ghanaian nationality found guilty of hunting without the necessary hunting licences and permits.

8 Cornu (2011: 815).

The protection provided by criminal law, therefore refers to a set of repressive legal means (legal and jurisprudential) adopted by a state or a community to ensure respect for public order in general and specifically for the elements that the law seeks to protect. Criminal law therefore has a key role to play in the environmental policy context, which is strongly imbued with the principle of prevention, insofar as it provides for the imposition of sufficiently dissuasive sanctions on possible offenders. As concerns environmental matters, criminal law, which deals with offences and sentences,[9] and the laws establishing them,[10] aims to enact legal and regulatory measures that prevent and sanction biodiversity offences. It thus covers a heterogeneous set of norms from parliament, government or international agreements. These are measures that address biodiversity protection, deal with offences and sanctions, and regulate the conservation, sustainable use or exploitation of biological resources and the fair and equitable sharing of benefits that stem from the use of genetic resources.[11]

The biological diversity,[12] or variability of living organisms of all origins (individuals and populations)[13] and the ecological complexes of which they are part, includes diversity among species and between species and ecosystems.[14] According to the Convention of Biological Diversity (CBD), biodiversity includes landscape diversity including an ecological[15] or cultural[16] sense of a given region.

However, this chapter focuses on protecting biodiversity in wildlife reserves through criminal law measures. The level of protection of different species depends on whether they are fully or partially protected. Section 2(8)(a) of Decree No. 95/PM/466 of 20 July 1995 lays down conditions for the implementation of wildlife regulations, underlining the preservation of endangered animal, plant and habitat species. This chapter, therefore, focuses only on "protected" threatened plant and animal species as well as the environment and habitats necessary for the life of these species.

---

9 Trousse (1956).

10 Haus (1873: 1).

11 Article 1 of the Convention on Biological Diversity.

12 Biodiversity, comes from the Greek word "bios" that means "life" or from Latin word "diversitas" which is the contraction of the biology diversity concept. However, the use of the term in its contracted form is from the biologist Wilson following a presentation in 1985, see <http://www.gnis.fr/index/action/page/id/233/title/> (accessed 12-7-2018).

13 De Sadeleer & Born (2004: 17).

14 Article 2 of the Convention on Biological Diversity. Ecosystem diversity refers to different habitats or environments that exist on earth like tropical or temperate forests, hot or cold deserts, wetlands, lakes, mountains, shrub steppes, and coral reefs.

15 In the ecological sense, the landscape refers to a portion of heterogeneous territory composed of interrelated sets of ecosystems, and is characterised by geomorphological and climatic constants.

16 A cultural landscape refers to a topographically defined territory whose aspect results from the combined action between the nature and man. Defined by the World Heritage Committee (No. 231), it refers to Category V of protected areas.

Today, environmental protection appears as an imperative towards which many policies[17] must converge in order to ensure their effectiveness.[18] From this point of view, criminal law seems to be an essential tool, at least when the sanctions it enacts are both dissuasive and proportionate in the protection of biodiversity. Environmental offences may be subject to both criminal and administrative sanctions. In fact, the Forestry Law of 1994 allows the administrative agents to impose sanctions against perpetrators of offences in the wildlife reserves and apply transactional fines with the authorisation of the State Counsel. These administrative and criminal sanctions have a punitive and restorative aim. This implies the possibility of imposing administrative fines for all environmental offences. In Cameroon, these administrative sanctions are implemented, not alongside criminal sanctions, but often in their stead. This is sometimes ambiguous because they mask the legibility and coherence of environmental policies. In this respect, the effectiveness of these sanctions in deterring prohibited conduct may be questioned, especially since criminal sanctions have a reputation of being ineffective, and even inappropriate.[19]

The perceptible contrast between criminal provisions and the persistence, or even aggravation, of environmental problems they are supposed to solve, raises the question of the role of criminal law in promoting sustainability. While the author partially agrees with the doctrine[20] linking this ineffectiveness to the disregard for local customs and practices, the fact remains that this ineffectiveness is primarily dependent on the very nature of repressive provisions that protect wildlife reserves in Cameroon, and especially their lax application by courts. Beyond the subjectivity of judgements concerning the state of criminal law,[21] legislative drafting today should look for a more rigorous approach taking into account the forms and causes of damages to the environment.

If the protection of certain aspects of forest biodiversity has already been examined in some works[22] in Cameroon, very few consider it in relation to the legal value of protected property.[23] Yet this vision would not only set the limits of criminal law protection but also guide the choice of the most adequate incrimination technique to ensure appropriate protection of biodiversity. Thus, the construction of incriminations as concerns environmental questions should, as a matter of priority, take into consideration biodiversity as a preserved social value, disconnected from all the links with human interests, while totally integrating man in everything that makes up the environment. This conception implies a global vision of biodiversity that promotes both the

17 Tunc (1977: 31-35).
18 We speak of effectiveness when the law enforcement bodies apply the criminal sanction.
19 Fossier (2017: 1).
20 Nguiffo & Talla (2010: 61).
21 Albertini (2015: 331).
22 Nguiffo (2001); Triplet (2009: 7); Bille & Picard (2007: 27); and WafoTabopba (2008: 9).
23 D'Ambrosio (2015: 90).

analysis of species and their habitat and which would include local residents as potential victims of the degradation of their living environment. The destruction of biodiversity has repercussions on all living things and necessarily affects the quality of life of humans, their health, feeding and that of their children, etc. With the disappearance of medicinal and consumable species, the first victims of destruction are the local residents who see their livelihoods becoming scarce[24] and their fundamental right[25] to a concrete and visible[26] quality environment violated.

The putting in place of a criminal policy in the domain of wildlife reserve management in Cameroon is at the heart of the dialectic between the will to preserve ecological balance and the generally preeminent desire to, in no way, disrupt the development of economic activities. This is surely what justifies the contrasted application of existing repressive norms.

2 A textual application of the criminal law protection of biodiversity in the wildlife reserves of Cameroon

The violation of the standards regulating use, exploitation and management of fauna resources within the protected areas is criminally punishable even if these standards remain bound to administrative law.[27] This category of administrative sanctions is apprehended more widely as one applied by the public administration.[28] The essential of the definition of the offence is dictated by administrative authorities and supplemented by an external definition.[29] In this respect, for the wrongful conduct to be sanctioned, it must necessarily be cumulated with non-compliance with an administrative regulation.[30] These sanctions are mainly aimed at protecting endangered animal species and secondarily at protecting the surrounding biodiversity.

---

24 Thus considered, it seems interesting to raise the awareness of local communities on the urgency and importance of their participation to the improvement of their condition, since it is up to them to gather all the necessary efforts to maintain and increase the productivity of protected species by adopting sustainable management methods.

25 Prieur (2003). The fundamental right to a quality environment refers to "the right for everyone to live in a balanced and healthy environment". This is an absolute necessity for Man whose existence on earth as well as the development goals seem seriously compromised by human activities.

26 Prieur (2005: 1160).

27 Ost (1995: 287).

28 Perrier (2017: 1).

29 Estupinal-Silva (2015: 66).

30 Deffairi (2016: 176).

2.1 An increased criminal law protection of endangered species

The Cameroonian legislator has chosen to map out geographic areas regulating access to and use of their resources. This technique is favourable for the survival of wildlife species and their development in their natural habitat.[31] This involves reserving part of the public domain by enacting police regulations in order to prevent damages to biodiversity[32] and, in certain cases, to reduce the sometimes irreversible,[33] pressure exerted by individuals on nature. With the creation of wildlife reserves, the legislator was more interested in things – in this case the endangered wildlife – that are not yet "patrimonialised"[34] or individualised in a certain manner, but that can be dynamic and/or changing. That is why the legislator has resorted to criminal sanctions as a guarantee for the application[35] of environmental standards.

The criminal norms for protecting the fauna are contained in various texts.[36] They criminalise behaviours that violate administrative and regulatory provisions related to the environment. In this respect, the law establishes a set of actions that are subject to strict prohibition or regulation, the violation of which becomes an offence; but as a general rule, it can be seen that the administrative authorities have the power to impose pecuniary sanctions in any case, to sanction either the lack of authorisation to hunt or the non-compliance to applicable rules.[37] It is for this reason that the company Saf Bois was sentenced to pay a fine of 3,980,000 FCFA for exploiting the national estate without authorisation.[38]

Traditional hunting is the only form of hunting that is carried out without a licence as long as it remains non-commercial. This right was acquired since colonial times[39] and concerns rodents, small reptiles, birds and other animals of Class C.[40] However, in order to limit its degrading effects[41] on biodiversity, it was regulated and limited to

---

31 Ly & Ngaide (2008: 89).

32 Martin (1995: 135); Martin (1992: 11); and Clay (2003: 1489).

33 For a research, see Fritz-Legendre (1998: 96); and Cans & de Klemm (1998: 119).

34 Tricot (2015: 145).

35 Beccaria (1856: 57).

36 Finally, hunting without prior authorisation of wildlife species classified on lists B and C which contain animals open to hunting is totally prohibited in accordance with the provisions of Section 15 of Decree No. 95/466/PM. Section 85 of the framework law of 5 August 1996 on the environment extends the competence of environmental sanctions to the Penal Code and to specific laws applicable to environmental protection.

37 Bush meat is subject to trade, but in addition to the existence of a list of protected animals contained in Order No. 0565/A/MINEF/DFAP/SDF/SRC, administrative authorities condition this activity to the respect of transparency and traceability standards contained in the Washington international convention of 3 March 1973 on the trade in endangered wildlife, ratified on 5 June 1981.

38 Ministry of Forests and Wildlife, press release No. 031/MINFOF/CAB/BNC of 5 July 2005.

39 Kamto (1996: 148).

40 Section 24 paragraph 2 of Decree No. 95/4466/PM.

41 Mafoua (1991: 122).

the slaughter of authorised games. All other forms of hunting, regardless of the method used, are either prohibited or subject to authorisation. This is the case with sport hunting usually carried out by tourists with weapons authorised by law.[42]

Administrative penalties that can be applied are of various types and levels of severity: they range from the suspension or revocation of the hunting permit or licence to the confiscation of the products harvested, or the restitution and even the injunction for the restoration of the degraded place.[43] Thus, Section 71(1) of Decree No. 95/466/PM of 20 July 1995 lays down the conditions for the implementation of wildlife regulations providing that the approval given to an operator can be suspended or withdrawn by the administrative authorities and suspension is pronounced in case of recidivism.[44] In this case, it is no longer the lack of authorisation, but the non-compliance with the rules governing the practice of hunting. In the same vein, Section 144 of the Forest Law allows the administration to sell the seized perishable products by public auction.[45] Section 142 of the same law provides that the sworn agents shall, upon the finding of the facts, seize the wrongly harvested products and the articles used to commit the offence and draw up a report. They exercise a right of action against offenders.

Under the system of administrative authorisation, the criminal law protection of wildlife reserves is "somewhat masked by the protection of administrative action"[46] exercised by officials of the Ministry of Forests. Through this mechanism of textual anticipation, the legislator incriminates offences against wildlife by establishing a presumption of risk with respect to certain human behaviours. This anticipation allows, at least ideally, the prevention of abusive infringements of protected species, but also, and above all, facilitates the incrimination procedure, especially through the insistence on the proofs of the offence. In this respect, it seems possible to conclude, that poor knowledge of environmental standards, even if it does not immediately cause damage to the wildlife environment, is likely to lead to the punishment of its perpetrator. This is how environmental offences are managed by the criminal law that ensures the protection of endangered species through monitoring and planning by the administration. In this regard, the application seems close to the repressive law of the environment through the severity of the means used[47] to protect endangered fauna species.

Given that they are pronounced very rapidly by the administration because of their simplicity and especially the immediate knowledge of the infringement, administrative sanctions generally precede criminal penalties. Once pronounced, and when the

---

42 According to the provisions of Section 29 of Decree No. 95/466/PM of 20 July 1995.

43 Prabhu (1994: 669).

44 In the commission of an offence punishable by a fine of at least 3,000,000 FCFA.

45 Or by mutual agreement, in the absence of a bidder, by the competent administration, except for those that are dangerous or damaged.

46 D'Ambrosio (2015: 90).

47 Estupinan-Silva (2015: 26).

measures they ordered enforced, or the lack of hunting permit regularised, criminal action is no longer necessary. But, on closer inspection, these measures are more regulatory than punitive. The punitive logic becomes secondary since the non-respect of these administrative measures may be subject to criminal sanctions.

In this regard, the law of 1994 sets up criminal sanctions for some offences committed in wildlife reserves in Cameroon and the penalties provided for are applicable without prejudice to confiscations, restitution, damages and remediation of the site as ordered by the administrative officials. These penalties are doubled in the event of recidivism or if it is a sworn officer of the competent administration or a judicial police officer with general jurisdiction who commit the corresponding offences, or if they are accomplices. This is without prejudice to the administrative and disciplinary sanctions. The penalties are also doubled for any hunting with the use of chemical or toxic products, violation of forest control barriers and in the event of a hit-and-run offence or refusal to comply with the injunctions of control officers. Furthermore, unauthorised traffic in a protected area is punishable with a fine of from 5,000 to 50,000 FCFA and/or imprisonment for ten days.[48] Section 155 of the 1994 Law provides for a term of imprisonment of from twenty days to two years and a fine of from 50,000 to 200,000 FCFA or one of these sentences, against any person engaged in hunting without the required licence or permit.[49] In addition, the sentences set out are in principle applied without a stay of execution or mitigating circumstances[50] as provided for by criminal law.[51]

However, Cameroonian jurisprudence rather seems lenient against offenders and imposes very light sentences, often whimsical and reduced by mitigating circumstances and stay of execution.[52] For instance, the Yabassi Court of First Instance, after finding the defendant guilty of slaughtering and moving around protected animals without a hunting permit, granted him mitigation circumstances.[53] Similarly, the Court of First Instance of Ebolowa by Judgement No. 480/COR of 6 September 2011, sentenced the defenders, found guilty of illegally keeping fully protected animals and capturing Class A species without a capture permit, to two months imprisonment and 150,000 and 100,000 FCFA fine respectively. This stand of Cameroonian jurisprudence is in contradiction with the repressive environmental provisions, in particular,

48 Section 154 of law No. 94/01 of 20 January 1994 to lay down forestry, wildlife and fisheries regulations.

49 Section 91 and following of the law of 20 January 1994.

50 Section 87 of the framework law of 1996 on environmental management in Cameroon.

51 Section 54 and 94 of Cameroon's new Penal Code of 2016.

52 The Judicial decisions sanction the capture of Class A species without licence (cf. the Yabassi Court of First Instance, Judgement No. 43/COR of 4 November 2003), the marketing of Class B animals without collection permit or certificate of origin, the slaughtering of protected animals without a hunting permit, the detention and illegal marketing of panther skin, etc.

53 Yabassi Court of First Instance, Judgement No. 43/COR of 4 November 2003.

Article 87 of the 1996 framework law. It is a position that is likely to encourage negligent or fraudulent behaviours or even the express violation of the law by offenders.

As it can be seen, repressive environmental law is multidimensional in nature.[54] It makes the distinction between administrative offences and purely repressive offences. The purely repressive offences consist of acts or omissions relating to the destruction of wildlife species, depletion or management of natural resources. The penal legislator does not necessarily require a material element of the result. To this end, the infringement is established when the existence of a behaviour endangering the life of the protected animal species is proven. Thus, the Court of First Instance of Yaounde administrative centre found a defendant guilty of illegally detaining ivory tusks and marketing game trophies[55] and sentenced him to a 30-day suspended prison sentence and a fine of 100,000 FCFA. The same sentence was applied to a person convicted of possessing and selling elephant trophies.[56]

If at first sight, such a position seems to violate the principle of *nullum crimen sine injuria* as denounced by the doctrine.[57] At the practical level it allows, however, for the rehabilitation of the object of the offence by annihilating the requirement of causality and result.[58] Criminal liability requires criminal intent,[59] but this intent is equated with gross negligence in environmental criminal law, for environmental crimes are not often isolated facts, but continuous facts where actions and omissions blend with a psychological aspect often linked to negligence rather than intent.

Wildlife liability may affect not only individuals but also legal entities. To this end, Article 150(1) of the law of 20 January 1994 states that: “Any individual or legal entity found guilty of violating the provisions of this law and its implementing instruments shall be liable and punishable in accordance with the penalties provided therefor”. Thus, Cameroonian environmental law is concerned with the criminal enterprise and henceforth permits the inclusion of legal persons and administrative agents involved in the commission of an offence within the circle of responsibilities.[60]

Furthermore, in providing for offences for failure to comply with legal requirements, the legislator sets a presumption of knowledge of the rules against the offender and, at the same time, excludes the error of law as a defence and retains only the factual error or lack of diligence. This solution of environmental criminal law seems interesting since it allows for proactive action, before the realisation of any hindrance, so as to prevent reprehensible behaviours.[61] Here, the penal legislator will not make the

54 Estupinan-Silva (2015: 26).

55 Yaounde Court of First Instance, Judgement No. 1201/CO of 17 December 2003.

56 Ibid.

57 Carraccioli (1994: 1013).

58 Minko-Ndongo (2015: 45).

59 Kalda (2014: 51).

60 Article 150 paragraph 2 the law of 20 January 1994.

61 It is an anthropocentric vision that considers environmental protection as a means of protection of the human interests and not as an intrinsically protected value by itself.

reprehensible behaviour disappear, but rather try to make it as respectful as possible of the critical state of biodiversity in the wildlife reserves. Consequently, protection and liability may present an apparent contradiction.[62] In fact, holders of permits or licences to hunt or slaughter protected species are exempted from the criminal responsibility, even when they capture an endangered species.

It is, however, regrettable that Cameroonian courts only marginally engage criminal actions against perpetrators of massive destruction of the wildlife. These jurisprudential hesitations may be indicators that could prompt legislative action for the acknowledgement of an autonomous place of repressive law within Cameroonian criminal law.

2.2 An indispensable protection of biodiversity in wildlife reserves

In order to preserve biodiversity in the wildlife reserves, the Cameroonian legislator has established a set of criminal rules to stop the threat of their impoverishment. Sustainable protection of species can only be guaranteed if living conditions are also guaranteed. In this respect, the preservation of the tropical fauna also implies the preservation of the living space of wild animals. It is within this perspective that, in defining the wildlife reserve, the legislator refers it to the natural habitat of species.[63] The legislator has made a choice of a conservation policy of natural ecosystems and habitats and a policy of maintaining and restoring viable populations in their natural environment.[64]

Although not explicitly specified by the legislator, it is conservation *in situ*,[65] which implies monitoring and protection of the wildlife found in a given space and which is of a certain interest for man. This conservation, entails less cost[66] than *ex situ* conservation[67] and extends to nearby zones to protected areas. This technique increases the limits of criminal law protection, by promoting sustainable and ecologically sound development. These areas are generally places where feed is available or that are suitable for nesting and mating.[68] Article 154 of the law of 20 January 1994 provides that contacts with neighbouring populations of wildlife reserves should be as little as possible.

62 Tricot (2015: 145).

63 Article 2(7) of Decree No. 95/466/PM 20 July 1995 to lay down the conditions for the implementation of wildlife regulations.

64 Article 2 of the 1992 Convention on Biodiversity.

65 It is not clearly stated in the text that wildlife reserves would be the subject of the *in situ* conservation, but there is no indication to the contrary; and according to Article 9 of the Convention on Biodiversity, measures adopted for the *ex situ* conservation complement those taken for *in situ* conservation.

66 Gonmadje et al. (2015: 46).

67 Guideline No. 2004/35/CE, Appendix II, Article 1(d).

68 ITIO Directive for the Conservation and Sustainable Use of Biodiversity in Tropical Timber-Producing Forests, Development Policy No. 17 OIBT/ITTO/UICN 2009 2.

To this effect, any provocation of wild animals is forbidden. Similarly, freedom of movement is also restricted.

In addition, the legislator sets up buffer zones[69] located at the periphery of wildlife reserves that enjoy the same criminal law protection as the overall biodiversity. The criminal law insists on the protection of endangered species and provides, to that effect, a set of measures that regulate all human activities likely to have an impact on them and their living environment. This is the case with the prohibition of bushfires and any activity that could affect, in one way or the other, the living environment of protected organisms within wildlife reserves. Indigenous and local populations cannot freely exercise their right of use on the preserved space. The exploitation of products of reserves is only allowed if it does not alter the course of forest productivity. The new Penal Code, in Articles 187, 187(1) and 227, as well as the law of 20 January 1994 in Articles 155 and 156 penalise fire, destructions and any other form of degradation. The penalty is doubled if the perpetrator or the accomplice is in a state of recidivism or belongs to the administrative body.

The protection of biodiversity in wildlife reserves seems essential insofar as it is necessary to protect the entire environment where the endangered species live. It is therefore important to provide an adequate response to environmental management as a whole by including all the components of the ecosystem because there is no sustainable development that does not take into account this essential fact, especially the one that wild flora and fauna are unpredictable natural elements. Forest degradation could have a negative impact on the communities that live within them and whose means of subsistence largely depend on products found in their living environment.

For this reason, the use of forest resources and space is subject to a strict legal framework that limits its duration and extent. Thus, all uses for economic purposes are subject to obtaining a permit from the forest administration and must comply with the objectives set by the latter. The law justifies this incursion into the private domain by ecological motivations, the imperative nature of which explains the necessity for the State to intervene, at the expense of the owner. Thus considered, the concessions authorising wildlife management are limited in time (15 years renewable once). They are also limited in space (200,000 ha) and material extent of the right transferred to the licensee. The legislator also regulates the prerogatives of the populations resulting from the appropriation and use of lands, keeping only those that allow for biodiversity conservation. Some of these prerogatives regulated include the mutilation of protected species, grazing, logging,[70] etc. The aim is to contribute to the protection of

69 Kamto (1996: 203).

70 Ibid: 200.

biodiversity by developing measures to regulate activities likely to have a negative impact on the survival of wild animal species[71] and their natural environment.[72]

Despite the existence of all the aforementioned conservation measures with criminal penalties for non-performance, the state of degradation of wildlife reserves of Cameroon continues to worsen. It seems that economic interests are taking precedence over environmental considerations. This is because it is difficult to reconcile what cannot be reconciled, in other words, to optimise the exploitation of wildlife resources while taking into account the imperative of sustainable development, and especially to fight against poverty effectively. The helplessness of the administrative agents, if not their inability to rigorously react after each serious attack to the biodiversity, bears witness to this reality. Therefore, the effective enforcement of the environmental criminal law in force in Cameroon is far from being a priority. However, penal sanctions play a considerable preventive role in environmental matters, because as Plato recalled in the antiquity:[73]

> He who cares to punish cleverly do not strike because of the past - what is done is done - but for anticipation of the future, so that neither the culprit nor the witnesses of this punishment be tempted to begin all over.

Repressive texts do set criminal sanctions against biodiversity offenders, but these texts are rarely applied to the intended extent. In any case, the lack of vitality of criminal law in environmental matters, and especially the side-lining of local residents in the drafting of criminal policy in the domain of biodiversity protection seems to explain the gap that still exists between the drafting of standards and their practical implementation.

3 A contrasted real application of repressive rules in the protection of biodiversity in wildlife reserves

Urbanisation, intensive exploitation of soils, mines and quarries, agriculture, the development of infrastructure[74] and demographic explosion are all causes of destruction of the habitats of species and consequently of the biodiversity crisis. Indeed, the fundamentally anthropocentric vision of the world pushes men to place their interests over those of non-human entities, despite the repressive measures that can be taken to ensure the conservation of the latter. Thus, infringements on biodiversity are commonplace in spite of penal sanctions provided for to this effect by the legislator. Several factors can justify this situation including the ambiguous and limited nature of the

71 Prieur (2004: 8).
72 Despax (1980: IX 8).
73 Plato (1984: 39).
74 de Sadeleer & Born (2004: 15).

penal provisions that regulate activities in the wildlife reserves of Cameroon and their inadequacy with the contemporary environmental requirements.

3.1 The ambiguity of repressive provisions for the protection of biodiversity in wildlife reserves

A reading of the repressive provisions punishing offences committed in Cameroon wildlife reserves reveal, at first glance, a lack of cohesion and above all a lack of convergence between the various sanctions provided for in cases of violation. This is likely to generate conflicts of the laws and especially a competitive dynamic between the various texts that can be applied. The competition is necessary with regard to the transaction that is easily proposed by the administration[75] since the 1996 framework law on environment provides that the public action shall cease when the perpetrator has fulfilled all the obligations resulting for him from the acceptance of the transaction within the time limit set.[76] This competition results in the termination of criminal proceedings following the execution of administrative sanctions. The transaction replaces criminal prosecution, since it is implemented in their stead.

This distinguishing effect of criminal prosecution is all the more disconcerting as the environmental transaction has a very wide field of application in Cameroonian law. In fact, pursuant to Article 91(1) of the framework law of 1996, the administrations responsible for environmental management have full power to make a deal.[77] Thus, it is possible for the administration to implement the transaction for any environmental offence provided for by the legislator. It should be noted that the Cameroonian legislator has not set any limit that would exclude the transaction for offences of particular gravity for the biodiversity either because of the consequences that they could engender, for example, the definitive extinction of a species protected or because of the *modus operandi*.

Owing to the fact that it allows a fine to be proposed to the offender, the amount of which may not be less than the minimum amount of the corresponding criminal fine,[78] it seems obvious that the environmental transaction is repressive. This is especially so since the transaction is most often the concertation between the prosecution and the competent administrative authority.[79] It allows the administration to propose a sanction of a punitive nature. The environmental transaction provides a simple, quick and inexpensive response to offences concerning biodiversity violations in wildlife reserves of

75 Mayer (2014: 523).
76 Section 146 and following of the law of 20 January 1994.
77 Also see the provisions of Articles 146 and 147 of law No. 94/01 of 20 January 1994.
78 Article 91 paragraph 2 of the framework law of 1996 on environmental management in Cameroon.
79 Perrier (2017: 2).

Cameroon. However, it is important to know whether these transactional measures are effective and dissuasive enough to ensure the prevention of damage to biodiversity.

While it is undeniable that environmental transaction provides a repressive response to the offence on biodiversity, its effectiveness in preventing such harm is questionable. Indeed, the transaction is not dissuasive. This lack of deterrence should encourage the Cameroonian legislator to limit the recourse to transaction only to minor infringements. For more serious offences, including illegal hunting of endangered species, it would be preferable to resort to sufficiently severe criminal sanctions. It is possible that the mere threat of imprisonment can help to achieve the prevention goal as sought for in international standards.

Moreover, it is not always obvious to have sufficient coherence in the penalties provided for by the Cameroonian legislator. The Penal Code provides for stronger penalties, with heavier prison sentences than the specific texts applicable to wildlife reserves. Thus, Section 155 of the Penal Code provides for, apart from the fine, an imprisonment term of 20 days to two months for the felling of protected trees. Section 184 of the Penal Code penalises a degradation of public or classified property by imprisonment from one month to two years. The same applies to the burning and destruction of property for which the Forest Law provides a prison sentence of six months, while the Penal Code sets a prison sentence from three to ten years. More so, when cases are brought to court, flexible sentences are often applied to offenders. The Ebolowa Court of First Instance, for example, sentenced a defendant to only two months in prison and a fine of 150,000 FCFA for illegal detention of fully protected animals and the capture of Class A species without a permit.

The discrepancies between the various criminal penalties are due to the fact that the forestry law focuses on taxation to the detriment of penal rigour. In fact, the legislator favours the pecuniary nature of penalties in disregard of the deterrent impact that could have more severe incriminations on the behaviour of those that the penal norms target. For example, Article 75 of Decree No. 95/466/PM favours the confiscation and auctioning of products from poaching, to the benefit of the administration. In practice, this criminal policy implemented in environmental matters does not have the desired effect on offenders because the amounts allocated for damages resulting from the commission of wildlife offences are often derisory in relation to the gravity of the offence. Imposing fines as the only criminal sanction applicable in the event of a violation of repressive environmental provisions does not seem judicious insofar as it seems insufficient compared to the severity of damages on the environment. In some cases, damage are irreversible, such as the complete disappearance of the western black rhino from Cameroonian territory in 2011.[80]

Generally, many factors contribute to the degradation of biodiversity in Cameroon. The role that criminal legislation should play is to adopt means and instruments that

80 For research see Prouteau-Lagrot (2007: 80).

can combat the daily delinquency that rages the wildlife reserves more effectively and promote the sustainable conservation of species and their habitat. An overhaul of criminal provisions in this domain seems urgent. Thus, in order to put an end to the profitability of environmental criminality and to strengthen the effectiveness of criminal responses, it seems essential that the state adopts sanctions that are equivalent to the gravity of environmental crimes. Penal sanctions should be defined according to the quality of the offenders and especially as regards the specificity of the offence. The individualisation of sentences would make it possible to apply the most appropriate sanction depending on the nature of the offence, the profile of the offender, the damage caused etc.[81]

3.2 Obsolescence of repressive provisions for the protection of wildlife reserves

In developing countries like Cameroon, local populations require opportunities to gain access to the resources which they need to survive. Environmental resources such as wildlife reserves often appear as a public utility that meets the criteria of non-exclusion.[82] The use of such utility is in principle free and not subjected to any formality or authorisation. It is a recognised subjective right[83] of local residents, that is justiciable[84] and opposable to third parties.[85]

This right of use, however, is nevertheless regulated in wildlife reserves. Damage to preserved species is allowed only in cases of self-defence.[86] Articles 82 and 83 of the law of 20 January 1994 exempt any person who kills or injures a classified animal in self-defence without provoking it from criminal liability. Similarly, the administration can proceed to controlled push-backs, when animals pose a danger to people or property. Apart from these protective measures, local populations whose survival depends on forest resources have largely been ignored by legal provisions.[87] The right of use of these communities within protected areas is subject to limitations (e.g. Article 5 of the decree of 20 July 1995).[88] These limitations at times generate conflicts between the

81 Fouchard & Neyret (2015: 415).

82 Bacache-Beauvallet (2008: 35).

83 Ibid.

84 Favoreau (2008: 1228-1230).

85 Nonaros (1996: 216); and Dabin (1952: 80-92).

86 Nevertheless, the person must prove the state of self-defence within 72 hours. If not they are liable to another offence punishable by a fine of 5,000 to 20,000 francs and/or 20 days to two months in prison (Article 155 of the law of 1994).

87 The legislator has voluntarily excluded the riparian population from the circle of people to be protected, even as the notion of environment is far from being an abstraction, but rather considered in its entirety.

88 These are the rights granted to the riparian population "to harvest all forest, wildlife and fisheries products freely for their personal use, except the protected species". See Article 8 of the law of 1994.

respect of the law on the one hand and ancestral practices on the other.[89] Indeed, the penalties imposed on members of indigenous communities often increases the hostility of these groups populations against the criminal law. In one case, for example, the Dschang Court of First Instance sentenced the defendants convicted of destroying a protected area to a six-month suspended prison sentence and a fine of 50,000 FCFA. By doing so, the court ignored the fact, that the defendants were not only poorly educated but also their state of necessity when exploiting environmental resources.

The local population's distrust of the law is exacerbated by the granting of exploitation rights to foreigners. An example is a case in the northern region, where the State transferred 19 out of 28 hunting areas to foreigners[90] to the detriment of local populations' pastures.

The exclusion of local populations from responsible protection of protected areas is one of the major flaws of the policy of conservation of wildlife biodiversity in Cameroon. Only participatory inclusion through the involvement (and not the exclusion or taxation) of local populations in the organisation, valorisation and management of wildlife reserves, can reduce the threat of extinction of vulnerable species. Residents of wildlife reserves live in a precarious situation, which requires improved dialogue and the consideration of their existential problems. The State should rather grant these groups subsidies to foster their enthusiasm about preserving the reserves linked to their ancestral heritage In addition, such grants could develop profitable alternative activities that enable local populations to take care of their most vital need and at the same time contribute to biodiversity protection in the form of payment for environmental services.[91]

Cameroonian environmental law is also drifting away from its international environmental law obligations. Despite a cautious introduction of innovative elements through the incorporation of international principles developed in 1992 in Rio, Cameroon's repressive laws attempt to make wildlife resources contribute to economic development at the cost of ecological, social and cultural concerns. Far from being a protective law, Cameroon's environmental criminal law largely focusses on use and exploitation of natural resources, providing economic privileges over sustainable ecosystems.

89 Barume (2004: 14).

90 Which moreover carries three parks of 730,000 ha and a vast ZIC of more than 2,000,000 ha. It is important to note that in 1986, there were 15 ZICs in the North for a total area of 729,390 ha. In 1996, this number rose to 27 and 28 in 1998. These 28 ZICs have a precise distribution: 23 are leased to hunting guides, three are managed by the state, one is allocated to the Lamido of Rey Bouba and one is intended for experimentation of a game-ranch.

91 Payments for environmental services (PES) are incentives that provide compensation in exchange for adopting practices that are conducive to the preservation of environment. They are based on contractual constructions that may involve private actors (landowners, companies, associations...) and public actors (the state, local authorities...).

While for instance the precautionary principle under the Rio Declaration was incorporated in various national texts (e.g. Article 9 of the framework law of 1996 on environmental management), Cameroon's forest criminal law is still contrary to principles of rational management of wildlife resources. In many cases, the forest administration continues to use unsustainable methods geared towards generating income for the national economy. The prescribed hunting season, for example, partially overlaps with the gestation periods for female animals, thereby promoting the interests of hunters over those of wildlife.

However, a more efficient management of protected areas should be adapted to conditions which best foster the protection of biological diversity. Protected sites could serve as an experimental approach to enhance the management, reproduction and protection of endangered species. Research students from different universities in Cameroon could benefit from scholarships to carry out field studies in the company of guards working in the reserves.[92] This would foster scientific knowledge on the one hand and strengthen a more cautious approach to the management of biodiversity on the other. Investigating commercial activities' impacts on forests and wildlife are equally essential. Although the implementation of certain environmental protection measures is costly, these could be funded by increasing returns from tourism. All of the aforementioned would contribute to an improved wildlife reserves governance in Cameroon.

4 Conclusion

There are many expectations regarding the repression of damages on biodiversity in Cameroon's protected areas. One of them is to enshrine ecocide[93] crimes in environmental penal law envisaging punitive damages.[94] Environmental offences are often lucrative in nature, committed voluntarily in the interest of commercial profit. In the same light, repressive biodiversity protection policies should not only consider the degradation of ecosystems but also the vulnerabilities of the poorest populations. Criminal law protection of biodiversity in wildlife reserves should be an ethical duty towards the threatened future and survival of both man and ecosystems.[95] As a proverb puts it so well, "when the last tree has been cut down, the last fish caught, the last river poisoned, only then will we realise that one cannot eat money."

---

92 In this sense, impact studies carried out by these reserves would enable MINFOF (the supervisory Ministry) to locate the difficult sectors and set up integrated study scenarios. Indeed, it is impossible that, on the field, MINFOF officials be the judge and party at the same time. The impact studies have the advantage of encouraging planning that goes along with monitoring and evaluation of the different projects initiated.

93 This involves the massive destruction of flora and fauna, as well as the implementation of any action that would cause an ecological disaster.

94 Lambert-Faivre (1998).

95 Thibierge (2013: 577).

References

Albertini, P (2015) *La crise de la loi: déclin ou mutation?*

Bacache-Beauvallet, M (2008) "Marché et droit, la logique économique du droit de l'environnement" 4 *Pouvoirs* 35-47.

Barume, AK (2004) *Cadre juridique et coutumier pour la protection des droits des peuples indigènes et tribaux (autochtones) au Cameroun: points d'entrée*, 2éme version initiale.

Beccaria, C (1856) *Des délits et des peines.*

Bille, R & R Picard (2007) *La conservation de la biodiversité dans le cadre de l'aide au développement: une synthèse critique*, at <https://www.iddri.org/sites/default/files/import/publications/an_0701_bille%26pirard_biodivetdevpmt.pdf> (accessed 20-7-2018).

Cans, C & C de Klemm (1998) "Un cas d'irréversibilité : l'introduction d'espèces exogènes dans le milieu naturel" *RJE* 119.

Carraccioli, I (1994) "La protection de l'environnement en droit pénal italien" 65 *RIDP* 1013.

Clay, J (2003) "Arbitrage et droit de l'environnement" 149 *Gazette du Palais* 10.

Cornu, G (2011) *Vocabulaire juridique* 9th ed.

Dabin, J (1952) *Droit subjectif.*

D'Ambrosio, L (2015) "Vers un droit pénal commun de l'environnement: critères et techniques d'incrimination" in L Neyret (ed.) *Des éco-crimes à l'écocide, le droit pénal au secours de l'environnement* 90.

Deffairi, M (2016) "Le recours aux instruments économiques; facteur de modernisation et/ou de simplification du droit de l'environnement" in I Doussan (ed.) *Les futurs du droit de l'environnement: simplification, modernisation, régression?* 176.

de Sadeleer, N & CH Born (2004) *Droit international et communautaire de la biodiversité.*

Estupinan-Silva, R (2015) "Report on the Ecocide Project" in L Neyret (ed.) *Des éco-crimes à l'écocide, le droit pénal au secours de l'environnement* 66.

Favoreau, L (2008) *Droit constitutionnel.*

Fossier, T (2017) "La nécessité et l'efficacité de la sanction pénale en droit de l'environnement" 12 *Energie-Environnement-Infrastructures* 11.

Fouchard, I & L Neyret (2015) "35 propositions pour mieux sanctionner les crimes contre l'environnement" in L Neyret (ed.) *Des éco-crimes à l'écocide, le droit pénal au secours de l'environnement* 415.

Fritz-Legendre, M (1998) "Biodiversité et irréversibilité" 96 *RJE* 79-100.

Gonmadje, CF, JB Donfack & J Kengue (2015) *L'état des ressources forestières mondiales – Cameroon National Report.*

Kalda, G (2014) *Contrat et droit pénal* Dissertation Master II, University of Yaounde II.

Kamto, M (1996) *Droit de l'environnement en Afrique.*

Lambert-Faivre, Y (1998) "L'Ethique de la responsabilité" *RTD civ* 1-22.

Ly, I & M Ngaide (2008) *Droit de l'environnement au Sénégal.*

Martin, G (1995) "La notion de responsabilité en matière de dommage écologique" *Droit et environnement : propos pluridisciplinaires sur le droit en construction PUAM* 135.

Martin, G (1992) "Dommage écologique en droit interne, communautaire et comparé" *Economica* 11.

Minko-Ndongo, MN (2015) *La problématique de la protection juridique des réserves de faune au Cameroun*, Dissertation, Master II, University of Yaounde II.

Nguiffo, S & M Talla (2010) "Législation relative à la faune sauvage au Cameroun: entre usage locaux et perception légale" 236(61) *Unasylva* 14-18.

Nguiffo, S (2001) "Cameroun: la réserve de la faune du DJA" *Peuples autochtones* 197-216.

Nonaros, M (1996) "L'évolution récente de la notion de droit subjectif" *RTD civ* 216.

ITTO / International Tropical Timber Organization (2009) *Guidelines for the conservation and sustainable use of biodiversity in tropical timber production forests policy development* No. 17 OIBT/ITTO/UICN 2.

Ost, F (1995) "La responsabilité, fil d'Ariane du droit de l'environnement" *Droit et société* 287.

Perrier, JB (2017) "La répression des infractions environnementales, à la recherche de sanctions proportionnées, efficaces et dissuasives" 12 *Energie-Environnement-Infrastructures* Dossier spécial 1.

Plato (1984) *Œuvres complètes* Tome III Les belles lettres.

Prabhu, M (1994) "Rapport général. Les atteintes à l'environnement: problèmes de droit pénal général" 65 *RIDP* 663-669.

Prieur, M (2003) "Vers un droit de l'environnement renouvelé" *RJE* 130-139.

Prieur, M (2005) "Les droits nouveaux" *AJDA* 1160.

Prouteau-Lagrot, I (2007) *Probable extinction du Rhinocéros Noir de l'Ouest (Diceros bicornis longipes) Etude de terrain 2006 au Nord Cameroun* Thesis National Veterinary School, Toulouse.

Remond-Gouilloud, M (1989) *Du droit de détruire: essai sur le droit de l'environnement.*

Tchindjang, M, SA Abossollo, J Armathée & VF Menga (2006) "Les difficultés de développement de l'écotourisme dans les aires protégées du Cameroun" 26(2) *Boletim Goiano de Geografia* 12-47.

Thibierge, C (2013) "Avenir de la responsabilité, responsabilité d'avenir" *RTD civ* 577.

Tricot, J (2015) "Eco-crimes et écocide: quels responsables" in L Neyret (ed.) *Des éco-crimes à l'écocide, le droit pénal au secours de l'environnement* 145.

Triplet, P (2009) *Manuel de gestion des aires protégées d'Afrique francophone.*

Trousse, PE (1956) *Les Novelles – Droit pénal* Vol. 1(1).

Tunc, VA (1977) "Un droit en miettes" XXII *La responsabilité, Archive de philosophie* 31-35.

Wafo Tabopba, G (2008) *Les aires protégées de l'extrême nord Cameroun entre politiques de conservation et pratiques locales* Thesis Orléa.

Chapter 12: Harnessing oil as natural resource wealth: a focus on the legal frameworks of Nigeria and Uganda

Lanre Aladeitan, Robert Alex Wabunoha & Chidinma Therese Odaghara

1 Introduction

Natural resources[1] are "a gift of nature and an endowment of comfort that makes the existence of mankind complete".[2] It is a matter of debate whether resource-rich states in Africa use the resources for the comfort of the majority of their citizens. Governance of natural resources is a broad issue that raises more questions than answers. This is despite society's longstanding desire for and institutionalisation of governance norms through law. Law serves three critical roles in the governance of natural resources. Firstly, states order the behaviour of individuals and organisations in the realm of natural resources through law and legal institutions, converting economic and social policies into outcomes.[3] Secondly, the law defines the structure of government by arranging and distributing political and economic interests and power. In the case of oil, legal authority to act, political and economic power are established and distributed among the state, local host communities and extractive companies as the major stakeholders in the exploration of the resource. Thirdly, the law provides space for public participation in governance through substantive and procedural tools that promote accountability.[4]

It is not enough to have a legal framework in a resource-rich state. A pragmatic legal framework in the realm of resource governance must seek to address issues that include, how rights and benefits are allocated among stakeholders; the rights and benefits of local host communities; requirements for linking investments to the economy or creating jobs; and environmental health and safety obligations of the extractive companies. Transparency, accountability and a clear sense of purpose, however, must accompany the making of law from the onset to the point of enforcement and

1 Natural resources in the context of this chapter refer to raw materials embedded in the soil, which are extracted and modified by man for his/her benefit and use. They can be thought of as natural capital assets, distinct from physical and human capital, in that they are not created by human activity. See World Bank (2010: 44-46).

2 Aladeitan (2013: 160).

3 See World Bank (2017).

4 Ibid.

implementation for such legal framework to shore up value realisation, revenue management and the creation of an enabling environment in oil resource governance.

This chapter examines the correlation between the resource-rich state and the content of its law focusing on performance level under three key components in the 2017 Resource Governance Index (RGI).[5] These include: value realisation; revenue management; and enabling environment. It focuses on the legal frameworks[6] of Nigeria and Uganda, which have been identified as part of the 81 states that together produce 8% of the world's oil and 78% of its gas.[7]

On a scale of 100, Nigeria scored 42 points and ranked 55 among 89 assessments in the 2017 Resource Governance Index (RGI). Nigeria has the largest oil and gas reserves in sub-Saharan Africa and has the ninth largest reserve in the world.[8] It, however, faces challenges that affect value realisation, revenue management and the enabling environment in the extractive decision-making chain.[9] Similar challenges bedevil the Ugandan oil and gas sector, which was rated 44 on a scale of 100 in the 2017 RGI, placing it at number 51of the 89 states assessed in the index.[10] Uganda has 2 billion barrels proven oil reserves, which attracted exploration interest during the commodity boom of the last decade.[11] According to the RGI Report, early years of exploration in Uganda have been marked by governance challenges that include a poor licensing regime, inadequate infrastructural development and investment conditions and hostility from the local communities.[12]

To analyse the correlation between the state and the content of its law, and the performance levels in the three key components of the 2017 RGI identified above, the chapter is divided into four sections. The first section comprises the introduction. The second section assesses selected laws dealing with oil resources law in Nigeria and

5 Natural Resource Governance Institute (2017a).

6 For each project to extract natural resources from the ground, there are rules that govern the rights and responsibilities of governments, companies and citizens. Together these rules are called a legal framework, or legal architecture. The legal framework that governs the extractive industry comprises a set of documents that include the constitution, legislation, regulations and contracts. See NRGI Reader (2015).

7 The 2017 RGI assesses how 81 countries, including Nigeria and Uganda govern their oil, gas and mineral wealth. The index composite score comprises of three components: value realisation; revenue management; and the enabling environment. According to the RGI report, the overall score for both Nigeria and Uganda in oil resource governance fall within the ranking for states that exhibit serious shortcomings. See <http://resourcegovernanceindex.org/> (accessed 5-3-2018).

8 OPEC (2017).

9 Value in Nigeria's oil resource industry is lost in licensing and in the state-owned enterprise's sales of government oil, as well as when revenues from oil and gas are disbursed and saved. See Natural Resource Governance Institute (2017b).

10 Natural Resource Governance Institute (2017c).

11 Ibid.

12 The 2017 RGI assesses how 81 resource-rich states govern their oil, gas and mineral wealth. See Natural Resource Governance Institute (2017c).

Uganda. In the Nigerian case, the focus is on: the 1999 Constitution of the Federal Republic of Nigeria (as amended); the Petroleum Act;[13] the Nigerian National Petroleum Corporation (NNPC) Act;[14] the Associated Gas Re-injection Act;[15] the Environmental Impact Assessment Act (EIAA);[16] and the Nigeria Extractive Industry Transparency Initiative (NEITI) Act.[17] In Uganda, the authors focus on the Constitution of Uganda (1995) (as amended); the Constitutional (Amendment) Act (2005); the Petroleum (Exploration and Production) (Conduct of Exploration Operations) Regulations;[18] the Petroleum (Exploration, Development and Production) Act;[19] and the Petroleum (Refining, Conversion, Transmission and Midstream Storage) Act.[20] The third section highlights some approaches, suggesting that there are components that may be built into the legal framework of both countries to boost sustainability in the harnessing of oil resource in Nigeria and Uganda. The fourth section comprises the conclusion.

2 Assessing the legal frameworks for oil resources in Nigeria and Uganda

2.1 Legal framework in Nigeria

2.1.1 The 1999 Constitution of the Federal Republic of Nigeria (as amended)

The legal framework in the Nigerian oil resources sector is discussed in light of the provisions of Sections 16(1) and (2)(b), 20 and 44(3) of the 1999 Constitution of the Federal Republic of Nigeria (as amended). Section 16(1) provides that:

> The State shall, within the context of the ideals and objectives for which provisions are made in this Constitution:
>
> (a) harness the resources of the nation and promote national prosperity and an efficient, a dynamic and self-reliant economy;
>
> (b) control the national economy in such manner as to secure the maximum welfare, freedom and happiness of every citizen on the basis of social justice and equality of status and opportunity;

Section 16(2)(b) further provides that the state shall direct its policy towards ensuring that the material resources of the nation are harnessed and distributed as best as possible to serve the common good. Under Section 20, the 1999 Constitution provides that

---

13 Petroleum Act 1969, CAP P 10, Laws of the Federal Republic of Nigeria 200419692004.

14 Nigerian National Petroleum Corporation Act No. 33 of 1977, Chapter N 123, Laws of the Federal Republic of Nigeria 2004.

15 Associated Gas Re-injection Act 1979.

16 Environmental Impact Assessment Act No. 86 of 1992.

17 Nigeria Extractive Industry Transparency Initiative (NEITI) Act 2007.

18 The Petroleum (Exploration and Production) (Conduct of Exploration Operations) Regulations (1993).

19 The Petroleum (Exploration, Development and Production) Act 2013.

20 The Petroleum (Refining, Conversion, Transmission and Midstream Storage) Act 2013.

the state shall protect and improve the environment and safeguard the water, air, land, forest and wildlife of Nigeria.

Section 44(3) of the 1999 Constitution, which refers to oil and other minerals, provides as follows:

> Notwithstanding the foregoing provisions of this section, the entire property in and control all minerals, mineral oils and natural gas in, under or upon any land in Nigeria or in, under or upon the territorial waters and the Exclusive Economic Zone of Nigeria shall vest in the Government of the Federation and shall be managed in such manner as may be prescribed by the national assembly.

The provision of Section 44(3) is reiterated by item 39 (part 1) of the second schedule to the 1999 Constitution, which vests exclusive powers to legislate on mines and minerals, (including oil fields, oil mining, geological surveys and natural gas) in the National Assembly of the state. The implication of these provisions is that only the federal legislature is vested with the prerogative to make laws in respect of mines and minerals, including oil fields, oil mining, geological surveys and natural gas.

Basically, any legal framework fashioned by the legislature should reflect a state's petroleum policy objective, establishing, maintaining and enforcing a system of competence to regulate petroleum activities in a manner consistent with the state's national petroleum objectives.[21] For a law to be effective, transparency, accountability and a clear sense of purpose accompanied by effective public participation should accompany the making of that law from the outset to the point of enforcement and implementation. Transparency and accountability are necessary if the national vision is to be realised and socioeconomic goals clarified. In this respect, the Nigerian 1999 Constitution is fundamentally flawed, as it does not encourage the inclusion of the input of the public through participatory processes.

The wording of Section 44(3) of the 1999 Constitution is at variance with the state's policy objectives laid out in Section 16(2)(b) because it restricts decision-making concerning the management of natural resources in Nigeria to the federal government, subject to the legislative competence of the National Assembly. Similarly, the provisions of Sections 16 and 20 of the 1999 Constitution, which appear to encompass the tenets of environmental justice and sustainability, as well as promote ideals that are synonymous with a sound legal framework for the governance of oil resources in Nigeria, are not enforceable by any court. The non-justiciability of Sections 16 and 20, which fall under Chapter II of the 1999 Constitution, is predicated on Section 6(6)(c) of the 1999 Constitution (as amended).[22] The practical implication of Section 6(6)(c) is to dismantle the aspirations of Section 16 and 20 in Chapter II of the 1999

21 Likosky (2010: 12).

22 Section 6(6)(c) provides that the judicial powers vested in the courts shall not except as otherwise provided by the Constitution, extend to any issue or question as to whether any act or omission by any authority or person or as to whether any law or any judicial decision is in conformity with the fundamental objectives and directives principles of state policy set out in Chapter II of the 1999 Constitution.

Constitution by ousting the jurisdiction of the Courts to entertain any "issue or question" relating to these sections.

2.1.2 The Petroleum Act, 1969 (as amended)[23]

The Petroleum Act provides for the exploration of petroleum from territorial waters and the continental shelf of Nigeria and vests the ownership of, and all on-shore and offshore revenue derived from petroleum resources in the federal government.[24] Section 1(1) of the Act reiterates the position of the 1999 Constitution as it vests the entire ownership and control of all petroleum in, under or upon any land in Nigeria in the federal government of Nigeria.[25]

The Office of the Minister of Petroleum Resources in Nigeria is a key unit of governance in the oil and gas industry by virtue of the Petroleum Act, which confers the Minister with wide powers including the power to grant and revoke licenses and make regulations. Section 2 of the Act provides that the Minister may grant:

- a licence, to be known as an oil exploration licence, to explore for petroleum;[26]
- a licence, to be known as an oil prospecting licence, to prospect for petroleum;[27] and
- a lease, to be known as an oil mining lease, to search for, win, work, carry away and dispose of petroleum.[28]

Under Section 3 of the Petroleum Act, no refinery shall be constructed or operated in Nigeria without a licence granted by the Minister in the prescribed form. Where no

23 Now known as Petroleum Act Cap. P10 (Laws of the Federation of Nigeria (LFN) 2004).

24 Section 14 of the Petroleum Act defines 'petroleum' as "mineral oil (or any related hydrocarbon) or natural gas as it exists in its natural state in bituminous shales or other stratified deposits from which oil can be extracted by destructive distillation", and 'natural gas' as gas obtained from boreholes and wells and consisting of hydrocarbons.

25 By virtue of Section 1(2) of the Act, this provision is deemed to apply to all land (including land covered by water) which is in Nigeria, under the Nigerian territorial waters, forms part of the continental shelf or forms part of the exclusive economic zone of Nigeria.

26 Oil exploration licences are no longer granted in practice. Presently, the Department of Petroleum Resources on behalf of the federal government of Nigeria has engaged the services of a seismic data-gathering services company, and this negates the need for exploration in the strict sense.

27 Oil prospecting licenses under the Petroleum Act appear to confer the rights to not only exploration but also exploitation of oil resources won during prospecting operations subject to the fulfilment of obligations imposed under the Act or by the Petroleum Profit Tax Act or any other law imposing taxation in respect of oil resources in Nigeria.

28 A lease is the grant to an applicant of the exclusive right to conduct exploration and prospecting operation and to win, get, work, store, carry away, transport export or otherwise treat petroleum discovered in or under the leased area. This is subject to any provision of the Petroleum Act and any special terms or conditions imposed in the grant of the lease.

form is prescribed, or no terms or conditions are prescribed, then the Minister has the discretion to decide or impose a form, terms and conditions. The Minister is equally vested with the power to regulate the downstream petroleum sector as no person is permitted to store, import, sell or distribute any petroleum products without a license granted by the Minister.[29] The consent of the Minister is also required for the assignment of any rights in licences or leases granted under the Petroleum Act.[30]

The provisions in the Petroleum Act on the assignment of rights in licences and leases initially seem to be straightforward. Practice in the oil industry, however, reveals a legal gap in the Act, widened by the advent of increasing acquisition, divestment and financing activities in the upstream petroleum sector. This gap lies in the definition of what constitutes "…interests therein or thereunder" in Paragraph 14 of the first schedule of the Petroleum Act. The Petroleum Industry Bill (PIB)[31] attempts to cure the lacunae in the Petroleum Act by expounding on the assignment of licence or lease.[32] The Bill, among other objectives, seeks to create new institutions to govern the operations of the industry, through the incorporation and privatisation of the state-owned enterprise, the Nigerian National Petroleum Corporation (NNPC). However, the PIB has been in draft form since 2008.

The Petroleum Act also includes provisions that promote safe operations, protection of the environment and conservation of natural resources. A fundamental challenge, however, persists because the Petroleum Act is outdated, and does not reflect contemporary realities. For instance, the state-owned enterprise might perform its commercial and operational duties through contractual arrangements, which presumably enjoy statutory authorisation by virtue of Paragraph 35(a) of the first Schedule of the Petroleum Act. The Minister is empowered to, if he considers it to be in the public interest, impose on a licence or lease terms and conditions not inconsistent with the Petroleum Act, participation by the Federal Government in the venture to which the licence or lease relates, on terms to be negotiated between the Minister and the applicant for the licence

---

29 Section 4 of the Petroleum Act.

30 Paragraph 14 of the First Schedule to the Petroleum Act provides that "[w]ithout the prior consent of the Minister, the holder of an oil prospecting licence or an oil mining lease shall not assign his licence or lease, or any right, power or interest therein or there under".

31 The PIB Draft Bill 2008 proposes: to establish the legal and regulatory framework, institutions and regulatory authorities for the Nigerian petroleum industry; to establish guidelines for the operation of the upstream and downstream sectors; and for purposes connected with the same.

32 Section 173 of the Petroleum Act provides that where a licence, lessee or production sharing or service contractor is taken over by another company or mergers, or is acquired by another company either by acquisition or exchange of shares, including a change of control of a parent company outside Nigeria, it shall be deemed to be, and treated as an assignment within Nigeria and shall be subject to the terms and conditions of the Petroleum Act. The PIB explicitly construes an assignment of a licence or lease or any rights, power or interest to include mergers, takeover and basically any other arrangement that results in a change of control of the licence or even a contract thereunder. See Sections 173 and 194 of the Petroleum Industry Bill (2008).

or lease.[33] The implication of this provision is that the NNPC undertakes its operation with extractive companies through various forms of contracts that do not maximise the benefits from oil and gas resource for the country. An examination of practice in the industry reveals that most contractual arrangements are usually fraught with frictions and conflicts between the respective committees, the Corporation's joint venture partners and production sharing contractors, over compliance with laid down legal and policy direction, accessibility to data and prompt and adequate reporting by the operating partners or contractors.[34]

2.1.3 The Nigerian National Petroleum Corporation (NNPC) Act

A discussion on the oil and gas governance framework in Nigeria is incomplete without discussing the NNPC and its enabling constitutive NNPC Act[35] with a view to show the lack of accountability and transparency in the Nigerian oil and gas sector. Statutorily, the affairs of NNPC are to be managed by a Board of Directors consisting of a chairman, who is the Minister of Petroleum Resources, and other members.

Section 5(2) is a far-reaching provision, which confers much latitude and flexibility to the President and the Corporation to undertake a general review of the affairs of the Corporation without legislative amendment. Of course, this provision is certainly not without consequences as such latitude has been susceptible to abuse, whims and caprices of the holders of the office of the President and the management of the Corporation over the years. The latitude may, no doubt, be responsible for the level of corruption and gross mismanagement of the country's number one foreign exchange earner; oil. It is equally imperative to note that this particular provision appears to be the basis on which the Corporation has undergone various changes by successive governments, from its inception in 1977 to present, without any significant amendment to the establishing Act.

The NNPC Act in Section 6(1) further confers wide-ranging discretionary power on the Corporation by providing that:[36]

> the Corporation shall have powers to do anything which in its opinion is calculated to facilitate the carrying out of its duties which includes but are not limited to holding, managing and alienating movable and immovable property; purchasing or otherwise acquiring or taking over all or any of the assets, business, properties, privileges, contracts, rights obligations and liabilities of any other Company, firm or person in furtherance of any business engaged in by the Corporation; entering into contracts or partnerships with any Company, firm or person which in the opinion of the Corporation will facilitate the discharge of its duties; establishing and maintaining

33 First Schedule, paragraph 35(a), of the Petroleum Act.

34 Aladeitan (2013: 160).

35 NNPC Act, 1977 (Decree No. 33, 1977), Cap. N. 123, L.F.N. 2004 and the NNPC (Amendment Act) of 2007.

36 Section 6(2) of the NNPC Act.

> subsidiaries for the discharge of such functions as the Corporation may determine, and; training managerial, technical and such other staff for the purpose of the running of its operations and for the Petroleum Industry in general.

With respect to the powers conferred on the NNPC by the Act, it is significant to point out that leaving the Corporation to exercise its powers as it may deem necessary, without setting parameters, guidance or performance standards comparable with international best practice of state-owned enterprises (SOEs) which must be complied with, appears to be a serious omission. This has resulted in the loss of value in licensing and a decline in sales of resources.

Although the NNPC Act requires the Corporation to keep proper accounts and records in accordance with best commercial standards[37] as well as appoint auditors with the approval of the President for purposes of auditing its accounts; it requires the auditors to submit its detailed observations and recommendations for that year to the Corporation.[38] The entire process for auditing the Corporation is flawed and defeats the essence of accountability, thus creating an avenue for reckless and unchecked excesses, which have characterised the Corporation over the years.

Another indication of lack of accountability and transparency in the management of the affairs and operations of the Corporation can also be observed from Section 7(4) and (5) of the NNPC Act which empowers the Corporation –

> to maintain a fund which consists of such monies as may from time to time be provided by the Federal Government for the purposes of the Act by way of grants or loans … and such monies as may be received by the Corporation in the course of its operations in relation to the exercise by the Corporation of any of its functions under the Act and from such fund [shall] defray all expenses incurred by the Corporation.

This provision gives the Corporation unfettered discretion in the application of monies accruing to it. The only check in the exercise of this wide power is the requirement of Section 7(5) of the NNPC Act which mandates the Corporation to submit to the President, not later than three months before the end of each financial year, estimates of its expenditure and income relating to the following financial year. What is required here is simply 'submission', and there is no requirement for approval by the President. This creates a gap that can be exploited and taken advantage of by the management board and officials of the Corporation.

The Corporation has an obligation to prepare and submit their schedule estimates of revenue and expenditure to the Minister of Finance under the Fiscal Responsibility Act (FRA) 2007.[39] What is clear from the provisions on the Corporation's borrowing powers[40] and disposal of surplus funds,[41] is the involvement of the President in issues relating to funds. It appears that the management of the affairs of the Corporation is more

37 Section 7(1) of the NNPC Act.
38 Section 7(2) & (3) of the NNPC Act.
39 Section 21 of the Fiscal Responsibility Act.
40 Section 8 of the NNPC Act.
41 Section 9 of the NNPC Act.

or less vested in the President, and if viewed from the fact that the NNPC Act was a product of the military interregnum in government, the drafting of the Act may not be surprising, having regard to the autocratic nature of the military rule. What is however surprising, is the fact that the succeeding civilian administration has not deemed it necessary to amend the Act to reflect contemporary realities that can promote value realisation and boost revenue management in a manner that translates to an enabling environment for investment in the oil resource sector.

Furthermore, the NNPC Act shields of the Corporation from legal proceedings through a limitation of suits and states that:[42]

> no suit against a member of the board or an employee of the Corporation for an act done in respect of an alleged neglect shall be instituted in any court unless it is commenced within 12 months next after the act or the neglect complained of

Before an action can be instituted or commenced against the Corporation, a notice of intention to sue is required to be served on it by the intending plaintiff or his agent one month prior to the suit.[43] This is an attempt to insulate the Corporation from being answerable for its neglect and defaults, bearing in mind that the discovery of acts of neglect or injury may be well after twelve months, and investigation to verify certain facts may take a longer period than a month.

Still on the issue of transparency and in what has been described as a measure of the Corporation's continuing importance to the calculus of political leadership,[44] is the regulation of public access to the Corporation's offices across the country. Regulation of access is so intense to the extent that there are extreme and extraordinary security arrangements in the Corporation's offices all over the country. Reasons other than security to ward off a physical attack, at least until the recent threat of 'Boko Haram' and attacks of the Niger-Delta militants, have been provided for the level of security. One reason is that public access to the Corporation is regulated for the purpose of securing and guarding its operational secrets.

Whereas the veracity or otherwise of this reason is not ascertainable, what is not in doubt is the fact that the NNPC Act actually enjoins the Corporation to prohibit and restrict the access of the public or of any class of members of the public to any premises vested in, occupied by or under the control of the Corporation etc.[45] The essence of this statutory restriction to a public corporation leaves much to be desired, but since it is not an outright prohibition, and with the enactment of the Freedom of Information Act[46], it is hoped that restriction of public access to the Corporation's premises may

42 Section 12(1) of the NNPC Act.

43 Section 12(2) of the NNPC Act.

44 Nwokeji (2007: 5).

45 Section 17 of the NNPC Act.

46 The Freedom of Information Act 2015 is an Act that makes public records and information more freely available. It provides for public access to public records and information, protect public records and information to the extent consistent with public interest and the protection of personal privacy.

be reduced to the barest minimum in order to bolster the dwindling image of the state as one that lacks the capacity to create an enabling environment.

2.1.4 The Associated Gas Re-injection Act, 1979

This is an Act made to compel every company producing oil and gas in Nigeria to submit preliminary programs for gas re-injection and detailed plans for implementation of gas re-injection by no later than 1 April 1980.[47] Section 3 of the Act prohibits any company engaged in the production of oil or gas to flare gas produced in association with oil without the written permission of the Minister. Under Section 3(2), the Minister may issue a certificate to a company engaged in the production of oil or gas, where he is satisfied that the utilisation or reinjection of the produced gas is not appropriate or feasible in a particular field.

The Minister is further vested with the discretion to specify the terms and conditions for the continued flaring of gas in the particular field or fields.[48] The Minister may also permit the company to continue to flare gas in the particular field or fields if the company pays such sum as the Minister may from time to time prescribe for every 28.317 standard cubic metre (SCM) of gas flared.[49] The Minister may, if satisfied, grant the permission subject to the payment of such a sum as the Minister may prescribe.[50] Section 4 penalises an offender with forfeiture of the concessions granted in a particular field in relation to which the offence was committed. The Minister may also withhold any entitlements of any offender towards the cost of completion or implementation of a desirable re-injection scheme.[51]

There are also the Associated Gas Re-injection (Continued Flaring of Gas) Regulations (1984), which are subsidiary legislation under the Associated Gas Re-injection Act. These stipulate conditions for the issuance of permits by the Minister under Section 3(2) of the Associated Gas Re-injection Act. Section 1 of the Regulations provide for the continued flaring of gas in a particular field or fields, provided anyone or more of the laid out conditions are met. The conditions include where more than 75 % of the produced gas is effectively utilised or conserved and where the produced gas contains more than 15% impurities, which render the gas unsuitable for industrial purposes. Other conditions include where an on-going utilisation programme is interrupted by

47 Sections 1 and 2 of the Associated Gas Re-injection Act.
48 Section 3(2)(a) of the Associated Gas Re-injection Act.
49 Section 3(2)(b) of the Associated Gas Re-injection Act.
50 There is a proviso to the effect that any such payment shall be made in the same manner and be subject to the same procedure as for the payment of royalties to the federal government by companies engaged in the production of oil. See Section 3(2)(b) of the Associated Gas Re-injection Act.
51 Section 4(2) of the Associated Gas Re-injection Act.

equipment failure; or where the ratio of the volume of gas produced per day to the distance of the field from the nearest gas line or possible utilisation point is less than 50,000 SCF/KM.[52]

These Regulations do not reflect contemporary realities and philosophy for transparency and accountability. There is an indication that the state lacks the political will to enforce its anti-gas flaring provisions in the Associated Gas Re-injection Act of 1979. The Act, which targets anti-gas flaring policies and requires companies to submit to the Minister detailed programs for reinjection of associated gas produced or programs for the use of such gas, is completely watered down by the provisions of Section 1 of the Associated Gas Re-injection (Continued Flaring of Gas) Regulations 1985.[53]

2.1.5 The Environmental Impact Assessment (EIA) Act, 1992

The EIA Act is a guide on the procedures to be undertaken in considering the likely impacts of any project, whether private or public, on the environment. The Act is described as a landmark in the Nigerian environmental protection regime because it is the first statute that allows public participation in the decision-making processes relevant to development.[54] Thus, members of the public have access to information on such projects and the right to participate in the decision-making process on the potential (negative or positive) impacts on their immediate environment.[55]

Under the EIA Act, companies engaged in extractive activities in the petroleum sector may not embark on projects without considering the environmental impacts at an early stage, except as permitted by law.[56] By virtue of Sections 2(2) and (3) of the EIA Act, "where the extent, nature or location of a proposed is likely to significantly affect the environment", oil companies are expected to undertake an environmental impact assessment of the intended project. Under Sections 4(d)-(e) of the EIA Act, an environmental impact assessment shall include a description of the proposed activities, assessment of the proposed activities, and an assessment of the likely environmental impacts and alternatives to mitigate any negative impacts of the project. Petroleum and

---

52 Section 1 of the Associated Gas Re-Injection (Continued Flaring Of Gas) Regulations.

53 Omeke (2011).

54 Section 7 of the EIA Act allows public participation in environmental impact assessment in Nigeria. It provides that "before the Agency gives a decision on an activity to which an environmental assessment has been produced, the Agency shall give opportunity to government agencies, members of the public, experts in any relevant discipline and interested groups to make comment on environmental impact assessment of the activity". The Review Panel accentuates public participation in environmental impact assessments in Nigeria. Under Section 37(b) of the EIA Act, proceedings in the review panel stage are expected to be conducted in public "in a manner that offers the public an opportunity to participate in assessment". See Omorogbe (2002: 577).

55 Ekhotor (2016: 43).

56 Section 2(1)(4) of the EIA Act.

mining are included in the list of industries deemed as subject to mandatory study activities under the schedule to the EIA Act.[57]

The Act has been a subject of criticism over the years due to limitations imposed by the provisions of Section 15(1) on exceptions to the performance of environmental impact assessment in certain projects. Section 15(1) of the EIA Act states that an environmental assessment of the project shall not be required where:

(a) in the opinion of the Agency the project is in the list of projects which the President, Commander-in-Chief of the Armed Forces or the Council is of the opinion that the environmental effects of the project is likely to be minimal;

(b) the project is to be carried out during national emergency for which temporary measures have been taken by the Government;

(c) the project is to be carried out in response to circumstances that, in the opinion of the Agency, the project is in the interest of public health or safety.

These provisions run contrary to the intentions of the EIA Act. For instance, based on the provisions, notwithstanding valid objections to a proposed project, the President of Nigeria has the discretion to evade the statutory requirements for an einvironmental impact assesement in projects relating to the petroleum sector. Consequently, corporate bodies with an extractive interest in the oil industry may through access or 'connections' to the President potentially influence him or her to give approval to their proposed projects, notwithstanding the negative environmental impacts of such projects.[58]

It is interesting to note that the Environmental Impact Assessment Bill (2017), which is presently under review, retains the provisions of Section 15. The Bill makes no significant clarification on what constitutes 'minimal' effect of a project as provided for in the EIA Act. Similarly, the Bill does not qualify the nature of projects which would be considered to be in the interest of the public, as laid down by Section 15 of the EIA Act. These are legal gaps that certainly deserve the attention of stakeholders in the field.

2.1.6 Nigeria Extractive Industry Transparency Initiative (NEITI) Act, 2007

The NEITI Act, as the title suggests, is enacted to ensure due process and transparency in the payments made by companies operating in the Nigerian extractive industry to the federal government.[59] The Act is intended to ensure accountability in the revenue receipts of the federal government from companies in the extractive industry and to

57 Under Section 25 of the EIA Act, in mandatory study activities projects, EIA reports shall be published and made available to the public in selected places and any person or individual can file comments on the conclusions and recommendations of such reports.

58 Osa (2016: 1).

59 Aladeitan (2015).

eliminate all forms of corrupt practices in the determination, payment, receipt and posting of revenue accruing to the federal government.[60] Having regard to the above functions, it is evident that the NEITI Act is a response to noticeable transparency and accountability gaps in the country's oil, and gas and solid minerals sectors.[61]

However, the Act is fraught with legal gaps. For instance, Section 2(c) of the Act empowers NEITI to "eliminate all forms of corrupt practices in the determination, payments, receipts and postings of revenue accruing to the Federal government from extractive industry companies".[62] This particular clause appears to be overly ambitious, and in fact, some of its terms of reference are already exercised by statutory government agencies such as the Federal Inland Revenue Service, Central Bank of Nigeria, and the Office of the Accountant General of the Federation. This clause can, however, be modified to give NEITI a clear coordinating role, limiting overlaps with other government agencies and departments in the performance of key functional mandates.

It is encouraging to note that the Petroleum Industry Governance (PIG) Bill addresses some of the gaps in the legal framework governing Nigeria's oil and gas industry.[63] For instance, by virtue of clause 86 of the Bill, all existing enactments, including but not limited to the Petroleum Act, the Pipeline Act and the Petroleum Profit Tax Act, are to be read with such modifications as to bring them into conformity with the Bill. In the event of any inconsistency between the provisions of the Bill and that of any other enactment, the provisions of the Bill shall prevail.[64] It is also instructive to note that although variation to all extant Acts covered by the Bill will take effect when the Bill is assented to by the President, the NNPC Act, the NNPC (Projects) Act and the NNPC Amendment Act will only be repealed when the Minister issues a legal notice vesting the assets and liabilities of the NNPC in the relevant successor entities.[65]

---

60 Section 2, Nigeria Extractive Industries Transparency Initiative (NEITI) 2007.

61 Aladeitan (2015).

62 This clause is similar to that of Section 3(c) of the NEITI Act which prescribes a function for NEITI to ensure transparency and accountability in the management of the investment of the Federal Government in all extractive industry companies.

63 The Senate only recently passed the PIG Bill into law in June 2017. The PIG Bill is just one of several components of the Petroleum Industry Bill which has been before the National Assembly for over a decade. The PIG Bill seeks to restructure the Nigerian. National Petroleum Corporation and the Department of Petroleum Resources, as well as remove the overlap of functions among the commercial, regulatory and policy institutions. Clause 2(1)(g) of the Bill curtails the discretion of the Minister by subjecting the exercise of his powers to grant, amend, renew, extend or revoke petroleum exploration and production licenses and leases under the Petroleum Act to the recommendation of a new commission to be created under the Bill; the Nigerian Petroleum Regulatory Commission.

64 See Clause 86 of the PIG Bill.

65 Ibid.

2.2 Legal Framework in Uganda

2.2.1 The 1995 Constitution of the Republic of Uganda (as amended)

The 1995 Constitution of the Republic of Uganda has elaborate provisions regarding environmental management. In the National Objectives and Directive Principles of State Policy, the Constitution requires the Government of Uganda to take measures to protect important natural resources, including land, water, wetlands, minerals, oil, fauna and flora on behalf of the people of Uganda.[66] The government is also required to promote and implement energy policies that will ensure that people's basic needs and those of environmental preservation are met. It is further required to promote the rational use of natural resources so as to safeguard and protect the biodiversity of Uganda.

In the substantive provisions, the 1995 Constitution makes specific provision for the right to a clean and healthy environment. Under Article 39, every Ugandan has a right to a clean and healthy environment. This provision is reiterated under Section 3 of the National Environment Act Cap 153 and Section 5(2) of the National Forestry and Tree Planting Act No. 8 of 2003, which similarly provide for the right to a clean and healthy environment. The breach of the right entitles any person or responsible body to bring an action in furtherance of the right. The 1995 Constitution further imposes on the state and citizens the duty to create and protect a clean and healthy environment.[67] These provisions imply that a party whose right to a clean and healthy environment is violated due to oil exploration and production, may institute legal action to seek redress against the extractive company responsible, or even the state.[68]

Over a decade ago, Uganda discovered commercial volumes of oil in the Albertine and Nile basin. Since then, a major concern for stakeholders in Uganda's natural capital sector has been oil resource governance and how much local content will be utilised in developing the sector. The oil resource sector in Uganda is budding, and most citizens are yet to enjoy the benefits of the resource through the creation of innovative

66 Principle XIII of the 1995 Constitution.

67 Article 17(1)(j) of the 1995 Constitution.

68 In the case of *Environmental Action Network v. British American Tobacco,* the applicant brought an application under Article 50(2) of the 1995 Constitution and rule 3 of the Fundamental Rights and Freedoms (Enforcement Procedure) Rules, for a court order compelling the respondent, a manufacturer of 'dangerous products' (cigarettes), to fully and adequately warn consumers of the health risks associated with its products. Although the order was ultimately denied, the court did confirm the *locus standi* of the applicant and that Article 50(2) enabled individuals to bring public interest matters to court on behalf of those who were not in a position to do so.

opportunities to build a new economy founded on upstream gas extraction activities, and the downstream linked value addition industries.[69]

The 1995 Constitution vests the ownership of all minerals and petroleum in the government, which is to hold the same in trust for the people of Uganda. This introduces the public trust doctrine in the management of oil and gas resources,[70] which is embedded in the Constitutional (Amendment) Act of 2005.

2.2.2 The Constitutional (Amendment) Act, 2005

This Amendment Act has significant implications for oil and gas management and control, and the sharing of royalties derived from oil and gas exploitation. Part XIII and specifically Section 43 amends Article 244 of the 1995 Constitution by replacement. Accordingly, the entire property in and the control of all minerals and petroleum in, on or under any land or waters in Uganda are vested in the government on behalf of the Republic of Uganda.

This is, however, subject to Article 26 of the 1995 Constitution, which emphasises the need to fairly and adequately compensate surface landowners before the government can take over the petroleum-rich lands. Just like Nigeria, the parliament in Uganda is mandated to make laws regulating the exploitation of minerals and petroleum; the sharing of royalties arising from mineral and petroleum exploitation; the conditions for payment of indemnities arising out of the exploitation of minerals and petroleum; and conditions regarding the restoration of derelict lands.

2.2.3 The Petroleum (Exploration and Production) (Conduct of Exploration Operations) Regulations, 1993

These Regulations were made under the repealed Petroleum (Exploration and Production) Act, Cap. 150. They however remain in force as long as they are not inconsistent with the repealing Act.[71]

Regulation 51(1) provides for the prevention of pollution of the environment in carrying out exploration, development, production and transportation of oil and gas.[72]

---

69 See <http://www.monitor.co.ug/Business/Prosper/What-Uganda-can-learn-from-other-oil-and-gas-producers/688616-3470538-item-00-jp6am5z/index.html> (accessed 9-12-2017).

70 Article 244.

71 Section 189 of the Petroleum (Exploration, Development and Production) Act, 2013.

72 Under Regulation 36, an application for the consent of the Commissioner to the construction or installation of a fixed platform should be made in writing and should state among others, the location at which it is intended to construct or install the fixed platform and the reasons for selection of that location.

Further, under Regulation 51(2), in the disposal of any waste material, a licence holder should not create any conditions, which may adversely affect public health, life, property, aquatic life, wildlife or vegetation. The Regulations further require that before drilling operations are commenced in any licensed area, the person-in-charge should submit a description of the procedure, personnel, equipment and materials that will be used in reporting, cleanup and prevention of the spread of any pollution resulting from exploration or development activities for approval. Regulation 56 also bars the disposal of drilling mud into any lake, river, stream, pond or other water bodies. Under Regulation 56(2), produced water may be disposed into an operating area after satisfying, with the commissioner's approval, that the oil content of produced waters discharged from offshore platforms has been reduced to an average of not more than 10 mg/l during normal operation.

The Regulations also make provisions for safety issues. Regulation 85(1) requires the operator to prepare a manual of instructions for safety in operations and bring it to the attention of every person who is about to be engaged in, or concerned with, the carrying out of operations or the execution of works in any licensed area. Regulation 112 further requires that all confined areas where operations could lead to the emission and accumulation of explosive mixtures or toxic gases should be provided with suitable means of ventilation and with a continuous ventilation monitoring system approved by the commissioner, which should be fitted with an audible warning device. Regulation 114 requires that at appropriate distances from every place where gases such as hydrogen sulphide are, or could be a hazard, the person-in-charge should cause to be displayed suitable signs warning of the presence of the gases, and any person observed approaching that place should be warned of the danger that exists. Regulation 115 prescribes that the exhaust gases from engines, motors or devices using gas in place of steam or air to operate pumps and other power-driven equipment, should be discharged in a direction and location where they will not create a health hazard to any person.

2.2.4 The Petroleum (Refining, Conversion, Transmission and Midstream Storage) Act, 2013

The Act seeks to operationalise the Oil and Gas Policy by establishing an effective legal framework to ensure that midstream operations are carried out in a sustainable manner that guarantees optimum benefits for all Ugandans, both the present and future generations; enabling the development of petroleum refining, gas conversion, pipelines, transmission and other activities in midstream operations.[73]

The Act provides that licensees, or any person exercising or performing functions, duties or powers thereunder, should take into account and comply with environmental

---

73 Section 1 of the Petroleum (Refining, Conversion, Transmission and Midstream Storage) Act.

principles prescribed in the NEA and other applicable laws. For these purposes, the Oil Authority of Uganda may grant a licence to an entity contracted by the licensee upon such conditions as are deemed fit by the National Environment Management Authority (NEMA), for the management of transportation, storage, treatment or disposal of waste arising out of midstream operations, and it is an offence for any such contracted entity to operate without such a licence.[74]

The Act prohibits venting and flaring of gases. Gas venting means the release of gases to the atmosphere, whereas flaring means combustion of hydrocarbons without application of the resulting heat or gases for any useful purposes.[75] These activities are prohibited by Section 38, which provides that a licensee is not allowed to flare or vent petroleum in excess of the quantities needed for normal operational safety without the approval of the Minister on the advice of the Oil Authority.[76] All facilities in the midstream stage should be planned and constructed in such way as to avoid gas flaring or venting under normal operating conditions. Hence, any disposal of gases by flaring or venting for normal operational safety should be with the written consent, of the Authority, where it is necessary for the safety of midstream operations or necessary to comply with a requirement imposed by or under any law in Uganda, or in case of an emergency.

However, even where flaring or venting is done without consent as an emergency, the licensee should ensure that the flaring or venting is kept at the lowest possible level, and submit a technical report to the authority detailing the nature and circumstances that caused the emergency situation. Part III of the Act provides that the process of licensing for midstream operations shall be kept open and transparent. Section12 provides that the Minister shall, within 45 days after receiving an application for a midstream licence, cause a notice of the application to be published in the Gazette and at least one newspaper of wide circulation in Uganda, and such notice must indicate: details of receipt of the application; description of the nature and location of the proposed facility or operation; inform the members of the public that the application may be inspected, within the limits of the laws governing intellectual property rights and commercial confidentiality; and invite parties and local authorities in the areas affected by the project who object to the granting of the licence, whether on personal, environmental or other grounds, to lodge their objections with the Minister.

According to Section 74, the Minister may, in accordance with the Access to Information Act, 2005, make available to the public: details of all agreements, licences and any amendments to the licences or agreements whether or not terminated or valid; details of exemptions from variations to, or suspensions of the conditions of a licence;

74 Section 3 of the Petroleum (Refining, Conversion, Transmission and Midstream Storage) Act.
75 Section 2 of the Petroleum (Refining, Conversion, Transmission and Midstream Storage) Act.
76 The Oil Authority of Uganda is established under Section 9 of the Petroleum (Exploration, Development and Production) Act.

and all assignments and other approved arrangements in respect of a licence. This section would ordinarily be very significant in ensuring transparency and accountability in midstream operations, but it seems the proceeding Sections 75 and 76, which impose very stringent clauses on confidentiality of data and prohibition against disclosure of information, respectively, curtail these guarantees.

2.2.5 The Petroleum (Exploration, Development and Production) Act, 2013

The Act is one of the newest enactments in the field of oil and gas. It was enacted basically to regulate the upstream sector and aims at giving effect to Article 244 of the 1995 Constitution of Uganda. It regulates petroleum exploration, development and production; establishes the petroleum authority of Uganda; provides for the establishment of the national oil company of Uganda; and regulates the licensing and participation of commercial entities in petroleum activities.

The major purpose of this Act is to operationalise the National Oil and Gas Policy. It aims to establish an effective legal framework and institutional structures to ensure that the exploration, development and production of petroleum resources is carried out in a sustainable manner that guarantees optimum benefits for all Ugandans, both the present and future generations and creating a conducive environment for the efficient management of petroleum resources.[77]

It also seeks to establish institutions to manage the petroleum resources and regulate petroleum activities; and regulate petroleum activities through licensing, exploration, development, production and cessation of activities or decommissioning. Public safety and protection of public health and the environment in oil activities; supporting the development of state participation and national content in the petroleum industry and ensure transparency and accountability in all activities regulated under the Act, are other strategic approaches laid out in the Act.[78]

To achieve this, a licensee is required to contract a separate entity to manage the transportation, storage, treatment or disposal of waste arising out of petroleum activities. However, the licensee shall remain responsible for all the activities of the entity so licensed. A person contracted by the licensee shall not undertake the above activities without obtaining a licence from NEMA.

The Act makes provision for punitive measures where a person violates the environmental principles contained in the Act. It further provides that a person shall not be granted a petroleum production licence unless their development plan takes proper account of best petroleum industry practices and safety factors.[79] This provision is largely

77 Section 1 of the Petroleum (Exploration, Development and Production) Act.

78 Ibid.

79 Section 74(1)(b) of the Petroleum (Exploration, Development and Production) Act.

vague because the Act does not satisfactorily define what amounts to 'best petroleum industry practices'.[80] The only reference to practice which might constitute 'best petroleum industry practice' is embedded in Section 76(1)(f) which states that a petroleum production licence granted under the Act must expressly require the licensee to undertake an environmental impact assessment prior to commencing any production activity.[81]

With respect to access to information by the public, the Act empowers the Minister, in accordance with the Access to Information Act (2005) to make available to the public: details of all agreements, licences and any amendments to the licences or agreements whether or not terminated or valid; details of exemptions from, or variations or suspensions of the conditions of a licence; approved field development plans; and all assignments and other approved arrangements in respect of a licence upon payment of the prescribed fee.[82] This seems to be a good guarantee for transparency and accountability in the sector. However, the stringent confidentiality provisions under Section 152 and other express restrictions in Section 153 have restricted it.

There are neither regulations on operational mechanisms of the Petroleum Fund, nor Regulations on sharing of revenues from royalties of oil and gas in the Petroleum (Exploration, Development and Production) Act (2013) or elsewhere.

Furthermore, although the National Oil and Gas Policy (2008) has transparency and accountability as some of its principles, and one of the actions in the policy is to participate in the processes of the extractive industries and transparency initiative (EITI), Uganda is yet to participate fully in the processes of the EITI as required under the Oil and Gas Policy.

A worrisome feature that cuts across most of the legal instruments in the oil governance sector for Nigeria and Uganda is the bureaucratic impediments hindering public participation in decision-making, access to justice and dispute resolution of aggrieved parties. The review of the legal framework for the management of the oil and gas sector in Nigeria and Uganda reveals that there is a variance between the law on paper and its implementation in practice.[83] It equally shows the prevalence of unfettered discretion in the management of the resource by the political leadership as opposed to a standardised approach for appropriate and effective management. It is submitted that unfettered discretion which gives far-reaching latitude and flexibility for the policy direction of a state's oil resources can be overwhelming and expose the

80 The Act merely defines 'best petroleum industry practices' to mean the best available practices that are generally accepted as good, safe, transparent and efficient in carrying out petroleum activities and that can be applied globally under similar circumstances, something which leaves a lot to be desired since environmental compliance is best achieved through strong regulation.

81 Section 76(1)(f) of the Petroleum (Exploration, Development and Production) Act.

82 Section 151 of the Petroleum (Exploration, Development and Production) Act.

83 See <http://resourcegovernanceindex.org/compare?country1=UGA_oil-gas&country2=NGA_oil-gas> (accessed 26-4-2018).

sector to undue interference and political consideration other than best operational and management practices.

3 Essential components of the legal framework for ensuring sustainability in the oil sector for Nigeria and Uganda

From the above examination of the Ugandan and Nigerian legal frameworks, the following elements of resource governance are suggested as components that should be highlighted and wholly integrated into the legal frameworks for improving sustainable governance of the oil industry in both coutries.

3.1 Value-based approach

Prior to building any legal framework for the oil and gas sector, a methodology must be adopted to guide decision-makers on the underlying prospects and challenges in the governance of natural resource in general, and oil resources in particular. Values imply a level of judgment about what is important. Through values, concrete principles like the actual value of the resource, human rights, social equity and legitimacy become synonymous with the emerging legal framework.

The emergence of values in resource governance is grounded on the understanding that whilst economic development is essential, not all values are monetary, as biodiversity has intrinsic and cultural values that go beyond economics.[84] The value-based approach attaches weight to oil resources, as well as connects the activities and decisions of key stakeholders in the sector. Based on values, key decisions can be made about oil resources and the impact of their extraction on the ecosystems.

The Nigerian and Ugandan legal frameworks have developed without clear values underpinning them. This failure has resulted in gaps that compromise the effectiveness of well-meaning legal provisions. While Uganda has a normative framework for ingraining the principles of accountability and transparency, it faces the same challenges that are faced in Nigeria. This raises the need for ensuring that when principles are adopted, they permeate all activities in the oil and gas industry. This will provide a context for dealing with corruption and other rent-seeking activities that are common in the oil and gas sector in both countries.

84 See <https://www.unep-wcmc.org/expertise/We-specialize-in/Valuing-natural-capital> (accessed 12-12-2017).

3.2 Value-addition approach

Most importantly, both states should seek to re-engineer their economic models to add value to their oil and gas resources.[85] Both states should shift from crude oil exports to intermediate and finished oil products by adding value and maximising their natural resource wealth. This shift is long overdue. Oil and gas industry governance in Nigeria and Uganda should include the use of legal provisions that buoy up national investment in the sustainable harnessing of environmental assets through industrialisation and reversing natural capital losses. These legal provisions should include developing and strengthening private and public partnerships for harnessing natural capital.

Similarly, there is a need for reform of the banking sector laws and regulations to ensure that investors rely extensively on company disclosures to evaluate environmental-related financial risks.[86] Presently, company quantification of natural resource use and pollution impacts is largely guided by the Global Research Index (GRI) sustainability reporting guidelines.[87] Increasingly, large companies and organisations are creating transparency reports and making considerable strides in building local communities through skills transfer and investment. As environmental, social and governance reporting become more commonplace, the corresponding monitoring systems are likely to improve.

3.3 Principles

Good governance, transparency, accountability, participation and responsiveness principles should be included in the laws of both states as they provide the architecture for the sustainable harnessing of oil and gas as well as a standard for measuring economic development in resource-rich states. Specifically, the principle of public participation goes beyond the typical state-driven approach by highlighting the central role of members of the public. Inclusive decision-making through the public participation principle implies a horizontal process in which power dynamics are re-balanced, and the views of groups at risk of marginalisation are clearly taken into account in decisions regarding natural resource governance, including through appropriate representation.

---

85 See <https://au.int/sites/default/files/newsevents/workingdocuments/12582-wd-agenda_2063_e_0.pdf> (accessed 21-12-2017).

86 UNEP (2015).

87 See Global Reporting Initiative (GRI) Sustainability Reporting Guidelines, which produce international framework for the sustainability reporting process to promote the drive towards greater transparency. The framework sets out principles and indicators that organisations can use to measure and report their economic, environmental, and social performance. CERES and the United Nations Environment Program (UNEP) founded GRI in the USA in 1997.

Recognition and respect for tenure rights, especially customary, collective rights of members of host local communities, is an important principle that should also be included in the laws of both Nigeria and Uganda. For instance, though the laws on oil and gas resources vest total ownership and control in the government in Nigeria and Uganda to the detriment of the local communities in the areas where the resources are situated, there is general consensus that the ownership of mineral resources by the federal government of Nigeria has been detrimental to the people of the oil producing areas of Nigeria.[88] This is likely to be replicated in Uganda. Recognising tenure rights of local communities in the oil and gas industry laws in both states can contribute to effective and equitable natural resource governance. More specifically, such recognition facilitates local stewardship of lands and resources, providing a foundation for sustainable livelihoods and contributing to the fulfilment of human rights and cultural survival. International frameworks such as the Voluntary Guidelines on the Governance of Tenure (Voluntary Guidelines),[89] the African Charter on Human and Peoples Rights (whose tenets are part of the law in both Nigeria and Uganda),[90] and the United Nations Declaration on the Rights of Indigenous Peoples[91] are all legal documents that reflect a global consensus on the need to recognise and respect all legitimate tenure rights. However, the Voluntary Guidelines and the UN Declaration on the Rights of Indigenous Peoples do not enjoy the force of law in Nigeria and Uganda. There are opportunities for including the principles in these documents in both countries, and these should be utilised.

Provision for devolution and subsidiarity through collaborative governance is also fundamental in improving the relevant legal frameworks of both countries. Devolution is defined as "a process by which state control over the use of natural resources is gradually and increasingly shared with local communities".[92] In the present context, devolution is closely linked to the principle of subsidiarity, by which decisions are taken at the lowest possible level. Devolution and subsidiarity are key elements that create flexible and adaptive processes for decision-making and management of natural resources. Accordingly, building devolution and the subsidiarity principles in the oil resource governance framework addresses access to justice, differentiated actions for specific situations of vulnerable groups and social and environmental accountability. The focus on devolution further reinforces the rights-based approach to natural resources governance, as members of the local community through their representatives are engaged in making decisions with respect to the extractive activities in their

88 Ekhator (2016: 43).

89 FAO (2012).

90 Article 21 of the African Charter provides that all peoples shall have the right to freely dispose of their wealth and mineral or natural resources.

91 United Nations Declaration on the Rights of Indigenous People (2007), at <http://www.un.org/esa/socdev/unpfii/documents/DRIPS_en.pdf> (accessed 20-01-2018).

92 Nakangu (2016).

environment. Both Nigeria and Uganda have work to do to ingrain devolution and subsidiarity principles within their oil and gas laws.

4 Conclusion

Nigeria and Uganda share similar historical antecedents in terms of laws that regulate certain sectors of their respective economies. Uganda's entrance into the group of oil resource extracting states is, however, relatively new compared to that of Nigeria, and the state is yet to fully participate in the EITI. Both states are making similar efforts to provide a responsive legal framework for oil resources governance.

This chapter does not dwell in-depth on the reasons for the poor performance of Nigeria and Uganda in the RGI Report. Based on the review of their legal frameworks, however, it is safe to posit that both states share similar governance challenges. The content of their respective laws and the role of the state as prescribed by these laws have contributed to the governance challenges the countries have experienced.

An assessment of the legal frameworks for oil resource governance in Nigeria and Uganda reveals gaps, which justify the 2017 RGI Report's conclusion that a governance deficit exists in the decision-making chain in the extractive industry in Nigeria and Uganda. Legal reforms to boost value realisation, improve revenue management and maintain an enabling environment are critical if Nigeria and Uganda are to harness oil wealth for the benefit of their people.

The existing legal instruments governing the management of oil resources in both states do not reflect contemporary realities and the principles of inclusiveness, transparency and accountability. This explains the mismanagement, lack of regard for the rule of law, poor regulatory quality and corruption associated with the governance of oil resources in Nigeria for instance.[93] It also explains the poor revenue management and corruption that undermines the development of an appropriate legal framework for the budding oil resource industry in Uganda.

Review of the content of laws in both states and their performance on the 2017 RGI, which places Nigeria and Uganda within the ranking for states that exhibit serious shortcomings in oil resource governance, leads us to conclude that there is a correlation between the content of the law, state presence and sustainable harnessing of oil resources. For any state, including Uganda and Nigeria, to govern its oil and gas sector sustainably, the principles of accountability and transparency outlined above, a value-based approach and the need for value addition must be incorporated into the legal framework.

93 See <http://resourcegovernanceindex.org/compare?country1=UGA_oil-gas&country2=NGA_oil-gas> (accessed 10-02-2018).

References

Ahmed, Z (2012) "NEITI: The prospects, issues and challenges" Presentation to the IMF Mission (21-3-2012), at <https://www.imf.org/external/np/seminars/eng/2012/kinshasa/pdf/za.pdf> (accessed 13-03-2018).

Aladeitan, L (2013) "Ownership and control of oil, gas, and mineral resources in Nigeria: between legality and legitimacy" 38 *Thurgood Marshall Law Review* 159-197.

Aladeitan, L (2015) *Natural resources and conflict in Nigeria: the legal framework for resource governance, peace and sustainable development* Ph.D. thesis, University of Abuja, Nigeria.

Ekhator, EO (2016) "Public regulation of the oil and gas industry in Nigeria: an evaluation" 21 *Annual Survey of International & Comparative Law* 43-93.

FAO / United Nations Food and Agricultural Organisation (2012) *Voluntary guidelines on the responsible governance of tenure of land, fisheries and forests in the context of national food security.*

Likosky, M (2010) "Contracting and regulatory issues in the oil and gas and metallic minerals industries" 18 *Transnational Corporations* 12.

Nakangu, BB (2016) *NRGF challenges and opportunities in eastern and southern Africa* NRGF Regional Scoping Report.

Natural Resource Governance Institute Reader (2015) "Legal framework navigating the web of laws and contracts governing extractive industries", at <https://resourcegovernance.org/sites/default/files/documents/nrgi_primer_legal-framework.pdf> (accessed 30-4-2018).

Natural Resource Governance Institute (2017a) "Resource governance index", at <http://resourcegovernanceindex.org/> (accessed 5-5-2018).

Natural Resource Governance Institute (2017b) "Nigeria: Oil and Gas, 2017 Resource Governance Index", at < http://resourcegovernanceindex.org/country-profiles/NGA/oil-gas> (accessed 8-4-2018).

Natural Resource Governance Institute (2017c) "Uganda: Oil and Gas, 2017 Resource Governance Index", at <http://resourcegovernanceindex.org/country-profiles/UGA/oil-gas> (accessed 8-4-2018).

Nwokeji, G (2007) *The Nigerian National Petroleum Corporation and the development of the Nigerian oil and gas industry: history, strategies and current directions* Policy Report of the Joint James Baker III Institute for Public Policy/Japan Petroleum Energy Centre on the Changing Role of National Oil Companies in International Energy Markets.

Omeke, CA (2011) *Critique on the legal regime governing gas flaring in Nigeria* unpublished LLM dissertation of the University of Nigeria Nsukka Nigeria.

Omorogbe, Y (2002) "The legal framework for public participation in decision-making on mining and energy development in Nigeria: giving voices to the voiceless" in DN Zillman, AR Lucas & G Pring (eds) *Human rights in national resource development: public participation in the sustainable development of mining and energy resource* 549.

OPEC / Organization of the Petroleum Exporting Countries (2017) Annual statistical bulletin, at <https://asb.opec.org/index.php/foreword> (accessed 29-4-2018).

UNEP (2015) *The financial system we need, aligning the financial system with sustainable development*, at <http://unepinquiry.org/wp-content/uploads/2015/11/The_Financial_System_We_Need_Policy_Summary_EN.pdf> (accessed 30-4-2018).

World Bank (2010) *Trade report*, at <https://www.wto.org/english/res_e/booksp_e/anrep_e/wtr10-2b_e.pdf> (accessed 10-3-2018).

World Bank (2017) *The role of law in World Development Report 2017*, at <https://openknowledge.worldbank.org/bitstream/handle/10986/25880/9781464809507_Ch03.pdf?sequence=35&isAllowed=y> (accessed 10-12-2017).

Chapter 13: Access and benefit sharing: beyond the Nagoya Protocol and its ideals

Andrew Muma

1 Introduction

This chapter analyses the utility of the Nagoya Protocol in the conservation and sustainable use of biodiversity resources, both flora and fauna. Sustainable development aims not only to conserve the resources that exist in the environment for the present generation but also generations to come.[1] This has a bearing on food sufficiency, preservation of heritage, intellectual property, climate change and sustainability.[2] Clear juridical rights of ownership in community-owned areas ensure that resources are not abused.[3] This chapter looks at community rights over land and resources on it as a possible tool for enhancing sustainable development.[4] Sustainable environmental management is important for life on earth.[5]

In this chapter, it is argued that one of the causes of environmental degradation is the crusade for private land ownership which has led to the neglect of values and principles of communitarianism that were geared toward sustainable resource utilisation.[6] This is premised on the fact that private property ownership is hedonistic and broods an attitude of total disregard for the impacts of current actions on the future.

The Nagoya Protocol restates principles of the past and proposes a bottom-up approach that puts communities at the centre of the ownership of biodiversity. By enhancing the status of communities' tangible rights over the finite resources, it has the potential to eradicate poverty and simultaneously to facilitate the reinvention of value systems needed for effective biodiversity management and that as a check against rapid resource depletion.[7]

---

1 Fimbel et al. (2005: 33).
2 Okoth Ogendo (2006: 65). Okoth argues that the formal regime ought to ensure that there is security of tenure for the juridical persons entitled to such rights if sustainable development is to be achieved in the larger society.
3 Nyukuri (2017: 266); and Seppälä et al. (2009).
4 Nyukuri (2017: 266).
5 Obare & Wangwe (2004); and Ogolla & Mugabe (1996: 85-86).
6 Ross (2009: 5).
7 Nnadozie (2003: 58).

2 Background

2.1 An ontological perspective on land ownership policies

It is becoming increasingly clear that the subjugation of traditional systems of property ownership occasioned by colonisation is no longer justifiable.[8] This is because the premise upon which the neglect was founded – the economic efficiency of private ownership of resources – is flawed.[9] Historical evidence shows that the introduction of private ownership of land and resources in Kenya was a ploy to dispossess indigenous communities and create room for the settler community.[10] Further, before the advent of colonisation, land and allied resources were owned by the community as a unit with different categories of rights granted to clans, families and individuals.[11] However, upon declaration of the Kenyan protectorate in 1897, Ordinances were introduced whose effect was to take away ownership of the land from the communities and vest it in the Crown – the equivalent of the state in modern day terms.[12]

Owing to the wrong perception that land and land-related resources could not be efficiently managed using communal/customary tenure, communities directly collided with the introduced 'formal' system of ownership.[13] The western ownership patterns, which had matured through the industrial revolution slowly, replaced the institutions that had been in existence for centuries and had sustained the communities.[14] Proponents of the market believed that only easily transferrable property rights were desirable[15] contrary to emerging literature.[16]

With the taking away of land rights, communities became squatters on their own land[17] and their access to flora and fauna was curtailed. They were forced into reserves, which were the only places in which they were allowed to roam.[18] Most forests, which were part and parcel of the traditional life, became state property and were fenced off. This curtailed access to wildlife, fruit, traditional shrines, areas demarcated for traditional rites, medicinal plants. Settlers were allowed access into some of the forests to

---

8 Kameri Mbote et al. (2013: 37).
9 Nyamu-Musembi (2006).
10 Odote (2017: 119-120). See also *Kalabri v. AG* (1938) 18 KLR.
11 Blackburn (1976).
12 Ghai & McAuslan (1970: 3). See also *Ole Njogo v. A.G of E.A.P*, (1914), 5 E.A.L.R. 70.
13 Kameri-Mbote et al. (2013: 40), argue that colonial and post-colonial policy was geared towards privatisation of land and customary tenure was neglected and ignored. See further Swynnerton (1995).
14 Kenyatta (1965: 38).
15 Kemboi (2015: 88).
16 Angeles (2011: 2).
17 Okoth Ogendo (1995).
18 Anderson (2000).

clear and commence farming. The colonial government required permits and licenses for hunting and gathering activities.[19]

Upon the attainment of independence, the emphasis on private property continued.[20] Some of the land taken away was sold back to the natives who could access credit in order to pay for the land.[21] Ownership of reserves where customary tenure operated was transferred to the county councils to hold as trust land on behalf of these communities.[22] It is important to note that before the advent of the wave of land reforms in the global south in the 1990s,[23] the Land (Group Representatives) Act was the only post-independence Act of Parliament in Kenya that recognised some form of community tenure. Nevertheless, Odote has argued that this was not the end, but a means to an end.[24] The alleged recognition was to facilitate the conversion of the ranches to private land holdings.

2.2 The history of natural resource management

The displacement of communities is clear from the foregoing discussion. Once the land was taken away, native communities were deprived of their sources of livelihood,[25] exacerbating poverty. Mborio et al.[26] note, discussing the future of the Khasigau, that upon the forceful taking away of land from the community, poverty struck and is still felt by the Kasighau relative to its neighbours in Taita Taveta County. Community resources in Kenya were taken away from communities for imperialist interests.[27]

The colonial government set up the Department of Forests to manage forests[28] after Kenya became a protectorate. This was done without a policy to guide the delineation of forests and highlight the goals and objectives of setting them aside. The communities living around the forests were, and still are, prevented from accessing the forest areas, and where access is allowed, utilisation is circumscribed to the extent of rendering their proximity to the forests' resources useless.

A policy was crafted in 1957, but by that time the areas gazetted as forests had already been set aside.[29] It is therefore likely that the demarcations were not based on

---

19 Peluso (1993); and Baker (1997).
20 Doyle (2016).
21 Mweseli (2000: 21-22).
22 Okoth-Ogendo (2000).
23 Knight (2010).
24 Odote (2010).
25 Sen (2001).
26 Mborio et al. (2016).
27 Lindholt (2005).
28 Ogada (2012).
29 See <http://www.kenyaforestservice.org/index.php?Option=com_content&view=article&id=406&Itemid=563> (accessed 28-11-2017).

equitable grounds but were meant to protect the interests of the regime. In 1968, another policy was crafted which continued the process of exclusion of communities from direct participation in the management and use of the forest resources. This revision happened at a time when the increasing population had inadequate land to settle on. A few changes were introduced such as the *shamba* system, to allow communities living around the forests to use land gazetted as forest areas for farming, as they also cultivated crops for domestic use. Members of the community remained squatters on land that originally belonged to them. Alarmingly, little has changed even with the Forest Management and Conservation Act No. 36 of 2016 and the Forest Policy of 2007. The depletion of forest cover continues at an alarming rate.

Other resources taken away from communities[30] include wildlife and extractives that form the *raison d'être* for the Convention on Biodiversity and its Protocols.[31] The case studies used by Kameri Mbote et al.[32] show that resources such as minerals, pasture and wildlife become the property of the state and their use is controlled by the state.[33] However, in the case of pasture in areas that are predominantly pastoralist, access is not limited. The challenge that arises is that in seasons of scarcity, there is a scramble for pasture on public land. In the case of minerals, exclusion fuels violent clashes and the minerals become a curse disguised as a blessing.[34]

In the case of genetic resources and the intellectual property of communities, exploitation is never brought to their attention. Furthermore, due to the sophistication with which such activities are conducted, the communities are totally excluded from the benefits that accrue. If such activities were brought to public light, communities could demand their entitlements. For instance, Lake Baringo residents benefitted from the use by a Japanese company of enzymes from the geysers in Lake Bogoria.[35]

Aquatic resources are also being depleted and degraded. The water hyacinth in Lake Victoria has really affected the ecosystem. The fish population in Lake Victoria is also dwindling, raising poverty levels and diminishing food sources for communities living around the lake. In terms of wildlife resources, continued deforestation has led to increased human-wildlife conflict owing to increased mobility of wildlife due to disturbed habitats. Communities that live near gazetted national parks do not often benefit directly from the revenue that accrues from such parks. It is channelled to national coffers thus making it difficult to convince communities living near the parks to participate in wildlife conservation.

30 Nyamwaya (2013).
31 Convention on Biological Diversity (1992) 31 I.L.M. 842.
32 Kameri-Mbote (2014).
33 See Article 71 of the Constitution of Kenya 2010.
34 Quinn & Conway (2008).
35 Muheembwa (2014).

3 Conceptual framework

3.1 Property rights and the management of biodiversity

3.1.1 Property rights

Property has different meanings to different people. To the layperson, property is a thing represented by physical resources. However, it is a legal concept, economic concept and a social relationship.[36] A right is a claim by an individual or institution-holder of a right on another upon whom there is a duty for an act or forbearance; and the failure to perform, entitles the right holder to use coercion to extract compliance or compensation in lieu thereof.[37]

Property represents a social relationship between the rights holder and persons amongst whom he lives.[38] It is a relationship between an individual and the community regarding the use and exploitation of resources, and is dependent on the enforcement mechanisms of the state.[39] It is the duty of the law, as the expression of the will of the people, to provide mechanisms to protect property in the interest of all citizens.

A property law system must protect and curtail the right of property holders to ensure an environment in which the rights of other property holders and the public interest are safeguarded. This view of property is very important for the discussion going forward because natural resource use that entails degradation affects the entire society. It is therefore important to emphasise the point that property is not just a commodity over which the owner has absolute rights. Choices on the use and regulation of property go beyond individuals to shaping social relationships generally.

Property is a legal relationship by virtue of a claim backed by law, a bundle of rights and expectations in a tangible or intangible thing that are enforceable against third parties including the government.[40] These are entitlements to possess, use, exclude, allow others to use, sell, give away, dispose of by will, recover from a thief and receive compensation in case of damage. With the encoding of these presumptions into law and policy, communal rights have been marginalised in Kenya since the official dogma openly supports private individual rights and actively encourages the transformation of community rights into private individual rights.[41] At the centre of all this property discourse is the maxim *cuis est solum eius est usque as coelom et ad infernos* – he who owns the land owns everything reaching up to the heavens and down the depths of the earth – which underscores the sacrosanct nature of land rights in English common

36 Bentham (1976: 133).
37 Becker (1977).
38 Kameri-Mbote (2007: 75).
39 Akech & Kameri-Mbote (2008: 15).
40 Cohen quoted in Sprankling (1991).
41 Kameri-Mbote et al. (2013: 37).

law.[42] Its subject matter includes the surface of the soil, the things on the soil enjoyed as part of the land (such as air, water, trees and animals); the things artificially attached to the land like buildings; and things found beneath the surface of the earth. It also includes biological resources.

There are three distinct property rights regimes that affect biodiversity management: individual/private property; communal/common property; and government control.[43] At the international level ownership of genetic resources have for a long time been a point of contention between developed and developing countries. A good case in point was the coining of the concept of farmers rights (FRs), a genus of intellectual property rights seeking to balance benefits enjoyed by donors of germplasm and technology versus the interests of farmers who preserve protect and conserve genetic resources and share them with others. Developing countries saw the abrogation of the common heritage of humankind concept as a step towards equity with developed countries in terms of genetic resource and commercialisation, but this has not been the case. Countries like Kenya have since moved to align their laws to regulate access to genetic material whilst neglecting land tenure arrangements, which are key to sustainable development. The result undermines the best interests of citizens.

Property rights are discussed under two headings at the national level: state regulation and market regulation. Both positions assume that human beings cannot use common pool resources in a sustainable manner without state regulation. In instances of state regulation, the state undertakes, through regulatory command and control mechanisms, to elicit behaviour conducive to biodiversity management. Market solutions, on the other hand, rely on personal motivation derived from granting private individual rights with the hope that it will provide incentive enough to right holders to maximise the benefits, thereby promoting sustainability.[44] The upshot of the foregoing campaign for private property rights in biodiversity conservation, both at the international and national level, is the view that property held in common encourages a rush by all having access to it to appropriate as much of it as possible while it lasts.[45] Food shortages and environmental degradation have led to disenchantment with command and control approaches to environmental regulation, raising the need to change the narrative. A change would call for an understanding of economics and property rights in addition to embracing relevant property rights regimes that work.

In biodiversity management, both real and intellectual property rights are relevant where real property comprises tangible commodities capable of exclusive possession and delineation.[46] Land exemplifies this form of property as it hosts an array of species and ecosystems, thus making land tenure arrangements central to biodiversity

42 Blackstone & Blackstone (1809).
43 Miller (1995).
44 Kameri-Mbote (2002: 20-25).
45 Ostrom (2015).
46 Swanson (1995: 118).

management. Land tenure defines the range of persons able to control and manage resources found on that land and the form of land management to apply to it. It also determines who may participate in resource extraction and to what degree.[47]

The value of intellectual property rights (IPRs), on the other hand, results from creating a shortage of information by limiting access to non-owners. IPRs have proven to be a challenge in communal setups as they are premised on the understanding that a creator has invested labour. This concept is akin to private property ownership and does not accommodate community knowledge developed over time and passed from generation to generation; knowledge that cannot be traced to a particular individual and which is available for use by all members of the community.[48] IPR regimes are, however, slowly warming up to the realisation that communities cannot be wished away and traditional knowledge and indigenous peoples property rights protection are taking centre stage in international debates.

3.1.2 The moral hazard theory

In the context of agency, an agent is seldom more concerned with the affairs of the principal than the principal would be. Therefore, an agent is likely to be less concerned with the long-term performance of the endeavours of the principal as long as the agent's short-term goals are catered for. In the context of corporate governance, a stakeholder other than the owner of an entity will likewise be less concerned with the performance of the affairs of the said entity. This rationalises the effort that is being expended in modern-day toward the creation of governance structure in entities, whether public or private, in order to protect the interests of the real owners of entities and to the factors of production.

Building on the argument above, stakeholders, other than the communities that live next to areas rich in natural resources, may theoretically not be the best institutional entities and/or persons to manage and conserve natural resources. This is because they do not bear first hand, the brunt of the mismanagement of such resources be they forests, aquatic resources, minerals or wildlife.[49] On this premise, it is therefore proposed to grant more pronounced rights to communities to enhance their chances of better biodiversity management.[50] Furthermore, the current system of vesting the rights of control, use and access to resources in the state has shown that the said powers are

47 Ochola et al. (2010: 399-406).
48 Mudiwa (2002).
49 Okidi Odidi & Odote (2017: 278).
50 Odote (2010).

prone to abuse.[51] Further, there has been continued depletion of the said resources and increased poverty for the people living around the natural resources.[52]

3.2 Commons as the institutional arrangement that may alter behavioural challenges

There is ample evidence that the current institutional arrangements fail because of the fallacy that common property regimes are inefficient. This, according to Okoth, was based on a lack of proper understanding of the nature of commons as a legitimate regime governed under customary law.[53] As opposed to private systems that are focused on individual advancement and optimal gain, commons are based on the understanding that individuals are interdependent. Therefore, the concept of mutual vulnerability is at the centre of societal development.[54] This is what other authors view as the requirement for reciprocity in dealings with property owned communally. From the foregoing, it is clear that the approach to property under customary or communal tenure had common interests as the chief goal of institutional arrangements.

On the other hand, under common property regimes, resources on land and in land were considered to be trans-generational assets.[55] Persons who were alive knew well that they were not exclusively entitled to benefit from the resources but to consider future generations as well.[56] This shows that under communal systems of ownership, sustainability of resource utilisation was paramount. This explains why communities would demand that once land that had been tilled for some time and had become depleted in terms of mineral richness, the land had to be left fallow for years before tilling would be allowed on it again.[57] The same applied to wildlife and forest resources, which were used under strict supervision.

Owing to the misunderstanding of the intrinsic nature of the commons, it has been argued by Hardin that due to a lack of restrictions on access, commons face a tragedy.[58] Musembi[59] has illustrated that such a theory is fallacious. Moreover, this is squarely because of the confusion of commons with open access. This position has been taken up by Akech who argues that there is a need to revive the commons as an alternative or complementary driving force to ensure sustainable use of not only land but other

51 Government of Kenya (2004).
52 Abwoli (2009: 315-333).
53 Okoth-Ogendo (2002: 7).
54 di Robilant (2011: 1363) discussed in Okoth Ogendo (1995).
55 Okoth Ogendo (1995).
56 Kameri-Mbote (2007).
57 Ibid.
58 Hardin (1968: 1243).
59 Musembi (2007).

resources too.[60] This position has been properly captured by Bromley and Cernea who have refuted the position that commons are wasteful in the following terms:[61]

> Resource degradation in developing countries while incorrectly attributed intrinsically to common property systems actually originates in the dissolution of local level institutional arrangements whose purpose was to give rise to resource use patterns that were sustainable.

3.3 Resource management decentralisation as a panacea

Irresponsible human activity is one of the main causes of resource degradation and depletion.[62] This explains why deforestation singularly accounts for between 12-18% of greenhouse gas emissions. It is noteworthy that globally, there is a push towards recognising community or indigenous rights. This recognition has converged with the growing importance of climate change and environmental degradation. Decentralisation places individual communities at the centre of resource management enabling them to individually and collectively manage the resources.[63] This ensures that they benefit from the resources and view them as a trans-generational asset. The results of this decentralisation range from the alteration of human behaviour in respect of resources to the improvement of livelihoods.[64]

The formal recognition of communities as juridical persons in law is a step in the right direction.[65] For instance, the Northern Rangelands Trust (NRT) was created to allow for proper use of pasture while at the same time conserving wildlife, which is a source of revenue.[66] Similarly, in Arabuko Sokoke, participatory forest management has been used to allow communities to access the forest resources while at the same time engendering conservation. This has contributed to changing the perception of communities toward natural resources and helped reduce human-wildlife conflict.

3.4 Access and benefit sharing: definition and importance in economic development

Access means obtaining, processing and using genetic resources, including derived products and where applicable, intangible components for purposes of research, bio-prospecting, conservation, industrial application or commercial use. Before the

60 Akech (2001).
61 Bromley & Cernea (1989: 47).
62 Adger et al. (2009).
63 Salick (2007).
64 Mariku et al. (2012).
65 Odote (2010).
66 Kameri Mbote et al. (2013: 54).

Convention on Biological Diversity (CBD)[67] came into effect in 1992, genetic resources were free to all humankind. They would be collected from countries of origin and taken to other countries without any regulation. This led to countries of origin seeking to share the benefits arising from the use of the resources sourced in their territory. Benefit sharing is a hotly debated topic in law, medical ethics and political philosophy. Its ordinary definition is the action of giving a portion of advantage or profit (monetary and non-monetary benefits) to others. However, for purposes of the international legal discourse, benefit sharing is used to mean giving a portion of advantage/profit derived from the use of genetic resources or related knowledge to resource providers.[68]

Economically, access and benefit sharing (ABS) regimes are important to channel benefits that accrue from the use of genetic material. Namibia, for example, exports the devil's claw, which is used as an analgesic anti-inflammatory drug. Export revenues are estimated at USD 2 million annually, but communities receive no benefit.[69] Similarly, Prunus Africana, used for boosting immunity and the treatment of prostate cancer, generates about USD 220 million annually, yet people who have nurtured it receive no benefit.[70] Industrial enzymes from microbes used for fading jeans are a trade worth USD 600 million annually, and the communities around Lake Bogoria in Kenya where the enzymes are sourced, do not benefit from the proceeds.[71] Communities living around Lake Ruiru in Kenya are also unaware of, and do not benefit from, the EUR 278 million generated from a diabetes drug processed from microbes sourced from the lake.[72]

4 Legal and regulatory framework governing natural resource management and conservation

From the foregoing, it is evident that community involvement in natural resource management has become necessary and ABS can facilitate it. ABS has achieved recognition in international treaties and protocols emphasising the need to legislate on ABS nationally. This part of the chapter looks at ABS treaties and the extent to which their provisions have been domesticated in Kenya.

67 Convention on Biological Diversity, 31 *International Legal Materials* opened for signature on 5 June 1992 and entered into force on 29 December 1993.

68 Carrizosa (2004).

69 Government of Namibia (2010).

70 Stewart (2003).

71 Lacey (2006).

72 Munyaradzi (2014: 117).

4.1 International framework for access and benefit-sharing

4.1.1 Convention on Biological Diversity

The CBD is a key instrument in discussions on ABS. It was opened for signature in 1992, entered into force in 1993 and has to date been ratified by 193 parties making it nearly universal. It has three objectives:[73]

- the conservation of biological diversity;
- the fair and equitable sharing of benefits arising out of the utilisation of genetic resources; and
- the sustainable use of the components of biological diversity.

Fair and equitable sharing of benefits arising from the use of genetic resources is addressed in Articles 15, 16 and 19 of the CBD. Article 15 provides for access to genetic resources on mutually agreed terms and subject to prior informed consent of the contracting party providing such resources. It requires contracting parties to take legislative, administrative and policy measures for fair and equitable sharing of the benefits; results of research and development; and the commercial and other use of genetic resources.

Article 16 focuses on access to, and transfer of, technology and requires contracting parties to undertake to provide both access to and transfer of technologies relevant to the conservation and sustainable use of biological diversity. Additionally, while recognising that patents and other IPRs may have an influence on the implementation of the CBD, it calls on parties to cooperate to ensure that IPRs support and do not run counter to its objectives.

Article 19 specifically addresses biotechnology and its benefits, emphasising the need for all parties to effectively participate in biotechnological research especially in developing countries. It also calls for practical measures to promote and advance priority access on a fair and equitable basis. Notably, it anticipates the need for and exhorts parts to consider a protocol with appropriate ABS procedures.

In a nutshell, the CBD represents a paradigm shift from the concept of common heritage of mankind to the concept of national sovereignty over genetic resources. While it lays a basis for ABS, it has been argued that it concentrates on access for chemical and pharmaceutical purposes and is difficult to apply to plant genetic resources used for food and agriculture.[74]

Implementation of the ABS provisions at the national level has been slow in Africa, owing to: a lack of 'user measures'; the absence of support for user compliance with ABS legislation in provider countries; and the difficulty in negotiating mutually agreed terms of ABS. According to the multi-donor ABS development capacity building

73 Article 1 of the Convention on Biological Diversity.
74 Santilili (2012: 56).

initiative, only six out of 54 African countries had developed ABS legislation by 2011.[75] While these few countries developed access oriented policies and legislation, the lack of corresponding benefit sharing policies and legislation in industrialised countries resulted in the adoption of the Nagoya Protocol in 2010 at the World Summit on Sustainable Development.[76]

4.1.2 African model law

The African Model Law for the protection of rights of communities, farmers and breeders, and the regulation of access to biological resources, was adopted in 1998 and provisions on plant breeder's rights (PBRs) included in 2001. This is not a law or agreement, but rather an information package for use in drafting national laws. It provides a framework for African Union member states to develop specific national legislation in compliance with their international commitments.[77] The African Model Law needs revision, but the question is whether it is useful within the context of a detailed international ABS instrument – the Nagoya Protocol.[78]

4.1.3 International Treaty on Plant Genetic Resources for Food and Agriculture (ITPGRFA)

The ITPGRFA,[79] adopted in November 2001 and which entered into force in June 2004, seeks to ensure the conservation and sustainable use of plant genetic resources for food and agriculture and the fair and equitable sharing of benefits arising out of their use, in harmony with the CBD. It only regulates access to plant genetic resources for food and agriculture (PGRFA) while access to other genetic resources is to be negotiated bilaterally in accordance with national ABS policies in the context of the CBD. Under the Treaty, ABS goals are to be achieved through a multilateral system where facilitated access is provided based on a standard material transfer agreement, which establishes benefit sharing obligations when PGRFA are commercialised.

---

75 GIZ (2011).

76 Paragraph 44 of the plan of implementation of the World Summit on SD A/Conf 199/20 (2002).

77 Munyi et al. (2012).

78 Nagoya Protocol on Access to Genetic Resources and the Fair and Equitable Sharing of Benefits Arising from their Utilization to the Convention on Biological Diversity, 29 October 2010, UNEP/CBD/COP/DEC/X/1.

79 International Treaty on Plant Genetic Resources for Food and Agriculture, adopted in November 2001 and which came into force in June 2004 <www.fao.org/3/a-i0510e.pdf> (accessed 30-5-2018).

4.1.4 Bonn Guidelines on Access to Genetic Resources and Fair and Equitable Sharing of the Benefits Arising out of their Utilisation

The Bonn Guidelines[80] were adopted in April 2002 by the sixth meeting of the Conference of Parties to the CBD. They apply to genetic resources covered by the CBD but not those covered by the ITPGRFA. The Guidelines are voluntary and flexible and were designed to guide countries in developing ABS legislation. They deal with the involvement of relevant stakeholders and capacity building; steps in the ABS process; elements of a prior informed consent system; potential monetary and non-monetary benefits; incentives; national monitoring and reporting; and accountability.[81]

4.1.5 Nagoya Protocol on Access to Genetic Resources and Fair and Equitable Sharing of Benefits Arising from their Utilization to the Convention on Biological Diversity (Nagoya Protocol)

This protocol to the CBD, adopted in Japan on 29th October 2010, sets out the rules and mechanisms for access to genetic resources and associated traditional knowledge (TK) and supports the fair and equitable sharing of benefits arising from their use. It draws significantly from the Bonn Guidelines. Articles 5 and 6 of the Protocol require that access to genetic resources by users be based on prior informed consent and that equitable benefit sharing must occur on mutually agreed terms.

4.1.6 Rights of indigenous people and local communities

Recognising that respect for indigenous knowledge, cultures and traditional practices contributes to sustainable development and proper resource management, several covenants and declarations have been signed, including: the Covenant on Intellectual Cultural and Scientific Resources; the Declaration of Principles of the World Council of Indigenous Peoples;[82] the UN Declaration on the Rights of Indigenous Peoples;[83] the Kari-Oca Declaration and the Indigenous Peoples Earth Charter;[84] the Charter of the

80 Secretariat of the Convention on Biological Diversity, Bonn Guidelines on Access to Genetic Resources and Fair and Equitable Sharing of the Benefits Arising out of their Utilization (2002).

81 Carrizosa et al. (2004).

82 World Council of Indigenous Peoples Declaration of Principles (CIRCA1984) adopted by the General Assembly of the WCIP at a gathering at Panama City, Panama (1984).

83 United Nations Declaration on the Rights of Indigenous Peoples, adopted by the General Assembly on 13th September 2007, A/RES/61/295.

84 KARI-OCA Declaration and Indigenous Peoples' Earth Charter, World Conference of Indigenous Peoples on Territory, Environment and Development KARI-OCA 25-30 May 1992.

Indigenous-Tribal Peoples of the Tropical Forests;[85] the Recommendations from the Voices of the Earth Congress;[86] the COICA/UNDP Regional Meeting on IPRs and Biodiversity basic points of agreement;[87] the UNDP Consultation on the Protection and Conservation of Indigenous Knowledge;[88] and the UNDP Consultation on Indigenous Peoples Knowledge and IPRs.[89] All these build momentum for communities' rights to participate actively in matters affecting their livelihood, including ABS relating to environmental management and conservation.[90]

4.2 National laws on ABS elements

Kenya signed the CBD in 1992 and ratified it in 1994 and the Nagoya Protocol in 2012. Kenya is also a party to the ITPGRFA. Some ABS elements are contained in some national laws, but their actual implementation is far from perfect.[91] Prior to CBD, there was little or no exchange of knowledge or compensation for access to resources. There is an urgent need to correct this position.

The ABS regime at the national level is fragmented with instances of role duplication, which makes enforcement difficult. Nyamwaya suggests the need for a comprehensive regime recognising the role of communities.[92] Internationally, the Universal Declaration of Human Rights recognises the rights of people to own property and natural resources, stating:[93]

> Indigenous peoples have the right to redress, by means that can include restitution or, when this is not possible, just, fair and equitable compensation, for the lands, territories and resources which they have traditionally owned or otherwise occupied or used, and which have been confiscated, taken, occupied, used or damaged without their free, prior and informed consent.

Community involvement in natural resource management ought to be embraced, and for this to be successful, it must be looked at both from a land ownership perspective and from the perspective of implementary ABS.

85 Charter of the indigenous and tribal peoples of the tropical forests (IAIP Charter), Penang, Malaysia (1992).

86 Recommendations from the Voices of the Earth Congress, Amsterdam, Netherlands, 10-11 November 1993. Cited in Posey and Dutfield (1996).

87 COICA/UNDP Regional Meeting on Intellectual Property Rights and Biodiversity, Santa Cruz de la Sierra, Bolivia, 28-30 September 1994.

88 UNDP Consultation on the Protection and Conservation of Indigenous Knowledge, Sabah East Malaysia (24-27 February 1995).

89 UNDP Consultation on Indigenous Peoples' Knowledge and Intellectual Property Rights, Suva (April 1995).

90 Posey & Dutfield (1996: 175-179).

91 Joseph (2012).

92 Nyamwaya (2013).

93 Article 28(1) of the Universal Declaration of Human Rights, proclaimed by the United Nations General Assembly in Paris on 10 December 1948 (General Assembly Resolution 217A).

4.2.1 Current legislation and regulations in Kenya

The Constitution of Kenya 2010,[94] the Land Act[95] and the Community Land Act[96] are of relevance here. The Community Land Act recognises, protects and provides for the registration of community land rights, and Sections 35 and 36 provide that natural resources found on community land shall be managed sustainably, with benefits accruing shared equitably subject to a clear agreement entered into between the investor and the community. However, the question is what happens to natural resources on public land held by the government that communities are entitled to? This is the issue graphically discussed in Kasighau in November 2011:[97]

> There is no land that is unclaimed. If we were to be told: each one to your positions go! There would be no vacant spaces left that anyone could point to and call 'ours' as everything would be labeled 'mine'. The government land is therefore what we are eyeing when we speak of community land.

On the other hand, natural resource laws include the Constitution of Kenya 2010, the Environmental Management and Coordination Act (EMCA),[98] the Forest Management and Conservation Act[99], the Fisheries Management and Development Act,[100] the Water Act,[101] the Wildlife Management and Conservation Act,[102] the Mining Act 2016,[103] and the Petroleum (Exploration and Production) Act.[104] The yet to be passed Natural Resources (County Royalties) Bill (2013)[105] and the Natural Resources (Benefit Sharing) Bill (2014)[106] which have a more direct bearing on sharing revenue from the use of natural resources, are yet to be passed.

Section 53 of EMCA deals with ABS and under it, the Environment Management and Co-ordination (Conservation of Biological Diversity and Resources, Access to

---

94 The Constitution of Kenya, 27th August 2010 <http://www.refworld.org/docid/4c8508822.html> (accessed 25-05-2018).

95 The Republic of Kenya, Laws of Kenya, Land Act No. 6 of 2012.

96 The Republic of Kenya, Laws of Kenya, Community Land Act No. 27 of 2016.

97 Mborio et al. (2016).

98 The Republic of Kenya, Laws of Kenya, Environmental Management and Co-ordination Act No. 8 of 1999. See furhter: Kenya Gazette Supplement No. 74 Act No. 5 of 3rd June 2015; and the Environmental Management and Co-ordination (Amendment) Act (2015).

99 The Forest Conservation and Management Act, Kenya Gazette Supplement No. 155 (Acts No. 34) of 7th September 2016.

100 The Republic of Kenya, Laws of Kenya, Fisheries Management and Development Act No. 35 of 2016.

101 The Republic of Kenya, Kenya Gazette Supplement No. 164, Water Act No. 43 of 2016.

102 The Republic of Kenya, Laws of Kenya, Wildlife (Conservation and Management) No. 47 of 2013.

103 The Republic of Kenya, Laws of Kenya, Kenya Gazette Supplement No. 71, Mining Act No. 12 of 2016.

104 The Republic of Kenya, Laws of Kenya, Petroleum Exploration and Production Act Chapter 308.

105 Republic of Kenya, Natural Resources (County Royalties) Bill 2013.

106 Republic of Kenya, Kenya Gazette Supplement No. 137 Senate Bills No. 34 of 2014.

Genetic Resources and Benefit Sharing) Regulations Legal Notice No. 160 of 2006 were made. The regulations provide for access at Part III and benefit sharing at Part IV, with implementation placed under National Environmental Management Authority (NEMA). All applications for permits are to be made to NEMA whose requirements include: payment of a fee; prior informed consent; mutually agreed terms; and minutes of meetings and research authorisation from the National Council of Science and Technology (NCST).[107] In the case of wildlife, prior informed consent should be sought from Kenya Wildlife Service (KWS);[108] and from the Kenya Agricultural and Livestock Research Organization (KARLO) in case of agriculture.[109]

Complaints about a lack of clarity in the systems, the multiplicity of regulators and a lot of paperwork abound with many seeing compliance with CBD lost as the obligation to pay fees imposed by NEMA takes centre stage. The expectation that communities would benefit has not been realised.[110] It is proposed in the draft National Biosciences Policy[111] that a National Biosecurity and Bioscience Research Authorization Committee be established to reduce the red tape. The involvement of the community in crafting access legislation is critical for progress to be made.

Section 5 of the Water Act[112] vests water resources in the government in trust for the people of Kenya. It also creates a Water Resources Authority to regulate the management and use of water resources, and grant and enforce permits for water abstraction, use and recharge. A Water Basin Committee has been established, with four to seven members including representatives of farmers/pastoralists. Its function is to advise the authority and county governments on conservation, use and apportionment of water resources, permit issuance and cancellation, equitable water sharing and related issues. There is an attempt at decentralisation in this Act, but ABS mechanisms for communities living around water bodies to motivate them to conserve the resources are absent. Benefits can be derived from bulk water revenues, tourism, water sports, energy generation, large-scale irrigation and aquatic resources. The Wildlife (Conservation and Management) Act[113] also makes no mention of ABS for communities living around the parks, only providing compensation for personal injury or death.

107 NEMA, ABS Brochure, Access and Benefit Sharing from Utilization of Biological Resources and Associated Traditional Knowledge in Kenya (2014). NCST is a semi-autonomous government agency established by the Science and Technology Act Cap 250 Laws of Kenya main role being research clearance and authorisation.

108 KWS is a state corporation established under the Wildlife Conservation and Management Act No. 47 of 2013.

109 KALRO is a corporate body created under the Kenya Agricultural and livestock Research Act of 2013.

110 Brink (2013: 45).

111 Science Technology and Innovation Act, 2013 Laws of Kenya, National Commission for Science, Technology and Innovation (NACOSTI), became the successor of NCST, currently developing the Bioscience Policy 2018.

112 The Republic of Kenya, Laws of Kenya, Water Act No. 43 of 2016.

113 Republic of Kenya, Wildlife Conservation and Management Act, No. 47 of 2013.

The Fisheries Management and Development Act[114] creates the Kenya Fisheries Advisory Council and Kenya Fisheries Service (KFS), whose functions are to ensure the development of standards on management, sustainable use, development and protection of the fisheries resources and aquaculture activities. Notably, Sections 35 and 36 of the Act provide for a working relationship between the county government and the KFS pursuant to the Constitution of Kenya 2010, Schedule 4. However, KFS retains a supervisory role over so many functions with the county government taking a back seat. Section 37 of the Act establishes Beach Management Units (BMUs) to ensure structured community participation in fisheries' management. The role of communities in the BMUs is left to future regulations.

The Forest Conservation and Management Act[115] establishes the Kenya Forest Service whose function is to conserve, protect and manage all public forests. Section 20 of the Act provides for a forest conservation area and a committee, which includes a community forest association nominee. It is worth noting that Part V of the Act provides for community participation in forest management through Community Forest Associations (CFA) with user rights in forests, which is meant to ensure sustainable forest management. However, it is not clear what their influence is on ABS relating to forest resources.

The Petroleum Exploration and Production Act[116] governs exploration of crude oil, natural gas and petroleum within Kenya and the continental shelf. It vests these resources in the government. There is no mention of community or benefit sharing anywhere in the Act even though communities can be occupiers of land with, or contiguous to, resources. The existence of these resources on land removes them from individuals and communities and vests them in the government. For private land, Section 10 provides that access will not be denied where a contractor intends to enter land to carry out petroleum operations. The Mining Act[117] also makes no mention of community rights and ABS in the exploitation of the natural resource and all decision approvals, permits licenses and benefits accrue to government through the Ministry, Mineral Rights Board and National Mining Corporation. The Energy Act,[118] which regulates electrical energy supply, petroleum and natural gas licensing and permits, renewable energy and energy efficiency and conservation, also has no ABS elements. This is despite the fact that communities live around windmills, hydroelectric power plants and geothermal plants.

The upshot of the above analysis is that CBD and Nagoya provisions on ABS are yet to be realised in Kenya. There is a need to review land ownership and natural

114 Republic of Kenya, Laws of Kenya, Fisheries Management and Development Act, No. 35 of 2016.

115 Republic of Kenya, Laws of Kenya, Forest Conservation and Management Act, No. 34 of 2016.

116 Republic of Kenya, Laws of Kenya, Petroleum Exploration and Production Act, Chapter 308.

117 Republic of Kenya, Laws of Kenya, Mining Act, No. 12 of 2016.

118 Republic of Kenya, Laws of Kenya, Energy Act, No. 12 of 2006.

resource laws to balance entitlements and restore public trust, which demands that we conserve our environment and right glaring wrongs.[119] Granting communities entitlements is one way of securing public trust.

5 Beyond the Nagoya Protocol

The government has a key role to play in biodiversity conservation if the current state of laws is anything to go by. The lacuna in law has caused the degradation of Kenya's natural resources, and it is, therefore, time to enhance community participation as a way of reducing government control over natural resources. This can be initiated through pilot projects.

There is also need to reduce the bureaucratic and complex nature of the existing ABS regulatory system. NEMA has already indicated a willingness to streamline procedures by developing templates for prior informed consent, mutually agreed terms and material transfer agreements; and introducing automating licensing. The idea of linking all institutions involved in ABS to create a one-stop shop for prospective users would certainly contribute to decreased complexity and reduced bureaucracy.

Raising awareness about ABS regulations amongst stakeholders is important. It should address issues such as the types of potential benefits, how to access these benefits and negotiation processes. Capacity building to enhance negotiation skills and meetings to align users' and providers' expectations should be convened. Better monitoring of compliance is key to the establishment of structures and the enhancement of expertise. Compliance, monitoring and enforcement should be strengthened in both the user and the provider countries. In addition, to ensure transparency and traceability and to guarantee compliance with the legal requirements in the country of origin, an international certificate of origin has been proposed.[120] Lastly, there is a need for greater coordination between ministries responsible for ABS in environmental resource sectors and agriculture. These recommendations can be addressed through the introduction of a *sui generis* ABS law, aligning relevant existing laws and anchored on stakeholder and community participation.

References

Abwoli, B (2009) "Emerging local economic dynamics shaping east African forest landscapes" in G Mery, P Katila, G Galloway, RI Alfaro, M Kanninen, M Lobovikov & J Varjo (eds) *Forest and society: responding to global drivers of change* 315-334.

119 Akech & Kameri-Mbote (2008: 15).
120 Wekundah (2012).

Adger, WN, I Lorenzoni & KL O'Brien (2009) *Adapting to climate change: thresholds, values, governance.*

Akech, M (2001) *Rescuing indigenous tenure from the ghetto of neglect.*

Akech, M & P Kameri-Mbote (2008) "Ownership and regulation of land rights in Kenya: balancing entitlements with the public trust" presentation at the Kenya Institute for Public Policy Research and Analysis Conference, Kenyatta International Conference Centre, Nairobi, 31 July 2008.

Anderson, D (2000) "Master and servant in colonial Kenya" 41 *Journal of African History* 459-485.

Angeles, L (2011) *Institutions, property rights, and economic development in historical perspective*, at <https://www.gla.ac.uk/media/media_189284_en.pdf> (accessed 26-11-2017).

Baker, JE (1997) "Trophy hunting as a sustainable use of wildlife resources in southern and eastern Africa" 5(4) *Journal of Sustainable Tourism* 306-321.

Becker, LC (1977) *Property rights. Philosophic foundations.*

Beinart, W (1984) "Soil erosion, conservationism and ideas about development: a southern African exploration, 1900-1960" 11(1) *Journal of Southern African Studies* 143-162.

Bentham, J (1864) *Theory of legislation.*

Blackburn, RH (1976) "Ogiek history" in BA Ogot (ed.) *Kenya before 1900* 53-84.

Blackstone W, E Christian & W Blackstone (1809) *Commentaries on the laws of England: In four books.*

Brink, M (2013) *Implementation of access and benefit sharing policies in sub-Sahara Africa: inventory, analysis and proposals.*

Bromley, D & M Cernea (1989) *The management of common property natural resources: some conceptual and operational fallacies* Discussion Paper No. 57.

Clarke, RA (2009) "Securing communal land rights to achieve sustainable development in sub-Saharan Africa: critical analysis and policy implications" 5(2) *Law, Environment and Development Journal* 130-151.

Doyle, K (2016) "Customary land rights in Kenya in the context of history: from colonialism through independence, from Jomo Kenyatta to Uhuru Kenyatta" in C Odote & P Kameri-Mbote (eds), *Breaking the mould: lessons for implementing community land rights in Kenya* 11-26.

Farbotko, C (2010) "Wishful sinking: disappearing islands, climate refugees and cosmopolitan experimentation" 51(1) *Asia Pacific Viewpoint* 47-60.

Fimbel, C, B Curran & L Usongo (2000) "Enhancing the sustainability of duiker hunting through community participation and controlled access in the Lobéké Region of Southeastern Cameroon" in J Robinson & E Bennett *Hunting for sustainability in tropical forests*, at <http://cup.columbia.edu/book/hunting-forsustainability-in-tropical-forests/9780231109772> (accessed 30-5-2018).

Fischer, C (2017) *International experience with benefit-sharing instruments for extractive resources* Paper done for Resources for the Future, World Bank.

Ghai, Y & J McAuslan (1970) *Public law and political change in Kenya: a study of the legal framework of government from colonial times to the present.*

Government of Kenya (2004), *Report of the Commission of Inquiry into illegal/irregular allocation of public land* (Ndung'u Commission Report).

Hardin, G (1968) "The tragedy of the commons" 162 *Science* 1243-1248.

Joseph, W (2012) *Why informal sector is important in food security* African Technology Policy Studies Network Special Paper Series No. 43.

Kameri-Mbote, P (2002) *Property rights and biodiversity management in Kenya: the case of land tenure and wildlife.*

Kameri-Mbote, P (2007) "Land tenure, land use and sustainability in Kenya: towards an innovative use of property rights in wildlife management" in N Chalifour, P Kameri-Mbote, L Heng Lye & JR Nolin (eds) *Land use for sustainable development* 132-160.

Kameri-Mbote, P (2014) "Community land rights: what exactly is at stake?" *The Star* (17-10-2014).

Kameri-Mbote, P & C Odote (eds) (2017) *The gallant academic: essays in honour of H.W.O Okoth Ogendo*.

Kameri-Mbote, P, C Odote, C Musembi & M Kamande (2013) *Ours by right: law, politics and realities of community property in Kenya*.

Kemboi, A (2015) *Resolution of community land disputes and the new constitutional order: a quest for the utilization of traditional justice systems* LLB Dissertation University of Nairobi.

Kenyatta, J (1965) *Facing Mount Kenya: the traditional life of the Gikuyu*.

Knight, SR (2010) *Statutory recognition of land rights in Africa: an investigation into best practices for law making and implementation*.

Lindholt, L (2005) *Human rights in development yearbook 2003: human rights and local/living law*.

Mariku P, M Caleb & O Callistus (2012) "Is participatory forest management an asset or liability to the local community households adjacent to Arabuko Sokoke Forest, Kenya?" 4(3) *Journal of African Studies and Development* 112-129.

Mborio, M, C Nyamu-Musembi, M Mwasaru & M Mwandigha (2016) "Kasighau: will constitutional recognition of community land reverse a history of extraction & marginalization?" in C Odote & P Kameri-Mbote (eds) *Breaking the mould: lessons for implementing community land rights in Kenya* 27-46.

Miller, MAL (1995) *The Third World in global environmental politics*.

Muheembwa, H (2014) "Kenyan community benefits from its genetic resources" *Intellectual Property Watch* (17-11-2014).

Munyi, P, M Tonye Mahop, P du Plessis, J Ekpere & K Bavikatte (2012) *A gap analysis on the African model law on the protection of the rights of local communities, farmers and breeders, and for the regulation of access to biological resources*.

Musembi, CN (2007) "De Soto and land relations in rural Africa: breathing life into dead theories about property rights" 28(8) *3rd World Quarterly* 1457-1478.

Mweseli, T (2000) "The centrality of land in Kenya: historical background and legal perspective" in S Wanjala, *Essays on land law: the reform debate in Kenya* 3-24.

Nnadozie, K (2003) *African perspectives on genetic resources: a handbook on laws, policies, and institutions*.

Nyamu-Musembi, C (2006) *Breathing life into dead theories about property rights: de Soto and land relations in rural Africa* Institute of Development Studies Working Paper No. 272.

Nyamwaya, C (2013) *Benefits sharing on extractive natural resources with society in Kenya*.

Nyukuri, E, (2017) "Land tenure and use among indigenous communities in Kenya: trade off with mitigation strategies" in P Kameri-Mbote & C Odote (eds) *The gallant academic: essays in honour of H.W.O Okoth Ogendo* 265-276.

Obare, L & JB Wangwe (2004) *Underlying causes of deforestation and forest degradation in Kenya*, at <http://www.wrm.org.uydeforestation/Africa/Kenya/html> (accessed 29-11-2017).

Ochola, WO, PC Sanginga & I Bekalo (2010) *Managing Natural Resources for Development in Africa: A Resource Book*.

Odote, C (2010) "Retracing our ecological footsteps: customary foundations for sustainable development and implications for higher education in Kenya" Paper prepared for the annual Strathmore

Law School Conference on Sustainable Development <http://www.strathmore.edu/ethics/pdf/collins-sustainable-devt.pdf> (on file with the author).

Odote, C (2010) *The legal and regulatory framework regulating community land tenure in Kenya: an appraisal.*

Odote, C (2014)"Benefit sharing in the extractive industry: which benefits? who shares? comparative analysis and lessons for Kenya" Presentation at the Law Society of Kenya Annual Conference 13-17 August 2014, at <http://kenyalaw.org/kenyalawblog/benefit-sharing-in-the-extractive-industry-comparative-analysis-and-lessons-for-kenya/> (accessed 20-12-2018).

Odote, C (2017) "The conundrum of institutional arrangements to govern community land in Kenya" in P Kameri-Mbote & C Odote C (eds) *The gallant academic: essays in honour of H.W.O Okoth Ogendo* 119-147.

Odote, C & P Kameri-Mbote (eds) (2016) *Breaking the mould, lessons for implementing community land rights in Kenya.*

Ogada, M (2012) *Forest management decentralization in Kenya: effects on household farm forestry decisions in Kakamega* Paper prepared for presentation at the International Association of Agricultural Economists (IAAE) Triennial Conference, Foz do Iguacu, Brazil, 18-24 August, (2012) (on file with author).

Ogolla, BD & J Mugabe (1996) "Land tenure and natural resource management" in C Juma & JB Ojwang *In land we trust: environment, private property and constitutional change* 85-116.

Okidi Odidi, C & C Odote (2017) "Developments in environmental governance in Kenya: experiences using the Owino-Uhuru case" in P Kameri-Mbote & C Odote (eds) *the gallant academic: essays in honour of H.W.O. Okoth Ogendo* 277-295.

Okidi, CO, P Kameri-Mbote & JM Akech (2008) *Environmental governance in Kenya: implementing the framework law.*

Okoth Ogendo, HWO (1995) *Tenants of the Crown: evolution of agrarian law and institutions in Kenya.*

Okoth Ogendo, HWO (2000) "Tragic african commons: a century of expropriation, suppression and subversion" in *Amplifying Local Voices for Environmental Justice: Proceedings of the African Public Interests Law and Community Based Property Rights Workshop.*

Okoth Ogendo, HWO (2007) "Climate change adaptation and mitigation: exploring the role of land reforms in Africa" in N Chalifour, P Kameri-Mbote, L Heng Lye & JR Nolin (eds) *Land use for sustainable development* 60-70.

Ostrom, E (2015) *Governing the commons: the evolution of institutions for collective action.*

Peluso, NL (1993) "Coercing conservation? The politics of state resource control" 3(2) *Global Environmental Change* 199-217.

Posey, DA & G Dutfield (1996) *Beyond intellectual property: toward traditional resource rights for indigenous peoples and local communities.*

Robilant, A di (2011) "The virtues of common ownership" 91 *Boston University Law Review* 1359-1374.

Quinn, J & R Conway (2008) "The Mineral resource curse in Africa: what role does majority state ownership play?" Paper prepared for The Center for the Study of African Economies (CSAE) Conference 16-18 March, Oxford University.

Salick, J (2007) *Indigenous peoples and climate change.*

Santilili, J (2012) *Agrobiodiversity and the law: regulating genetic resources, food security and cultural diversity.*

Sedjo, RA & RD Simpson (1995) "Property rights, externalitites and biodiversity" in TM Swanson (ed.) *The economics and ecology of biodiversity decline: the forces driving global change.*

Sen, A (1999) *Development as freedom.*

Sen, A (1999) *Reason before identity: the Romanes Lecture for 1998* delivered before the University of Oxford on 17 November 1998.

Seppälä, R, A Buck & P Katila (2009) *Adaptation of forests and people to climate change: a global assessment report.*

Sprankling, JG (1991) *Understanding property law.*

Swynnerton, RJM (1955) *The Swynnerton Report: a plan to intensify the development of African agriculture in Kenya.*

Wekundah, JM (2012) *Why protect traditional knowledge?*, at <https://www.africaportal.org/publications/why-protect-traditional-knowledge/> (acceseed 20-7-2018).

Chapter 14: Ecosystem services: legal issues on Nigeria's wetlands

Erimma Gloria Orie

1 Introduction

This chapter deals with the Nigerian legal framework relevant to wetlands as an ecosystem service. At the outset, it is necessary to define concepts such as 'ecosystem' and 'wetlands'. In Nigeria, ecosystems provide general and environmental services such as flood attenuation, water purification, soil stabilisation and erosion reduction, food, groundwater recharge, and climate change mitigation. In this functional context, an ecosystem can be defined as:[1]

> a dynamic complex of plant, animal and micro-organism communities and their non-living environment interacting as a functional unit.

In other words, an ecosystem is a complex set of relationships among the living resources, habitats, and residents of an area. It is a community of living and non-living things that work together. Ecosystems vary in size and composition, although each ecological community is considered a functioning unit. An ecosystem may include animals, birds, fish, micro-organisms, plants, soil, water and people. When all the elements in an ecosystem live in balance, the ecosystem is said to be healthy, sustainable and rich in biodiversity.[2]

Ecosystem services, on the other hand, are the direct and indirect contributions ecosystems provide to human well-being. They are the outcomes from ecosystem functions that are to the benefit of humans.[3] They support human survival and quality of life (directly or indirectly).[4] According to the UN Millennium Ecosystem Assessment,[5] ecosystem services can be classified into four types, namely: supporting service, regulating service, cultural service, and provisioning service. Within the European Union (EU), a conceptual framework for mapping and assessment of ecosystems and their services (MAES) has been developed to steer a more harmonised approach to

---

1 See Article 2 of the Convention on Biological Diversity, at <https://www.cbd.int/convention/articles/default.shtml?a=cbd-02> (accessed 29-7-2018).
2 See <http://www.nhptv.org/natureworks/nwepecosystems.htm> (accessed 3-3-2018).
3 Miller & Tangley (1991: 268).
4 Orie (2018).
5 WRI (2005: v).

ecosystem and ecosystem services assessments.[6] More recently, the idea of a common international classification is gaining ground as it has been recognised that if ecosystem accounting methods are to be developed and comparisons made, then some regularisation is desirable. Some ecosystems are accorded special protection by international and domestic laws. These include wetlands, which are defined in Article 1.1 of the Ramsar Convention on Wetlands of International Importance, 1971[7] (the Ramsar Convention) as:

> areas of marsh, fen, peatland or water, whether natural or artificial, permanent or temporary, with water that is static or flowing, fresh, brackish or salt, including areas of marine water the depth of which at low tide does not exceed six metres.

Wetlands "may incorporate riparian and coastal zones adjacent to the wetlands, and islands or bodies of marine water deeper than six metres at low tide lying within the wetlands".[8] More broadly, wetlands can be categorised into five types, namely marine, tidal, lacustrine, palustrine and riverine.[9] Wetlands provide many ecosystem services including sewage treatment,[10] pollination,[11] and provision of hydro-electricity. In Nigeria, wetlands perform strategic functions such as cultural,[12] supporting[13] and provisioning[14] services amongst others. Wetlands are recognised as a precious part of the ecosystem. Notably, a reasonable percentage of Nigeria's over 170[15] million

6 For further information see <https://biodiversity.europa.eu/maes> (accessed 29-7-2018).

7 Convention on Wetlands of International Importance, Especially as Waterfowl Habitat (1972) II ILM 963.

8 Article 2.1 of the Ramsar Convention.

9 See <https://www.ramsar.org/sites/default/files/documents/library/info2007-01-e.pdf> (accessed 29-7-2018).

10 With regard to global water scarcity, wetlands are remarkable for their non-provisioning ecosystem services like water purification and waste water treatment. See Russi et al. (2013: 2).

11 Orie (2017).

12 Cultural services include non-material benefits derivable from the ecosystems like intellectual development, spiritual, archaeological and/or emblematic enrichment, recreation and aesthetic values. Wetlands provide these to varying degrees. Emblematic plants and animals, e.g. national symbols such as American eagle, British rose, Welsh daffodil; Spiritual, ritual identity, e.g. holy places; sacred plants and animals and their parts as in southern part of Nigeria; on the Coburg Peninsula (the world's first Ramsar site), traditional Aboriginal owners still conduct an active ceremonial life and undertake semi-traditional hunting and gathering in this coastal wetland. See <http://wwf.panda.org/about_our_earth/about_freshwater/intro/value/#culture> (accessed 3-1-2017).

13 Wetlands support nutrient cycling and soil formation. They also support agriculture through maintenance of water tables and nutrient retention in floodplains, for example, rice, a common wetland plant, is an important agricultural product in Southern European countries, Asia and Nigeria. US AID (2008: 10).

14 Conceptually, wetlands and other freshwater habitats provide food, fiber and fuel, freshwater, biochemical and genetic materials for the benefit of humankind. They are important sources of wild game fish and other aquatic food items agrarian for people. They provide habitat for a myriad of other diverse species.

15 See <http://www.worldbank.org/en/news/press-release/2016/03/15/nigerias-booming-population-requires-more-and-better-jobs > (accessed 3-1-2017).

population derive their livelihood from wetland resources, albeit in an unregulated manner.[16] Nevertheless, wetlands are increasingly threatened and degraded mainly due to unsustainable anthropogenic exploitation activities and situations like oil and gas installations, sand mining and channelisation, Nypa palm dispersion, population, dredging and reclamation, and coastal urbanisation among other things that change the water quality, quantity or flow rates, increasing pollution and change the make-up of species.

In Nigeria, this situation is exacerbated by a lack of effective national law for wetland management, a weak institutional framework, improper wetland valuation,[17] etc. These deficiencies do not only result in the depletion of existing wetlands, loss of biodiversity and unsustainable ecosystems, but also in lack of incentives and financing mechanisms for achieving conservation goals. Such negative impacts reduce the capacity of wetlands to provide significant ecosystem services and ensure sustainable ecosystems. The key legal question, therefore, is whether the law can be used to improve or ensure sustainable wetlands in Nigeria. Consequently, this chapter examines the relevance of wetlands in the ecosystem services, the issues and challenges associated with the regulation of wetlands and strategies for conserving wetlands in Nigeria.

Nigeria's marine and coastal environment is rich in resources and species diversity. The mangroves in this environment are the largest remaining tract in Africa[18] and also the third largest in the world covering about 9,723 km^2.[19] The mangrove ecosystem provides a nursery and breeding ground for many of the commercial fishery species obtained in the Gulf of Guinea.[20] The coast of Nigeria is said to have about 199 species of finfish and shellfish, a large number of which are used commercially.[21] The shrimp fisheries of the country are exceptionally strong, and their produce is being exported to other countries, including the United States of America. Artisanal fisher folk harvest a large variety of fish, crustaceans, and molluscs from the estuaries and channels and utilise mangrove and swamp forest products for different kinds of domestic uses.[22]

Similarly, a variety of birds,[23] mammals, and reptiles, including a few endemic species like the Sclater's guenon and the Nile Delta red colobus monkey, inhabit the mangroves and swamp forests of the coast. Although a few species of sea turtles lay eggs

16 Orie (2017).

17 Wetland valuation is a way to estimate ecosystem benefits and it allows financial experts to carry out a cost benefit analysis. It is therefore an important tool for environmental managers and decision makers to justify public spending on conservation activities and wetland management.

18 Federal Republic of Nigeria (2015).

19 US AID (2008: 10).

20 Ibid.

21 Ibid.

22 Ibid.

23 It was the response to international bird conservation concerns that resulted in the first major international agreement on wetlands, the Ramsar Convention. Wetlands are among the key areas in migration flyways of birds. See Copernicus (2015).

on the beaches, they are rare and under threat from human predation.[24] The wetlands are also used for the cultivation of different staples like plantain (*Musa sapientumvar paradisiacal*), banana (*Musa sapientum*), sugarcane (*Saccharumofficinarum*), bitter leaf (*Vernoniaamygdalina*), red spinach/plumed cock's comb/silver cock's comb, locally called *Soko* (*Celosia argentea*), and West African mallow leaves, locally called *Ewedu* (*Corchorusolitorius*), cocoyam (*Colocasiaesculenta*), fruits and vegetables. The production of logs, fuel-wood, peat, fodder, extraction of medicines and other materials for biota, genes for resistance to plants pathogens, and ornamental species are also aspects of the provisioning services.

2 Effects of loss of wetlands

Wetlands are some of the Earth's greatest anchor productive ecosystems and incredibly biodiverse. Yet, wetlands are also among the world's most threatened ecosystems with 50% of all wetlands having disappeared in the last century.[25] For example, corals are the lynchpin of the entire undersea ecosystems but have been suffering from a severe warming climate in recent years. In the same vein, the kelp harbours communities of diverse types of fish and other living organisms and in turn provides significant value to humans through their contribution to fisheries.[26] In fact, kelp is worth Australian $10 billion to the Australian economy annually due to its contribution to tourism and fishery.[27] Specifically, the kelp supports an entire ecological community such that when "we lose the kelp we lose a biological engine that controls or dominates temperate reefs."[28] However, more recently, there has been the massive death of giant kelp around Tasmania.[29] About 100 km of the forests were wiped out due to a marine heat wave, upsetting marine biodiversity, while about 90% of the kelp forest off the western coast of Australia has been wiped off between 2011 and 2013.[30] These threats to the ecosystem lead to loss and wetland degradation, leaching of soil nutrient, and acidification ultimately.

There is evidence that the loss and degradation of wetlands increase hazards from coastal storms and tidal surges, loss of shelter from fast-moving currents, loss of hiding place from predators, and loss of reproduction site (spawning and nursery sites) for aquatic, amphibian and terrestrial life forms.[31] The loss of the remaining wetlands

24 Copernicus (2015).
25 European Comission (2007).
26 Matthiesen (2015).
27 Wernberg (2015).
28 Mooney (2016a).
29 Mathiesen (2016).
30 Wahlquist (2016).
31 Adegun et al. (2014).

would result in the loss of refugia for the biotic communities inhabiting the wetlands and, in particular, to the loss of recovery from natural hazards such as flood. The cumulative result is that the ecosystem services that wetlands provide to people are compromised, leading to unintended but foreseeable consequences for the environment. For instance, it was reported that whenever the Oyan Dam in Nigeria was 'opened', the storm usually affected the floodplains and wetlands covering about 2,800 ha of River Ogun catchment within Lagos comprising Ikosi-Ketu, Mile 12, Agiliti, Thomas Laniyan Estate, Owode-Onirin, Agboyi, Owode-Elede, Maidan and Isheri North Scheme.[32] On 10 July 2011, the entire Lagos State was flooded. In some areas of the state, the flood water-mark on the houses was about 3.5 m. Conservatively, about 25 persons reportedly lost their lives in the Lagos flood which caused the state to close down schools.

In 2012, about 21 states were declared disaster zones by the Federal Government of Nigeria, because of severe flooding which destroyed both farmlands and wetlands.[33] The year 2017 saw about 27 states also submerged due to massive flooding. In adding, an unknown number of oil wells submerged, especially in the Forcados area of Delta State.[34] Besides, some hydrological modelling opined that three feet of sea level rise could put nearly all the Delta's onshore oil fields in Nigeria under water.[35] Such immersion would translate into a massive loss of wetlands and invaluable species.

Interestingly, there tends to be realisation in some quarters that the greatest impacts of climate change may not be the direct effects of warming on one species as compared to the effects of warming on the way species interact with each other.[36] Indeed, some scientists have submitted that warming does not kill the coral itself, but it actually breaks the relationship between the coral and the symbiotic algae in the same way that the changes in the ecosystem processes have serious negative impacts on artisanal fisheries of Nigeria.[37] All these losses (real and potential) are the outcome of an unconcerned attitude of both the people and government to protect the wetlands, which are incessantly converted to uses with economic gains.

3 The regulation of wetlands in Nigeria: issues and challenges

Three issues need to be analysed in the context of the regulation of wetlands in Nigeria, namely, the policy, legal and institutional frameworks that support the federal government's strategic mission to secure, conserve and manage the country's rich biological

32 Ajibola et al.(2016).
33 Orie (2013).
34 Orie (2015).
35 Awosika (1995).
36 Barton & Ives (2014).
37 Mooney (2016b); Mustapha (2013: 130).

endowment together with the diverse ecosystems sustainably. This section reviews the major past and present efforts of the government in biodiversity conservation, especially, as it concerns Nigeria's wetlands.

3.1 Policy framework

The 1999 National Policy on the Environment, among other objectives, focuses on securing a quality environment that is adequate for good health and well-being, the conservation and use of the environment and natural resources for the benefit of present and future generations, and the restoration, maintenance and enhancement of the ecosystems and ecological processes for the conservation of biological diversity. The policy is complemented by the Policy on Biodiversity.[38] Some other policies that have a bearing on the protection of wetlands include:

- The National Forest Policy (2006): the purpose of this policy is to ensure sustainable forest management, promote participatory process of development, facilitate private sector forestry development and adopt an integrated approach to forestry development.
- The National Policy on Erosion, Flood Control and Coastal Zone Management (2005).
- Nigeria's National Agenda 21 (1992) which integrates environment into development planning at all levels of government – the private sector and the non-governmental sector.
- The Climate Change Policy (2017) approved by the federal government recently.

3.2 Legal framework

Section 20 of the 1999 Constitution[39] of the Federal Republic of Nigeria (as amended) provides the fundamental legal principles for environmental protection in Nigeria. It provides that the state shall protect and improve the environment and safeguard water, air, land, forest and wildlife.[40] In an effort to achieve environmental sustainability, the Nigerian government established the Federal Environmental Protection Agency (FEPA), which was scrapped in 1999. In another development, the National Environmental Standards and Regulations Enforcement Agency (NESREA) Establishment Act (2007) was enacted. The latter supersedes the FEPA Act (1988). Section 8(k) of

38 Federal Republic of Nigeria (2015).
39 The Constitution of the Federal Republic of Nigeria 1999 as amended.
40 Ibid.

the statute mandates NESREA to present for the Minister's approval proposals for guidelines, regulations and standards on environmental matters (excluding the oil and gas sector) such as: atmospheric protection, air quality, ozone-depleting substances, noise control, effluent limitations, water quality, waste management and environmental sanitation, erosion and flood control, coastal zone management, dams and reservoirs, watersheds, deforestation and bush burning.

NESREA's authority extends to the enforcement of environmental guidelines and policies like the National Policy on the Environment, 1999. The Agency is charged with the responsibility of the protection and development of the environment, biodiversity conservation and the sustainable development of the country's natural resources as well as environmental technology. The federal government, through NESREA, has developed 24 environmental regulations that have been gazetted and are now in force. Six of these regulations are (directly or indirectly) linked to the management of wetlands in various capacities. These regulations include:[41]

- the National Environmental (Wetlands, River Banks and Lake Shores) Regulations, 2009, S. I. No. 26. They provide for the conservation of wetlands and their resources in Nigeria;
- the National Environmental (Watershed, Mountainous, Hilly and Catchments Areas) Regulations, 2009, S. I. No. 27. They make provisions for the protection of water catchment areas, identification of major watersheds; restriction on the use of watersheds, mountainous and hilly areas, delineation of roles, prevention of fires in watersheds, afforestation and reforestation, as well as grazing of livestock;
- the National Environmental (Access to Genetic Resources and Benefit Sharing) Regulations, 2009, S. I. No. 30. These regulate the access to and use of genetic resources;
- the National Environmental (Soil Erosion and Flood Control) Regulations, 2010, S. I. No. 12. These make provision to check all earth-disturbing activities, practices or developments for non-agricultural, commercial, industrial and residential purposes to protect human life and the environment;
- the National Environmental (Desertification Control and Drought Mitigation) Regulations, 2010, S. I. No. 13. They seek to provide an effective and pragmatic regulatory framework for the sustainable use of all areas already affected by desertification and the protection of vulnerable lands; and
- the National Environmental (Protection of Endangered Species in International Trade) Regulations, 2010, S. I. No. 16. These provide for the protection of endangered wildlife species of fauna and flora.

41 Abere & Jasper (2010).

Furthermore, there are some existing laws at the federal and state levels that complement the federal laws on the conservation of natural resources. These include:

- the Natural Resources Conservation Act (1989) which is the most recent legislation on natural resources conservation. The Act establishes the Natural Resources Conservation Council which is empowered to address soil, water, forestry, fisheries and wildlife conservation by formulating and implementing policies, programmes and projects on conservation of the country's natural resources;
- the Environmental Impact Assessment Act (No. 86 of 1992). This Act requires that environmental impact assessment must first be carried out before any project likely to impact the natural environment could be undertaken;
- the Endangered Species (Control of International Trade and Traffic) Act (No. 11 of 1985). This Act makes provision for conservation and management of the country's wildlife and protection of some of the rare and endangered species;
- the National Parks Services Act, Cap N65 Laws of the Federation of Nigeria 2004, one of the principal laws on biodiversity conservation, was promulgated to provide for the conservation and protection of natural resources and plants in national parks.

Nigeria is a signatory and a party to several international agreements for the conservation and sustainable use of biodiversity, which demonstrates the country's commitment to the conservation of natural resources. The country is a signatory to the Ramsar Convention which provides the framework for national action and international cooperation for the conservation and wise use of wetlands and their resources. The Convention covers all aspects of wetland conservation, recognising wetlands as ecosystems that are extremely important for biodiversity conservation in general and for the well-being of human communities. The country also took an active part in all the negotiation processes leading to the adoption of the Convention on Biological Diversity in Rio de Janeiro in 1992. Subsequently, Nigeria ratified the Convention in 1994 and thereafter, started the process of preparing her Biodiversity Strategy and Action Plan. In 1993, a report of a country study compiled by FEPA acknowledged the position of Nigeria's biological diversity, policies, laws, and conservation programmes.[42] Additionally, the Convention on International Trade in Endangered Species of Wild Fauna and Flora (CITES) was ratified in 1974.

An overview of the legal framework reveals that it comprises both laws and regulations. In Nigeria, an Act is a bill that has been enacted by the National Assembly and assented to by the president. On the other hand, a regulation could be a mere creation

42 Myada (2015).

of a minister in charge of a particular sector.[43] It is a subordinate legislation that is associated with an Act of Parliament. It is more descriptive than an Act because, in many cases, most of the details of the Act are mentioned in the regulations. Thus, regulations indicate how a certain law has to be implemented step by step. The NESREA Act (2007) is the environmental law in Nigeria. Nonetheless, the Act merely mandates NESREA (the implementing agency) to present for the minister's approval proposals for guidelines, regulations and standards on environmental matters including wetlands. Obviously, there is no specific law that gives direction on the regulation of wetlands.

3.3 The institutional framework

Presently, despite the importance wetlands and the ecosystem portend, the lead agency is not one of the few institutions the President heads. Instead, the Federal Ministry of Environment implements and enforces the provisions of the National Environmental Standards Regulation (NESREA) Act, its supporting regulations, and other relevant laws.

Apart from the above structure, there are several linkage centres in Nigerian institutes and universities created in 2001 as part of the activities undertaken in support of the Convention for Biological Diversity. These include the Linkage Centres for Arid Environments (Maiduguri), Freshwater Environments (Minna), Highlands/Montane Environments (Jos), Delta Environments (Port Harcourt), Marine and Coastal Environments in conjunction with the Nigerian Institute for Oceanography and Marine Biology (Lagos), and Forests, Conservation, and Biodiversity at the University of Agriculture (Abeokuta), which is designed to focus on coordinating data and research relevant to biodiversity conservation. Regrettably, there is very little information on how well these centres have done in fulfilling their mandates. Ordinarily, these institutions are expected to assist in the management of the Nigerian wetlands for the benefit of the immediate community and country at large. However, the reverse is the case due to some of the challenges discussed in the subsequent section.

43 For example Section 34 of the NESREA Act empowers the Minister of Environment to create several regulations on various aspects of the environment. National Environmental (Wetlands, River Banks and Lake Shores) Regulations, 2009, National Environmental (Watershed, Mountainous, Hilly and Catchments Areas) Regulations, 2009. S. I. No. 27.

4 The legal issues and strategies for conserving Nigeria's wetlands

The main legal issues and strategies pertinent to Nigeria's wetlands and its ecosystem are outlined in the following subsections.

4.1 The absence of law

Nigeria has ratified the Ramsar Convention but is yet to transmit it into its body of laws. By virtue of Section 12 of the Nigerian Constitution, such conventions cannot have the full force of law until they are domiciled.[44] The above section provides that "…no treaty between the federation and any other country shall have the force of law except to the extent to which such a treaty has been enacted into law by the National Assembly."[45] Thus, there is presently no legal basis to implement the Ramsar Convention for the protection of wetlands in Nigeria. Although there are some related laws on the subject matter, the absence of a specific law on the protection of wetlands is a major challenge to the institution charged with enforcement. Related to this is the fact that some other related laws on the subject matter, like the Land Use Act, are neither consistent with relevant government policies on forestry and biodiversity nor are they comprehensive.[46]

In addition, the absence of unique and vulnerable wetlands geographical information system (GIS) maps for each community and technical training on how to use the maps for stormwater management planning is a major challenge. These maps identify the locations of the vulnerable wetlands in relation to developed sites which makes it easy to determine and plan for the appropriate type and placement of stormwater control options to protect these resources better and reduce phosphorus loading to the river.[47] These challenges are aggravated by lack of a national law on climate change which has made it possible for other impacts of climate change to equally affect the management of ecosystems.

44 Orie (2014).

45 The Supreme Court of Nigeria in the *locus classicus* case of *General Sani Abacha and 3 others v. Chief Gani Fawehinmi* (2000) NWLR (pt4) 533 at 585-586, held that no international treaty can be said to have come to effect in Nigeria except the provisions of such treaty have been enacted into law by the Nigerian National Assembly and that it is such law that breathes life into such treaty in Nigeria.

46 The Policy on Forestry and Biodiversity recognises the need for local communities to own or at least be active stakeholders in the management of the protected areas. On the other hand, Sections 5, 6, 21 and 22 of the Land Use Act divest individuals and communities of rights of ownership and to that extent are inconsistent with the objectives of both the forestry and biodiversity policies of the government.

The ratification of the Convention is not enough. There is an urgent need to integrate the Convention into the Nigerian body of laws. The point being canvassed here is that the absence of laws in areas like climate change mitigation is affecting the health of the environment, which in turn impacts on the quality of wetlands. For instance, in some remote areas in China, where laws on the mitigation of the impacts of climate change are not yet effective, climate change has led to the change in the movement of the bees in that environment. This resulted in a situation where the farmers lacked the requisite population of bees to pollinate plants, and were compelled to engage in manual cross-pollination exercises.[48]

4.2 Valuation of wetlands

Wetland valuation is used to build local and political support for their conservation and sustainable use. It helps to diagnose the causes of environmental degradation and biodiversity loss. It also allows more balanced planning and decision-making, and develops incentive and financing mechanisms for achieving conservation goals.[49] However, in Nigeria, this is not the case. A study by Ajibola[50] reveals that valuing wetland resources is fraught with challenges such as lack of data, complex wetland ecosystems, inadequate government policy, sophisticated survey design and hostility from residents within and around wetlands. Egbenta[51] adds that the inadequacy of legal regulations is a major challenge frustrating wetland valuation.[52]

Strategically, markets need to capture values of ecosystem services and to improve the understanding of the various services and their potential trade-offs. Collaboration between the government, professional bodies and various stakeholders to provide data banks for the valuation of wetland resources is equally necessary. In addition, the multinational oil companies need to be compelled to adopt contemporary (environmental) valuation methods in the determination of compensation payable to claimants, understand the link between various services and to various components of biodiversity. Also, there is the need to analyse the role that an economic institution, specifically, 'the market', plays in promoting the adoption of ecosystems management in both public and private domains. Ecosystem service approaches provide an opportunity to link ecosystem functions with social values, but in reality, the essential role that social dynamics play in the delivery of outcomes remains largely unexplored. Social factors

48 Liess (2015).

49 Barbier et al. (1997).

50 Ajibola (2012: 34).

51 Egbenta (2010). For further reading see Turpie et al. (2010).

52 After a comprehensive review of the various statutory provisions for compensation, Egbenta (2010) is of the view that there is no comprehensive statutory provision for assessing compensation resulting from oil spills/pollution in the petroleum industry.

such as management regimes, power relationships, skills and values can dramatically affect the definition and delivery of ecosystem services. The rationale for this is founded on the fact that, ultimately, services must support individual or societal values.

4.3 Recognition of market or economic value

Although the commercial value of biological diversity in Nigeria exceeds the cost of conservation measures by more than US$3 billion at 1993, biodiversity conservation has not been recognised as a feasible investment in Nigeria's economic development.[53] Consequently, biological diversity valuation has not been fully incorporated into the national economic planning. The challenge, therefore, is that until biodiversity conversion is accorded such recognition, it may be difficult to incorporate it into national economic planning. Unfortunately, unlike some jurisdictions like Peru and the Czech Republic,[54] the Nigerian legislations do not actually provide for the payment for ecosystem services (PES).[55] In Peru, the high-level political commitment and the multi-stakeholder participation in monitoring results, transparency and verifiability are some of the success factors of the PES system.[56] In contrast, the individuals and other use right holders in Nigeria do not benefit from the sale of specified ecosystem products derived from their lands. The implication is that individual and community landowners do not adjudge themselves as stakeholders of the ecosystems who, therefore, should be involved in the protection of the respective wetlands and ecosystems.

Generally, regulating ecosystem services is a complex process, and the specific relationship will look different for different services. The main challenge is how to manage the various service relationships, potential trade-offs, and stakeholders' interactions among others. Part of the strategy Nigeria needs to adopt is to recognise biodiversity conservation as a feasible investment in Nigeria's economic development and consequently incorporate natural resources valuation fully into the national economic planning. Thus, in line with Article 6 of the Convention on Biodiversity, the Federal Ministry of Environment initiated the strategy and action planning process in order to guarantee the conservation of Nigeria's biological diversity. This strategy should be adopted by other ministries and the communities. Embracing and capturing economic values of ecosystem services in mainstream decision-making tools and indicators. For

53 See the Fourth National Biodiversity Report, Federal Republic of Nigeria (2010). The Fifth National Biodiversity Report has been submitted in 2014.

54 The Czech Republic legislation provides possibilities on how to compensate forest owners providing ecosystem services.

55 This is clear from a combined reading of the Land Use Act and the National Conservation Act. For further reading see Orie (2016).

56 Fagbohun & Orie (2015).

example, a national income and growth matrix can help in designing effective policies for sustainable growth and societal well-being.

4.4 Wetland rehabilitation and recreation

A major strategy for Nigeria is to restore its wetlands as a way of checkmating its loss of ecosystem services and the consequent loss of biodiversity. This can be achieved through partnerships with some expert organisations like LIFE-Nature. Nigeria should learn from the experience of Hungary's Hortobágy region where the LIFE-Nature organisation was able to restore the wetlands of the region. In addition, with the help of terrestrial arthropod monitoring, the organisation proved that the high intensity of grazing in the wetland areas could be beneficial for the improvement of the fauna in such wetland area and also the communities.[57] Similarly, in Spain, LIFE-Nature was able to reverse decades of environmental damage by recreating the wetlands of Lake Banyoles. These projects are good examples of collaboration among different administrations (local, national and regional) and private entities (Foundation *Territori IPaisatge*) working together for the conservation of a natural site. However, to ensure that the results of the restoration work would be preserved, the Nigerian government as beneficiary should introduce traditional cattle grazing in restored areas.

4.5 Capacity building and lack of awareness

Nigeria lacks capacity mostly in the areas of finance, human and technical resources. The various complimentary laws on wetland are not properly understood by many of the enforcement agencies and even the communities. There are few trained and qualified people in the field to enforce compliance. In addition, oversight function at all levels is sorely lacking, making way for 'entrepreneurial opportunities' to make money through the unsustainable use of the wetlands, such as over-harvesting of seafood and conversion of wetlands for construction purposes. Effective management of wetlands requires the allocation of more financial resources to acquire and collect accurate data on the distribution and abundance of the resources involved, the ecological parameters of sustainability for each, the amount harvested from year to year, the benefits of the wetlands to Nigeria and other relevant factors. There is no such information on Nigeria's wetland; no data on the actual content of the wetlands, their peculiarities and the challenges of the habitats. Without a proper understanding of existing regulations and

57 The intensive grazing of cattle keeps the grass short and gives the competitively weak plant associations such as the *Puccinellio-Salicornetea* the space to spread in suitable soil areas.

information about the status of most habitats and species, effective management becomes extremely difficult.

Critical to the conservation of biodiversity and the sustainable management of wetlands, in particular, is the need for a systematic and long-term approach to building the knowledge base of Nigerians and the integration of this knowledge into the decision-making process to ensure the prudent use of wetlands.[58] One major way of doing this is through an ecosystem management approach (EMA),[59] which encourages cost-efficient policies and development strategies that blend short-term needs with long-term targets that place conservation and management of ecosystems at the centre[60] in a way devoid of major challenges. To achieve this, the Ramsar Convention Secretariat, over the years, developed handbooks as guidelines to assist those with interest in, or directly involved with the implementation of the Convention at the international, regional, national, subnational or local levels. One of the latest is the Ramsar handbook for the wise use of wetlands.[61]

There is need to provide more ecosystem sensitive infrastructure, and to pursue the transfer and uptake of appropriate technologies, improve the knowledge of change in wetland areas in Nigeria, as well as improve the consistency of data on change in wetland areas in published papers and reports. Participation in global ecosystems agreements will also attract overseas ecosystems management assistance (OEMA) to Nigeria. Another means to protect wetlands is to educate the public about the benefits of wetlands. According to the NBSAP,[62] by 2020, 30% of Nigeria's population should be aware of the importance of biodiversity to the ecology and economy of the country. This government strategy appears not to be sufficiently proactive. In a country of over 170 million people, and considering the benefits that Nigeria stands to lose from such lack of awareness exacerbated by the impact of climate change, the 30% awareness by 2020 is a far cry. If the public does not recognise the benefits of wetland preservation, wetlands will not be preserved.

Furthermore, there is a need to change the content and character of awareness creation and information dissemination to be in tandem with the times. The law should specifically incorporate a framework for promoting awareness. Such framework should also preclude the following practices: physical draining of wetland water; draining of streams and watercourses feeding the wetlands; mining in wetlands, human settlements and their related infrastructural developments in wetlands, and disposal of

58 Ramsar COP3 (1987) defined wise use of wetlands as "their sustainable utilisation for the benefit of mankind in a way compatible with the maintenance of the natural properties of the ecosystem." (This definition was updated in 2005 by Resolution IX.1, Annex A, to "Wise use of wetlands is the maintenance of their ecological character, achieved through the implementation of ecosystem approaches, within the context of sustainable development").

59 For further discussion on EMA see Lackey (1998).

60 UNEP (2012).

61 Ramsar Convention Secretariat (2010).

62 Target 1 of the NBSAP.

solid waste and effluents in wetlands. On the other hand, the framework should seek to promote the use of wetlands for farming, grazing, fishing, timber production and salt-winning in a manner that promotes the conservation of the ecosystem, biodiversity and sustainable productivity of the wetlands. Another more proactive measure will be to incorporate this information into the schools' curricula from primary to tertiary education.

4.6 The top-down approach

Wetlands in Nigeria are owned by the government of Nigeria.[63] The top-down approach of government to biodiversity management and in particular wetland conservation is a big challenge to the system. Despite the current limited recognition of wetland benefits, there still exist many potentially conflicting interests such as between the interests of landowners (the government),[64] the local community (the original owners of the land before the advent of the Land Use Act which divested them of such ownership rights), and the general public; and between developers and conservationists. Part of the challenge is also how to integrate biodiversity concerns in sectoral policies and programmes and modify existing government policies and regulation to achieve consistency, for instance the Land Use Act, the National Policy on Forestry and the Policy on Biodiversity Conservation.

In terms of strategy, many conservationists are of the view that the best hope for protecting and conserving natural resources is through a public participatory approach which will entail carrying the local communities along and also by compensating them for preserving the wetlands.[65] Communities near protected areas and any other remaining wild areas in Nigeria rely on these resources for their existence, and it is to their advantage to conserve them for future uses. Carrying the local communities along will require the establishment and formalisation of the 'Development Triumvirate' that will comprise the government, the private sector, and other stakeholders like the indigenous community, the civil society, to name a few. For example, in Costa Rica and Peru, the governments adopted the payment for environmental service system which entails paying the community members compensation for forest conservation, reforestation and agroforestry.[66] The system was such a huge success that it was recommended for other

---

63 Regulations 1-4 and 8 of the National Environmental (Wetlands, Rivers Banks and Lake Shores) Regulation, 2009.

64 A person who desires to carry out regulated activity listed in the schedule to the National Environmental (Wetlands, Rivers Banks and Lake Shores) Regulation, 2009 on wetlands shall apply to NESREA in line with Regulations 8 and 9. Regulation 14 provides that even landowners, occupiers or users of property contiguous to a wetland have a duty to prevent the degradation or destruction of such wetlands.

65 Orie (2016).

66 See <http://www.fao.org/docrep/006/y5305b/y5305b01.htm> (accessed 13-01-2016).

countries.[67] Protection can be accomplished only through the cooperative efforts of citizens.

Efforts to manage ecosystems divorced from ownership realities are equally ineffectual. Therefore, to implement integrated ecosystem management, there is a need for the inclusion of individual and community landowners. An institutional mechanism for managing ecosystems across the various states in Nigeria is required, and cooperation among a broad range of interests.

4.7 The impact of climate change

According to the Millennium Ecosystem Assessment,[68] climate change will not only further worsen the loss and degradation of many wetlands and cause the extinction of or decline in their species,[69] but the human populations that are dependent on their services will also be negatively impacted. The main challenge is that there is currently no climate change law in Nigeria, although the country is a signatory to the United Nations Framework Convention on Climate Change (UNFCCC) and the Paris Agreement.

A major step in the fight for a sustainable ecosystem through the protection of wetlands is the protection of the ecosystem against the impacts of climate change. This strategy calls for the enactment of a law on climate change. This will invariably ensure the protection of wetlands and ultimately a sustainable ecosystem.

5 Conclusion and recommendations

This chapter examined wetlands issues in Nigeria. It attempted to proffer legal strategies to overcome the challenges associated with management of wetlands. Wetlands are indispensable for the countless benefits or ecosystem services that they provide to humanity globally and Nigeria in particular, ranging from regulating, provisioning, supporting to cultural services. These wetlands are consistently over-exploited, albeit, in an unregulated manner leading to several challenges for the ecosystem. It was found that, although Nigeria is a signatory to the Ramsar Convention, it is yet to incorporate it into the Nigerian body of laws.

The piecemeal complementary laws and regulations on land management are neither consistent with relevant government policies nor are they comprehensive. In

---

67 Fagbohun & Orie (2015).

68 WRI (2005).

69 Rise in temperature will lead to drought, loss or reduction of the species of the wetland and even disappearance of the wetlands.

addition, the institutional framework for the enforcement of the laws is weak and ineffective due to inadequate inter-ministerial cooperation at the federal level which also affects state and local government levels. The institutional framework should be strengthened through capacity building of enforcement operators and collation of relevant data to ensure effective management of the Nigerian wetlands. Furthermore, the management of ecosystems when divorced from landownership realities is equally ineffectual. Therefore, to implement an integrated ecosystem management, there is a need for the inclusion of community landowners. The chapter, therefore in answer to the legal question whether the law can be used to improve or ensure sustainable wetlands in Nigeria, advocates for the establishment of a national law and a strong institutional framework for the regulation of wetlands in Nigeria and for a consideration of the critical role that social dynamics play in generating outcomes between the social and the ecological link which the ecosystem services framework provides.

In the light of the above discussion, the chapter, therefore, makes a case for:

- The establishment of a national law on the regulation of Nigerian wetlands. Such law should incorporate ecosystem management concerns like building capacity and data, wetland rehabilitation and recreation, perpetuating wetland areas, valuation of wetland, and payment for ecosystem services. The law, when established, should work in synergy with other relevant and complementary laws and regulations in Nigeria. For instance, wetlands conservation issues should be integrated into Nigeria's national land-use planning policies.
- A strong institutional framework for effective management of the Nigerian ecosystems and wetlands in particular. This will entail having the correct mix of infrastructure and facilities necessary for such management operations, proper funding, capacity development, data availability, collaboration with sister ministries or agencies as well as ensuring that other relevant/complementary laws and regulations like the Environmental Impact Assessment Act are co-opted as part of the enforcement mechanism.
- The establishment of a law on climate change to indirectly address the protection of wetlands.

References

Abere, SA & E Jasper (2010) "Evaluation of forest resources conservation laws in Nigeria" 2(5) *Mediterranean Journal of Social Sciences* 49-54.

Adegun, O, S Odunuga & Y Appia (2014) "dynamics in the landscape and ecological services in system I drainage area of Lagos" 6 *Ghana Journal of Geography* 75-96.

Ajibola, MO (2012) "Challenges of valuing wetlands resources for compensation in the Niger Delta, Nigeria" 2(11) *Transnational Journal of Science and Technology* 34-49.

Ajibola, MO, BA & KC Ijasan(2016) "Effects of urbanisation on Lagos wetlands" 3(17) *International Journal of Business and Social Science* 310-318.

Awosika, L (1995) "Impacts of global climate change and sea level rise on coastal resources and energy development in Nigeria" in JC Umolu *Global climate change: impact on energy development.*

Barbier, EB, M Acreman, & D Knowler (1997) *Economic valuation of wetlands*, at <http://archive.ramsar.org/pdf/lib/lib_valuation_e.pdf> (accessed 29-7-2018).

Barton, BT & AR Ives (2014) "Direct and indirect effects of warming on aphids, their predators, and ant mutualists" 95(6) *Ecology* 1479-1484.

Copernicus (2015) *Wetlands – unexpected treasures* Brief No. 55, at <http://www.copernicus.eu/sites/default/files/documents/Copernicus_Briefs/Copernicus_Factsheet_Wetlands_Issue55_November2015.pdf> (accessed 29-7-2018).

Egbenta, RI (2010) *Application of contingent method to valuation of non-market goods damaged by oil pollution for compensation* Unpublished Ph.D Thesis, Department of Estate Management, University of Nigeria, Nsukka (Enugu Campus).

European Comission (2007) *LIFE and Europe's wetlands*, at <http://ec.europa.eu/environment/life/publications/lifepublications/lifefocus/documents/wetlands.pdf> (accessed 29-7-2018).

Fagbohun, AO & EG Orie (2015) "Nigeria: law and policy issues in climate change" *Environmental Law Research Institute Monograph Series* 18-20.

Federal Republic of Nigeria (2010) *Fourth national biodiversity report*, at <https://www.cbd.int/doc/world/ng/ng-nr-04-en.pdf> (accessed 29-7-2018).

Federal Republic of Nigeria (2015) *National biodiversity strategy and action plan*, at <https://www.cbd.int/doc/world/ng/ng-nbsap-v2-en.pdf > (accessed 29-7-2018).

Lackey, RT (1998) "Seven pillars of ecosystem management" 40(1-3) *Landscape and Urban Planning* 21-30.

Liess, S (2015) "After bee die-off, Chinese apple farmers resort to hand pollination" *Epoch Times* (25-4-2015), at <https://www.theepochtimes.com/after-bee-die-off-chinese-apple-farmers-resort-to-hand-pollination_1321746.html> (accessed 29-7-2018).

Mass.gov (2015) *Mapping and protecting vulnerable wetlands and stormwater management planning project*, at <https://www.mass.gov/guides/mapping-and-protecting-vulnerable-wetlands-and-stormwater-management-planning-project> (accessed 29-7-2018).

Mathiesen, K (2016) "Ocean heatwave destroys Tasmania's unique underwater jungle" *Climate Home News* (14-10-2016), at <http://www.climatechangenews.com/2016/10/14/ocean-heatwave-destroys-tasmanias-unique-underwater-jungle/> (accessed 29-7-2018).

Miller, K & L Tangley (1991) *Trees of life: saving tropical forests and their biological wealth.* 268

Mooney, C (2016a) "Global warming could be breaking up this 200 million year old relationship" *Washington Post* (2-11-2016), at <https://www.washingtonpost.com/news/energy-environment/wp/2016/11/02/how-climate-change-could-be-breaking-up-a-200-million-year-old-relationship/?utm_term=.562a7b6ac2f7> (accessed 29-7-2018).

Mooney, C (2016b) "Scientists say climate change wiped out an entire underwater ecosystem. Again" *Washington Post* (15-11-2016), at <https://www.washingtonpost.com/news/energy-environment/wp/2016/11/15/scientists-just-found-another-case-of-climate-change-wiping-out-an-underwater-ecosystem/?noredirect=on&utm_term=.fc1a2b45b408> (accessed 29-7-2018).

Mustapha, MK (2013) "Potential impacts of climate change on artisanal fisheries of Nigeria" 4(1) *Journal of Earth Science and Climate Change* 130-136.

Myada, SW (2015) *Nigeria's biodiversity and the Nagoya Protocol* Master Thesis, University of Cologne, at <https://www.researchgate.net/publication/278678078_Nigeria%27s_Biodiversity_and_the_Nagoya_Protocol> (accessed 29-7-2018).

Orie, EG (2013) *The clean development mechanism as a tool for sustainable development: a case for regulatory action* Unpublished Ph.D Thesis, Nigerian Institute of Advanced Legal Studies, University of Lagos Nigeria.

Orie, EG (2014) "Environmental protection and fundamental human right to life: a review of the Nigerian constitutional provision and the judicial posture" 4 *NOUN Current Issues in Nigerian Law* 148-196.

Orie, EG (2015) "Climate change and sustainable development: the Nigerian legal experience" 5 *NOUN Current Issues in Nigerian Law* 68-114.

Orie, EG (2016) "Climate change and sustainable forest management in Nigeria: a case for regulatory action" 1 *National Open University of Nigeria Law Journal* 31-53.

Orie, EG (2017) "Sustainable wetlands and biodiversity conservation: Nigeria's Lagos Lagoons in focus" in U Tandon, M Parasaran & S Luthra (eds) *Biodiversity: law, policy and governance* 11-35.

Ramsar Convention Secretariat (2010) *Wise use of wetlands: concepts and approaches for the wise use of wetlands* 4th ed, at <https://www.ramsar.org/sites/default/files/documents/library/hbk4-01.pdf> (accessed 30-7-2018).

Russi, D, P ten Brink, A Farmer, T Badura, D Coates, J Förster, R Kumar & N Davidson (2013) *The economics of ecosystems and biodiversity for water and wetlands*, at <http://www.zaragoza.es/contenidos/medioambiente/onu/1024_eng_teeb_water_and_wetlands.pdf> (accessed 25-9-2018).

Turpie J, K Lannas, N Scovronick & A Louw (2010) *Wetland ecosystem services and their valuation: a review of current understanding and practice* Report to the Water Research Commission (WRC) Report No. TT 440/09 March 2010.

UNEP / United Nations Environment Programme (2012) *Putting ecosystem management in the vision of Africa's development*, at <https://europa.eu/capacity4dev/unep/document/putting-ecosystem-management-vision-africa's-development-towards-sustainable-green-economy> (accessed 30-7-2018).

US AID (2008) *Nigerian biodiversity and tropical assessment*.

Votteler, TH & TA Muir (2002) *Wetland protection legislation water resources of the United States* United States Geological Survey Water Supply Paper 2425, at <https://water.usgs.gov/nwsum/WSP2425/legislation.html> (accessed 30-7-2018).

Wahlquist, C (2016) "Australias vast kelp forests devastated by marine heatwave, study reveals" *The Guardian Weekly* (7-7-2016), at <https://www.theguardian.com/environment/2016/jul/07/australias-vast-kelp-forests-devastated-by-marine-heatwave-study-reveals> (accessed 30-7-2018).

Wernberg, T (2015) "Australia's 'other' reef is worth more than $10 billion a year – but have you heard of it? *The Conservation* (16-8-2015), at <http://theconversation.com/australias-other-reef-is-worth-more-than-10-billion-a-year-but-have-you-heard-of-it-45600> (accessed 29-7-2018).

Wilen, BO, C Virginia & JR Jones (2002) *Wetland mapping and inventory* United States Geological Survey Water Supply Paper 2425, at <https://water.usgs.gov/nwsum/WSP2425/mapping.html> (accessed 30-7-2018).

WRI / World Resources Institute (2005) *Millenium ecosystem assessment – Ecosystems and human well-being: wetlands and water*, at <https://www.millenniumassessment.org/documents/document.358.aspx.pdf> (accessed 30-7-2018).

Chapter 15: The role of the Environment and Land Court in governing natural resources in Kenya

Collins Odote

1 Introduction

Kenya's 2010 Constitution reformed the structure of the judiciary to enhance access to justice.[1] One of the innovations was the creation of a specialised court with the status of the High Court to "hear and determine disputes relating to the environment and use and occupation of, and title to land".[2] With the establishment of this court, Kenya joined countries that have adopted specialised courts and tribunals to respond to environmental challenges. The main goals in establishing specialised courts are two-fold. The first is as a case management tool to improve the quantity and quality of cases handled, when compared to general courts.[3] The second imperative is to develop an alternative jurisprudence that moves from the traditional 'legalistic' adjudications to a more 'problem-solving', 'therapeutic' or 'interdisciplinary' approach.[4] Consequently, environment courts and tribunals –[5]

> are looked to as one solution for fairly and transparently balancing the conflicts between protecting the environment and promoting development; for managing cases more efficiently and effectively; for supporting greater public information, participation, and access to justice; and for achieving more informed and equitable decisions.

The court has been operative for close to six years. While its adoption, set in the context of a progressive, transformative and 'green' constitutional architecture, was hailed as progressive, its rollout and performance have been a mixed bag. The country's environmental challenges continue and arguments about the inconvenience of a court dedicated to environmental and land matters abound. There is also concern about the quantity and quality of cases focussing on the environment dealt with by the court, and questions have been raised about the court's design. All these beg the question as to whether the court's presence is positive and its impact demonstrable, or whether the

1 See generally Akech et al. (2011); and Kameri-Mbote & Akech (2011).
2 Article 162(2), Constitution of Kenya (2010).
3 Ibid.
4 Nolan (2009); and Rottman (2000).
5 Pring & Pring (2009).

continued existence of the court as a mechanism for dealing with Kenya's intractable environmental challenges is an unnecessary inconvenience.

This chapter argues that while the existence of the court is essential for improved environmental governance, its utility has been hampered by structural and normative challenges. First, the operationalisation of the court has suffered a conceptual flaw occasioned by a misinterpretation by the judiciary of the nature of a specialised court, its status in the judicial hierarchy and its rationale. The second hindrance has been the attitude of the judges of the court and the quality of the natural resource governance jurisprudence it has produced.

Based on a review of key decisions on the functioning of the Environment and Land Court (ELC), the author argues that despite recent court decisions clarifying the position of the ELC as a specialised court and further granting magistrates courts powers to determine land and environmental matters, there is need to improve the quality of jurisprudence on land and environmental matters so as to promote sustainable management of natural resources and the environment in Kenya.

2 Courts and sustainable development realisation

From its early antecedents,[6] the sustainable development principle has gained tremendous traction, leading to its current central position in the global discourse. In 2015, the global community adopted the Sustainable Development Goals (SDGs)[7] to foster the realisation of sustainable development. Comprising of 17 goals and 169 clear targets, SDGs are geared toward transforming the world.[8]

Implementing sustainable development requires action at several levels and the involvement of many actors, including the judiciary.[9] The discussion on the role of the judiciary should be set within the broader context of the role of law in protecting the integrity of the environment. Ojwang[10] has argued that environmental integrity focuses on three interrelated issues: "prudence in the use of environmental resources – to the intent that they may, as the capital base for the economy, not be exhausted"; "effective control and management of social and economic activities – so that they may not generate harmful levels of pollution and waste";[11] and "ecological planning and management – so as to achieve and maintain an aesthetic and healthful arrangement of the structures, features, assets and resources surrounding us".[12]

---

6 Case Concerning *Gabcikovo Nagymaros*, ICJ Rep. 1997, 7.
7 UNGA (2015).
8 See <https://sustainabledevelopment.un.org/?menu=1300> (accessed 23-4-2018).
9 Preston (2005); and Kameri-Mbote & Odote (2009-2010).
10 Ojwang (2007: 19).
11 Ibid.
12 Ibid.

There are several steps and agencies involved in the process of ensuring environmental integrity. Laws as a set of rules are developed to define environmental goals and prescribe the necessary action to realise those goals. As one of the three arms of government, the judiciary plays the role of adjudicating disputes. This is a critical cog in the wheel of promoting a sustainable environment and natural resources management. The international recognition of the judiciary's critical contribution was acknowledged at the World Summit on Sustainable Development in Johannesburg in 2002.[13] Before the Summit, chief justices and senior judges met at the Global Judges Symposium on the Role of Law and Sustainable Development,[14] where they adopted a set of Principles on the Role of Law and Sustainable Development,[15] affirming that:[16]

> ... an independent Judiciary and judicial process is vital for the implementation, development and enforcement of environmental law, and that members of the Judiciary, as well as those contributing to the judicial process at the national, regional and global levels, are crucial partners for promoting compliance with, and the implementation and enforcement of, international and national environmental law.

Further, the judges underscored that:[17]

> the fragile state of the global environment requires the Judiciary as the guardian of the Rule of Law, to boldly and fearlessly implement and enforce applicable international and national laws, which in the field of environment and sustainable development will assist in alleviating poverty and sustaining an enduring civilization, and ensuring that the present generation will enjoy and improve the quality of life of all peoples, while also ensuring that the inherent rights and interests of succeeding generations are not compromised.

These resolutions formed the launching pad for enhanced discourse on the judiciary's contribution to the realisation of sustainable development. Subsequent developments at the national and international level both clarified the content and normative character of sustainable development and the framework for their achievement. This culminated in the Rio+20 Declaration on Justice, Governance and Law for Environmental Sustainability[18] at the World Congress in Rio in 2012. The declaration recognised that since the Johannesburg Summit:[19]

> ... the importance of the judiciary in environmental matters has further increased and resulted in a rich corpus of decisions, as well as in the creation of a considerable number of specialized

13 The Conference was convened by the United Nations in Johannesburg from 26 August to 4 September 2002. At the end, the Johannesburg Declaration on Sustainable Development was adopted, A/CONF.199/20. <http://www.un-documents.net/jburgdec.htm> (accessed 12-5-2018).

14 UNEP (2005: 54).

15 See <https://www.eufje.org/images/DocDivers/Johannesburg%20Principles.pdf> (accessed 31-7-2018).

16 Ibid.

17 Ibid.

18 See <http://wedocs.unep.org/bitstream/handle/20.500.11822/9969/advancing_justice_governance_law.pdf?sequence=1&isAllowed=y.> (accessed 20-4-2018).

19 UNEP (2012).

courts and green benches, and a lasting effect on improving social justice, environmental governance and the further development of environmental law, especially in developing countries.

The above developments eventually led to the evolution of the concept of the environmental rule of law and tremendous work by the United Nations Environment Programme (UNEP) on the environmental rule of law. While scholars have long been familiar with the concept of the rule of law and its place in orderly affairs in society, in the environmental field, the rule of law approach to environmental management was only recently recognised. In a description on the UN website, the essence of the concept is captured in the following terms:[20]

> Environmental rule of law is central to sustainable development. It integrates environmental needs with the essential elements of the rule of law and provides the basis for improving environmental governance. It highlights environmental sustainability by connecting it with fundamental rights and obligations. It reflects universal moral values and ethical norms of behavior, and it provides a foundation for environmental rights and obligations. Without environmental rule of law and the enforcement of legal rights and obligations, environmental governance may be arbitrary, that is, discretionary, subjective, and unpredictable.

The concept of the environmental rule of law was originally coined by the UNEP Governing Council in 2013, when, in Decision 27/9 on Advancing Justice, Governance and Law for Environmental Sustainability, it requested the executive director of UNEP to –[21]

> lead the United Nations system and support national Governments upon their request in the development and implementation of environmental rule of law with attention at all levels to mutually supporting governance features, including information disclosure, public participation, implementable and enforceable laws, and implementation and accountability mechanisms including coordination of roles as well as environmental auditing and criminal, civil and administrative enforcement with timely, impartial and independent dispute resolution.

The above decision was arrived at against the background acknowledgement that –[22]

> the violation of environmental law has the potential to undermine sustainable development and the implementation of agreed environmental goals and objectives at all levels and that the rule of law and effective governance play an essential role in reducing such violations…

The realisation of sustainable development is accordingly a cooperative endeavour and effective judiciaries are an integral component of the institutional architecture that every country must put in place, equip and utilise so as to ensure the realisation of sustainable development.

---

20 See <https://www.unenvironment.org/explore-topics/environmental-governance/what-we-do/strengthening-institutions/promoting> (accessed:12-05-2018).

21 UNEP Governing Council Resolution 27/9 of 2013, at https://www.informea.org/en/decision/advancing-justice-governance-and-law-environmental-sustainability> (accessed 23-4-2018).

22 Ibid.

3 The evolution of the Environment and Land Court (ELC)

Until the adoption of the 2010 Constitution, environment and land matters were handled within the normal court structure. Consequently, the general complaints about courts as being too technical, case delays, executive influence and corruption that were the key drivers for judicial reform, also affected the disposal of land and environmental matters.

While environmental matters are largely public-spirited in nature, the traditional adjudicative process and philosophy are characteristically private rights focused. This hampers the performance of courts in environmental matters with many cases being dismissed on technicalities as a result of the failure of those seeking redress from courts to demonstrate their specific private rights under threat. The Kenyan Nobel Laureate and one-time assistant Minister for Environment became the point of reference in this restrictive approach by courts when her attempts to protect the county's most famous recreational park in the centre of Nairobi, Uhuru Park, was dismissed. The judge famously quipped that Professor Mathai:[23]

> has strong views that it would be preferable if the building of the complex never took place in the interests of many people who had not been directly consulted. Of course, many buildings are being put up in Nairobi without many people being consulted. Professor Wangari apparently thinks this is a special case. Her personal views are immaterial. The Court finds that the Plaintiff has no right of action against the defendant company and hence she has no locus standi.

This negative attitude by the judiciary on litigating environmental matters in the public interest has changed gradually starting with the enactment of a facilitative framework environmental law in Kenya: the Environmental Management and Coordination Act (EMCA). The Act was "enacted by Parliament after a lengthy but cordial debate, in 1999".[24] Its history, however, started much earlier and is traceable to the Stockholm Conference in 1972 and Kenya's hosting of UNEP.[25]

The Act sought to provide "an appropriate legal and institutional framework for the management of the environment in Kenya".[26] The implication from this preambular statement was that the hitherto existing framework was deficient. The deficiency arose from several factors including a sectoral and uncoordinated approach to managing the environment, a purely command and control legislative architecture and excessive executive discretion in enforcing environmental prescriptions. On the contrary, "EMCA is based on the recognition that improved coordination of the diverse sectoral initiatives is necessary for better management of the environment".[27]

23 HCCC 5403 of 1989 reported in (2006) 1 Kenya Law Reports (Environment and Land) 170.
24 Okidi (2008: 126).
25 Ibid. See also Okidi & Kameri-Mbote (2001).
26 Preamble, Act Number 8 of 1999 Laws of Kenya.
27 Angwenyi (2008: 143).

From a dispute resolution standpoint, EMCA recognised the role of the court in environmental management. Section 3 provides the right and duty of every citizen to a clean and healthy environment, and grants access to courts for resolution of disputes in relation to violations of this right, stipulating that:[28]

> If a person alleges that the entitlement conferred under subsection (1) has been, is being or is likely to be contravened in relation to him, then without prejudice to any other action with respect to the same matter which is lawfully available, that person may apply to the high court for redress and the High Court may make such orders, issue such writs or give such directions as it may be deem appropriate.

In addition to the High Court's powers, the Act also creates environmental offences, which according to Kenya's judicial structure are resolved by subordinate courts. By the time EMCA was enacted there were already complaints about the performance of courts in resolving environmental disputes. Consequently, EMCA established two other dispute resolution fora:[29]

> ...the public complaints committee, which is in the nature of an environmental ombudsman, whose function is to receive complaints and petitions of a technical or non-technical character, and the National Environment Tribunal whose function is to review administrative decisions.

These two bodies provided quick and expeditious options for resolving environmental disputes but suffered from several challenges, notably the structuring of the public complaints committee (PCC) as a committee of the National Environmental Management Authority, yet it was supposed to also investigate the Authority.

While Kenya had a progressive law in the form of EMCA, the existing constitutional architecture did not deal with environmental issues. This was despite the recognition of the need to elevate environmental matters to the constitutional level and the existence of environmental provisions in several constitutions across the continent.[30] As a result, courts relied on the constitutional right to life, as it was the only avenue for addressing violations of environmental rights. This, however, happened in a single case before the adoption of the 2010 Constitution. In that case, the court held that:[31]

> Under Section 71 of the Constitution all persons are entitled to the right to life - in our view the right to life is not just a matter of keeping body and soul together because in this modern age that right could be threatened by many things including the environment. The right to a clean and healthy environment is primary to all creatures including man, it is inherent from the act of creating, the recent restatement in the Statues and the Constitutions of the world notwithstanding.

Environmental rights and management received extensive treatment in the 2010 Constitution.[32] Not surprisingly, the Kenyan 2010 Constitution has been labelled as a "green Constitution"[33] for elevating environmental management and the realisation of

28 Section 3(3), EMCA.
29 Mumma (2007: 259-260).
30 See Bruch et al. (2001: 187).
31 *Peter K. Waweru v. Republic* (2006) eKLR.
32 Odote (2012).
33 Kaniaru (2011-2012: 581).

sustainable development to constitutional status.[34] The establishment of the ELC by the Constitution as one of the two specialised courts within the judicial structure and its positioning at the level of the High Court was also trailblazing. Writing in the early days of the adoption of the Kenyan 2010 Constitution, one writer stated that:[35]

> How soon the court is in place and the type of results it turns out may well determine whether this lead is taken or not taken by the many African countries currently engaged in constitutional reviews in their phase of maturity since independence.

The court was operationalised by the enactment of the ELC Act in 2011 and the appointment of an initial 16 judges to the court in 2012. Consequently "(a) at the end of 2012, the ELC was fully operational. Many expect(ed) that the court will be able to develop a sound jurisprudence on environment and land matters and address the many challenges facing the country".[36]

The creation of the court was the culmination of increasing efforts to enhance the judiciary's role in environmental management and to facilitate its departure from the largely negative and restrictive reputation captured in the approach taken in the *Wangari Mathaai* case.[37] The initial efforts were made by UNEP in fulfilment of the declaration at the global Judges Symposium in Johannesburg in 2002, when a call was made for dedicated capacity building for judiciaries across the world. However, the turning point for Kenya was between 2005 and 2007, when the University of Nairobi partnered with the Institute for Law and Environmental Governance and the National Environment Management Authority to mount a capacity building programme for the judiciary on environmental law. Through a series of colloquia and symposia, all judges of the High Court and Court of Appeal and senior magistrates were introduced to the concepts and principles of environmental law, highlights of the national and legal framework governing environmental management and the role of the judiciary in promoting sustainable development.[38]

One of the experts at the training session for judges was the Chief Judge of the Land and Environment Court of New South Wales, the pioneer specialised environmental court in the world. In his presentation, Judge Preston shared the experience of their courts and courts in Asia and Pacific in promoting sustainable development.[39] He argued that "the role of the judiciary in relation to the law of sustainable development is thus of the greatest importance".[40] Consequently, "it is up to the judiciary to clearly define the circumstances of application and the means of implementation of the principles of sustainable development so that this body of law can continue to develop".[41]

---

34 Ibid.
35 Ibid.
36 Odote (2013: 177).
37 HCCC 5403 of 189 reported in 1 Kenya Law Reports (Environment and Land) 2006, 164-171.
38 These fora run for three years and included several presenters. See for example, Okello (2006).
39 Preston (2005).
40 Preston (2005: 210).
41 Ibid: 211.

In the Kenyan context, these words challenged the judiciary leadership resulting in the Chief Justice establishing a division of the High Court responsible for land and environmental matters.[42] This laid the early foundations for the ELC. It also led to challenges relating to jurisdiction, when following the promulgation of the 2010 Constitution and the establishment of the ELC, the Chief Justice appointed a judge of the High Court and not one of the ELC to act as the presiding judge of the Court. This was changed following a case,[43] canvassing the jurisdiction of the court.

Kenya borrowed from the design of New South Wales to combine both environment and land matters. The Land and Environment Court of New South Wales was the first to be established as a specialised superior court of record focusing on land and environmental matters. The importance of land and the responsibility for the judiciary to be able to deliver on the constitutional imperative of sustainable development led to the creation of the Kenyan Environment and Land Court.[44] Land forms the backbone of the country and a direct nexus exists between land tenure and use, on the one hand, and environmental management on the other. Consequently, the manner in which the judiciary handles land and environment cases has direct and fundamental impacts on the majority of the population who rely on land for their livelihoods. The performance of the ELC is thus an important determinant of the judiciary's contribution to socio-economic development in the country. As Judge Brian Preston, the Chief Judge of the Land and Environment Court pointed out:[45]

> The judiciary has a role to play in the interpretation, explanation and enforcement of laws and regulations. …Increasingly, it is being recognised that a court with special expertise in environmental matters is best placed to play this role in the achievement of ecologically sustainable development.

4 Jurisdictional challenges

The question of jurisdiction has dogged the ELC since its establishment. To be fair, this jurisdictional issue is part of the rationale for the inclusion of both the employment and labour relations court and the ELC in the 2010 Constitution. Before the 2010 Constitution, the country had an Industrial Court to determine labour disputes. However, there continued to be a jurisdictional challenge between the High Court and the Industrial Court, with the High Court entertaining appeals from the Labour Court much to the disquiet of the labour movement, which argued that this reduced the utility of the Industrial Court. Consequently, the 2010 Constitution sought to put a stop to this.

---

42 See <https://www.standardmedia.co.ke/article/2000074719/cj-shuffles-judges> (accessed 12-5-2018>.

43 *Karisa Chengo & 2 others v. R*, CA No. 44,45 and 76 of 2014.

44 Preston (2005); and Kameri-Mbote & Odote (2009-2010).

45 Preston (2008: 386).

For the ELC, the 2010 Constitution provides for the establishment of the court "with the status of the High Court"[46] and further that the jurisdiction and function of the court would be determined by the Parliament.[47] These provisions have raised operational challenges for the ELC. The main challenge resulted from the fact that by granting the court the jurisdiction to handle disputes relating to "the environment and the use and occupation of, and title to, land"[48] in a country where the majority of disputes relate to land, there was the fear that the ELC would be clogged. Secondly, the ELC could hear and determine disputes relating to the right to a clean and healthy environment.

A lot of debate revolved around what was meant by a court of the status of the High Court. Did this mean that it is part of the High Court or distinct from the High Court? The ELC Act gave the court several adjudicative functions relating to environment and land matters, including an original, supervisory and appellate jurisdiction. Clarifying its exact jurisdiction became controversial. How would one handle succession cases involving land? Were these land cases or succession cases? The importance of this issue derives from the importance of jurisdiction to the functioning of courts. The *locus classicus* for this was laid down years ago by the Kenyan Court of Appeal in the case of *Owners of Motor Vehicle "Lilian S" v. Caltex Oil Kenya Limited*[49] where it held:[50]

> Jurisdiction is everything. Without it, a court has no power to make one more step. Where a court has no jurisdiction, there would be no basis for a continuation of proceedings pending other evidence. A court of law downs its tools in respect of the matter before it the moment it holds the opinion that it is without jurisdiction.

Delineating the proper contours of the jurisdiction of the ELC would consequently help in its performance. As the Court of Appeal argued in *Karisa Chengo and others v. Republic*:[51]

> Land in Kenya is an emotive issue and for good reasons; agriculture is the backbone of the country's economy. In our view there was need to have expeditious disposal of land and environment matters and a specialized court would ensure that was done as well as provide jurisprudence on adjudication of land and environment disputes. The need therefore for preserving the objective of creating the specialized courts contemplated under Article 162(2) of the Constitution cannot be gainsaid. We have already stated that the matters handled by these courts are extremely important and sensitive which have an impact on socio-economic well being. Consequently, it is important to empower those courts in dealing with their mandate.

This case epitomises and also resolves the jurisdictional challenge of the ELC. However, the actual jurisdictional confusion was created by the actions of the former Chief Justice of the Republic of Kenya. In 2012, he issued practice directions clarifying the

46 Article 162(2), Constitution of Kenya.
47 Article 162(3), Constitution of Kenya.
48 Article 162(2)(b), Constitution of Kenya.
49 (1989) KLR 1653(CA).
50 Ibid.
51 Criminal Appeals Numbers 44, 45 and 76 of 2014.

jurisdiction of the ELC.[52] The first practice directions issued in September 2012 vested the Court with jurisdiction to hear succession cases. This was, however, corrected in November 2012, but the jurisdictional confusion would continue for much longer.

The rationale behind this confusion was the intention, for administrative convenience, to avoid drawing a fine distinction between judges of the High Court and those of the ELC. *Karisa Chengo v. Republic*[53] demonstrates this jurisdictional separation between the judges. On 4 October 2013, Dr. Willy Mutunga, the then Chief Justice gazetted[54] judges to hear and determine criminal appeals following his declaration of a service week to clear the backlog of criminal cases in the country between 14 and 18 October. Magistrates courts had convicted Karisa Chengo and others of the offence of robbery with violence. Their appeal was heard during the service week by a panel comprising a High Court judge and a judge of the ELC. The bench dismissed the appeal. He appealed to the Court of Appeal, which held that the panel lacked jurisdiction because of the inclusion of an ELC judge.

On subsequent appeal to the Supreme Court, the latter upheld the Court of Appeal decision, finally resolving the jurisdictional problem. It delved into the history of the establishment of the courts, especially the record of the committee of experts, which drafted the country's 2010 Constitution. In the words of the Supreme Court:[55]

> The Committee of Experts in its Final Report thus, adverted to three main factors in securing anchorage in the Constitution for the specialized Courts. These were, first, setting out in broad terms the jurisdiction of the ELC as covering matters of land and environment and of the ELRC as covering matters of employment and labour relations but leaving it to the discretion of Parliament to elaborate on the limits of those jurisdictions in legislations. Secondly, and more fundamentally, the establishment of the ELC was inspired by the objective of specialization in land and environment matters by requiring that ELC Judges were, in addition to the general criteria for appointment as Judges of the superior Courts, to have some measure of experience in land and environment matters. Lastly, the Committee of Experts ensured the insertion in the Constitution of a statement on the status of the specialised Courts as being equal to that of the High Court, obviously to stem the jurisdictional rivalry that had hitherto been experienced between the High Court and the Industrial Court.

The Supreme Court also dealt with the double issue of status and jurisdiction clarifying that while the High Court and the ELC were of the same status, meaning same level, their jurisdictions were distinct. The ELC is a "special cadre of courts with sui generis jurisdiction".[56]

The above decision has settled a limitation on the ELC, which sadly had been administratively created by the judiciary. Another administrative hurdle was evidenced

---

52 Practice Directions on Proceedings relating to the Environment and the use and Occupation of, and Title to Land *Gazette* Notice Number 13573, dated 20 September 2012 and published on 28 September 2012.

53 High Court Criminal Appeal Number 49 of 2012.

54 *Gazette* Notice Number 13601.

55 *Republic v. Karisa Chengo and others* Supreme Court Petition No. 5 of 2015.

56 Ibid.

by the decision to designate the head of the ELC as a Principal Judge when the courts were being operationalised. The designation was later changed to Presiding Judge.

The 2010 Constitution envisaged that the ELC would be a court with the same status as the High Court. It contemplated a clear system of administration of the judiciary where leadership would not be the preserve of the Chief Justice. The establishment of an independent Judicial Service Commission and provision for leadership of each court evidences this. The Chief Justice is the head of Supreme Court as its President, while the Court of Appeal also has a President. The High Court has a Principal Judge, elected by judges of the High Court from amongst themselves.[57] The link between the status of the ELC and its leadership is critical.

While the establishment of the court followed appreciation of the importance of land and environmental issues in the country's governance and development arena, its distinction from the High Court is still subject to debate within the judiciary.[58] When the 2010 Constitution was adopted, the Employment and Labour Relations Court and ELC were by dint of Article 162 created as separate superior courts with the same status as the High Court. It is important to point out that the Employment and Labour Relations Court had a successor in the Industrial Court. This had always operated as a separate court from the High Court. The only debate was whether it was inferior to the High Court or not. The ELC on the other hand, used to be a High Court Division. The 2010 Constitution placed these two courts at the same level and removed matters within their jurisdictions from the High Court.

When the enabling legislation was enacted, a Principal Judge was contemplated for both the Employment and Labour Relations Court and for the ELC. However, through an amendment in 2011, the term Principal Judge was replaced with Presiding Judge. The ELC Act provides that "The Presiding Judge shall have supervisory powers over the Court and shall report to the Chief Justice".[59]

It is important to debate the rationale for the change of the title for the head of the ELC from Principal Judge to Presiding Judge. While one may argue that this was to avoid confusing it with the Principal Judge of the High Court and also that there is nothing in a name, practice does not support this argument. If the head of the Employment and Labour Relations Court is designated as a Principal Judge and that court is of the same status as that of the ELC, why should the ELC have a Presiding Judge? Secondly, divisions of the High Court have presiding judges. For example, the civil division of the High Court has a Presiding Judge. Does the designation of the head of the ELC not make the court be seen as a division of the High Court?

57 Article 165(2), Constitution of Kenya (2010).

58 The jurisdiction challenge outlined above and the initial appointment of a head for the court and not election evidences this.

59 Section 6(3), ELC Act.

This is not a futile debate. Since its establishment, the status and jurisdiction of the ELC has been the subject of heated debate. Initially, the Chief Justice established a division of the High Court headed by a High Court before the Act operationalising the ELC was enacted. Then the court had three judges. When the fifteen judges of the court were hired by the Judicial Service Commission and appointed by the President, the High Court judge continued serving as the head of the ELC. This is despite her not being appointed as an ELC judge. Secondly, this happened despite the express provisions of the Environment and Land Court Act providing for the manner of appointing the Presiding Judge for that court. When the Court of Appeal ruled in the *Karisa Chengo* case, the High Court Judge was transferred to Machakos and a judge appointed under the ELC Act appointed as the ELC Presiding Judge, despite the provisions of the Act for elections.[60] This issue was only resolved when elections were held for the position in 2017.

The related question of the powers of the Presiding Judge versus those of the Principal Judge needs to be ventilated and resolved. The ELC Act does not define either the Principal or Presiding Judge. Before the 2012 amendments it had defined a Principal Judge. The 2012 amendment replaced Principal Judge with Presiding Judge. The High Court (Organization and Administration) Act[61] may help here but it is important to point out that this Act gives effect to Articles 165(1)(a) and (b) of the 2010 Constitution by providing for the organisation and administration of the High Court, which the ELC is neither a part nor a division of. The Act defines a Principal Judge as one elected under Article 165(2) of the 2010 Constitution, while a Presiding Judge is one appointed by the Chief Justice to preside over a station or division. Designating the head of the ELC as Presiding Judge therefore envisages that they are heading a division or station but not a court. Secondly, if one compares the provisions of Section 6 of the ELC Act, they are on all fours with Section 5(2) to (5) of the Employment and Labour Relations Act.[62] Curiously though, the head of the Employment and Labour Relations Court is designated "Principal" while that of ELC is "Presiding".

The designation has implications for both authority and management. While Section 6 of the ELC Act states that the Presiding Judge of the Court is answerable to the Chief Justice, the High Court (Organization and Administration) Act envisages that a Presiding Judge shall be answerable to the Principal Judge and shall rank lower in precedence than a Principal Judge.

A Principal Judge has support staff including a Chief Officer and such other staff as designated by the Chief Registrar,[63] while a Presiding Judge does not. Currently, the Presiding Judge of the ELC only has a secretary like other judges. In addition, the

60 Section 6, ELC Act.
61 Act No. 27 of 2015.
62 Chapter 234B, Laws of Kenya.
63 Section 6(5), Act No. 27 of 2015.

Presiding Judges do not have a distinct budget. This limits the discharge of their management responsibility and ability to supervise the performance of the court. Further, while Section 9 of the ELC Act provides for a Registrar of the Court to be appointed by the Judicial Service Commission, to date no substantive Registrar has been appointed. The court operates with a Deputy Registrar.

The leadership of the ELC needs to be enhanced bearing in mind both its unique status and that judges of the court are spread throughout the country. They sit in the same stations with their High Court colleagues, but are not part of the High Court in organisation and administration.

5 Linkages to lower courts and tribunals

The ELC has supervisory and appellate jurisdiction over lower courts and tribunals. However, questions have continued to abound as to the implications of this on the benefits of specialisation which these courts were expected to herald with their establishment. While tribunals by their nature provide for expedited disposal of cases, the ELC was established with the same rationale. Questions, therefore, arise on the necessity for having both the ELC and the National Environment Tribunal (NET) established under the Environment Management and Coordination Act.[64] The retention of the NET when the ELC was adopted was not, and has not been, properly thought through, especially considering ongoing efforts to reform tribunals in the country to bring them within the ambit of the judiciary and rationalise their numbers. NET also experienced challenges when at the end of 2017 both the Judiciary Service Commission and the Ministry of Environment had a back and forth regarding the powers over appointment and supervision of the tribunal. With a specialised court, and innovations on its procedures, there is a need to reconsider the necessity for and continued relevance of the NET, which is centralised in Nairobi, while there are ELC courts across the country.

The second aspect relates to the role and jurisdiction of Magistrates Courts over environmental matters. Because of a lack of initial clarity over the jurisdictional powers of the ELC, controversy also arose as to whether Magistrates' Courts could handle environmental matters. This, in my view, is one place where the controversy was unwarranted. First, accorded the status of the High Court implied that there would be matters that would not necessarily need to be brought to the ELC. In addition, Kenya's environmental management approach combines both civil and criminal tools. Criminal enforcement of environmental law is necessary to protect the integrity of the regulatory system, prevent harm to the environment, protect public health and welfare, and to punish culpable violations. Clarity on the criminal jurisdiction in environmental cases

64 Odote (2013: 177). See also Mcleod (1997); and Stein (1997).

is therefore as necessary as in civil cases. The ELC does not have a jurisdiction to handle criminal matters. Magistrates Courts are consequently relevant in the resolution of environmental disputes in criminal cases.

Despite this, and because of conflicting interpretations on the role of Magistrates' Courts in environmental matters, amendments were made to the law in 2015 to clarify the jurisdiction of Magistrates' Courts in environmental matters. First, the ELC Act was amended by introducing Section 26(3), which provided that "(t)he Chief Justice may, by notice in the Gazette, appoint certain magistrates to preside over cases involving environment and land matters of any area of the country".[65] Section 26(4) of the same Act also provided that subject to Article 169(2) of the Constitution, the magistrate appointed under sub-section (3) shall have jurisdiction and power to handle:[66]

> (a) disputes relating to offences defined in any Act of Parliament dealing with environment and land; and
>
> (b) matters of civil nature involving occupation, title to land, provided that the value of the subject matter does not exceed the pecuniary jurisdiction as set out in the Magistrates' Courts Act.

In addition, a new Magistrates' Court Act[67] was enacted in the same year. The Act included a comprehensive section focusing on the jurisdiction of environment and land matters by Magistrates' Courts. It stated that Magistrates' Courts:[68]

> in the exercise of the jurisdiction conferred upon it by section 26 of the Environment and Land Court Act (Cap. 12A) and subject to the pecuniary limits under section 7(1), hear and determine claims relating to – (i) environmental planning and protection, climate issues, land use planning, title, tenure, boundaries, rates, rents, valuations, mining, minerals and other natural resources; (ii) compulsory acquisition of land; (iii) land administration and management; (iv) public, private and community land and contracts, choses in action or other instruments granting any enforceable interests in land; and (v) environment and land generally.

These amendments, however, became the subject of court disputes involving members of the Law Society of Kenya (LSK). In a suit filed by the LSK Malindi Branch, the lawyers argued that this section was unconstitutional. A three-judge bench in Malindi heard the case and held the amendments unconstitutional. At this stage, the LSK Nairobi Branch, which had not been a party to the proceedings at the initial stage, sought to join the case by filing an appeal against the judgment. While they were allowed to prosecute the appeal, the case raised two interesting procedural issues. The first was the fact that a party that was not part of the proceedings at all in the initial case could file an appeal against such a decision. This precedent had the potential of encouraging people to sit out litigation until judgment is delivered even if they feel they will be affected by such a decision, only to wake up and argue that they are unhappy with the decision and must appeal it; yet they could have ventilated their concerns at the trial

65 Act No. 5 of 2015.
66 Act No. 25 of 2015.
67 Act No. 26 of 2015.
68 Section 9(a) Act No. 26 of 2015.

stage. Secondly, although the LSK has branches in several parts of the country, it is one statutory body established in law. In addition, as a representative body of lawyers in the country, it is assumed that there is consultation before they take a position on a public matter. This litigation pitted two branches against each other, with the parent body in the midst of both of them. The courts, by allowing the appeal, also ignored this aspect of corporate governance.

Substantively on the issue of jurisdiction of the Magistrates' Courts, the Court of Appeal held that that the courts had jurisdiction over environment and land matters, arguing that:[69]

> In our view, conferring jurisdiction on magistrates' courts to hear and determine does not diminish the specialization of the specialized courts considering that appeals from the magistrates' courts over those matters lie with the specialized courts. As urged by Mr. Kanjama, under the doctrine of judicial precedent, the decisions of the specialized courts would bind the magistrates' courts and the specialized courts would therefore undoubtedly imprint the "specialized jurisprudence" on the magistrates' courts.

The above decision followed an earlier judgment by Justice Lenaola in the High Court even before the 2015 amendments. Although his decision was just one of the contending views then, the above sentiments by the Court of Appeal have now settled the law and agreed with his position that:[70]

> In that context, looking at Section 13 (1) of the Act it is clear that Parliament did not intend that the Environmental and Land Court should have exclusive jurisdiction to hear and determine matters related to the environment, and the use and occupation of, and title to land. ...It therefore follows that the Magistrates' Courts have jurisdiction to determine matters falling within the jurisdiction of the Environment and Land Court Act and their decisions will be subject to appeals preferred to the Land and Environment Court. I would not attribute any other meaning to the above provisions. Sadly, therefore I do not think that the Applicants can sustain the argument that the Environment and Land Court has exclusive jurisdiction to hear and determine disputes, actions and proceedings concerning land and the environment because the law does not bear them out.

6 A review of emerging jurisprudence

As the Court of Appeal alluded to, it is imperative that the ELC imprints its specialised jurisprudence. This will give guidance to Magistrates' Courts, clarify many legal issues and help assert the role of the court in the management of environmental matters. Since its establishment, the courts have made numerous judgments in both environmental and land cases. While there is no comprehensive statistics on the cases handled to date and how many of these are land matters versus environmental mattters, anecdotal and preliminary review of the cases demonstrates that the majority of the

69 *Law Society of Kenya (Malindi Branch) v. Malindi Law Society of Kenyan and others* Malindi Civil Appeal, 287 of 2016.

70 *Edward Mwaniki Gaturu & another v. Hon. Attorney-General & 3 others* (2013) eKLR.

decisions from the court are land, and even for these there is a disproportionate high number addressing itself to injunctive and preliminary relief.

There are, however, several cases that signal that the court is alive and is setting a positive trajectory with its jurisprudence on environmental matters.

6.1 Environmental impact assessment (EIA)

The ELC has dealt with the question of EIA as a tool for environmental management. The EMCA clearly provides that EIA exists to help ensure that in designing and undertaking development projects, environmental considerations are taken into account and integrated in the entire process. It provides for an elaborate process of identifying negative environmental and social impacts of any proposed projects, determining what mitigation measures are necessary and whether if such action is undertaken, the project could proceed without negatively impacting on the environment.

While EIA has been subject of several cases before the ELC, the jurisprudential approach by the court is demonstrated by the case of *Kwanza Estates Limited by Kenya Wildlife Services.*[71] The case arose out of the action of the defendant to construct public toilets, which the plaintiff, a registered owner of land in Wakame where he had constructed a resort, argued was causing adverse environmental effects to his resort hence devaluing the property. In determining whether to grant an injunction against the construction of the toilets, the court was guided by the place of EIA in sustainable development since the plaintiff had complained that no EIA was undertaken before the toilet was constructed. The court held that while "it is in the public interest that every public beach must have toilets accessible to the members of the public",[72] compliance with EIA processes was necessary. In the courts' words the "protection of the environment for the benefit of the present and future generations is supposed to be done in a structured manner".[73] On EIA, the court held that its necessity was justified, both on the need to ensure sustainable development and due to the need to comply too with the constitutional stipulation of public participation, which would be actualised by conducting an EIA and compiling a report for approval by the NEMA. The court ruled that EIA was an important process, pointing out that:[74]

> EIA is a tool that helps those involved in decision making concerning development programmes or projects to make their decisions based on knowledge of the likely impacts that will be caused on the environment. Where the impacts are negative and likely to result in significant harm, decisions markers will be able to decide what kind of mitigating measures should be taken to eliminate or minimize the harm. The projects that are potentially subject to EIA are specified in the

71 2013 eKLR.
72 Ibid.
73 Ibid.
74 Ibid.

> second schedule of EMCA and they include an activity out of character with its surrounding, any structure of a scale not in keeping with its surrounding and change in land use...

Consequently, for failing to demonstrate that there had been public participation, the court granted an injunction against the construction arguing that this was a denial of public participation. In the courts' view, it prevented them from raising any concerns they had with the proposed project:[75]

> The importance of public participation in decision making in environmental matters is highlighted by the requirement that EIA study report be published for two successive weeks in the Gazette and in a newspaper circulating in the area of the project and the public to be given a maximum of sixty days for submissions of oral or written comments on the same. EIA process gives individuals like the Plaintiff in this case, a voice in issues that may bear directly on their health and welfare and entitlement to a clean and healthy environment.

6.2 Relationship between NEMA and lead agencies

Environmental enactments adopt a framework approach to deal with the sectoral and uncoordinated approaches of the past. EMCA is designed as a framework law with NEMA designated as the agency to coordinate environmental management. In practice though, turf wars are discernible between NEMA and sectoral agencies established under sectoral environmental laws, in regulations promulgated under these laws and in the implementation of the institutions' environmental mandate.[76] The relationship between NEMA and lead agencies was addressed in the case of *Republic versus National Environmental Management Authority and another Ex parte Phillip Kisia and Another.*[77] NEMA charged the Nairobi City Council Town Clerk for failing to perform environmental obligations. The court held that lead agencies have an obligation to co-operate with NEMA in environmental management but –[78]

> the buck stops with NEMA as regards environmental matters. NEMA assists and guides lead agencies in the preservation and protection of the environment but when a lead agency fails to comply with the directives given by NEMA then NEMA has no option but to engage the powers granted to it by EMCA.

6.3 Access to information and public participation

Procedural rights are critical to realising the right to a clean and healthy environment. ELC has demonstrated the importance of procedural rights, making decisions, which underscore that failure to involve the public in environmental decisions or to provide

75 Ibid.
76 Akech (2008: 334).
77 2013 eKLR.
78 Ibid.

access to environmental information, are a violation of environmental rights and hinder sustainable environmental and natural resources management. Consequently, courts will give relief to enforce these guarantees.

Two cases demonstrate this approach. *Joseph Leboo & 2 others v. Director Kenya Forest Services & Another*[79] involved an application by Lembus Council of Elders Committee Members against the Director of Kenya Forest Service and the Baringo County Forest Coordinator, for alleged illegal allocation of rights to pre-qualified and unqualified saw millers to harvest timber and fuel materials from Lembus forest, without involving the community and against the laid down procedure. The court held that public participation is a key prerequisite for sound environmental management. The second case, *Friends of Lake Turkana v. Attorney General and others*[80] related to an alleged memorandum of understanding between the Government of Kenya and the Government of Ethiopia, entered into in 2006, to purchase of 500 MW of electricity from Gibe III as well as an $800 million grid connection between Kenya and Ethiopia. To generate electricity, the Ethiopian Government constructed dams on River Omo, a principal source of water for Lake Turkana. A civil society organisation – Friends of Lake Turkana – sued, arguing that the construction of the dam would adversely affect the environment and Lake Turkana. The failure of the Government of Kenya to provide access to information on the nature of agreement with the Government of Ethiopia was also raised. The court held that access to information was important for public participation and monitoring government actions.

6.4 The precautionary principle and environment management

Section 3 of the EMCA incorporates international environmental law principles as subsets of the principle of sustainable development and requires courts to rely on them in the management of the environment. One such principle is the precautionary principle,[81] captured in the Rio Declaration as follows:[82]

> In order to protect the environment, the precautionary approach shall be widely applied by States according to their capabilities. Where there are threats of serious or irreversible damage, lack of full scientific certainty shall not be used as a reason for postponing cost-effective measures to prevent environmental degradation.

The principle was popularised in the famous case of *Shehla Zia v. WAPDA*[83] where the court held that in appropriate cases it would grant injunctions in instances of threat to environment even if the state of scientific knowledge was uncertain. This approach

79 Ibid.
80 2014 eKLR.
81 Preston (2005).
82 Principle 15, Rio Declaration.
83 Supreme Court of Pakistan, *Shehla Zia v. WAPDA*, PLD 1994 SC 693 (12-2-1994).

was approved by the ELC in a case involving the decision of the Cabinet Secretary for environment and natural resources to ban plastic bags. In the case of *Kenya Association of Manufacturers v. Cabinet Secretary for Environment for Natural Resources*[84] the court held that:[85]

> At this stage of determining whether the applicant has established a prima facie case or not, the court's role will entail an examination of the relevant legal framework to establish if the 1st Respondent had the requisite powers to issue the legal notice. Section 3 of the Act echoes the constitutional framework on the right to a clean environment. It also provides a broad framework on environmental governance principles and access to justice in environmental disputes. One of the environmental governance principles emphasised by this legal framework is the principle of public participation in the development of policies, plans and processes for the management of the environment and natural resources. The other key principle set out in this section is the precautionary principle. This principle requires that where there are threats of damage to the environment, whether serious or irreversible, immediate, urgent and effective measures be taken to prevent environmental degradation notwithstanding the absence of full scientific certainty on the threat to the environment.

7 Conclusion

From the review, the ELC is setting a path which favours sustainability in the management of natural resources and which demonstrates the benefits of a specialised environmental court.[86] However, several issues need to be resolved to enhance the role of the court in sustainable natural resources management.

First is the quantity and quality of jurisprudence. There are very few substantive cases on the environment that have established sound jurisprudence from the court. The majority of the cases revolve around temporary relief. While these signal sound knowledge of environmental law, the lack of depth and analytical focus needs to be addressed going forward. The plans by the Judiciary Training Institute to develop a bench book on environmental law is a useful starting point for providing the foundations for a rigorous analysis of the emerging jurisprudence and challenging the courts to explore and provide guidance on critical and emerging environmental challenges. The success of this will, however, require that many more environmental cases are brought before the ELC. In an adversarial system like Kenya's, courts can only make judgments based on matters brought before them.

It is also important that the relationship between NET and ELC be revisited. Additionally, the use of experts in environmental matters should be considered so that courts can benefit from scientific advice in their determinations. This will improve both the substantive investigation of issues and the quality of judgments.

---

84 2017 eKLR.

85 Ibid.

86 Preston (2005).

On the issue of jurisdiction, despite the clarification by the courts, there are still the outstanding issues: how to determine which case is environmental and which is land; and relatedly, how to deal with issues of mixed jurisdiction. How does one determine the jurisdiction in a case having both land and environmental issues and other questions of law? This arises both in the context of constitutional issues and normal civil litigation. The case of *Tasmac Limited v. Shalin Chitranjan Gor*[87] had elements of land and company law and the court held that either the High Court or the ELC had jurisdiction. This approach has the potential of encouraging forum shopping, as it does not clarify jurisdictional competence. Judge Ngugi in *Suzanne Achieng Butler v. Redhill Heights Investments Limited and Another*[88] adopted a better approach. He argued that the consideration of competence should be based on the "predominant purpose test" entailing the determination of the predominant purpose of the transaction and the gravamen of the dispute. Thus, while a case may involve several issues, the approach is to determine what is at the heart of the dispute. In this way, it will be possible to determine which court has jurisdiction as opposed to the first court to be approached as happened in *Tasmac*.

In the final analysis, the ELC has made movement, although baby steps, in its quest to enhance sustainable development in the country.

References

Akech, M (2008) "Governing water and sanitation in Kenya" in CO Okidi, P Kameri-Mbote & M Akech (eds) *Environmental governance in Kenya: implementing the framework law* 305-333.

Akech, M, P Kameri-Mbote, C Odote & G Mwangi (2011) *Judicial reforms and access to justice in Kenya: realizing the promise of the new Constitution.*

Angwenyi, AN (2008) "An overview of the Environmental Management and Coordination Act" in CO Okidi, P Kameri-Mbote & M Akech (eds) *Environmental governance in Kenya: implementing the framework law* 142-182.

Bruch, C, W Coker & C VanArsdale (2001) "Constitutional environmental law: giving force to fundamental principles in Africa" 26 *Columbia Journal of Environmental Law* 131-212.

Kameri-Mbote, P & M Akech (2011) *Kenya justice sector and rule of law.*

Kameri-Mbote, P & C Odote (2009-2010) "Courts as champions of sustainable development: lessons from East Africa" 10(1) Fall, *Sustainable Development Law and Policy* 31-38, and 83-84.

Kaniaru, DW (2011-2012), "Environmental courts and tribunals: the case of Kenya" 29 *Pace Environmental Law Review* 566-581.

Mcleod, G (1997) "Do we need an environmental court in Britain" in D Robinson & J Dunkley (eds) *Public interest perspectives in environmental law* 274.

Mumma, A (2007) "The Role of administrative dispute resolution institutions and processes in sustainable land use management: the case of the national environment tribunal and the public

87 *Tasmac Limited v. Shalin Chitranjan Gor* 2014 eKLR.
88 High Court Kiambu Commercial case No. 2 of 2016.

complaints committee" in N Chalifour, P Kameri-Mbote, L Heng Lye & JR Nolin (eds) *Land use for sustainable development* 253-265.

Nolan Jr, JL (2009) *Legal accents, legal borrowing: the international problem-solving court movement.*

Ojwang, JB (2007) "The role of the judiciary in promoting environmental compliance and sustainable development" (1) *Kenya Law Review* 19-29.

Okidi, CO (2008) "Background to Kenya's framework environmental law" in CO Okidi, P Kameri-Mbote & M Akech (eds) *Environmental governance in Kenya: implementing the framework law* 126-142.

Okidi, CO & P Kameri-Mbote (2001) *The making of a framework environmental law and policy.*

Odote, C (2012) "Kenya constitutional provisions on the environment" 1 *IUCN Academy of Environmental Law* 136-145.

Odote, C (2013) "The new Environment and Land Court" 4 *IUCN Academy of Environmental Law* 171-177.

Preston, BJ (2005) "The role of the judiciary in promoting sustainable development: the experience of Asia and the Pacific" 9(2&3) *Asia Pacific Journal of Environmental Law* 109-212.

Preston, BJ (2008) "Operating an environment court: the experience of the Land and Environment Court of New South Wales" 25 *Environmental and Planning Law Journal* 385-409.

Preston, BJ (2012) "Benefits of judicial specialization in environmental law: the Land and Environmental Court of New South Wales as a case study" 29(2) *Pace Environmental Law Review* 396-440.

Pring, G & C Pring (2009) *Greening justice: creating and improving environmental courts and tribunals.*

Rottman, DB (2000) "Does effective therapeutic jurisprudence require specialized courts (and do specialized courts imply specialized judges)?" 37 *American Judges Association Court Review* 22-27.

Stein, P (1997) "A Specialist Environmental Court: An Australian Experience" in D Robinson & J Dunkley (eds) *Public interest perspectives in environmental law* 255-273.

UNEP / United Nations Environment Programme (2005) *UNEP global judges programme*, at <http://wedocs.unep.org/bitstream/handle/20.500.11822/8406/-UNEP%20Global%20Judges%20Programme-20053747.pdf?sequence=3&isAllowed=y> (accessed 31-7-2018).

UNEP / United Nations Environment Programme (2012) *Advancing jusitce, governance and law for environmental sustainability*, at <http://wedocs.unep.org/bitstream/handle/20.500.11822/9969/advancing_justice_governance_law.pdf?sequence=1&isAllowed=y.> (accessed 31-7-2018).

UNGA / United Nations General Assembly (2015) *Transforming our world: the 2030 Agenda for Sustainable Development* A/RES/70/1, at <http://www.un.org/ga/search/view_doc.asp?symbol=A/RES/70/1&referer=/english/&Lang=E> (accessed 31-7-2018).

Chapter 16: Public participation in environmental decision-making in Cameroon – myth or reality?

Jean-Claude Ashukem

1 Introduction

There seems to be an apparent parallel reality between the legal provision of the right to public participation and its actual implementation in Cameroon. The country's rules, procedures and processes of public participation in environmental matters are flawed to the extent that they seem to be void of effective participation by local communities. In this regard, it is doubtful whether local communities participate in environmental decision-making at all; or whether their views are ever taken into consideration prior to the implementation of development activities. Several examples are apparent to substantiate this assertion, and these form the focus of this chapter. Two examples are mentioned briefly below by way of introduction.

Firstly, several commentators have argued that in the context of forest governance, forest management plans are often approved without due regard to legal prescriptions that provide for public participation by local communities.[1] This is contrary to the objective of the Law on Forestry, Wildlife and Fisheries Regulation[2] of 1994. Secondly, public participation in decision-making relating to the approval of development activities under the Ordinance on the Management of State Lands[3] of 1976 seems flawed. The Ordinance provides for public participation in the guise of the composition of the Land Consultative Board (LCB), but – as will be explored later in the chapter – several problems have been identified regarding the composition and function of this LCB. Examples such as this have led commentators to question whether public participation in environmental matters in Cameroon is a mere symbol of intent rather than a meaningful and powerful right designed to oblige the government to ensure the effective

1 Fuo & Semie (2011: 84-85); Alemagi et al. (2013: 9); and Ashukem (2016a: 242). For a detailed critique of the forest management plans in Cameroon, see Cerutti et al. (2008).

2 Law No. 94/01 of 20 January 1994 to lay down Forestry, Wildlife and Fisheries Regulation in Cameroon (Law No. 94/01).

3 Ordinance No. 76/166 of 25 April 1976 laying down the Management of State Lands in Cameroon (Ordinance 76/166).

involvement and full participation of local communities in environmental decision-making processes.[4]

The aim of this chapter is to critically appraise the legal framework on public participation in environmental decision-making in Cameroon. It assesses whether it empowers local communities to participate in environmental decision-making processes effectively; and whether or not their views and aspirations are taken into account in the decisions that emanate from these processes. The chapter is organised into four discrete but interrelated parts. Part 2 provides an overview of public participation in environmental decision-making and a synoptic perspective of its provision and use in relevant international and regional legal instruments. Part 3 outlines Cameroon's relevant legal framework with particular emphasis on the following: the Constitution of the Republic of Cameroon, 1996 (the Constitution); Law No. 94/1 on Forestry, Wildlife and Fisheries Regulation; Ordinance No. 76/166 on the Management of State Lands; Law No. 96/12 on Environmental Management; and Law No. 2003/006 on Biotechnology. Part 4 contains a critical appraisal of Cameroon's legal framework regarding public participation in environmental decision-making. This is followed by the conclusion and a set of recommendations for improving the current regime.

2 Public participation in environmental decision-making: an overview

Generally, public participation is a multi-layered activity that involves participation in decision-making and policy-making, proceedings to challenge the outcome of decision-making and governance processes. Since the 1970s, there have been calls for a 'bottom-up' more people-centred approach to socio-economic development,[5] and for stronger environmental protection.[6] This collectively gave impetus to public agitation for more democratic and participatory approaches in the environmental context.[7] Public participation can be divided into two components: capacity building; and the process of participation. Capacity building relates to and focuses on environmental education and raising awareness. The participation process deals with transparent and consultative processes that provide an opportunity for concerned individuals to express their views, linked with some assurance that their views will be taken into account in the final decision-making process.[8]

Public participation, which must be backed by transparency, access to information, and access to justice, is considered one of the most recognised principles for achieving sustainable development, since it helps to balance the three conflicting and interwoven

4 Ashukem (2016a: 247).
5 Spyke (1999: 269); Morrow (2011: 140); and Ashukem (2016a: 128).
6 Barton (2002: 81-83); Kiss & Shelton (2007: 102); and Foster (2008: 225).
7 Ashukem (2016a: 128-129).
8 Du Plessis et al. (2016: 100).

dimensions of sustainable development.[9] This has led to public participation becoming an indelible feature of modern environmental regulatory systems. It involves not only the engagement of state entities, but also the role of non-governmental organisations (NGOs), local communities and other interested and affected parties[10] in environmental decision-making processes prior to the implementation of development projects impacting on the environment. Legislation in many countries incorporates the principle of public participation as a necessary catalyst to spur environmental protection measures.[11] This enables and promotes both state and non-state actors (including local communities and other interested and affected parties) to engage, deliberate and take meaningful decisions relating to the protection of the environment, ultimately seeking to improve the environment for the benefit of both present and future generations.[12]

At the international level, Principle 10 of the Rio Declaration on Environment and Development[13] (1992) provides the basis for the use of a participatory approach in environmental decision-making. It advocates that every person should have access to information, an ability to participate in decision-making processes and access to justice in environmental matters. Similarly, both the Convention on Access to Information, Public Participation in Decision-Making and Access to Justice in Environmental Matters[14] (Aarhus Convention) of 1998 and the Guidelines for the Development of National Legislation on Access to Information, Public Participation and Access to Justice in Environmental Matters (Bali Guidelines) of 2010 provide for and reiterate the importance of public participation in environmental decision-making as a necessary catalyst for environmental protection.

The Aarhus Convention provides for the right of the public to participate at an early stage in a wide range of environmentally-related activities; places an obligation on public authorities to consider a participatory approach when preparing plans and/or issuing decisions that permit certain activities that may significantly affect the environment; and recognises the need for the public to participate during the preparation of executive regulations and other generally applicable legally binding rules that may

---

9 Segger & Khalfan (2004: 156-158); Segger et al. (2003: 54); Charnovitz (1997: 183); Robinson (2011: 18-19); Steele (2001: 426); and Morrow (2011: 140).

10 Morrow (2011: 139).

11 See, for example: Section 2(4)(f) of the National Environmental Management Act 107 of 1998 (South Africa); Section 2(2)(b) of the Ugandan National Environment Act Cap of 1998; and Section 9(e) of the Law No. 96/12 on Environmental Management in Cameroon.

12 Petkova et al. (2002: 66-67); Ebbesson (2007: 684); and Razzaque (2007: 587).

13 United Nations Conference on Environment and Development (1992) 31 ILM 874.

14 The Convention on Access to Information, Public Participation in Decision-making and Access to Justice in Environmental Matter (1998) 38 ILM 517. Although African states, including Cameroon, are not signatory to the Convention, it provides international benchmarks in terms of the observance and respect for the right to access to information, public participation in decision-making and access to justice in environmental matters.

have a significant impact on the environment.[15] The Bali Guidelines call on states to: ensure, facilitate and provide opportunities for early and effective public participation in environmental decision-making; recognise their responsibility to undertake efforts to ensure proactive public participation operates in a transparent and consultative manner, including efforts to ensure that the concerned are given an adequate opportunity to express their views; ensure that relevant environmental information is made available to the public to facilitate their effective participation in decision-making processes; take due account of public comments received; and make sure that the final decision is made public.[16] The Bali Guidelines furthermore call on states to: ensure public participation in review processes of previously unconsidered environmental sensitive issues; consider appropriate ways of ensuring public input into the preparation of legally binding rules that might have a significant effect on the environment and into the preparation of policies, plans and programmes relating to the environment; and finally, to provide measures that encourage and support capacity-building, including environmental education and awareness-raising and measures that serve to promote public participation in environmental decision-making.[17] At the African regional level, public participation is enshrined in the African Charter on Human and People's Rights[18] (African Charter) of 1982. It provides a broad approach to public participation and bestows an obligation on state parties to respect the right of all citizens, whether individually or through their chosen representatives, to freely participate in the governance of their country.[19] This broad approach to public participation under the African Charter, it is argued, is not limited only to environmental decision-making processes and extends to participation in the formulation of laws, policies and implementation.[20] The right has been given serious attention by the African Commission on Human and Peoples' Rights (African Commission) in the case of *Centre for Minority Rights Development (Kenya) and Minority Rights Group International on behalf of Endorois Welfare Council v. Kenya*, 2010 (*Endorois* case),[21] where the African Commission stated:[22]

> This duty requires the State to both accept and disseminate information, and entails constant communication between the parties. These consultations must be in good faith, through culturally appropriate procedures and with the objective of reaching an agreement.

15 See Articles 6-8 of the Aarhus Convention. Also see Ebbesson (2002: 3); and Kravchenko (2006: 110).

16 Bali Guidelines (2010) 9-11.

17 Bali Guidelines (2010) 12-14.

18 African Charter on Human and People's Rights (1981) 21 ILM 58.

19 African Charter on Human and People's Rights (1981), Article 10.

20 Ashukem (2016a: 194).

21 Also see the *Social and Economic Rights Action Centre and the Centre for Economic and Social Rights v. Nigeria,* African Commission on Human and People's Rights, Comm. No. 155/92 (2001).

22 *Endorois* case, para. 289; and Du Plessis et al. (2016: 101).

The African Commission emphasised that an equal bargaining position is a necessary requirement for effective participation and that public participation must include local communities and other interested and affected parties having the opportunity to influence the outcome of a project's implementation on the environment. In terms of the *Endorois* case, it follows that merely noting an impending project as a *fait accompli* would not amount to effective public participation, since the local communities and affected stakeholders would not have had the chance to influence the outcome of the project.[23] The essential elements for effective and full public participation in environmental matters for the purposes of this chapter, are those set out in the *Endorois* case and include: effective public participation before the project is a *fait accompli*; an equal bargaining position must be established; literacy and an understanding of the project must be promoted; effective public participation must be made in good faith; effective and full participation of local communities has to be based on, and be facilitated by access to information and other procedural entitlements; and measures that facilitate public participation must be culturally sensitive.[24]

The author has previously distilled relevant characteristic features from relevant international and regional instruments (including soft laws and multilateral environmental treaties) that are necessary for effective public participation in environmental matters.[25] It is important to bear in mind that the rationale for public participation is to attempt to influence policies and individual decisions made by government bodies relating to the protection of the environment.[26] This concerns, for instance, the ability to have access to, to understand, to evaluate, to formulate and to comment on proposals, plans and programmes that may impact on the environment. Generally, and within an environmental context, public participation takes various forms.[27] These include broad-based participation through representative bodies such as NGOs which speak on behalf of individuals and affected communities; and stakeholder participation through which formulated proposals are circulated for comment to parties interested in and affected by a development project.[28] It can also take the form of deliberative participation that entails agreeing the rules of decision-making. According to Richardson and Razzaque,[29] public participation in environmental decision-making has been rationalised from two perspectives: a process perspective and a substantive perspective. The process perspective is based on the argument that public participation improves the substantive outcome of decision-making; while the substantive perspective supports

23 *Endorois* case, para. 281; and Ashukem (2016a: 128).
24 *Endorois* case, para. 289; and Ashukem (2016a: 137).
25 Ashukem (2016a: 212-213).
26 Bell & McGillivray (2008: 311).
27 See generally: Arnstein (1969: 216); and Du Plessis et al. (2016: 100).
28 Bell & McGillivray (2008: 311-312); and Arnstein (1969: 216).
29 Richardson & Razzaque (2006: 170).

the view that public participation "bolsters the democratic legitimacy of decision-making".[30]

The law plays a crucial role in all of these approaches and perspectives, especially as it "creates a structure for participation that helps crystallise and protect environmental objectives".[31] This is because the law stipulates participatory procedures in environmental impact assessment (EIA) processes, for example, and considers public participation a necessary element for effective EIA decision-making. The proper implementation of public participation generally, and in EIA processes in particular, has the potential to ensure and promote environmental justice and human well-being, as it helps to balance the needs of both present and future generations in governmental decisions, to integrate environmental consideration within decisions, and to implement and enforce environmental standards.[32] In sum, public participation in environmental decision-making provides a platform where voices meet and are heard. Whether this is the case in Cameroon's legal framework is considered in the next section of this chapter.

3 The legal framework of public participation in Cameroon

Provisions relating to the right to public participation in Cameroon can be found in the Preamble of the Constitution, Law No. 94/1, Law No. 96/12, Law No. 2006/2003 and Ordinance No. 76/166. The relevant provisions of these laws are examined below.

3.1 The Constitution of the Republic of Cameroon, 1996

Although the Constitution of Cameroon has no direct provision on the right to public participation, the right could implicitly be inferred from the Preamble of the Constitution. In terms of Article 65 of the Constitution, the Preamble is part and parcel of the Constitution, with enforceable rights. The Preamble requires the state to harness its land and environmental resources in such a way as would benefit all Cameroonians. Furthermore, in guaranteeing the right to a healthy environment, the Preamble requires that the "protection of the environment shall be the *duty and responsibility* (emphasis added) of every citizen". Finally, the Preamble affirms the duty and responsibility of the state to safeguard the effective protection of vulnerable populations, including *inter alia*, local communities, minority populations and indigenous communities. The foregoing suggests that the participation of the public is essential to ensure effective

30 Ibid.
31 Ibid: 167.
32 Birnie & Boyle (2002: 261); Verschuuren (2004); and Ashukem (2016a: 136).

environmental protection, the protection of the rights of vulnerable populations, and the harnessing of land and environmental resources for the benefit and prosperity of all Cameroonians. The reverse would be true if the decision-making processes of large-scale land investment activities were void of public participation.

3.2 Law No. 94/01

Section 1 of Law No. 94/01 provides a framework for the integrated and sustainable use of forests, wildlife and fisheries. This vision is also reflected in its Decree of Implementation.[33] According to the law, a *cahier de charges* (specifications) must be included in concession forest contracts which specifies the concessionaire's obligations. These contracts must be negotiated between local administrative authorities and the local community concerned, for which the latter would be provided an opportunity to be involved and participate in decision-making.[34]

Section 23 of Law No. 94/01 provides that forest management plans (FMPs) must be submitted to the Minister of Forestry for approval. This compels logging companies to ensure the participation of local communities during the preparation of such plans so as to ensure the sustainability of forest resources. FMPs seem to provide a platform for agreements between logging companies and local communities where the latter could be involved and participate in decision-making insofar as the exploitation of forestry resources is concerned,[35] as without such participation, the FMPs may not be approved by the Minister. Hence, the involvement and participation of local communities and affected stakeholders in FMPs of forestry activities relating to carbon offset projects, for example, has the potential to enhance and ensure the sustainable use and exploitation of forest resources and their management. The participation of local communities in forest carbon offset projects may also promote the conservation of permanent value forest, which according to Sections 20 to 22 of Law No. 94/01, must constitute 30% of the national territory.[36] In this regard, the responsibility lies on the Minister to actually ensure that logging companies adhere to a participatory approach, thereby providing local communities and affected stakeholders with the right to be actively and fully involved in FMPs relating to forestry activities.

33 Decree No. 95/531/PM of 23 August 1995 setting the Modalities for the Implementation of Forests Regulations; and Decree No. 95/466/PM of 1995 setting the Modalities for the Implementation of Wildlife Regulations.

34 Alemagi et al. (2013: 9).

35 Ibid.

36 Fuo & Semie (2011: 84); and Ashukem (2016a: 241).

3.3 Ordinance No. 76/166

Ordinance No. 76/166 provides a framework for land management in Cameroon and creates a Land Consultative Board (LCB) to discharge this responsibility. In terms of the Ordinance, the LCB must consist of representatives of government, a Senior Divisional Officer (or Prefect), the chief and two village elders, and decisions on matters relating to land investment must be made with the participation of all the members.[37] The fact that decision-making on land-related matters must take place in this manner, is an indication that a land-related development activity cannot commence without the full and effective participation of local communities and affected stakeholders, who in terms of Article 12 of Ordinance No. 76/166, are members of the LCB.[38]

3.4 Law No. 96/12

As with most national legislation that incorporates certain principles for effective and efficient environmental governance, Law No. 96/12 follows the same trend.[39] Section 9 of Law No. 96/12 provides for the principle of public participation, which entails, among other things, the right and responsibility of everyone to safeguard the environment and to contribute to its protection, where decisions concerning the environment shall be taken after the full and effective consultation and participation with other actors concerned, or through public debate.[40] Thus, to properly safeguard and protect the environment, local communities and interested and affected parties have to be actively involved in decision-making, plans and programmes of environment-related processes and procedures in order to properly assert protection of their environmental and other related rights. This means, therefore, that for local communities and interested and affected parties to be actively involved in environmental protection measures, they should be allowed to be part of environmental decision-making processes, as their participation could provide a necessary platform for public authorities to enhance environmental protection and other related human rights-based interests. Section 72 of Law No. 96/12 obliges the state to encourage and allow for public participation insofar as environmental governance and protection is concerned. The state is also required to create appropriate mechanisms to ensure the dissemination of environmental information through training, research and education about environmental issues.[41]

Law No. 96/12 also provides for an environmental and social impact assessment (ESIA) regime, which makes provision for the involvement and participation of local

---

37 Article 12 of Ordinance 76/166.
38 Ashukem (2016a: 242).
39 Section 9 of Law No. 96/12.
40 Ibid.
41 Section 72(i)-(iv) of Law No. 96/12.

communities in decision-making processes of activities impacting on the environment. For example, in *FEDEV v. China Road and Bridge Corporation* (FEDEV case),[42] the Court of First Instance in Widikum, Cameroon, granted FEDEV *locus standi* to institute legal proceedings in the public interest, with a view to compelling the respondents to engage local communities in the ESIA process.

3.5 Law No. 2003/006

Law No. 2003/006 reinforces public participation with respect to genetically-modified organisms (GMOs). In terms of the law, the competent national authority is required to foster and facilitate active and effective public participation with regard to the safe movement, manipulation and use of GMOs.[43] Part III of the law, titled "Open testing and use of genetically modified organisms", provides for public participation in matters relating to the use and release of GMOs. It expressly requires the competent national authority to hold a sufficient number of consultative and participatory meetings with the public in the context of the use, release and sale of GMOs and products containing GMOs.[44] The competent national authority is further required to ensure that there is adequate public consultation and participation in applications for the open testing of GMOs for risk assessment in order for an environmental safety attestation to be issued.[45] The foregoing means that any environmental safety attestation that is approved without full and effective public participation, is void and contrary to the law.

4 The myth or reality of public participation in environmental decision-making in Cameroon: a critical appraisal

Rules, procedures and processes governing public participation in Cameroon are flawed and do not often align with governance practices that provide for the effective involvement and participation of local communities during decision-making processes.[46] At worst, their views and opinions are rarely considered.[47] For example, during the regulation of the BioPalm palm oil project, a government official clearly disregarded public opinion and is quoted as saying that "I did not come to ask the opinion of the populace. The forest is the forest of the state".[48] Such derogatory remarks

42 2009 Unreported decision No. CFIB/004M/09; and Fuo & Semie (2011: 89).
43 Section 35 of Law No. 2003/006.
44 Section 42(1) of Law No. 2003/006.
45 Section 42(2) of Law No. 2003/006.
46 Ashukem (2016a: 247-248).
47 Ashukem (2016b: 17).
48 Freudenthal et al. (2013: 348); and Ashukem (2016a: 229).

succinctly illustrate the top-down approach to environmental governance in Cameroon. It also highlights lack of transparency and accountability, and underlines the authoritarian nature of the governance structure in the country devoid of democratic norms and principles such as public participation. The BioPalm palm oil scenario illustrates that public participation in Cameroon is nothing short of a formality as opposed to a desire of the state to promote a culture of inclusive and participatory governance of natural resources generally, and in environmental decision-making specifically.

Law No. 94/1 could be criticised for failing to have an all-inclusive provision on public participation that guarantees the right of local communities and affected stakeholders to effectively participation in decision-making processes. Considering the fact that the prime objective of the law is to promote and ensure "the involvement of local communities in the management and protection of the forest",[49] it would have been laudable if the law were to have a specific provision(s) obliging the state to facilitate and ensure the effective participation of local communities and affected stakeholders within this context. Without such a specific legal guarantee, it is hard to imagine how local communities and affected stakeholders can effectively participate in decision-making in the context of forestry-related projects. It has been argued that in practical terms, local communities rarely exercise this right because FMPs are often approved without due regard to legal prescriptions such as those providing for the participation of local communities.[50] Instead, concession-based forest, which clearly excludes local communities from decision-making processes, has been the order of the day with regard to the exploitation and management of forestry resources. In reality, local communities are generally not consulted and do not participate in decision-making processes about logging permits and other forestry-related investment.[51] This lack of effective involvement and participation by local communities in decision-making processes relating to forestry activities is in direct contrast to the laws prime objective indicated above. It has been argued that in tandem with the Policy Document: National Forestry Action Programme of Cameroon[52] (1995), the intention of the government to enhance sustainable and inclusive forestry governance has turned out to be nothing but a mirage,[53] since it is void of effective involvement and participation of local communities and affected stakeholders in the governance of forestry resources.

---

49 Section 23 of the 1994 Forestry Law. See further: Egbe (2001: 25-26); and Explanatory Statement to Parliamentary Bill No. 54/PJL/AN of November 1993.

50 Ashukem (2016a: 242); Fuo & Semie (2011: 85); Cerutti et al. (2008); and Alemagi et al. (2013: 9).

51 Dupuy & Bakia (2013: 6); and Ashukem (2016a: 248).

52 Ministry of Environment and Forestry (1996: 1-4 and 35).

53 Egbe (2001: 26).

It has been indicated that public participation suffers from a 'decision-making hiccough'.[54] This is predicated on the fact that the right to participate in environmental decision-making in Cameroon is heavily characterised by bribery and corruption,[55] with a corroberation and affirmation of decision-making processes largely amounting to carefully thought, planned and already considered governmental decisions. It is common for the public to have a superficial outline of the final form of some project or development as per prior agreement by government bodies, developers and other decision-makers.[56] Still, it has been warned that since such practices have the potential to negatively undermine the very essence of public participation, they must be prevented at all cost in order for public participation to be truly exercised from the outset of the decision-making process.[57] This is essential as people with *mala fide* intentions, who are usually paid, often partake in decision-making processes to the extent that it is only fair to question the merit of their inputs, as this could greatly affect the final outcome of the decision.[58] In fact, during the negotiation of the Herakles Farm palm oil project, it was reported that some chiefs and elders were paid large sums of money in order to support the project.[59] Freudenthal et al.[60] noted a similar problem during the regulation of the Biopalm palm oil project in Cameroon and reported that some chiefs had close personal links with the company from which they received payment in return for supporting the project's approval.

Although the FEDEV case may seem to indicate the realisation of public participation in environmental decision-making in Cameroon, it must be noted that the substantive merits of the case focussed on the broad locus standi provision contained in Law No. 96/12. In fact, the case could be hailed as the first of its kind to set a precedent for the effective implementation of the locus standi provision in Cameroon. It did not, however, specifically deal with the issue of public participation.

Turning to consider the composition of the LCB, as prescribed by Article 12 of Ordinance No76/1 discussed above. It feasibly provides for and supports a participatory approach to land governance. However, Article 15 appears to bar the effectiveness of this right, particularly as it provides that "[T]he Commission's recommendation are adopted by a simple majority of members present and valid if the head of the village or the community is present". This undermines the intent of Article 12 in that decision-making on land matters should surely not be made without the presence of all members of the LCB being present. In this context, it could be possible for the Government of Cameroon to rely on the provision of Article 15 to restrain the effective participation

54 Oyono et al. (2005: 357).
55 Freudenthal et al. (2013: 350).
56 Du Plessis (2008: 7).
57 Ibid.
58 Ibid: 8; Ashukem (2016a: 137).
59 Mousseau (2013: 4); Ashukem (2016a: 186); and Ashukem (2016b: 17).
60 Freudenthal et al. (2013: 350).

of local communities and affected stakeholders in decision-making processes in order to approve internationally financed land-related-investment projects. It has been reported that the Herakles Farms land deal was implemented without proper consultation with, and the participation of, local communities.[61] Concerns were raised by representatives of the village of Ebanga, who expressed dissatisfaction with the composition and functions of the LCB, and the demarcation of areas to be developed between Ebanga and Ndonga villages with respect to the Herakles Farm palm oil plantation.[62]

Similarly, during the negotiation of the Nanga-Eboko rice project, it was reported that local communities and the local municipality were not consulted and did not participate in the decision to lease community land for the project. This was confirmed by the Mayor of Nanga-Eboko, who is alleged to have stated that "…the municipality and our administration had not been consulted in the selling of the land".[63] As mentioned above, the lack of public participation by local communities restricts their ability to make informed decisions on activities that have the potential to negatively impact on their rights. The lack of effective consultation and participation by local communities in decision-making clearly runs counter to the precepts of good governance.

It is argued that there is a glaring and complete absence of involvement and participation of local communities in ESIA processes relating to large-scale development activities in Cameroon.[64] It has been reported that there were flaws in the implementation of the Chad-Cameroun Oil Pipeline project, including for example, huge problems with the ESIA monitoring and control regime, and issues of institutional democracy and governance (or perhaps rather a lack thereof).[65] An empirical study by Alemagi et al.[66] highlighted that local communities from eight villages in the south-west region of Cameroon were entirely excluded from public participation processes relating to huge forest development projects. Commentators have also argued that the ESIA regime neither provides for, nor requires, prior consultation with local communities and interested and affected parties during the early phases of project development.[67] It furthermore does not explicitly stipulate that their views and opinions should be taken into account during decision-making processes relating to project plans.[68] Interestingly, the ESIA regime does not state whether or not an ESIA is required for the expansion of projects in Cameroon, and if local communities have a right to participate in the decision-making process relating to them. Given the fact that the expansion of

---

61 Dupuy & Bakia (2013: 6); and Ashukem (2016a: 229).

62 See <http://www.sciencespo.fr/ecole-de-droit/sites/sciencespo.fr.ecole-de-droit/files/Analysis%20of%20Some%20Contested%20Legal%20Issues%20Reviewed%20FINAL%20VERSION.pdf> (accessed 19-2-2018); and Ashukem (2016a: 229).

63 See: <http://www.afronline.org/?p=2908> (accessed 19-11-2017).

64 Alemagi et al. (2013: 10).

65 Eyong (2010: 36); and Bekhechi (2012: 78-80).

66 Alemagi et al. (2013: 8-24).

67 Foti & Silva (2010).

68 Alemagi (2013); Nguene et al. (2012); and Bitondo (2000).

already existing projects such as the Cameroon Development Corporation project[69] is a common phenomenon in Cameroon, one would have expected the ESIA regime to have subjected such expansions to additional ESIAs preceded by public consultation.[70] However, this does not seem to be the case and supposedly, their impact on the environment and on people's environmentally-related rights will be unidentified, unassessed and unmitigated, which amounts to a contradiction of the environmental management principles contained in Law No. 96/12.

According to a study undertaken by Eyong,[71] over 68 ESIA reports have been processed by the Department of Environmental Assessment. Of these, 54 have been environmentally assessed and most of the ESIAs carried out were sponsored by international finance corporations including the World Bank. It therefore remains unclear whether these ESIAs, which should in principle promote and facilitate public participation in these projects, actually reflect a genuine response on the part of the Government of Cameroon to ensure and enhance the right to a healthy environment espoused in the Constitution.[72] Perhaps they rather provide a mere guise designed to aid and abet the approval and implementation of these vast internationally-financed projects, notably for example, the Chad-Cameroon Oil Pipeline project mentioned above.

In Cameroon, the right of the public to participate in ESIAs is restricted to reviewing the ESIA report. It does not extend to the screening, scoping, decision-making and follow-up stages of the process.[73] This further demonstrates and supports the argument that local communities and affected stakeholders are rarely participate in decision-making processes relating to activities with great potential to impact on the environment. In terms of Article 16 of Law No. 96/12, developers of authorised projects must submit biannual reports about the implementation of their environmental management plans to the Ministry of Environment and Nature Protection, the authorising agency. Pragmatically, the Ministry is the sole monitoring institution of ESIAs, an indication that developers of projects must be accountable only to the Ministry and not other stakeholders, such as local communities and civil society organisations. This holds potential to undermine the essential independent scrutiny public participation can bring to the ongoing monitoring of projects post their commencement.

The above seeks to outline that effective public participation in the ESIA process may not occur.[74] This reality was clearly illustrated in the Cobalt Nickel Mining project where there was no effort to engage with local communities (the Pygmies and the Bantu).[75] There was also no input sought from those most closely affected by the

69 See <http://cdc-cameroon.net/new2014/expansion-projects/> (accessed 19-2-2018).
70 See, for example, the environmental management principles of Law No. 96/12.
71 Eyong (2010: 26-27).
72 See the Preamble of the Constitution of the Republic of Cameroon, 1996.
73 Sama (2017: 215).
74 Kravchenko (2009: 36).
75 Ibid: 9-10.

destruction of natural resources associated with the mining project, negatively impacting on the local communitie's land and tenure rights, right to food and environmental rights. This example raises two concerns, namely: it shows the apparent fundamental disrespect by the government of the procedural rights of participation of local communities; and it impedes the protection of the environment and the environmentally-related rights of these local communities.[76]

As with public participation in the forestry sector, it may be correct to submit that ESIAs in Cameroon only serve as a formality for the approval of proposed development projects, and not necessarily a need to promote, facilitate and ensure effective involvement and full participation of local communities in decision-making processes with the hope of enhancing environmental governance and promoting justifiable sustainable development. For the latter to be a reality, the ESIA process would need to ensure the effective involvement and participation of local communities at all stages of the ESIA process. The proper implementation of public participation generally, and in ESIA processes particularly, has the potential of ensuring and promoting environmental justice and human well-being, as it helps to balance the needs of both present and future generations in government decisions, integrate environmental consideration in decisions, and implement and enforce environmental standards.[77]

5 Conclusion

This chapter has sought to canvas public participation in environmental decision-making in Cameroon, and to highlight apparent serious problems with its enforcement and implementation. Despite having certain legal provisions aimed at promoting and facilitating public participation in environmental governance, the implementation of the relevant legal framework is very problematic. Local communities appear to be mere observers to the relevant environmental decision-making processes as opposed to meaningful and active participants in them. This supports the contention that public participation in Cameroon is just a formality that only exists on paper. In this light, it is apposite to say that the right to public participation in environmental decision-making processes in Cameroon is more of a myth than a reality. As demonstrated above, in Cameroon there is a top-down approach to environmental decision-making and this is not tempered by processes advocating public participation. Public participation processes are further characterised by intimidation, bribery and corruption. They furthermore often exclude vital role players such as local communities and other interested and affected parties, thereby undermining their environmental and related rights.

76 Ibid: 36; and Ashukem (2016a: 185).
77 Birnie & Boyle (2002: 261); and Verschuuren (2004: 29-48).

In light of the above, it is strongly recommended that the government of Cameroon respect its citizens' rights of access to information in order to facilitate their effective involvement and participation in decision-making relating to activities that have a direct bearing on their rights. It is furthermore suggested that the government should refrain from influencing the views and opinions of local communities through bribery and intimidation. Instead, it should commit to providing a platform where local communities can freely participate and make informed decisions on their own volition.

There is equally a need to revise the ESIA regime to include mandatory requirements for ESIA processes and the effective participation of local communities for project expansions, aligned with the environmental management principles prescribed in Law No. 96/12 on environmental management. It is also recommended that Article 15 of Ordinance 76/166 be repealed since it conflicts with Article 12 and appears to be an inherent barrier to the effective involvement and participation of local communities and affected stakeholders in decision-making processes relating to land-development projects.

Furthermore, it is recommended that with the proposed revision of Law No. 94/1, attention should be given to include provisions that allow an all-inclusive participatory approach designed to include and involve indigenous people and local communities in decision-making processes in forestry-related projects, while implementing public views and opinions during participatory processes in order to effectively attain the objective of the law as set out in its preamble. Finally, the government should ensure, promote and facilitate a platform of public participation where voices meet and are heard, without which the relevant rights of its citizens will remain a myth in Cameroon.

References

Alemagi, D & R Kozak (2010) "Illegal logging in Cameroon – causes and the path forward" 12(8) *Forest Policy and Economics* 554-556.

Alemagi, D, R Hajjar, Z Tchoundjeu & R Zozak (2013) "Cameroon's environmental impact assessment decree and public participation in concession-based forestry – An explanatory assessment of eight forest-dependent communities" 6(10) *Journal of Sustainable Development* 8-24.

Arnstein, S (1969) "A ladder of citizen participation" *Journal of American Institute of Planning* 216-224.

Ashukem, J (2016a) *A rights-based approach to foreign agro-investment governance in Cameroon, Uganda and South Africa* LLD thesis, North-West University.

Ashukem, J (2016b) "Included or excluded? – an analysis of the application of the free prior and informed consent principle in land grabbing cases in Cameroon" *Potchefstroom Electronic Law Journal* 1-29.

Barton, B (2002) "Underlying concepts and theoretical issues in public participation in resource development" in D Zillman, A Lucas & G Pring (eds) *Human rights in natural resource development: public participation in the sustainable development of mining and energy resources* 77-121.

Bekhechi, M (2012) "The Chad-Cameroon pipeline project: some thoughts about the legal challenges and lessons learned from a World Bank-financed large infrastructure project" in D Zillman, M Roggenkamp, L Barrera-Hernanndez & I del Guayo (eds) *Energy networks and the law: innovative solutions in changing markets* 78-101.

Bell, S & D McGillivray (2008) *Environmental law* 7th Ed.

Birnie, P & A Boyle (2002) *International law and the environment.*

Bitondo, D (2000) "Environmental assessment in Cameroon: state of the art" 18(10) *Impact Assessment and Project Appraisal* 33-42.

Cerutti, P, R Nassi & L Tacconi (2008) "Sustainable forests management in Cameroon needs more than just forests management plan" *Ecology and Society* 1-13.

Charnovitz, S (1997) "Two centuries of participation: NGOs and international governance" *Michigan Journal of International Law* 183-286.

Creighton, J (2005) *The public participation handbook-making better decisions through citizen involvement.*

Du Plessis, E, A Mugadza, N Lubbe, J Ashukem, S Malan, M Parramon-Gurney & C Bocchino (2016) "South Africa: participation principle and protected areas" in P Martin, B Boer & L Slobodian (eds) *Framework for assessing and improving law for sustainability: a legal component of a natural resource governance framework* 42-45.

Du Plessis, A (2008) "Public participation, good environmental governance and fulfilment of environmental rights" *Potchefstroom Electronic Law Journal* 2-34.

Dupuy, J & A Bakia (2013) *Fact finding mission on Herakles Farm (SGSOC) oil palm plantation project.*

Ebbesson, J (2007) "Public participation" in D Bodansky, J Brunnée & E Hey (eds) *The Oxford handbook of international environmental law* 681-703.

Ebbesson, J (2002) *Information, participation and access to justice: the model of the Aarhus Convention* Background Paper No. 5 presented at the Joint UNEP-OHCHR Expert Seminar on Human Rights and the Environment, 14-16 January 2002 Geneva 1-7.

Egbe, S (2001) "The concept of community forest under Cameroonian law" *Journal of African Law* 25-50.

Eyong, M (2010) *environmental assessment tools as a framework for decision-making: a comparative study between EIA theory and practice in Cameroon and Sweden* Masters thesis, Stockholm University.

Foster, S (2008) "Public participation" in M Gerrard & S Foster (eds) *The law of environmental justice: theories and procedures to address disproportionate risk* 2nd Edition 225-263.

Foti, J & L Silva (2010) *A seat at the table-including the poor in decisions for development and environment.*

Freudenthal, E, T Lomax & M Venant (2013) "The biopalm oil palm project-a case study in the department of ocean, Cameroon" in M Colchester & S Chao (eds) *Conflict or consent? The oil palm sector at a crossroads* 337-354.

Fuo, O & S Semie (2011) "Cameroon's environmental framework law and the balancing of interests in socio-economic development" in M Faure & W Du Plessis (eds) *The balancing of interests in environmental law in Africa* 75-93.

Kiss, A & D Shelton (2007) *Guide to international environmental law.*

Kozak, R, W Stetic, H Harshaw, T Maness & S Sheppard (2008) "Public priorities for sustainable forest management in six forest-dependent communities of British Columbia" 38(12) *Canadian Journal of Forest Research* 3071-3084.

Kravchenko, S (2006) "The Aarhus Convention: a work in progress" *South African Journal of Environmental Law and Policy* 105-113.

Kravchenko, S (2009) "The myth of public participation in a world of poverty" *Tulane Environmental Law Journal* 34-55.

Morrow, K (2011) "The court and public participation in environmental decision-making" in J Benidickson, B Boer, A Benjamin & K Morrow *Environmental law and sustainability after Rio* 138-157.

Mousseau, F (2013) *Herakles exposed – the truth behind Herakles farms false promises in Cameroon.*

Nguene, F, C Fonocho, J Enjoh, L Taza-Asaba & S Nien Ngapout (2012) *Role and level of stakeholders involvement in the EIA practice in Cameroon-case of EIAs of the upstream energy sector.*

Oyono P, C Kouna & W Mala (2005) "Benefits of forests in Cameroon: global structure, issues involving access and decision-making hiccoughs" 7 *Forest Policy and Economics* 357-368.

Petkova, E, C Maurer, N Henninger & F Irwin (2002) *Closing the gap: information, participation and justice in decision-making for the environment.*

Pring, G & S Noé (2002) "Emerging international law of public participation affecting global mining, energy and resources development" in D Zillman, A Lucas & G Pring (eds) *Human rights in natural resource development* 11-76.

Razzaque J "Linking human rights, development, and environment: Experiences from litigation in South Asia" (2007) *Fordham Environmental Law Review* 587-608.

Rehbinder, E (2006) "Promoting and enforcing environmental law and sustainable development" *South African Journal of Environmental Law and Policy* 1-72.

Richardson, B & J Razzaque (2006) "Public participation in environmental decision-making" in B Richardson & S Wood (eds) *Environmental law for sustainability* 165-194.

Robinson, N (2011) "Reflecting on Rio: environmental law in the coming decades" in J Benidickson, B Boer, A Benjamin & K Morrow *Environmental law and sustainability after Rio* 9-30.

Sama, S (2017) *Harnessing environmental justice to protect against land-grabbing in Cameroon* PhD thesis, University of Ottawa, Canada.

Segger, M, A Khalfan, M Gehring & M Toering (2003) "Prospects for principles of international sustainable development law after WSSD: common but differentiated responsibilities, precaution and participation" *RECEIL* 54-68.

Segger, M & A Khalfan (2004) *Sustainable development law: Principles, practices and prospects.*

Spyke, N (1999) Public participation in environmental decision-making at the new millennium: structuring new spheres of public influence" *Boston College Environmental Affairs Law Review* 263-315.

Steele, J (2001) "Participation and deliberation in environmental law: exploring a problem solving approach" *Oxford Journal of Legal Studies* 415-442.

Verschuuren, J (2004) "Public participation regarding the elaboration and approval of projects, in the EU after the Aarhus Convention" in T Etty & H Somsen (eds) *Yearbook of European environmental law* 29-48.

Wilkinson, P (1976) "Public participation in environmental management – a case study" *Natural Resource Journal* 117-135.

Chapter 17: Utilising Kenya's marine resources for national development

Kariuki Muigua

1 Introduction

This chapter discusses how Kenya can maximise the use of its marine resources to spur economic growth and development for the betterment of its citizens' livelihoods. While it has been observed that oceans provide a substantial portion of the global population with food, livelihoods and are the means of transport for 80% of global trade, Kenya cannot arguably boast of securing as many benefits from its related resources.[1] Furthermore, the marine and coastal environment also constitutes a key resource for the important global tourism industry, supporting all aspects of the tourism development cycle from infrastructure and the familiar 'sun, sand and sea' formula to the diverse and expanding domain of nature-based tourism.[2] Tourism is one of Kenya's key economic sectors, but its potential has not been fully exploited.[3] It has also been documented[4] that the seabed currently provides 32% of the global supply of hydrocarbons with exploration expanding and advancing technologies opening new frontiers of marine resource development from bio-prospecting to the mining of seabed mineral resources. The sea offers vast potential for renewable blue energy production from wind, wave, tidal, thermal and biomass sources.[5] While Kenya has made some progress in this regard, it is yet to fully tap into these resources. This source of energy would be key in boosting Kenya's efforts towards meeting its energy requirements for national development and realising its Vision 2030.[6]

The main livelihoods for the majority of Kenyans are agriculture, livestock, fishing and forestry. In addition, tourism is Kenya's greatest foreign exchange earner, and one of the largest sources of employment.[7] The moist sub-humid to humid lands are classified as the high potential areas of Kenya, supporting rain-fed agriculture; while the

---

1 UN (2014); and *Capital Business* (2016).
2 UN (2014: 2).
3 Ruwa (2006).
4 UN (2014: 2).
5 Ibid.
6 Republic of Kenya (2014).
7 UNFAO & Republic of Kenya (2006: 5).

dry sub-humid lands have medium potential and are mainly used for agro-pastoralism.[8] The rest of Kenya, which includes arid and semi-arid lands (ASAL), is suitable for pastoralism and wildlife and supports nearly half of the country's livestock population.[9] In light of these variations in climatic conditions, Kenya needs to make use of all the natural resources within its territory to promote development. This includes the living and non-living marine resources in Kenya's territorial waters. This chapter discusses ways in which Kenya can take advantage of its location as a coastal state to fully exploit its marine resources for national development and to achieve sustainable livelihoods for its people.

2 The sovereign right to exploit natural resources

The sovereign right of states to exploit natural resources lying within their territories is recognised in various international and regional legal instruments. This recognition, however, comes with responsibilities such as respecting the rights of other states to exploit their resources and the environmental obligation to take care of the various ecosystems.

The International Covenant on Civil and Political Rights provides that all people have the right of self-determination. By virtue of that right, they freely determine their political status and freely pursue their economic, social and cultural development.[10] Furthermore, all people may freely dispose of their natural wealth and resources without prejudice to any obligations arising out of international economic cooperation, based upon the principle of mutual benefit and international law. In no case may a person be deprived of their own means of subsistence.[11]

The Protocol Against the Illegal Exploitation of Natural Resources (2006),[12] concluded by the International Conference on the Great Lakes Region, has the following objectives: to promote and strengthen, in each member state, the development of effective mechanisms to prevent, curb and eradicate the illegal exploitation of natural resources; to intensify and revitalise cooperation among member states with a view to achieving more efficient and sustainable measures against the illegal exploitation of natural resources; and to promote the harmonisation by member states of their national legislations, policies and procedures against the illegal exploitation of natural

8 Ibid.
9 Ibid: 4.
10 Article I(1) of the International Covenant on Civil and Political Rights.
11 Article I(2) of the International Covenant on Civil and Political Rights.
12 Available at <https://www.google.com/search?client=safari&rls=en&q=Protocol+Against+the+Illegal+Exploitation+of+Natural+Resources,&ie=UTF-8&oe=UTF-8#> (accessed 30-7-2018).

resources.[13] Under this Protocol, the illegal exploitation of natural resources is considered a violation of the right of member states to permanent sovereignty over their natural resources, and contrary to the spirit and principles of the following international and regional instruments:[14] the United Nations Charter; the Declaration on the Right to Development; the Constitutive Act of the African Union; and the African Charter on Human and Peoples' Rights.

The fundamental principle of the African Convention on the Conservation of Nature and Natural Resources is that contracting states should undertake to adopt measures necessary to ensure the conservation, use and development of soil, water, flora and faunal resources in accordance with scientific principles and with due regard to the best interests of the people.[15]

The principles of sovereignty and the right to exploit natural resources within a state's jurisdiction govern the use of resources falling within their marine territories. Unless countries allow other states or foreigners to exploit such resources through licensing, the international law regime prohibits such affront to the sovereignty of an independent state.

3 Rights and duties of coastal states in the exclusive economic zone

Article 55 of the United Nations Convention on the Law of the Sea (UNCLOS) defines the exclusive economic zone (EEZ) as an area beyond and adjacent to the territorial sea, subject to the specific legal regime established in this part, under which the rights and jurisdiction of the coastal state and the rights and freedoms of other states are governed by the relevant provisions of this Convention. Article 56 further provides for the rights, jurisdiction and duties of the coastal state in the EEZ. Specifically, it provides that in the EEZ, the coastal state has:[16]

- sovereign rights for the purpose of exploring and exploiting, conserving and managing the natural resources, whether living or non-living, of the waters superjacent to the seabed and of the seabed and its subsoil, and with regard to other activities for the economic exploitation and exploration of the zone, such as the production of energy from the water, currents and winds;
- jurisdiction as provided for in the relevant provisions of the Convention with regard to the establishment and use of artificial islands, installations and

13 Article 2 of the Protocol on the Illegal Exploitation of Natural Resources.

14 Article 4 of the Protocol on the Illegal Exploitation of Natural Resources.

15 Article 2 of the African Convention on the Conservation of Nature and Natural Resources (1968).

16 Article 56(1) of UNCLOS.

structures; marine scientific research; the protection and preservation of the marine environment; and

- other rights and duties provided for in the Convention.

However, in exercising its rights and performing its duties in the EEZ, the coastal state should have due regard to the rights and duties of other states and should act in a manner compatible with the provisions of the Convention.[17] The rights relating to the sea-bed and subsoil should also be exercised in accordance with the provisions contained in Part VI.[18]

Article 76(1) of the UNCLOS defines the continental shelf of a coastal state as comprising the sea-bed and subsoil of the submarine areas that extend beyond its territorial sea throughout the natural prolongation of its land territory to the outer edge of the continental margin, or to a distance of 200 nautical miles from the baselines from which the breadth of the territorial sea is measured where the outer edge of the continental margin does not extend up to that distance.

These provisions apply to Kenya, which is a coastal state located on the eastern coast of the African Continent, between latitudes 5°4'S north and 4°40'S and between longitudes 33°50'E and 41°45'E. It has a total land surface area of 582,644 km^2[19] and a coastline of about 640 km extending from latitudes 1°41'S to 4°30'S and forming part of the western border of the Indian Ocean marine eco-region.[20]

Kenya's Maritime Zones Act (1989) was enacted to consolidate the law relating to Kenya's territorial waters and the continental shelf. It provides for:[21]

- the establishment of the EEZ of Kenya;
- the exploration and exploitation and conservation and management of the resources of the maritime zones; and
- other connected purposes.

Section 4 of the Maritime Zones Act establishes and defines Kenya's EEZ.[22] It is noteworthy that Section 5 of the Act provides that:

> Kenya shall, within the exclusive economic zone, exercise sovereign rights with respect to the exploration and exploitation and conservation and management of the natural resources of the zone and without prejudice to the generality of the foregoing, the exercise of the sovereign rights shall be in respect of –
>
> (a) exploration and exploitation of the zone for the production of energy from the tides, water currents and winds;
>
> (b) regulation, control and preservation of the marine environment;

17 Article 56(2) of UNCLOS.
18 Article 56(3) of UNCLOS. Part VI has provisions dealing with the continental shelf.
19 UNFAO & Republic of Kenya (2009: 13).
20 Anam & Mostarda (2012).
21 Preamble of the Maritime Zones Act (1989).
22 Section 4 of the Maritime Zones Act (1989).

(c) establishment and use of artificial islands and offshore terminals, installations, structures and other devices; and

(d) authorisation and control of scientific research.

The First Schedule to the Act describes Kenya's territorial waters. The foregoing provisions define the area within which Kenya should be seeking to exploit resources to spur the growth and development of its economy. However, this may not be entirely possible at the moment due to a number of challenges. The Kenyan marine habitats support a wide variety of species, most of which are harvested by artisanal fishers operating mostly between the shoreline and the reef.[23] It is estimated that the annual economic value of goods and services in the marine and coastal ecosystem in the blue economy in the western Indian Ocean today is a little over $22 billion, with Kenya's share being slightly over $4.4 billion and the tourism sector taking the lion share at over $4.1 billion.[24]

The 1985 Nairobi Convention for the Protection, Management and Development of the Marine and Coastal Environment of the Eastern African Region (Nairobi Convention) requires state parties, including Kenya, to take all appropriate measures to prevent, reduce and combat pollution of the convention area (Article 4), particularly pollution from ships (Article 5), dumping (Article 6), land-based sources (Article 7), exploration and exploitation of the seabed (Article 8), and airborne pollution (Article 9). States parties undertake to protect and preserve rare or fragile ecosystems as well as the habitat of depleted, threatened or endangered species and other marine life in specially protected areas (Article 10); and to cooperate in dealing with pollution emergencies in the convention area (Article 11). Article 12 also requires parties to take all appropriate measures to prevent, reduce and combat environmental damage resulting from dredging, land reclamation, and other engineering activities in the convention area. Moreover, they are to develop guidelines for the planning of major development projects in the convention area, assess the environmental effects of development projects likely to cause significant adverse changes in the convention area and develop procedures for dissemination of information and consultation among the parties in such assessments.[25] Parties are also encouraged to cooperate in scientific research and monitoring in the convention area, to exchange collected data[26] and to develop rules and procedures to govern liability and compensation for damage caused by pollution in the convention area.[27] The Nairobi Convention spells out more practical obligations for coastal states in the East African coastal region that can go a long way in boosting the conservation and exploitation of the resources within this region.

---

23 Anam & Mostarda (2012: 1).
24 *Freight Logistics* (2018).
25 Article 13 of the Nairobi Convention.
26 Article 14 of the Nairobi Convention.
27 Article 15 of the Nairobi Convention.

This chapter covers both the living and non-living resources lying within Kenya's marine territory. While it may highlight rights of other actors as provided for under Article 56(1), the main focus is on Kenya's sovereign rights to explore and exploit, conserve and manage living or non-living natural resources in the waters superjacent to the seabed and of the seabed and its subsoil. It also addresses other activities relating to the economic exploitation and exploration of the zone, such as the production of energy from the water, currents and winds.

4 The place of the blue economy in the sustainable development agenda

The blue economy concept is generally used to cover both aquatic and marine spaces, including oceans, seas, coasts, lakes, rivers and underground water. It encompasses a range of productive sectors, including fisheries, aquaculture, tourism, transport, shipbuilding, energy, bioprospecting and underwater mining.[28] A United Nations Blue Economy Concept Paper[29] captures the importance of the blue economy in national development. It acknowledges that the coastal and island developing countries have remained at the forefront of the blue economy advocacy, recognising that the oceans have a major role to play in humanity's future; and that the blue economy offers an approach to sustainable development that is better suited to their circumstances, constraints and challenges.[30] It also highlights the fact that cutting-edge technologies and rising commodity prices are opening up new realms of opportunity for submarine exploitation; that the high seas constitute the last global commons; and urgent attention is required to enable the sound management of ocean resources to realise sustainable development.[31]

Investing in the long-term health of coastal and marine resources is vital to the sustainability of the global economy. This is because oceans provide economic wealth from minerals, fisheries, transport and numerous other uses for food security and national development.[32] Investment in the sector is therefore needed to take advantage of the opportunities offered by the blue economy. However, many of the ocean habitats are deteriorating, species in them are threatened with extinction, their chemical nature is changing due to pollution and ocean acidification, and much of their value and that of coastal ecosystems has been lost due to poor management and overuse.[33] Conservation of the environment should therefore be an integral part of resource exploitation.

28 UNECA (2016: 1).
29 UN (2014: 2).
30 Ibid.
31 Ibid.
32 Svensson & Pendleton (2014: 25).
33 Ibid: 5.

Offshore oil and gas production pose some of the greatest risks to the sustainable development agenda due to potential pollution. Countries seeking to explore offshore oil and gas production need to invest heavily in the sector and develop capacity to ensure that while they benefit from the resultant products, the environmental concerns are fully addressed. The next section of this chapter highlights the challenges facing Kenya in managing its EEZ and the exploitation of the resources lying therein.

5 Kenya's marine resources and exploitation challenges

Kenya has a rich diversity of marine and coastal ecosystems, which include mangrove wetlands, coastal forests, estuaries, sandy beaches, sand dunes, coral reefs and seagrass beds that support a host of marine and coastal species.[34] With the exception of mangrove swamps, which have been studied in detail, there is currently limited taxonomical information on the marine biota of Kenya, and species lists for coastal and pelagic environments are incomplete.[35] There are twelve patches of mangrove forests along the Kenya coast, with an estimated total area of between 53,000 and 61,000 ha, with 67% occurring in the Lamu district and 10% each in the Kilifi and Kwale Districts.[36] Mangrove forests are nutrient-rich environments supporting a variety of food chains and functioning as a nursery and feeding ground for fish and invertebrates. Many of these species spend part of their life cycle in coral reefs, seagrasses and open waters. Mangrove trees are also important for shoreline stabilisation and provide resources for both rural and urban coastal populations.[37]

Kenya enjoys a reputation as one of the world's great big game sports fishing destinations.[38] Its marine waters contain most of the major target game species, including billfishes, sailfish, swordfishes, marlins, sharks and some tunas.[39] Sports fishers are registered in several sport-fishing clubs, which coordinate fishing activity and record data.[40] The peak sports fishing season is from September to March, and the popular sport-fishing areas are Malindi, Watamu, Shimoni and Lamu.[41] In 2005, 30 sport-fishing clubs were registered.[42]

The marine fisheries are classified into two subsectors: the coastal artisanal fishery; and the EEZ fishery.[43] A basic feature of the coastal fishery is the largely subsistence

34 Tuda & Omar (2012: 43).
35 Anam & Mostarda (2012: 1).
36 Ibid: 3.
37 Ibid.
38 Ibid.
39 Ibid.
40 Ibid: 4.
41 Ibid.
42 Ibid.
43 UNFAO (2016).

and artisanal nature of the fishers who operate small craft propelled by wind sails and manual paddles.[44] The EEZ fishery, on the other hand, is characterised by distant-water fishing vessels which exploit target species mainly with purse-seines and long-lines.[45] It is also estimated that the maximum sustainable yield of Kenya's marine and coastal waters is between 150,000 and 300,000 metric tonnes, while the current production level is only about 9,000 metric tonnes per annum.[46]

Most fishing in Kenya is artisanal, with a little industrial fishing by prawn trawlers. It is estimated that approximately 80% of the total marine products come from shallow coastal waters and reefs, while only 20% are from off-shore fishing.[47] Distant Waters Fishing Nations (DWFN) currently fish in the EEZ through a licensing system, and only a small quantity of catch from the EEZ is landed in Kenya, primarily tuna for export.[48] The local fishers lack the capacity to exploit deep water resources. Overfishing in inshore areas has continued to cause a decline in fish catches, while the deeper territorial waters remain underexploited.[49]

As for the mineral resources within the territorial waters of the country, these remain largely untapped, due to technological challenges. However, it is noteworthy that the Kenyan territorial waters also fall under the exploration blocks allocated to foreign companies licensed to carry out oil and mineral exploration in the country. For instance, from August 2014, there has been an ongoing boundary dispute before the International Court of Justice (ICJ) between the Republic of Kenya and the Federal Republic of Somalia regarding maritime delimitation in the Indian Ocean.[50] Somalia contends that both states "disagree about the location of the maritime boundary in the area where their maritime entitlements overlap", and asserts that "[d]iplomatic negotiations, in which their respective views have been fully exchanged, have failed to resolve this disagreement".[51] Somalia requested the Court:[52]

> to determine, on the basis of international law, the complete course of the single maritime boundary dividing all the maritime areas appertaining to Somalia and to Kenya in the Indian Ocean, including the continental shelf beyond 200 [nautical miles].

Somalia further asked the Court "to determine the precise geographical coordinates of the single maritime boundary in the Indian Ocean".[53] It is arguable that the main reason

44 Ibid.
45 Ibid.
46 Ibid.
47 Fondo (2004: 6).
48 Ibid.
49 Anam & Mostarda (2012: 3).
50 See <http://www.icj-cij.org/docket/files/161/18360.pdf> (accessed 12-5-2017).
51 International Court of Justice, *Dispute Concerning Maritime Delimitation in the Indian Ocean (Somalia v. Kenya)* (2014) para. 17.
52 Ibid: paras 36 and 37.
53 Ibid.

for disputes such as this one is the vast resources found in these areas.[54] This may be supported by the fact that Kenya has already awarded some of its petroleum blocks in the disputed area to potential investors for oil prospecting. The outcome of this dispute will have an impact on the exploration and exploitation of the marine resources lying in the contested areas.

Kenya has been a party to UNCLOS since March 1989 and to the 1995 UN Fish Stocks Agreement since July 2004. Kenya also signed the Port State Measures Agreement in November 2010, is a member of the Committee for Inland Fisheries of Africa (CIFA), a founding member of Aquaculture Network for Africa (ANAF), a member of the FAO Indian Ocean Tuna Commission (IOTC), and a member of the FAO South West Indian Ocean Commission for Fisheries (SWIOFC). These bodies generally advocate for sustainable management and exploration of marine resources for development, conservation and protection.

6 Using Kenya's marine resources for national development

It is estimated that the fisheries sector presently accounts for approximately 0.5% of Kenya's gross domestic product (GDP), where revenues from inland fisheries make up 95% of this contribution and marine fisheries only 5%.[55] Kenya can take full advantage of its diverse marine resources in order to boost the livelihoods of the coastal area's communities as well as the overall national income. There is, however, a need to adopt or strengthen a number of approaches to the management and exploitation of marine resources for this to be achieved.

6.1 Adopting an integrated coastal zone management approach to promote effective co-management

Integrated coastal zone management (ICZM) has been described as a dynamic, multidisciplinary and iterative process to promote the sustainable management of coastal zones. It is one of the integrated marine and coastal area management approaches that cover the full cycle of information collection, planning (in its broadest sense), decision making, management and implementation monitoring. ICZM uses the informed participation and cooperation of all stakeholders to assess the societal goals in a given coastal area and to take actions toward meeting these objectives. ICZM seeks, over the long-term, to balance environmental, economic, social, cultural and recreational objectives, all within the limits set by natural dynamics. 'Integrated' in ICZM refers to

54 Farah (2015) *Horseed Media* (31 July 2015).
55 KCDP (2013: 9).

the integration of objectives and also to the integration of the many instruments needed to meet these objectives. It means integration of all relevant policy areas, sectors and levels of administration. It means integration of the terrestrial and marine components of the target territory in both time and space.[56]

Integrated management has also been described as –[57]

> an approach that provides policy direction and a process for defining objectives and priorities, and planning development beyond sectoral activities. This is because it adopts a systems perspective and multi-sectoral approach which takes into account all sectoral interests and stakeholder interests, and deals with economic and social issues as well as environmental and ecological issues ... by employing a holistic, ecosystem perspective recognising the interconnections between coastal systems and uses, ICZM avoids traditional sectoral management approaches.

While it is true that Kenya has already adopted ICZM in the management of various environmental issues,[58] there is need to not only fully exploit the resources but also to actively and meaningfully involve communities in ICZM implementation. It has rightly been argued that the great diversity of ecosystems and species situated along the Kenyan coastline and the widespread dependence of communities on these natural resources, require that attention be paid to promoting the sustainable use of these natural resources.[59] Proponents of the full and active implementation of ICZM argue that it would go a long way to promoting such sustainable use if it dealt with problems such as: the modification of habitats/ecosystems that results in reduced capacity to meet basic human needs (food, fuel, shelter) for the local communities; loss of cultural heritage; loss of existing income and foreign exchange, and high costs of restoring modified ecosystems; overexploitation of fisheries and other living resources that causes reduced economic returns and threatens inter-generational equity; microbiological pollution, beach erosion and siltation of the inshore lagoon waters causing increased costs of shoreline protection, increased water treatment costs, as well as problems in the tourism business; and biodiversity loss, collapse of cultural values and poverty.[60]

Kenya's marine protected areas (MPAs) are considered essential components of an ICZM program because they protect biodiversity and ecological processes on which humans residing in the coastal zone depend.[61] There is a need for the meaningful inclusion and the active participation of coastal communities in the conservation and exploitation of marine resources to realise enhanced conservation and productivity from these resources. For instance, while MPAs can benefit local communities through empowerment, improved governance, alternative livelihoods, improved fisheries, and social, educational, and cultural benefits;[62] it has been argued that they can also be

---

56 European Commission (1999).
57 Meltzer (1998: 9).
58 Republic of Kenya (2013).
59 Ochiewo (2001: 1).
60 Ibid: 3. See also generally, Clark (1992: 167).
61 Tuda & Omar (2012: 45).
62 Bennetta & Dearden (2014).

used to deny local communities means of livelihood, where it is reported that due to the high number of MPAs already in place in the Kenyan coastal area, there is resistance from fishers to the introduction of additional protected areas.[63] It is suggested that good governance is promoted through legitimacy, transparency, accountability, inclusiveness or participation, fairness or equity, integration or coordination, capability and adaptability.[64] As such, an effective MPA management requires adequate capacity and resources, effective communication of rules and regulations (such as boundaries), extensive programs of education and outreach, participatory processes to create management structures, consideration of the values of all stakeholders, relationships built on trust, coordination with other management institutions, integration of scientific and traditional knowledge, and mechanisms for conflict resolution and to ensure transparency and accountability.[65]

The Fisheries (Beach Management Units) Regulations (2007) establish the Beach Management Units (BMUs) whose objectives include to: support the sustainable development of the fisheries sector; help alleviate poverty and to improve the welfare and livelihoods of members through improved planning and resource management, good governance, democratic participation and self-reliance; strengthen the management of fish-landing stations, fishery resources and the aquatic environment; recognise the various roles played by different sections of the community including women in the fisheries sector; and to prevent or reduce conflicts in the fisheries sector.[66] BMUs are also part of efforts to promote fisheries co-management in Kenya. Past research[67] on the operation of BMUs has indicated that they have not been operating efficiently and optimally. It has been recommended that to improve performance, there is a need to: expand and strengthen existing BMU financial and technical resource bases; register BMUs as fisheries co-management institutions; confer fishing rights through a co-management policy; secure land for BMU infrastructural development; improve fish production, marketing and distribution channels; and improve post-harvest practices and technologies through training and provision of appropriate equipment.[68]

6.2 Investing in science and technology for marine resource exploration and exploitation

As already pointed out, much of the artisanal fishing and exploitation of marine resources along the Kenyan coast happens within the shallow waters of Kenya's

63 Fondo (2004: 8).
64 Bennetta & Dearden (2014).
65 Ibid.
66 Regulation 3(3) of the Fisheries (Beach Management Units) Regulations (2007).
67 Kanyange et al. (2014).
68 Ibid.

territorial waters. This means that there are still deep-sea resources within the country's national jurisdiction that are yet to be exploited for the benefit of the Kenyan coastal communities and the country at large.

The offshore fisheries zone is mainly exploited by licensed fishing DWFN vessels targeting highly migratory tuna species in the Kenyan EEZ, with no obligations to land, trans-ship or declare catches in the country.[69] This arrangement limits the country's benefits derived from its EEZ fisheries, especially from value addition activities associated with trans-shipment, landing for processing or even from trade in by-catch. This situation is attributable to the fact that there are no local fishing fleets and or locally-based foreign fishing fleets targeting these offshore resources.[70]

There is need to invest in science and technology as a means of enhancing management of marine resources in Kenya, and to enable local communities, in general, to access marine resources currently unavailable to them due to technological challenges.

It is also suggested that in the context of a blue economy, higher fish production with lower environmental damage is possible through polyculture, species diversification, optimal feeds and feeding, prevention of diseases and countries embracing the blue economy focusing more on developing sophisticated technologies for farming, conservation and processing of species.[71] The role of small-scale aquaculture by native fishing communities is also considered paramount from the perspective of food security and boosting their livelihood by selling surplus fish in the urban markets.[72] Furthermore, it is suggested that by having enabling policies on pricing, certification, labelling and marketing, the fishing sector in the context of the blue economy can be more organised and regulated.[73]

There is also a need for the state to equip artisanal fishermen with more advanced fishing vessels through providing grants and loans to them to purchase or hire these advanced vessels. They should also be equipped with knowledge on sustainable fishing practices and environmental conservation to ensure the exploitation of the marine resources on a sustainable basis. Investing in science and technology for the preservation of harvested marine resources for longer and safer storage for marketing will also help the fishing communities to minimise losses, increase their profit margin, and enhance food security locally and nationally.

69 KCDP (2013: 9).
70 Ibid.
71 Mohanty et al. (2015: 11).
72 Ibid.
73 Ibid.

6.3 Regulating foreign vessels in Kenya's deep seas and high seas territories

It has been observed that due to the nature of the high seas activities, supervision of the fishing area is a big problem and it is likely that unlicensed fishing vessels could easily poach fish from Kenyan territorial waters. It is also difficult to get accurate information about the fish caught by foreign-owned vessels.[74] There is therefore a need to enforce the fishing regulations governing such activities in order to ensure that the country does not lose its resources and foreign exchange revenue derived from these resources.

Illegal, unregulated and unreported (IUU) fishing is identified as one of the major challenges facing developing countries due to inadequate or total lack of relevant technological capacity. The fight against IUU fishing activities has even gained international attention in the international fisheries management agenda.[75]

6.4 Ecosystem-based approach to marine resources management

The ecosystem approach in the context of marine resource management has been defined as:[76]

> the comprehensive integrated management of human activities based on the best available scientific knowledge about the ecosystem and its dynamics, in order to identify and take action on influences which are critical to the health of marine ecosystems, thereby achieving sustainable use of goods and services and maintenance of ecosystem integrity.

The ecosystem approach has been heralded as a key framework for delivering sustainable development in both the terrestrial and the coastal and marine environment, as it provides an important framework for assessing biodiversity and ecosystem services, and evaluating and implementing potential responses.[77] Ecosystem-based management is seen as a place – or area –focusing on a specific ecosystem and the range of activities affecting it. It implies that after a certain area has been defined, sustainable development and use will be established for all activities in the whole area.[78] In addition, its application involves a focus on the functional relationships and processes within ecosystems, attention to the distribution of benefits that flow from ecosystem services, the use of adaptive management practices, the need to carry out management actions at multiple scales, and inter-sectoral cooperation.[79] There is a need to make this approach

74 Fondo (2004: 6).
75 Le Gallic & Cox (2006); and Agnew et al. (2009).
76 Douvere & Ehler (2009: 78).
77 Douvere (2008: 764).
78 Ibid.
79 Ibid. See also Port & Indian Ocean Commission (1997).

fully operational in Kenya in order to attain the goals of sustainability ensure that all stakeholders get to participate and benefit from the use of marine resources.

6.5 Capacity-building for stakeholders

It is noteworthy that the efficiency of Kenya's fisheries and marine sector is dependent on the institutions and the stakeholders behind it. While there are a number of state-controlled management institutions driving the sector, there is a need to ensure that they are led by people who are competent and knowledgeable as far as implementation of the existing framework is concerned. The capacity of institutions such as the Kenya Marine and Fisheries Research Institute (KMFRI)[80] and the State Department for Fisheries and the Blue Economy[81] should be enhanced. They should be well equipped not only to enable them to carry out their mandates more efficiently, but also to reach out and cooperate more effectively with all other stakeholders in the sector.

One of the recognised principles of the ecosystem approach to management is that it should consider all forms of relevant information, including scientific, indigenous and local knowledge, innovations and practices.[82] It is therefore imperative to build the capacity of stakeholders to effectively participate in the implementation of the ecosystem approach.

6.5.1 Human resource capacity development

There is a need to ensure that there is a synergy between the various institutions, especially if management responsibilities are decentralised. One of the ways that cooperation can be achieved is through the development and adoption of mechanisms for integrated planning. There is also a need for human resource development through training of administrative staff, observers on board fishing vessels, enforcement officers,

---

80 Kenya Marine and Fisheries Research Institute (KMFRI), a State Corporation under the Ministry of Agriculture, Livestock and Fisheries, has a mandate to undertake research in marine and freshwater fisheries, aquaculture, environmental and ecological studies, in order to provide scientific data and information for sustainable exploitation, management and conservation of Kenya's fisheries resources, and contribute to national strategies of food security, poverty alleviation, clean environment and creation of employment as provided for under vision 2030. See <http://www.kmfri.co.ke/index.php/careers/vacancies> (accessed 10-6-2017).

81 The State Department for Fisheries and the Blue Economy was created by Executive Order No. 1/2016 under the Ministry of Agriculture Livestock and Fisheries. It is mandated to facilitate the exploration, exploitation, utilisation,management, development and conservation of fisheries resources as well as aquaculture development and to undertake research in marine and freshwater fisheries, see <http://www.kilimo.go.ke/fisheries/index.php/about-us/mandate/> (accessed 10-6-2017).

82 AID Environment & National Institute for Coastal and Marine Management (2004: 5).

scientists and advisers, and fishers, to optimise their interaction in the participatory processes.

Sustainable development also requires establishing functional interconnections between administrations dealing with fisheries and the environment within the ecosystem boundaries.

6.5.2 Effective framework for negotiations involving multiple stakeholders

As a way of achieving sustainable management of resources, equitable benefit sharing and the effective management of potential conflicts, there is a need to establish an effective framework for conducting negotiations between multiple stakeholders. This will not only be useful in achieving the principles of participation and transparency, but will also ensure that all the relevant stakeholders collectively participate in the management of marine and fisheries resources along Kenya's coastline. Ultimately, this will promote social and economic development within the confines of the principles of sustainable development.

6.5.3 Scientific research capacity development

It has been suggested that ways of improving efficiency and productivity in the marine and fisheries sector include: strengthening research; improving data collection, integrated analysis and communication; developing a better understanding of the ecosystem's functioning; evaluating policy and management options; identifying trade-offs; ensuring the use of appropriate assessment methodologies (including management performance and risk assessment); and identifying relevant indicators and reference points.[83] Well-functioning information systems are important to support indicators for different fisheries and ecosystems, including large-scale multi-criteria descriptions of ecosystems such as GIS.[84]

7 Conclusion

Coastal areas throughout the world are under stress, with various anthropogenic factors such as population growth, pollution, habitat degradation, multiple resource use conflicts, and over-exploitation of resources causing marine environmental degradation

83 Garcia & Cochrane (2005: 315).
84 Ibid.

and depletion of coastal resources.[85] Marine resources, especially along Kenya's coast hold great potential to contribute to national development. However, for this to be a reality, the foregoing anthropogenic factors ought to be addressed. Notably, some of these factors such as population growth, multiple resource use conflicts and over-exploitation of the resources can most effectively be addressed through the adoption of more efficient management approaches. Some of the approaches suggested in this chapter could go a long way in achieving this since they bring all stakeholders on board in their mode of operation. They are also likely to gain the acceptance and credibility that can only come with addressing the interests and concerns of all, while at the same time achieving sustainability. Kenya's economic blueprint, Vision 2030, requires the mobilisation of all national resources for sustainable national development. It is therefore important that measures are put in place to maximise the benefits accruing from Kenya's coastal marine and fisheries sector to boost social and economic development. As part of its efforts to realise Vision 2030, Kenya should fully utilise its marine resources to improve the livelihoods of its people and to boost the national economy generally.

References

Agnew, DJ, J Pearce, G Pramod, T Peatman, R Watson, JR Beddington & TJ Pitcher (2009) "Estimating the worldwide extent of illegal fishing" 4(2) *Plos one* e4570, at <http://journals.plos.org/plosone/article/file?id=10.1371/journal.pone.0004570&type=printable> (accessed 3-8-2018).

AIDEnvironment & National Institute for Coastal and Marine Management (2004) *Integrated marine and coastal area management (imcam) approaches for implementing the Convention on Biological Diversity* CBD Technical Series No. 14, at <https://www.cbd.int/doc/publications/cbd-ts-14.pdf> (accessed 10-6-2017).

Anam, R & E Mostarda (2012) *Field identification guide to the living marine resources of Kenya, FAO Species Identification Guide for Fishery Purposes.*

Bennetta, NJ & P Dearden (2014) "Why local people do not support conservation: community perceptions of marine protected area livelihood impacts, governance and management in Thailand" 44 *Marine Policy* 107-116.

Capital Business (2016) "Let's expand fishing in Indian Ocean, President urges coastal counties" *Capital Business* (1-9-2016), at <http://www.capitalfm.co.ke/business/2016/09/lets-expand-fishing-indian-ocean-president-urges-coastal-counties/ (accessed 1-4-2016).

Clark, JR (1992) *Integrated management of coastal zones* FAO Fisheries Technical Paper No. 327, at <http://campusdomar.es/observatorio/_documentos/ordenacion_del_litoral/doctrina/integrated_management_of_coastal_zones.pdf> (accessed 12-5-2017).

Douvere, F (2008) "The importance of marine spatial planning in advancing ecosystem-based sea use management" 32(5) *Marine Policy* 762-771.

85 Meltzer (1998: 8).

Douvere, F & CN Ehler (2009) "New perspectives on sea use management: initial findings from European experience with marine spatial planning" 90 *Journal of Environmental Management* 77-88.

European Commission (1999) *Towards a European Integrated Coastal Zone Management (ICZM) Strategy: general principles and policy options*.

Farah, H (2015) "Why Somalia has to withdraw case against Kenya at the ICJ?" *Horseed Media* (31-7-2015), at <https://horseedmedia.net/2015/07/31/why-somalia-has-to-withdraw-case-against-kenya-at-the-icj/> (accessed 12-5-2017).

Fondo, EN (2004) *Assessment of the Kenyan marine fisheries from selected fishing areas*, at <http://www.unuftp.is/static/fellows/document/estherprf04.pdf> (accessed 14-5-2017).

Freight Logistics (2018) "Major boost for 'blue economy' as Kenya hosts global maritime conference" (24-2-2018), at <http://feaffa.com/magazine/2018/02/24/major-boost-for-blue-economy-as-kenya-hosts-global-maritime-conference/> (accessed 8-5-2018).

Garcia, SM & KL Cochrane (2005) "Ecosystem approach to fisheries: a review of implementation guidelines" 62(3) *ICES Journal of Marine Science: Journal du Conseil* 311-318.

Kanyange N, P Kimani, P Onyango, S Sweenarain & Y Yvergniaux (2014) *Performance assessment of beach management units along the coastlines of Kenya and Tanzania*, at <www.fao.org/3/a-az413e.pdf> (accessed 1205-2017).

KCDP / Kenya Coastal Development Project (2013) *Draft monitoring, control and surveillance (MCS) standard operating procedures (SOPs) for the marine and coastal fisheries of Kenya*, at <http://www.kcdp.co.ke/en/reports/project-documents/draft-monitoring-control-and-surveillance-mcs-standard-operating-procedures-sops> (accessed 12-5-2017).

Le Gallic, B & A Cox (2006) "An economic analysis of illegal, unreported and unregulated (IUU) fishing: key drivers and possible solutions" 30(6) *Marine Policy* 689-695.

Meltzer, E (1998) *International review of integrated coastal zone management*, at <http://www.dfo-mpo.gc.ca/Library/253987.pdf> (accessed 12-5-2017).

Mohanty, SK, P Dash, A Gupta & P Gaur (2015) *Prospects of blue economy in the Indian Ocean*, at <http://www.ris.org.in/sites/default/files/Final_Blue_Economy_Report_2015-Website.pdf> (accessed 3-8-2018).

Ochiewo, J (2001) *The Kenyan coastal and marine resources management: a case study of the socio-economic setting of Mida Creek* Proceedings of the 12th Biennial Coastal Zone Conference Cleveland 15-19 July 2001, at <http://webapp1.dlib.indiana.edu/virtual_disk_library/index.cgi/4916229/FID3790/pdf_files/ochiewoj.pdf> (accessed 14-5-2017).

Port & Indian Ocean Commission (1997) *Integrated coastal area management: the role of the regional environment programme of the Indian Ocean Commission*, at <http://ec.europa.eu/development/body/publications/fish/pe039715.pdf> (accessed 10-6-2017).

Republic of Kenya (2013) *Integrated coastal zone management (ICZM) policy*.

Republic of Kenya (2014) *Kenya vision 2030*, at <www.vision2030.go.ke/vision/> (accessed 14-5-2016).

Ruwa, RK (2006) *Coastal and offshore marine fisheries of Kenya: status and opportunities* KMFRI Technical Report.

Svensson, LE & L Pendleton (eds) (2014) *Transitioning to a new blue economy: proceedings of the December 2013 economics of the ocean summit* Nicholas Institute for Environmental Policy Solution Conference Proceedings.

Tuda, A & M Omar (2012) "Protection of marine areas in Kenya: the Lenya wildlife service in the 21st century" 29(1) *The George Wright Forum* 43-50.

UN / United Nations (2010) *Resumed review conference on the Agreement Relating to the Conservation and Management of Straddling Fish Stocks and Highly Migratory Fish Stocks*, at

<http://www.un.org/depts/los/convention_agreements/reviewconf/FishStocks_EN_C.pdf> (accessed 25-6-2017).

UN / United Nations (2014) *Blue economy concept paper*, at <https://sustainabledevelopment.un.org/content/documents/2978BEconcept.pdf> (accessed 14-5-2016).

UNECA / United Nations Economic Commission for Africa (2016) *Africa's blue economy: a policy handbook.*

UNFAO / United Nations Food and Agricultural Organization (2016) *Fishery and aquaculture country profiles: Kenya country profile fact sheets*, at <http://www.fao.org/fishery/facp/KEN/en> (accessed 20-5-2016).

UNFAO / United Nations Food and Agricultural Organization & Republic of Kenya (2006) *Kenya: national integrated natural resources assessment*, at <www.fao.org/forestry/download/16259-07d9f8a278081dbc73fa0030fc0182bce.pdf, > (accessed 4-5-2016).

UNFAO / United Nations Food and Agricultural Organization & Republic of Kenya (2009) *Final project report on pilot zones in the coastal, eastern and Lake Victoria regions of Kenya 2007-2008* Draft Three.

Chapter 18: The Environmental Management Act (2017) and natural resource regulation in Malawi: opportunities for and limitations to effective enforcement

Gift Dorothy Makanje

1 Introduction

Malawi's first significant policy document on environmental issues was the National Environmental Action Plan[1] (NEAP) published in 1994. The NEAP was set out to document and analyse all the major environmental issues and proposed measures to alleviate them as well as to promote the sustainable use of natural resources in Malawi. The NEAP highlighted that one of the greatest challenges to effective environmental protection and management was poor enforcement of the legal framework. In particular, NEAP highlighted that the legislative framework was uncoordinated and had several gaps, inconsistencies, duplications and conflicts all of which made enforcement difficult. This was the main reason for the adoption of the National Environmental Policy[2] (NEP) in 1996 (revised in 2004) and the subsequent enactment of a framework environmental law, the Environmental Management Act[3] (EMA) in 1996. The EMA (1996) provided for an elaborate institutional framework for implementing the environmental and natural resource management provisions prescribed in the Act, expanded opportunities for stakeholder consultations and enabled coordination. However, there is little indication that it improved environmental management in general or sector coordination to any significant degree.[4]

In an attempt to address the above concerns, a second Environmental Management Act (EMA) was assented to by the President in February 2017. EMA (2017) provides for a coordinated and comprehensive future legal framework for environmental protection and management as well as the conservation and sustainable use of natural resources. EMA (2017) will replace EMA (1996), when the former commences by way of notice in the future. Until this occurs, EMA (1996) remains the applicable law.

1 Republic of Malawi (1994).
2 Republic of Malawi (1996).
3 Act 23 of 1996.
4 Banda (2004).

The enforcement of environmental laws remains a challenge in many jurisdictions. In Malawi, environmental degradation and the unsustainable exploitation of natural resources continue to occur notwithstanding the existence of several laws regulating these issues. What guarantee is there that the introduction of EMA (2017) will remedy the situation? This chapter examines EMA (2017) in a bid to highlight the opportunities and limitations it presents with respect to improving enforcement in the natural resource sector, particularly relating to forest, fish and wildlife resources. It critically evaluates the enforcement mechanisms provided for in EMA (2017) and highlights outstanding barriers to enforcement, and opportunities for reform.

2 Overview of Malawi's environment

Malawi is one of the most densely populated countries in Africa which imposes significant pressure on its limited natural resources. The Malawi State of Environment and Outlook Report[5] (2010) outlines the following key environmental problems: soil erosion; deforestation; water resources depletion and degradation; high population growth; depletion of fish stocks; threats to biodiversity; human habitat degradation; climate change; and air pollution. Similar problems were identified in the NEAP (1994) and the NEP (2004). Malawi's high population density and its over-dependence on agriculture are the main causes of continued environmental degradation. These problems are exacerbated by poverty since a high proportion of the population relies on natural resources, like firewood and fish stocks, for survival.[6]

Over 90% of Malawi's exports stem from the natural resource sector, most notably from agriculture.[7] Malawi's economy is therefore very much linked to its environment, and environmental degradation threatens its social and economic development. The importance of domestic legislation regulating environmental protection, environmental management and the conservation and sustainable use of natural resources is therefore critical.

3 Forestry, fisheries and wildlife regulation in Malawi

Malawi continues to suffer tremendous declines in forest, fishery and wildlife resources.[8] The unsustainable exploitation of forest resources and land clearing associated with agricultural expansion due to rapid population growth have largely

5 Ministry of Natural Resources, Energy and Environment (2010).
6 Ibid: iii.
7 Commission of the European Communities (2006).
8 Dobson & Lynch (2003).

contributed to acute deforestation in Malawi. Constant power outages plaguing the country since 2015 have worsened forest degradation as the demand for firewood and charcoal rises even in urban areas. The threat to fish resources is largely due to increased numbers of fishermen, fishing undertaken during breeding seasons, the use of inappropriate fishing methods, encroachment of water weeds (water hyacinth), reduction in water flow, increased sedimentation in rivers and water pollution.[9] With respect to wildlife, encroachment and poaching are common.[10] The degradation of natural resources therefore continues to be a major threat to socio-economic development in Malawi.

The Forestry Act[11] provides for participatory forestry, forest management, forestry research, forestry education, forest industries, protection and rehabilitation of environmentally fragile areas, and international cooperation in forestry. The Fisheries Conservation and Management Act[12] (FCMA) makes provision for the regulation, conservation and management of the fisheries; while the National Parks and Wildlife Act[13] (NAPWA) consolidates the law relating to national parks and wildlife management. All these statutes have various provisions to ensure the conservation and sustainable use of forests, fish and wildlife in Malawi. However, enforcement has always been weak with the sad result that natural resource degradation continues unabated. It therefore becomes imperative to examine whether EMA (2017) will improve the regulation of natural resources in Malawi.

4 Environmental Management Act (2017) – enforcement mechanisms

As indicated above, EMA (2017) is the integrated and comprehensive future legal framework for environmental and natural resource management in Malawi. It is the coordinating statute on all environmental and natural resource matters in Malawi. When it commences, it will repeal EMA (1996) and hopefully provide a more responsive legal framework for protecting and managing the environment and conserving and sustainably using natural resources. This is its prescribed purpose. 'Sustainable utilisation' has been defined in the Act as "the use or exploitation of natural resources which guards against the extinction, deletion or degradation of any natural resource of Malawi and permits the replenishment of natural resources by natural means or otherwise"; while 'conservation' has been defined as "the preservation of natural resources and their protection from misuse, fire or waste".[14]

9 Kalima (2011: 219).
10 Ibid.
11 Act 11 of 1997.
12 Act 25 of 1997.
13 Act 15 of 2004.
14 Section 2 of the EMA (2017).

Section 6 highlights its supreme status by providing that any environment and natural resource law that is inconsistent with the provisions of EMA (2017) shall, to the extent of such inconsistency, be invalid, thereby making this law subject only to the Constitution of the Republic of Malawi (1994) (the Constitution). EMA (2017) makes provision for the following substantive enforcement mechanisms: the right to a clean and healthy environment and the issue of *locus standi*; the establishment of the Malawi Environmental Protection Authority (MEPA); accountability and institutional arrangements; local community participation; the establishment of an environmental tribunal; environmental and social impact assessments, monitoring and auditing; environmental protection orders; inspection, analysis and records; administrative penalties and offences. Each of these mechanisms and the opportunities they present for effective enforcement are addressed below.

4.1 The right to a clean and healthy environment and the issue of *locus standi*

Section 4(1) of EMA (2017) affords every person the right to a clean and healthy environment and the corresponding duty to safeguard and enhance the environment. The Constitution does not explicitly provide for an environmental right which undermines its value in environmental protection. In Section 13, the Constitution merely provides for principles of national policy which include that the state shall actively promote the welfare and development of the people of Malawi by progressively adopting and implementing policies and legislation aimed at achieving specified goals which include the environment. In this regard, the goal is to manage the environment responsibly in order to: prevent degradation of the environment; provide a healthy living and working environment for the people of Malawi; accord full recognition to the rights of future generations by means of environmental protection and the sustainable development of natural resources; and to conserve and enhance the biological diversity of Malawi.[15] However, this provision is merely directory in nature and not justiciable.

While Section 4 of EMA (2017) may not have the same status as a constitutional right, it is nevertheless an essential provision for the enforcement of environmental and natural resource regulation. EMA (1996) contains a similar provision, but its implementation has been frustrated by restrictive interpretations of the requirement of *locus standi*.[16] EMA (2017) has addressed this problem and expanded the right significantly in two respects.

Firstly, Section 4(4) of EMA (2017) enables MEPA, any concerned environmental agency or any person to bring an action against any person whose activities or omissions have or are likely to have a significant impact on the environment to: prevent or

15 Section 13(d)(i-iv) of the Constitution of the Republic of Malawi (1994).

16 Kalima (2009: 235).

stop any act or omission which is deleterious or injurious to any segment of the environment or likely to accelerate unsustainable depletion of natural resources; procure any public officer to take measures to prevent or stop any act or omission which is deleterious or injurious to any segment of the environment for which the public officer is responsible under any law; require that any on-going project or other activity be subject to an environmental audit or monitoring in accordance with the act; and seek a court order for the taking of other measures that would ensure that the environment does not suffer significant harm. EMA (1996) accords no similar power to the coordinating institution or other lead environmental institutions to take action on behalf of the public. Hence the public is currently compelled to rely on the Attorney General's office which is problematic as this office is understaffed and environmental concerns are regarded as peripheral. Section 4(4) of EMA (2017) is accordingly a significant addition in the context of enforcement.

Secondly, Section 4(5) of EMA (2017) provides that:

> …any person proceeding under section 4(4) shall have capacity to bring an action notwithstanding that the person cannot show that the defendant's act or omission has caused or is likely to cause him any personal loss or injury: provided that the legal action –
>
> (a) is not frivolous or vexatious; or
>
> (b) is not an abuse of the court process;
>
> provided further that in every case the determining factor shall be whether such person is acting in the best interest of the environment and in exercise of the duty to safeguard and enhance the environment.

Legal actions are a powerful tool for compelling compliance and imposing sanctions for violations of environmental laws. However, a person wishing to bring an action before court to enforce a right is required to demonstrate that they have *locus standi* (in other words sufficient interest in the matter). *Locus standi* is critical to the exercise of the right of access to court since the more liberal the interpretation given to the rules of standing, the more individuals are guaranteed access to the courts.[17] One of the most commonly lamented barriers to the enforcement of environmental law under EMA (1996) has been the issue of *locus standi*. The Malawian judiciary has historically adopted a very restrictive approach to *locus standi* which commentators have argued has in turn limited the growth of public interest litigation in the country.[18] Public interest litigation has, however, been recognised as a key tool for promoting the interests of the poor, vulnerable and marginalised sectors of Malawi's population who cannot access the courts on their own.[19]

17 Chirwa (2011: 70).

18 Nkhata (2008). The article compares the treatment of the *locus standi* requirement in decisions of the High Court and the Supreme Court of Appeal. The Supreme Court of Appeal required to establish a personal interest or substantive interest surpassing that of other citizens in order to be held to have sufficient standing to commence an action.

19 Gloppen & Kanyongolo (2007: 258).

EMA (2017) is therefore to be commended for settling this question in clear terms. It has not only granted the right to a clean and healthy environment to all citizens, but has also made enforcement of the right possible. In a country where poverty and illiteracy levels are high, and political interference spans many sectors, non-governmental organisations (NGOs) and other interested stakeholders are often best positioned to enforce environmental rights through public interest litigation. These parties can help in detecting violations, notifying the authorities, applying public pressure and bringing suits to enforce the law. The recent case of *State v. Lilongwe Water Board, Minister of Agriculture, Irrigation and Water Development, the Director of Environmental Affairs, the Minister of Natural Resources Energy and Mining Ex parte the Malawi Law Society*[20] (*Salima-Lilongwe Water Pipeline* case) emphasises the relevance of interested stakeholders in enforcing environmental law. It involved the Malawi Law Society bringing action to secure compliance with the environmental impact assessment (EIA) provisions contained in EMA (1996). Section 4(5) of EMA (2017) is broad enough to allow persons or organisations to commence court actions in the sole interest of the environment and natural resources. Such persons would only be required to establish that they were acting in the best interests of the environment as required by the proviso contained in Section 4(5). This provision should therefore go a long way in encouraging much needed public interest litigation and with it effective enforcement of legislation regulating natural resources.

4.2 The Malawi Environmental Protection Authority

As indicated above, the main motivation for the enactment of EMA (1996) was that Malawi's environmental legal and institutional framework was too diffuse for effective coordination and enforcement. Although EMA (1996) attempted to improve stakeholder consultation and provides for sectoral coordination, it has not been successful in this regard.[21] The Act fails to outline clearly the functions of lead agencies and provided no workable mechanisms for promoting coordination. In addition, too many powers were given to the Minster and the fact that the coordinating agency, the Environmental Affairs Department (EAD), is a government department could be seen to compromise its independence and professionalism.

EMA (2017) addresses the above concerns. Section 7 establishes an autonomous body, MEPA, which shall be the principal agency for the protection and management of the environment and sustainable use of natural resources. MEPA shall have powers to coordinate, monitor, supervise and consult with all stakeholders on all activities

20 Judicial Review Case No. 16 of 2017, High Court (Zomba District Registry) (unreported). This case is more fully discussed in part 4.6 below.

21 Banda (2004).

relating to the use and management of the environment and natural resources. Functions currently vested in the Minister for Environmental Affairs under EMA (1996) will be transferred to MEPA in the future.

Some of MEPA's key functions are outlined in Section 9, and include: to advise the Minister for Environmental Affairs on the formulation and implementation of policies for environmental protection and management; to initiate legislative proposals, standards and guidelines; to enforce the right to a clean and healthy environment; to monitor and enforce compliance with environmental and natural resource related policies and legislation by lead agencies (in this case MEPA has been given powers to direct lead agencies to submit regular reports on their activities); to review and approve environmental and social impact assessments; to receive and investigate complaints; and to prepare and publish a national state of the environment report every five years and an annual report on the status of the environment. MEPA shall accordingly be a critical enforcement institution for environmental policies and legislation in Malawi in the future.

EMA (2017) also contains provisions that enable MEPA to strengthen coordination, implementation and enforcement of environmental and natural resources management laws. Being an independent institution means MEPA can work efficiently and professionally with minimal political interference. The only hiccup may relate to the appointment of persons to it. Section 10 of EMA (2017) states that MEPA shall consist of a chairperson, vice-chairperson and five other members all of whom shall be appointed by the President. The Secretary for Environmental Affairs and the Solicitor General shall be ex-officio members of MEPA. Presidential appointments can negatively impact on the autonomy and professionalism of the authority and eliminate any hopes of non-political interference in MEPA. Presidential appointees have not historically inspired confidence as they are perceived to owe allegiance to the appointing authority which might affect their efficiency. However, this remains to be seen.

4.3 Accountability and institutional arrangements

One of the biggest challenges to effective environmental management in Malawi has been the uncoordinated legislative framework that has several gaps, inconsistencies, duplications and conflicts thereby making enforcement difficult.[22] The EMA (2017) addresses this problem. It refers to institutions like the forestry directorate, the fisheries directorate and the wildlife directorate as lead agencies. 'Lead agency' has been defined in the Act as "any public office or organisation including a ministry or government department which is conferred by any written law or policy with powers and functions for the protection and management of any segment of the environment and

22 See generally: Department of Research and Environmental Affairs (1994).

the conservation and sustainable utilisation of natural resources in Malawi".[23] Section 23 provides that MEPA shall, in consultation with lead agencies, issue guidelines for the elimination of gaps, conflicts, inconsistencies and duplications in environmental and natural resource policies and legislation and their implementation. This is especially important for interconnected natural resource sectors like forestry, fisheries and wildlife.

MEPA will have an oversight role over all the lead agencies and can delegate functions to any of them.[24] Under Section 22, MEPA has the power to direct any lead agency to perform, within such time and such manner as it shall specify, any of the duties imposed on the lead agency by the Act or any written law. If the lead agency fails or neglects to comply with such directions, MEPA may itself perform, or cause to be performed, the duties in question. This will hopefully guard against neglect of duties on the part of the various natural resource institutions and ensure that even where duties have been neglected, the omission is not left unattended to.

Section 23 of EMA (2017) indicates that the Act should not be construed as divesting any lead agency of the powers, functions, duties or responsibilities conferred or imposed on it by any written law relating to the protection and management of the environment and the conservation and sustainable use of natural resources; or limiting such powers. Lead agencies shall perform functions and responsibilities as provided under relevant written laws and EMA (2017), and shall ensure sustainable realisation of national development by preventing activities that degrade the environment; undertake appropriate precautionary measures and enforcement of standards applicable to their sector; and report on their implementation and enforcement activities to MEPA.[25] Lead agencies will also be required to report on their operations, the state of their sector and the measures taken by the lead agency to maintain or improve the environment.[26] Considering that enforcement is currently weak under the various natural resource institutions, requiring them to report on enforcement to MEPA should compel them to strengthen their enforcement mechanisms. It will also create a mechanism for holding them accountable, which has not historically been available.

Accountability in environmental and natural resource management should accordingly be strengthened under EMA (2017). Even MEPA shall be required to publish and lay before parliament (through the minister) a report on the exercise and performance of its functions annually.[27]

23 Section 2 of EMA (2017).
24 Sections 20 and 21 of EMA (2017).
25 Section 23(3) of EMA (2017).
26 Section 24 of EMA (2017).
27 Section 18 of EMA (2017).

4.4 Local community participation

Failure of existing regulatory management institutions to conserve natural resources has led to the recognition of the value of stakeholder involvement in natural resource management.[28] In Malawi, the current policy and legislative framework shows a clear shift from the command-and-control approach to participatory environmental and natural resource governance, which has the local communities at its core.[29] Under the Forestry Act (1997), this has been done through the creation of village forest areas and village natural resource management committees for the purpose of promoting the participation of local communities and the private sector in forest conservation and management. Under the NAPWA (2007), this has been done through the creation of wildlife management authorities which are local community organisations tasked with promoting local community participation in the conservation and management of wildlife. The FCMA (1997) also creates beach village committees with similar purposes. However, the creation of these committees creates needless proliferation and duplication at the local level.

The EMA (2017) attempts to address this problem while retaining an emphasis on the importance of local community participation. Section 5 provides that for the purpose of ensuring effective public participation and the enforcement of rights and duties created under the Act, the MEPA shall promote the right of every person to participate in environmental decision-making processes directly or through representative bodies. It also compels lead agencies to create mechanisms for effective, direct and indirect public participation. MEPA is further obliged, in consultation with local authorities, to issue guidelines for the establishment of a committee on the environment for each district known as the district environment sub-committee. The functions of these committees include to coordinate the activities of a local authority relating to the management of the environment and natural resources.[30] Each local authority shall, on the advice of the district environment sub-committee, establish a Local Environment and Natural Resources Committee (LENRC) responsible for undertaking environmental and natural resource management activities in their jurisdiction.[31]

The LENRC has been defined as:[32]

> the village and area development committees as established under the Local Government Act to initiate, coordinate and mobilise local community participation in environmental and natural resource management issues and to represent interests of such local communities and includes any local community institution participating in the management and protection of the environment and natural resources under any written law.

28 Dobson & Lynch (2003).

29 Banda & Ngwira (2007: 38).

30 Section 26 of EMA (2017).

31 Section 27 of EMA (2017).

32 Section 2 of EMA (2017).

The LENRC must, among other things, mobilise local communities in its jurisdiction to sustainably manage and conserve the environment and natural resources, and restore degraded environmental resources through self-help.[33] Section 27(2) of EMA (2017) provides that the LENRC must be established with special recognition of the roles and responsibilities of traditional leaders; and the need to integrate traditional knowledge in environmental and natural resource strategies, plans programs. This is another advantageous provision for enforcement considering that the committees created under the Forestry Act (1997), FCMA (1997) and NAPWA (2007) overlooked the critical role of traditional authorities in the rural areas.

4.5 The Environmental Tribunal

Effective dispute resolution mechanisms greatly impact on the enforcement of any law. The EMA (1996) makes provision for the establishment of an Environmental Tribunal. The Tribunal, however, is granted very limited administrative jurisdiction under the Act and its role is largely limited to considering appeals against decisions and actions of the minister, director or inspectors under the Act. Some 21 years since the enactment of EMA (1996), this Tribunal is yet to be established.

The EMA (2017) also makes provision for an Environmental Tribunal.[34] It has, however, considerably expanded the jurisdiction and powers of the Tribunal. The Tribunal can hear and determine petitions on violations of the right to a clean and healthy environment, any other provision under the Act or any written law relating to environmental and natural resource management; and receive complaints from any person, lead agency, private sector and NGOs relating to the implementation and enforcement of environmental and natural resource management policies and legislation.[35] Decisions of this Tribunal will have the same force and effect as High Court decisions.[36]

Given its wide jurisdiction, the Tribunal should become an essential institution in the enforcement of environmental law, especially considering the cost and delays that come with taking matters to court in Malawi. The Tribunal has the potential to quickly and efficiently deal with environmental disputes and enforce the law accordingly. A further advantage of this Tribunal is that it shall be chaired by a legal practitioner who is conversant with environmental law and who shall be appointed by the Malawi Law Society.[37] This differs from the provisions in EMA (1996) that provide for the Tribunal to be chaired by a person appointed by the President. This may address the political interference concerns raised above. The Tribunal also has the advantage of non-rigid

33 Section 27(4)(c) of EMA (2017).
34 Sections 107-115 of EMA (2017).
35 Section 107 of EMA (2017).
36 Section 115 of EMA (2017).
37 Section 107(2)(a) of EMA (2017).

compliance with common law rules of procedure and evidence, which may lead to the more cost-effective and expedient disposal of cases,[38] something of great advantage to the protection of natural resources.

Nevertheless, considering the extensive delays in establishing the similar Tribunal under EMA (1996), there is no guarantee that the government will establish the Tribunal under EMA (2017) without delay. Perhaps EMA (2017) should have prescribed deadlines by which the Tribunal should be established.

4.6 Environmental and social impact assessments, monitoring and auditing

Part VI of EMA (2017) makes extensive provision for environmental and social impact assessments, monitoring and auditing. EMA (1996) only made provision for an EIA without the social element.[39] An 'environmental and social impact assessment' (ESIA) is defined in EMA (2017) as "a systematic evaluation of a project to determine its impact on the environment and the conservation of natural resources".[40] These are powerful mechanisms for the enforcement of environmental and natural resource policies and legislation as they ensure that developmental projects should not be implemented at the expense of the environment. However, although EMA (1996) contains similar provisions for EIAs, environmental audits and monitoring are scarcely used, the challenge being the lack of personnel, technical expertise and funding in the enforcement agency. As long as there is no commitment to address these issues, these mechanisms though good on paper, will prove ineffective in practice.

The recent *Salima-Lilongwe Water Pipeline* case[41] is relevant. It involved the need for an EIA in the Salima-Lilongwe/Lake Malawi Water Supply Project. Khatho Civils Proprietary Limited was contracted by the Lilongwe Water Board and Malawi Government to install a water pipeline pumping water from Salima to Lilongwe (a distance of about 130 kilometres). The Malawi Law Society was of the view that the contractor had commenced the project without an EIA and initiated judicial review proceedings against the Lilongwe Water Board, Minister of Agriculture, Irrigation and Water Development, Director of Environmental Affairs and the Minister of Natural Resources Energy and Mining to compel them to undertake an EIA. The parties agreed that the project was of such magnitude that the contractor could not commence with it in the absence of an EIA and ESIA. The contentious question was whether the project had commenced. The court of first instance and the Supreme Court of Appeal, however, both never had an opportunity to deal with the substantive issue as the matter was

38 Sections 110 and 116 of EMA (2017).

39 Section 24 of EMA (1996).

40 Section 2 of EMA (2017).

41 Judicial Review Case No. 16 of 2017, High Court (Zomba District Registry) (unreported).

disposed of on procedural grounds. Nonetheless, this case highlights the fact that there is a potential danger to sacrifice environmental concerns in the implementation of developmental projects perceived as beneficial to the country. This makes mandatory requirements for ESIAs so critical. The case also illustrates how interested stakeholders and NGOs are essential in addressing environmental concerns and ensuring accountability of the relevant authorities.

4.7 Environmental protection orders

Part XI of EMA (2017) gives MEPA the power to issue environmental protection orders against any person whose acts or omissions have, or are likely to have, adverse effects on the protection and management of the environment and the conservation and sustainable use of natural resources. This, if efficiently utilised, is another powerful enforcement mechanism.

4.8 Inspection, analysis and records

Section 81 of EMA (2017) states that MEPA must establish an inspectorate with the necessary technical staff and facilities to administer, monitor and enforce measures for the protection and management of, and for the prevention and control of, pollution to the environment. Inspectors play a very important role in the enforcement of environmental and natural resource standards. Subject to adequate availability of technical staff and facilities (which is not the case now), inspectors can prevent the occurrence or aggravation of actual environmental harm and also facilitate the conviction of offenders by providing the necessary proof in environmental and natural resource cases.

4.9 Administrative penalties

Section 108 of EMA (2017) has introduced various administrative penalties. These include written warnings, monetary penalties, directing the wrongdoer to do or refrain from doing an act, directing wrongdoers to remedy the effects of contravention or to compensate victims. The prescribed monetary penalties are reasonably hefty.

Of all the current laws regulating the forestry, fisheries and wildlife sectors, only the FCMA (1997) makes provision for administrative penalties for offences of a minor nature. These are, however, very limited in scope. Provision in EMA (2017) for more extensive administrative penalties is a welcome development and is in line with principles of environmental law since they allow preventive action to be taken before environmental damage occurs. The introduction of these administrative penalties should hopefully ensure that recourse to legal action is the last option thereby reducing the number of matters that go into the court system with its attendant costs and delays. If used efficiently, these penalties should complement the criminal sanction that has been popular in the enforcement of environmental law in Malawi, and help in eliminating the problems associated with criminal enforcement.

4.10 Penalties

Part XV of EMA (2017) provides for various criminal offences in relation to environmental and natural resource protection and management. Criminal sanctions are commonly used to enforce environmental law. However, it has often been lamented that fines provided under EMA (1996) are too weak to have any deterrent effect.[42] Similarly, weak sanctions are available under the Forestry Act (1997), FCMA (1997) and NAPWA (2007). EMA (2017) attempts to address this concern by providing for reasonably hefty fines. The Act also fortunately provides for recurring offences and an additional fine for each day that environmental harm continues after conviction. This may motivate offenders to expeditiously remedy environmental harm and offending behaviour. Criminal offences are commonly prosecuted by the Malawi Police Service prosecutors and officers from the Director of Public Prosecution's chambers. However, these officers may not have the requisite expertise in technical environmental matters. Coordination between these departments and MEPA is therefore imperative for the successful prosecution of these offences.

5 Barriers to enforcement and possible solutions

With the exception of the significant differences noted above, most of the enforcement mechanisms contained in EMA (2017) are currently also provided for under EMA (1996). Barriers like poverty, lack of alternative income and energy options, illiteracy and attitudinal problems, resource constraints, institutional weaknesses and political interference greatly undermined the success of EMA (1996). These issues remain today and may accordingly also stifle the success of EMA (2017) if they are not effectively addressed. Each of these barriers and solutions to possibly overcome them are discussed in turn below.

---

42 See, for example, *R v. Maria Akimu* (Revision Case No. 9 of 2003).

5.1 Poverty

Poverty remains the primary cause of the unsustainable use of the environment and natural resources, and an underlying challenge to effective enforcement. Related to this is the overdependence of Malawi's energy economy on biomass fuels like firewood and charcoal, a factor which has significantly contributed to environmental degradation in Malawi. Poverty also reduces motivation among people to care about environmental degradation or pursue environmental justice, with their primary concern being about survival. While there are many poverty alleviation policies and schemes in Malawi, many of them remain in form rather than substance, and until serious efforts are made to actually alleviate poverty and provide alternatives to biomass fuels, this will remain a challenge to the conservation and sustainable use of the country's natural resources.

5.2 Lack of alternate income generating activities and energy options

Lack of alternative income generating activities remains a challenge that drives most people to unsustainably exploitat natural resources, especially fish and forest resources. The Malawi Labour Force Survey[43] (2013) indicated that Malawians are predominantly engaged in informal work with 45% of the labour force engaged in skilled agricultural, forestry and fishery occupations. As regards fishing, limiting access as a solution to conserving diminishing fish stocks was once considered by the government, although subsequently rejected owing to the extreme poverty of many people who depend on fishing for survival.[44] The incessant electricity outages being experienced in Malawi since 2015 have also increased the demand for charcoal even by those in urban areas. This in turn contributes to forest degradation. For the urban population, improving electricity supply can help. However, for the majority living in rural areas, it is essential that the government eases the overdependence on biomass fuels by providing alternatives. As long as the demand for firewood and charcoal is high, suppliers will always be available in the presence or absence of law. Alternative income generating activities must also be encouraged.

5.3 High illiteracy levels and attitudinal problems

Another barrier to effective enforcement of environmental law is the high illiteracy levels coupled with societal attitudes to environmental wrongs. The extent to which

43 National Statistics Office (2013).
44 Dobson & Lynch (2003: 235).

people regard environmental crimes as being morally wrong will determine their demand for justice, reporting and identification. Unfortunately, most Malawians do not seem to consider environmental crimes as moral wrongs as can be evidenced by brazen littering across the country. Another example is the case of *R v. Maria Akimu*,[45] where officials of the National Parks and Wildlife Department, posing as would-be purchasers of ivory, met the defendant at her house. They agreed to buy some pieces of ivory at the defendant's house, at the defendant's father's house and another person's house. They eventually arrested the defendant and recovered the ivory, but not without stiff resistance from the defendant's neighbours and relations who could not understand why an individual should be prosecuted for selling animal products. There have also been media reports of forestry officials being assaulted for confiscating charcoal from sellers.

To overcome this, implementing intensive public awareness campaigns and making environmental and natural resource education an integral part of primary and secondary education can help to impress upon children the importance of these resources and help them grow into adults who utilise natural resources responsibly. Primary education has already assisted with HIV awareness even among young children, and if well integrated into the education curriculum, natural resource management issues may also benefit. A complete change of mentality is imperative if Malawi is to move toward conserving and sustainably using its natural resources.

5.4 Resource constraints

Related to the poverty challenge, is the fact that government allocates minimal resources to environmental and natural resource matters. Lack of resources, material and human, is a significant challenge for all natural resource enforcement institutions. In the area of wildlife, most national parks and wildlife reserves lack personnel, vehicles, fuel, guns and ammunition, and this causes ineffective policing and increased poaching.[46] The Environmental Affairs Department remains underfunded and understaffed and this negatively impacts on their enforcement mandate. For instance, inspectors cannot efficiently enforce environmental standards because they are very few in number and lack technical expertise as well as other necessary facilities. Adequate budgetary support to MEPA and lead agencies is therefore critical if EMA (2017) is to make much impact.

45 Revision Case No. 9 of 2003.
46 Kalima (2009: 235).

5.5 Delays in establishing institutions

Although EMA (2017) makes provision for essential enforcement institutions like MEPA and the Environmental Tribunal, delays in their establishment may undermine their potential. It is hoped that the MEPA and Environmental Tribunal do not take 21 years to establish, as has been the case for the latter institution under EMA (1996). As mentioned above, perhaps EMA (2017) should be amended to include minimum periods within which these key institutions should be created.

5.6 Political interference

Political interference has proven to be a constant challenge to enforcing laws in Malawi. One way this happens is through political appointments. Practice has shown that most presidential appointees are prone to political manipulation. Consequently, though MEPA has been given autonomy as an environmental enforcement agency, it is a cause for concern that Section 10 of EMA (2017) places the appointment of its chairperson, vice-chairperson and remaining members in the hands of the President. Presidential appointments have the potential to compromise the autonomy and professionalism of MEPA and with it effective enforcement. The proposed composition and appointment process therefore bears rethinking.

6 Further recommendations

6.1 Optimising criminal sanctions

Malawian environmental law places more reliance on the criminal sanction than any other sanction for environmental protection, and criminal sanctions will accordingly remain an important device for securing compliance with the law.[47] Criminal sanctions are either applied as a primary sanction or as a supporting sanction where administrative measures fail. However, this is not ideal since the criminal law is reactive not proactive. It is furthermore contrary to one of the fundamental principles of environmental law, the preventive principle, which requires that environmental damage should as much as possible be prevented in advance rather than rectified or punished retrospectively. Since most environmental disputes will culminate in criminal cases, there is a need to optimise benefits from the use and outcome of criminal sanctions, such as depositing fines paid for environmental offences into an environmental fund to be used to remediate current and prevent future environmental degradation. Strengthening the

47 Kalima (2006).

involvement and technical expertise of public prosecutors, investigators and courts in enforcing environmental laws also warrants serious consideration.

6.2 Judicial activism

Some 21 years have passed since the enactment of EMA (1996) and very few cases have been brought before the High Court praying for relief in terms of its provisions. This is a lost opportunity for the courts to articulate and enforce the right to a clean and safe environment. Given the chance, which might arise with the broad *locus standi* provisions now contained in EMA (2017), Malawi's judiciary should be encouraged not to be conservative and use their role to develop the law as a mechanism for environmental and natural resource protection. Furthermore, it has been argued that one reason why activists have been discouraged from bringing environmental matters to court is the fear of adverse cost orders.[48] While EMA (2017) is silent on cost orders, it is encouraging to note the approach of the Supreme Court of Appeal in the *Salima-Lilongwe Water Pipeline* case[49] where the court said:

> We are a big believer of public interest litigation. We have therefore always done our part to encourage it by especially being careful with how we deal with matters of costs. At the same time we think it our duty to urge all that find it necessary to resort to public interest litigation to do so responsibly so that it does not lead to needless waste especially of treasury.... Because costs must follow the event we were minded to award costs against the Society. We are mindful however of the role, in many ways via litigation, the Society plays in safeguarding, promoting and protecting our people's rights. An award for costs against the Society might put a dampener on their activities and enthusiasm. Such an award would also not sit comfortably with our belief in the benefits to be had from public interest litigation.

The court then proceeded to order each party to pay their own costs. It is therefore recommended that courts should do their part in responsibly encouraging environmental litigation by making proactive cost orders.

7 Conclusion

The enforcement of environmental law remains a challenge in Malawi. An attempt was made to address this problem through the enactment of EMA (1996). This Act has, however, been rather unsuccessful, which has triggered the introduction of EMA (2017). The latter is an integrated and comprehensive legal framework for environmental and natural resource management in Malawi. This chapter examined this law in a bid to highlight the opportunities and limitations that it presents with respect to

---

48 Kalima (2009: 223).

49 MSCA Civil Appeal No. 59 of 2017.

effective enforcement in the natural resources sector. It has been highlighted that while EMA (2017) presents tremendous potential for natural resource conservation and sustainable use, the outstanding limitations discussed above must be addressed to improve enforcement.

References

Banda, GZ (2004) *Report on the revision of the Environmental Management Act.*

Banda, GZ & T Ngwira (2007) *Introduction to environmental law in Malawi.*

Chirwa, D (2011) *Human rights under the Malawian Constitution.*

Commission of the European Communities (2006) *Country environmental profile for Malawi.*

Department of Research and Environmental Affairs (1994) *National environmental action plan (Malawi).*

Dobson, T & K Lynch (2008) "As nearshore stocks drop, Malawi begins a return to local fisheries management" 29(2) *Journal of Great Lakes Research* 232-242.

Gloppen, S & F Kanyongolo (2007) "Courts and the poor in Malawi: economic marginalisation, vulnerability and the law" 5(2) *International Journal of Constitutional Law* 258-293.

Kalima, J (2006) *The effectiveness of environmental law in Malawi: an analysis of the principal legal tools for achieving environmental protection with emphasis on the criminal sanction* PhD Thesis, University of Kwazulu-Natal.

Kalima, J (2009) "A critique of the legal framework for wildlife protection in Malawi" 3(2) *Malawi Law Journal* 199-235.

Kalima, J (2011) "Environment and development in Malawi – any balancing of interests" in M Faure & W Du Plessis (eds) *The balancing of interests in environmental law in Africa* 219-260.

Ministry of Natural Resources, Energy and Environment (2010) *Malawi state of the environment and outlook report.*

National Statistics Office (2013) *Malawi labour force survey.*

Nkhata, M (2008) "Public interest litigation and *locus standi* in Malawian constitutional law" 2(2) *Malawi Law Journal* 209-225.

Republic of Malawi (1994) *National environmental management plan.*

Republic of Malawi (1996) *National environmental policy.*

PART III:

WATER GOVERNANCE, MANAGEMENT AND USE

Chapter 19: Pollution of water in South Africa by untreated sewage: addressing the governance issues

Michael Kidd

1 Introduction

Anyone who follows developments in the water sector in South Africa will be aware of the pervasive problem of pollution of South Africa's water resources by untreated sewage over recent years. Not only is this acknowledged by the government in the Green Drop Reports (discussed further below), but the media has been replete with stories relating to this problem,[1] the number of news items reflecting the seriousness of the situation. The primary cause of the problem is municipal mismanagement of water treatment and sewage reticulation, which in most cases involves non-compliance with applicable laws. This creates compliance and enforcement complications due to the intra-governmental nature of the relationship between regulator and 'offender' and the South African laws relating to cooperative government; or, perhaps more accurately, interpretations of these laws. While recognising that there are elements other than law that play a role in this scenario, this chapter uses a legal lens to consider the relevant governance framework in relation to water treatment and recommends ways of clarifying and addressing poor governance, as a first and necessary step in addressing the problem.

Having described the problem in more detail, the chapter will then consider the governance structure in relation to water treatment in South Africa. This will be followed by an evaluation of how water governance is failing in the country. The chapter concludes with a set of recommendations, based on existing applicable law, on how to address the concerns. In all cases the focus on governance will be limited to the legal aspects of governance, as explained in more detail later.

---

1 See, for example, Bronkhorst (2014); van der Rheede (2015); Kings (2015); Qukula (2015); Kings (2017); and *The Citizen* (2017).

2 Sewage pollution in South Africa: highlighting the problem

The 2009 Green Drop Report[2] released by the national Department of Water (DWS)[3] indicated that, of the 449 water treatment plants assessed for the report (53% of the total number in the country), only 65 (14.5%) were in compliance with legal standards applicable to the release of treated effluent. It is likely that very few of the plants not assessed were compliant either.[4] The 2009 Green Drop Report provided a significant amount of detail in relation to the performance of individual treatment plants, but this level of detail was absent from subsequent reports.

In the 2011 Green Drop Report[5] there was far wider coverage: 821 of the 852 waste water systems were assessed, from all 156 municipalities in the country.[6] Details of compliance with applicable legal standards were not provided in this Report, but the overall results (based on a combination of factors affecting the risk involved with the plant, including legal compliance) indicated that only 44% of the plants managed to score over 50% in the rating.

The third, and last available, Green Drop Report, from 2013,[7] assessed a total of 824 waste water treatment works (WWTWs) from 152 municipalities,[8] and there was a slight improvement to 50.4% of the plants scoring over 50%.[9] A total of 248 systems received scores of less than 30%, which the Report labels as 'systems in crisis'.[10]

More recent reports have not been published, although widespread evidence of continuing problems with sewage contamination suggest little if any improvement. It has been suggested by the main opposition political party (the Democratic Alliance) that one of the reasons for non-publication of more recent reports is avoidance of publishing information which would embarrass local governments ahead of the 2016 local government elections throughout the country.[11] This would probably also go some way to explaining why the reports after 2009 contained little detailed information about individual WWTWs.

---

2 Department of Water Affairs (2010).

3 The acronym DWS is used in this chapter to refer to the current name of the Department, the Department of Water and Sanitation. It has previously been called the Department of Water Affairs (DWA) and before that the Department of Water Affairs and Forestry (DWAF).

4 For further detail on the 2009 Green Drop Report, see Kidd (2011).

5 Department of Water Affairs (2012).

6 Ibid: 11.

7 Department of Water Affairs (2013). All that was released for public consumption was the Executive Summary of this Report.

8 The total number of municipalities in the country had been reduced from 156 to 152 over that period.

9 Department of Water Affairs (2013: 2).

10 Ibid.

11 See report at <https://www.da.org.za/2016/01/mokonyane-withholding-blue-and-green-drop-reports-to-hide-poor-anc-performance/> (accessed 9-4-2018).

As implied by the information set out above, the vast majority of the WWTWs assessed in these reports (which assess the overwhelming majority of those actually operating in the country) are managed by local government bodies and not by private operators. The legal provisions relating to this governance arrangement are explained in the next part of the chapter.

3 Legal governance structure for water in South Africa

3.1 Water governance generally

According to the Food and Agriculture Organization of the United Nations (FAO), water governance:[12]

> relates to the enabling environment in which water management actions take place: that is, the overarching policies, strategies, plans, finances and incentive structures that concern or influence water resources; the relevant legal and regulatory frameworks and institutions; and planning, decision-making and monitoring processes.

Where the entity that is primarily responsible for water governance is the government, and the government is one that operates in accordance with the rule of law, the 'relevant legal and regulatory frameworks and institutions' are the keystone of the governance framework. It is the legal framework that provides the authority for the government to make the underlying policy decisions relating to water issues, to carry out the necessary planning, strategising and decision-making, make provision for and mobilise the necessary finances, and ultimately ensure that there is compliance with the legal requirements by all players in the water sector. It is because the legal framework is the most important aspect of the governance framework, that it forms the focus of this chapter.

The legal framework operates in (at least) two relevant dimensions in relation to water governance. The first is the law on paper. This (decided and publicised laws) is clearly a prerequisite for any water governance worthy of the description. Its overall quality (on paper) will be determined by how well it provides (on paper) for the other aspects of governance – planning, strategising, decision-making, finances, monitoring and securing compliance with the laws. But it is trite that paper laws are not sufficient. The second dimension is how these laws are utilised: how they are implemented by the relevant legal institutions and how compliance with the laws is secured in practice by a combination of monitoring and enforcement, whatever form the latter takes. Underpinning this second dimension is the way in which the relevant legal institutions understand their legal mandates in relation to water governance. This is an important

12 FAO (2018).

theme in the South African situation discussed in this chapter, as will become apparent below.

3.2 The relevant legal framework in South Africa

South Africa's constitutional structure involves three spheres of government: national, provincial and local. It is important to understand these spheres not as levels in a hierarchical sense, but as individual spheres of government that each have their own 'functional areas' (the term used in the Constitution)[13] of legal authority. In the functional area of water, the overall governance of water is an exclusive national competence in terms of the Constitution, and this responsibility is carried out by the national Department of Water and Sanitation (DWS). Although this is not explicitly indicated by the Constitution, all those functional areas that do not appear on either of Schedule 4 (functional areas of concurrent national and provincial legislative competence) or Schedule 5 (functional areas of exclusive provincial competence) are regarded as being of exclusive national competence.

Local government (municipal) powers and functions are provided for in Section 156 of the Constitution, which provides that a municipality has executive authority in respect of, and has the right to administer the local government matters listed in Part B of Schedule 4 and Part B of Schedule 5; and any other matter assigned to it by national or provincial legislation. Part B of Schedule 4 includes the item: Water and sanitation services limited to potable water supply systems and domestic waste-water and sewage disposal systems. Consequently, the governance and management of water resources generally is legally provided for by the National Water Act,[14] and exercised by the national DWS. The latter has provincial branches but these are branches of the DWS located in provinces, not part of provincial departments, provinces having no constitutional competence – neither legislatively nor administratively – for water matters. Governance and management of water services (in relation to provision of domestic water supplies and sanitation) is the responsibility of local government in terms of the Water Services Act.[15] Related to this, access to water 'services' (such as household and domestic use) is the responsibility of local government whereas access to water 'resources', for productive use such as irrigation, industry and bulk supply to local government, is the responsibility of the DWS.

The Water Services Act deals with the provision of water supply services and sanitation services, the ambit of which includes the operation of WWTWs. Every 'water

---

13 Constitution of the Republic of South Africa, 1996.

14 Act 36 of 1998.

15 Act 108 of 1997.

services authority', defined in the Act as a municipality,[16] is under a duty to all consumers or potential consumers in its area of jurisdiction to progressively ensure efficient, affordable, economical and sustainable access to water services.[17] A 'water services provider' is "any person who provides water services to consumers or to another water services institution",[18] and most water services authorities are also water services providers. In other words, most municipalities play the role of water services providers in terms of the Act in their areas of jurisdiction. This is why most WWTWs are operated by municipalities, as observed above.

Juxtaposed with this governance arrangement is the explicit recognition in the National Water Act's preamble that water is a scarce and unevenly distributed national resource which occurs in many different forms which are all part of a unitary, interdependent cycle. In line with this, Section 3 of the Act provides –

> (1) As the public trustee of the nation's water resources the National Government, acting through the Minister, must ensure that water is protected, used, developed, conserved, managed and controlled in a sustainable and equitable manner, for the benefit of all persons and in accordance with its constitutional mandate.
>
> (2) Without limiting subsection (1), the Minister is ultimately responsible to ensure that water is allocated equitably and used beneficially in the public interest, while promoting environmental values.
>
> (3) The National Government, acting through the Minister, has the power to regulate the use, flow and control of all water in the Republic.

How are the responsibilities in Section 3 of the National Water Act reconciled with the constitutional distribution of water governance functions outlined above? The answer is complicated, first, by the Constitution's provisions relating to the competencies of the spheres of government and how these have been interpreted by the courts, and, second, by the Constitution's provisions relating to cooperative government.

Focusing on local government, the following provisions are instructive. Section 151(4) of the Constitution states that the national or a provincial government may not compromise or impede a municipality's ability or right to exercise its powers or perform its functions. The objects of local government, in terms of Section 152, are:

> (a) to provide democratic and accountable government for local communities;
>
> (b) to ensure the provision of services to communities in a sustainable manner;
>
> (c) to promote social and economic development;
>
> (d) to promote a safe and healthy environment; and
>
> (e) to encourage the involvement of communities and community organisations in the matters of local government.

While the Constitution provides for local government to pursue its objects without interference, there are provisions which allow for oversight and intervention in certain

---

16 Section 1 of the Water Services Act (1997).

17 Section 11 of the Water Services Act (1997).

18 Section 1 of the Water Services Act (1997).

circumstances. In terms of Section 154(1) of the Constitution, the national government and provincial governments, by legislative and other measures, must support and strengthen the capacity of municipalities to manage their own affairs, to exercise their powers and to perform their functions. Section 155(6)(a) of the Constitution states that each provincial government must provide for the monitoring and support of local government in the province. Moreover, Section 139, headed 'Provincial supervision of local government', provides –

> (1) When a municipality cannot or does not fulfil an executive obligation in terms of legislation, the relevant provincial executive may intervene by taking any appropriate steps to ensure fulfilment of that obligation, including –
>
> (a) issuing a directive to the Municipal Council, describing the extent of the failure to fulfil its obligations and stating any steps required to meet its obligations; and
>
> (b) assuming responsibility for the relevant obligation in that municipality to the extent necessary –
>
> (i) to maintain essential national standards or meet established minimum standards for the rendering of a service;
>
> (ii) to prevent that Municipal Council from taking unreasonable action that is prejudicial to the interests of another municipality or to the province as a whole; or
>
> (iii) to maintain economic unity.

In short, local government has specific functions that are within its constitutionally-defined authority, and "the national and provincial spheres are not entitled to usurp the functions of the municipal sphere except in exceptional circumstances, but only temporarily and in compliance with strict procedures".[19]

The Constitution's provisions relating to the powers of the three spheres of government are reinforced by those dealing with cooperative government. Section 41(1) of the Constitution provides that all spheres of government and all organs of state within each sphere must, inter alia –

> (g) exercise their powers and perform their functions in a manner that does not encroach on the geographical, functional or institutional integrity of government in another sphere; and
>
> (h) co-operate with one another in mutual trust and good faith by –
>
> (i) fostering friendly relations;
>
> (ii) assisting and supporting one another;
>
> (iii) informing one another of, and consulting one another on, matters of common interest;
>
> (iv) co-ordinating their actions and legislation with one another;
>
> (v) adhering to agreed procedures; and
>
> (vi) avoiding legal proceedings against one another.

19 *City of Johannesburg Metropolitan Municipality v. Gauteng Development Tribunal* 2010 (6) SA 182 (CC) para. 44.

This is in turn reinforced by the Intergovernmental Relations Framework Act[20] which provides for a suite of mechanisms and procedures to promote relations between different spheres of government. In Section 40(1), it provides that all organs of state must make every reasonable effort to avoid intergovernmental disputes when exercising their statutory powers or performing their statutory functions; and to settle intergovernmental disputes without resorting to judicial proceedings.

Before considering these governance provisions' impact on water governance in the country, particularly in relation to water treatment by municipalities, it remains to consider relevant compliance and enforcement provisions. In terms of the National Water Act, Section 19 provides –

> (1) An owner of land, a person in control of land or a person who occupies or uses the land on which-
>
> (a) any activity or process is or was performed or undertaken; or
>
> (b) any other situation exists, which causes, has caused or is likely to cause pollution of a water resource, must take all reasonable measures to prevent any such pollution from occurring, continuing or recurring.
>
> ...
>
> (3) A catchment management agency may direct any person who fails to take the measures required under subsection (1) to –
>
> (a) commence taking specific measures before a given date;
>
> (b) diligently continue with those measures; and
>
> (c) complete them before a given date.

Although the power to issue directives in Section 19 vests in a catchment management agency, the Act provides that, in areas for which a catchment management agency is not established or, if established, is not functional, all powers and duties of a catchment management agency vest in the Minister.

Finally, there are provisions in the Water Services Act for dealing with water services institutions that fail to carry out their responsibilities. Section 62(1) provides that the Minister and any relevant Province must monitor the performance of every water services institution in order to ensure compliance with all applicable national standards prescribed under the Act; compliance with all norms and standards for tariffs prescribed under the Act; and compliance with every applicable development plan, policy statement or business plan adopted in terms of the Act. Section 63 provides that:

> (1) If a water services authority has not effectively performed any function imposed on it by or under this Act, the Minister may, in consultation with the Minister for Provincial Affairs and Constitutional Development, request the relevant Province to intervene in terms of section 139 of the Constitution.
>
> (2) If, within a reasonable time after the request, the Province –
>
> (a) has unjustifiably failed to intervene; or

20 Act 13 of 2005.

(b) has intervened but has failed to do so effectively, the Minister may assume responsibility for that function to the extent necessary-

(i) to maintain essential national standards;

(ii) to meet established minimum standards for providing services; or

(iii)to prevent that Province from taking unreasonable action that is prejudicial to the interests of another province or the country as a whole.

...

(4) After assuming responsibility for a function under subsection (2), the Minister may issue a directive to the water services authority to perform that function effectively.

(5) If the water services authority fails to comply with that directive, the Minister may intervene-

(a) by taking appropriate steps to facilitate the performance of that function, including giving financial, managerial and technical advice and assistance; or

(b) on notice to the water services authority, by taking over that function.

...

(9) In the interests of co-operative government, a Province must immediately inform the Minister of its intention to intervene by taking over any function of a water services authority under section 139 of the Constitution.

(10) In considering the manner and implementation of any intervention under this section, the Minister must consider –

(a) the reasons for the extent and the period of non-compliance by the water services authority concerned;

(b) the attempts made to achieve compliance;

(c) the effect of the non-compliance; and

(d) any other relevant matter.

In light of these legal provisions, their use (or non-use) in the context of pervasive non-performance in terms of the water legislation will now be assessed.

4 Evaluation of current water governance in relation to water treatment and sewage pollution

As observed in the discussion of the Green Drop Reports above, there are many municipalities that are not complying with their responsibilities under (at least) the Water Services Act. As I have observed elsewhere,[21] the reasons for this are not confined to a lack of conscientiousness in relation to compliance with the law. There are problems with resources (both physical and human) and often historical shortcomings inherited by current municipalities. In 2010, it was estimated that it would cost over R500 billion (about US$41 billion) to repair and increase the capacity of infrastructure – 30% to

21 See further: Kidd (2011); and Kidd (2016: 157).

40% of which was not working.[22] It is unlikely that most municipalities in the country will have the resources (given current funding sources) to meet the infrastructural costs necessary to address water treatment problems. In 2015, the Auditor-General of South Africa "rated the financial health of 65% of the municipalities as either concerning or requiring intervention".[23] Moreover, in total, "27% of municipalities were in a particularly poor financial position by the end of 2015-16, with material uncertainty with regard to their ability to continue operating in the foreseeable future".[24] In January 2017, municipalities owed Eskom (the country's electricity supplier) a total of R10.2 billion[25] and in November 2017, there were 29 municipalities facing water supply cut off by the DWS due to non-payment of costs amounting to R10.7 billion.[26] This shows that a substantial number of municipalities are in no financial position to spend sufficient money on water infrastructure to address the water treatment problems, irrespective of whether they are directed to do so by the DWS or whether there is intervention in terms of Section 63 of the Water Services Act.

The response of the DWS to non-performing municipalities following the 2013 *Green Drop Report* evaluation is that those scoring less than 30%[27]

> ...have 30 days in which to implement a corrective action plan. If they do not comply they subsequently receive a directive from DWS. If there is still no compliance it becomes very difficult for the Department to take action against them because of the principle of co-operative government in the South African Constitution.

The approach of issuing a directive (in terms of Section 19 of the National Water Act as outlined above), is only likely to be effective when there are no serious budgetary constraints to compliance; for example, where the municipal manager refuses to approve the payment for chlorine for water treatment because 'chlorine is very expensive' and expenditure was prioritised elsewhere,[28] as opposed to having to carry out a capital upgrade of the entire WWTW. Issuing a directive to address a problem that requires several million rand to fix when there is no budget for WWTW repairs is pointless.

The cooperative government impediment to taking further action against defaulters mentioned in the quote above may attract two responses. The first is that the requirements of cooperative government do not prohibit absolutely legal proceedings between

---

22 CDE (2010).

23 Auditor-General of South Africa (2017: 7).

24 Ibid: 8. See also Monteiro (2018).

25 Njobeni (2017).

26 *Business Tech* (2017).

27 Ntombela et al. (2016: 708). The Executive Summary of the 2013 Green Drop Report indicates that "...systems scoring under 30% are placed under regulatory surveillance, in accordance (sic) the Water Services Act (108 of 1997) Sections 62 and 63" (Department of Water Affairs (2013: 4)). As Section 63 envisages intervention, it appears that this is not being carried out in practice, as no municipalities have been subject to intervention for failures in the water treatment responsibilities.

28 Stacey (2016).

organs of state, but requires them to use this, in effect, only as a last resort. But it appears as if the DWS's response outlined in the quote above is the *only* response; not a last resort response having exhausted other avenues. According to Ntombela et al, the engagement of the DWS with municipalities scoring poorly in the *Green Drop* analysis is confined to Departmental officials involved with compliance and enforcement actions and who are not equipped to offer support to the municipalities.[29] This may be exacerbated by lack of capacity and skills to offer the requisite support.[30] This suggests that the DWS is ignoring the essence of cooperative government – that organs of state must work together (cooperate) in order to meet mutual objectives (in this case, effective water treatment and clean water) – and jumping straight to the last resort (command and control) and then complaining that this approach does not work because of the impediment of cooperative government. If one recalls the 'public trusteeship' mandate in Section 3 of the National Water Act, the DWS is required to –

> ensure that water is protected, used, developed, conserved, managed and controlled in a sustainable and equitable manner, for the benefit of all persons and in accordance with its constitutional mandate.

Nobody can claim that this mandate is being respected when half of the WWTWs in the country are not performing adequately, and when the state of sewage pollution in the country is as reflected in the media articles cited in the introduction.

The (more desirable) alternative is to take both the Section 3 exhortation and cooperative government seriously and for DWS to cooperate with and support municipalities in order to improve the performance of water treatment. It is clear that many municipalities will not be able to improve the situation acting alone because of a lack of resources. Requiring the non-performing municipality to implement a corrective action plan without DWS support seems to be a classic case of passing the buck. Proponents of cooperation may face the possible argument that DWS support of municipalities contravenes those provisions of the Constitution (outlined above) that prohibit national government interference in (or usurpation of) matters of municipal competence. But that is ignoring the difference between 'support' and 'interference'. Section 3 of the National Water Act, in my view, requires such support.

DWS's apparent failure to appreciate the difference between support and interference was evident in the case of *Federation for Sustainable Environment and Another v. Minister of Water Affairs and Others*[31] where it was argued on behalf of the DWS that, although national and provincial government were 'committed' to providing financial assistance to a municipality suffering from a water supply contaminated with acid mine drainage (which finance had been provided), "they are debarred from

29 Ntombela et al. (2016: 708).

30 Ibid.

31 Unreported case 35672/12 (NG), see <http://www.saflii.org/za/cases/ZAGPPHC/2012/128.html> (accessed 9 April 2018).

interfering and imposing their will on the local government".[32] The court appeared to agree with this argument and decided, in effect, to absolve them of any responsibility in the case, although there is no express wording to this effect in the judgment. The approach of the DWS in this case appears to be one of "let's give the municipality some money which may address the problem" rather than the one which would be required by Section 3 of the National Water Act of cooperating (not only in relation to finance) to address the problem – "how can we solve this together"?

If the DWS were to put more effort into support of municipalities in their water services functions, this could assist in appropriate municipal planning (for example, upgrades of existing facilities that have not kept track with increasing populations), which in turn could provide insight for the DWS in regulating municipal expenditure on water treatment (by means of norms and standards envisaged by Section 9 of the Water Services Act, for example). Another potential benefit of national-municipal co-operation could arise from economies of scale in relation to procurement of supplies for WWTWs. Procurement is currently seen as a problem facing municipalities,[33] both in relation to identification of appropriate technologies and in relation to the reliability of suppliers, and the facilitation of DWS in this regard could be of great assistance.

Potentially the most ideal instrument in providing for a cooperative response to sewage pollution problems is the catchment management agency (CMA), provided for in the National Water Act. The Act envisages division of the country into nine (previously 19) water management areas and each has a CMA with governance jurisdiction over that water management area. The functions of CMAs are set out in Section 79(4) of the Act, and these include that a CMA must strive towards achieving cooperation and consensus in managing the water resources under its control.[34] The development of catchment management agencies has been slow and, at this stage, only two have been established. Upon the establishment of a CMA, its initial functions are –[35]

- to investigate and advise interested persons on the protection, use, development, conservation, management and control of the water resources in its water management area;
- to develop a catchment management strategy;
- to coordinate the related activities of water users and of the water management institutions within its water management area;
- to promote the coordination of its implementation with the implementation of any applicable development plan established in terms of the Water Services Act…; and

---

32 *Federation for Sustainable Environment and Another v. Minister of Water Affairs and Others* (Unreported case 35672/12 (NG), see <http://www.saflii.org/za/cases/ZAGPPHC/2012/128.html> (accessed 9-4-2018)) para. 19.

33 Ntombela et al. (2016: 707-708).

34 Section 79(4)(b).

35 Section 80.

- to promote community participation in the protection, use, development, conservation, management and control of the water resources in its water management area.

These functions appear to be tailor-made for cooperative solutions to sewage pollution problems in areas under the governance of CMAs, and the establishment of the remaining CMAs ought ideally to be expedited as much as possible. This may, however, not materialise because of a proposal in late 2017 to establish only one CMA for the entire country,[36] which appears to undermine the entire purpose of CMAs. The reasons provided for such a move are wholly unconvincing and, as pointed out by former Director-General of DWS, Mike Muller, proper implementation of the existing Act is what is necessary, not tinkering with the legal framework.[37]

The functions of the CMA also highlight the role played in community participation, which is largely absent, other than complaints made by citizens, in the sewage pollution crisis. Part of the reason for this is the lack of transparency, in relation to the Green Drop Reports that followed the first one.[38] Other than a series of unreported cases brought by the NGO Save the Vaal Environment against the Ngwathe Municipality,[39] there are no examples of 'citizen suit' applications to require municipalities to clean up their act in relation to water treatment. Despite liberal environmental laws (which include water laws) permitting relatively easy access to courts, there has been a somewhat perplexing shortage of cases of this type. Perhaps one of the reasons is that citizens are aware that the problem is often not merely a case of recalcitrant municipal officials and that the appropriate remedy is therefore a difficult one to mould. Be this as it may, increasing participation by citizens, including by means of litigation if necessary, would appear to be a prerequisite for improvement of the situation. This in turn is dependent on adequate access to information which, as has been pointed out, is deficient at present.

In wrapping up this section, it is worth observing that the apparent desire by the DWS to address failures of implementation of the water laws by amending the legislation rather than improving the existing laws' implementation makes it somewhat difficult to make recommendations for addressing the sewage pollution governance issues. The following recommendations, nevertheless, assume that the law remains as it is.

36 *Government Gazette* 41321 GN 1415 of 15 December 2017.
37 Muller (2018).
38 Ntombela et al. (2016: 708).
39 Stacey (2016).

5 Recommendations

In the light of the preceding discussion, the following recommendations are apposite.

First, there must be a change in emphasis by the DWS from command-and-control to cooperative attempts at finding a solution to the problems of inadequate water treatment. Municipalities must not be regarded as adversaries but an important part of the solution and the DWS needs to provide appropriate support in line with the true objective of laws relating to cooperative government.

Secondly, in this regard, it is important that the DWS appreciates the difference between support or assistance of municipalities in carrying out their water services functions on the one hand and interference in these functions on the other. The latter is constitutionally impermissible; but 'support' is not only consistent with the Constitution but required by Section 3 of the National Water Act, which must be regarded as a guiding light in dealing with the problem of sewage pollution.

Thirdly, in addition to support of municipalities, the DWS must regulate water treatment appropriately based on the nature of the existing failures and identified needs of municipalities, whether in relation to forward-planning; compulsory ring-fencing of funds required for WWTWs; norms and standards relating to maintenance and upgrade requirements; or similar aspects.

Finally, there needs to be significant improvement in transparency. Maximum detail of which municipalities are performing or not, and in which ways they are deficient, must be made available to all stakeholders, including affected citizens. This will facilitate citizen involvement which, as argued above, will contribute to reaching solutions.

All of these recommendations, however, depend on a strong DWS that is functioning optimally and consistently with its constitutional and statutory mandate. Unfortunately, the current situation of the DWS appears to be far from what is required, with the Standing Committee on Public Accounts reportedly describing the 'complete collapse' of the DWS, involving claims of instability and financial mismanagement.[40] The onus thus is on national government to strengthen the Department, ensuring capable leadership and employment of the requisite skills in order to be able to follow these recommendations. It is clear that most municipalities are incapable of stemming the ineffable flow of untreated sewage by acting on their own and the participation and support of a strong and competent DWS is vital if this crisis is to be averted.

---

40 Tandwa (2018). The 'Mokonyane' referred to in the title of the article is the erstwhile Minister of Water and Sanitation, who has been moved to another Cabinet position after a reshuffling early in 2018.

References

Auditor-General of South Africa "Auditor-general reports marginal improvements in local government audit results" *Media Release* (21-6-2017), at <http://www.agsa.co.za/Portals/0/Reports/MFMA/201516/MR/2015-16%20MFMA%20 media%20release.pdf> (accessed 9 April 2018).

Bronkhorst, E (2014) "Millions set aside for Bloemhof water crisis" *ENCA* (9-6-2014), at <http://www.enca.com/millions-bloemhof-water> (accessed 9-4-2018).

Business Tech (2017) "All the municipalities facing water cuts over non-payment" *Business Tech* (27-11-2017), at <https://businesstech.co.za/news/government/213231/all-the-municipalities-facing-water-cuts-over-non-payment/> (accessed 9-4-2018).

CDE / Centre for Development and Enterprise (2010) *Water: a looming crisis?*, at <http://www.cde.org.za/water-a-looming-crisis/> (accessed 9-4-2018).

Department of Water Affairs (2010) *Green drop report 2009.*

Department of Water Affairs (2012) *Green drop report 2011.*

Department of Water Affairs (2013) *Green drop report 2013.*

FAO / Food and Agriculture Organization of the United Nations (2018) "Water governance", at <http://www.fao.org/land-water/water/watergovernance/en/> (accessed 9 April 2018).

Kidd, M (2011) "Poisoning the right to water in South Africa: what can the law do?" *International Journal of Rural Law and Policy*, at <http://epress.lib.uts.edu.au/journals/index.php/ijrlp/article/view/2604/2834> (accessed 9-4-2018).

Kidd, M (2016) "Muddied water: (un)cooperative governance and water management in South Africa" in J Gray, C Holley & R Rayfuse (eds) *Trans-jurisdictional water law and governance*, 157-174.

Kings, S (2015) "Sewage in Gauteng's drinking water" *Mail & Guardian* (24-7-2015), at <https://mg.co.za/article/2015-07-23-sewage-in-gautengs-drinking-water> (accessed 9-4-2018).

Kings, S (2017) "50 000 litres of sewage flows into SA's rivers every second" *Mail & Guardian* (21-7-2017), at <https://mg.co.za/article/2017-07-21-south-africas-shit-has-hit-the-fan> (accessed 9-4-2018).

Monteiro, A (2018) "SA cities on brink of collapse – Nene's dire warning" *Biznews* (9-4-2018), at <https://www.biznews.com/undictated/2018/04/09/sa-cities-brink-collapse-nene-warning/?acid=TNRlfeBjf0AeZeuwhd4cWQ%3D%3D&adid=vlf1wfKX3q0Q9pc0JfeOsA%3D%3D &date=2018-04-10> (accessed 9-4-2018).

Muller, M (2018) "South Africa needs good water management – not new water laws" *The Conversation* (2-2-2018), at <https://theconversation.com/south-africa-needs-good-water-management-not-new-water-laws-91253> (accessed 9 April 2018).

Njobeni, S (2017) "Eskom forecasts debt due of R12 million" *IOL Business Report* (6-1-2017), at <https://www.iol.co.za/business-report/energy/eskom-forecasts-debt-due-of-r12bn-7340635> (accessed 9 April 2018).

Ntombela C, N Funke, R Meissner, M Steyn & W Masangane (2016) "A critical look at South Africa's Green Drop Programme" 42(4) *Water SA* 703-710.

Qukula, Q (2015) "Poor sewage treatment may see SA on brink of 'catastrophe' – water expert" *702* (29-10-2015), at <http://www.702.co.za/articles/6074/high-volume-of-sewage-flows-could-see-sa-on-brink-of-catastrophe-says-expert> (accessed 9-4-2018).

Stacey, R (2016) "Falling short of constitutional norms: does 'normative (in)congruence' explain the courts' inability to promote the right to water in South Africa?" *Law & Social Inquiry*, at <https://ssrn.com/abstract=3070999> (accessed 9 April 2018).

Tandwa, L (2018) "Mokonyane lambasted for 'collapsing' water dept: Scopa decries reshuffling and calls for charges" *News 24* (27-2-2018), at <https://www.news24.com/SouthAfrica/News/mokonyane-lambasted-for-collapsing-water-dept-scopa-decries-reshuffling-and-calls-for-charges-20180227> (accessed 9 April 2018).

The Citizen (2017) "Joburg North residents warned of sewage" *The Citizen* (1-11-2017), at <https://citizen.co.za/news/south-africa/1711594/joburg-north-residents-warned-of-sewer-contaminated-water/> (accessed 9 April 2018).

van der Rheede, C (2015) "SA municipalities are discharging raw sewage into our river systems and wetland areas" *Health 24* (26-3-2015), at <https://www.health24.com/Lifestyle/Environmental-health/News/SA-municipalities-are-discharging-raw-sewage-into-our-river-systems-and-wetland-areas-20150326> (accessed 9-4-2018).

Chapter 20: Kenya's Water Act (2016): real devolution or simply the 'same script, different cast'

Elizabeth Gachenga

1 Introduction

The debate surrounding the enactment of Kenya's Water Act (2016) and its relationship with its predecessor, the Water Act (2002), brings to mind the lyrics of a contemporary pop duet, 'Same script, different cast'.[1] As the jilted girl attempts to forewarn the current girl of the hurtful ways of her former boyfriend, the latter resists arguing he has changed. To persuade the impressionable new girl to see beyond the façade of the apparent change, the ex-girlfriend uses the expression 'same script, different cast' repeatedly, to demonstrate that all that has changed is the actors. In a bid to align the Water Act (2002) with the Constitution of Kenya (2010) (Constitution) and particularly to achieve the devolution enshrined in the Constitution, the Water Act 2016 was enacted following a long drawn out process beginning with the first draft Water Bill of 2012. Despite the amendments brought about by the new Act, critics argue that the Water Act (2016) is at most a superficial modification of the Water Act (2002) albeit with renamed institutions, thus evoking the parallel with the song.

Among the greatest critics of the Water Act (2016) are the county governments to which the Constitution devolves water provision and sewerage services. The Council of Governors has even moved to court to stop the implementation of the Water Act (2016), arguing that it is unconstitutional because it excludes county governments from water governance and perpetuates a centralised framework for provision and regulation of water and sanitation services.[2] These criticisms seem to suggest that the Water Act (2016) has failed to achieve its purpose, which is "to provide for the regulation, management and development of water resources and water and sewerage services in line with the Constitution".[3]

1 Cox & Houston (2000).

2 *Council of County Governors v. Lake Basin Development Authority & 6 others* (2017) eKLR in which a preliminary objection against this petition was dismissed. The main matter is yet to be determined.

3 Section 3 of the Water Act (2016).

The mismatch between the content of the Water Act (2016) and the expectations of its stakeholders also brings to the fore some underlying assumptions that have driven water sector reforms over the last 20 years. For instance, an overriding principal driver of water sector reforms in Kenya has been the conviction that the governance problem facing the water sector is attributable to the lack of decentralisation. It was hoped that devolution, introduced by the Constitution, would entirely cure this ailment. While the Water Act (2016) revamps the institutional water governance framework to provide for national and county functions, critics are of the view that the framework largely comprises of a multiplicity of institutions at the national level as was the case with the Water Act (2002), albeit with these institutions being renamed under the new Act.

2 Analysis of the Water Act (2016)

In order to determine the merits or otherwise of the criticism meted against the Water Act (2016), it is paramount to conduct a comparative analysis between the provisions of the two laws. The analysis is based on the main provisions of the water law on ownership of water resources, the human right to water and water rights, and the institutional frameworks for water governance at the national and county levels. The analysis is anchored on the provisions of the Constitution, which the new Act should be aligned with.

2.1 Overall alignment with the Constitution of Kenya (2010)

Kenya's Water Act (2002) was premised on the notion that a successful water governance framework should address three main issues: delineation of roles; devolution of water and sewerage services; and privatisation. This thesis also informed the National Water Master Plan 2030 launched in 2014.[4]

The Water Act (2016) is based on a similar premise, with the additional goal of aligning the water law to the Constitution. To this end, the Act contains an overarching provision requiring its administration or application to be guided by relevant constitutional provisions.[5] These include Article 10 on the national values and principles of governance; Article 43 outlining economic and social rights in the Bill of Rights; Article 60 on equitable, efficient, productive and sustainable management of land resources; and Article 232 on the values and principles of the public service.

4 Government of Kenya (2014).
5 Section 4 of the Water Act (2016).

2.2 Ownership of water resources

The Constitution contains some fundamental provisions in relation to the ownership of water resources and the rights of Kenyans to water and sanitation. One of the expected outcomes of the revision of the Water Act (2002) was thus the alignment of the Act to the letter and spirit of the Constitution.

In a bid to emphasise the sovereignty of the people, the Constitution clearly vests all resources of the country in the people of Kenya. Water resources, including rivers, lakes and other water bodies as defined by an Act of Parliament are included in the definition of public land.[6] According to the Constitution, "all land in Kenya belongs to the people of Kenya collectively as a nation, as communities and as individuals" and consequently the people of Kenya essentially own the country's water resources.[7]

The Water Act (2002) vested the ownership of water resources in the state subject to any other rights of use granted by law. In keeping with the spirit of the Constitution, the Water Act (2016) makes it clear that while the state, and more specifically national government, is the custodian of resources, it holds them in trust for the people of Kenya.[8] This is a fundamental departure from the Water Act (2002) and has some interesting implications to water resource governance.

Firstly, defining rivers, lakes and other water bodies as public land puts them under the mandate of the National Land Commission (NLC). Arguably, this provides a framework for sustainable governance of all-natural resources, including water.

While the Water Act (2016) contains no explicit recognition of this oversight role of the NLC, it is replete with references to other land laws including the Land Act[9] and the Community Land Act.[10] Further, in recognition of the central nexus between land and water resources, the Act provides for representation of the Principal Secretary responsible for land or his/her representative in the membership of the Water Resources Authority Management Board. Interestingly, the Water Act (2016) includes a provision subordinating its provisions pertaining to community land to the Community Land Act.[11]

Secondly, the Water Act (2016) clarifies the effect of a devolved governance framework for water resources. During stakeholder meetings preceding the enactment of the Act, counties raised the possibility of counties hosting water resources, to charge other counties for the use of the water sourced from their county. This is for instance, Murang'a County's contention with respect to water supply from Ndakaini Dam in Murang'a to Nairobi County. Section 6 of the Water Act (2016) debunks this notion by

6 Article 62(1)(i) of the Constitution of Kenya (2010).
7 Article 61 of the Constitution of Kenya (2010).
8 Section 5 of the Water Act (2016).
9 Section 8(4) of the Water Act (2016).
10 Section 138 of the Water Act (2016).
11 Ibid.

assigning the Water Resources Authority the role of regulating the management and use of water resources as an agent of the national government.

Water basins in Kenya, as in other jurisdictions, cut across various county boundaries and thus the vesting of ownership in specific counties would have resulted in the need for complex inter-county arrangements for sharing of water resources. Australia's water governance framework is a good example of the complexities that arise when ownership and management of water resources is vested in state governments as opposed to the federal government.[12]

The Water Act (2016) also includes any water works that relate to cross-cutting water resources or works whose objective is to serve national government in the definition of national public water works. This further clarifies the issue of ownership and management of water resources.[13] In the fourth schedule of the Constitution, public works constitute a function of the national government in contrast with county public works, which are a function of county governments.[14] The Act also grants wide-ranging powers to the national government in relation to public water works including powers to acquire land required for these national public water works. Arguably, this seems to go against the spirit of devolution and subsidiarity, as it gives a blank cheque to the national government in relation to designating certain water resource infrastructure as national public water works, thus taking away the powers of county governments over these.

2.3 Water: a human right or still an economic good?

The Water Act (2002) treated water primarily as an economic good, a common trend in water sector reforms globally.[15] Consequently, under the Act, water rights were vested in the Minister in charge of the sector and could only be granted through permits or other means anticipated in the Act. The Act had no provisions explicitly recognising the nature of water as a public good or considering the governance of water resources in the context of public trusteeship.

Apart from vesting the ownership of water resources in its people, the Kenyan Constitution is a progressive one with an enriched Bill of Rights incorporating the economic, social and cultural rights in the list of fundamental rights. The Constitution, by explicitly recognising the human right to water, emphasises an important and fundamental dimension of water resources. The Constitution additionally requires the government to take affirmative action to ensure that minorities and marginalised groups

12 Kildea & Williams (2010: 595).
13 Section 8, Water Act (2016).
14 Fourth Schedule Section 19 of the Constitution of Kenya (2010).
15 Cullet (2006: 206).

have reasonable access to water.[16] The responsibility for 'progressively' realising this lies with the national government.[17] Counties are, however, very critical in this regard as they are responsible for water service provision. One primary objective of the Water Act (2016) is to align the water law to the Constitution's recognition of water as a human right. The realisation of this objective calls for cooperation and collaboration between the national and county governments.

2.3.1 Right to water and the Water Act (2016)

The Water Act (2016), in alignment with the Constitution, explicitly recognises the fundamental right of every person in Kenya to clean and safe water in adequate quantities and to reasonable standards of sanitation.[18] Further, the Act clearly stipulates that the role of regulating the management and use of water resources lies with the national government through its agent, the Water Resources Authority.[19]

Arguably, the recognition by the state of the right to water and reasonable sanitation standards provides a basis for obliging the state to put in place measures to redress issues of underserviced rural populations and the urban poor. However, the recognition by a Constitution or a water law of the right to water and sanitation in and of itself does not ensure the realisation of the right. It is necessary to define the normative content of the right so as to provide a basis for making the right justiciable. Justiciability of the right depends on a clear agreement on the minimum core constituting the right as evidenced by case law from other jurisdictions with similar rights in their legal frameworks.[20] In the case of Kenya's Constitution, the provisions relating to the enforcement of the Bill of Rights seek to ensure the justiciability of the rights.[21]

Apart from recognising the right to water and sanitation, the Water Act (2016) attempts to flesh out some normative content constituting the government's obligation relating to the progressive realisation of the right. For instance, the Act requires the Cabinet Secretary responsible for water to prepare a five-year National Water Services Strategy which will include the plans in place for the progressive realisation of this right to water and sanitation to all. The Water Services Regulatory Board (WASREB) is also obliged to make regulations, which should among other issues, address the progressive realisation of the right to water services.[22] In addition, the Act requires that Water Service Providers (WSPs) that hold county or national public assets, to refrain

16 Article 56(e) of the Constitution of Kenya (2010).
17 Section 64(2) of the Water Act (2016).
18 Section 63 of the Water Act (2016).
19 Section 6 of the Water Act (2016).
20 *Mazibuko and Others v. City of Johannesburg and Others* (2009) 28 ZACC.
21 Articles 20-22 of the Constitution of Kenya (2010).
22 Section 72(1)(n) of the Water Act (2016).

from paying dividends or making any other payments as long as the universal rights of access to safe and clean water have not been achieved in the designated service areas.[23]

From the foregoing, it is evident that the Water Act (2016) contains substantive provisions that distinguish it from the Water Act (2002) in relation to the right to water and sanitation. The Water Act (2002) contained no provisions on the human right to water and sanitation.

2.3.2 Water rights

The Water Act (2016) clarifies the distinction between 'water right' and the right to water. The Act defines the term 'water right' as the right to have access to water through a water permit. The human right to water under the Act recognises the right of all its citizens to access safe drinking water and reasonable sanitation under the Constitution.

The Water Act (2002) vested the right to use water in the Minister, except to the extent that this right was alienated under the Act or under any other law.[24] The Water Act (2016) does not contain a similar provision. It vests ownership of all water resources in the people of Kenya. In relation to water rights, the Water Act (2016) provides that after its commencement, all rights in respect of any water resources can only be granted pursuant to provisions of the Act.[25] The primary mode of granting water rights under the new Act continues to be through permits from the Water Resources Authority (WRA), the successor to the Water Resources Management Authority (WRMA), thus suggesting that not much has changed. However, the Water Act (2016) recognises the concept of public trusteeship by vesting the ownership of water in citizens, with the state, through the national government, playing the role of administration of the water resources.[26] This is consistent with the Constitution.

The provisions on requirements for water permits and exemptions from the need to obtain a permit in both Acts are generally similar. However, the Water Act (2016) introduces some minor changes that could have important ramifications.

The inclusion of requirements for a permit and the water charges for abstraction of water resources in the Water Act (2002) was criticised for being prejudicial to the rural poor, as it implied the privatisation of water rights and their control by those who could afford land and the charges for acquiring and maintaining permits under the Act.[27] Further, the separation of water resource management from water service provision at

23 Section 131(3) of the Water Act (2016).
24 Section 5 of the Water Act (2002).
25 Section 7 of the Water Act (2016).
26 Section 9 of the Water Act (2016).
27 Mumma (2008).

the local level, was faulted as working against integrated customary law systems for water governance already in existence in some rural areas, which systems played both roles of regulation and service provision.[28] The fact that the new Act adopts the same system of permits and of delineating institutional roles seems to confirm the suspicion that there has been no real change to the script.

Further confirming the apparent lack of change, is the manner in which the Water Act (2016) links permits to land or undertakings on land. This approach to water governance has been criticised on the basis that groundwater is often the main source of drinking water for most people, and thus tying water rights to land rights does not contribute to a social perspective to water or to the realisation of the human right to water.[29] It has been argued that in fact, this linkage serves to privatise water rights and in so doing, limit the right to acquire such rights to those who have rights to land or the potential to acquire these rights.[30] Poor rural communities end up disadvantaged because they do not often have title to the community land to which their water resources are appurtenant. They can thus not acquire water rights under the Act.

While the Water Act (2016) largely seems to adopt the approach of the Water Act (2002), it provides some reprieve to poor rural communities. The contemporary Act explicitly recognises the existence of community land rights as demonstrated by its subordination of the application of its provisions to any written laws relating to community land.[31] Arguably, the import of this provision is to limit the extent to which the Water Act (2016), including its provisions relating to water permits, are applicable to community landowners.

Paradoxically, the envisaged written law relating to community land, alluded to above and that is given precedence over the Water Act (2016), seems to take away some of this privilege. The Community Land Act (2016) provides that the management of community land shall be subject to national and county government laws and policies in relation to, among other matters, water protection, securing sufficient residual water, hydraulic engineering and dams safety.[32] A broad interpretation of this provision implies that the Community Land Act is subordinate to the provisions of the Water Act (2016), in so far as most, if not all, the provisions of the latter Act are ultimately intended to ensure water protection, secure sufficient residual water, hydraulic engineering and safety of dams.

In relation to Water Resource Users Associations (WRUAs), the Water Act (2016) introduces a proviso recognising that agreements between the WRA and a WRUA may make available a portion of the water use charges for use to finance regulatory

28 Gachenga (2012).
29 Cullet (2006: 206).
30 Mumma (2008).
31 Section 138 of the Water Act (2016).
32 Section 38(2)(c) of the Community Land Act (2016).

activities undertaken by the WRUA on behalf of WRA.[33] This provision expands the mandate of the WRUAs, by anticipating their potential to conduct some of the activities of the WRA. Arguably, this could to some extent be regarded as an implicit recognition of the regulatory role played by communities in their community-based water governance systems.

A further minor change introduced in the Water Act (2016) is in relation to objections to permit applications. Under the Act, parties opposed to the grant of a permit, may object in writing to the Water Tribunal, within thirty days of publication of the notice of application.[34] Under the previous Act, parties' objections were addressed to the WRMA.[35] The transfer of the mandate to the Water Tribunal established under Section 119 of the Water Act (2016) helps to distinguish the role of the regulator (WRA) from the role of the adjudicator, the Water Tribunal.

The amendments discussed above confirm that the Water Act (2016) is aligned to the Constitution in so far as ownership of water resources and the recognition of the rights to water and reasonable sanitation services are concerned. However, the extent to which the rest of the Act makes provision for the implementation of the human right to water and sanitation is debatable given the maintenance of the permit system as the mode of acquiring water rights. Nonetheless, there are opportunities for challenging the implementation of the Act by the national or county government where the realisation of the human right to water is hindered. The development of case law in this area will, with time, hopefully help to interpret the extent to which the Water Act (2016) can be deemed to conform to the Constitution.

3 Devolution and the water laws

Among the fundamental governance changes introduced by the 2010 Constitution was the creation of a devolved government, with clear separation of roles between the national and county governments. Kenya's devolved government is based on the division of the country into 47 geographical units referred to as counties. In accordance with the concept of integrated water resources management, Kenya is divided into five main river basins: Lake Victoria Basin; Rift Valley Basin; Athi River Basin; Tana River Basin; and Ewaso Ngiro Basin. These basins traverse across the various county boundaries.

In relation to devolution of water governance, the Constitution, in its fourth schedule, identifies and sets out the role of the national government to protect the environment and natural resources, including water resources, with the objective of

33 Section 42(3) of the Water Act (2016).
34 Section 40(5) of the Water Act (2016).
35 Section 29(5) of the Water Act (2002).

"establishing a durable and sustainable system of development".[36] This specifically encompasses the management of national public works, water protection, securing sufficient residual water, hydraulic engineering and safety of dams.[37] The county government is responsible for the implementation of national water policy and the management of county public works and services, which include stormwater management systems and the provision of water and sanitation services.[38]

3.1 Institutional frameworks of the 2002 and 2016 Water Acts: 'same script, different cast?'

Among the most lauded reforms introduced by the Water Act (2002) was the establishment of a clear institutional framework with clearly defined and delineated roles. The Act separated the role of policy formulation, water resource regulation and planning on the one hand, from that of direct water and sanitation service provision on the other. It provided for a twofold institutional structure that respected this delineation of roles separating management and regulation from service provision. The rationale for this clear delineation of roles was to avoid a potential conflict of interest arising where only one institution is vested with ownership of water resources, the roles of resource allocation and management and service provision. Any other approach would be tantamount to turning such an authority into the judge and jury in their own case.

The Water Act (2002) was thus intended to achieve subsidiarity and decentralisation, allowing for decision making to happen at the lowest appropriate level. The implementation of the principle of subsidiarity and the pro-poor approach in sector policies and strategies, it was believed, would result in greater equity. The subsidiarity envisioned would provide sector institutions with the autonomy necessary to function efficiently, while ensuring greater transparency and accountability in sector institutions.

Delineation of roles and subsidiarity were intended to provide the founding pillars for a decentralised water governance framework. Ownership and management under the Water Act (2002) was to be left to national government and that of service provision devolved to local government, communities and the private sector. In comparison to other service sectors, Kenya's water sector reforms leading to the Water Act (2002), arguably gave the sector a considerable head start in the devolution anticipated by the Constitution.

The legal and institutional framework established under the Water Act (2002) incorporated the key principles driving modern global water reforms. Supporters of the

---

36 Fourth Schedule Part 1(22) of the Constitution of Kenya (2010).

37 Ibid.

38 Fourth Schedule Part 2(11) of the Constitution of Kenya (2010).

Water Act (2002) point out that it had all the ingredients for a successful modern water law in so far as it considered water as primarily an economic good, but managed in an integrated way that catered for poverty orientation, sustainability, cost recovery and human rights.[39] However, these water sector reforms confirm that an ideal legal framework is insufficient for successful water governance, as demonstrated by some persistent centralisation challenges that still gnaw at the Kenyan water sector. Kenya's overall legal framework, prior to the enactment of the 2010 Constitution, was largely state-centric.

Despite the separation of the role of service provision from regulation and management, institutions established to focus on the latter role also suffered various challenges due to the lack of autonomy from central government. Corruption and unethical practices such as bribing to obtain permits or cover up abstraction, skewed water allocations in exchange for money or political support, kickbacks to regulatory officials to overlook pollution incidents or distort environmental impact assessments and generally weak accountability and inadequate capacity to enforce regulations also affected the effectiveness of the institutions.[40] Further, problems such as irregular tendering and procurement continued to undermine the successful implementation of projects. The provisions of the Water Act (2002) seeking to decentralise functions thus lacked an enabling environment. Indeed, critics of the Water Act (2002) argued that the decentralisation under the Act was merely nominal as its approach to water governance was largely state-centric.

Given the above challenges, the greatest expectation of the people of Kenya and of county governments, following the promulgation of the 2010 Constitution, was that the Water Act (2016) would make the devolution of water resources governance a reality. Unfortunately, the Water Act (2016) seems to maintain the same institutional framework as its predecessor, albeit with some change of names. While a deeper scrutiny of the provisions of the Water Act (2016), reveals some substantive changes to the institutions, the question that still needs to be answered is whether these changes are sufficient to result in a change in script moving forward.

3.2 Water policy, resource management and regulation

As noted above, the Water Act (2002) introduced an institutional framework for managing water resources that distinguished between water resource management and regulation on the one hand, and water and sewerage service provision on the other. Further, the Act provided for a few national institutions such as the Water Appeals Board, the National Water and Conservation Pipeline and the Water Services Trust Fund. In

39 GIZ (2012).
40 Ibid.

relation to regulating and managing water resources, the Act provided for the Water Resources Management Authority (WRMA), the Catchment Areas Advisory Committees (CAAC) and WRUAs.

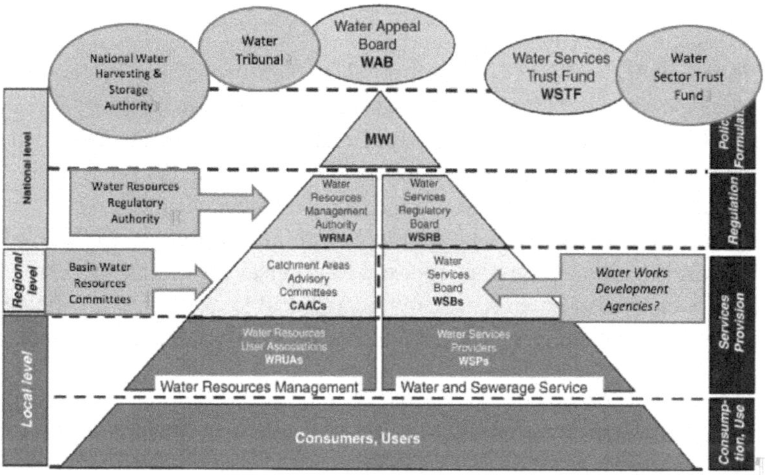

Figure 1: Institutional Framework Water Act 2002, modified to incorporate changes in the Water Act 2016[41]

The Water Act (2016) maintains a similar institutional framework, replacing a few of the institutions of the Water Act (2002), or renaming and redefining their membership and roles as discussed in the following sub-sections.

3.2.1 The Water Tribunal

The Water Act (2002) established a Water Appeal Board (WAB) consisting of a chairman, with the qualification of a judge of the High Court, appointed by the President on the recommendation of the Chief Justice and two other persons appointed by the Minister. The WAB heard appeals by holders of water rights affected by a decision or order of the Minister, WRMA or WASREB, concerning a permit or licence granted under the Act.[42] The judgement of the WAB was final save for matters of law, which could be appealed to the High Court.[43]

41 Ministry of Water and Irrigation (2007).
42 Section 84 of the Water Act (2002).
43 Section 87 of the Water Act (2002).

Under the Water Act (2016), the Water Appeal Board has been replaced by the Water Tribunal.[44] Appeals from decisions of the WRA in relation to applications for permits lie to the Water Tribunal.[45] Unlike under the previous Act, the Chairperson of the Tribunal and other staff shall be appointed by the Judicial Service Commission and not by the President or the Minister.

The jurisdiction of the Water Tribunal is wider than that of the Water Appeals Board. Any person directly affected by the decision or order of the Cabinet Secretary, WRA, WASREB or any person acting under their authority, can appeal to the Tribunal despite not having a right or proprietary interest.[46] Appeals from decisions of the Tribunal in matters of law lie to the Land and Environment Court.[47]

Arguably, the change in the appointing authority of the Chairperson and staff of the tribunal will result in professional as opposed to political appointments. Further, it provides a more conducive environment for the Tribunal to exercise professionalism and independence in executing its mandate, including in determining appeals against decisions of the Cabinet Secretary.

3.2.2 The National Water Harvesting and Storage Authority

The Water Act (2016) establishes the National Water Harvesting and Storage Authority, whose role is to act on behalf of the national government in developing policy and implementing strategies relating to national water harvesting and storage and the development and management of the related national public water works.[48] Under the Water Act (2002), the National Water Conservation and Pipeline Corporation was responsible for development works and managing assets for purposes of state schemes for storage and impounding of water for purposes of bulk water supplies.[49]

The establishment of the National Water Harvesting and Storage Authority more closely aligns the constitutional provisions on the role of the national government with the institutional framework established by the Water Act (2016). One of these roles is the national government's obligation to secure sufficient residual water, which task is assigned to this Authority. It is hoped that the Authority will address problems of lack of water harvesting plaguing Kenya. Currently, approximately 43% of the total water generated in the country is either lost or unaccounted for.[50] Further, the National Water Harvesting and Storage Authority is expected to be instrumental in ensuring that the

44 Section 119 of the Water Act (2016).
45 Ibid.
46 Section 121 of the Water Act (2016).
47 Section 124 of the Water Act (2016).
48 Section 30 and 32 of the Water Act (2016).
49 Section 22(4) of the Water Act (2002).
50 Water Services Regulatory Board (2016).

national government meets its obligation to secure the human right to water of all Kenyans. Currently, Kenya's per capita consumption stands at approximately 43 litres per person per day.[51]

3.2.3 The Water Sector Trust Fund

A Water Services Trust Fund was established under the Water Act (2002) to assist in financing the provision of water services to areas of Kenya without adequate water services. This was intended to provide a mechanism for redressing the common problem of underserved populations.[52]

The Water Sector Trust Fund established under the Water Act (2016) may, on the face of it, seem to be a mere replacement of the Water Services Trust Fund.[53] However, the renaming of the institution in the new Act helps demonstrate the wider mandate of the Fund. The 2016 Act also includes more detailed provisions on the composition and functions of the Board of Trustees for the Fund.

Further, the Water Act (2016) includes provisions allowing for funding of counties through conditional and unconditional grants, to assist in financing their development and management of water services in marginalised or underserved areas. Such financing extends beyond direct service provision activities to include community-level initiatives for sustainable management of water resources and research activities in the areas of water resource management.[54]

Under the Water Act (2016), the Water Sector Trust Fund is critical for successful implementation of devolved water governance. The Act provides for the various sources of money for the Fund, which include an allocation from the national budget and from the Equalization Fund, and proceeds from any levies imposed on consumers of piped water from licensed water service providers.[55]

3.2.4 The Water Resources Regulatory Authority

Under the Water Act (2002), WRMA was responsible for the overall management of water resources at the national level. Under the Water Act (2016), WRMA has been replaced by Water Resources Authority (WRA). The change in name lays emphasis of its role as regulator apart from manager. The Water Act (2016) provides that the WRA

51 Ibid.
52 Section 83 of the Water Act (2002).
53 Section 113 of the Water Act (2016).
54 Section 114 of the Water Act (2016).
55 Section 117 of the Water Act (2016).

shall serve as the agent of the national government and so regulate the management and use of water resources.[56]

While the objective of WRMA and WRA are significantly similar, the composition of the governance board of the WRA and its mode of operation is more developed in the Water Act (2016).[57] Under the Water Act (2002), WRMA was ultimately responsible for: developing and enforcing standards relating to the management and use of water resources; the planning and issuing water permits; and collecting permits and water use fees.

The Water Act (2016) provides for a Management Board and sets out the composition of the members of this Board,[58] while the previous Act simply provided for the existence of a Governing Board comprising of a Chairman, appointed by the President, and ten other members appointed by the Minister. The composition of the Management Board in the Water Act (2016) reflects the recognition of the need for coordination between related sectors such as finance, environment and land. The detailed list of the members of the Governing Board and the requirement that all members of the Management Board hold relevant professional qualifications and experience,[59] is a response to the challenges faced under the Water Act (2002). The wide discretion enjoyed in selecting the ten members of the Governing Board and the lack of specification on the qualification and competencies of the members resulted in political appointments of persons without the requisite skills.

Further, the provisions on appointing the Chief Executive Officer (CEO) of the WRA under the Water Act (2016) differ from those on appointing the WRMA CEO. The Act provides for an appointment by the Cabinet Secretary on recommendation of the Management Board,[60] rather than the previous position, where the Authority, with approval of the Minister, appointed the CEO.[61] The qualifications and term of office for the CEO of WRA are also specified under the new Act.[62]

The mandate of the WRA is largely similar to the mandate of WRMA, with a few modifications. For instance, while WRMA was previously responsible for the preparation of the National Water Resources Strategy, this is the responsibility of the Cabinet Secretary under the Water Act (2016).[63] Further, the role of WRA has been extended to include the classification of water resources for purposes of determining water resources' quality objectives.[64] This was previously the role of the Minister.[65] WRA

56 Section 6 of the Water Act (2016).
57 Section 14 of the Water Act (2016).
58 Section 14(1) of the Water Act (2016).
59 Section 14(3) of the Water Act (2016).
60 Section 17 of the Water Act (2016).
61 Section 9(1) of the Water Act (2002).
62 Section 17 of the Water Act (2016).
63 Section 10 of the Water Act (2016).
64 Section 24 of the Water Act (2016).
65 Section 49 of the Water Act (2002).

is also responsible for ensuring the presence of a national monitoring and geo-referenced information system for water resources.[66] The Water Act (2016) provides that information on water resources shall be accessible to the public at a prescribed fee.[67] This is in accordance with Article 35 of the Constitution, which provides for the right of access by the public to information held by the state.

3.2.5 The Basin Water Resources Committees

The Water Act (2016) uses the term 'basin area' to refer to a defined area from which rainwater flows into a watercourse.[68] The term catchment area under this Act means an area that is part of a basin.[69]

Catchment Advisory Committees under the Water Act (2002) are replaced by Basin Water Committees under the Water Act (2016).[70] The Basin Water Resources Committees are responsible for managing water resources within their respective basin areas. The composition of these Committees and their mode of operation are provided for in detail under the Act. The Catchment Areas Advisory Committees under the Water Act (2002) played a merely advisory role.

While the Water Act (2002) provided for a maximum of 15 members, the Water Act (2016) caps the maximum number of members at seven.[71] Under the latter Act, a representative appointed by the WRA after approval by the County Assembly, shall represent county governments whose area is within the basin in the respective Basin Water Resources Committee. Arguably, this provision offers the opportunity for devolved county governments to play a greater role in the management of water resources falling within their counties. The provisions of the Water Act (2016) in relation to the composition of these committees also demonstrate the balance sought between inclusion and technical expertise as well as the effort to guard against capture.[72]

3.2.6 The Water Resources Users Associations

Under the Water Act 2002, Water Resources Users Associations (WRUAs) could be established for cooperative management of water resources in catchment areas and for

66 Section 21(1) of the Water Act (2016).
67 Section 21(3) of the Water Act (2016).
68 Section 24 of the Water Act (2016).
69 Section 2(1) of the Water Act (2016).
70 Section 25 of the Water Act (2016).
71 Section 26(1)(a) of the Water Act (2016).
72 Section 26(3) and (4) of the Water Act (2016).

conflict resolution.[73] The Water Act (2016) contains provisions similar to those of the Water Act (2002) but adds that Basin Water Committees may contract WRUAs as agents to perform certain duties in water resource management.[74] The use of the words "may contract" and "as agents" could arguably mark the beginning of a more formal and expanded mandate of WRUAs in the management of water resources at the sub-basin level. However, the extent to which WRUAs will be formally engaged to act as agents of the Basin Water Committees at the grassroots level is dependent on the extent to which the challenges faced by WRUAs in exercising their mandate are addressed.[75]

3.3 Water and sewage service provision

Under the Water Act (2002), the Water Services Regulatory Board (WASREB), the Water Services Board (WSB) and the Water Service Providers (WSPs) addressed water service provision. The Water Act (2016) maintains, to a large extent, this institutional framework for water service provision. Further, contrary to the expectations of county governments, the Act does not explicitly or immediately devolve the provision of water and sanitation services to counties as would have been anticipated given the provisions of the Fourth Schedule of the Constitution.

3.3.1 The Water Services Regulatory Board

On the face of it, the Water Act (2016) seems to maintain the status quo in so far as the Water Services Regulatory Board is concerned. Under the Water Act (2002), the WASREB had the overall role of regulating water service provision, thus taking responsibility for issuing licences, setting service standards and guidelines for tariffs and prices; and providing mechanisms for handling complaints. Under the Water Act (2016), WASREB continues to be the agent of national government with wide-ranging powers in relation to water service provision, thus calling into question the extent to which service provision under the Act has been devolved to county governments as anticipated by the Constitution. However, some apparently subtle changes in the contemporary Act significantly alter the landscape for water service provision.

Under the Water Act (2002), the Chairman of WASREB was a presidential appointee and the Minister appointed the other ten members of the Board.[76] The Chief Executive Officer (CEO) of the Board was appointed by the Board and would be

73 Section 15(5) of the Water Act (2002).
74 Section 29(4) of the Water Act (2016).
75 Aarts (2012).
76 Section 46(3) of the Water Act (2002).

responsible for the management of WASREB.[77] The Water Act (2016) provides for a leaner WASREB comprising of a Chairperson appointed by the President, four members appointed by the Cabinet Secretary and the CEO.

Apart from setting national standards for water service provision, the Water Act (2016) expands the functions of WASREB to include the evaluation and recommendation of water and sewerage tariffs to county water service providers; setting of licence conditions; accrediting WSPs; and developing a model memorandum and articles of association for use by water companies applying to be registered as WSPs.[78]

Under the Water Act (2016), the role of county governments in the context of water service provision seems to be limited to establishing water service providers, whose function it is to provide water services within the specified areas and to develop county assets for water service provision.[79] In what seems to be an attempt to safeguard water service provision from political capture, the Act stipulates that members of the Board of Directors of WSPs must possess qualifications that meet the standards set by WASREB and cannot be serving as elected members of a county government, holding office in a political party, or be members of Parliament.[80]

One of the challenges faced under the Water Act (2002) was the delay in the transfer of ownership of water services' assets from local authorities to Water Service Boards (WSBs). Under the Water Act (2016), ownership of water services' assets of county-owned or cross-county owned WSPs established as public institutions are vested in the public with the WSPs holding them on behalf of the public.[81] The Act further requires the Cabinet Secretary to make regulations for the transfer of national public assets to the county WSPs, which regulations should include arrangements to protect public assets in the event of private sector participation, through for instance, the separation of operations from asset holding and development.[82] This provision is consistent with the public trust doctrine, where the government or its agents hold public property in trust for the public.

3.3.2 Water Works Development Agencies

Under the Water Act (2002), the responsibility for providing water services was vested in Water Service Boards (WSBs), which were issued with licences to supply water services and regulated by WASREB. WSBs were responsible for the efficient and economical provision of water services authorised by licence. The ownership of plant,

77 Section 48 of the Water Act (2002).
78 Section 72(1) of the Water Act (2016).
79 Sections 77 and 78 of the Water Act (2016).
80 Section 80 of the Water Act (2016).
81 Section 83 of the Water Act (2016).
82 Section 84 of the Water Act (2016).

equipment or other assets, with or without associated liabilities, in connection with water services previously held by the government were by law to be transferred to WSBs.[83] The members of WSBs were ministerial appointees.

The Water Act (2002), provided for the requirement of a licence for any person supplying more than twenty-five thousand litres of water a day for domestic purposes; or more than one hundred thousand litres of water a day for any other purpose; with an exception for provision of water to employees or on the premises of certain settings such as hospitals, schools, hotels and research institutions.[84]

The Water Act (2002) envisaged that WSBs would exercise and perform their powers and functions under licence through one or more agents referred to as Water Service Providers (WSPs).[85] The WSB could, however, also perform direct service provision of water services, where it was not possible to do so through an agent. The Minister had residual powers under the Act to provide water services to consumers with the assistance of the National Water Conservation and Pipeline Corporation under certain conditions.[86] WSPs could be private firms, non-governmental organisations, companies owned by the local authorities or community groups.

A report compiled in 2012 aptly describes how the autonomy sought from central government, intended to reduce bureaucracy and improve efficiency, was undermined under the Water Act (2002) regime.[87] Local authorities delayed the transfer of assets and equipment to WSBs, hampering their effectiveness and their capacity to ring-fence funds for re-investment as anticipated by the Act.[88] The lack of autonomy was further exacerbated by the politicisation of the appointment of officers by the Minister, leading to patronage, nepotism, conflict of interest and opportunism, as demonstrated by board expenses constituting a great percentage of total expenditure.[89]

With the enactment of the Water Act (2016), it was presumed that the WSBs, along with their powers and mandate, would automatically be devolved to county governments. However, the Water Act (2016) takes a slightly different approach. The Act does not provide for WSBs, though the Water Works Development Agencies (WWDAs) seem to be the equivalent of the old WSBs, albeit renamed. The Water Act (2016) confirms this by providing that all assets and liabilities formerly held by WSBs will be deemed to belong to the WWDAs, subject to the provisions of the 2012 Transition to Devolved Government Act.[90] The former Tanathi Water Services Board also confirms this by describing its mandate as per Section 68 of the Water Act (2016),

83 Section 113(2) of the Water Act (2002).
84 Section 56 of the Water Act (2002).
85 Sections 53 and 55 of the Water Act (2016).
86 Section 67 of the Water Act (2016).
87 GIZ (2012).
88 Ibid.
89 Ibid.
90 Section 152 of the Water Act (2016).

which provision relates to the role of a WWDAs.[91] However, a closer scrutiny of the provisions relating to the WWDAs indicates certain pertinent differences between this institution and the WSB envisaged by the Water Act (2002).

The Water Act (2016) provides for the possibility of the Cabinet Secretary establishing, by a Gazette notice, one or more WWDAs with a defined geographical area of jurisdiction. Although the WWDAs are corporate bodies as were the WSB, the composition of the formers' members is different. The WWDA Board comprises of a Chairperson, appointed by the Cabinet Secretary, and four other members also appointed by the Cabinet Secretary from counties within the basin area and the Chief Executive Officer.[92] In contrast, the Water Act (2002) gave the Minister discretion in determining the number of members of a WSB through a Gazette notice.[93]

Section 68 of the Water Act (2016) sets out the functions and powers of the WWDAs which include undertaking the development, maintenance, management and operation of national public water works in their jurisdiction. A national public water work is defined, under Section 8, as one designated as such by the Cabinet Secretary by Gazette notice. The provision further sets out the basis for its designation, which is the fact that the water resource on which it depends is cross-cutting, is financed by the national government and is intended to serve a function of the national government, or a function which has been transferred to the national government by agreement between the national and county government. WSBs, on the other hand, were responsible for the efficient and economical provision of water services through an agent.[94]

WWDAs are mandated to act as a WSP until the responsibility for operation and management of the waterworks are handed over to a county government or their respective WSPs. They are also tasked with providing reserve capacity, technical services and capacity building to county governments and WSPs in their respective areas.[95]

The Water Act (2016) provides for the handing over of national public works from WWDAs to the county government, the joint committee or authority of the county governments within whose area the water works fall, or to the relevant WSP for purposes of provision of water services.[96] Nevertheless, the same provision in the Act makes this transfer of the ownership of the assets to the county government subject to the payment of any outstanding liabilities. Further, the Act provides that should a county government or its agent default on the repayment of any outstanding loans arising from the development, rehabilitation or maintenance of the works, the WWDA can

91 See <www.tanathi.go.ke> (accessed 20-5-2018).
92 Section 66 of the Water Act (2016).
93 Section 51 of the Water Act (2002).
94 Section 53 of the Water Act (2002).
95 Section 68 of the Water Act (2016).
96 Section 69 of the Water Act (2016).

petition WASREB to order a transfer of the WSPs functions back to the WWDA until full repayment of the loan.[97]

A further confirmation of the caution exercised in the transfer of assets, is the Gazette notice from the Cabinet Secretary for Water and Irrigation that established the date of commencement of the Act as 21 April 2017. This notice excludes from this date of commencement: Sections 152 and 155, which relate to transfer of assets from WSBs to WWDAs and from the Water Appeals Board to the Water Tribunal; and Section 153 which relates to the transfer of assets from WSBs to cross county WSPs.[98] Further, the revocation of Section 156(3) relating to the transition period for the institutions under the Water Act (2002) to institutions under the Water Act (2016) stipulated that such revocation did not extend to the Water Appeals Board and to WSBs.[99]

The above provisions seem to delay the devolution of ownership and management of county public works as implied by the Constitution. However, the prudence exercised seems justified in view of the experience of the devolution of health services in Kenya which has been characterised by challenges arising from capacity gaps, rampant corruption, inadequate allocation of county funds to the sector and conflicts between national and county governments.[100]

3.3.3 Water service providers

Under the Water Act (2002), WSPs, which could be companies, non-governmental organisations of other persons or bodies, were responsible for providing water services under a licence agreement with a WSB. One main challenge of the Water Act (2002) was the political capture of WSPs. It was not uncommon to find among the list of approved registered WSPs, names of politicians in central government or their agents, either as individuals, companies or non-governmental organisations.[101] The registered WSPs also lacked financial capacity and technical expertise to provide water services.

In accordance with the Constitution, the Water Act (2016) transfers the responsibility of water service provision to county governments.[102] County governments are responsible for establishing WSPs (public limited companies under the Companies Act 2015), which shall be responsible for providing water services within the specified area and also for developing county assets necessary for water service provision.[103]

97 Section 69(3) of the Water Act (2016).
98 Legal Notice No. 59 of 2017.
99 Legal Notice No. 60 of 2017.
100 Kimathi (2017: 55).
101 GIZ (2012).
102 Section 77 of the Water Act (2016).
103 Ibid.

The Water Act (2016) attempts to mitigate the risk of political capture of WSPs by setting out clear conditions for WSPs when applying for licences. Members of the Board of a WSP cannot at the time of nomination for appointment be serving as elected members of a county government; hold office in a political party; or be serving members of Parliament.[104] The Act further requires that the application for a licence as a WSP, made to WASREB, must be publicised and subjected to the input of stakeholders including the county government. The Act includes clear provisions on the requirements for an application and grounds for revocation or suspension of a licence. An application for a licence must include, among other things, evidence of a business plan, financial capability and plans for infrastructural development as a safeguard against the financial and technical challenges faced under the Water Act (2002), and which they continue to battle with to date.[105]

4 Same old law or a water law for sustainability?

The comparative analysis above of the substantive law and institutional frameworks under both Acts suggests that although the changes introduced by the Water Act (2016) might appear at a cursory glance to result in a similar script with a few changes to the institutions, some fundamental changes have been made to Kenya's water law.

Further, the true basis for evaluating the effectiveness or failure of the Water Act (2016) ought to be its capacity to achieve its primary purpose, which is "to provide for the regulation, management and development of water resources and water and sewerage services in line with the Constitution".[106] Whereas the county governors and the Council of Governors have focused on devolution as the principal goal of the Constitution, a more holistic reading of the Constitution, particularly in the context of management of natural resources, demonstrates that the principle of sustainable development is equally critical.

4.1 Devolution in the context of subsidiarity

Arguably, the Water Act (2016) has maintained, at least in broad terms, the institutional framework of the Water Act (2002). The framework under the Water Act (2002) was founded on the principal of delineating and decentralising the roles of water management and service provision. Consequently, the fact that the Water Act (2016) does

---

104 Section 80 of the Water Act (2016).
105 Kanda (2018: 19).
106 Section 3 of the Water Act (2016).

not depart radically from this main framework does not undermine its alignment with the constitutional requirement for devolution.

The failure of the Water Act (2002) to achieve the decentralisation intended was not the result of fundamental flaws in the Act itself, but rather challenges in implementing the law. These challenges included the lack of technical expertise and financial capacity at the local level to which roles had been decentralised. Political capture of positions in the institutions established by the Act also undermined the capacity of these institutions to achieve their mandate.

The Water Act (2016) has attempted to devolve certain aspects of water resource governance to county governments. However, the analysis of the Act also demonstrates a cautionary approach, supporting a gradual devolution rather than an immediate devolution. Further, the Act seems to introduce safeguards to mitigate the risk of facing similar challenges to those characterising the Water Act (2002) decentralisation process.

Such caution is not averse to the principle of subsidiarity, which requires that the functions of government be performed at the lowest level possible provided that they can be performed adequately.[107] Where the lower levels of government cannot perform these functions, a failure to intervene on the part of the national government would amount to shirking its responsibility to its people.

4.2 Sustainable development as a national principle of governance under the Constitution

The Constitution of Kenya includes sustainable development as one of its governance principles.[108] In the context of natural resource governance, the national government is required to "ensure sustainable exploitation, utilisation, management and conservation of the environment and natural resources, and ensure the equitable sharing of the accruing benefits".[109] This function is further reiterated in the fourth schedule of the Constitution in relation to water protection, securing sufficient residual water, hydraulic engineering and the safety of dams.

The Water Act (2016), like the Water Act (2002) ascribes the role of regulation, policy development, management of water resources, as well as national water harvesting and storage to the national government. This is to be expected as sustainable water resource management for Kenya can be best achieved if the role is pitched at the national level.

---

107 Marshall (2005).
108 Article 10(2)(d) of the Constitution of Kenya (2010).
109 Article 69(1)(a) of the Constitution of Kenya (2010).

As noted above, the Act seems to have adopted a prudent and slow approach to devolving water service provision to county governments. The experience of the health sector in which a rapid devolution of health service provision to county governments resulted in a crisis supports the wisdom of taking a staggered and prudent approach. The rushed devolution in the health sector was characterised by duplication of roles by national and county governments, inadequate support and financing of systems and processes at county government levels, and delays in accessing resources resulting in a failure by county governments to manage their health units.[110] Given the critical need for sustainable water management in Kenya, there may be some wisdom in retaining some control of water services' management and provision at the national level to avoid a similar scenario as that faced in the health sector.

Further, given the intra-county geographical extension of water resources, the management of water resources and even water service provision in some cases ought to remain within the mandate of the national government to ensure the sustainability of these water resources. As the experience of other countries demonstrates, the challenges faced in achieving sustainable management of basin areas that cut across states and territories has led to an increased move towards greater control by the federal government.[111]

From the foregoing, it appears that the comparison between the Water Acts 2002 and 2016 reveals that this is not entirely a case of 'same script different cast'. Further, even where the script is the same, then the adage that 'if it ain't broke don't fix it' applies.

References

Aarts, J (2012) *Will community-based water management solve Africa's water problems? The performance of water resource user associations in the upper Ewaso Ng'iro river basin, Kenya* PhD Thesis Radboud University Nijmegen.

Cox, D & W Houston (2000) *Same script, different cast* Pop song performed as a duet.

Cullet, P (2006) "Water law reforms – analysis of recent developments" 48(2) *Journal of the Indian Law Institute* 206-231.

Gachenga, EW (2012) "integrating customary and statutory law systems of water governance for sustainable development: the case of the Marakwet of Kenya", at <http://handle.uws.edu.au:8081/1959.7/524487> (accessed 15-5-2018).

GIZ / *Gesellschaft für Internationale Zusammenarbeit* (2012) Good governance in the Kenyan water sector. Policies, pipes and the participation of the people-water governance practices on the ground.

110 Kimathi (2017: 55).

111 McKay & Madsen (2009).

Government of Kenya (2014) *National water master plan 2030*, at <www.wasreb.co.ke> (accessed 20-05-2018).

Kanda, E, O James, VO Lutta & BT Ong'or (2018) "Challenges facing small and medium water service providers in Kenya: a case of Amatsi Water Services Company, Vihiga County" 4(1) *Journal of the Civil Engineering Forum* 19-27.

Kimathi, L (2017) "Challenges of the devolved health sector in Kenya: teething problems or systemic contradictions?" XLII(1) *Africa Development* 55.

Kildea, P & G Williams (2010) "The Constitution and the management of water in Australia's rivers" 32 *Sydney Law Review* 595-616.

Marshall, GR (2005) *Economics for collaborative environmental management: regenerating the commons*.

McKay J & S Marsden (2009) "Australia: the problem of sustainability in water" in JW Dellapenna & J Gupta (eds) The *Evolution of the Law and Politics of Water*.

Ministry of Water and Irrigation (2007) *The national water services strategy (NWSS) 2007-2015*.

Mumma, A (2008) "Kenya's *New Water Law: An Analysis of the Implications for the Rural Poor*" in M Giordano, BV Koppen & J Butterworth (eds) *Community-based water law and water resource management reform in developing countries*.

Water Services Regulatory Board (2016) *A performance review of Kenya's water services sector 2014-2015*.

Chapter 21: Improving the legal protection of strategic water source areas: a South African perspective

Amanda Mkhonza

1 Introduction

South Africa is a water scarce country with an average annual rainfall of 490 mm per annum – half that of the world's annual rainfall.[1] The need to secure South Africa's water supply for current and future generations is a grave concern and challenge. Heeding this concern, the government revised the country's water legislation and introduced the National Water Act[2] (NWA) in 1998. The NWA contains comprehensive provisions governing, among other things, water management strategies, water management institutions, measures to protect water resources generally and the use of water.[3] It is complemented by the Water Services Act[4] that governs the provision of water services to the population through various water service institutions.[5]

Notwithstanding the introduction of the above legislation specifically designed to deal with water management and provision in a water scarce country, South Africa's water security is perilous. The country is experiencing its worst drought in the past 30 years. In order to manage this, the government has taken measures to declare eight of the country's nine provinces as drought disaster zones in the past few years under the Disaster Management Act.[6] More recently, it has declared a national drought disaster throughout the country due to ongoing droughts.[7] This has triggered debates about whether South Africa is adequately equipped to deal effectively with the current and

1 WWF-SA (2013: 29).
2 Act 36 of 1998.
3 For a comprehensive explanation of water law, see generally: Glazewski (2014); and Thompson (2006).
4 Act 108 of 1997.
5 Section 1 of the Water Services Act: This means a water services authority (a district or local municipality), a water services provider, a water board and a water services committee.
6 Act 57 of 2002.
7 *Government Gazette* 41439 GN 107 of 13 February 2018. Some provinces have gone a step further to restrict water use from certain dams in terms of the NWA in order to deal with the disaster locally and introduce stringent water restrictions on users. The Western Cape, for example, placed this restriction on one of its water supply schemes in terms of *Government Gazette* 40279 GN 1057 of 16 September 2016.

future droughts? These debates have raised questions concerning the ability of the country's current water regime to conserve and manage scarce water resources and the capacity of its institutions to implement it. Are there certain water management mechanisms or approaches which could be introduced to improve the country's water security? If so, what are these mechanisms and approaches and how can they be implemented? Do they require new legislation, or can they be implemented through existing legislation?

South Africa's water regime historically focused on supply management before moving into more contemporary times to focus on demand management. One particular mechanism or approach that seems to have been somewhat overlooked is area-based management adopted in other water-scarce countries to manage, conserve and protect areas globally known as 'water towers',[8] better known in South Africa as strategic water source areas (SWSAs). This term specifically denotes a link to a geographical area containing the very ecological infrastructure from whence the water originates, but cleverly uses the word 'strategic' to imply that it is not an exhaustive identification of all water source areas.[9]

The identification of SWSAs began in 1959 when South Africa's principal mountain catchment areas were identified and mapped by the Soil Conservation Board.[10] From this knowledge came the study and development of national climate and hydrological spatial databases (based on mean annual runoff) that were used in preparing the National Spatial Biodiversity Assessment (2004).[11] Due to their limitations, the National Freshwater Ecosystem Priority Areas (NFEPA) Project (2011) set to build on existing knowledge and identified 'high water yield areas' – areas which produced up to three times higher than the mean annual runoff.[12] The NFEPA Project was a multi-partner collaborative project between various government departments, their technical advisors, scientists and non-governmental organisations.[13] Through recent refinement and scientific adjustments to that knowledge, South Africa's 22 SWSAs were identified as part of a collaborative project between the Council for Scientific and Industrial Research (CSIR) and the World Wide Fund for Nature-South Africa (WWF-SA).[14]

Described as the 'crown jewels' of South Africa's water resources, SWSAs comprise only 8% of the country's landscape, yet provide more than 50% of its surface water. [15] These areas are undeniably crucial as they mark the first part of the 'journey of water'. Once vast amounts of rain waters are caught, SWSAs distribute them

8 WWF-SA (2013: 8).
9 Nel et al. (2017: 252).
10 This process has led to the identification of 109 mountain catchment areas, cf. WWF-SA (2013: 9).
11 WWF-SA (2013: 9).
12 Ibid.
13 Nel et al. (2011: v).
14 Nel et al. (2017: 253 and 255).
15 Ibid: 255; and WWF-SA (2013: 6).

through rivers, streams and other watercourses into the country's dams. From there, water is transported through engineered infrastructure and distributed for domestic, industrial and agricultural use through the country's extensive national, provincial and municipal water reticulation system. Although located in only six of the country's nine provinces, most of South Africa's SWSAs provide water nationally, supporting growth and development needs that are often a far distance away. Research conducted by the CSIR indicates that SWSAs support about 50% of the population, 64% of the economy and about 70% of irrigated agriculture.[16] Their invaluable ecological function therefore qualifies them as being 'strategic' and rightfully worthy of a customised and dedicated legal regime to manage, conserve and protect them.

At this juncture, it is crucial to distinguish SWSAs from the more commonly known water management areas (WMAs). WMAs are "established as a management unit in the national water resource strategy within which a catchment management agency (CMA) will conduct the protection, use, development, conservation, management and control of water resources".[17] There are currently nine WMAs which have been identified[18] in South Africa which span the entire landscape of the country. Being regional management units which do not provide water nationally or support the country's population and economy significantly, they are distinguishable from SWSAs which are far smaller pockets of land found within (and sometimes straddling numerous) WMAs.

Currently, there are 22 SWAs in the country. The South African government has also "endorsed and acknowledged [SWSAs] as strategic national assets at the highest level in all sectors" by way of policy, particularly in the context of water resource protection.[19] It is disconcertingly anomalous that the NWA, being the country's main freshwater management legislation, contains no express measures specifically designed to manage, conserve and protect this crucial ecological infrastructure is disconcerting and anomalous. Adding to this confusion is the fact that area-based approaches to freshwater management are not a new legal phenomena. In the 1970s, the country introduced the Mountain Catchment Areas Act[20] (MCAA) which enabled the government to declare mountain catchment areas and subject them to various forms of control and regulation. This Act is now exceptionally outdated, and rather fortuitously, in the absence of a contemporary mechanism contained in the NWA, approximately 13% of the country's SWSAs are situated within protected areas[21] declared under the National

16 Nel et al. (2017: 255).

17 Section 1 of the NWA.

18 *Government Gazette* 40279 GN 1056 of 16 September 2016. The Minister recently announced a proposal for the establishment of a single catchment management agency (*Government Gazette* 41321 GN 1415 of 15 December 2017). This is in direct opposition to existing national water policy that provide for decentralisation and public participation in water governance.

19 Department of Water Affairs (2013: 44).

20 Act 63 of 1970.

21 For a breakdown of the percentage of protection for each SWSA, see Nel et al. (2017: 256).

Environmental Management: Protected Areas Act[22] (NEMPAA). This, however, leaves by far the majority of the country's crucial SWSAs outside of formal legal area-based protection. These 'unprotected' SWSAs face a range of threats from coal mining, the plantation of alien and invasive species within and around them, and land degradation caused by poorly managed farming practices.[23] Even though some threats, like mining, might appear minimal at a national scale, studies show that the extent of the threat posed by mining activities to SWAs on a provincial scale is vast.[24] The need for more concerted efforts to improve the protection of South Africa's SWSAs is a clear priority.

This chapter begins by briefly outlining South Africa's current environmental regime with a view to identifying possible area-based management measures that could be used to fill the current apparent regulatory vacuum when it comes to managing, conserving and protecting the country's SWSAs. This survey spans South Africa's framework environmental law (the National Environmental Management Act[25] (NEMA)); freshwater management laws (NWA and MCAA); protected areas laws (the NEMPAA); forestry and biodiversity laws (the National Forests Act[26] (NFA)) and National Environmental Management Biodiversity Act[27] (NEMBA)); and mineral resource laws (the Mineral and Petroleum Resource Development Act[28] (MPRDA)). In respect of each of these laws, the author canvasses the possibly relevant existing legal provisions and then critically reviews their utility. It must be highlighted at the outset that this survey is expressly limited to the framework environmental management laws and natural resources laws, focussing on those tools promoting area-based management for conserving surface water in the country's identified SWSAs. The scope of this chapter unfortunately does not provide an opportunity to include a discussion of other potentially relevant laws within its remit, such as those governing land-use planning.

Having outlined and critically reviewed the legal possibilities inherent within South Africa's current domestic legal regime and the constraints facing their implementation in the context of SWSAs, the chapter then turns to consider the Australian context, specifically New South Wales' state laws that contain specific area-based management measures aimed at managing, conserving and protecting the scarce water resources in this Australian state. This analysis is undertaken with a view to scoping possible legal reform for South Africa's water legislation in the concluding part of this chapter.

22 Act 57 of 2003.

23 For a detailed discussion on all threats faced by SWSAs, see WWF-SA (2013: 16).

24 Less than 1% of water source areas are currently mined; however, 70% of the areas in Mpumalanga are under either a prospecting or mining license and this is cause for particular concern, see: WWF-SA (2013: 14).

25 Act 107 of 1998.

26 Act 84 of 1998.

27 Act 10 of 2004.

28 Act 28 of 2002.

Finally, it should be noted that the discussion of SWSAs in this chapter refers strictly to those providing surface water, and not those providing groundwater.

2 Existing South African environmental legal mechanisms for promoting SWSAs

As should be evident from the list mentioned in the introduction, several laws in South Africa are of possible relevance to promoting area-based management of surface water in the country's identified SWSAs. These laws span framework environmental laws, water management laws, protected areas laws, forestry and biodiversity laws, and mineral resource laws. The relevant laws and their potential utility in promoting the management, conservation and protection of the country's SWSAs are discussed in turn below.

2.1 Framework environmental laws

NEMA enables the Minister of Environmental Affairs and relevant provincial environmental ministers to list activities which may not be undertaken without an environmental authorisation issued by the competent authority.[29] Prior to granting an environmental authorisation, the competent authority must consider either a basic assessment report or a scoping and full assessment report submitted by the applicant.[30] The lists of activities[31] and regulations governing the relevant assessment process[32] have been published under NEMA. A few of the listed activities constitute activities highlighted in the introduction to this chapter as those potentially threatening SWSAs, and, therefore, while not an area-based management measure, this mechanism may go some way to mitigating the negative impact of activities on SWSAs.

Since December 2014, NEMA accords the Minister of Environmental Affairs the power to:[33]

> ...prohibit or restrict the granting of an environmental authorisation... for a listed or a specified activity in a specified geographical area for such period and on such terms and conditions as the Minister may determine, if it is necessary to ensure the protection of the environment, the conservation of resources or sustainable development.

This power provides several opportunities for improving the protection of the country's SWSAs. First, the effect of this provision is that the responsible authority "must not accept any further application for an environmental authorisation for the identified

29 Section 24(2) of the NEMA.
30 Section 24(1) of the NEMA.
31 *Government Gazette* 38282 GNR 982 of 8 December 2014.
32 *Government Gazette* 38282 GNs 983-985 of 4 December 2014.
33 Section 24(2A)(a) of the NEMA.

listed or specified activity in the identified geographical area until such time that the prohibition has been lifted" and "must deem all pending applications to have been withdrawn".[34] This is a proactive mechanism as it requires the responsible minister to exercise his or her power in accordance with the cautious and risk-averse approach set out in the NEMA's national environmental management principles.[35] It is also a mechanism that deals with both future and existing applications. This is the first provision of its kind in South African environmental legislation.

Secondly, this mechanism provides flexibility in two ways. It gives the Minister a discretion to link certain activities to certain geographical areas, and discretion to remove the restriction or prohibition should the circumstances change. Understanding that each SWSA is different and the shifting science around the determination of these areas,[36] flexibility becomes vital in providing nuanced protection instead of creating blanket protection for all SWSAs. This mechanism is yet to be used generally or in the context of protecting SWSA, and its practical utility accordingly remains uncertain.

2.2 Freshwater management laws

The MCAA has been on South Africa's statute book since 1970. Although the purpose of protecting mountain catchment areas does not make explicit reference to water resource (or source) protection, the 1961 Report of the Interdepartmental Committee on the Conservation of Mountain Catchments in South Africa specifically highlighted the protection of water resources as the main driver behind controlling mountain catchments.[37] Mountain catchment areas are therefore beneficial for maintaining water yield and ensuring water quality, whilst contributing to nature conservation, recreation and agriculture simultaneously.[38] The MCAA provides for the declaration of mountain catchment areas[39] and their regulation through the issuing of directions presribed in the Government Gazette.[40] These directions can relate to "the conservation, use, management and control of such land, the prevention of soil erosion, the protection and treatment of the natural vegetation and the destruction of vegetation which is … intruding vegetation".[41] The MCAA, although being one of the obvious statutes of refuge for SWSAs, is problematic for several reasons. The Act is exceptionally outdated as it

34 Section 24(2A)(b) of the NEMA.
35 Section 2(4)(a)(vii) of the NEMA.
36 For an explanation on the process undertaken in mapping the SWSAs and the changes that were subsequently made in that process, see: Nel et al. (2017: 253-254). A more in-depth discussion of refinement of the list of SWSAs is detailed in see Le Maitre et al. (2018: 67-78).
37 Rabie & Burgers (1997: 356).
38 Ibid: 351.
39 Section 2 of the MCAA.
40 Section 3 of the MCAA.
41 Section 3(1) of the MCAA.

was passed before the coming into effect of the Constitution of the Republic of South Africa, 1996. While it was updated in 1996, the Act largely does not align to the country's post-constitutional dispensation. Furthermore, the directions providing for the conservation, use, management and control of these areas are yet to be published. Regarding governance, the Act places the authority to declare and administer mountain catchment areas in the hands of the provincial government,[42] which is not ideal given the desirability and probable need for nationally declared SWSA to be determined and managed by national authorities. Lastly, mountain catchment areas are overwhelmingly present in the Western Cape, and a few regions of the Eastern Cape and Mpumalanga.[43] This Act will most likely achieve limited protection for SWSAs, particularly in relation to those located in other provinces.

The NWA, on the other hand, generally does not have an area-based focus in its mechanisms toolbox of legal mechanisms. It makes no mention of the term 'SWSAs' and therefore arguably provides a single possible option for SWSA protection: the Minister's power to make regulations for the protection of a water resource, an instream habitat or a riparian habitat.[44] The definition of these features will most likely encompass most of a SWSA's physical features and can thus be used to secure some level of protection, at least for those specific features. These regulations, however, are yet to be enacted, and similar to the provisions in NEMA discussed above, the nature and extent of protection they can possibly offer are currently unknown. Should the Department of Water and Sanitation now undertake a process to develop these regulations, the time-consuming process prescribed in the NWA[45] could defeat the objective of improving protection for SWSAs because this process would run parallel to a process currently being undertaken by the Department to completely overhaul the NWA.[46] In other words, drafting regulations based on an Act that is being reviewed may only create more confusion once the new Act is passed.

---

42 *Government Gazette* 16346 GNR 5485 of 7 April 1995. There are issues raised with this assignment of powers and it has caused a great deal of confusion in the provinces, see: Rabie & Burgers (1997: 355).

43 Rabie & Burgers (1997: 354).

44 Section 26 read with Section 1 of the NWA defines 'water resource' to include "a watercourse, surface water, estuary or aquifer"; an 'instream habitat' to include "the physical structure of a watercourse and the associated vegetation in relation to the bed of the watercourse", and a 'riparian habitat' to include "the physical structure and associated vegetation of the areas associated with a watercourse which are commonly characterised by alluvial soils, and which are inundated or flooded to an extent and with a frequency sufficient to support vegetation of species which a composition and physical structure distinct from those of adjacent land areas".

45 Section 69 of the NWA. It prescribes a lengthy process that involves both provincial and national Parliament for the drafting and finalising of regulations.

46 Department of Water and Sanitation (2017: 36). This process provides a great opportunity for the development of customised protection for SWSAs and will form the core of the discussion in the last part of this chapter.

Three other possible options in the NWA – although precarious – may provide some form of protection for SWSAs. The first is by way of definition and regulation of watercourses[47] through licensing.[48] Licences are granted with conditions attached to them to ensure that the licence holder uses the watercourse in such a way that the holder does not pollute it and exercises a general duty of care towards the watercourse at all times.[49] Those watercourses that form part of SWSAs and that are used by licence holders are potentially protected through the licensing mechanism (assuming that the licence holder complies with the licence conditions). However, although watercourses indeed form part of SWSAs, they still need to be distinguished from SWSAs. First, SWSAs are of strategic national significance due to their contribution to the country – economically, socially and environmentally. Secondly, their physical attributes also consist of other natural features (e.g. forests and mountains) which are not watercourses. Reliance on watercourse regulation for SWSA protection is thus insufficient and extremely narrow.

The second option is the Minister's powers to regulate activities of a detrimental nature towards water resources through the declaration of controlled activities.[50] The four named controlled activities do not include, or purport to include, any SWSA-specific measures. Although the NWA allows the Minister to extend this list,[51] it has not been extended for 20 years. The regulation of the four controlled activities will not suffice in deterring the most detrimental impacts to SWSAs that prevail in varying mining, forestry and agricultural activities. Similar to the development of regulations under the NWA, undertaking a process to extend this list of activities would create a process parallel to the review of the NWA that may result in a wasted duplication of effort. Moreover, the regulation of controlled activities adopts a blanket approach in that it applies one set of rules to all water resources in which these activities are being undertaken, failing to consider the unique differences in threats and protection levels required for each SWSA.

---

47 Section 1 of the NWA defines a 'watercourse' as "(a) a river or spring; (b) a natural channel in which water flows regularly or intermittently; (c) a wetland, lake or dam into which, or from which, water flows; and (d) any collection of water which the Minister may, by notice in the Gazette, declare to be a watercourse, and a reference to a watercourse includes, where relevant, its bed and banks".

48 Section 22(1)(b) of the NWA provides that "a person may only use water if that water use is authorised by a licence under this Act". Section 21 of the NWA lists a number of water uses which include impeding or diverting the flow of water in a watercourse, altering the bed, banks, course or characteristics of a watercourse, and other activities involving the water resource (which by definition, includes watercourses).

49 Sections 28 and Section 29 of the NWA.

50 Section 37 of the NWA identifies four controlled activities: the irrigation of land using water containing waste generated through industrial activity; activities which modify atmospheric precipitation; a power generation activity that changes the flow of a water resource; and intentional recharging of an aquifer with waste water.

51 Section 38 of the NWA.

The third option is the possibility of SWSAs being managed by catchment management agencies (CMAs) that manage those WMAs within which SWSAs exist. Contrarily, it can be argued that the national significance of these areas would not be best managed regionally, particularly when considering the extent of the powers of CMAs.[52] Due to their powers being assigned and/or delegated before they can be exercised, CMAs have experienced challenges in exercising their powers in recent years due to the Minister revoking powers that had been previously assigned or delegated.[53] Thus, it would not appear wise for SWSA to be managed regionally by CMAs whose powers and functions have been undermined and crippled in the past few years.

2.3 Protected areas laws

Different categories of protected areas[54] can be declared[55] to achieve specific purposes[56] under NEMPAA. These include national parks, marine protected areas, special nature reserves, nature reserves and protected environments. Certain protected areas are declared and regulated under specific Acts, such as the declaration of mountain catchment areas under the MCAA.[57] However, as the framework legislation for the management of protected areas generally, certain provisions of NEMPAA still apply to all types of protected areas.

The benefit of including SWSAs within South Africa's protected areas network is the protection they would gain from mining-related activities generally.[58] There is also

52 Section 79 of the NWA sets out the general powers and duties of CMAs. Section 73 of the NWA provides that the Minister can also assign further powers to CMAs, including those listed in Schedule 3 of the Act. None of these powers are specifically related to SWSAs.

53 South African Water Caucus (undated: 19-20). This report was released in November 2017 and amongst other things, it highlights pertinent issues around the delegation and subsequent revocation of the CMAs powers by the Minister, as well as uncertainty as to the role of CMAs generally. This report was widely publicised in numerous news articles and radio interviews, see: Arendse (2017); Matthews (2017); Makhowana (2017); and Fraser (2017).

54 Section 9 of the NEMPAA.

55 Depending on whether it is a national or provincial protected area, either the national Minister of Environmental Affairs or a relevant provincial environmental minister can declare the area.

56 The general purpose for declaring protected areas is set out in Section 17 of the NEMPAA. The purpose for declaring special nature reserves is set out in Section 18 of the NEMPAA. The purpose for declaring national parks is set out in Section 20 of the NEMPAA. The purpose for declaring nature reserves is set out in Section 23 of the NEMPAA. The purpose for declaring protected environments is set out in Section 28 of the NEMPAA.

57 See the discussion on mountain catchment areas in part 2.2 above.

58 Section 48(1)(a) and (c) of the NEMPAA provide that prospecting, mining, exploration and production is expressly prohibited within special nature reserves, national parks, nature reserves, world heritage sites, marine protected areas and forest protected areas. Section 48(1)(b) provides that the Ministers of Mineral Resources and Environmental Affairs can give consent for mining-related activities to continue within a protected environment. The Act is silent on mining-related

wide scope for regulating and managing protected areas more closely. The Minister of Environmental Affairs or relevant provincial environmental minister has the power to regulate a variety of activities that may negatively affect SWSAs found in protected areas, such as the use of land and water in protected areas, and prohibiting or restricting land uses in protected areas that are harmful to the environment.[59] These regulations are strengthened by the offences and penalties that may be meted out for contravention thereof.[60] Furthermore, the Minister may generally assign the management of protected areas to any suitable person or organ of state.[61] Should the management authority fail in its duties or underperform, the Minister similarly has the power to terminate its management authority.[62]

The challenges with protected areas, however, are also dire. Mining-related activities may still be conducted in protected environments.[63] This legislative anomaly results in protected environments being targeted as 'low hanging fruit' for mining companies.[64] Although other types of protected areas are explicitly protected from mining-related activities, there has been a tide of applications for mining activities in and around protected areas that were indeed authorised, causing a flood of litigation in an attempt to review and set aside these decisions in the recent years.[65] So even though approximately 13% of South Africa's SWSAs currently enjoy formal legal protection in the form of protected areas,[66] even these are not sterilised from mining-related activities in the true sense. To add a layer of complexity to the matter, more than 80% of South Africa's landscape that is critical for the country's water security and supply still remains unprotected. This statistic alone should drive the urgent need for dedicated legislation aimed at protecting the country's SWSAs.

---

activities being conducted within mountain catchment areas. Nonetheless, the latter two types of protected areas pose challenges for SWSA protection, which will be discussed below.

59 Section 86(1)(c)(vi) and (d)(iii) of the NEMPAA. Municipalities also have the power to regulate local protected areas in terms of their by-laws (Section 49(c) of the NEMPAA).

60 Section 89(3) of the NEMPAA.

61 Section 38(1)(a), (aB) and (b) of the NEMPAA. The management of national parks more specifically must be assigned to the South African National Parks Authority in terms of Section 38(1)(aA) of the NEMPAA. The management authority has powers to also create internal rules for the proper administration of the protected area in terms of Section 52 of the NEMPAA. The Minister has passed regulations which assign powers to certain management authorities whilst simultaneously detailing the manner in which protection of these declared areas should be exercised. See for example: *Government Gazette* 39891 GN 15 of 1 April 2016 (for Mountain Zebra Camdeboo Protected Environment); *Government Gazette* 39379 GN 1074 of 6 November 2015 (for Dwesa-Cwebe Marine Protected Area); and *Government Gazette* 32797 GN 1175 of 11 December 2009 (for Knysna Protected Environment).

62 Section 44 of the NEMPAA.

63 Section 48(1)(b) of the NEMPAA requires the permission of both the Ministers of Mineral Resources and Environmental Affairs in this case.

64 See generally: Centre for Environmental Rights (2016: 28); WWF-SA (2017); and Davies (2015).

65 See further Davies (2015).

66 For a breakdown of the percentage of protection for each SWSA, see Nel et al. (2017: 256).

2.4 Forestry and biodiversity laws[67]

The NFA provides for the declaration of forest protected areas.[68] Once declared, layers of protection apply to the forest protected area that would be advantageous for SWSAs that fall within such areas. Considering the extent to which SWSAs have forests within them or even fall into forest protected areas,[69] this tool advances protection for SWSAs. First, the forest may not be cut, disturbed, damaged or destroyed except by way of licence, in terms of an exemption from the Minister, in terms of the rules for the proper management of the forest protected area, in terms of a right of servitude, or with consent of the registered owner in the case of a protected forest area situated outside a State forest.[70] Furthermore, the Minister has the power to declare a 'controlled forest area':[71]

> if the Minister is of the opinion that urgent steps are required to prevent the deforestation or further deforestation of; or rehabilitate a natural forest or woodland which is threatened with deforestation, or is being or has been deforested.

Forest protected areas must be managed by making rules to achieve the purpose for which the area was declared.[72] As an overarching protected areas framework, Chapters

---

67 For a detailed explanation on forestry and biodiversity laws, see generally Paterson (2014a and b).

68 Section 8 of the NFA gives the Minister the power to make such a declaration. Section 18 of the NFA read with regulation 17 of the Regulations of the National Forest Act (published in *Government Gazette* 32185 GNR 466 of 29 April 2009) also give any person, organisation or organ or state the right to apply to the Minister to have a forest declared protected. The same applies to an owner of private land who wishes to have a forest on their own land declared protected. They too may apply to the Minister in terms of regulation 18 of the Regulations of the National Forest Act.

69 Plantation forestry is the major land-use in the Mpumalanga Drakensberg, Upper Usutu, Mbabane Hills, Wolkberg and Mfolozi Headwaters and also occupies a substantial proportion of the Enkangala Grassland, Southern Drakensberg, Outeniqua and Amatole SWSAs. See Le Maitre et al. (2018: 151).

70 Section 10(1) of the NFA.

71 Section 17(2) of the NFA. This declaration may stop any person from using their right of access into the area, prohibit a person from removing forest produce from the area, suspend licences issued in respect of this area (a forward-looking mechanism, in the author's opinion), require the owner to take steps to prevent deforestation or rehabilitate the natural forest/woodland, and require the owner to submit and comply with a forest management plan. See, for example, *Government Gazette* 33734 GN 1032 of 12 November 2010, where the Minister declared the Declaration of Phase 2A of the Olifants River Water Resources Development Project Offsite Mitigation Area as Controlled Forest Area. In this declaration, the Minister prohibited grazing, unauthorised removal of forest produce, cultivation, any activities which, may cause deforestation or prevent rehabilitation and transplanting for a fixed period of three years, and simultaneously suspended any licences that had been granted in respect to this area. The Minister also required the following steps to be taken: rehabilitation; transplanting of vegetation; and the submission of a sustainable management plan for the area.

72 Section 11(2) of the NFA. These rules need not be created by the Minister where they already exist.

1 and 2 of NEMPAA[73] and Section 48 NEMPAA,[74] also apply to forest protected areas declared under the NFA.[75] The overall challenge in using this tool for SWSA protection would arise when attempting to regulate an area that comprises many features through a law that deals with a single aspect thereof. The limited application to forests would result in the rest of the SWSA (their watercourses, mountain catchments, etc. that fall outside the forest area) not enjoying the same protection. Furthermore, forestry plantations of alien and invasive species are one of the major threats to SWSAs as they use more water than natural forests and if not properly managed, the invasive plantations pose a risk to water availability within the SWSAs.[76] Although not dealt with in the NFA, the regulation of alien and invasive species is governed by the country's biodiversity legislation.

Measures for protecting biodiversity in NEMBA are potentially effective but currently ineffective. The identification of ecosystems that are threatened and in need of protection[77] has been done by the Minister,[78] but the identification of the corresponding threatening activities which may not be commenced within such areas without an environmental authorisation being granted under NEMA[79] has not. Although some of the key threats against SWSAs are already identified and are being regulated in terms of the authorisations process in NEMA,[80] it does not deal with all threats, particularly those pertaining to biodiversity issues such as plantations of invasive and alien species. This tool's utility is therefore in a state of limbo as far as the ecosystems approach is concerned. Biodiversity planning tools also provide some level of guidance in decision-making processes affecting certain areas, but do not provide offences and penalties for those who fail to comply with them. Relevant biodiversity planning tools would include the National Biodiversity Framework[81] which identifies priority areas for conservation action and the establishment of protected areas.[82] Unlike the National Water Resource Strategy which is grounded in the NWA and which explicitly "endorsed and acknowledged [SWSAs] as strategic national assets at the highest level in all

73 These chapters deal with the objectives of the Act, state trusteeship of protected areas, application of the Act, application of NEMA, application of NEMBA, conflicts with other legislation, status of provincial legislation on provincial and local protected areas, kinds of protected areas, register of protected areas, norms and standards, provincial protected areas, world heritage sites, continued existence of marine protected areas, specially protected forest areas, and mountain catchment areas.

74 This section deals with the prohibition of mining-related activities in forest protected areas.

75 Section 15 of the NFA.

76 WWF-SA (2013: 16).

77 Section 52 of the NEMBA.

78 *Government Gazette* 34809 GN 1002 of 9 December 2011.

79 Section 53 of the NEMBA.

80 Such as forestry plantations and mining activities.

81 Section 38 and 39 of the NEMBA. The National Biodiversity Framework is published in *Government Gazette* 32474 GNR813 of 3 August 2009.

82 Section 39(1)(c) of the NEMBA.

sectors",[83] the National Biodiversity Framework which is grounded in NEMBA falls short of such an endorsement. Instead, one of its strategic objectives is the expansion of the protected areas network and conservation areas.[84] Although SWSAs may possibly be protected through this measure, grave shortcomings persist.[85] Declaring SWSAs as bioregions is an alternative method of reinforcing their protection. Unfortunately, only a very few bioregions have been declared to date in South Africa.[86] Their practical effectiveness is therefore currently difficult to determine. Moreover, the characteristics of a bioregion[87] do not align with the characteristics of an SWSA.[88] Using this measure even innovatively would still not satisfy the need for customised legal protection of SWSAs. Fortunately though, the declaration of a bioregion simultaneously requires the publication of bioregional plan "for the management of biodiversity and components of biodiversity in such a region"[89] which could potentially be used to detail SWSA protection. Lastly, SWSAs falling within an ecosystem declared as either being in threat or requiring protection[90] would also benefit from being managed in terms of a biodiversity management plan, which aims to ensure the long-term survival of the ecosystem.[91] However, of all the biodiversity management plans published to date, none of them relate to ecosystems (area-based) management.[92]

---

83 Department of Water Affairs (2013: 44).

84 Paragraph 4.5 of the National Biodiversity Framework.

85 See discussion on protected areas in part 2.3 above.

86 These are bioregional plans for: Nelson Mandela Metropolitan Municipality (*Provincial Gazette* 3362 PN13 of 20 March 2015); and West Rand District Municipality and Ekurhuleni Metropolitan Municipality (*Provincial Gazette* 2684 PN390 of 2 September 2015).

87 Section 40(1) of the NEMBA provides that a bioregion is a "region which contains whole or several nested ecosystems and is characterised by its landforms, vegetation cover, human culture and history".

88 SWSAs often only occupy a small fraction of the land surface area but supply a relatively high amount of water to the surrounding region, see: Nel et al. (2017: 251).

89 Section 40(1)(b) read with Section 41 of the NEMBA. This plan is required to be reviewed at least every five years in terms of Section 42 of the NEMBA.

90 In terms of Section 52 of the NEMBA.

91 Section 43 read with Section 45(a) of the NEMBA. The plan is required to be reviewed at least every five years in terms of Section 46 of the NEMBA.

92 Instead they relate to species protection. See for example: *Government Gazette* 31968 GNR 214 of 2 March 2009; *Government Gazette* 34388 GNR 416 of 24 June 2011; *Government Gazette* 36096 GNR 49 of 25 January 2013; *Government Gazette* 36411 GNR 433 of 26 April 2013; *Government Gazette* 40793 GN 305 of 21 April 2017; *Government Gazette* 40883 GN 423 of 2 June 2017; and *Government Gazette* 41498 GN 214 of 16 March 2018. There is only one draft plan relating to ecosystems protection, which is yet to be finalised (*Government Gazette* 39922 GN 427 of 15 April 2016). However, Norms and Standards for Biodiversity Management Plans for Ecosystems have been published (*Government Gazette* 37302 GN 83 of 7 February 2014).

2.5 Mineral resource laws

The MPRDA prohibits mining activities within 'no-go mining areas'[93] (amongst other areas), which the Minister of Mineral Resources is empowered to declare by restricting or prohibiting the granting of a reconnaissance permission, prospecting right, mining right or permit within an identified geographical area.[94] However, the Minister is also allowed to issue these permits, rights and permissions within the 'no-go' areas based on certain grounds.[95] This exception can only be made subject to Section 48 of the NEMPAA.[96] This means that if the 'no go' area is indeed a declared protected area, mining and mining-related activities are completely prohibited therein, despite the Minister wishing to invoke the grounds of exception. The sole benefit of the Minister using this tool to protect SWSAs is the plausibly strong political message associated with it – it is far more convincing for the Minister of Mineral Resources to publicise an intention to protect a certain environment 'from' mining, when their mandate is to ensure the development of mineral resources 'through' mining. Unfortunately, the disadvantages of this legal mechanism far outweigh the advantages. First, the purpose of declaring 'no-go mining areas' is based on "the national interest, the strategic nature of the mineral in question and the need to promote the sustainable development of the nation's mineral resources".[97] This intention generally does not consider the need to protect the environment or SWSAs within these environments.[98] As expected, it relates to a law completely juxtaposed to environmental protection. Secondly, even if so declared, it would protect SWSAs from only one of many threats posed thereto,[99] leaving SWSAs exposed to a plethora of inherent risks. Lastly, on the very limited occasions that the Minister has made such declarations, the period of application has generally

93 Section 48 of the MPRDA.

94 Section 49 of the MPRDA.

95 Section 48(2) of the MPRDA: A reconnaissance permission, prospecting right, mining right or mining permit may be issued in respect of the land contemplated in subsection (1) if the Minister is satisfied that (a) having regard to the sustainable development of the mineral resources involved and the national interest, it is desirable to issue it; (b) the reconnaissance, prospecting or mining will take place within the framework of national environmental management policies, norms and standards; and (c) the granting of such rights or permits will not detrimentally affect the interests of any holder of a prospecting right or mining right.

96 Section 49 read with 48(1)(d) of the MPRDA.

97 Section 49(1) of the MPRDA.

98 Very few exceptional cases do exist. For example: *Government Gazette* 38004 GN 718 of 12 September 2014 had "regard to the national interest to protect the sensitive environment of areas within the buffer zone of the Mapungubwe World Heritage Site". *Government Gazette* 34051 GN of 4 March 2011 had "regard to the national interest to protect the sensitive environment of areas around Lake Chrissie, commonly known as the Chrissiesmeer Biodiversity Site".

99 For example, forestry plantations of invasive and alien species, poorly managed agricultural land due to overgrazing, amongst others. For a detailed discussion on all threats faced by SWSAs; see WWF-SA (2013: 16).

been short and applicable to certain parts of the country,[100] which results in an unco-ordinated approach to ensuring meaningful protection, regulation, management (and sometimes rehabilitation, where required) of SWSAs.

Having analysed the possible opportunities inherent in South Africa's current legal regime for promoting the management and protection of the country's SWSAs, and concluded that by far the majority fails to provide a coherent and integrated solution, it would now seem prudent to consider possible approaches adopted in other water-scarce countries, such as the state of New South Wales in Australia. The purpose of this enquiry is to determine whether they provide examples of more feasible and dedicated regimes for protecting SWSAs from which South Africa's policy-makers could learn.

3 The protection of water source areas in Australia: a comparative analysis

Similarities between South Africa and Australia's legal water context are eloquently summarised by one commentator below:[101]

> Australia and South Africa both inherited legal systems with water laws developed in response to well-watered European climatic conditions. Thus the common law systems for regulating water use reflected non-indigenous environmental contexts. As a consequence, these water laws imported regulatory forms with many inappropriate constructs and assumptions. As statutory regimes developed the focus was upon water supply and physical infrastructure development with little consideration of the consequent environmental modifications. Recent reforms in both countries have been predicated on identified social and economic goals and the objectives of environmental protection that more clearly take into account prevailing physical and social contexts.

The utility of a comparison between South Africa and Australia's water laws flows naturally from this premise.[102] Globally, Australia is the second driest continent (to

100 The following are examples. *Government Gazette* 40277 GN 1014 of 15 September 2016 applied in a certain part of the Eastern Cape for 18 months and was further extended by another 18 months by *Government Gazette* 40898 GN 546 of 9 June 2017. *Government Gazette* 38004 GN 718 of 12 September 2014. *Government Gazette* 38128 GN of 31 October 2014 is one of the rare declarations which apply for an indefinite period but only in the Free State. *Government Gazette* 36490 GN 367 of 24 May 2013 applied for 10 years to certain portions of land. *Government Gazette* 33511 GN 768 of 31 August 2010 applied nationally, but only for six months. It was later extended by another six months in respect to Mpumalanga and by 12 months for the rest of the country in *Government Gazette* 34057, GN 160 of 28 February 2011. This notice was again extended by another two weeks (to the extent that it applied nationally) by *Government Gazette* 34171 GN 287 of 31 March 2011. *Government Gazette* 28216 GN 1118 of 18 November 2005 applied in a certain part of Limpopo.

101 Godden (2005: 182).

102 However, unlike South Africa, the Commonwealth of Australia was formed by the federation of six states (New South Wales, Queensland, South Australia, Tasmania, Victoria and Western Australia), which retained their powers to create and execute its own laws. It also comprises of ten territories (areas which are not claimed by any of the states), some which are governed purely

Antarctica)[103] and the driest continent that sustains a permanent human population,[104] with an average rainfall of 430 mm per year.[105] Most of this water is lost to evaporation and on average, about 383,000 gigalitres remain for Australia's water environments and approximately 70,000 to 95,000 gigalitres provide for Australia's annual consumptive water needs.[106] These statistics are similar to South Africa's water situation. In Australia's worst drought since the 1900s, however, it suffered sustained impacts during what was then coined as the 'Millennium Drought' during 2001-2009.[107] Similar to South Africa, dam levels dropped significantly throughout the country,[108] lessening water available for supply and ultimately resulting in water restrictions being put in place coupled with large-scale technological interventions to manage the drought.[109]

The Water Act (2007),[110] a Commonwealth law, was enacted as a response to the prolonged pressures of the Millennium Drought.[111] The Act mainly regulates, manages and protects the use of Australia's largest water catchment (the Murray-Darling Basin[112] (MDB)) amongst other things. The MDB stretches over 14% of Australia's landscape which consists of four states and a single territory.[113] Approximately 77,000km of rivers (23 rivers in total)[114] flow through it, which include Australia's three largest river systems.[115] It also provides about 40% of the Commonwealth's agricultural output and houses 65% of its irrigated land.[116] Acknowledging its importance and significant contribution towards socio-economic and environmental factors, the Water Act (2007) establishes the Murray-Darling Basin Authority,[117] which developed the

---

by Commonwealth laws and others which are self-governing. Australia is therefore a federal government system whereby the Commonwealth is governed by national legislation passed by the Parliament of the Commonwealth, and each of the six states are further governed by state laws passed by State Parliament. States are only permitted to pass laws which are not controlled by the Commonwealth in terms of Section 51 and 122 of the Commonwealth of Australia Constitution (1900).

103 Argent (2017: 5).

104 Godden (2005: 183).

105 Argent (2017: 5).

106 Ibid.

107 van Dijk et al. (2013: 1040-1041).

108 Lindsay & Supski (2017: 51).

109 Ibid.

110 For a discussion on the historical development of the Water Act 2007 and the extent to which it gives powers to the Commonwealth to manage water resources, see generally: Fisher (2009: 154-160).

111 Loch & Adamson (2015: 1432).

112 For more information and a general overview on the Murray-Darling Basin, see: Murray Darling Basin Authority (2014: 1-5).

113 Bischoff-Mattson & Lynch (2017: 42)

114 Loch & Adamson (2015: 1431).

115 Murray Darling Basin Authority (2014: 1 and 4).

116 Loch & Adamson (2015: 1431).

117 Part 9 of the Water Act (2007).

Murray-Darling Basin Plan.[118] It also establishes a Commonwealth Environmental Water Holder whose main function is to manage the Commonwealth's environmental water, in order to protect and restore the environmental assets of both the MDB and those outside the MDB where the Commonwealth owns water.[119] The Water Act (2007) does not, however, provide further protection, regulation and management laws for SWSAs within the MDB at a Commonwealth level.[120] New South Wales' state laws pertaining to water source protection and regulation that do so are studied in turn below.

3.1 State laws of New South Wales: water catchment regulation

3.1.1 Declared areas

The Water NSW Act (2014) (the Water Act) provides for the declaration of three types of areas: declared catchment areas;[121] special areas;[122] and controlled areas;[123] Currently, the Sydney Catchment Area is the only declared catchment area and it is critical for the supply of water to Sydney, as well as the Blue Mountains, the Illawarra, the Southern Highlands and parts of the Shoalhaven area.[124] The catchment extends about 16,000 square kilometres and although forming only 2% of New South Wales, it provides 60% of the inhabitants' drinking water.[125] Due to its undeniably critical role, the Water Act specifically provides that the size of the catchment shall not be reduced, and an order to revoke the catchment's declaration can only be made by an Act of Parliament.[126]

---

118 Part 2(1) of the Water Act (2007). This plan is a legislative instrument and any amendment thereto is a legislative amendment (Section 33 of the Water Act (2007)). The purpose of the plan is to provide for the integrated and sustainable management of water resources in the MDB (Section 20 of the Water Act (2007)). This plan was passed as law in November 2012.

119 Part 6(2) of the Water Act (2007).

120 This is expected due to the Commonwealth, but for one major exception (the MDB) historically having refrained from managing Australia's water resources. States are left to do so, and where water resource traverse more than one State, they enter into interstate agreements pertaining to that resource, see Fisher (2009: 154).

121 Part 4(2) of the Water NSW Act (2014).

122 Part 4(2) of the Water NSW Act (2014).

123 Part 4(3) of the Water NSW Act (2014).

124 Alluvium Consulting Australia (2017: 4). This is the most recent audit as catchment audits are required every three years from the last publication date, see: Section 42(4) of the Water NSW Act (2014).

125 See generally: Water NSW and Office of Environment and Heritage (2015: 9); and <https://www.waternsw.com.au/water-quality/education/learn/catchment> (accessed 9-12-2017).

126 Section 40(3) of the Water NSW Act (2014).

Special areas located within the catchment are declared for purposes of ensuring that good quality of stored water is maintained (be it that it is used for drinking or other purposes) and that the ecological integrity of the declared area is maintained.[127] Similar to catchment areas, they may not be reduced in size except by way of an Act of Parliament.[128] A management plan must also be developed[129] to grant varying levels of access into the respective special areas, which must be carried out and given effect to by law.[130] Statistically, special areas form about 23% of the broader Sydney Catchment Area. They are pockets of mixed land types which may comprise of legally protected areas, land owned by Water NSW (i.e. state-owned land) and privately owned land.[131] Mimicking this type of composition would provide much-needed flexibility when regulating South Africa's SWSAs, which too comprise of protected areas, state-owned land and private land. Except to say that controlled areas may be declared, the Water Act itself is very discreet about the management and regulation thereof.[132] Once declared though, regulations may be made to provide for the management of different activities within controlled and special areas, such as abstracting, using, polluting or contaminating waters therein.[133] For purposes of furthering this discussion, controlled areas will not be dealt with in great detail.

3.1.2 Objectives

The Special Areas Strategic Plan of Management (2015) (SASPoM) is grounded in the Water Act.[134] It lays down a set of strategic management objectives to give guidance for planning and prioritising projects and programs within special areas, which address issues of water quality, water quantity, maintenance of the hydrological integrity of surface and groundwater sources, fire management, maintenance of ecological integrity of biodiversity, and policy, planning and evaluation amongst others. Some key objectives include:[135]

- pollutants are controlled so that impacts on water quality and natural and cultural values are minimised;

127 Section 47(2) of the Water NSW Act (2014).

128 Section 47(3) of the Water NSW Act (2014).

129 Section 52 of the Water NSW Act (2014). The Special Areas Strategic Plan of Management has been developed and will be discussed below.

130 Section 53 of the Water NSW Act (2014).

131 For a detailed breakdown on the land composition of each special area in the Sydney Catchment Area, see: Water NSW and Office of Environment and Heritage (2015: 6).

132 Section 54 of the Water NSW Act (2014).

133 Sections 55 of the Water NWS Act (2014). The Water NSW Regulations (2013) are in place and will be discussed below.

134 Section 53 of the Water NSW Act (2014).

135 Nine objectives are set out, see: Water NSW and Office of Environment and Heritage (2015: 21).

- surface and groundwater sources and their interactions will be better understood so decisions are made that seek to minimise impacts on Special Areas hydrological integrity;
- access to the special areas is controlled to protect water quality and ecological integrity while providing for appropriate visitor opportunities; and
- ecological integrity including threatened plant and animal species, endangered populations, endangered ecological communities, geodiversity and other natural values are maintained.

Through the achievement of these objectives, all issues faced within special areas are intended to be managed appropriately. Again, considering threats faced by SWSAs[136] (such as forestry plantations of alien and invasive species, fires, and impacts arising from mining activities), objectives of this nature form a workable framework within which measures could be taken to ensure the most comprehensive form of protection for SWSAs.[137]

3.1.3 Regulating activities and developments within declared areas

The Water NSW Regulation (2013) (the Regulations) divides special and controlled areas into Schedules 1 and 2 land.[138] Schedule 1 land consists of both special areas and controlled areas immediately surrounding water storages, and public entry therein is prohibited.[139] Schedule 2 land consists only of special areas that form a buffer to Schedule 1 land, to which restricted public access is allowed to encourage recreational activities by the public.[140] The Regulations deal with many aspects of, and threats to, SWSAs in very clear and direct terms. No one may interfere with water in a special or controlled area either by damming, diverting or taking such water.[141] The disposal of waste in a special or controlled area is prohibited, as well as land or water pollution therein.[142] Stock control,[143] intensive livestock agriculture[144] and the lighting of fires[145] are all dealt with separately.

---

136 For a detailed discussion on all threats faced by SWSAs, see: WWF-SA (2013: 16).

137 These objectives are also subject to review at each review cycle and therefore offer flexibility in terms of providing for other (perhaps currently unforeseen) issues to be dealt with accordingly in future. See further: Water NSW and Office of Environment and Heritage (2015: 21).

138 For a full list of these areas, see: Schedules 1 and 2 of the Water NSW Regulation (2013).

139 Water NSW and Office of Environment and Heritage (2015: 13).

140 Ibid.

141 Regulation 12 of the Water NWS Regulation (2013).

142 Regulation 13 of the Water NWS Regulation (2013).

143 Regulation 14 of the Water NWS Regulation (2013).

144 Regulation 28 of the Water NSW Regulation (2013).

145 Regulation 22 of the Water NSW Regulation (2013) completely prohibits the lighting of fires in Schedule 1 land. Regulation 23 of the Water NSW Regulation (2013) restricts the lighting of fires in Schedule 2 land.

Mining impacts are monitored by Water NSW in terms of the SASPoM. Although not having any legislated powers to prevent mining within special areas, Water NSW's partial ownership of land in the special areas gives them the platform to make recommendations to the State, regulators and mining companies on any proposed mining activities within the catchment.[146] The Minister of Industry, Resources and Energy has, surprisingly, ensured that no coal seam gas mining licences are granted within the special areas of the catchment through an initial moratorium placed on such mining in 2013,[147] followed by a once-off petroleum exploration licences buy-back process from December 2014-September 2015 in terms of the NSW Gas Plan.[148] This is an excellent example of cooperative governance in matters affecting the environment.

When it comes to development (be it agricultural, residential or commercial) within catchment areas, special areas and controlled areas, reliance is placed on the Environmental Planning and Assessment Act (1979) that provides the statutory framework for planning and environmental impact assessment. It sets a higher threshold for development applications to be granted within the Sydney Catchment Area (which includes special areas and control areas located therein) by providing that:[149]

> Provision is to be made in a State Environmental Planning Policy requiring a consent authority to refuse to grant consent to a development application relating to any part of the Sydney drinking water catchment unless the consent authority is satisfied that the carrying out of the proposed development would have a *neutral or beneficial effect* on the quality of water. (own emphasis)

Clause 3 of the State Environmental Planning Policy (Sydney Drinking Water Catchment) (2011) includes this provision in its aims,[150] as well as in the context of the assessment and approval of development and activities.[151] This golden rule is applied even in cases of existing developments for which extension or expansion applications are brought before the state,[152] therefore being implemented as a 'double-edged sword' in its regulation of both new and existing applications within the catchment. This is a

---

146 See <https://www.waternsw.com.au/water-quality/catchment/mining/sca-role> (accessed 24-5-2018).

147 Validakis (2013).

148 NSW Government (2014). This process resulted in the buying back of 16 petroleum exploration licences and the reduction of the coal seam gas footprint from more than 60% of the state to just 8.5%.

149 Section 3.26 (2) of the Environmental Planning and Assessment Act (1979).

150 Clause 3 of the State Environmental Planning Policy (Sydney Drinking Water Catchment) (2011). The three aims of this policy are: to provide for healthy water catchments that will deliver high quality water while permitting development that is compatible with that goal; to provide that a consent authority must not grant consent to a proposed development unless it is satisfied that the proposed development will have a neutral or beneficial effect on water quality; and to support the maintenance or achievement of the water quality objectives for the Sydney drinking water catchment.

151 Clause 10 of the State Environmental Planning Policy (Sydney Drinking Water Catchment) (2011).

152 Clause 11A of the State Environmental Planning Policy (Sydney Drinking Water Catchment) (2011).

particularly beneficial tool for detrimental activities currently continuing within SWSAs, such as mining; the rights and permits of which are subject to renewal. This important requirement is further detailed in the Neutral or Beneficial Effect Water Quality Assessment Guideline (2015),[153] which decision-makers are legally compelled to take into account. It gives meaning to the neutral or beneficial effect (NorBE) requirement as follows:[154]

> A neutral or beneficial effect on water quality is satisfied if the development: (a) has no identifiable potential impact on water quality, or (b) will contain any water quality impact on the development site and prevent it from reaching any watercourse, waterbody or drainage depression on the site, or (c) will transfer any water quality impact outside the site where it is treated and disposed of to standards approved by the consent authority.

The NorBE Guideline also prescribes the manner in which one would achieve this requirement and how to assess an application against it.[155] It provides a clear, straightforward and practically manageable way of ensuring the ecological integrity and optimal hydrological functioning of the catchment and all special areas within it, as it clearly indicates to all potential applicants that in the first instance, all developments are strictly prohibited within the catchment. It also rids the decision-makers of confusion as to whether or not certain activities may, or may not be, permitted within certain boundaries of the catchment, as it provides a clear method for proving the NorBE requirement and assessing a development against its prescripts. The NorBE requirement is also strategically worded so that it prevents the granting of applications that would cause any level of harm to the catchment. It therefore precludes authorities from having to ensure that applicants have security in place to later rehabilitate the environment once the damage has been done. In this way, a proactive approach is taken when protecting the Sydney Catchment Area from possible deterioration.

3.2 Lessons for South Africa: towards SWSA protection

The South African government has endorsed SWSAs "as strategic national assets at the highest level in all sectors" in the National Water Resource Strategy,[156] a policy which is grounded in the NWA.[157] Why the NWA, the country's main freshwater management legislation, contains no express measures specifically designed to manage, conserve and protect these acknowledged SWSAs is puzzling? Instead, it focuses mostly on managing, protecting and regulating water as a resource. A broader application of the NWA is therefore necessary to go beyond the management of water

153 Sydney Catchment Authority (2015: 1-70).
154 Ibid: 6.
155 Ibid.
156 Department of Water Affairs (2013: 44).
157 Sections 5-7 of the NWA.

resources and catchments, to include the management of those key areas from which vast amounts of water resources originate. So how can this be achieved, drawing from lessons learnt through the Australian experience?

3.2.1 Declared areas

Firstly, recognition must be given in the NWA to the term 'strategic water source areas', to distinguish them from catchments and WMAs. This can be achieved by defining what an SWSA is and then making provision for their formal designation by way of publication of notices and associated maps in the *Government Gazette*.[158] Given that SWSAs are of strategic national significance, perhaps the authority to declare these areas should vest in the national Minister of Water and Sanitation. The NWA should perhaps also preclude the reduction of the size of SWSAs except by way of formal amendment by the Minister.

Provisions on water source management that contextualise SWSAs within the catchments that they fall into and that enable the adoption of rules to regulate these areas need to be developed, similar to the management rules for special areas adopted in New South Wales. Area-based management is no new concept in South African environmental law.[159] However, it needs to be translated into water-focussed area-based measures. Just as New South Wales declares special areas through its Water NSW Act (2014) and controls them through regulations and management plans, so should South Africa declare SWSA through the NWA, ensuring that it similarly provides the necessary regime to manage and control activities undertaken in these areas once designated. Furthermore, given that the land potentially falling into SWSAs may span state-owned and privately-held land, the NWA should ideally provide for the designation of both forms of land tenure as SWSAs.

3.2.2 Objectives

The current objectives of the NWA are to ensure that: [160]

> the nation's water resources are protected, used, developed, conserved, managed and controlled in ways which take into account [the following] factors:
>
> (a) meeting the basic human needs of present and future generations;
>
> (b) promoting equitable access to water;

---

158 Ideally, the definition should not be scientific but rather descriptive so as to provide clarity to any lay person as to the specific types of geographical areas that are ring-fenced as SWSAs.

159 Section 24 of NEMA.

160 Section 2 of the NWA.

(c) redressing the results of past racial and gender discrimination;

(d) promoting the efficient, sustainable and beneficial use of water in the public interest;

(e) facilitating social and economic development;

(f) providing for growing demand for water use;

(g) protecting aquatic and associated ecosystems and their biological diversity;

(h) reducing and preventing pollution and degradation of water resources;

(i) meeting international obligations;

(j) promoting dam safety;

(k) managing floods and droughts.

As is, these objectives are well crafted and well suited for SWSA protection, except in so far as they still require slight revision to reflect the needs and aims specifically relevant to area-based protection measures.

3.2.3 Regulating activities and developments within declared areas

Should the NWA equip the Minister with authority to declare SWSAs, it is recommended that provision should also be made to regulate all threatening activities within SWSAs. The latter could be achieved through the identification of threatening activities in the NWA itself;[161] by cross-referencing the already identified activities in the 2014 NEMA EIA Regulations Listing Notices to make them applicable to SWSAs declared under the NWA;[162] or by providing the Minister of Water and Sanitation with regulatory powers to identify activities that may not commence within SWSAs except if they meet a certain standard. The last of these approaches is strongly encouraged in that it can be specifically tailored to suit SWSAs and the threats posed to them. It is suggested that the standard constitute a 'golden rule' similar or identical to New South Wales' NorBE requirement. The standard should be briefly described within the NWA itself for legal backing, and fleshed out if necessary in appropriate policies and guidelines. The standard would ideally need to be defined and be capable of measurement so as to enable authorities to implement reporting and monitoring requirements. In this way, similar to New South Wales, South Africa would be in a position to apply a single, clear and practical rule to all applications made for the commencement of identified activities within SWSAs through the NWA, its regulations and policy documents.

161 The amendment of an Act is a far slower and more burdensome process to undertake, should there be a need to amend these identified activities over time.

162 Given that the NWA is a specific environmental management Act listed under the NEMA, it would be relatively easy to make all listed activities applicable in SWSAs too. This would result in the commencement of such activities in SWSAs requiring environmental authorisation from the Minister of Environmental Affairs.

4 Conclusion

The need for robust legal protection of South Africa's SWSA goes without saying. The NWA seems to be an obvious home for the potential regulation, conservation and management of the country's SWSAs. It would be constitutionally sensible as the mandate to realise everyone's right of access to sufficient water[163] is that of the Minister of Water and Sanitation "as the public trustee of the nation's water resources".[164] However, as seen above, the NWA currently focuses on protecting water as a 'resource' without extending its application to protecting the 'source' from where the resource originates. It currently presents very limited mechanisms to do this but current legislative reform being undertaken in the water sector seems to provide an opportune moment for SWSAs to finally receive much-desired attention.

The objectives for protecting SWSAs can easily be formulated by tweaking the current objectives prescribed in the NWA so as to widen their scope to area-based measures. The desired legal provisions would, as an initial step, require a workable definition for 'strategic water source areas', which would give a broad, general description of the area's features and characteristics (without being too prescriptive, bearing in mind the evolving nature of science). These areas would need to be formally declared under the NWA, based on the purpose and objectives thereof. An identification of threatening activities would need to be clearly spelt out, preferably in a set of regulations. Regulatory mechanisms for these activities would need to be developed in such a way that they ensure flexibility as each SWSA may have its own unique characteristics and features; and face different threats to varying degrees. A proactive approach is also critical to deal with both current and future activities within SWSAs. By setting out a standard in the NWA (together with a detailed policy on this standard) that must be met before allowing any identified activity to commence within an SWSA, government authorities (and prospective applicants) would be placed in a position where they would know from the outset that activities are *prima facie* prohibited, except if proven to have met the golden standard.

Without ensuring that the country's 'headwaters' are protected against threats, the South African government's countless attempts to otherwise ensure water security and water supply seem futile. Building more dams and managing demand will not provide South Africans with more water if SWSAs are not providing those dams with the necessary water to meet the increasing demand.

163 Section 27(1)(b) of the Constitution of the Republic of South Africa, 1996.
164 Section 3(1) of the NWA.

References

Alluvium Consulting Australia (2017) *2016 Audit of the Sydney Drinking Water Catchment*, at <https://www.parliament.nsw.gov.au/lc/papers/DBAssets/tabledpaper/WebAttachments/71475/Sydney%20Catchment%20Audit%20Vol%201.pdf> (accessed 23-5-2018).

Arendse, N (2017) "Damning new report reveals Department of Water and Sanitation in crisis" *Moneyweb*, at <https://www.moneyweb.co.za/moneyweb-radio/damning-new-report-reveals-dws-in-crisis/> (accessed 10-5-2018).

Argent, R (2017) *Australia – state of the environment 2016: inland water*, at <https://soe.environment.gov.au/sites/g/files/net806/f/soe2016-inlandwater-final-web-v2.pdf?v=1495087097> (accessed 21-5-2018).

Bischoff-Mattson, Z & AH Lynch (2017) "Integrative governance of environmental water in Australia's Murray-Darling Basin: evolving challenges and emerging pathways" 60(1) *Environmental Management* 41-56.

Centre for Environmental Rights (2016) *Zero hour: poor governance of mining and the violation of environmental rights in Mpumalanga*, at <https://cer.org.za/wp-content/uploads/2016/06/Zero-Hour-May-2016.pdf> (accessed 23-6-2016).

Davies, T (2015) "Mining – coming to a protected area near you" *GroundUp*, at <https://www.groundup.org.za/article/mining-coming-protected-area-near-you_3094/> (accessed 15-5-2018).

Department of Water Affairs (2013) *National water resource strategy* 2nd Ed.

Department of Water and Sanitation (2017) *Annual report (2016/17).*

Fisher, D (2009) *The law and governance of water resources.*

Fraser, J (2017) "New report slams water department" *The Messenger*, at <http://www.themessenger.global/2017/11/28/new-report-slams-water-department/> (accessed 10-5-2018).

Glazewski, J (2014) "Water law and the environment" in J Glazewski & L du Toit (eds) *Environmental law in South Africa.*

Godden, L (2005) "Water law reform in Australia and South Africa: sustainability, efficiency and social justice" 17(2) *Journal of Environmental Law* 181-205.

Le Maitre, DC, H Seyler, M Holland, L Smith-Adao, JA Nel, A Maherry & K Witthüser (2018) *Identification, delineation and importance of the strategic water source areas of South Africa, Lesotho and Swaziland for surface water and groundwater. Final integrated report on project K5/2431.*

Lindsay, J & S Supski (2017) "Changing household water consumption practices after drought in three Australian cities" 84 *Geoforum* 51-58.

Loch, A & D Adamson (2015) "Drought and the rebound effect: a Murray-Darling Basin example" 79(3) *Natural Hazards* 1429-1449.

Makhowana, S (2017) "Drinking water quality deteriorates: Report" *IOL News*, at <https://www.iol.co.za/dailynews/drinking-water-quality-deteriorates-report-12192516> (accessed 10-5-2018).

Matthews, C (2017) "Water and sanitation department in a mess, says report" *Business Day*, at <https://www.businesslive.co.za/bd/national/2017-11-28-water-and-sanitation-department-in-a-mess-says-report/> (accessed 10-5-2018).

Murray Darling Basin Authority (2014) *The Murray-Darling Basin: Australia's largest and most diverse river system.*

Nel, JL, DC Le Maitre, DJ Roux, C Colvin, JS Smith, LB Smith-Adao, A Maherry & N Sitas (2017) “Strategic water source areas for urban water security: making the connection between protecting ecosystems and benefiting from their services” 28 *Ecosystem Services* 251-259.

Nel JL, KM Murray, A Maherry, CP Petersen, DJ Roux, A Driver, L Hill, H van Deventer, N Funke, ER Swartz, LB Smith-Adao, N Mbona, L Downsborough & S Nienaber (2011) T*echnical report for the national freshwater ecosystem priority areas project.*

NSW Government (2015) “NSW Gas Plan PEL Buy Back Scheme” *Media Release*, at https://www.resourcesandenergy.nsw.gov.au/__data/assets/pdf_file/0005/534830/NSW-Gas-Plan.pdf> (accessed 24-5-2018).

Paterson, A (2014a) “Biodiversity, genetic modification and the law” in J Glazewski & L du Toit (eds) *Environmental law in South Africa.*

Paterson, A (2014b) “Protected areas” in J Glazewski & L du Toit (eds) *Environmental law in South Africa.*

Rabie, A & C Burgers (1997) “The Mountain Catchment Areas Act and its implementation” 12(2) *SA Public Law* 351-371.

South African Water Caucus (undated) *Report on the state of the Department of Water and Sanitation*, at <http://www.emg.org.za/images/downloads/water_cl_ch/SAWC_State-of-DWS-Report.pdf> (accessed 20-3-2018).

Sydney Catchment Authority (2015) *Neutral or beneficial effect on water quality assessment guideline*

Thompson, H (2006) *Water law.*

Validakis, V (2013) “CSG work banned from water catchment areas” *Australian Mining*, at <https://www.australianmining.com.au/news/csg-work-banned-from-water-catchment-areas/> (accessed 24-5-2018).

van Dijk, AIJM, HE Beck, RS Crosbie, RAM de Jeu, YY Liu, GM Podger, B Timbal & NR Viney (2013) “The millennium drought in Southeast Australia (2001-2009): natural and human causes and implications for water resources, ecosystems, economy, and society” 49 *Water Resources Research* 1040-1057.

Water NSW and Office of Environment and Heritage (2015) S*pecial areas strategic plan of management*, at <https://www.waternsw.com.au/__data/assets/pdf_file/0020/71093/Special-Areas-Strategic-Plan-of-Management-2015_v7-Final_single_pages.pdf> (accessed 9-12-2017).

WWF-SA / World Wide Fund for Nature-South Africa (2013) *An introduction to South Africa's water source areas: the 8% land area that provides 50% of our surface water.*

WWF-SA / World Wide Fund for Nature-South Africa (2013) *Defining South Africa's water source areas.*

WWF-SA / World Wide Fund for Nature-South Africa (2017) *Decision to allow coal mining in Mabola protected environment of deep concern*, at <http://www.wwf.org.za/?20201/Coal-mining-in-Mabola-Protected-Environment-of-concern> (accessed 15-5-2018).

Chapter 22: Institutional and legal challenges to realising clean and safe water for all in Uganda

Phiona Muhwezi Mpanga

1 Introduction

Water resources are one of the key natural resources slated to drive Uganda's economic progress from a least developed economy to middle-income status.[1] In the country, water is important for a variety of uses: domestic, production, hydropower generation, and transport, among others. Uganda is not a water scarce country. It has both trans-boundary and internal water sources. The country's rivers and lakes, including wetlands, cover about 18% of the total surface area of the country.[2] Uganda receives ample rainfall, which also enhances available water sources.[3] The country's most significant hydrological features include Lake Victoria and the River Nile.[4] Nearly all of Uganda lies within the River Nile basin which charts its course through eleven African countries, many of which are water scarce.[5] Despite the fact that water is readily available, the realisation of the human right to water and sanitation has not been achieved, particularly for the most vulnerable sectors of the population. At the same time, Uganda has not escaped the effects of climate change, which threatens its freshwater resources. Within this context, it is appropriate to interrogate Uganda's institutional and legal framework of relevance to the provision of water and sanitation services in order to identify the opportunities and challenges that impede the realisation of the right to water and sanitation.

This chapter critiques the institutional framework governing water distribution, identifying the challenges, opportunities and prerequisites for establishing a sustainable water delivery system. It argues that while existing institutions have enhanced

---

1 Government of Uganda (2016: 4).

2 According to the Uganda Water Supply Atlas 2017, the country comprises a total area of 241,550 km^2, of which 41,028 km^2 are covered by fresh water bodies, permanent and seasonal swamps. See Government of Uganda (2017a).

3 See <http://www.nationsencyclopedia.com/Africa/Uganda-CLIMATE.html> (accessed 17-5-2018).

4 See <http://countrystudies.us/uganda/18.htm.> (accessed 17-5-2018).

5 The river Nile basin area is shared by Burundi, Rwanda, Tanzania, DRC, Uganda, South Sudan, Sudan, Ethiopia, Eritrea, Kenya and Egypt.

access to water and sanitation services, on the whole, there remains a deficit of unserved citizens. This may be due to the fragmentation of institutions and institutional mandates. It is argued that a radical shift from the operative legal and administrative mechanisms that are influenced by neoliberalism, to a more human rights-based system, would facilitate and meaningfully improve water and sanitation delivery to Ugandan citizens. The chapter attempts to draw linkages between the human rights and environmental discourse in order to identify impediments to achieving SDG 6 in Uganda, which calls for clean water and sanitation for all people by 2030.

2 The human right to water and sanitation

The human right to water is defined as the "right of everyone to sufficient, safe, physically accessible and affordable water for personal and domestic uses".[6] These constitute the five key elements of the human right to water and establish specific legal obligations for states parties to the International Covenant on Economic, Social and Cultural Rights (ICESCR). According to the United Nations Committee on Economic and Social Cultural Rights (UNCESCR), the right to water also includes freedoms and entitlements. The freedom pertains to the autonomy of access to water supply; and entitlement relates to water supply and management that provides the equality of opportunity for people to enjoy the right to water.[7]

Access to sufficient water is likely to pose a challenge to many individuals because of the high demand for water for production. It is clear that most industrial undertakings require huge amounts of water. For a developing country that hopes to hasten industrial development, it is of concern that ultimately, the demand for water for domestic consumption particularly for vulnerable citizens, will remain unmet.

Similarly, access to water of a quality that is safe for consumption remains a challenge when water sources are frequently flooded with sewage, chemical substances and radiological hazards contaminating the water available for domestic use.[8] Research indicates that changes in groundwater levels substantially change the quality of water and changes in weather patterns have a negative impact on the quality of water delivered to citizens within the context of the World Health Organization's standards of quality.[9] For instance, where long droughts have exhausted water resources, even where the infrastructure exists, it becomes difficult for a government to meet its obligation to deliver water to its citizens. In such instances, the right to physical access to

6 General Comment 15, para. 2; and General Comment 14 para. 15.
7 General Comment 15, para. 10.
8 United Nations (2010: 3).
9 Bates (2008: 2).

water services is inadvertently at risk due to the effects of climate change.[10] Further extreme weather events such as flash floods damage water infrastructure set up along rivers and lakes, posing a threat to the affordability of water services in many areas.[11] The rise and fall of groundwater levels threaten the acceptability of water services delivered to citizens as it makes the colour and taste of water unacceptable to its intended users.[12]

Conversely, the enjoyment of a right to water and sanitation envisages a role for the state, which has obligations to respect, protect and fulfil the human rights of its citizens, including the right to water under international law. First, the right to water demands that states respect the right to water by refraining from acts that would cause unlawful pollution or contamination of water.[13] Within this context, a state must take measures to ensure that access to water is not interfered with or denied unjustly.

Secondly, the obligation to protect the human right to water and sanitation enjoins state parties to adopt necessary and effective legislative measures to restrain third parties, including individuals, groups, corporations and their agents from inequitably dealing with water resources.[14] Within this context, states must avert acts of third party water operators that are likely to compromise equality, affordability and physical accessibility of sufficient safe and acceptable water, by establishing an effective national regulatory system. Such a system should ideally include institutions that provide independent monitoring, a framework for genuine public participation and potential penalties for non-compliance on the part of water suppliers.[15]

The obligation to fulfil the right to water and sanitation entails facilitating, promoting and providing water.[16] Access to information is an important aspect of the obligation to fulfil the right to water. To satisfy the requirement of accessibility of water resources, the state ought to enhance access to information.[17] This entails ensuring that citizens are able to seek and receive information useful to enable them to make informed choices about water services. Conversely, the state ought to take steps to impart information concerning water issues to citizens.

---

10 For instance, see <http://theugandan.com.ug/exceptionally-dry-river-rwizi-leads-mbarara-water-warnings-nwsc/> (accessed 17-5-2018).

11 United Nations (2010: 3).

12 Ibid: 4.

13 Also refer to General Comment 14, para. 34; Bourquain (2008: 141-142); General Comment 15 para. 21; Mwebaza (2009); and Twinomugisha (2009).

14 General Comment 15, para. 23

15 General Comment 15, para. 24. Also see General Comment 14, para. 35 on the right to health which describes the obligation to protect to include equal access to health-related services provided by third parties. Bourquain (2008: 148).

16 General Comment 15, para. 25; and General Comment 14, para. 37.

17 General Comment 15, para. 12(c)(iv).

3 An overview of the legislative and institutional framework pertaining to water and sanitation services in Uganda

Within the context of governance and the institutional framework, water and sanitation is a shared responsibility of the central government and local government. The local government is based on the district as the main administrative unit. The Constitution of the Republic of Uganda, 1995 (1995 Constitution) stipulates that:[18]

> ...the system of local government in Uganda shall be based on the district as a unit under which there shall be such local governments and administrative units as Parliament may by law provide.

Article 189 of the 1995 Constitution stipulates that the functions of the central government and other functions and services not specified in the sixth schedule are the responsibility of local governments; local district councils are mandated to execute water and sanitation services functions. To enable the functioning of local governments, the 1995 Constitution further provides that the applicable principles to the local government system shall include appropriate measures to enable local government units to plan, initiate and execute policies in respect of matters falling within their jurisdiction.[19]

In the exercise of its constitutional powers, the Parliament of Uganda is required to make laws on any matter for the development and good governance of the country.[20] Objective XIV of the National Objectives and Directive Principles of State Policy (NODPSP) stipulates that:[21]

> The State shall endeavour to fulfil the fundamental rights of all Ugandans to social justice and economic development and shall in particular, ensure that –
>
> ...
>
> All Ugandans enjoy rights and opportunities and access to education, health services, clean and safe water, work, decent shelter, adequate clothing, food, security and pension and retirement benefits.

Objective XXI further stipulates that the state shall take all practical measures to promote a good water management system at all levels.[22] Article 8A of the 1995 Constitution envisages that the state shall fulfil its obligations by enacting laws to give effect to the rights enumerated in the NODPSP. The bill of rights in the 1995 Constitution explicitly guarantees a right to a clean and healthy environment to all citizens.

There are three primary laws that directly impact on water delivery, supply and sanitation. These are the Water Act (and its attendant regulations), the National Water and Sewerage Corporation Act (NWSC Act) and the National Environment Act (NEA), all

18 Article 176(1) of the Constitution of Uganda, 1995.
19 Article 176(2)(e) of the Constitution of Uganda, 1995.
20 Article 79(1) of the Constitution of Uganda, 1995.
21 1995 Constitution.
22 Ibid.

of which were promulgated in 1995.[23] The Water Act, the NWSC Act and the NEA were promulgated pursuant to the 1995 Constitution, and as part of broader environmental protection reforms.

Two considerations provide an important background to the motivation behind these water and environmental law reforms. One is that prior to the enactment of these laws, principles regulating water resources and water delivery were scattered in several outdated and inadequate laws.[24] The new legislation sought to harmonise the water regime bringing water resource management under one comprehansive law. Secondly, the state had ratified the Ramsar Convention relating to the protection of wetlands, but there was no domestic law protecting wetlands.[25] Given the emphasis on environmental rights within the NODPSP and the main body of the 1995 Constitution, it would seem that at the time of promulgating the Constitution, its drafters were more intent on articulating principles for the protection and management of the environment.[26] The above neither underscored strengthening the water management institutions as a vehicle for improving water and sanitation services delivery within an inclusive model, nor did they envision propagating a rights-based approach to water delivery. Given that the constitutional protection of socio-economic rights typically enhances their enforcement by other State institutions, the failure to explicitly spell out the nature and scope of a right to water and sanitation within the 1995 Constitution was reflected in subsequent statutes enacted by Parliament, after its promulgation.[27] Four examples are provided below to demonstrate this.

First, the conceptualisation of water and sanitation services within Uganda's water regime remains problematic. The term 'water' is defined by the Water Act as including:[28]

- (i) Water flowing or situated upon the surface of any land;
- (ii) Water flowing or contained in-
  - (A) Any river, stream, watercourse or other natural course for water;
  - (B) Any lake, pan, swamp, marsh or spring, whether or not it has been altered or artificially improved;
- (iii) Ground water;
- (iv) Such other water as the Ministry may from time to time declare to be water.

As a result, water that is subject to the Water Act regulatory framework appears to be slightly different from that conceptualised within the context of international human

23 The Water Act (Chapter 152, Laws of Uganda) and the NWSC Act (Chapter 317, Laws of Uganda) were promulgated in 1995. The former commenced in 1997 and the latter in 1995.

24 Water service delivery was governed by NWSC Decree, 34 of 1972. Water management was governed through Public Lands Act 1969 and Rivers Act, Chapter 357, 1907.

25 Uganda acceded to the Ramsar Convention in March 1988.

26 At about the same time that the Water Act and NWSC Act were promulgated, Parliament also promulgated the NEA (Chapter 153, Laws of Uganda) in 1995.

27 Mpanga (2015: 164).

28 Section 1 of the Water Act.

rights law, the UNCESCR's General Comment 15 and SDG 6. In the author's view, while this definition suits an understanding of water resources within the environmental law context of conservation and management, it does not aptly contemplate 'water' within the context of a right to access clean and safe water for domestic use. As mentioned above, it is important to conceptualise water rights within the dual context of environmental and human rights law.

Historically, access to water, particularly in rural areas and non-serviced urban areas, was based on customary practices. This meant that those within the precincts of a spring or well would simply collect water from this source without necessarily seeking permission or consent. The Water Act maintains customary rights to water.[29] To this end, it stipulates that:[30]

> ... a person may –
>
> (a) while temporarily at any place; or
>
> (b) being the occupier of or a resident on any land, where there is a natural source of water use that water for domestic use, fighting fire or irrigating a subsistence garden.

Beyond the customary right to access water, the Water Act also embraces the international law understanding of a right to water set out in the General Comment 15 and referred to earlier in this chapter. First, the Act has as one of several objectives, "to promote the provision of a clean, safe and sufficient supply of water for domestic purposes to all persons".[31]

Second, within the context of addressing rights and freedoms to water and sanitation, the Water Act stipulates that:[32]

> ... the occupier of land or resident on land may, with the approval of the authority responsible for the area, use any water under the land occupied by him or her on which he or she is resident or any land adjacent to that land.

In relation to sewerage services, the Water Act stipulates that a sewerage authority may "connect any land to its works on application by the owner or his or her agent, in a form prescribed by regulation or the authority".[33] Such an application cannot be

29 Customary rights to water refer to the traditional understanding that natural water sources on land can be impliedly accessed by any member of the community.

30 Section 7(1)(a) and (b) of the Water Act.

31 Section 4(b) of the Water Act. Under the definition contained in Section (1), 'domestic use' includes, use for the purpose of human consumption, washing and cooking by persons ordinarily resident on the land where the use occurs; watering not more than 30 livestock units; irrigating a subsistence garden; and watering a subsistence fish pond.

32 Section 7(2) of the Water Act. Domestic use is defined in Section 1(1) of the Water Act in substantially the same manner as General Comment 15. It includes purposes of human consumption, washing and cooking by persons ordinarily resident on the land where the use occurs; watering not more than 30 livestock units; irrigating a subsistence garden; and watering a subsistence pond.

33 Section 63(3)(b) of the Water Act.

unreasonably rejected. Where a private sewerage connection is more appropriate, the Water Act stipulates that:[34]

> (1) A person who wishes –
>
> (a) to construct a private sewer within that sewerage area; or
>
> (b) to connect a private sewer to the authority's sewer,
>
> may apply to the relevant sewerage authority in a manner prescribed by regulations or the authority.

While the Water Act goes to great lengths to promote the standards through which water can be maintained in a clean and safe state, through regulating who and how water can be abstracted, the Act does not explicitly grant citizens a right to access water services. The statutory right relating to access to sewerage services is far more explicit than any provision relating to water services.

On the other hand, when analysed through the context of state responsibility to realise the rights to water and sanitation, it would seem to fall short. The Water Act stipulates that: "All rights to investigate, control, protect and manage water in Uganda for any use is vested in the Government…".[35] Even though the content of the Water Act goes so far as to set out explicit statutory provisions relating to the respect and protection of the right. It spells out very little about the promotion and fulfilment of the right in concrete terms.

Third, it should be noted that within the context of a sound institutional framework, the legal and policy framework establishes various institutions that appear to remove power from local government.[36] Given that the constitutional provisions relate to decentralising water and sanitation service delivery, it is arguable that the establishment of these institutions may be problematic when viewed from this perspective.

The Water Act establishes several structures that are responsible for the investigation, use, control, protection, management or administration of water resources. Section 43 envisages that the minister responsible for water will exercise his or her powers and functions with regard to the objectives of the Act; any relevant international agreements regulating the use of water to which Uganda is a party, and any policy of government concerning decentralisation of powers and functions.

The Water Act elaborates the institutional framework within which water is supplied.[37] For instance, the Act envisages the creation of water supply areas delineated along local government borders. The local governments that constitute water supply areas, are required to establish water supply authorities, and it is these water supply authorities that are ultimately mandated to deliver water to households.[38] In urban

34 Section 65 of the Water Act.

35 Section 5 of the Water Act.

36 Section 16 of the NEA; Government of Uganda (2012: 4); and Nabaho (2013).

37 Sections 45-61 of the Water Act.

38 Section 45 and 46 of the Water Act. In reality this chain of supply applies to a fraction of the population, 69% in urban areas and 64% in rural areas. The rest of the population rely on

areas, the water supply authority is the NWSC, while in rural areas, the mandate is held by the local government or municipal council.[39] Umbrella organisations have also been gazetted as water authorities.[40]

The Water Act sets out the various institutions for planning and managing water resources. The Water Policy Committee established under the Act is responsible for planning for water resource management nationally. At lower levels, local governments are mandated to make plans for the delivery of water services in their respective districts. The Act also establishes water user associations and water supply and sanitation boards where water is sourced from boreholes, wells and springs or piped water schemes respectively.[41] From the foregoing, it is clear that the Water Act seeks to shift from a national to a local government based water delivery system and creates an institutional set up to support the shift.

There are several agencies that deal with the different components of water as defined above that include: the Ministry of Water and Environment as the parent agency; with the Directorate for Water Development, Water Resources Management; semi-autonomous agencies such as NWSC and the National Environment Management Agency (NEMA). In practice, management and conservation aspects have conflicted with urgent demands for water supply. It can be argued that the institutional framework does not appropriately synthesise human rights and environmental law principles through which the right to water for consumption may be universally enjoyed by citizens.

As part of the strategy to improve access, the water sector established several institutions responsible for water services, namely: the Ministry of Water and Environment units (Directorates); private water operators; six umbrella organisations; four water management zones and 15 catchment management organisations; and water and sanitation development facilities at the regional level.[42] Each of these institutions has been established to serve a specific purpose within the strategic goals prescribed by the Ministry as indicated in table 1 below. The Directorates are established to play a strategic role in the actual implementation of the programs. The umbrella organisations support the local water authorities to improve their functionality in terms of promoting the delivery of water services' ensuring the financial viability of projects and promoting the sustainability of projects.[43] The water and sanitation development facilities were established to bring services closer to the target communities and ensure

naturally existing water sources and do not benefit from the efficient quality control mechanisms available to those who access piped water supply. Government of Uganda (2013: 1 and 11).

39 Within the capital city, Kampala Capital City Authority Act mandates the institution to take responsibility for public water sources and public sanitation services.

40 *Gazette* of 14 July 2017 in Vol. CX No. 39, General Notices No. 577-582.

41 Sections 50 and 51 of the Water Act.

42 Government of Uganda (2017b).

43 Government of Uganda (2017b: 8).

equitable distribution of resources within the decentralised framework.[44] The water management zones were created to ensure that water resources are managed more broadly beyond the administrative structures since many of the water resources are shared by more than one district.[45] The catchment management organisations were designed to oversee and protect catchment areas that ultimately affect water resources.[46] Finally, the private water operators provide water delivery services at the very lowest household-level, where piped schemes have been established.[47]

Table 1: Institutions in the water and sanitation sector[48]

Institution	Number of structures	Names of structures	Institutional Mandate
Directorates within the Ministry of Water and Environment	2	Directorate of Water Resources Management. Directorate for Water Development	Managing and developing water resources of Uganda in an integrated and sustainable manner in order to provide water of adequate quantity and quality. Overall technical oversight for planning, implementing of delivery of urban, rural water and sanitation services.
Semi-autonomous agencies	2	National Water and Sewerage Corporation; National Environment Management Authority	Water supply and sanitation across the country. Coordinating, monitoring, regulating and supervising environmental management in the country.
Water & Sanitation Development Facility	4	WSDF (North), WSDF (East), WSDF (Central), WSDF (Southwest)	To bring services closer to target communities and ensure equity in the decentralising process.
Umbrella Organisations	6	Southwest, Midwest, Centre, North, East and Karamoja	Support the local water authorities/ boards to improve functionality, financial viability and sustainability of small piped water schemes.
Catchment management organisations	15		To plan and implement plans for the water management zones.

The NWSC Act established the NWSC, whose mandate is primarily water and sanitation delivery in a commercial context. The Act stipulates that the objects of the NWSC

44 Ibid.
45 Ibid.
46 Ibid: 118.
47 Ibid: 9.
48 Government of Uganda (2017b).

include the provision of water supply services for domestic and other uses.[49] The Act specifically provides that the NWSC must develop the water and sewerage systems in urban centres and big national institutions.[50] Inevitably, the NWSC operates within a limited scope of urban centres and state-owned institutions. Other provisions of the NWSC Act deal with the corporation's management, providing that it shall be managed as a commercially viable entity.[51]

The NEA establishes a framework that envisages that the National Environment Management Agency will work with districts in setting and implementing environmental goals.[52] For instance, the NEA stipulates that the local government system shall on the advice of a district environment committee, appoint local environment committees whose functions include preparing a local environment work plan, consistent with a national environmental action plan.[53]

More than twenty years after the enactment of the 1995 Constitution, the institutional setup is still not delivering and is dogged by several contradictions that impede its ability to deliver desired reforms. On the one hand, decentralisation is endorsed; while on the other, a centralised approach is promoted. Consequently, it is plausible to argue that the institutionalised exclusion of citizens identified within Uganda's pre-1995 constitutional dispensation continues to inadvertently surface through the multitude of institutions that have varied mandates.[54]

One consequence of varied institutional mandates within the same sector relates to the cost of water and sanitation services. While the individual's autonomy to access water services through the NWSC is guaranteed, the use of water derived from the water authorities' supply infrastructure attracts charges/fees for service provision.[55] Such charges have implications. First, the NWSC is allowed by law to index its water

49 Section 5(2)(b)(i) of the NWSC Act.

50 Section 5(2)(d) of the NWSC Act.

51 The NWSC has several institutional guidelines relating to the manner in which water supply will be managed. Some of these relate to water quality standards and a customer service charter. But these are non-enforceable standards which do not further a possibility for citizens to vindicate claims for a human right to water.

52 Section 14 of the NEA.

53 Section 14 and 16(2) of the NEA.

54 Prior to 1962, the NWSC served a few towns, which were predominantly occupied by Europeans and Asians.

55 See Section 32 of the Water Act. Fees charged to consumers of water services include: 1) monthly service charges; and 2) in case of disconnection, reconnection fees. See further Section 94 of the Water Act that enables the authority to fix rates and charges for the services it provides. Regulation 28(1), Water Supply Regulations 1999, determines that charges are payable within a period of 14 days from the date of receipt of notice. Charges may be assessed on the basis of quantity of water supplied, or any other manner approved by the Minister. According to Section 94(4) of the Water Act, a water authority is authorised to establish the minimum charges to be paid for water supplied, and the charges to be paid per unit of water supplied, albeit with the prior approval of the Minister. See further Section 5(2)(b) of the NWSC Act, that mandates the NWSC to set tariffs and charges.

service rates to prevailing market prices. For instance, the Water Act (General Rates) Instrument determines that the rates payable are subject to annual indexation against the domestic price index, the exchange rate, the foreign price index and the electricity tariff.[56] It is arguable that, even where water authorities set out to price water at an affordable rate, such annual indexation would negate affordability if it is accepted that other determining factors of the water price consistently rise sharply annually.[57] Moreover, in other instances, the poor pay more for water services.[58] The Ministry of Water and Environment's annual sector report[59] highlights this challenge noting that an average tariff charged by private service providers was three times higher than the tariff charged for household connections.[60]

In semi-urban and rural areas, the nature of water use is distinct and covers multiple uses. Besides water requirements for basic human consumption and sanitation, many individuals need water for both livestock and crop farming. In many parts of Uganda, subsistence agriculture is practised. This means that the volume of water consumed may be much higher than those consumed in a typical urban household. Indeed, most rural households rely on the springs, wells, boreholes, valley dams and water harvesting from water bodies as a source of water for their livestock and crop farming. [61] Subsequently, the matter of fees and their negative impact on the affordability of water appears to determine how far out of the urban setting the NWSC can extend its network. It is clearly difficult to extend the piped water supply system to areas where the community cannot afford the service, and would rather rely on natural sources.

While it must be acknowledged that some amount of control and regulation is required to manage and supply water services, the provisions in the NWSC Act appear to identify the collection of revenue and avoidance of loss, as the core functions of the institution. This approach is manifestly neo-liberal. While the NWSC has been planning to realise the goal of delivering water to all by 2040, it may face challenges because of its institutional structure and mandate. The mandate of the NWSC does not entirely lend itself to a rights-based approach to water and sanitation services' delivery needed for the realisation of the SDGs by 2040. This means that the ministry responsible for water must also continue to take on a larger role in supporting service delivery for rural-based consumers.

---

56 Regulation 3 of the Water Act (General Rates) Instrument, Statutory Instrument No. 30 of 2006.

57 In an interview with the NWSC-Kampala Water Legal Services Manager in September 2013, the author learned that at that time, the NWSC paid Uganda shillings 2 billion (equivalent to US $750,000) each month towards electricity charges for supplying water within Kampala alone (The interview transcript is on file with author).

58 As of 2016, the average tariff at a public stand pipe of Ug.shs. 150/= per 20 litre container was three times higher than the tariff at household connections. Government of Uganda (2017b: 177).

59 Government of Uganda (2017b: 177).

60 Ibid.

61 Ibid: 6.

When the provisions of the Water Act and the NWSC Act are considered together, the conclusion is that the legal and institutional frameworks are presently inadequate to deliver water to all by 2040. To date, citizens still rely on self-help mechanisms to access water. Sometimes, rainwater is harvested during the rainy seasons and stored in large quantities; boreholes may be used; or an individual with a standing tap may sell water at a small premium.[62] In some urban areas, mobile water trucks may sell water to locals, or a local entrepreneur may collect water from a spring and traverse the neighbourhood selling jerry cans from a bicycle. While these provide some relief to citizens, the methods appear unsustainable. At the district level, the local governments have been given conditional grants to develop water and sanitation facilities within each district. Due to the demand for water supply services, many of these are still being spent on developing and maintaining infrastructure within the towns and rural growth centres.

In addition, the trend seems to have shifted from a devolved to a more centralised system. Even though the 1995 Constitution envisaged devolving powers to local authorities, studies show that twenty years after the promulgation of the 1995 Constitution, local governments are still weak and lack the skills and know-how to effectively plan and execute suitable water and sanitation service delivery programs.[63] As a result, the NWSC's proven success has led to an arrangement where local water and sanitation services are handed over to the NWSC for efficient management when they reach optimum capacity. With the growth of more towns, it remains to be seen whether the institutional advantages of a post-privatisation NWSC will be replicated at a larger scale if it takes over all the existing 111 local government supply schemes. The limitations of scaling up include inefficiency. Therefore, while it may present an example of a success story, the challenges of inefficiency that affect reliable access to water and sanitation services, may foster future tensions.

4 The underlying challenges related to poverty

Poverty is another enduring problem that affects the context in which water is delivered in Uganda. 70.3% of Uganda's population was reported to be multi-dimensionally poor in 2016.[64] As in other developing countries where water is scarce, women and

62 The cost of tapping large amounts of rainwater still remain prohibitively high because of the high cost of safe reservoirs. For example to be able to set up a rain water harvesting system and store 40,000 litres of water in a plastic and easy to clean tank may cost up to USD 2,000.

63 Government of Uganda (2012: 3).

64 According to the 2016 Human Development Indicators profile for Uganda, the country ranked below the trends in sub-Saharan Africa. The indicators provide a composite measure of three dimensions: health, education and income. Uganda's HDI was 0.493, ranking 163 out of 187 countries with comparable data. In comparison the HDI of sub-Saharan Africa was 0.497.

children in Uganda are burdened with collecting water. A large percentage of the population still spend significant amounts of their productive time walking long distances to collect water.[65] To compound this, owing to the long distances travelled, even the water collected may end up contaminated due to unhygienic water handling and storage practices.[66] This implies that there are still many citizens who need support in enhancing their enjoyment of the right to good quality water and whose social context ought to be taken into account when planning and implementing water delivery programs.

The development of water and sewerage infrastructure is a costly investment and is therefore categorised as an infrastructure project rather than as a social service. Funding for water and sewerage infrastructure development is therefore an essential determinant in how the state approaches water delivery services. In Uganda's case, water infrastructure has been funded through the World Bank, IFC, the European Union, DANIDA, the Austrian government and the African Development Bank, among others. Most of the funding is in the form of long-term development loans and grants.[67] Where the funding is a loan, it has to be repaid, and a business case has to be made in order to acquire the loan. For instance, there must be an indication of the demand for the water services, which will eventually begin to pay off the loan. Where grants are given, there must be an indication of demand and willingness to pay for the services so that the grant facility is put to optimum use. Yet the majority of citizens who lack access to water and sanitation services are poor and unable to pay consistently for water services.

The governance system at the local authority level is weak and unable to mobilise revenues efficiently for the services. Even where the central government subsidises local governments to support infrastructure development, funding to the entire water and environment sector remains low, at 3% of the national budget, even as the population and its needs increase.[68]

While the state has made progress in enhancing access to water supply from an economic perspective, the underlying problems surrounding substantive enjoyment of the human right to water remain.[69] Given that the poorest and most vulnerable may be

---

Sourced from <http://hdr.undp.org/sites/all/themes/hdr_theme/country-notes/UGA.pdf> (accessed 23-3-2018).

65 Government of Uganda, *Sector Performance Report* (2017b:3) 70% of citizens in rural parts of the country walk at least one kilometre to reach an improved water source. This implies that about 30% may walk a longer distance.

66 United Nations (2006: 61).

67 Government of Uganda (2017b: 26).

68 Government of Uganda (2016: 7 and 28).

69 Over the last 20 years, Uganda moved from implementing a Poverty Eradication Action Plan (PEAP I and PEAP II), which was intended to provide a framework for national planning; to a National Development Plan (NDP I and presently II). While the country is essentially still struggling to alleviate poverty, the NDP provides a more comprehensive agenda covering all areas likely to impede development.

unable to compete for water in circumstances of scarcity, it seems that the state's initiatives may perpetuate the inequity existing in water delivery models. It would therefore seem that while Uganda does not suffer from water scarcity, the enjoyment of access to water is impeded by the weak water governance regime. This raises the question of whether approaching water delivery issues from a human rights paradigm may lead to a better enjoyment of water services by the entire population.

5 Opportunities: towards an environment and human rights-based approach to water and sanitation delivery

The notion that rights are a tool for social transformation is viewed with cynicism in some circles.[70] It has, for instance, been argued that law, by design, protects and entrenches the interests of the few who have or control resources. Some have argued that the conceptualisation of human needs within the human rights framework only serves to legitimise the interests of the wealthy and effectively to maintain the status quo, given that there are often laws through which the poor are excluded from enjoying access to basic needs.[71] Moreover, it has been argued that through the liberties that come along with rights' recognition, a rights framework prevents the redistribution of resources in any manner that would likely improve the social status of the poor and vulnerable.[72] In short, the argument is that law serves the interests of those with power, and therefore the human rights model cannot improve the lived realities of the poor and vulnerable.

But these arguments have been countered and have mostly been found to be erroneous. Scholars arguing for the application of a rights-based approach within the domestic context advance the view that a rights-based approach empowers those who are poor and vulnerable to secure their freedom and entitlement to enjoy certain rights through direct claims made against the state.[73] Within the context of access to water services, it is increasingly accepted that a rights-based approach can inform decisions in the climate change context.[74] The approaches that have been recognised as being rights-based include participation, accountability, non-discrimination and equality, empowerment and legality. In 2015, the Ministry of Water and Environment undertook to incorporate a human right to water and sanitation among the indicators against which its performance should be measured.[75]

70 Tushnet (1984: 1363).
71 Ibid.
72 Ibid. See also Pieterse (2007).
73 O'Connell (2012: 4).
74 United Nations (2010: 3).
75 Government of Uganda (2017b: 6).

During the course of 2013, the Ministry of Water and Environment initiated proposals for broad reforms to the country's water legislation. Although these proposals are yet to be implemented, it is clear that the need for reform is acknowledged. The proposals for reform have been motivated by the need to incorporate many of the developments in water resource management and water delivery that have taken place over the past 14 years. Since these proposals have not come into force, they are not yet applicable within the legal regime governing water.[76] Nonetheless, two significant proposals should be mentioned, namely the draft National Water Policy[77] and the draft Water (Amendment) Bill.[78]

The draft National Water Policy proposes six guiding principles for reformulating the domestic water supply policy. These are: to prioritise protection of the environment; to enhance participation of women in water service delivery; to strengthen communities to implement and sustain water and sanitation programs; to enhance financial viability of public utilities; and to ensure the allocation of public funds for water supply development activities in a manner that prioritises those segments of the population who are presently inadequately served or not served at all.[79] The draft Policy appears to have considered a re-conceptualisation of water delivery in a manner that incorporates the human right to water and its implications for domestic water supply.

Within the draft Water (Amendment) Bill, the significant proposal is to extend the right to access water to include a clause to the effect that residents are entitled to access water through the use of rainwater harvesting techniques, such that an owner or occupier of land may construct any works for rainwater harvesting or for the recycling of used water for domestic purposes without having to seek approval or a permit from the water authority.[80] While this may elaborate on an entitlement to use water, it also raises some challenges. An individualistic approach may subsequently affect water reservoirs in the wetlands and rivers where such rainwater would naturally drain into. This would ultimately reduce available shared water resources.

Whereas these proposals for reform are welcome, it appears that they will change little in terms of the substantive enjoyment of a human right to water and sanitation, to the extent that the scope of the right remains vague and the obligations attaching to the State for realising the right are absent. The proposals do not go far enough to articulate an enforceable right to water and sanitation.

In a nutshell, water delivery for most citizens in Uganda is effected by self-help mechanisms, with minimal state intervention, both within urban and rural areas. The

76 This information arose from a personal communication with an official with the Ministry of Water and Environment. Important to note is that neighbouring states such as Kenya (2016) and Tanzania (2009) have amended the relevant Water services legislation.

77 Proposed National Water Policy (draft of July 2013) 1, 29. On file with author.

78 Proposed Water (Amendment) Bill, Section 7A (draft of June 2013). On file with author.

79 Proposed National Water Policy (draft of July 2013) 1, 29. On file with author.

80 Proposed Water (Amendment) Bill, Section 7A (draft of June 2013). On file with author.

term self-help implies that individuals take responsibility to ensure that water is available for their households. In many instances, citizens still depend on customary riparian rights to share water resources and their own geographic knowledge of the city or rural area to determine where and how to reach water resources and the use to which water should be put. As noted above, rainwater is harvested during the rainy seasons or boreholes are used when they are functional. For others, the state water supply system may reach their homes or schools to supply water at a charge. This shows that the majority of water delivery arrangements are unregulated and operate outside the national policy and legislative framework governing the use and distribution of water. It is therefore necessary to work towards a policy and legislative framework that applies to the majority of citizens.

In addition to these legislative proposals, experts in water resource management have encouraged a transition towards integrated water resources management.[81] This would mean that the process of formulating and implementing management strategies for sustainable water resources development takes into consideration various dimensions and temporal interdependencies among natural processes and human and ecological water uses. This means that the knowledge required to protect and sustain these water resources would be drawn from various disciplines, including various disciplines within the law itself. This could bridge the gap between the law and practice.

Under the framework for integrated catchment-based water resource management, Uganda presently has five water management zones located in the central, eastern, western, northern and southern parts of the country. It aims to ensure that water extraction from catchment areas is coordinated to serve the surrounding areas.

Water user groups and associations, which are provided for within the Water Act, are a formidable mode of enhancing meaningful participation. The Water Act stipulates that: "A set of individuals or households may form a water user group and collectively plan and manage the point source water supply system in their area".[82] In 2017, the Ministry of Water and Environment's Sector Performance Report[83] indicated that 88% of rural areas and 72% of urban areas had actively functioning water and sanitation committees. The Sector Performance Report also indicated that many of these committees had included women in their membership. A 2014 study on the performance of water user associations, carried out by an independent organisation, found that water user associations performed poorly on administrative and accountability mechanisms, operation and maintenance.[84] While the government's study indicates progress, the benefits of public participation in decision making within the realms of

81 Government of Uganda (2017b: 14).

82 Section 50(1) of the Water Act.

83 Government of Uganda (2017b: 162).

84 See <https://www.ircwash.org/sites/default/files/2014_10_ts-uganda-pb_assessment_service_delivery_models.pdf> (accessed 6-5-2018).

environmental law and human rights may not have been adequately realised within the context of water and sanitation delivery institutions.

6 Conclusion

This chapter set out to critically explore the impact of the legislative and institutional frameworks on water and sanitation delivery within Uganda. It argues that the legislative and institutional frameworks significantly set the tone for the conceptualisation of water and sanitation as a commercial service rather than as both a human right and a natural resource. The chapter demonstrates that the legislation predominantly focuses on the preservation of water resources and provides little ground for realising a human right to water and sanitation as envisaged within international law and the general comments of the UNCESCR. Uganda has not harmonised the two frameworks.

Notably, the legislative framework creates a myriad of institutions but has not allowed for the strengthening of local governments to plan and execute water and sanitation delivery in a sustainable manner. The local governments consequently remain weak and unable to fulfil and promote a human rights-based approach to water and sanitation service delivery. While the current government statistics relating to the coverage of clean and safe water and sanitation are impressive, this has remained led by the central government. Actual access to water and sanitation services remains impeded by legislative requirements and a corporate institutional framework that venerates payment and enhancing revenues. For the more impoverished communities, the situation is dire as their demands for water cannot be met due to the costs of accessing water. The institutional limitations will continue to impede efforts to reach the SDG Goal 6 – to provide clean and safe water to all by 2030. There is a need for more meaningful public participation, decentralisation and catchment-based approaches that enhance water and sanitation services for Uganda's citizens.

References

Bates, BC, ZW Kundzewicz, S Wu & JP Palutikof (2008) *Climate change and water* Technical Paper VI, International Panel on Climate Change.

Bourquain, K (2008) *Fresh water access from a human rights perspective*.

Government of Uganda (2012) *Draft national local government capacity building policy*.

Government of Uganda (2013) *Joint water and environment sector strategic plan final programme document (2013-2018)*.

Government of Uganda (2016) *The national development plan 2016/17-2021/22*.

Government of Uganda (2017a) *Water supply atlas*, at <http://mwe.go.ug/index.php?option=com_docman&task=cat_view&gid=59&Itemid=55> (accessed 10-1-2015).

Government of Uganda (2017b) *Uganda water and environment sector performance report*.

Mpanga, MP (2015) *Conceptualising, realising and enforcing a human right to water for Uganda: comparative perspectives* PhD thesis, University of the Witwatersrand.

Mwebaza, R (2009) "Climate change and the international human rights framework in Africa" in R Mwebaza & LJ Kotzé (eds) *Environmental governance and climate change in Africa: legal perspectives* 227-261.

Nabaho, L (2013) "Recentralization of local government chief administrative officers appointments in Uganda: implications for downward accountability" *Commonwealth Journal of Local Governance* 17-29.

Twinomugisha, B (2009) "Implications of climate change for the right to health in Uganda" in R Mwebaza & LJ Kotzé (eds) *Environmental governance and climate change in Africa: legal perspectives* 267-268.

O'Connell, P (2012) *Vindicating socio-economic rights international standards and comparative experiences.*

Pieterse, M (2007) "Eating socioeconomic rights: the usefulness of rights talk in alleviating social hardship revisited" 29(3) *Human Rights Quarterly* 796-822.

Tushnet, M (1984) "An essay on rights" 62(8) *Texas Law Review* 1363-1403.

United Nations (2010) *Climate change and the human rights to water and sanitation*, at <http://www2.ohchr.org/english/issues/water/iexpert/docs/ClimateChange_HRtWS.pdf> (accessed: 15-3-2018).

United Nations (2006) *2nd World water development report.*

Chapter 23: The conflict between privatisation and the realisation of the right to water in Kenya

Nerima Akinyi Were

1 Introduction and background

In 2009, figures released by the World Bank indicated that there was an estimated 42%-59% of nationally piped water coverage in Kenya.[1] These figures, which remain the most recent estimates, are supported by Water Sector Strategic Plan[2], which indicates that water coverage in rural areas is estimated at 40% and in urban areas at 60%. These figures show that millions of Kenyans have inadequate water supply.[3] Within urban areas, informal settlements have proven difficult to reach in terms of water supply and in rural areas women and girls are most affected, as they have to spend disproportionate amounts of time and travel long distances to fetch water at the expense of other activities including school.[4] 2010 figures comparing poor and non-poor households in Kenya's major cities (Nairobi, Mombasa and Kisumu) revealed that a minimum of 30% of poor households were forced to rely on small-scale water providers[5] for water, while a maximum of 32% of non-poor households were in the same position.[6] There is also significant water deprivation with 57% of low-income households surveyed consuming less than the water poverty line of 20 litres per capita per day and about 62% of households spending above their affordability threshold on water.[7]

The inadequacy of water access in Kenya goes beyond the government's laxity in water provision. The major cities are poorly planned and populations exceed the capacity of the cities. Even with this consideration in mind, one must note the fairly low estimates of piped water coverage. However, piped water is not the only source of water. In August 2011, the Guardian[8] reported that, in 2007, the Water and Sanitation

---

1 Uwazi InfoShop (undated).
2 Government of Kenya (2010).
3 Water and Sanitation Programme (undated: 8); and Government of Kenya (2009).
4 Government of Kenya (2010).
5 There are different types of small scale water providers these are tap water vendors, water kiosks (a kiosk is a small usually makeshift shop), borehole water vendors, pushcart vendors and tanker trucks.
6 Uwazi InfoShop (undated).
7 UNDP (2011).
8 Mugo (2011).

for the Urban Poor Project began to implement a project to help nearly 100,000 poor peri-urban dwellers in Naivasha access portable, affordable, accessible and reliable drinking water. This project resulted in certain consumers reliant on kiosks paying Ksh. 50 per cubic meter of water, a Ksh. 200 reduction from previous prices. An encouraging drop at the time but an indictment to the plight of many people because the cost of water remains high in a country where more than 58% of the population lives on less than 2 dollars (USD) per day.

However, it is encouraging to note that there have been significant investments in water resource management and water services. The state, through the Ministry of Water, almost tripled the budget spent on water infrastructure from Kshs.6.9 billion in 2004/2005 to Kshs. 18.6 billion in 2008/2009.[9]

2 The privatisation of access to water or water services in Kenya

This chapter explores the privatisation of water in Kenya and begins by defining privatisation and contextualising it in Kenya. Privatisation has been defined as:[10]

> the entire process of expanding the sphere of the market through a host of regulations that create an enabling environment for free enterprise to operate as a strategy for sustainable economic development.

Kenya's water policy after independence was founded on the country's landmark post-colonial nation-building and socio-economic development blueprint, Sessional Paper No. 10 on African Socialism and its Application to Kenya (1965), which emphasised political equality, social justice and human dignity.[11] Its principles were grounded on state control of the economy, defining the state as the entity that implements social and economic programmes to address historical and social inequalities. The logical consequence of this was that the government delivered basic services including water and health at no cost and other actors were minimally involved in service delivery.[12]

While alleviating poverty through the provision of safe drinking water formed part of the political agenda, the government's ambitious target to provide water freely for all was not realised. Water service provision coverage remained low in the years after independence.[13] Issues identified to explain this shortfall included lack of cost-efficient recovery mechanisms and operation and maintenance systems, and the government's failure to renew existing systems leading to many becoming non-operational.[14] In seeking to deal with these shortfalls, the responsibility for water service provision

9 Uwazi InfoShop (undated).
10 Moyo & Kinuthia-Njenga (1998: 6).
11 Government of Kenya (1965).
12 Notley et al. (2010).
13 Ibid: 16.
14 Ibid.

shifted from the state, and a call was made to individuals to take on the mandate to help themselves. This was followed initial by increased investment through donor funding and thereafter privatisation ensued.

The state's inability to deliver on Sessional Paper No. 10 became apparent with growing disillusionment among government actors from the mid-1970s and the early 1980s.[15] The government used *Harambee* (the spirit of pooling resources together) as a vehicle for the country's social and economic development.[16] Communities and individuals were encouraged to consider their role in service provision and urged to help themselves.[17] *Harambee* was used to shift the control of water resources, including the implementation of development projects, to local communities with minimum input and control from the state.[18] While the policy was well intended, it achieved little in the water sector due to limited financial resources, lack of skilled human resources and limited investment in new projects.[19]

The development of the National Water Master Plan in 1974 signalled a shift in the proposal for the development of water supply and sanitation, with the underlying goal of providing water for all by 2000. Development partners worked with the government to implement the plan, which resulted in water service coverage growing rapidly in many provinces as a result of large regional or provincial projects being supported by donor partners.[20] While coverage rapidly increased, there were glaring weaknesses in the model. The most notable one was sustainability. The large projects were donor driven and had the dual effect of undermined the state's role in service provision, particularly at the local level. This reduced political buy-in and ownership of the projects within the government, which had deteriorated by the time their management was handed over and could therefore not meet the needs of the project.[21]

The decade between the mid-80s and the mid-90s marked a shift in the provision of water services in Kenya. Relying on the liberal state ideology, the World Bank and the International Monetary Fund strongly marketed the limitation and undesirability of the state's role in the provision of basic services and provided both loans and aid conditions to support a shift along these lines.[22] The role of the state was continuously redefined with strong arguments for limitating the role of the state in service provision. The role of the state was to be facilitative and was relegated to the creation of an enabling environment for free market operations.[23] Other services, such as healthcare, were also affected by the introduction of user fees for both inpatient and outpatient

15 Ibid.
16 Ogendi & Ong'oa (2009: 186).
17 Notley et al. (2010).
18 Ogendi & Ong'oa (2009: 186).
19 Swallow et al. (2003).
20 Notley et al. (2010: 16); and Mwega (2009).
21 Notley et al. (2010: 16).
22 Chuma & Okungu (2011).
23 Jaglin (2002: 232); and Wambua (2004: 4-7).

services at health facilities. Patients were required to subsidise healthcare service financing to address budgetary constraints within the government.[24]

Liberal policies were introduced through the Fourth Kenya National Development Plan (1979-1983), which made provision for greater reliance on markets and for improved efficiency of the public sector.[25] Detailed policy reforms came with the Sessional Paper No. 1 on Economic Management for Renewed Growth.[26] This set up the framework for liberalisation of markets by introducing cost sharing for public services; reducing human resources in public service through retrenchments; selling state firms (parastatals) and privatising some government functions; removing price and import controls that protected agricultural enterprise; and removing some government subsidies and budget allocations away from social programmes.[27]

In 1988, the National Water Conservation and Pipeline Corporation was established.[28] Its primary objective was to commercialise water sector operations and achieve financial autonomy in water operations. In 1992, the state conducted a Delineation Study of the Water and Sanitation Sector in Kenya, which strongly recommended institutional reforms for the water sector, highlighting the inefficacies in the existing system, particularly the slow shift to business like operation, inefficient service production and the low-cost recovery within the sector.[29]

During the early 1990s, the political atmosphere in Kenya was stagnant, a trend that continued in varying degrees until the end of the Moi regime despite the developments and changes in policy and institutional arrangements. Notably, water and sanitation services in Kenya remained inadequate, and though coverage grew rapidly in the early 1990s, it slowed as the decade progressed and came to a standstill.[30] Coverage figures stayed level or even declined after this period.[31]

The Water Act (2002) is perhaps the first law to set a framework for both the privatisation and commodification of water coherently, and to set the legislative framework for the shift of water from a public good to a commodity.[32] The Water Act (2002) separated the management of water resources, the supply of water and the provision of water services.[33] The Water Resource Management Authority was established to regulate water resources, and the Water Services Regulatory Board was established to

24 Chuma & Okungu (2011).
25 Government of Kenya (1979). See also K'Akumu & Appida (2006: 317).
26 Government of Kenya (1986).
27 Ibid.
28 It was established under the State Corporations Act, Chapter 446 of the Laws of Kenya through Legal Notice No. 270 of 24 June 1988.
29 Government of Kenya (1992).
30 Notley et al. 2010: 19).
31 Ibid: 16. See also K'Akumu & Appida (2006: 315).
32 Water Act No. 8 of 2002.
33 Shurie et al. (2017: 6).

regulate the supply of water.[34] Section 113(1) of the Water Act (2002) provided the legislative authority for the transfer of the management and operation of water services to the Water Services Boards, shifting water services to water service providers regulated by Water Services Boards.

While the framework of the Water Act (2002) provided the legislative environment for shifting water service provision from the state to private hands, Section 57(5)(d) of the Act highlighted the shift to commodification and commercialisation of water services. This Section provided the following requirement for licensees for water services:

> …the application shall not be granted unless the Regulatory Board is satisfied that … the applicant, or any water service provider by whom the functions authorized by the licence are to be performed will provide the water services authorized by the licence on a commercial basis and in accordance with sound business principles.

Licensing was thus required for the commercial provision of water, which had to be in accordance with sound business principles. Water was, as a consequence, to be treated as a commodity that had to be supplied in a profitable enterprise. The commodification and privatisation of water services illustrate the failure to treat water as a human right, particularly because in this instance, there is a legislative requirement to supply water on a commercial basis by non-state parties.

The Water Act (2016)[35] replaced the Water Act (2002). It recognises that water is a human right and that every person in Kenya has the right to clean and safe water in adequate quantities and to reasonable standards of sanitation.[36] The Water Act (2016), like its predecessor, separates the management of water resources from the supply of water services. It also takes cognisance of the devolution of water services in line with the provisions of the Constitution of Kenya (2010) which creates two levels of government: national and county governments. Under the Constitution, functions have been apportioned to both government levels and in the case of water; water services' provision is the function of county governments.[37] Water resource management and trans-county issues, such as pollution and the protection of water resources, are functions of the national governments.[38]

The Water Act (2016) establishes Water Services Development Boards, which are mandated to provide water services as water service providers until the operation, and management of waterworks is transferred to county governments.[39] Section 86(5)(e) of the Water Act (2016) almost mirrors Section 57(5)(e) of the Water Act (2002) and requires that water services be provided on a commercial basis in accordance with

34 Ibid.
35 Water Act No. 43 (2016).
36 Section 63 of the Water Act 2016.
37 Kameri-Mbote & Kariuki (2015: 108).
38 Ibid.
39 Section 68(b) of the Water Act (2016).

sound business principles. Additionally, Section 88(a) requires an applicant seeking to be a Water Services Provider to provide evidence that water services shall be provided on a commercial basis. Another provision speaking to commercialisation is Section 96 of the Water Act (2016) that requires the prescribed area for water services provision shall not be less than the area required for commercial viability. The Act goes even further in Section 97:

> Where it appears necessary to the Regulatory Board, for the purpose of securing a commercially viable water service, it may, by notice in the Gazette, order a joint provision of water services or a transfer of water service and vary the relevant licenses accordingly.

While the Water Act (2002) also required water to be provided on a commercial basis, this was only mentioned once in the Act. In the Water Act 2016, however, commercial viability is a running theme and seems to form one of the determinants for the provision of water services as it is emphasised throughout the Act and plays a more prominent role than it did in 2002. Further, and this is also a criticism of the Water Act (2002), commercial viability or commercial basis are not defined.[40] However, what is apparent is that the Water Services Regulatory Board, in terms of the Water Act (2016), is required to provide standards of commercial viability, which county governments are required to adhere to.[41]

There is a positive shift in the Water Act (2016) besides the concern with commercial viability as a worrying running theme. Section 94(1) of the Act states that: "Nothing in this Act shall deprive any person or community of water services on the grounds only that provision of such services is not commercially viable". The Act goes further and establishes a Water Services Sector Trust Fund, which has a number of objectives including the provision of conditional and unconditional grants to assist in the financing of the development and management of water services in marginalised areas.[42]

The Water Act (2016) specifically highlights rural areas, which have been historically disadvantaged on the provision of water services, and requires that county governments put in place measures to provide water services in rural areas not considered to be commercially viable.[43] This may ameliorate the harsh impact of the focus on commercial viability. It is worth noting that one of the objectives of the Water Services Sector Trust Fund is to provide financing for the development of water services in rural areas and under-served poor urban areas.[44]

In a nutshell, the Water Act (2016) has shifted from the approach of its predecessor: firstly, by recognising that water is a human right; secondly by taking into account historic injustices in the provision of water services; thirdly by making provision for

---

40 K'Akumu (2004: 217).
41 Section 77(2) of the Water Act (2016).
42 Section 114 of the Water Act (2016).
43 Section 94(2) of the Water Act (2016).
44 Section 114(b) and (c) of the Water Act (2016).

the devolution of water services; and finally, by promoting commercial viability as a basic requirement for the provision of water services.

3 Normative framework for the right to water

3.1 International framework for the right to water

The human right to water and sanitation has gone through a process of evolution from implicit responsibility, to explicit obligation and to an independent right.[45] While the right to water and sanitation is not explicitly mentioned in the International Covenant on Economic Social and Cultural Rights (ICESCR),[46] it has been recognised by the Committee on Economic, Social and Cultural Rights (the Committee) through General Comment No. 15: The Right to Water (Articles 11 and 12 of the Covenant).[47] The Committee relied on Articles 11 and 12 of the ICESCR on the right to adequate standard of living including adequate food, clothing and housing and the right to the highest attainable standard of health respectively. The Committee opines that the right to water is inextricably linked to these rights given that it is one of the most fundamental conditions for survival.[48]

The right to water has also been recognised in other international instruments. Article 14 of the Convention for the Elimination of All forms of Discrimination Against Women recognises that women have the right to enjoy adequate living conditions particularly in relation to water supply. Article 24 in paragraph 2 of the Convention for the Rights of the Child also places a positive obligation on states to combat disease and malnutrition through the provision of adequate nutritious foods and clean drinking water. Additionally, Article 28 paragraph 2 of the Convention on the Rights of Persons with Disabilities requires that persons with disabilities have an adequate standard of living and social protection, which includes an obligation on the state to ensure equal access by persons with disabilities to clean water services. It is worth noting that due to the nature of these conventions, they only apply to specific segments of the population. This underscores the importance of General Comment No. 15, which covers all persons.

In 2010, the United Nations General Assembly declared safe and clean drinking water and sanitation a human right under international law[49] by adopting a Resolution

45 Gupta et al. (2010: 294).

46 Wekesa (2013: 3). While General Comments are not binding they do have persuasive authority and give states guidance as to the normative content of the rights enshrined in relevant instruments. See Blake (2008).

47 CESCR (2003: 4). See Tully (2005: 35) for a critical analysis of General Comment No. 15.

48 CESCR (2003: paras 3 and 4).

49 UNGA Resolution: 64/292 of 28 July 2010.

on the Human Right to Water and Sanitation. Water and sanitation were thus recognised as a singular, composite, independent right obliging states to ensure the provision of water and sanitation. The Resolution recognises both water and sanitation as a human right essential for the full enjoyment of life and all human rights and calls upon states to provide resources to scale up efforts to provide safe, clean, accessible and affordable drinking water and sanitation for all.

General Comment No. 15 elaborates the normative content of the right to water noting that it must be adequate for human dignity, life and health.[50] Adequacy, the Committee notes should not be interpreted narrowly and further, water should be treated as a social and cultural good and not primarily as an economic good.[51] The Committee further notes that while adequacy of water may vary as dictated by circumstances, water must be available, accessible and meet a certain quality (that is, be safe) in all circumstances.[52]

What is noteworthy in contextualising the right to water and sanitation internationally, is that the UN Resolution makes reference to clean and safe drinking water while General Comment No. 15 is broader. The latter provides that this right applies to personal and domestic use which includes drinking, personal sanitation, washing clothes, food preparation, personal and household hygiene.[53] This is a much broader scope of what the right to water entails than what the General Assembly committed to in 2010.

3.2 The African human rights system

The African Charter on Human and Peoples' Rights (the Charter) makes no mention of the right to water in the way other international instruments do. The African Charter on the Rights and Welfare of the Child (Child's Charter), however, recognises that state parties have an obligation to provide safe drinking water for children.[54] This is not a stand-alone right but a component of the child's right to health as guaranteed in Article 14 of the Child's Charter. While the right to water is included in this Charter, its ambit is limited in that it only guarantees safe drinking water (does not recognise other water needs) for children and only within the context of their right to health. Similarly, the African Protocol on Rights of Women in Africa (Maputo Protocol), through Article 15, recognises the state's obligation to provide women with access to

50 CESCR (2003: para. 11).
51 Ibid.
52 Ibid: para. 12.
53 Ibid: para. 11.
54 Article 14(2)(c) of the African Charter on the Rights and Welfare of the Child.

clean drinking water as a component of women's rights to nutrition and adequate food.[55]

The human right to water has been recognised in the African human rights system primarily due to the judicial innovation of the African Commission on Human and Peoples' Rights (The Commission).[56] The Commission has 'read in' the right to water by purposively interpreting the scope of other rights and including water as a subset of these rights. In *Free Legal Assistance Group and Others v. Zaire*,[57] the Commission found that the State's failure to provide safe drinking water constituted a violation of the right to health. Similarly, and more expansively, in the landmark case of *Social and Economic Rights Action Centre (SERAC) & Another v. Nigeria*,[58] the Commission held that the contamination of sources of drinking water was a violation of the right to health and the right to a satisfactory environment as guaranteed in the Charter.

Until 2015, the Commission treated the right to water as an auxiliary right subject to the protection of more explicit rights, being hesitant to explicitly recognise water as a right and shying away when invited to do so.[59] Thus while water was not recognised as an independent right in the African human rights system, the Commission has taken cognisance of the fact that rights such as health, housing and dignity cannot be realised without adequate access to water.[60] However, in 2015, the Commission adopted a resolution on the Right to Water Obligations, which urges member states to meet their obligations to provide clean drinking water for all their populations.[61] The resolution makes reference to a number of obligations on states including the obligation to guarantee the justiciability of the right to water and to build the capacity of populations in human rights education including the right to water. However, while this Resolution shows the development of the right to water, it does fall short of recognising water as an independent right.

---

55 See Hellum et al. (2015: 32) for a robust discussion of the recognition of the right to water in the Maputo Protocol and CEDAW.

56 Bulto (2017: 344).

57 ACHPR: *Free Legal Assistance Group and Others v. Zaire* 4 April 1996 ACHPR 25/89-47/90-56/91-100/93 para. 47.

58 ACHPR: *Free Legal Assistance Group and Others v. Zaire* 4 April 1996 ACHPR 25/89-47/90-56/91-100/93 paras 49, 50-54, 57 & 66.

59 In ACHPR: *Sudan Human Rights Organisation & Another v. Sudan* 27 May 2009 279/03-296/05 despite an emphatic request that the Commission recognises the independent right to water, it failed to do so without reasons.

60 Bulto (2017: 344).

61 ACHPR Resolution 300 (EST.OS/XVII) of 25 February 2015.

3.3 The Kenyan framework for the right to water

Article 2(6) of the Constitution of Kenya (2010) provides that any treaty or convention ratified by Kenya shall form part of the law of Kenya. Kenya has acceded to the ICESCR, [62] the Convention of the Elimination of all Forms of Discrimination Against Women,[63] the Convention for the Rights of the Child[64] and the Convention on the Rights of Persons with Disabilities.[65] The provisions combined in these instruments form part of Kenyan law.

Article 43(1) of the Constitution of Kenya (2010) provides that "every person has the right to clean and safe water in adequate quantities". This is understood within the context of the state's obligation to respect, protect, promote and fulfil the rights enshrined in the Bill of Rights.[66] Further, there is an obligation imposed on the state to take legislative, policy and other measures, including the setting of standards, to achieve the progressive realisation of the right to water.[67] The state has both negative and positive obligations to ensure that the right to water is realised. The state is at the very least required to desist from preventing and impairing the right to water while positively, the state is required to provide a legislative and policy framework for the right, achieve the progressive realisation of the right and do so within available resources.[68]

The obligation to fulfil the right to water requires that appropriate legislative, administrative, budgetary, judicial and other measures be undertaken to ensure the full realisation of the right.[69] The Kenya National Commission on Human Rights (KNCHR) has pointed out measures necessary for the realisation of the right to water in Kenya. It recommends the adoption of a national water policy that prioritises water management for essential personal and domestic use; identifies resources available to meet the obligation to fulfil the right to water; specifies cost-effective ways to use the resources; and outlines the responsibilities and timeframes for the realisation of this right.[70] Essentially, the KNCHR advocates for a rights-based approach to water that prioritises domestic use and avails resources necessary for the realisation of this right in an equitable, non-discriminatory and inclusive manner.[71]

62 Acceded to on 1 May 1972.
63 Acceded to on 9 March 1984.
64 Ratified on 30 July 1990.
65 Ratified on 18 May 2008.
66 Article 21(1) of the Constitution of Kenya (2010).
67 Article 21(2) of the Constitution of Kenya (2010).
68 Wekesa (2013).
69 Kenya National Commission on Human Rights (2017).
70 Ibid.
71 Ibid.

3.3.1 Normative context of Article 43(1)(d)

Three issues are primarily underscored in Article 43(1)(d) which guarantees the right to water. Firstly, everyone has the right to "clean and safe water", which refers to the quality of water provided. General Comment No. 15 can serve as guidance in this regard as it states that water must be free from microorganisms, chemical substances and radiological hazards that constitute a threat to a person's health.[72] However, it does remain a matter of legislative or policy directive for the state to determine what clean and safe water means in the context of Kenya. It may be sufficient for the state to adopt international standards but this is a question that is commonly determined in legal systems by balancing exposure-based health assessments with economic cost-benefit analyses.[73]

Secondly, Article 43(1)(d) makes reference to water in adequate quantities. This, of course, begs the question of what would constitute adequate quantities of water. General Comment No. 15 makes reference to the World Health Organisation Guidelines on "Domestic water quantity, service level and health: what should be the goal for water and health sectors", which provide for minimum water requirements but allows for flexibility. The Committee insists that states do not interpret adequacy narrowly with reference to volumetric quantities, but also to consider the social and cultural context of water. Additionally, the Kenya National Commission on Human Rights discusses adequacy and notes that this connotes:[74]

> … continuous supply of an amount sufficient for drinking, food preparation, personal and household hygiene and washing. Basic access is defined as 20 litres per person per day, while 50-100 litres per person per day is needed to maintain a basic level of health 7.5 litres per person per day will provide sufficient water for survival needs.

Thirdly, and inevitably, for the right to water to be realised it must be both accessible and available. Availability refers to a continuous and sufficient water supply for personal and domestic use.[75] Accessibility requires that water, water facilities and services are accessible to everyone without discrimination.[76] According to the Committee, accessibility has four overlapping dimensions: physical accessibility; economic accessibility; non-discrimination; and information accessibility.[77]

72 General Comment No. 15 makes reference to WHO (1993).
73 Wekesa (2013: 3).
74 Kenya National Commission on Human Rights (2017).
75 CESCR (2003: para. 12).
76 Ibid.
77 Ibid.

3.3.2 Progressive realisation

Article 21(2) of the Constitution of Kenya (2010) states that the state shall take legislative, policy and other measures, including the setting of standards, to achieve the progressive realisation of the rights guaranteed under Article 43. What is progressive realisation? How does one define it? How is it quantified? How can citizens hold the state accountable?

The Committee, in General Comment No. 3: The Nature of the State Parties' Obligations, unpacks this term as follows:[78]

> The concept of progressive realization constitutes a recognition of the fact that full realization of all economic, social and cultural rights will generally not be able to be achieved in a short period of time…Nevertheless, the fact that realization over time, or in other words progressively, is foreseen under the Covenant should not be misinterpreted as depriving the obligation of all meaningful content. It is on the one hand a necessary flexibility device, reflecting the realities of the real world and the difficulties involved for any country in ensuring full realization of economic, social and cultural rights. On the other hand, the phrase must be read in the light of the overall objective, indeed the raison d'etre, of the Covenant, which is to establish clear obligations for States parties in respect of the full realization of the rights in question. It thus imposes an obligation to move as expeditiously and effectively as possible towards that goal. Moreover, any deliberately retrogressive measures in that regard would require the most careful consideration and would need to be fully justified by reference to the totality of the rights provided for in the Covenant and in the context of the full use of the maximum available.

In *Mitubell Welfare Society v. The Attorney General & 2 Others*[79] the court held that:

> The argument that socio-economic rights cannot be claimed at this point two years after the promulgation of the Constitution ignores the fact that no provisions of the Constitution is intended to wait until the state feels it is ready to meet its constitutional obligations. Article 21 and 43 require that there should be "progressive realization" of socio-economic rights, implying that the state must be seen to be taking steps, and I must add be seen to take steps towards realization of these rights.

The Constitution of Kenya (2010) recognises that with limited resources some rights may not be immediately achieved in their entirety. However, that should not be interpreted in a manner that leads to the deprivation of the right. This has been recognised by the CESCR and the High Court of Kenya. The challenge does not lie in understanding that the steps must be taken; it lies in quantifying whether or not the steps taken are adequate. The Constitution of Kenya (2010) goes a step further in Article 20(5)(a) providing that:

> In applying any right under Article 43, if the State claims that it does not have the resources to implement the right, a court, tribunal or other authority shall be guided by the following principles – it is the responsibility of the State to show that the resources are not available.

Therefore, the burden of proof is on the state to provide evidence that resources are not available to provide adequate quantities of clean and safe water. A measure of

---

78 CESCR (1990).

79 High Court of Kenya *Mitubell Welfare Society v. The Attorney General & 2 Others* Petition No. 164 of 2011.

progressive realisation was noted by the Constitutional Court of South Africa in *Mazibuko and Others v. the City of Johannesburg and Others*[80] which held that this concept recognises that "policies formulated by the State will have to be reviewed and revised to ensure that social economic rights are progressively being achieved". While this may serve as a meaningful marker, the Constitutional Court did not go further to explore what the revisions entail and if such revisions translated to increased access to water. Thus, a more meaningful interrogation of both the continued revision of policy and legislation and the increased access to water within the resources available may result in a more meaningful assessment of steps taken by the state.

3.3.3 Jurisprudence on the right to water

Since the Constitution of Kenya (2010) was promulgated, two significant cases on the right to water have been adjudicated on. In seeking to contextualise these cases, it must be noted that both cases were founded on evictions and thus a number of violations alleged primarily related to the right to accessible and adequate housing.[81]

The first case is that of *Ibrahim Sangor Osman v. Minister of State for Provincial Administration and State Security*[82] where government officials evicted 1,123 persons from their land to make way for constructing a road. The petitioners had occupied the land since the 1940s and were forcefully evicted without notice through a violent process using tear gas and bulldozers. The petitioners were rendered homeless and forced to live in makeshift structures or in the open, and thus were exposed to the elements of nature, health risks and could not access basic necessities like food, water and sanitation. Another result was that several children were forced to drop out of school and elderly members of the community endured unbearable conditions.

The court in coming to its conclusion relied on ICESCR, the Universal Declaration on Human Rights and the International Covenant on Civil and Political Rights. The court found that the purpose of recognising and protecting rights and fundamental freedoms is to preserve the dignity of individuals and communities.[83] Furthermore, the court in reference to the women, children and elderly persons affected by the eviction, found that the state had an obligation to address the needs of vulnerable persons in the society.[84] The court found that the fundamental rights of the petitioners had been violated, including the right to water.

---

80 Constitutional Court of South Africa *Mazibuko and Others v. the City of Johannesburg and Others* 2010 (4) SA 1 (CC).

81 This is guaranteed in Article 43(1)(b) of the Constitution of Kenya (2010).

82 High Court of Kenya *Ibrahim Sangor Osman v. Minister of State for Provincial Administration and State Security* Petition No. 2 of 2011.

83 Ibid: 7.

84 Ibid: 11.

While this court found a violation of the right to water, this was an inevitable consequence of finding that the right to access adequate housing had been violated by the brutal eviction and displacement of an entire community. The court did not meaningfully dissect the right to water, but the decision has jurisprudential value in establishing the inextricable link between the right to water and other rights including housing, health and food.

The second case discussed, *Satrose Ayuma & 11 Others v. The Registered Trustees of the Kenya Railways Staff Retirement Benefits Scheme* (the *Muthurwa* case),[85] is more significant for its deliberation than for its finding. While the court found that the right to water was not violated, it provided an incisive discussion on the right to water in similar circumstances, namely where petitioners had been evicted from their homes.

Justice Lenaola looked at the normative context of the right to water and considered General Comment No. 15 and rulings from the African Commission on Human and Peoples' Rights that found that state failure to provide basic services such as drinking water constituted a violation of the right to the highest attainable standard of health.[86] Justice Lenaola recognised that Kenyans are in a fortunate position because the right to water is recognised in the Constitution of Kenya (2010), thereby avoiding the gaps in the international normative framework are avoided.[87] He did, however, note that the mere recognition of the right is not sufficient to ameliorate the plight of those without access to water.[88]

Justice Lenaola's rather grim view on the violation of this right is explained in the judgment as follows:[89]

> ... all Kenyan Municipalities are obliged to manage and operate water services on business and corporate lines and must embrace the full cost of recovery in the provision of water services. The Nairobi Water and Sewage company falls under this category and it is supposed to operate the provisions of water as a business and it ought to make profits, such that the failure of the Petitioners and other persons to pay for the water they have consumed to the tune of Kshs.13 Million necessarily called for disconnection. I will say something about the water bill later in this Judgment but the water supply system as I understand it, demands for payment of a fee to access water. The Petitioners cannot fail to pay for that supply and now be heard to complain about their denial of water when somehow they accepted for the years that they have been tenants that it is their contractual obligation to pay for consumption of water.

---

85 High Court of Kenya *Satrose Ayuma & 11 Others v. The Registered Trustees of the Kenya Railways Staff Retirement Benefits Scheme* Petition No. 65 of 2010. See also East African Centre for Human Rights (undated 8-9 and 33-34) on the horizontal application of the Bill of Rights and for an analysis of the *Muthurwa* case.

86 ACHPR *Free Legal Assistance Group and Others v. Zaire* 4 April 1996 ACHPR 25/89-47/90-56/91-100/93; ACHPR: *Sudan Human Rights Organisation & Another v. Sudan* 27 May 2009 279/03-296/05; and ACHPR: *Minority Rights and Minority Rights Group International (on Behalf of Endorois Welfare Council) v. Kenya* 25 November 2009 276/03.

87 High Court of Kenya *Satrose Ayuma & 11 Others v. The Registered Trustees of the Kenya Railways Staff Retirement Benefits Scheme* Petition No. 65 of 2010 para. 96.

88 Ibid: para. 97.

89 Ibid: para. 100.

The court concluded that the existing legislative framework was problematic as it had commercialised the provision of water services, required payment for water services and allowed for disconnection from the piped water system where payment was not made. Justice Lenaola, however, went further and held that:[90]

> Suffice it to say in any event that it is time the water suppliers and the State adopts a rights based approach with regard to the provision of water services and I suggest that we should borrow a leaf from the South African water laws regime. Section 4(3)(c) of South Africa's Water Services Act states that procedures for the discontinuation of water services must not result in a person being denied access to basic water services for non-payment, where that person proves that he or she is unable to pay for such basic services. Section 4(3) of the Water Services Act further provides that procedures for the limitation or discontinuation of water must be fair and equitable and should provide for reasonable notice of intention to terminate water services and most significantly, for an opportunity to make representations. This, in my view, is what a progressive and realistic realization of social economic rights including the right to water should be.
>
> I must add that it is time that the Kenyan Water Act is amended as it was enacted 8 years before the promulgation of the Constitution, 2010 and it does not expressly provide for the right to water and there is a clear need to have it amended and brought into conformity with the present realities which include the new constitutional dispensation and the devolution of services including the provision of water by County Governments.

This critique is insightful as it provides the executive with directive steps that may be taken towards progressively realising of the right to water, particularly maintaining the provision of access to basic services for persons who are unable to pay for such services. This is a lesson from the South African context and while it is accepted that the judiciary cannot give the executive or legislature direction on policy, this may guide what progressive realisation would mean.

While the court critiqued the situation with regard to the provision of water services, it is disappointing that the court did not make a finding on the violation of the right. This is because firstly, a violation was not found and therefore the court's *dictum is* merely persuasive and not binding. Secondly, and perhaps more significantly, is the fact that the Constitution of Kenya (2010) had already been promulgated and a normative framework was available at the regional and international levels, yet the primary factor considered in making a determination was the economic value of water (illustrated by the ability to pay for services). The judgment explained its finding as based on the fact that the legislative framework favoured commercialisation. However, it remains a hard pill to swallow considering the right to water is enshrined in the Constitution of Kenya (2010) and the legislation relied on was pre-constitutional.

90 Ibid: paras 102-103.

4 Critique of privatisation as a model for delivering on human rights

One of the more ardent advocates against privatisation of water is Vandana Shiva and in her book, *Water Wars: Privatisation, Pollution and Profits*,[91] she lists nine principles underpinning water democracy. These principles are significant for understanding water and its privatisation: water is nature's gift; water is essential to life; life is interconnected through water; water must be free for sustenance needs; water is limited and can be exhausted; water must be conserved; water is a commons; no one holds a right to destroy, and water cannot be substituted.

Significant reasons for the recognition of water as a human right are highlighted – it is essential to life and a source of life for all species not just humans. Shiva's criticisms of privatisation are founded on the belief that commodification of water has and shall continue to lead to conflict.[92] She quotes Ismail Serageldin, vice president of the World Bank: "if wars of this century were fought over oil, the wars in the next century will be fought over water".[93] Shiva argues that commodification: is non-democratic and centralises the control over decision making and resources; destroys natural resources and erodes the democratic control of natural resources, means of production undermine the cultural identity; and erodes the democratic base of politics because these are hijacked by the World Bank, International Monetary Fund and other players that push the privatisation agenda.[94]

The privatisation of water services has not been coherent in Kenya and prior to 2002, there was no clear legislative framework for the privatisation of water services. However, as noted above, this is not an indication that the water supply was not privatised. Small-scale water vendors, including kiosks and pushcart vendors, have been providing water services outside of the realm of regulation with the implication that neither price nor quality is regulated. This is of course necessitated by the low water supply coverage, which creates a gap in the provision of services and places people at the mercy of vendors.

Certain criticisms were raised at the onset of systematic privatisation of water in Kenya through the Water Act (2002). While privatisation had been pushed as the only option to address public sector mismanagement, there are other options available for reform in the water sector.[95] K'Akumu argued that privatisation does not necessarily

91 Shiva (2002).

92 Ibid: 7. She notes that water wars are not a thing of the future but they already surround us although they are not always recognised as water wars.

93 Ibid.

94 Ibid: 9.

95 Renzetti & Dupont (2003: 19) note that empirical data does not unambiguously support the notion that privatisation leads to improved performance. See also studies conducted in the United States of America where there was no difference in performance between privately owned or public enterprises or where public enterprises performed better: Byrnes et al. (1986: 337); Lambert et al. (1993: 1573); and Bhattacharyya et al. (1994: 197).

provide an advantage over public enterprise and is not a precondition for efficient management.[96] Many experiences with water privatisation in low and middle-income countries have proved to be disappointing, particularly with regard to extending coverage to lower-income groups.[97] He further argued that privatisation had failed to attract private capital, reduce corruption and protect the interests of the poor.[98]

The negative effects of privatisation of water have been experienced in a number of countries such as Chile,[99] South Africa,[100] Australia,[101] Britain[102] and Argentina[103]. While the drive for privatisation of water in abovementioned countries has been systematic, initiated by the International Monetary Fund and World Bank,[104] privatisation of water supply in Kenya has been both systematic and unsystematic. In instances of unsystematic privatisation, this gap has led to a sort of entrepreneurship, which can also be described as exploitation. The overall effects of privatisation have, however, been the same as in the countries listed above and include high costs and reduced quality of water supplied.

Legislation including the Water Act (2016) recognises that water belongs to the state and is to be managed and supplied for the benefit of the people, which is a step in the right direction with regard to equity. However, the negative incidences of privatisation discussed above point to the contrary. In Kenya, privatisation does not benefit the marginalised and vulnerable groups.

Another argument against privatisation is that it shifts the state obligation for the fulfilment of a human right for its citizens to private actors, and also directly violates some basic principles particularly those that provide that water must be free for sustenance needs and that water is a common pool resource. There is a counter to this, which notes that this shift does not negate the nature of the human right because the state still has an obligation to develop a system of equity and justice to ensure that such rights are not violated.[105] Further, it has been contended that the recognition of water as a human right does not necessarily imply that the public sector has to be the provider of these services.[106] This leads to the following question: does the system for the provision of water in Kenya ensure that the right to water is not violated? The history of

96 K'Akumu (2004: 217).

97 Ibid.

98 Ibid.

99 In Chile, Suz de Lyonnaise insisted on a 35% profit for supplying water, Shiva (2002: 100).

100 In South Africa, Johannesburg's water supply was overtaken by Suez Lyonnaise des Eaux. Water soon became unsafe, inaccessible, and unaffordable. Thousands of people were disconnected and cholera infections became rampant. See Shiva (2002: 100-101).

101 Hrudey & Hrudey (2004).

102 In Britain, water and sewage bills increased 67% between 1989-90 and 1994-95. The rate at which people's services were disconnected rose by 177%. See Shiva (2002: 101).

103 Hacher (2004).

104 Ibid.

105 K'Akumu (2006: 540).

106 Budds & McGranahan (2003: 94-95).

privatisation discussed above is illustrative of an incoherent system that has failed to meaningfully consider not only the needs but the views of citizens. The drive for privatisation was mostly a reaction either to state failure to provide services or donor pressure, and thus any argument of justice and equity may be nullified by a process driven outside of the will of citizens.

A further concern is the opaque nature of the terms commercial basis and commercial viability, as used in the Water Act (2002) and the Water Act (2016). It is accepted that there are costs associated with the provision of water services. However, what remains unclear is what it means to be commercially viable and what profit margins are allowed? To what extent is water provided simply as a commodity and not a right? There is not much literature on the licensing practices of the Water Services Regulatory Board and thus it is not clear to what extent economic, commercial and other factors are considered relevant.

Significantly, what the private sector takes to be a commercially viable opportunity may differ from the criteria a state would employ when providing a public service.[107] The former may have very little to do with developmental goals for the country or a human rights-based approach to the provision of services.[108] Private service providers are likely to be guided by their investors and market conditions and it remains to be seen whether these guiding factors can translate into the realisation of a human right to water or the implementation of a rights-based approach.

It is encouraging that both the Water Act (2002) and the Water Act (2016) have tariff controls and the Water Services Regulatory Board provides Tariff Guidelines. However, these only seek to regulate water as a commodity. The other factors discussed in terms of adequacy by the CESCR; such as water being treated as a social and cultural good, are not apparent in the legislative framework.[109] Further, non-discrimination and information availability in the water services' sector are not canvassed in the legislative framework and in practice. The Water Act (2016) has made provision for addressing marginalisation and historical injustices, but there are no explicit requirements for non-discrimination in the provision of water services.

5 Conclusion and recommendations

There is a constitutional responsibility to ensure that residents have access to safe and adequate water. Firstly, Kenya needs to address the regulatory lacuna in the cities by prescribing clear standards for water supply and guidelines on allowable amounts to be charged by small-scale water services providers. Secondly, the principles of free

107 Ibid: 102.
108 Ibid.
109 See <https://wasreb.go.ke/downloads/Tariff%20guidelines.pdf> (accessed 16-12-2017).

market cannot apply to the supply of water, because water is necessary for life. Where a model of privatisation is adopted, due consideration to democratic principles of transparency, accountability and public participation must be advanced to allow communities to have a voice in water service provision. Kenya's target is to ensure that every person has access to improved water and sanitation services by 2030. For this to be realised, some hard truths on the intended and unintended consequences of privatisation and commodification have to be honestly addressed before deciding that privatisation is indeed the ideal model for the delivery of human rights.

Water is a human right and water is life. The significance of water to the continuation and development of life on earth, not just human life, cannot be underscored. However, like all other basic needs, there are cost implications in the provision of water services and these costs must be offset. However, meeting costs and making a profit are two separate concepts and privatisation and commodification, as has been discussed in this chapter, are geared towards making profit and not merely meeting the cost of service provision. This raises both moral and legal questions around the commodification of basic human rights. Is it right? Does the state maintain its obligation? To what extent can private actors be held accountable for the provision of human rights? These and many other questions must be answered, as privatisation becomes a model of choice for the provision of services.

The Constitution of Kenya (2010) provides for devolved government in Chapter 11. County governments, in order to accommodate both cultural and societal diversity associated with the use of water, can play a significant role. The framework for the transfer of water services provided to county governments is provided for under the Water Act (2016). There is a need to define commercial viability and allow county governments to develop context-specific standards of commercial viability. There is no applicable one size fits all set of standards for all counties. Similarly, tariffs should not be set nationally, but rather counties should be allowed to determine tariffs in accordance with the needs and affordability level of their constituents.

The concept of social tariffication suggested by K'Akumu, where tariffs are determined on a social rather than commercial basis, remains significant. It would ensure that low-income or poor households connected to the main water network but who cannot afford the market price have tariffs designed to alleviate this difficulty.[110] K'Akumu suggested that the social tariff be set for the first block of consumption (referring to basic needs) with the cost increasingly progressively with movement up the consumption blocks.[111] This can also be used as a conservation method because households may limit themselves to their basic needs to minimise their cost.[112]

110 K'Akumu (2004: 220).

111 Ibid.

112 Ibid.

In line with the above thinking and Justice Lenaola's decision in the *Muthurwa* case, Kenya should adopt the approach in South Africa's Water Services Act (108 of 1997) that provides that discontinuation of services shall not result in a person losing access to basic services for nonpayment where such a person can prove they are unable to pay for such basic services.[113] As already noted, water is life and therefore if one cannot afford to pay for it, that alone should not be a reason for denying the right to it. Kenya should include a similar provision in its legislation to protect the most vulnerable persons' rights to water irrespective of their economic status.

The government should develop stop-gap measures to address unintended consequences of privatisation and predatory practices of unregulated water service providers. Literature has shown that it is the poor and marginalised persons, particularly in peri-urban settlements, that fall prey to these practices and a significant portion of their income is used towards accessing a human right.[114] These stop-gap measures can be put in place while the Water Services Boards work toward increasing coverage and connecting more residents to piped water. Regulations should be developed to address unlicensed water service providers and a framework put in place for the Water Services Regulatory Board, to manage the quality and price of the services provided.

References

Bhattacharyya, A, E Parker & K Raffiee (1994) "An examination of the effect of ownership on the relative efficiency of public and private water utilities" 70(2) *Land Economics* 197-209.

Blake, C (2008) *Normative instruments on international human rights law: locating the general comment* Centre for Human Rights and Global Justice Working Paper No. 17.

Byrnes, P, S Grosskopf & K Hayes (1986) "Efficiency and ownership: further evidence" 68(2) *Review of Economics and Statistics* 337-341.

Budds, J & G McGranahan (2003) "Are the debates on water privatization missing the point? Experiences from Africa, Asia and Latin America" 15(2) *Environment & Urbanization* 87-114.

Bulto, TS (2017) "The human right to water in the corpus and jurisprudence of the African human rights system" 11(2) *African Human Rights Law Journal* 341-367.

CESCR / International Covenant on Economic, Social and Cultural Rights (1990) *General Comment No. 3: The Nature of State Parties' Obligations (Article 2, Para 1, of the Covenant)*, at <http://www.refworld.org/pdfid/4538838e10.pdf> (accessed 26-3-2018).

CESCR / International Covenant on Economic, Social and Cultural Rights (2003) *General Comment No. 15: the right to water (Articles 11 and 12 of the International Covenant on Economic, Social and Cultural Rights*, at <http://www2.ohchr.org/english/issues/water/docs/CESCR_GC_15.pdf> (accessed 15-12-2017).

---

113 Section 4(3)(c) of the Water Services Act (1997).

114 UNDP (2011). See also K'Akumu & Appida (2006: 315); and K'Akumu (2007: 534) on the exclusion of poor and marginalised communities from water services and the inevitable effect of using water services vendors.

Chuma J & Okungu V (2011) "Viewing the Kenya health system through and equity lens: implications for universal coverage" (26-05-2011) 10(22) *International Journal for Equity in Health*, at <https://equityhealthj.biomedcentral.com/articles/10.1186/1475-9276-10-22> (accessed 5-06-2017).

East African Centre for Human Rights (undated) *Compendium on economic and social rights cases under the Constitution of Kenya, 2010*, at <http://eachrights.or.ke/wp-content/uploads/2017/12/A_Compendium_On_Economic_And_Social_Rights_Cases_Under_The_Constitution_Of_Kenya_2010.pdf> (accessed 25-5-2018).

Government of Kenya (1965) *African socialism and its application to Kenya* Sessional Paper No. 10.

Government of Kenya (1979) *Fourth national development plan (1979-83)*.

Government of Kenya (1986) *Economic management for renewed growth* Sessional Paper No. 1.

Government of Kenya (1992) *Delineation study of water and sanitation sector in Kenya*.

Government of Kenya (2009) *Sector investment plan for the water and sanitation sector in Kenya*.

Government of Kenya (2010) *Water sector strategic plan (WSSP) 2009-2014*.

Gupta, J, R Ahlers & L Ahmed (2010) "The human right to water: moving towards consensus in a fragmented world" 19(3) *Review of European Community & International Environmental Law* 294-305.

Hacher, S (2004) "Argentina water privatization scheme runs dry" *Corpwatch* (26-2-2004), at <http://www.corpwatch.org/article/argentina-water-privatization-scheme-runs-dry> (accessed 11-11-2017).

Hellum, A, I Ikdahl & P Kameri-Mbote (2015) "Turning the tide: engendering the human right to water and sanitation" in A Hellum, P Kameri-Mbote & B van Koppen (eds) *Water is life: women's human rights in national and local water governance in southern and eastern Africa* 32-80.

Hrudey, EJ & SE Hrudey (2004) *Safe drinking water: lessons from recent outbreaks in affluent nations*.

Jaglin, S (2002) "The right to water versus cost of recovery: participation, urban water supply and the poor in sub Saharan Africa" 14(1) *Environment & Urbanization* 231-245.

Lambert, D, D Dichey & K Raffiee (1993) "Ownership and sources of inefficiency in the provision of water services" 29(6) *Water Resources Research* 1573-1578.

Kameri-Mbote, P & F Kariuki (2015) "Human rights, gender and water in Kenya: law, prospects and challenges" in A Hellum, P Kameri-Mbote & B van Koppen (eds) *Water is life: women's human rights in national and local water governance in southern and eastern Africa* 81-117.

Kenya National Commission on Human Rights (2017) "Framework for monitoring the realization of the rights to water and sanitation in Kenya", at <http://knchr.org/Portals/0/EcosocReports/PHE-Framework.pdf?ver=2018-05-16-082038-583> (accessed 25-5-2018).

K'Akumu, OA (2004) "Privatisation of the urban water supply in Kenya: policy options for the poor" 16(2) *Environment & Urbanization* 213-222.

K'Akumu, OA (2006) "Privatisation model for water enterprise in Kenya" 8(6) *Water Policy* 539-557.

K'Akumu, OA (2007) "Toward effective governance of water services in Kenya" 9(5) *Water Policy* 529-543.

K'Akumu, OA & PO Appida (2006) "Privatisation of urban water service provision: the Kenyan experiment" 8(4) *Water Policy* 313-324.

Moyo, S & C Kinuthia-Njenga (1998) *Privatisation of municipal services in East Africa: a governance approach to human settlements management*.

Mugo, K (2011) "Partnership working brings safe water to Kenya's poor" *The Guardian Sustainable Business* (9-8-2011), at https://www.theguardian.com/sustainable-business/revolutionised-kenya-water-supply-business (accessed 11-11-2017).

Mwega, FM (2009) *A case study of AID effectiveness in Kenya: volatility and fragmentation of foreign AID, with a focus on health* Wolfensohn Centre for Development Working Paper No. 8, at <https://www.brookings.edu/wp-content/uploads/2016/06/01_kenya_aid_mwega.pdf> (accessed 29-5-2018).

Notley, J, C Gathuthi, J Murage, B Junker & C Katee (2010) *Lessons learned and good practices from support to the Kenyan water sector*, at <https://www.ircwash.org/sites/default/files/Notley-2010-Lessons.pdf> (accessed 17-12-2017).

Ogendi, GM & IM Ong'oa (2009) "Water policy, accessibility and water ethics in Kenya" (7)1 *Santa Clara Journal of International Law* 177-196.

Renzetti, S & D Dupont D (2003) "Ownership and performance of water utilities" 42 *Greener Management International* 9-19.

Shiva, V (2002) *Water wars: privatization, pollution, and profit.*

Shurie, M, B Mwaniki & P Kameri-Mbote (2017) *Project country report: water permit systems, policy reforms and implications for equity in Kenya*, at <http://africa.iwmi.cgiar.org/wp-content/uploads/sites/2/2017/04/Water-Permitting-Kenya-Country-Report-PI_IWMI-March-2017.pdf> (accessed 17-12-2017).

Swallow, B, NA Okono, C Ong & F Place (2003) "TransVic: improved land management across the Lake Victoria Basin" in RR Harwood & AH Kassam (eds) *Research towards intergrated natural resources management: examples of research problems, approaches and partnerships in action in the CGIAR* 65-78.

Tully, S (2005) "A human right to access water? a critique of general comment No. 15" 23(1) *Netherlands Quarterly of Human Rights* 35-63.

UNDP / United Nations Development Programme (2011) *Small-scale water providers in Kenya: pioneers or predators?*

Uwazi InfoShop (undated) "It's our water too! Bringing greater equality in access to water in Kenya", at <http://www.uwazi.org/24D5E300-20A1-40D5-BEE5-6065ECD7D289/FinalDownload/DownloadId9548731E84A4A0092EEA01B8AE31BD64/24D5E300-20A1-40D5-BEE5-6065ECD7D289/uploads/files/KE%20english%20It%20is%20Our%20Water%20Too%20.pdf> (accessed 11-11-2017).

Wambua, S (2004) "Water privatization in Kenya" 8 *Global Issues Papers* 1.

Water and Sanitation Programme (undated) *Water supply and sanitation in Kenya: turning finance into services for 2015 and beyond*, at <http://wsp.org/sites/wsp.org/files/publications/CSO-Kenya.pdf> (accessed 25-05-2018).

Wekesa, S (2013) "Right to clean safe water under the Kenyan Constitution 2010" 14(3) *Economic and Social Rights Review* 3-6.

WHO / World Health Organization (1993) *Guidelines for drinking water quality* 2nd Ed.

Chapter 24: Policy, regulatory and institutional frameworks relevant to Ethiopian water governance

Mekete Bekele Tekle

1 Introduction

Ethiopia is a country with varied geographical, hydrological and climatological characteristics with a strategic location in the Horn of Africa region. It receives a substantial amount of rain annually that flows to its rivers, lakes and reservoirs. It has about 100 rivers and 27 lakes and reservoirs, including the Grand Ethiopian Renaissance Dam (GERD), that are found in the 12 river basins of the country. Most of Ethiopia's surface waters flow to the low-lying plains of the neighbouring countries. Ethiopia has a great potential for hydroelectric power generation that could be used for national consumption and export to neighbouring countries in the region. For these reasons, it is considered to be the water tower Horn of Africa.[1] Regardless of receiving sufficient rainfall going by the national average, Ethiopia remains a water scarce country by the international standard of consumable water availability for its population. The cause of the water shortage in the country is not lack of water, but rather lack of proper management and effective administration of the available water resources.

Ethiopia has a population of about 106 million people.[2] More than 80% of the population live in rural areas and are engaged in agricultural activities that mostly depend on seasonal rains. The use of irrigation is minimal and any change in the rainfall pattern always causes food shortages in the country. Failure of seasonal rains in different parts of the country has in the past caused drought and famine where millions of people had to rely on international food aid for survival. One of the persistent challenges in Ethiopia is ensuring food security, and the Government has adopted different national policies, plans and strategies[3] to deal with the root causes of recurring food insecurity.

Ethiopia has many institutions working on water management. These include the: Federal Ministry of Water, Irrigation and Electricity; Water Bureaus of the Regional States and Zonal Administration; River Basins High Councils; Basins Authorities; and

---

1 See <https://www.bmiresearch.com/blog/ethiopia-the-water-tower-of-africa> (accessed 30-11-2017).
2 See <http://countrymeters.info/en/Ethiopia> (accessed 26-1-2018).
3 FDRE (1996); FDRE (1997); and FDRE (2005).

municipal water supply utilities. Even though the Federal Government is responsible for administering the shared water resources among the regional states, it is very difficult to determine whether a given water resource is within the exclusive jurisdiction of a regional state. In the absence of properly managed resource allocation, it would be problematic to avoid the overlapping mandates of the regional states among themselves or between a regional state and the Federal Government.[4] As the water resources are public property and as the Federal Government is duty bound to make water available to all citizens of Ethiopia, it is necessary to transfer water from one basin to another basin or within different regions in the same basin. The Federal Government has the duty to balance the water deficits in the regions with the view of bridging the disparity between the regions.

2 The policy framework for Ethiopian water resources governance

2.1 The Constitution of Ethiopia

The Government of Ethiopia is structured on a federal principle of power-sharing between the central and the constitutive regional states, and the power-sharing modality is indicated in the Federal Democratic Republic of Ethiopia (FDRE) Constitution of 1995. The legal framework for water resource administration in Ethiopia reflects the federal system that allows governance at two levels. The FDRE Constitution, which lays the primary legal foundation for federal and state governments' power, has several provisions that have direct legal and institutional significance for the management of the country's water resources. Article 40(3) of the FDRE Constitution exclusively vests the rights of ownership of both rural and urban land, as well as all natural resources, in the state and peoples of Ethiopia.

The FDRE Constitution also defines the powers and functions of the Federal Government and regional states respectively, with respect to the management and administration of the country's water resources. Accordingly, the Federal Government has the mandate to enact laws for the use and conservation of land and other natural resources, including water resources.[5] More specifically, the Federal Government is exclusively vested with the power to "determine and administer the utilization" of the waters or rivers and lakes linking two or more states or crossing the boundaries of the national territorial jurisdiction.[6]

4 The 1995 Constitution of the Federal Democratic Republic of Ethiopia gives the Regional States the mandate to administer natural resources that are within their exclusive territory.

5 Article 51(5) of the FDRE Constitution.

6 Article 51(11) of the FDRE Constitution.

Article 51(11) of the FDRE Constitution vests the power to "determine and administer the utilization" of those water resources such as rivers and lakes and that are linking two or more states or crossing the national territorial jurisdiction to the Federal Government. All the powers that are not expressly given to the Federal Government are the residual powers of the respective regional states within which such resources are found. Accordingly, water resources such as ground waters or lakes that do not link two or more states would fall within the residual power of regional states, since powers that are not expressly given to the Federal Government are reserved for the regional states.[7] As per Article 52(2)(d) of the FDRE Constitution, regional states have to abide by the laws of the Federal Government in administering the water resources within their regions.

Federalism by its very nature is a system of administration where there has to be a certain level of coordination and cooperation between the central and regional states to administer shared natural resources. According to the FDRE Constitution, the Federal Government has the duty to ensure that national wealth is equitably distributed among the citizens. The FDRE Constitution states that: "Government has the duty to ensure that all Ethiopians get equal opportunity to improve their economic conditions and to promote equitable distribution of wealth among them".[8] Furthermore, the social objective of the Federal Government is stated in broad terms as to provide necessary facilities and all possible amenities within its reach, including clean water, to the public. Article 90(2) of the FDRE Constitution provides: "[T]o the extent the country's resources permit, policies shall aim to provide all Ethiopians access to public health and education, clean water, housing, food and social security". The Government has the duty to administer land and other natural resources (including water) in the common interest of the people.[9] Accordingly, it is possible for the Federal Government to facilitate the transfer of water resources from one state to another to make it available to the needy people of the respective states.

On the other hand, the regional states may issue laws on the administration and management of the water resources falling within their exclusive territorial jurisdiction, and some of the regional states have already enacted such laws.[10] Though the regional states are given the power to enact laws on the management of natural resources falling within their jurisdiction, there are restrictive provisions put in place in the regional states' constitutions to avoid a potential conflict of laws.[11]

---

7 Article 52(1) of the FDRE Constitution.

8 Article 89(2) of the FDRE Constitution.

9 Article 89(5) of the FDRE Constitution.

10 For example, Afar Regional State Water Works Construction Enterprise (Proclamation No. 27/1998, Article 6(4)), and the Oromia Irrigation development Authority (Proclamation No. 199/2008, Article 39) deal with issues of water resources utilisation for irrigation purposes.

11 For example, the provisions of Article 47(2.3) of the Revised Amhara National Regional State Constitution (2001) and Article 47(2)(c) of the Tigray National Regional State Constitution

2.2 Environmental policy and development plans of Ethiopia

Ethiopia has ratified many international treaties and adopted the common principles of the sustainable use of natural resources that are enshrined in the national laws and policies. There are a series of strategy documents developed by the government that can be used as sources for the preparation of laws and policies. The Conservation Strategy of Ethiopia (CSE)[12] of 1996 is one of the documents that deal with the country's natural resource base. The strategy document is organised in five volumes and was prepared to serve the purpose of developing future national resource policies for the country. One of the national policies that arose through this process is the Environmental Policy of Ethiopia (EPE),[13] which contains a section on water resource management. Some of the most important policy guidelines on water resource use and conservation are stated under Section 3.4 of the EPE:

1) To ensure that the control of environmental health hazards be a necessary condition in the design, construction and use of dams and irrigation systems;
2) To ensure that any proposed introduction of exotic species into water ecosystems be subject to detailed ecological studies and environmental impact assessment;
3) To promote the protection of the interface between water bodies and land (e.g. lake shores, river banks and wetlands);
4) To subject all major water conservation, development and management projects to the environmental impact assessment process and to include the costs and benefits of protecting watershed forests, wetlands and other relevant key ecosystems in the economic analysis of such water projects; and
5) To promote, through on-site training, effective water management techniques at the farm level for improved performance of medium to large-scale irrigation schemes.

The EPE also steers the monitoring and evaluation of policies towards community participation and the protection of the available natural resources, including water.[14] It also envisages public and state institutions' cooperation in monitoring and evaluating processes to enhance the review of the policy itself.

The other important national policy is Ethiopia's Climate-Resilient Green Economy (CRGE) Strategy[15] adopted in 2011, which aims at achieving middle-income status in

---

indicate that the Regional State shall administer land and natural resources in accordance with the laws enacted by the federal government.

12 See generally, Environmental Protection Authority and Ministry of Economic Development (2001). Volume I of the strategy document establishes the setting by evaluating the state of the natural resources, the environment and development in Ethiopia and examining the interconnected causes and effects of the existing situation. Volume II presents a policy and strategy framework aimed at ensuring a sustainable use and management of natural resources. Volume III deals with institutional arrangements to implement the strategies. Volume IV deals with a plan of prioritised actions within the framework of cross-sectoral and sectoral programmes. Volume V gives a listing of projects with estimated costs.

13 FDRE (1997).

14 Ibid: Section 5.3(e).

15 FDRE (2011).

the country by 2025 while developing a green economy. The CRGE Strategy is a blueprint for development activities to achieve the predetermined targets of the government. In relation to water management, the CRGE provides that:[16]

> This category includes the promotion of terracing, particularly in hilly regions with high soil erosion hazards, and the improvement of water harvesting and irrigation structures, such as providing supplementary irrigation by focusing on increased water use efficiency, which can enhance carbon storage in soils through enhanced yields and residue returns.

Ethiopia is running a series of successive national development plans. The current plan series is the Growth and Transformation Plan (GTP), being the second five-year-plan period, (i.e. GTP-II). The transformation plans are geared toward moving the country from an agrarian economy to moderate industrialisation within the successive GTP planning periods. GTP-II has relevant provisions on watershed management that set targets to be achieved by the end of the plan period. The following major targets are set for watershed management during GTP-II:[17]

1) The number of community watersheds within a development plan is projected to increase from 19,748 in 2014/15 to 93,713 by the end of the plan period;
2) The area of land rehabilitated through area closure is projected to increase from 10.86 million hectare in 2014/15 to 22.54 million hectare by the end of the plan period;
3) The area of watersheds supported with physical soil and water conservation structures is projected to increase from 8.12 million hectare in 2014/15 to 27.23 million hectare by the end of the plan period; and
4) 1.5 million jobs are to be created for citizens through development works in watershed management.

Since the GTP documents are dealing with development targets, the water sector of the plan of GTP-II has set the abovementioned goals. Accordingly, building on the achievements gained by GTP-1, GTP-II set targets for urban and rural potable water supply, irrigation developments and industrial water supply. The major targets of GTP-II with regard to water resource management provide are to:[18]

1) increase access to clean water from 84% in 2014/15 to 100% at national level during the GTP II period;
2) increase rural water supply coverage from 59% in 2014/15 to 85% by 2019/20;
3) increase national water supply coverage from 58% to 83% in the same period;
4) increase groundwater exploration coverage from 13% to 25% during the period;
5) expand integrated catchment and degraded land rehabilitation from 922,520.7 ha to 2,304,801 ha; and
6) increase basins and hydrological information systems from 25% to 63% and hydrological mapping coverage to reach 95% during the plan period.

16 Ibid: 141.
17 FDRE (2016).
18 Ibid: 183.

Regarding the water sector development, the current growth and transformation plan envisages a wider scope of cooperation and understanding among the stakeholders. This plan states that "capacity development as well as coordination efforts will be undertaken by all executive agencies and relevant stakeholders" to achieve the targets.[19]

2.3 Ethiopian water resources management policy

The Ethiopian Water Resources Management Policy (EWRMP)[20] has specific goals, objectives and principles. The overall goal of the policy is "to enhance and promote all national efforts towards the efficient, equitable and optimum utilisation of the available water resources of Ethiopia for significant socioeconomic development on a sustainable basis".[21] Efficiency, equity and optimum and sustainable utilisation of water are main elements of the goals that have to be achieved through the objectives of the policy. The objectives of the EWRMP are enumerated in Section 1.2 of the document. These are:

1) development of the water resources of the country for economic and social benefits of the people, on an equitable and sustainable basis;
2) allocation and apportionment of water, based on comprehensive and integrated plans and optimum allocation principles that incorporate efficiency of use, equity of access, and sustainability of the resource;
3) managing and combating drought as well as other associated slow onset disasters through, inter alia, efficient allocation, redistribution, transfer, storage and efficient use of water resources;
4) combating and regulating floods through sustainable mitigation, prevention, rehabilitation and other practical measures; and
5) conserving, protecting and enhancing water resources and the overall aquatic environment on a sustainable basis.

In addition to the objectives listed above, the EWRMP contains a set of fundamental principles and rules which are derived from the different laws, including the FDRE Constitution. The first fundamental principle is the recognition of public ownership of water, along with other natural resources, which has already been entrenched in the FDRE Constitution. The EWRMP further states that the Government of Ethiopia shall make every effort to provide every citizen with water of sufficient quality and quantity. What has been emphasised in the policy is the fact that "water shall be recognized both as an economic and a social good"[22] under the Ethiopian legal system. The importance of this principle is to facilitate and to determine the modalities of providing the

19 Ibid: 184.
20 Ministry of Water Resources (1999).
21 Ibid: Section 1.1.
22 Ibid: Section 1.3(2).

resource depending on the type of water use in question. Accordingly, water can be supplied at a production cost price, a subsidised price or for free, depending on conditions of water availability or scarcity in a given area of its provision. The general direction of the national policy in this regard is stated as follows:[23]

> Although all water resources development ought to be based on the "economic value" of water, the provision of water supply services to the underprivileged sectors of the population shall be ensured based on a special "Social Strategy".

The core principle of the EWRMP is the principle of integrated water resources management (IWRM). There are various conceptual definitions of IWRM submitted by different writers. One author defines it as a "systematic process for the sustainable development, allocation and monitoring of water resource use in the context of social, economic and environmental objectives".[24] The EWRMP, being a guiding instrument for any water management activity, defines IWRM as a concept that "addresses the interdependence of the different uses and users of water resources".[25] The EWRMP recognises hydrologic boundary or 'basin' as the fundamental planning unit for water resources management in Ethiopia.[26] This includes management aspects such as water tariff setting and watershed management plans. Taking into account the fact that the country is a federal state, the policy promotes the integration and institutionalisation of "meteorological and hydrological services at all levels (from the centre up to the lowest administrative structure)" and ensures that the agricultural sector receives the utmost benefit from these services, and the services are monitored by the appropriate organs of the regional states. It is also possible to transfer water from one basin to another, as necessary. To this effect the EWRMP provides that:[27]

> As deemed necessary, promote that inter-basin transfer of water is to be one of the basic principles for the development of water resources, in view of the disparity of available water amongst the different basins and the erratic devastations due to the extremities of drought and floods.

The IWRM principles mentioned in the EWRMP give clues for the transfer of water from a water-abundant basin to a water-scarce basin. This principle is applicable in the inter-basin and intra-basin contexts where a meaningful and mutually fair cooperation is expected between the Federal Government and the concerned regional states for equitable use of the water resources located in the basins.[28] For the equitable use and fair sharing of costs and benefits among the water users, a basin is an important aspect of good governance. There are dry river basins where the water resources are scarce and insufficient to satisfy the development activities in the area. The IWRM activities

23 EWRMP, Section 2.1.1(12).
24 CAP-Net, Global Water Partnership & UNDP (2005: 7).
25 Ministry of Water Resources (1999: Glossary section).
26 Ibid: Section 2.1.1(6).
27 Ibid: Section 2.1.1(10).
28 Ibid: Section 2.2.7(4).

in such dry basin areas must be geared toward rainwater harvesting and protecting the groundwater in the hydrological area.

The EWRMP provides for water use priorities. First priority is given to home consumption, which is considered as the basic minimum requirement in any water allocation plan.[29] The water use for home consumption includes uses such as drinking, cooking, sanitation and watering cattle. The other types of water uses are prioritised on the basis of their impact on socioeconomic benefits.[30] Special consideration is made for drought-prone areas while allocating water based on the prevailing conditions within the given basin, sub-basin and other hydrological boundaries.[31] It is believed that water management can be best handled if it is done at the local level and if a proper maintenance framework that provides reliable and sustainable water supply systems is put in place in all regions. Encouraging community participation in the operation and maintenance of water systems, and promoting operation and maintenance of water systems at lower levels, is an additional policy consideration in water resources allocation and apportionment.[32] It is believed that managing water based on a decentralised system will enhance its sustainability.

The EWRMP considers water as a natural resource with an economic value and clearly state that users of the services should be charged. The policy also suggests striking a balance between high and low water price settings. The policy suggests that "the price for water should be neither too high (and discourage water use) nor too low (and encourage abuses and over-use of water)".[33] There is also a consideration of the provision of water for free to those communities that cannot afford to pay for the water used for basic human needs. The policy emphasises the importance of this economic consideration and includes the following statement:[34]

> Ensure that the basic human needs of water for disadvantaged rural communities, who cannot afford to pay for development of water systems, shall be borne by the government, as appropriate, and in so far as the communities are able and willing to cover the operation and maintenance costs on their own.

The enabling environment for water resources management include: developing institutions at both federal and regional levels; building capacity at all levels for the personnel involved in water management; creating a legislative framework for the formulation of water resources laws and regulations that enable citizens to have access to water; facilitating participation of all stakeholders (including water users' associations, the community and particularly women) to play a central role in water resource management activities; and creating the necessary legal framework for the citizens to get

29 Ibid: Section 2.2.1.
30 Ibid.
31 Ibid.
32 Ibid: Section 2.2.3 (D).
33 Ibid: Section 2.2.5(B)(4).
34 Ibid: Section 2.2.5(B)(6).

access to water resources.[35] There are specific sectoral policies for different types of water use that are addressed under separate subheadings in the EWRMP. Section 3 of the EWRMP has detailed paragraphs on: water supply and sanitation (including sub-sectoral policies on drinking water, livestock water supply, water supply for industry and other uses, sanitation and integrated water supply); an irrigation policy; and an hydropower policy.[36]

3 The legal framework for water resources governance

The legal framework for water resource administration in Ethiopia reflects the federal arrangement of the country with a shared responsibility of governance between the federal and state governments. The FDRE Constitution, which lays the primary legal foundation for federal and state governments' power, has several provisions that have direct legal and institutional significance for the management of the water resources of the country. Article 40(3) of the Constitution exclusively vests the rights of ownership of both rural and urban land as well as all natural resources, including water resources, in the state and peoples of Ethiopia. In addition to the constitutional provision that governs the allocation of natural resources, there are specific laws and regulations that have been issued to regulate water resources utilisation. The main water resources governance laws and regulations will be discussed in the subsections below.

3.1 Ethiopian water resources management laws

The main water governance law is the Ethiopian Water Resources Management Proclamation No. 197/2000. The key purpose of the Proclamation is to ensure that the water resources are put to the highest social and economic benefit for all people through appropriate protection and diligent management.[37] The Proclamation reaffirms that water resources are under public and state ownership. Article 6 of the Proclamation sets out the fundamental principles that should guide the management of water resources. One of the fundamental principles is to introduce integrated basin master plan studies. The other fundamental principle is to establish a supervising body to administer the water resources in accordance with the water policy and to subject the management of water resources to a permit system.[38] The Proclamation provides that domestic use "shall have priority over and above any other water uses".[39] The Proclamation also

35 Ibid: Section 2.2.13.
36 Ibid: Section 2.3.1 to 2.3.3.
37 FDRE (2000).
38 Ibid: Article 6(3) and (4).
39 Ibid: Article 7(1).

puts an end to any claim of having an existing allocated or planned use when it comes to the prioritisation of domestic use.

As opposed to the previous practice in the country, the Proclamation provides for the establishment of the Supervising Body[40] for water resources administration and subjects certain types of water uses to a permit system. According to the relevant provisions of the law, activities such as waterworks construction, supply of water, and release or discharge of waste into water resources shall not be performed without obtaining a permit from the Supervising Body.[41] Though hand-dug wells and traditional irrigation may not be subject to the permit system, the Supervising Body may issue directives to prevent inappropriate use and wastage of water whenever it appears necessary to do so. The Supervising Body has the power to suspend or revoke a water use permit at any time.[42] The permit system requires the applicant to hold a certificate of competence to become engaged in the waterworks envisaged in the submitted application.

The Proclamation provides for the payment of a service fee (charge) for any water use type, except for certain prescribed exempt types of use. The Supervising Body may also allow a discharge or release of waste into water resources by fixing the amount to be paid. Accordingly, the Council of Ministers of Ethiopia issued the Water Resources Management Regulation No. 115/2005. The Regulation provides for the protection of the environment by imposing an obligation on the applicant for the permit to: install and use a waste treatment method; discharge only the type and volume of treated waste permitted; and to allow the Supervising Body to take a treated waste discharge sample at any time.[43]

The Ministry of Water, Irrigation and Electricity (MoWIE) is a federal body established to undertake the management of water resources, water supply and sanitation, large and medium scale irrigation and electricity. MoWIE is a regulatory body that governs: the planning, development and management of resources; and the preparation and implementation of guidelines, strategies, policies, programmes, sectoral laws and regulations.[44] It is a supervising authority for all national (federal) water resource matters with the mission of playing a significant role in the socio-economic development of Ethiopia through the development and management of its water and energy

---

40 Ibid: Article 8.

41 Ibid: Article 11(1).

42 The Supervising Body may, at any time, suspend or revoke a permit in whole or partially where the holder fails to observe or fulfil his/her obligations. The details shall be determined by the regulations to be issued for the implementation of this proclamation (Article 17 of Proclamation No. 197/2000).

43 The opening statement of Article 12(1) of Council of Ministers of Ethiopia, which issued the Water Resources Management Regulations No. 115/2005, enumerates sets of obligations that any person using water for industry or for any other purposes which may cause pollution shall have.

44 See <http://www.mowie.gov.et/Overview> (accessed 9-12-2017).

resources in a sustainable manner, and the provision of quality and equitable supplies to the entire country.[45]

3.2 Sectoral laws on water resources

In addition to MoWIE, there are other federal institutions that are directly or indirectly involved in water resource management. The Ministry of Agriculture and Natural Resources is tasked with expanding small-scale irrigation schemes development and the Ministry of Livestock and Fisheries is obliged to "follow up the expansion of water resources, infrastructure necessary for livestock resource development[46] in the pastoral areas and establish a system for natural and irrigated rangeland development and utilization."[47]

Furthermore, the Ethiopian Construction Works Corporation (ECWC) is established and responsible for "construction, upgrading and maintenance of works relating to dams, irrigations, hydro power generations, water supply systems, sewerage system, drainage, deep water wells, reclamations, and river diversions…".[48] The ECWC is specifically entrusted "to acquire, own and administer irrigation dams, deep water wells and as may be necessary water supply canals constructed and to be constructed by the federal government budget and collect charges from the beneficiaries of such dams".[49] The same scheme is prescribed in the legal framework regulating the construction of waterworks by the Afar Regional State Water Works Construction Enterprise.[50]

Water for irrigation could also be provided through private investments in the development of irrigation and related water works.[51] Investors are allowed to engage in irrigation development activities that may cover more than 50 hectares.[52] The purpose of the Regulation to Provide for Irrigation Development Investment Incentives is to provide incentives "to investors engaging in irrigation development to bring about an accelerated economic development of the country by increasing the role of private sector in developing irrigation through utilizing the huge available irrigable land and water resources of the country".[53] Regulation No. 162/2009 stipulates incentives to be granted to include "exemptions from water use charges and making available for

45 See <http://www.mowie.gov.et/Vision> (accessed 8-12-2017).
46 Proc. No. 916/2015, Article 19(1)(o).
47 Proc. No. 916/2015, Art. 20(1)(i).
48 ECWC Establishment Council of Ministers Regulation No. 366/2015, Article 5.
49 Ibid: Article 5(3).
50 Proclamation No. 27/1998, Article 6(4).
51 Council of Ministers Regulation to Provide for Irrigation Development Investment Incentives (No. 162/2009).
52 Ibid: Article 2(3).
53 Ibid: Article 4.

further development of major irrigation structures such as dams, main canals and access roads at government cost".[54]

The federal regulation of water resource management provides legal frameworks for the registration of water users' cooperative societies established to undertake medium- or large-scale irrigation. These water users' cooperative societies established to undertake small-scale irrigation are registered by an organ established by law at regional or city administration level. However, the regional or city administration organs that organise and register small-scale irrigation water users' cooperative societies must transmit information to the Supervising Body.[55]

The Irrigation Water Users' Association Proclamation No. 841/2014 governs the management of farmers' of irrigation and drainage systems "which are formed on irrigation infrastructures constructed by the federal government throughout Ethiopia".[56] This Proclamation envisages that irrigation water users five or more may form an association.[57] Irrigation water users' associations may be formed through two procedural mechanisms. The Water Resources Management Proclamation No. 197/2000 entrusts the Supervising Body with facilitating the establishment of water users' associations.[58]

The guiding principles for the operation of water users' associations envisaged under the Irrigation Water Users' Proclamation include:[59]

- ensuring fairness and equity in decision making and the allocation of irrigation water;
- preventing wastage and the pollution of water;
- applying transparency and participatory decision-making processes; and
- complying with a system of cost recovery and the efficient use of resources.

Each association is expected to operate within a defined service area without overlapping with other service areas. The charge payable by an association to a service provider for the delivery of water shall be determined by the Supervising Body.[60]

The Ethiopian Water Resources Development Fund Establishment and its Administration Proclamation No. 268/2002 (as amended by Proclamation No. 581/2008) has the objective of enabling institutions engaged in water supply and sanitation services to be efficient in their service to the community and make a contribution towards attaining food self-sufficiency by expanding irrigation development.[61] The Public Health Proclamation No. 200/2002 prohibits the provision of water of which the quality is not

---

54 Regulation No. 162/2009, Article 6(1)(3).

55 Council of Ministers Ethiopian Water Resources Management Regulations (No. 115/2005), Article 29.

56 Irrigation Water Users' Association Proclamation No. 841/2014, Article 3.

57 Ibid: Article 10(1).

58 Ethiopian Water Resources Management Proclamation No. 197/2000, Article 27.

59 Irrigation Water Users' Association Proclamation No. 841/2014, Article 5.

60 Ibid: Article 55(1)(2).

61 Water Resources Development Fund Establishment Proclamation No. 268/2002 (as amended), Article 4.

verified by the relevant health authority and into which untreated liquid waste is discharged from polluting sources.[62] The Food, Medicine and Health Care Administration Proclamation No. 661/2009 also refers to the assurance of the quality of transregional water supply for the public.[63] According to this law, violations of water supply quality standards are offences punishable by imprisonment and fines.[64] The Environmental Pollution Control and Environmental Impact Assessment Proclamations No. 299/2002 contain important provisions dealing with the protection of water resources. Both Proclamations provide for the protection of water and the need for setting water quality standards for different users.[65] The Federal Ministry of Health is directly responsible for the verification of water quality standards in Ethiopia as stated in the National Water Quality Monitoring and Surveillance Strategy document.[66]

3.3 Ethiopian river basin laws

The management of water resources at basin level is said to be the most logical approach for the "planning and optimum utilization of available water resources" in a given river basin.[67] Both the EWRMP and the Water Resources Management Proclamation emphasise water management plans and strategies to be developed at basin level. Regarding the relevance of a basin master plan, the Proclamation states that:[68]

> The social and economic development programmes, investment plans and programmes and water resources development activity of any person, shall be based on the country's Water Resources Policy, the relevant Basin Master Plan Studies and Water Resources laws.

A basin is defined by the Proclamation as: "a geographical area, described by the watershed limits of a water system including surface and underground water flowing into a common terminus".[69] Additional laws and regulations have been issued to implement the IWRM principles in the context of river basin water-use planning and administration. All recent water resources-related legal documents focus on the equitable and efficient use of the available water resources of the country. In line with EWRMP, the River Basin Councils and Authorities Proclamation No. 534/2007 has been issued. This Proclamation defines the term 'basin' in exactly the same manner as it is defined

62 Public Health Proclamation No. 200/2000, Article 10.
63 Food, Medicine and Health Care Administration and Control Proclamation No. 661/2009, Article 4(20).
64 Ibid: Article 53(i).
65 Environmental Impact Assessment Proclamation No. 299/2002, Article 2(20); and Environmental Pollution Control Proclamation No. 300/2002, Article 6(1)(a).
66 FDRE (2011: 5).
67 Awulachew et al. (2007: 4).
68 Ethiopian Water Resources Management Proclamation No. 197/2000, Article 6(2).
69 Ethiopian Water Resources Management Proclamation No. 197/2000, Article 2(15).

by the Water Resources Management Proclamation, and lists the 12 river basins of the country under Article 2(1).[70]

The River Basin Councils and Authorities Proclamation No. 534/2007 is a framework law that facilitates the establishment of basin high councils and basin authorities across the river basins. The Council of Ministers is mandated to establish river basin high councils and river basin authorities for each basin. According to the River Basin Councils and Authorities Proclamation, two or more river basins may be under the jurisdiction of a single basin high council and a basin authority.[71] Ethiopia has so far established three basin high councils (BHCs) and basin authorities (BAs), all of which have been made accountable to the Council of Ministers.[72] The remaining nine basins do not as yet have basin high councils and authorities. The water resources management activities in these basins are being carried out by the water bureaus of the respective regional states in these basins. The objectives, powers and duties of the basins so far established are somewhat similar to the provisions of the River Basin Councils and Authorities Proclamation. Article 4 of this Proclamation prescribes the objectives of the BHCs and BAs as:

> The overall objectives of river basin High Councils and Authorities shall be to promote and monitor the integrated water resources management process in the river basins falling under their jurisdictions with a view to using of the basins' water resources for the socio-economic welfare of the people in an equitable and participatory manner, and without compromising the sustainability of the aquatic ecosystems.

The EWRMP emphasises the need to "develop long term water balances/drought models with different scenarios including interventions like inter-basin water transfer".[73] Taking into account the disparity of water availability and severe scarcity in many of the areas, the promotion of inter-basin transfer of water is considered to be one of the important basic principles for the development of water resources to manage the devastation caused by the extremes of drought and floods among the different basins.[74] The establishment of the BHCs and BAs may help create a common understanding of the IWRM system across the basins and thereby alleviate the calamities that may arise as a result of water scarcity.

70 The 12 basins of Ethiopia established by the River Basins Councils and Authorities Proclamation No. 534/2007 are: Abbay; Aisha; Awash; Baro-Akobo; Danakil; Genale-Dawa; Mereb; Ogaden; Omo-Ghibe; Tekeze; Rift Valley Lakes; and Wabi-Shebelle basins.

71 River Basins Councils and Authorities Proclamation No. 534/2007, Article 3(2).

72 Abbay Basin High Council and Authority Establishment Regulation No. 151/2008; Awash Basin High Council and Authority Establishment Council of Ministers Regulation No. 156/2008; and Rift Valley Lakes Basin High Council and Authority Establishment Council of Ministers Regulation No. 253/2011.

73 Ministry of Water Resources (1999: Section 2.2.7(4)).

74 Ibid: Section 2.1.1(11).

3.3.1 Basin High Councils

The River Basin Councils and Authorities Proclamation provides for two sets of organisations, namely Basin High Councils (BHCs) and Basin Authorities (BAs), institutions of vital importance for the implementation of IWRM principles in the basins. The BHCs and BAs have detailed powers and duties in the management of the water resources within their respective jurisdictions. Generally, the BHCs have powers and duties to:[75]

1) provide policy guidance and planning oversight to ensure a high level of coordination among stakeholders for the implementation of integrated water resources management in the basin;
2) direct the preparation of the river basin plan and submit same for approval by the Government;
3) propose to the Government the rate of the water charges to be paid by water users in the basin;
4) examine and decide on the appropriateness and prioritization of major water works in the basin;
5) examine and decide on water allocation rules and principles in normal times and in times of water shortage as well as in times of drought or flooding;
6) manage water use disputes between Regional States in the basin;
7) provide information and advisory support to the body in charge of negotiating with neighbouring countries with respect to the basin where the basin is part of a transboundary basin; and
8) establish standing or ad hoc committees necessary for discharging specific activities.

The accountability of the BHCs is said to be determined by the regulations to be issued to implement the Proclamation in the river basin. According to Article 5(2) of the Proclamation, it appears that each river basin may be accountable to different state organs.[76] For example, all the three BHCs established to date (Abbay, Awash and Rift Valley Lakes basins) are accountable to the Council of Ministers of the Federal Republic of Ethiopia. The Proclamation and the Regulations envisage the possibility of the establishment of BHCs for different basins, either a BHC for each basins or one BHC for two or more basins.[77] It is stipulated that the appointment of members of BHCs shall be made by the Government, but no such appointment has been made so far.[78] There is, however, one national High Basins Council, composed of the high-ranking Federal Government and regional state officials, whose role it is to oversee the activities of all river basin authorities and to make decisions for all the basins in the

75 River Basins Councils and Authorities Proclamation No.534/2007, Article 6.

76 Ibid: Article 5(2) which reads: "The accountability of a BHC shall be determined by a Regulation to be issued b) the Council of Ministers". But the basin authorities are accountable to the respective BHCs (Article 10(1)).

77 Article 3(2) of River Basins Councils and Authorities Proclamation No. 534/2007; Article 5 of the Abbay Basin, the Awash Basin and the Rift Valley Lakes Basin establishment regulations, respectively.

78 Tamrat (2008); and Mosello et al. (2015).

country.[79] This is a clear deviation from the law and policy framework that advocates "basin-based management" decentralised administration of water resources.

3.3.2 Basin authorities

Parallel to the BHCs, there are basin authorities (BAs) that serve as the secretariat of the respective BHCs. BAs are accountable to their associated BHCs with respect to issues falling under the latters' powers and duties. BAs are also accountable to the MoWIE with respect to other issues falling under its jurisdiction. BAs are headed by director generals appointed by the Government, who oversee the functions of their staff carrying out the day-to-day activities in each basin.[80] Some of the powers and functions of the BAs are to:[81]

- initiate policy measures for a conducive environment for the implementation of IWRM in the basin…;
- ensure that projects, activities and interventions related to water in the basin are, in their content, schedule, impacts and management, in line with the IWRM process;
- prepare, and submit to the BHC, the basin's plan and monitor its implementation upon approval;
- collect, compile, analyse and disseminate information for proper planning, administration and steering of water resources in the basin;
- give advice… to BHC and the Ministry on dispute resolution [on] allocation and use of water resources;
- set up a forum for effective networking among stakeholders; [and] collect water charges from users; and
- undertake studies, surveys and researches that are deemed necessary to carry out its functions.

The list of powers and duties of the BAs provided above is indicative of the trend to devolve the main powers and duties of water resources management from the central administration system to the BAs. According to the current trend of devolution of powers, MoWIE is assisting these newly emerging institutions in terms of budget allocation, human resources allocation and overall technical capacity building.[82] The devolution of powers to the BAs is a gradual and time-consuming process as the new institutions require time to build their own management capacities. As a responsible federal body for water resources administration, MoWIE undertakes basin studies and verifies the country's ground and surface water resource potential in terms of volume and

---

79 The Nation Basins High Council of Ethiopia is currently chaired by the deputy prime minister of Ethiopia and has several ministers and all the presidents of the Regional States within the three already established basins, i.e. Abbay, Awash and Rift Valley Lakes, as its members.

80 River Basins Councils and Authorities Proclamation No. 534/2007, Article 11.

81 Ibid: Article 9.

82 The MoWIE is the supervising organ for the BAs. Plans and programmes prepared by the BAs must be approved by the MoWIE.

quality, and facilitates the use of these until such time that the BAs can have the capacity to take up the task.[83] These powers can be delegated to the BAs when they are capable of handling the tasks in the future.

3.4 River basin establishment regulations

The EWRMP and water resources laws and regulations promote the principle of IWRM in the context of Ethiopia's river basins. The River Basins Councils and Authorities Proclamation also reaffirms the need to reconcile the different uses of water within a river basin to achieve their balanced and sustainable development. For IWRM to function in a basin, all stakeholders must have good relationships and work in harmony, notwithstanding their differences in approach, interests and perceptions of the effects of their decisions, plans and activities on the hydrological cycle and other users.[84]

Ethiopia has initiated decentralised water resources management by transferring most of the water resources management powers of the MoWIE to river basin-based institutions. The Council of Ministers Regulations on BHCs and BAs govern the powers and duties of the authorities, while the powers and duties of the BHCs are inferred from the River Basin Councils and Authorities Proclamation. Each of the regulations has its own specific objective and confers detailed powers and duties on the relevant BHCs and BAs. For instance, the Abbay Basin Regulation[85] has its own list of powers and duties. The Abbay Basin accounts for about half of the total annual discharge of surface freshwater of the country and about 62% of the total discharge that drains into the Aswan Dam in Egypt. The basin is accordingly of both national and international importance.[86] Article 3 of the Regulation for the Abbay Basin Authority states the overall objective of the authority as promoting and monitoring the implementation of the IWRM process in an equitable and participatory manner. Some of the powers and duties of the Abbay Basin Authority are to:[87]

- undertake activities necessary for, and facilitate, the implementation of IWRM in the basin;
- ensure that projects, activities and interventions related to water in the basin are, in their content, schedule, impacts and management, in line with the IWRM process;

83 Definition of Powers and Duties of the Executive Organs of the Federal Democratic Republic of Ethiopia Proclamation No. 916/2015, Article 28(b).

84 Opening paragraphs of the Preamble of the River Basin Councils and Authorities Proclamation No. 534/2007.

85 Regulation No. 151/2008 Council of Ministers Regulation to Establish Abbay Basin High Council and Authority.

86 FDRE (2016: 4).

87 Regulation No. 151/2008 Council of Ministers Regulation to Establish Abbay Basin High Council and Authority, Article 6.

- prepare, and submit to the BHC, the basin's plan and monitor its implementation upon approval;
- issue permits applicable to the basin's water use and water works..., without prejudice to the power given to Regional States by law, ;
- set up a forum for effective networking among stakeholders; and
- provide information for negotiations with other countries concerning transboundary river basins.

The Abbay Basin is part of the bigger Nile Basin that contributes about 85% of the water flowing to neighbouring countries, such as South Sudan, the Sudan and Egypt. The ongoing construction of the Grand Ethiopian Renaissance Dam (GERD) is becoming a major concern to some of the riparian countries, particularly Egypt, regardless of the many advantages that may emanate from the GERD project, including hydropower generation for the region and water conservation of the Nile Basin.[88] The Abbay Basin Authority is compelled to balance the competing interests of the stakeholders in the basin, by taking care of the right of regional states in the process of issuing permits[89] and providing the Government with necessary information about transboundary management aspects in the basin.[90] As part of its obligation under the international treaties and on the basis of its own national law, Ethiopia is bound to abide by the principles of shared water resource management that involves all stakeholders in the process of decision making dealing with or impacting on water resources situated in the basin.

There are about ten riparian states along the Nile Basin that are party to the Comprehensive Framework Agreement (CFA).[91] The Regulation establishing the Abbay Basin Authority is in line with the provisions of the Nile Basin's CFA,[92] which refers to "[t]he principle that each Nile Basin State has the right to use, within its territory, the waters of the Nile River System in a manner that is consistent with...basic principles referred to herein".[93] There are many principles that are developed by the Nile

88 Salman (2018).

89 The Regional States have constitutions and other laws that deal with water resources administration in their locality. The Abbay Basin Authority is expected not to tamper with the rights of the Regional States to manage their water resources as they think fit.

90 As the negotiations with foreign countries are being handled by the Federal Government, the Abbay Basin is obliged to supply the necessary information to the Federal Government to aid it in any potential negotiation.

91 These states are: Burundi; DR Congo; Egypt; Ethiopia; Kenya; Rwanda; South Sudan; Sudan; Tanzania; and Uganda. All these countries are members of the Nile Basin Initiative (NBI) and expected to be signatories to the CFA.

92 Agreement on the Nile River Basin Cooperative Framework or Comprehensive Framework Agreement (CFA), at <https://www.internationalwaterlaw.org/documents/regionaldocs/Nile_River_Basin_Cooperative_Framework_2010.pdf> (accessed 15-12-2017).

93 CFA Agreement on the Nile River Basin Cooperative Framework or Comprehensive Framework Agreement (CFA), Article 3 paragraph 6.

Basin Initiative (NBI)[94] and adopted by the CFA. The main principle is a shared vision to achieve sustainable socio-economic development through the equitable utilisation of the basin and benefits from the common Nile Basin water resources.[95] The only significant project undertaken by Ethiopia in the Abbay Basin so far is the GERD which aims to generate about 6,000 megawatt of electric power. However, Egypt has raised concerns about the size of the GERD Project, which may pose challenges to the project's success.[96] Almost all Nile riparian countries are developing projects along the river and Egypt is reviving its old claim of a monopoly over the Nile's waters, an action that may not be accepted by other riparian states which want to have their fair share of the flow of the Nile.

The other basin that has a BHC and BA is the Awash Basin. This is the most used basin in Ethiopia and it covers parts of Afar Regional State, Amhara Regional State, Oromia, Somali Regional States, Southern Nations, Nationalities and Peoples Regional State, and Addis Ababa and Dire Dawa Administrative Councils. The Awash Basin is fed by several tributaries, but part of the catchment in the eastern part of the basin does not contribute any significant surface runoff to the river.[97] The Regulation for the Establishment of the Awash Basin High Council and the Basin Authority provides the power and duties of the Authority that enable it to function as a water resource governance institution. Most of the provisions are similar to that of the Abbay Basin Authority. The focus in the Awash Basin is on irrigation as there are several irrigation schemes in the basin.[98] As part of its duty, the Awash Basin Authority advises the Basin High Council and MoWIE on dispute resolution in relation to the allocation and use of water resources in the basin, and it may also provide advice and technical support whenever necessary.[99]

According to the Water Management Proclamation No. 197/2000 and its Regulation No. 115/2005, most uses of the water resources and wastewater discharge in the Awash Basin require a permit. The permit system is, however, not well established within the basin as the Awash Basin Authority has not yet been able to implement a basin-wide

94 The NBI is managed from three Centres: the Secretariat (Nile-SEC) based in Entebbe; Uganda; the Eastern Nile Technical Regional Office (ENTRO) based in Addis Ababa, Ethiopia; and the Nile Equatorial Lakes Subsidiary Action Program Coordination Unit (NELSAP-CU)-based in Kigali, Rwanda. NBI implements three core programs, namely: Basin Cooperation; Water Resource Management; and Water Resource Development.

95 Mekonnen (2010).

96 Lawson (2017).

97 See <http://www.awba.gov.et/?page_id=8> (accessed 16-12-2017).

98 For instance, Article 6(11) and (12) of the Awash Basin High Council and Authority Establishment Council of Ministers Regulation No. 156/2008 has provision dealing with irrigation management issues.

99 Awash Basin High Council and Authority Establishment Council of Ministers Regulation No. 156/2008, Article 6(8).

permit system.[100] The Awash Basin spans several regional states and requires an equitable allocation of water resources among the regional states and other water users within the basin as per the basin-wide master plan.[101] Moreover, there is some confusion regarding the demarcation between the mandate of the Federal Government, the regional states and the Awash Basin Authority[102] on water resources management issues. For example, the mandate of the Awash Basin Authority with respect to water charge setting is very limited and it may not be possible for the Authority to impose a charge or collect charges without consulting or obtaining consent from these other institutions.

The Rift Valley Lakes Basin is the other basin for which a BHC and BA have been established. This basin has four sub-basins, namely: the Ziway-Shala Sub-basin; the Awasa Sub-basin; the Abaya-Chamo Sub-basin; and the Chew Bahir Sub-basin.[103] The Regulation for the Establishment of the Rift Valley Lakes BHC and BA gives similar powers and duties to administer the water resources of the basin area as those given to the Abbay and Awash basins.[104] Even though the Rift Valley Lakes Basin Authority has been established by regulation, it has not yet come into operation. This basin is a water-scarce basin when compared with the two basins mentioned above. The growing number of industries and other water-intensive activities in the basin has caused serious water management challenges in the area, including siltation and pollution of the lakes and groundwater systems.

Regional, Zonal and Woreda Water Bureaus[105] within the basins are also involved in water administration. MoWIE is actively engaged in capacity-building programmes and strategies for all the basins to enable them to embark on IWRM implementation in their areas, including assisting private service providers that are allowed to provide services in the water sector. As a matter of policy, water supply services are handled entirely by public organisations and the private sector may only engage in the provision of professional services such as consultancy and maintenance services.[106] There are, however, certain practices which do not adhere to the above functional division. For instance, the companies Karuturi Global Ltd and Saudi Star Agricultural

---

100 Water Governance Centre, (Issue Paper) *Water Governance Capacity: Awash Basin, Central Ethiopia*, The Hague, The Netherlands (April 2013) 15.

101 Water Governance Centre (2013: 17).

102 There is a tendency of the MoWIE to continue the centralised system of managing the water resources in the basins. For instance, the MoWIE wants to have a minimum national average water charge for water abstraction, whereas the water policy and the water laws consider the basins as the planning units for such management.

103 Raventós Vilalta (2010).

104 Rift Valley Lakes Basin High Council and Authority Establishment Council of Ministers Regulation No. 253/2007.

105 The hierarchical of administrative structure in Ethiopia comprises of the following, from the highest to the lowest level: Federal Ministry, Regional State Bureaus, Zonal State Bureaus and Woreda Bureaus.

106 Defere (2015).

Development, which concluded large-scale agricultural land lease agreements with the Ethiopian Government, have been allowed to use both ground and underground water in the areas they lease.[107]

4 Water resources-related disputes

Conflict or dispute over water resources can take various forms and can occur at any level of governance. There can be horizontal and vertical conflicts at the local and national levels on the use and management of water resources. There are also certain complaints or disputes by Ethiopia's neighbouring states over the water resources situated in some of the basins. Despite recognition of the principle of the equitable utilisation of shared water resources and the need for international cooperation among countries, there are always conflicts over shared water resources – unless the concerned countries enter into fair water sharing agreements. The need for IWRM arises from the simple fact that different uses of water resources are interdependent.[108] All Ethiopian water resource laws and regulations emphasise the importance of IWRM. However, the existing water resources system is facing actual and potential conflict at the international and domestic level.

4.1 Disputes at the national and local level

Disputes over water resources at the local level usually arise in areas subject to water scarcity. They are often triggered by non-compliance with water permits, creating conflict between permit holders and third parties. These conflicts should be resolved in terms of the relevant legal framework.[109] Any dispute relating to water resource use that is within the jurisdiction of the first instance court must be entertained by the Supervising Body. If the disputes are between the Supervising Body and the permit holder, the matter will be handled by an arbitration process where the arbitrators shall be nominated by the parties. Any party that is aggrieved by the decision of the arbitrators may appeal to a regular court of jurisdiction.[110]

Conflicts are common when pastoral communities in water-scarce areas migrate to other areas in search of water and other resources for their livelihood. This kind of migration is common among communities in the Oromia Regional State, Somali

107 GRAIN (2012).

108 Cap-Net et al. (2008).

109 Ethiopian Water Resources Management Proclamation No. 197/2000, Article 9; and Council of Ministers Ethiopian Water Resources Management Regulations No. 115/2005, Article 35.

110 Ibid: Article 36.

Regional State and the Afar Regional State.[111] These kind of conflicts have on several occasions led to all-out wars between competing resource users.[112] A case in point is the recurring conflicts over water and grazing areas in the Ogaden Region of Ethiopia.[113] Though not properly institutionalised, there are local dispute resolution mechanisms including using elders to settle the disputes.[114] The transregional or transboundary transfer of water may also cause conflict among regions and states. The best strategies to be followed in IWRM would be resorting to transparent, democratic and accountable decision-making processes that include all relevant stakeholders,[115] so that they feel that decisions are influenced by their inputs.

4.2 International disputes over water resources

The River Basin Council and Authorities Proclamation envisages negotiation as a method of dispute resolution on water use.[116] As a major stakeholder in one of the most shared basins in the region, the Nile Basin, Ethiopia has ratified the CFA of the Nile Basin, and has committed itself to abiding by the terms of the agreement not to cause significant harm to the interests of the lower riparian states. The lowest riparian state, Egypt, is, however, raising issues that are related to old treaties.[117] Egypt is particularly concerned about Ethiopia's construction of the GERD Project, a mega hydropower dam, along the course of the Blue Nile (Abbay). Egypt views this project as a potential threat to its water security. It is hoped that Egypt and Sudan will eventually agree to the terms of the CFA on water security and drop their demand for the recognition of their existing use and resource rights to the waters of the Nile River.[118] It is also hoped that all parties to the CFA will finally agree on all terms of the agreement, including a peaceful settlement of disputes as per Article 3 paragraph 12 of the CFA.

There are other transboundary river basins that provide fresh surface water to countries neighbouring Ethiopia.[119] The Omo-Gibe River Basin, whose waters flow from

111 Tigist (2014). For inter-regional conflicts and the Somali Region in particular see <https://openaccess.leidenuniv.nl/bitstream/handle/1887/13839/chapter%20eight.pdf?sequence=7> (accessed 18-12-2017).

112 See <https://www.africaportal.org/documents/5266/ethiopia-2002-2.pdf> (accessed 16-12-2017).

113 Flintan & Tamrat (2002: 251-253).

114 Edossa et al. (2007).

115 Carr (2015).

116 Article 6(7), River Basins Councils and Authorities Proclamation No. 534/2007.

117 The old treaties over the Nile waters include the 1902 Anglo Ethiopian Agreement, the 1929 Agreement signed between Britain and Italy and the1952 Agreement.

118 Salman (2017).

119 Baro-Akobo Basin; Genale-Dawa Basin; Omo-Gibe Basin and Wabi Shebele Basin are the river basins with water resources of transboundary nature and calling for the involvement of the relevant stakeholders as per the principles of IWRM system.

the western Ethiopian highlands into its terminus Lake Turkana on the border with Kenya, is one of the Ethiopian river basins assailed with conflict. The construction of hydropower dams and the diversion of the river for irrigation of sugarcane plantations have caused displacements and water shortages for the local population. This has resulted in an uproar by communities concerned with diminution of the lake's water level.[120] The construction of massive hydropower dams along the basin is stirring constant disputes. There is a fear of possible landslides and even an earthquake of huge magnitude as a result of the construction of Gibe II Dam. The dispute between Ethiopia and Kenya relating to the receding water resource along their common border has led to further conflict over land, livestock and other resources.[121] Since the Omo-Gibe Basin Authority has not yet been formally established by regulations of the Council of Ministers of Ethiopia, the responsibility for administering water resources in the basin rests with the MoWIE or the relevant water bureaus.

5 Conclusion

Ethiopia has embarked on a comprehensive process to restructure its existing water management institutions and amend its existing laws and regulations in order to promote IWRM. This is reflected in the EWRMP and other national documents. The Ethiopian Water Management Proclamation and its Regulations significantly improve the country's water governance system. The establishment of BHC and BAs for better and decentralised governance of the water resources is a wise approach to promote the equitable use of the available water resources in the country. The planning of water resources management at a basin level and the establishment of basin and sub-basin level institutions for decentralised water resources management is a commendable undertaking. The most important task ahead is the implementation of the principles, policies, laws and regulations in order to achieve the sought after goals and objectives.

The water resource management laws do not have clear provisions on the transfer of water from one basin to another. The actual and potential overlaps of powers and duties of the Federal Regional States in the context of water resources administration and use may create unnecessary institutional duplication. The accountability of BAs to BHCs, on the one hand, provided that they might be established as stipulated, and to MoWIE, on the other, may create dual accountability, which may weaken the mandate of the river basin organisations to make effective decisions on water management issues. As fresh water resources are dwindling owing to climate change and population

120 See generally University of Oxford (2012); Carr (2017).

121 Hathaway (2010); see also <http://www.colinmayfield.com/waterhealth/course5/content/concepts/extra/LakeTurkana/LAKE%20TURKANA%20WATER%20CONFLICT_2015.pdf> (accessed 16-12-2017).

pressure, the conflict over these resources will increase. Accordingly, there must be an appropriate dispute settlement system or a mechanism to prevent conflicts over water resources arising in the first place.

The existing and planned water governance institutions in Ethiopia need to be re-examined with the view to avoiding the problems of overlapping mandates and the bottlenecks that are likely to cause the malfunctioning of the laws and institutions. As the power-sharing between the Federal Government and the regional states is extended to water governance, amending some of the laws that appear to cause overlapping powers and duties among the administrative organs and legislative jurisdiction of the two levels of government may be necessary.

References

Awulachew, SB, AD Yilma, M Loulseged, W Loiskadl, M Ayana & T Alamirew (2007) *Water resources and irrigation development in Ethiopia* International Water Management Institute Working Paper No. 123.

CAP-Net, Global Water Partnership & UNDP (2005) *Integrated water resources management: training manual and operational guide.*

Cap-Net, UNDP & International Network for Capacity Building in Integrated Water Resources Management (2008) *Conflict resolution and negotiation skills for integrated water integrated water resources management* Training Manual, at <http://www.gwp.org/globalassets/global/toolbox/references/conflict-resolution-and-negotiation-skills-from-iwrm-capnet-2008.pdf> (accessed : 16-12-2017).

Carr, CJ (2017) *River basin development and human rights in Eastern Africa: a policy crossroads.*

Carr, G (2015) "Stakeholder and public participation in river basin management – an introduction" 2(4) *WIRE's Water* 393-405, at <http://wires.wiley.com/WileyCDA/WiresArticle/wisId-WAT21086.html> (accessed 24-12-2017).

Defere, E (2015) *Private sector landscape for WASH in Ethiopia: bottlenecks and opportunities* One WASH plus Programme Report.

Edossa, DC, SB Awulachew, RE Namara, MS Babel & AD Gupta (2007) "Indigenous systems of conflict resolution in Oromia, Ethiopi" in B van Koppen, M Giordano & J Buttersworth (eds) *Community-based water law and resource management in developing countries* 146 at: <http://publications.iwmi.org/pdf/H040692.pdf> (accessed 16-12-2017).

Environmental Protection Authority and Ministry of Economic Development and Cooperation (2001) *Conservation strategy of Ethiopia phase III project (1996-2001) final evaluation report* Vol. 1, at <https://www.iucn.org/downloads/cons_strategy_ethiopia_final.pdf> (accessed 9-8-2018).

FDRE / Federal Democratic Republic of Ethiopia (1996) *Ethiopia's food security strategy.*

FDRE / Federal Democratic Republic of Ethiopia (1997) *Environmental policy of Ethiopia.*

FDRE / Federal Democratic Republic of Ethiopia (2000) *Ethiopian water resources management proclamation No. 197/2000.*

FDRE / Federal Democratic Republic of Ethiopia (2005) *A plan for accelerated and sustained development to end poverty (PASDEP) 2005/06-2009/10*, at <https://extranet.who.int/nutrition/gina/en/node/7935>, (accessed 10-7-2018).

FDRE / Federal Democratic Republic of Ethiopia (2011) *Ethiopia's climate-resilient green economy: green economy strategy.*

FDRE / Federal Democratic Republic of Ethiopia (2011) *National drinking water quality monitoring and surveillance strategy.*

FDRE / Federal Democratic Republic of Ethiopia (2016) *Growth and transformation plan II (GTP II) (2015/16-2019/20)* Vol. I: main text.

FDRE / Federal Democratic Republic of Ethiopia (2016) *The Great Ethiopian Renaissance Dam*, at <http://www.aba.gov.et/Portals/0/Abbay Basin Book Let.pdf> (accessed 15-12-2017).

Flintan, F & I Tamrat (2002) "Spilling blood over water? The case of Ethiopia" in J Lind & K Sturman (eds) *Scarcity and surfeit: the ecology of Africa's conflicts* 251.

GRAIN (2012) *Squeezing Africa dry: behind every land grab is a water grab*, at <https://www.grain.org/Article/entries/4516-squeezing-africa-dry-behind-every-land-grab-is-a-water-grab> (accessed 24-12-2017).

Hathaway, T (2010) *Fighting for Lake Turkana: why Kenyan communities are resisting Gibe 3 Dam*, at: <https://www.internationalrivers.org/sites/default/files/attached-files/laketurkanatripreport0610.pdf> (accessed:26-12-2017).

Lawson, FH (2017) "Egypt versus Ethiopia: the conflict over the Nile Metastasizes" 52(4) *The International Spectator* 129-144, at <http://www.tandfonline.com/doi/full/10.1080/03932729.2017.1333272> (accessed 15-12-2017).

Mekonnen, DZ (2010) "The Nile Basin Cooperative Framework Agreement Negotiations and the adoption of a 'Water Security' paradigm: flight into obscurity or a logical cul-de-sac?" 21(2) *European Journal of International Law* 421-440.

Ministry of Water Resources (1999) *Ethiopian water resources management policy.*

Mosello, B, R Calow, J Tucker, H Parker, T Alamirew, S Kebede, T Alemseged & A Gudina (2015) *Building adaptive water resources management in Ethiopia*, at <https://www.odi.org/sites/odi.org.uk/files/odi-assets/publications-opinion-files/9648.pdf> (accessed 8-8-2018).

Raventós Vilalta, E (2010) *Water resources management in the Central Rift Valley of Ethiopia* MSc Thesis in Civil Engineering, Universitat Politècnica de Catalunya, at <https://nilebdc.wikispaces.com/file/view/Anteneh_Dejenie_IWMI_NBDC_Symposium.pdf> (accessed 15-12-2017).

Salman, M.A. (2018) "Agreement on the declaration of principles on the GERD: levelling the Nile Basin playing field" in Z Yihdego, A Rieu-Clarke & AE Cascão (eds) *The Grand Ethiopian Renaissance Dam and the Blue Nile Basin: the Implication for transboundary water cooperation.*

Salman, MA (2017) "The Nile Basin Cooperative Framework Agreement: The impasse is breakable!" *Sudan Tribune* (22-7-2017), at <http://www.sudantribune.com/spip.php?article62804> (accessed 8-8-2018).

Tamrat, I (2008) "Policy and legal framework for water resources management in Ethiopia" International Conference on Water Management in Federal and Federal Type Countries, at <http://www.forumfed.org/libdocs/SpainWater2008/Imeru%20Tamrat%20_%20final%20en.pdf> (accessed 23-12-2017).

Tigist, KF (2014) *Conflicts among pastoralists in the Borana Area of Southern Ethiopia: the case of Borana and Garri* Master Thesis University of Tromsø.

University of Oxford, African Studies Centre, (2012) *Lake Turkana and the Lower Omo: hydrological impacts of the Major Dam and irrigation development report* Vol. 1.

Water Governance Centre (2013) *Water governance capacity: Awash Basin, Central Ethiopia* Issue Paper.

Chapter 25: Water resources management and environmental sustainability in west and central Africa

Joseph Magloire Ngang

1 Introduction

Shaken by decades of crisis, water resource management around the world is feeding pessimism; and, instead of appearing as a benchmark of good governance, the issue of water remains largely addressed within the context of poverty alleviation. It is through this fight that states have renewed their commitment especially in favour of the achievement of the Sustainable Development Goals[1] (SDGs) and in the pursuit of new horizons set within the framework of the water decades, [2] the latest of which (2018-2028) was proclaimed on 21 December 2016 by the United Nations General Assembly under the theme: "Water and Sustainable Development".[3]

Sub-Saharan African Countries are among the most affected: A World Bank analysis of international river basins reveals that in 1995, eight river basins were already facing water stress while four were experiencing water shortages and the number of river basins to face water stress will increase to sixteen by the year 2025. This means that a growing number of Africans will live in an environment characterised by water scarcity. [4] The same sources mention, that Africa had experienced an improvement in the water supply during the 1980-1990 water decade as coverage increased from 32% to 46%, while sanitation improved from 28% to 36%. Since the end of the decade, however, there has been stagnation, and probably more people lack adequate water and sanitation services today than in 1990. In 1994, 381 million people (then

---

1 On 25 September 2015, on the side-lines of the UN General Assembly, 193 world leaders took the engagement on 17 global goals known as the Sustainable Development Goals (SDGs) aimed to achieving the three key objectives during the 2015-2030 period, namely: eradicate extreme poverty fight against inequalities and injustice, resolve the problem of climate change. Clean water and sanitation is the 6th objective of the SDCs.

2 The United Nations Conference on water, held on 14 March 1977 in Mar del Plata, launched the first international decade of water (1980-1990), under the theme: "Drinking Water and Sanitation"; 2005-2015 was proclaimed as the second decade of water with the theme: "Water, a source of life".

3 Resolution (A/RES/71/222) International Decade of action on the theme: Water and Sustainable Development (2018-2028).

4 African Development Bank (2009: 3).

approximately 54% of the African population) did not have access to safe drinking water, while 464 million (then 66%) did not have access to sanitation facilities.[5]

Today, the observation that emerges and which is partly true is that several decades after independence the challenge remains the same. Until recently, only a few African countries had implemented national policies on the management of water resources. This in turn was a result of the fact that environmental issues were still of secondary concern. Poorer countries, for the most part, predominantly focused their economic development on the exploitation of natural resources. As a result, the water sector continues to be affected - both quantitatively and qualitatively. With the combined effects of climate change, this led to the depletion of water resources. These developments also had dramatic repercussions on the grassroots' social sectors.

There are many problems across the world which have urged the international community to lay the essential legal bases for improved water protection. Thus for instance a consensus was reached for Integrated Water Resources Management (IWRM), a cherished formula that emerged from two successive international mechanisms. The first, referred to as the Dublin Principles[6], emanated from the international conference on water held in Dublin in January 1992. The second was Agenda 21[7], which was an outcome of the 1992 Earth Summit in Rio de Janeiro. Like any decision adopted on a global scale, the recommendations of these summits were to be translated into local realities. But in the absence of national legislative efforts, many states' control of water still remains doomed to failure, as the principles of sustainable and ecological management are not yet in place.

The term governance commonly refers to the way in which institutions operate to meet social needs. The latter is often determined by the positive or negative relationship between the management of natural resources and economic development. In the context of the ongoing water crisis, it has been argued that it is not so much water that is "in crisis" as it is the governance of this valuable resource.[8] While the demand for water is constantly rising, states fail to make water available to the people despite its abundance. Moreover, freshwater is being polluted and wasted shamelessly.[9]

Water is a vital human need, it touches on economic activities, it affects environmental protection, it influences regional development and is most relevant to public health. It is therefore essential that African countries improve their water governance structures in order to ensure the success in international cooperation efforts. What is needed are effective institutions, standards and procedures, which internalise and respect the principles of IWRM.

---

5 Ibid.

6 Dublin Principles derived from the Dublin Declaration on water in the view of a sustainable development (ICWE 1992). See also African Development Bank (2009: 3).

7 UN Agenda 21, Chapter 18.

8 See Julien (2012: 4) with further references.

9 Ibid.

2 Available water resources and the problem of bad governance

The soils and subsoils of many African countries equally abound in rich water resources. The paradox is that these are very often poorly managed. In 2009, a study carried out by the African Development Bank demonstrated that sub-Saharan Africa consisted of many least developed countries where less than half the population has adequate access to sufficient drinking water.[10] Nearly a decade later, this observation still remains valid. Several factors account for this failure, which is increased by unplanned population growth and related urbanisation as many states are unable to develop their water services.[11] A more in-depth analysis revealed, that besides legally inappropriate frameworks, factors such as poverty and conflict exacerbate the situation, especially in arid zones.

2.1 Poverty, climate change, conflict and pollution

The period of decolonisation of Africa was also one of gaining sovereignty over natural resources of the countries concerned. Despite the relative progress regarding the protection of natural resources, the current conditions still demand more sustainable social and economic development efforts in the interest of all segments of the population.[12]

Although Africa is credited with better prospects for growth, it remains at the centre of deep concerns when it comes to the governance of water resources, in particular, because supply capacities continue to dwindle below the scarcity threshold of 1,700 m^3/year according to the international standard.[13] In 2018 people without access to safe drinking water increased all over Africa, both in the rich countries (South Africa) and the poorer countries of the continent (Somalia, Sudan, Central Africa).

While it is true that water resources are a global asset, each society is responsible to make its own contribution. While we experience an increase in dry and polluted water reserves, catastrophic floods, declining quality of drinking water, states are equally responsible to counter the water crisis.[14]

Unfortunately, in Africa more than elsewhere, the water crisis is nurtured by inadequate policies and poverty, which both keep states below their capacity to develop their potential to provide training and to equip themselves with better water infrastructure. Climate variability greatly increases the cost of the required infrastructure.[15]

10 See African Development Bank (2009).
11 Mardini (2009: 4).
12 Republic of Cameroon (2014: 4).
13 On the scarcity threshold, see Jemmali (2013).
14 IAEA (2018).
15 Blanchon (2001: 118).

Meanwhile, deforestation continues, deserts keep advancing and drought periods are becoming longer and longer. Phenomena such as the gradual drying up of Lake Chad are a sad reflection of ecological disasters on the continent.

When the pressures on natural resources endanger various aspects of human security, it becomes necessary to delimit the risks of conflict[16] as have been recorded in recent years in Africa: In the Nile river basin between Egypt and Ethiopia (1979 and 1991); around the Okavango river, between Namibia and Botswana (1989-1993) until the establishment of a Joint Commission of the Okavango Basin; around the Senegal river, with violent uprisings in Mauritania (1989) triggering the exodus of black populations towards Senegal; at the Mauritania-Mali border (1999), where there are recurrent conflicts among villagers; around the Tana river in Kenya (2001) regarding access to water and pasture; around the wells in the El Bur region, north of Mogadishu (Somalia) between 2004 and 2006 (more than 250 deaths among others).[17]

The reasons for these water-related conflicts are numerous. Some are, however, undeniably associated with the unequal distribution of the resource:[18]

> Hydrologically, the subcontinent is clearly divided between the West, with limited resources, and the East, which has much more water. This contrast is strengthened by a very strong segmentation of river basins, inherited from the colonial boundaries. Through the interplay of agreements between colonial powers and decolonisation processes, some States, such as Malawi or Namibia, have found themselves poor in this resource.

Moreover, the unsafe quality of water is also a given fact:[19]

> Africa is regularly hit strongly by remarkable droughts (...). Water reserves dry up and the fear of an economic standstill is real. Variability is also shown by catastrophic floods. In some regions such as southern Africa, the climate follows natural cycles of ten to fifteen years, the effects of which are still poorly measured, but which are clearly incompatible with the requirements of economic development.

Another reason for conflict is the geographical distance between the water resources and developed zones, which is often "due to the continent's development pattern, based on underground resources".[20] Yet, nothing prevents states from developing a more effective normative and institutional infrastructure, where water management benefits the population and favours sustainable development.

16 Ibid.
17 Lasserre & Boutet (2002).
18 Hellendorf (2013: 117).
19 Ibid: 118.
20 Ibid: 119.

2.2 The coexistence of significant differences between the available resource and satisfying the right to water

Water as a priority need is included in the category of social rights. Water security is often seen as a right which should be based on the principle of universal access. Unfortunately, in contrast to the objective of universality, many realities still stand in the way of the realisation of water as a human right. In many poor countries the lack of water often attains the humanitarian emergency threshold of 70% of the population without having access to water.[21] OECD reports that, mostly in developing countries, in addition to the 2.2 million people who die every year from diseases linked to poor sanitary conditions and unsafe water, knowledge of water resources, uses, discharges, as well as the functioning of the environment remain very insufficient to achieve global and sustainable water management.[22] This is a reality in Cameroon, Cote d'Ivoire, Niger, Togo or Mali, among others. These countries experience urbanisation coupled with population growth. Related problems concern both rainwater and wastewater[23] among others. The lack of technical capacities can be measured by the urban water supply rates, which remain low: below 41% on average, barely above 55% in large cities (of more than 1 million inhabitants) and only 27% for the urban poor.[24]

At the end of the Millennium Development Goals (2000-2015) implementation period, it was largely agreed that the global water situation had progressed while Africa was still lagging behind. This shortcoming was newly addressed in the SDG-framework in order to guarantee access to safe water and sanitation, by improving water resources management in a sustainable manner.[25] Weather this goal can be reached by the 2030 deadline is doubtful.

The CICOS basin (International Commission of the Congo-Oubangui-Sangha Basin) is the second largest hydrological basin in the world with its backbone, the Congo River, whose flow rate is 42,000 m³/s, in high season and 38,000 m³/s in the dry season. The basin comprises six countries (Angola, the Democratic Republic of Congo, Congo-Brazzaville, Cameroon, Gabon and the Central African Republic). While most of these countries are facing water crises, the DRC which holds the greatest water resources of the continent –[26]

> is facing an acute crisis in the supply of drinking water. Indeed, only 26 per cent of Congolese have access to safe drinking water, an estimate that falls way below the 60 per cent average for all of sub-Saharan Africa.

21 Central African Republic Humanitarian Fund (2017: 7).
22 OECD (undated).
23 Tchotsoua et al. (1992).
24 Jaglin (2005: 5-22).
25 Sustainable Development Goals, Goal Number 6.
26 UNEP (2011: 27).

To address water shortages, the city of Yaoundé, Cameroon for example, started a project to supply drinking water from the Sanaga River (PAEPYS). The objective was to supply an additional 300,000 to 400,000 m^3/d by 2020. Ambitious projects such as this have been undertaken in various countries. Senegal, for example, has completed the implementation of the Long-Term Water Programme (2002-2009) and the Millennium Drinking Water and Sanitation Programme (2005-2015).[27] The cumulative effects of many projects should be sufficient in the long-term to reduce water shortages, but a problem solved often gives rise to another. Given the very high cost of water supply projects, the repercussions are felt on the water price by the consumer. In addition, public institutions, leasing companies or private concessions that revolve around the water sector generally lack the means to ensure maintenance considering the quality of the infrastructure acquired. While channels are built across the cities, it is not uncommon for water service providers to use tankers to supply water to the population. Sometimes, it could be the people themselves, who, disappointed by the regular failure of services, resort to rudimentary methods of water supply, such as accessing natural wells or springs.

The aforementioned examples reflect the complexity of environmental and natural resources, management problems, which often relate to multisector involvement, high uncertainty and a lack of know-how to address the problems. It is in those countries with high water potential that water resources suffer more losses through deficient management marred by a lack of civic behaviour, informality, a lack of scientific knowledge and the absence of public investment. As concerns the failure to anticipate the effects of climate change, which is a real structural problem, many countries have opted for an investment-raising approach whereas they do not have a national water policy. This is a major handicap because it is the policy that serves as the foundation for legislation, strategic planning and operational management.[28] Even where such policies exist, they are often inadequate, and water legislation is poorly developed in many cases. Legislative efforts have emerged at national levels through the adoption of water laws such as in Cameroon (14 April 1998), Chad (July 1998), Burkina Faso (8 February 2002), Senegal (4 March 1981), and the Democratic Republic of Congo (31 December 2015). At the regional community level several instruments have been designed: the Water Charter for the Lake Chad Basin (April 2012), the Water Charter of Niger Basin (30 April 2008), and the Water Charter of the Organisation for the Development of the Senegal River (28 May 2002).

Many of the aforementioned instruments were developed out of improvisation and need to be connected to local realities on the ground. Like customs and traditions, governance is an empty concept without the transmission of ethical values that respect the environment. Therefore, in order to take cross-cutting issues into account, the

27 Law No. 2009-24 of 8 July 2009 on the Sanitation Code, Explanatory note.
28 African Development Bank (2009: vi).

education component should not be left out of the package of measures, which would enable states not only to optimise water management but also contribute to the overall health situation of their populations.

3 Guaranteed sustainability through the dissemination of IWRM Principles

Despite the immense challenges that still exist for many African countries, they are not so oblivious as to ignore the real threats to their sovereignty over natural resources. Sustainable development is the core of the options taken on the continent and a solution for continuity named IWRM was adopted between a crisis period and the beginning of a new process of economic and social emergence. Burkina-Faso and Senegal are examples that show that water management prospects, as far as quality is concerned, are much better than before. Other countries like Cameroon, if their current efforts are sustained, could attain a sufficient level of production, to significantly reduce the water deficit, at least in the major cities, upon completing structuring projects which target the water sector. For the most part, the results achieved do not yet offer an objective comparison with other countries, while the value placed on improved water management has been amply demonstrated, at least in terms of developing national and community management schemes featuring regulations, procedures and standards with minimum requirements and guidelines for sustainable management of water. One of their qualities and not the least is the adoption of specific taxation based on water uses.

3.1 Normative and institutional dissemination

IWRM is a conceptual tool for equitable and rational management to achieve the SDGs. The link between water and environment has been established in line with the principles affirmed both in the context of the 1992[29] Dublin Declaration and the UN Agenda 21.[30] Many regional instruments were inspired by these international law instruments as for instance also applies to the African Convention on the Conservation of Nature and Natural Resources, adopted on 11 July 2003 in Maputo, Mozambique.

It is from the International Conference on Water and the Environment, held in Dublin in January 1992, that the world witnessed a declaration of the four principles considered as fundamental in the field of resource management. These principles state that freshwater is a limited and vulnerable resource, essential for sustaining life, development and the environment. Water exploitation and management must be based on a

29 International Conference on Water and Environment (ICWE) Dublin, Ireland, 26-31 January 1992.

30 Agenda 21, Chapter 18.

participatory approach, involving users, planners and decision-makers at all levels; women play a crucial role in the supply, management and preservation of water. Water has an economic value in all its competing uses and must therefore be acknowledged as an economic good.[31]

Agenda 21 emerged from the 1992 Earth Summit in Rio de Janeiro, laying down priorities for the sustainable and efficient use of freshwater resources. The measures proposed concern the integrated exploitation and management of water resources; assessment of water resources; protection of water quality and aquatic ecosystems; provision of safe drinking water, food production, rural development and sanitation; understanding and monitoring the impacts of climate change on water resources.[32]

As an expression of sectoral progress in global governance, both instruments have provided an opportunity for a collective shift towards considering solutions to local water problems. In the light of their recommendations and apart from the specific legislation that has spread as a sign of attachment to international mechanisms, African countries have engaged in joint initiatives such as the Lagos Action Plan (1980). This plan incorporates an environmental protection component adopted on the basis of a strategy to strengthen local economies, sovereignty over natural resources, food self-sufficiency, industry development and the mobilisation of the population.[33] The Plan is a continental approach based on regional cooperation. It mobilised the continent's largest financial institution, the AfDB to encourage its implementation. In so doing, the Plan served as a framework for the beginning of an organisation that enabled African states to look towards the future. To go even further and beyond the stage of mere political rhetoric that does not generally yield any results, states adopted a Convention on the conservation of nature and natural resources that displays both the ambition to do everything possible to better promote the integrated management of water resources stemming from the principles resulting from the new developments at the international level, and also to provide specific answers that fall under the continent's own options. The convention has the merit of being part of a process based on the achievements of the international meetings that precede it. Article VII, dealing with "Waters", is based on the satisfaction of three main conditions.

The first, which is conservation, recommends to states to manage their water resources in such a manner as to maintain the quality and quantity of these resources at the highest possible level. To this end, parties should take measures to maintain essential hydro-ecological processes and to protect human health against waterborne diseases; prevent any damage that could endanger human health or natural resources in

31 Dublin Principles emanating from the Dublin Declaration on Water for sustainable development (ICWE 1992). See also African Development Bank (2009: 3).

32 Agenda 21, Chapter 18.

33 Robert (2015).

another state as a result of pollutant releases; and prevent excessive extractions of these resources for the benefit of downstream communities and states.[34]

The second condition, which is planning, relies on the policies of conservation, management, use and development of groundwater and surface water, as well as the collection and use of rainwater. This condition which aims at ensuring adequate and continuous supply of sufficient water to the population, is largely dependent on specific studies of water cycles and watershed inventories; integrated water resources management; conservation of forest areas and other watershed areas and the coordination and planning of water resource development projects; inventory and management of all water resources including the administration and control of all forms of water use; controls which help to better prevent and check water pollution by establishing effluents and water quality standards.[35]

Finally, the third condition is cooperation: where surface or groundwater resources and related ecosystems, including wetlands, are cross-border to two or more parties (states), they should consult each other and, where appropriate, establish inter-state commissions responsible for their fair use, the settlement of disputes relating to the use of these resources and their collaborative development, their cooperative management and conservation.[36] Similarly, parties should undertake, individually or within sub-regional arrangements, to cooperate in the rational management and conservation of water in irrigated agriculture, with a view to ensuring greater food security and sustainable agro-industrialisation. Achieving all these goals requires a good vision, which is also a step that has been taken since the adoption of the Africa Water Vision 2025, which embodies the continental ambition for "an Africa where water resources are used and managed in a fair and sustainable manner for poverty alleviation, socio-economic development, regional cooperation and environmental protection".[37]

Even in the absence of national policies on water at the local level, African states had adopted international mechanisms to make a number of internal adjustments, despite the economic context that was not conducive for a genuinely sustainable and ecological water management. Could this be the reason why the 2002 World Summit on Sustainable Development held on African soil, in Johannesburg, examined on the ground, the realities of sustainable development and proposed the adoption of national action plans for the integrated management of water resources; a number of African countries that had adopted a water policy instrument before this date. These included South Africa, Egypt, Malawi, Mozambique, Nigeria, Uganda, the Seychelles and Zambia.[38] Today, this number has increased whether in terms of the states that have national

34 African Convention on the Conservation of Nature and Natural Resources, Maputo 2003, Article VII(1)(a)(b)(c).
35 Ibid: Article VII(2)(a)(b)(c)(d)(e).
36 Ibid: Article VII(3).
37 UN Water/Africa (2000).
38 African Development Bank (2009: 94).

policies or those that have simply developed comprehensive water resources instruments for home use or for livestock, fisheries or irrigation purposes.

The fact that there was no 'water sector' *per se*, and that water-related activities were spread across various sectors and managed by the institutions of these sectors led to inconsistencies in the management of water resources. Today, institutions are more and more working together. Consequently, there are signs of improvement even if the results achieved are still far from the expectation and from reaching the global targets. At least, two positive things have been achieved. The first is the considerable mobilisation of resources with the support of development partners who help governments to densify and significantly expand their sanitation networks, and the second is the capacity building of local stakeholders. In Senegal, for instance, Law No. 2009/24 of 8 July 2009 provides that every municipality must have a master plan for wastewater and rainwater treatment. Every rural community must also have a local water and sanitation plan. The master and local plans, in their sanitation component, define the short and medium-term[39] sanitation policy of the local community. In Burkina Faso, the General Code of Local Authorities has transferred powers to municipalities to establish, manage and develop local public services, including water and sanitation. As a matter of fact, since 2004, local authorities have become the country's competent authorities in matters of water and electricity, and since 2009, the state's powers and resources pertaining to drinking water supply and sanitation have been gradually transferred to these authorities.[40]

Cameroon has adopted an economic policy instrument that commits the country to an infrastructure equipment programme in order to become an emerging country by the year 2035. This vision is a bet on the future, for which objectives have been previously set and for which strategies have been adopted accordingly. An integrated water resources management plan was validated in December 2009 to guide state action in the area of water resources management. Important missions are central to the role assigned to certain administrative institutions set up such as the Ministry of Water and Energy, the Ministry of the Environment and Nature Protection, among others. Also in the context of decentralisation, a role has been transferred to municipalities in the maintenance of public water supply networks. These are based, in particular, on rural engineering for the promotion of village water supply.

Decentralisation remains a good solution for tackling the water crisis and is even one of the new options that generally relates to the reform of this sector. This has resulted in the design of the IWRM, which has as an advantage to synergise stakeholders in order to facilitate the management of problems whose scope is most often beyond the capacity of a single state. The problem that community instruments are keen to solve is to allow each state to organise water management on its territory while taking

39 Law No. 2009-24 of 8 July 2009 on the Sanitation Code of Senegal, Article 8.

40 Réseau Rhône Alpes d'Appui à la Coopération (2010: 3).

account of its neighbours. To illustrate this expanding form of co-management, several agreements can be cited, beginning with that of 6 November 1999 in Brazzaville, whereby the International Commission of the Congo-Oubangui-Sangha Basin (CICOS) was established. This commission draws on the tradition of cooperation as regards the use of international rivers.[41] For its part, the Water Charter for the Lake Chad Basin was the first milestone in sub-regional cooperation around a shared natural resource, Lake Chad. This initial legal framework, whose main merit is being among the first conventions on river basins in Africa, soon proved, however, obsolete because it did not include the most important rules of international rivers and lakes. This situation has been an impediment to the willingness of states to legitimately engage in a new era of cooperation to strengthen their 'community of interest' through the sustainable management of this shared lake. To remedy this situation of legal insufficiency, member states of the Lake Chad Basin Commission (LCBC), at the beginning of the 1970s, took the initiative of drawing up an additional treaty instrument to the basic convention.[42] Despite efforts dating back several decades, Lake Chad had shrunk by almost half, by the time the "Lake Chad Vision by 2025" was drawn up. This vision attempts to move up an already downward curve, by shedding light on the common guidelines of the member states and by emphasising the objective of sustainable conservation of the Lake and other wetlands by 2025 in order to ensure the economic security of the member states. [43]

Other initiatives also depict such shared vision. The three state signatories (Mali, Mauritania and Senegal) to the Charter of the Organisation for the Development of the Senegal River have moved in a similar direction of promoting a policy of optimal and sustainable use of the river's resources, involving the responsibility of users and an asserted policy in the field of water saving through integrated and equitable management for the benefit of present and future generations.[44] While the Organisation for the Development of the Senegal River itself has existed since 1972, the adoption of its Water Charter in 2002 enabled it to settle the issue of the method of distribution of water between uses. This method was supposed to be based on the principles of the obligation to guarantee the balanced management of water resources, the equitable and reasonable use of the river's water, the obligation to preserve the environment and to negotiate in the event of conflicts.[45] The application of the Charter is thus submitted to the Standing Committee on Water, made up of representatives of the member states.

Lastly, among the examples that can be retained, is the Water Charter of the Niger Basin, which musters its nine signatory states[46] around the objective of promoting

41 Ngodi (2012: 48).
42 Ibid.
43 Lake Chad Vision 2025, drafted in 2000 by the Lake Chad Basin Commission (LTBC).
44 Water Charter of the Senegal River (2002), Preamble.
45 Ibid: Article 4.
46 Benin, Burkina Faso, Cameroon, Côte d'Ivoire, Guinea, Mali, Nigeria, Niger and Chad.

cooperation based on solidarity and reciprocity for equitable and coordinated use of the water resource of the Niger River basin.[47] This instrument shows that the parties pledge to take action on the basis of participation and the equitable use of resources. To that effect, the signatories took immediate measures within the framework of the implementation of the precautionary and preventive principles making it possible to prevent and remedy, as a priority, environmental damage at source.[48] As regards accountability, the Charter lays down the obligations of the parties, the most fundamental of which are the maintenance of the quality and quantity of water resources and the adoption of a policy for the planning, conservation, management and development of water resources.[49] The Charter focuses on the essential questions of costs and pricing applied to natural and legal persons who pollute or draw water. At the level of standards and procedures alone, a more sustainable water resources management framework is being tested.

3.2 Taxation: a deterrent and financial resource mobilisation tool

Environmental taxation, which is defined as a doctrine whose main objective is the protection of the environment,[50] demonstrates a certain degree of effectiveness in some fields of environmental protection such as forestry, by introducing the use of appropriate economic instruments to influence consumer behaviour. It is clear, that pricing plays a key role in improving water resources management by developing tariffs and levying structures based on economic, ecological, financial and social considerations. Social protection and efficient resource allocation are maximised when water prices are equal to the economic cost of its production. By influencing prices, governments are sending signals and encouraging good water use. They also encourage producers to provide water at optimal levels.[51]

Agenda 21 states that, depending on the situation in each country and where resources permit, water taxes should be introduced taking into account the marginal and opportunity costs of water, particularly when it is used for production activities.[52] A number of sub-Saharan states have introduced water taxes into their domestic legal systems through environmental codes, water policy laws or specific tax laws. Chadian law, for example, defines the general principles of environmental protection through a system of financial and fiscal incentives aimed at encouraging investment and

47 Water Charter of the Senegal River, Article 2.
48 Ibid: Articles 6 and 7.
49 Ibid: Article 10.
50 Caudal (2014: 29).
51 African Development Bank (2009: viii).
52 Agenda 21, Chapter 18, para. 59(b).

operations to clean up and preserve the environment.[53] In Senegal, various laws, including Law No. 2001/01 of 15 January 2001 on the Environment Code, introduce a pollution tax that is determined according to the degree of pollution or pollution load.[54] Senegal's Law on the Sanitation Code provides that taxes and fees for the discharge of water into the natural environment are collected under the conditions set by the Environment Code.[55]

The objective of regulating water uses is linked to a whole chain of specific privileges granted to the administration through authorisations and declarations as well as policing measures that provide competent services with the means to ensure the control of activities carried out on water. Burkinabe Law No. 002-2001/AN of 8 February 2001 on the Water Management Policy Act provides, *inter alia*, that hydraulic installations and, in general, installations, facilities, works and activities carried out by any natural or legal person, whether public or private, and resulting, as the case may be, in withdrawals of surface or underground water, whether or not restored, resulting in a change in the level or mode of water flow, spills, discharges or direct or indirect, chronic or episodic, even non-polluting discharges[56] or deposits are subject to authorisation or declaration. Besides, installations, facilities, works and activities likely to endanger public health and safety, reduce water resources, substantially modify water levels, flow patterns or regimes, or seriously affect the quality or diversity of aquatic ecosystems are subject to authorisation. Such authorisation shall, where necessary, lay down requirements imposed on the beneficiary with a view to eliminating, reducing or offsetting hazards or impacts on water and aquatic ecosystems.[57]

The practice of authorisations leads to the collection of application fees and levies.[58] All these resources are used to finance the construction, maintenance and operation of water treatment facilities or installations and recurrent charges.[59] The peculiarity of the authorisation lies in its precariousness, that is, it is revocable if justified by public interest or in the event of non-compliance with one of the conditions laid down by it.[60] Since water is not a non-commercial good, states thus find in liberalisation an incentive to private funding and the best way to dissuade and, at the same time, offset the losses suffered by the resource.

---

53 Law No. 14/PR/98 laying down the general principles of environmental protection in Chad, 17 August 1998.

54 Law No. 2001/01 of 15 January 2001 on the Environment Code in Senegal, Article L73.

55 Law No. 2009-24 of 8 July 2009 on the Sanitation Code in Senegal, Article L73.

56 Law No. 002-2001/AN of 8/2/2001 (OG 2001 No. 23) on the orientation law on water management in Burkina Faso, Article 24.

57 Law No. 002-2001/AN of 8 February 2001 (OG 2001 No. 23) on the orientation law on water management in Burkina Faso, Article 26.

58 Law No. 81-13 of 4 March 1981 on Water Code in Senegal, Article 61.

59 Law No. 81-13 of 4 March 1981 on Water Code in Senegal, Article 62. This text states, in addition, that the financial system shall define the use of the funds provided.

60 Law No. 81-13 of 4 March on Water Code in Senegal, Article 21.

"The fear of the gendarme is the beginning of honesty". In line with this saying, water authorities have been endowed with a repressive arsenal targeting the various cases of violation of the water policy. These concern surface waters, groundwater, waters of territorial sea and waters of the exclusive economic zone.[61] The repressive arsenal punishes all discharges, spills, direct or indirect deposits, any act in general likely to pollute continental or marine waters, all discharges from the water banks and all waste substances, industrial waste, all solid substances.[62]

Water does not only require scientific knowledge but also good legislation and practices, which contribute to an education of mentalities in relation to the environment. Policing measures and fiscal incentives all result in the imposition of forms of levy on both the uses of water and its polluting activities. The combination of these elements places the sector on a field of innovation enabling it to preserve the quality and quantity of water suitable for human consumption, while regulating competing uses likely to generate the financial resources that enable the sector to withstand economic constraints.

4 Conclusion

The proliferation of ecological and safety threats affects water resource management in Central and West Africa and links states to a common ambition of sustainable development. Surpassing their economic difficulties to satisfy the demand for a resource directly linked to life, states have embarked on improving the governance of water resources when it comes both to supply and sanitation. The water crisis on the African continent has been a key factor in this awareness. Sustainable water management is far from being a natural phenomenon. The water crisis in sub-Saharan Africa is a social issue.

References

African Development Bank (2009) *Politique de gestion intégrée des ressources en eau.*

Blanchon, D (2001) "Les nouveaux enjeux géopolitiques de l'eau en Afrique australe" 3(102) *Hérodote.*

Caudal, S (2014) *La fiscalité de l'environnement.*

Central African Republic Humanitarian Fund (2017) *Annual report 2017*, at <https://www.unocha.org/sites/unocha/files/CAR%20HF%20-%20Annual%20Report%202017.pdf> (accessed 8-8-2018).

61 The Burkinabe Law No. 002-2001/AN of 8 February 2001 on the orientation law on water management, Article L74.

62 Ibid: Article R56.

Ebodé, JVN (ed.) (2012) *La gestion coopérative des ressources transfrontalières en Afrique centrale: Quelques leçons pour l'intégration régionale*, at <http://www.fes-kamerun.org/documents/ntudaebode.pdf> (accessed 8-8-2018).

Hellendorff, B (2013) *Water, conflicts, and cooperation-water management in West Africa: risks and opportunities*.

IAEA / International Atomic Energy Agency (2018) "Achievements in Africa and Latin America" 34 *Water and Environment* 6, at <https://www-pub.iaea.org/MTCD/Publications/PDF/Newsletters/we-34.pdf> (accessed 8-8-2018).

Jaglin, S (2005) *Services d'eau en Afrique subsaharienne. La fragmentation urbaine en question*.

Jemmali, H (2013) "Mesure de la pauvreté en eau: analyse comparative et développement de pauvreté en eau" 13(2) *Vertigo – la revue électronique en sciences environnementales*.

Julien, F (ed.) (2012) *La gestion intégrée des ressources en eau en Afrique subsaharienne, paradigme occidental, pratiques africaines*.

Lasserre, F & A Boutet (2002) "Le droit international réglera-t-il les litiges du partage de l'eau? Le bassin du Nil et quelques autres cas" 33(3) *Études Internationales* 497-514.

Mardini, R (2009) *Water and war: ICRC response*.

OECD Environment Programme (undated) *Improving water management: recent OECD experience*, at <https://www.oecd.org/env/resources/2715072.pdf> (accessed 8-8-2018).

Republic of Cameroon (2014) *Human rights action plan for* 2015-2019.

Réseau Rhône Alpes d'Appui à la Coopération (2010) *Comprendre la politique publique de l'eau au Burkina Faso*.

Robert, AC (2015) "Le plan d'action de Lagos" *Le Monde Diplomatique* (June/July), at <https://www.monde-diplomatique.fr/mav/141/ROBERT/53043> (accessed 8-8-2018).

Tchotsoua, M, JP Ndame, A Wakponou & J Bonvallot (1992) "Maîtrise et gestion des eaux a Ngaoundéré (Cameroun), Problèmes et esquisses de solutions" 23 *Geo-eco-Trop* 91-105.

UN Water/Africa (2000) *Africa water vision 2025*, at <https://www.afdb.org/fileadmin/uploads/afdb/Documents/Generic-Documents/african%20water%20vision%202025%20to%20be%20sent%20to%20wwf5.pdf> (accessed 8-8-2018).

UNEP / United Nations Environment Programme (2011) *Water issues in the Democratic Republic of the Congo, challenges and opportunities*, at <https://postconflict.unep.ch/publications/UNEP_DRC_water.pdf> (accessed 8-8-2018).

Chapter 26: Water security and environmental justice in Nigeria and South Africa: achievable concord or discordant alliance?

Irekpitan Okukpon

1 Introduction

As the world seeks responses to converging risks from inequality and environmental change, attention is placed on the role of improved governance for sustainable development. The way in which ecosystems and natural resources are currently governed often results in deprivation, marginalisation and structural inequality.[1] In many contexts, "environmental degradation generates further poverty by the exhaustion of natural resources and creates prejudice to the exercise of basic rights".[2] Poor and vulnerable communities suffer from various forms of environmental injustice, often unable to fight back and reverse trends, which keep them mired in a state of exclusion.[3] Without a paradigm shift in how natural resources and the environment are valued and governed, inequality will deepen and post-2015 developmental goals will be threatened, if not reversed.[4]

The concept of environmental justice has arisen, in this context, as a mechanism of accountability and legal transformations aimed at curbing abuses of power that result in the poor and vulnerable suffering disproportionate impacts of pollution and lacking equal opportunity to access and benefit from natural resources.[5] Environmental justice emerged as a self-conscious movement in the 1980s,[6] originally focused on the inequity of the distribution of toxics and hazardous waste in the United States of America, but has now moved far beyond this.[7] A major focus of the environmental justice scholarship has always been a move beyond the simple description and documentation of inequity into a thorough analysis of the underlying reasons for that injustice.[8] It also involved participatory justice, namely speaking for ourselves or a seat at the table; a

1 UNDP (2014).
2 IUCN (2007: 1). See also UNHRC (2011).
3 UNDP (2014: 5).
4 Ibid.
5 Ibid: 6.
6 Kaswan (2012).
7 Schlosberg (2013: 41).
8 Ibid: 4.

'justice' encompassing not only equity, recognition and participation, but more broadly, the basic needs and functioning of individuals and communities.[9] In its latest incarnation, environmental justice is also about the material relationship between human disadvantage and vulnerability and the condition of the environment and natural world in which that experience is immersed.[10] Currently, the environmental justice movement challenges the exclusive nature of environmental decision-making, working to ensure that the voices of those most affected get attention in transparent environmental decision-making processes.[11]

The inequities of water security in developing countries have become a global environmental justice issue. Water security has been described as:[12]

> adequate protection from water related disasters and diseases and access to sufficient quantity and quality of water at affordable cost to meet the basic food, energy and other needs essential for leading a healthy and productive life without compromising the sustainability of vital ecosystems.

Accordingly, water embodies the link between human needs and sustainability of resources that is very present in environmental justice debates.[13] Decision-making regarding accessibility of water and its management is deeply political and contested,[14] with the water domain being dominated by top-down and closed decision-making processes, where the concerns of the marginalised and disenfranchised citizens have not been taken seriously.[15]

This chapter discusses water security from an environmental justice perspective, highlighting inequities that arise from water management in general. It emphasises the need to apply an adaptive governance approach to water security issues, exploring the extent to which such an approach has been segued into developing countries like South Africa and Nigeria, which are both plagued with water inequities. The chapter further discusses South Africa in comparison with Nigeria because of the inequities of apartheid experienced in the former and the continued evolution of legislation and environmental justice to address any form of inequities, particularly, in relation to water and other basic human needs. Hence, the chapter examines existing legislation on water in both jurisdictions with a view to proffering a reconstructive theory of the concept of water security and what it should entail in a continuously changing world. The chapter further reflects on the importance of the right to water in both jurisdictions and how this right accords each jurisdiction the momentum and tools to entrench the concepts of environmental justice and adaptive governance in achieving water security.

---

9 Ibid: 5.
10 Ibid: 16.
11 Chiro (1996); and Vanderwarker (2012).
12 Pachova et al. (2008).
13 Agyeman et al. (2002); and Allouche et al. (2014).
14 Zeitoun (2013).
15 Mehta et al. (2007).

2 The concept of water security

The global recognition of the human right to water is fundamental to the concept of water security. The globally endorsed human right to water has been the result of intense global struggles for decades until November 2002, when the United Nations Committee on Economic, Social and Cultural Rights adopted a General Comment on the Right to Water.[16] It provided an authoritative, but not legally binding interpretation of the right to water under the International Covenant on Economic and Social Rights.[17] General Comment 15 states:[18]

> The human right to water is indispensable for leading a life in human dignity. It is a prerequisite for the realization of other human rights.

The central hypothesis behind General Comment 15 is summarised in the second paragraph:[19]

> The human right to water entitles everyone to sufficient, safe, acceptable, physically accessible and affordable water for personal and domestic uses. An adequate amount of safe water is necessary to prevent death from dehydration, to reduce the risk of water-related disease and to provide for consumption, cooking, personal and domestic hygienic requirements.

Through much lobbying and struggle, access to clean water and sanitation was finally recognised by the General Assembly of the United Nations as a human right in July 2010.[20] Later that year, the UN Human Rights Council affirmed by consensus that the right to water and sanitation is derived from the right to an adequate standard of living, which is contained in several international human rights treaties and that it is both justiciable and enforceable.[21] The official recognition of the right to water was a great victory for the global water justice movement and has been used as a powerful mobilising tool for water struggles around the world.[22] In global climate circles, one hears the expression 'water security' used with ever-increasing frequency together with declarations about the urgency to increase water security in these times of unprecedented global change and future uncertainty.[23] There is no agreement among experts on the terminology and some show little concern over its precise meaning, but it is generally conceived as the interaction between physical stress on water resources, the risk of

16 OHCR General Comment No. 15: The Right to Water (Arts 11 and 12 of the Covenant) Adopted at the Twenty-ninth Session of the Committee on Economic, Social and Cultural Rights, on 20 January 2003, Document E/C.12/2002/11 (Geneva: CESCR).

17 Langford (2005: 275).

18 OHCR General Comment No. 15.

19 OHCR General Comment No. 15: para. 2; Hardberger (2005-2006: 348).

20 Mehta et al. (2007: 160).

21 United Nations News (2010).

22 Mehta et al. (2007: 160).

23 Foster & MacDonald (2014: 1489).

water-related hazards and the coping capacity in water management of the society concerned.[24]

Traditionally, water security had two meanings which apply both to the rights of an individual or to the claims of a state on behalf of its citizens. The first meaning is a firm water right, which can be judicially or diplomatically enforced against those who interfere with it.[25] Domestic water law is a structure to channel and minimise conflict and competition because the object of all water law is to allow the acquisition of firm, quasi-exclusive rights to the use of water.[26] It does this by minimising but not eliminating the risks inherent in the use of water.[27] The second traditional meaning of security is a physically dependable supply which can be tied to a legal allocation or it can be simply based on capture and a low risk that any other party can interfere with the capture. In both arid and humid areas, water rights are provided by a right backed up by carry-over storage, dams and reservoirs.[28] Thus, as a result of increasing uncertainty about future supplies, the concept of water security today is being expanded beyond these traditional definitions to include the guarantee of sufficient water for a nation's sustainable food production.[29] The concept has received increased attention over the past decade in both policy and academic communities.[30] The assumption is that unless sufficient water exists for this and related health purposes, the lack of water will become a source of social insecurity or violence.[31]

Multiple definitions of the concept of water security exist, promoted by a variety of governments and international organisations. Domestic water management agendas in the past decade have embraced water security, leading some to characterise the concept as "a key objective of a range of governmental and non-governmental agencies across the spectrum of governance levels".[32]

3 Defining water security from a global perspective

The water security paradigm re-orients the goals of natural resource and environmental law and policy to achieve "an acceptable quantity and quality of water" with acceptable costs and risks.[33] Water lies at the heart of human conflict and cooperation. Water

24 Ibid.
25 Tarlock (2008: 715).
26 This characterisation of a water right was adopted by the New Mexico Supreme Court in *Walker v. United States,* 162 P.3d 882, 888 (N.M. 2007).
27 Tarlock (2008: 715).
28 Ibid.
29 Postel (1999).
30 Cook & Bakker (2016: 19).
31 Tarlock (2008: 715).
32 Cook & Bakker (2016: 19).
33 Grey & Sadoff (2007: 547-548); and Tarlock & Wouters (2009: 53).

security is the most integrated and accessible paradigm needed to move natural resource law and policy forward.[34] Interest in water security has expanded since the United Nations (UN) Ministerial Declaration of The Hague on Water Security in the 21st Century was issued at the World Water Forum in 2000.[35] The Ministerial Declaration led to wide use of the term in global policy development and science agendas over the past 15 years.[36] In response, definitions have proliferated, generating both convergence and confusion about the concept and options for measuring and managing water security.[37] The Ministerial Declaration describes the water security challenge as:[38]

> ensuring that... ecosystems are protected and improved; that sustainable development and political stability are promoted, that every person has access to enough safe water at an affordable cost to lead a healthy and productive life, and the vulnerable are protected from the risks of water-related hazard.

In multilateral policy circles, the most widely quoted definition appears to be that of the Global Water Partnership (GWP), which defines water security as "a common goal" where "...every person has access to enough safe water at affordable cost to lead a clean, healthy and productive life, while ensuring that the environment is protected and enhanced".[39]

The water security and growth session at the fourth World Water Forum in 2006 was an important milestone in recent science and policy agendas. Grey and Sadoff[40] examined the relationship between water security and human development, yielding a definition of water security based on water's productive uses and potential destructive impacts. They describe water security as the "availability of an acceptable quantity and quality of water for health, livelihoods, ecosystems and production, coupled with an acceptable level of water-related risks to people, environments and economies".[41]

Although this definition is more encompassing because it embraces both a risk-based perspective and addresses the role of water as both source of services and a source of threat, what is 'acceptable' is subject to different interpretations by different groups.[42] This definition raises a number of key challenges: what does acceptable mean for health, livelihoods, environment and production and how can this be determined? How should one determine an 'acceptable quantity' in different contexts? How should

34 Larson (2017: 164).

35 United Nations Ministerial Declaration of The Hague on Water Security in the 21st Century (2000).

36 Garrick & Hall (2014: 613).

37 Cook & Bakker (2012); Garrick & Hall (2014: 614); Obani & Gupta (2016: 201).

38 United Nations Ministerial Declaration of The Hague on Water Security in the 21st Century (2000: 1).

39 Global Water Partnership (2000).

40 Grey & Sadoff (2007).

41 Ibid.

42 Pahl-Wostl et al. (2013: 676).

one determine an 'acceptable quality' for different users and different uses? How should one assess 'water-related risks' acceptable 'to people, environments and economies' in the face of multi-decadal changes in water extremes (floods and droughts) and uncertainties in future climates?[43] These issues are a pointer that enhancing water security is first of all a governance challenge.[44]

Most recently, UN-Water used a dialogue process to define water security based on the multiple interests tied to it.[45] The resulting working definition describes water security as the:[46]

> capacity of a population to safeguard sustainable access to adequate quantities of and acceptable quality water for sustaining livelihoods, human well-being, and socio-economic development, for ensuring protection against water-borne pollution and water-related disasters, and for preserving ecosystems in a climate of peace and political stability.

This chapter adopts the following definition of Jun Xia et al.[47]

> ... water security includes: (a) population-wide security, that is, everyone can obtain secure water for domestic use; (b) economic security, namely water resources can satisfy the normal requirements of economic development; (c) ecological security, namely water resources can meet the lowest water demands of ecosystems without causing damage.

Similarly, the United Nations Development Programme (UNDP) views water security as an integral part of the broader conception of human security:[48]

> In broad terms, water security is about ensuring that every person has reliable access to enough safe water at an affordable price to lead a healthy, dignified and productive life, while maintaining the ecological systems that provide water and also depend on water. When these conditions are not met, or when access to water is disrupted, people face acute human security risks transmitted through poor health and the disruption of livelihoods.

These definitions reflect in part, the influence of different conceptions of security and the implications of these differences for water management.[49] Thus, four dimensions of water security were noted in the debate of Cook and Bakker:[50] water stress and availability; vulnerability to hazards, human development needs, and sustainability. Wouters et al.[51] have also identified three core constituent elements of water security: availability (controlled supply of quality and safe water); access (enforceable rights to water for a range of stakeholders); addressing conflicts of use (where competing uses occur, a mechanism to avoid and/or address disputes is needed. Flowing from this,

43 Ibid: 676.
44 Ibid: 677.
45 Garrick & Hall (2014: 614).
46 UN-Water (2013).
47 Xia et al. (2007).
48 UNDP (2006).
.49 Allouche et al. (2011: 160).
50 The first three can be understood through a risk lens. Hall & Borgomeo (2013: 371); and Cook & Bakker (2012).
51 Wouters et al. (2009).

water security appears to be a societal issue, and, thus, a political concern,[52] which has become increasingly important both at the national and international levels. Through the concept of water security, states seek to respond to the increasing threats to their water supply and quality and also to the potentially increasing conflicts and tensions arising between states.[53]

It therefore appears that understandings of the different requirements for achieving water security will vary between different regions and different countries, especially, between 'mature' and developing water management regimes. Any global water security framework must cater for different regions having different water security issues: for example, regional flood control, reducing drought disaster, water pollution control, and ecosystem conservation.[54] Although there are differing demands for understandings of water security in different regions, different countries at different levels of development, regional water security strategies could be developed under the framework of global water security. This global framework could emphasise the most important water security issues in each region, as the ones mentioned above, by linkage of hydrological cycle, while maintaining the goal of global water security.[55] The important thing is to recognise the underlying systemic nature of water security, so that the impacts or consequences of water security activities are considered in the light of human welfare and environmental responsibility, namely sustainable development.[56] This chapter, therefore, argues that the key to achieving an effective water security framework in developing jurisdictions is through the concept of adaptive governance. An exposition of this encompassing concept geared towards consolidating legal, social, economic and political processes in relation to natural resources like water is carried out below.

3.1 Using adaptive governance to achieve water security in developing countries

The introductory part of this chapter highlighted the role of environmental justice as one concerned with legal transformations aimed at ensuring that the poor do not lack equal opportunity to access and benefit from natural resources such as water.[57] Beyond mere revisions of strategies and regulations, empowering the poor requires broad systemic changes to laws and institutions that help overcome exclusion of the poor from their right to a healthy environment and support equal opportunity to access and benefit

---

52 Foster & MacDonald (2014: 1489).
53 Soyapi & Honkonen (2017: 2).
54 Allan et al. (2013: 630).
55 Ibid.
56 Ibid.
57 UNDP (2014: 6).

from natural resources.[58] Hence, adaptive governance entails the ability to generate long-term sustainable policy solutions to complex and dynamic environmental problems through collaboration among diverse stakeholders.[59] Governance is viewed as adaptable, flexible and repetitive; it extends from natural systems to human organisations.[60] Improved governance is seen as a force to regulate social, environmental and economic trade-offs in the process of development, and supporting an enabling environment of institutions that engender 'triple win' solutions for goals of sustainability, inclusion and resilience.[61] It reacts to change in ecological and human institutions and systems as science continues to evolve.[62] The concept can ensure flexibility in regulation[63] on water to ensure accessibility, affordability and availability of the resource to all. Hence, water governance is viewed as "the political, social, economic and administrative systems that are in place, and which directly affect the use, development and management of water resources and water service delivery at different levels of society".[64]

Accordingly, for adaptive governance to be applied to water-related issues in any jurisdiction, such political, social, economic and administrative systems on water must support the adaptive capacity of society, often, with an iterative approach to policy-making, stressing flexibility of the regulatory instruments.[65] The application of adaptive governance to water governance requires policymakers to act despite uncertainties.[66] Experimental interventions require resilience, supervisory and accountability mechanisms, and the assurance that adaptive management interventions do not risk unacceptable and irreversible outcomes.[67] The hope is that the technique of these scientific interventions will permit decision-makers to avoid the paralysis that scientific uncertainty creates by viewing management as an experiment that can progressively reduce scientific uncertainty over time.[68] Adaptive governance favours impermanent policy interventions and adoption of strict oversight mechanisms to encourage

58 Ibid.

59 Scholz & Stiftel (2005: 5).

60 Onzivu (2013: 625).

61 'Triple win' solutions in the sustainable development context covers economic, social and environmental 'pillars' to be thought of as synergistic and integrated stands that 'lend' themselves to inter-weaving and linkages. For more information, see <http://www.undp.org/content/dam/undp/library/Cross-Practice%20generic%20theme/Triple-Wins-for-Sustainable-Development-web.pdf> (accessed 14-12-2017).

62 Ruhl (1997: 933); Folke et al. (2005: 441); and Oglethorpe (2002).

63 Onzivu (2013: 625).

64 See <http://watergovernance.org/whatiswatergovernance> (accessed 12-12-2017); and Pahl-Wostl et al. (2013: 677).

65 Honkonen (2017: 3).

66 Onzivu (2013: 626).

67 Armitage et al. (2007: 83); and Gunderson (1999: 7).

68 Tarlock (2008: 728).

flexibility.[69] Dietz et al.[70] propose the first general list of criteria necessary for adaptive governance: inclusive dialogue between resource users – analytic deliberation – (complex); redundant layered institutions (nesting); mixed institutional types (such as market and state-based); and institutional designs that facilitate experimentation, learning and change. Thus, policy-making in adaptive governance is an iterative process of review and revision, requiring no rest for actors in a complex adaptive system.[71] The smooth functioning of this iterative process depends critically on the progressive development of mechanisms for the regular monitoring of specificity of processes and outcomes of policy interventions. Outcomes of monitoring processes routinely feed back into the policy process to re-assess policy goals, assumptions and objectives themselves.[72] Such self-conscious monitoring and feedback mechanisms facilitate learning, fine-tune policy instruments, highlight knowledge gaps, reveal the shortcomings of problem definition and knowledge, and create a culture of openness and experimentation in the conduct of policy.[73]

The process of adaptive governance to water systems also incorporates the intertwining of environmental justice in order to achieve water security in developing jurisdictions. If disputes over water management or the inequalities associated with water arise, it is expected that the network of systems in place (social, economic, political, legal and administrative) ensures that access to justice is available to stakeholders and that the public administration of water remains within legal bounds.[74] These stakeholders should, therefore, be able to enforce their right to public participation and to challenge acts, administrative decisions and omissions in the implementation of water plans and programmes of measures.[75]

Environmental justice movements often challenge dominant systems and global understandings of the environment-development balance, and systems of rights and justice. This is particularly the case in traditional and indigenous communities where cultures and ways of life are uniquely tied to the environment, and which have faced especially harsh forms of alienation and environmental dispossession for centuries.[76] Standing as the poorest and most socially excluded communities in the world, indigenous and tribal communities also host much of the planet's remaining reserves of natural resources[77] like water.

69 Hornstein (2005: 929-933).
70 Dietz et al. (2003).
71 Ruhl (2009: 903); and Onzivu (2013: 626).
72 Cooney & Lang (2007).
73 Ibid. See also Onzivu (2013: 626).
74 Keesen & van Rijswick (2012: 43).
75 Ibid.
76 UNDP (2014: 10).
77 Ibid.

4 Water security in South Africa

South Africa is a water-stressed country with a high proportion of arid land. More than 90% of South Africa is categorised as arid, semi-arid or sub-humid.[78] South Africa's economy is highly dependent on natural resource use, even though the economy has latterly become diversified.[79] There are strong links between agricultural land uses and high levels of water use in South Africa.[80] 86% of the land area in South Africa is used for agriculture.[81] While large parts of the population is heavily dependent on agriculture, much of the country is marginal in terms of dryland agriculture.[82] Consequently, water for irrigation purposes accounts for a major proportion of water consumption. In this manner, water is regarded as both an environmental 'limit' and a key component for economic prosperity.[83] The agricultural sector, while maintaining self-sufficiency in most basic food items, has a 'dual structure'. It has a commercial component but has many more subsistence level farmers.[84] The dual structure is marked by differential access to, and use of, water resources.

As a legacy of the apartheid regime, many black South Africans are concentrated in the rural areas, often living below the international poverty line, and with many having only limited access to water.[85] The demise of apartheid and the election of the first non-racial and democratic government in South Africa in 1994 remains a major landmark for political and socio-economic development in the country.[86] Since then, public policy reform discourses have gained more visibility in various sectors of the economy (water sector included). Inequality of access to water resources marked South Africa's history profoundly.[87]

The water law framework was overlain by the apartheid system characterised by a disparity of access to water that operated along racial lines with significant differences in water availability for racial groups in urban and rural areas.[88] The system of riparian rights, especially in rural regions, tended to favour an inequitable allocation of water as the right to water was tied to landownership. Particularly in the more productive agricultural regions, there were major inequalities as landownership was disproportionately skewed towards the white minority population.[89] Non-land holders who

78 See <http://www.gcis.gov.za/docs/publications/yearbook.htm> (accessed 18-12-2017).
79 Kasrils (2003: 2).
80 Godden (2005: 185).
81 Willis et al. (2000: 189).
82 Ibid; see also <http://www.gcis.gov.za/docs/publications/yearbook.htm> (accessed 4-12-2017).
83 Peart & Govender (2001: 51).
84 See <http://www.gcis.gov.za/docs/publications/yearbook.htm> (accessed 4-12-2017).
85 Stein (2000: 285).
86 Chikozho et al. (2017: 270).
87 Ibid.
88 Apartheid legislation distorted access to natural resources, denying the majority of South Africans the use of land, water, fisheries, minerals, wildlife and clean air. See DWAF (1997: 28).
89 Godden (2005: 196).

required water had to make an application to the Water Court. Any access to water so granted was premised on the use not interfering with the existing allocations to riparian owners. The other option was to become a landowner – a status from which many black and coloured South Africans were precluded.[90] The Water Act 54 of 1956 addressed some water allocation problems as it allowed for Government Water Control Areas in which, in certain circumstances, the Minister could override riparian allocations. Nonetheless, the focus remained on water supply and the 1956 Act failed to respond effectively to issues of environmental degradation, equity of distribution or the downstream effect of water allocations.[91] The apartheid lawmaker harnessed the law, and the water in the interests of the mostly white dominant class and groups who had privileged access to land and economic power.[92] Thus, the resulting body of laws and policies and the varied forms of infrastructure that were developed to harness water for multiple social practices over time constituted a complex political ecological terrain that was difficult to redress.[93]

The current vision for water governance in South Africa is, therefore, a product of radical changes in the national socio-economic and political environment.[94] Redistribution of water rights to redress the results of past discrimination became an explicit purpose of post-apartheid water governance, policy and the legislative regime.[95] Desired reforms in the water sector were translated into policy documents (a White Paper on National Water Policy 1997) and legislation (the Water Services Act 1997 and the National Water Act 1998). These legislations were geared towards the promotion of equity, sustainability, representativeness and efficiency through decentralisation of water management, new local and regional institutions, water users' registration and licensing and the emergence of a water rights market.[96] Therefore, the new water policy and law represented a fundamental legal reform in the country as it shifted the focus of formal water control from riparian water title holders, largely consisting of the white minority, to the new government as the custodian of the nation's water resources. Government is now the manager of the nation's limited water resources and not an administrator of a system of rights as in the past.[97] Towards this end, the effectiveness of these water legislations are analysed below to determine the extent to which it facilitates water security in South Africa.

---

90 Ibid.
91 Perkins (2003: 148).
92 MacKay et al. (2003: 29); Schreiner et al. (2004: 178); Pienaar & Van der Schyff (2007); and Woodhouse (2008).
93 Willis et al. (2000: 189).
94 Tewari (2009: 710).
95 MacKay et al. (2003: 29); and Gowlland-Gualtieri (2007).
96 Backeberg (2005: 123); and Chikozho et al. (2017: 270-271).
97 Chikozho et al. (2017: 271).

4.1 Water sector reforms in South Africa and water security paradigms

The Constitution of the Republic of South Africa[98] ushered in two central provisions that arguably form the backbone of water law in the country.[99] It contains a Bill of Rights (Chapter 2) intended to ensure the rights of individuals to a clean environment and safe water.[100] The first provision (Section 24) gives individuals a right to a safe environment that is not harmful to his/her health and well-being and to have the environment protected through reasonable legislative and other measures that prevent pollution, ecological degradation and secure ecological sustainable development. The second provision (Section 27) provides for access to health care services and sufficient food, water and social security. The right to water is provided in Section 27(1)(b): "everyone has the right to have access to sufficient food and water". The Constitution also provides that "the state must take reasonable legislative and other measures within its available resources, to achieve the progressive realisation of each of these rights".[101] These rights refer to the rights contained in Chapter 2 of the Bill of Rights, including the right to water.

The 1997 White Paper on Water Policy sets out fundamental principles for water law in South Africa. It provides that:[102]

> [t]he quantity, quality and reliability of water required to maintain the ecological functions on which humans depend shall be reserved so that the human use of water does not individually or cumulatively compromise the long term sustainability of aquatic and associated ecosystems.

The White Paper also introduced the necessity of a Reserve:[103]

> after providing for the basic needs of citizens, the only other water that is provided as a right is the Environmental Reserve – to protect the ecosystems that underpin our water resources, now and into the future.

Additionally, the White Paper recognises certain principles including: (a) water required to meet basic human needs and for the environment shall be identified as the Reserve and shall enjoy priority of use by right. Other uses of water shall be subject to authorisation;[104] (b) national government has a duty to assess the needs of the Environmental Reserve and ensure that the amount of quality water is set aside;[105] (c) where the needs of the environmental reserve cannot be met because of existing developments, there must be provision for active intervention to protect the water resources.[106]

98 Act 108 of 1996.
99 Chikozho et al. (2017: 274).
100 Ibid: 270.
101 Section 27(2), 1996 Constitution
102 DWAF (1997: Appendix 1, Principle 7); and Takacs (2016: 80).
103 Takacs (2016: 80).
104 DWAF (1997: Appendix 1, Principle 10).
105 Ibid.
106 Ibid.

It must also be noted that Schedule 4A to the Constitution provides for the functional areas of concurrent national and provincial legislative competence, whereas Schedule 4B affords the local governments executive authority with regards to provision of water and sanitation services. In other words, the water cycle is administered by two separate spheres of government, that is, national government, which is responsible for the management of water resources, and local government, which is responsible for water services with national government playing a regulatory and oversight role.[107]

As a means to emphasise the importance of water law reforms via legislation, the National Water Act (NWA) 1998 recognises in its Preamble that:[108]

> water is a scarce and unevenly distributed resource which occurs in many different forms… [and] that while water is a natural resource that belongs to all people, the discriminatory laws and practices of the past have prevented equal access to water, and use of water resources….

Too often in South Africa, water managers appear to frame the problem of water scarcity/unavailability of water as people not paying enough for the water they receive, thus wasting it.[109] This assertion appears to be reflected in the NWA 1998, which provides that:[110]

> water use charges will be used as a means of encouraging reduction in waste, and provision is made for incentives for effective and efficient water use. Non-payment of water use charges will attract penalties, including the possible restriction or suspension of water supply from a water work or of an authorization to use water.

Larson argues that:[111]

> a provision right to water framed in a manner opposed to water pricing and cost recovery is not only counter-productive to its presumed end of protecting disadvantaged communities, but also poses risks to ecological sustainability and human health.

This chapter argues that if water security envisages the provision of adequate water to meet basic human needs, particularly those of previously disadvantaged individuals in a particular jurisdiction, charges for water uses should not be discounted but must be at a rate, which is affordable to all, whether rich or poor.

Similarly, the Water Services Act provides that every water services authority has a duty to all consumers or potential consumers in its area of jurisdiction to progressively ensure efficient, affordable, economical and sustainable access to water services, subject to equitable allocation and regulation of access to water services.[112] The National Water Resource Strategy 2 (NWRS2) of South Africa reiterates that:[113]

107 Chikozho et al. (2017: 274).
108 Paras 1 and 2, Preamble to the National Water Act (NWA), Act No. 36 of 1998.
109 Takacs (2016: 73).
110 Chapter 5.1, NWA 1998.
111 Larson (2013); and Takacs (2016: 73).
112 Section 11(1) and (2), Water Services Act.
113 DWAF (2013: 47).

> the first objective is to ensure that sufficient quantities of raw water are available to provide for the basic water needs of people. In terms of current policy, a quantity of 25 litres per person per day has been incorporated into the Reserve determination. Even though this is the minimum volume, this will be progressively increased where appropriate.

The NWRS2 recommends that "…the management activities required to ensure the provision of sufficient water for the ecological reserve must be paid for by all registered and billable users…".[114]

The extent to which the combined provisions of the Constitution, the National Water Act and the NWRS2 translate to the need for availability, accessibility and affordability of water, which is what the concept of water security envisages. This was also subject of determination in a 2008 case, which sought to provide environmental justice for residents of Phiri, a township in Soweto, Johannesburg, South Africa. The aforementioned case and its implications for environmental justice and water security in South Africa is examined below.

4.2 The implications of *Mazibuko* on environmental justice and water security in South Africa

Phiri is a township in Soweto (the largest of Johannesburg's suburbs with a population that is 98.5% Black) with many impoverished residents living in overcrowded conditions.[115] As is the case in many similar communities in South Africa, few households have in-home running water.[116] Johannesburg Water Ltd, the state-owned company responsible for delivering water to Phiri residents, was charged both with delivering a scarce resource to a growing population and recouping its costs under a 'full cost recovery' model.[117] Johannesburg Water claimed that whereas Sowetans consumed one-third to one-quarter of all water delivered by the company, only one per cent of their revenue came from there; both because residents did not pay their bills and because antiquated infrastructure led to leaking pipes and other water waste.[118] To conserve water and recover expenses, the company instituted a plan where citizens who wanted water piped onto their property would have to install a prepaid water meter. However, after twenty-five litres per person of free basic water flowed, if the residents had not paid fees, their water would be turned off with no advance notice.[119]
Five Phiri residents sued the City of Johannesburg, Johannesburg Water and the Ministry of Water Affairs and Forestry. They alleged that the provision of six kilolitres per household per month did not meet constitutional standards in terms of the right to

114 Ibid: 88.
115 Magaziner (2008: 512-516).
116 Humby & Grandbois (2010: 526); and Wesson (2011: 394).
117 Daniels (2006: 63).
118 *Mazibuko v. City of Johannesburg* 2010 (4) SA 1 (CC) 12 (S. Afr.).
119 Ibid: para. 3; and Wesson (2011: 395).

water, requesting that the amount be doubled. The plaintiffs also alleged that the installation of pre-paid water meters, which would shut off without notice if bills were not paid, was unconstitutional, violating provisions of the rights to dignity (Section 7); equality (Section 9) and water (Section 27 (b)) of the South African Constitution.[120] The plaintiffs also alleged that the installation of pre-paid metres in black/poorer communities was discriminatory as this was not the norm in predominantly white communities. They also contended that when the metres were installed, Johannesburg Water gave citizens enough time to pay bills before disconnection, unlike in Phiri.

Accordingly, the Constitutional Court held that the obligation of progressive realisation of water rights imposed a duty upon the state to review its policies continually to ensure that the achievement of the right is realised progressively.[121] In light of the evidence presented, it could not be said that the provision of six kilolitres of free water per household per month was unreasonable,[122] especially as the applicants failed to establish that the introduction of prepaid water metres was unlawful.[123] In a move, which is reflective of how adaptive governance should work with regards to effective utilisation and security of water, the Constitutional Court held that when the state is challenged judicially as to its socio-economic policies, the agency in question must explain why the policy is reasonable; and must disclose what it did (including its investigation and research) to formulate the policy, where alternatives were considered and the reasons why the option underlying the policy was selected. The state may then be challenged judicially to account for its decisions and must accordingly demonstrate that the policy selected was reasonable and in due consideration of its obligation to progressively realise the relevant socio-economic right[124] – in this case, the right to water.

The case has been criticised by various scholars worldwide. Roithmayr[125] states that the Constitutional Court "found it constitutional to ration access to water based on the ability to pay, even for the country's poorest black residents" and in doing so, the court "took as its implicit baseline of reasonability...apartheid inequalities of race and class...that target the poor". In effect, finding "these inequalities constitutionally permissible, even though cost recovery from the poor serves to reinforce the legacy of apartheid".[126] She argues further that the court could have ruled that the city should refrain from aggressive cost recovery-targeted towards the country's poorest via prepaid meters.[127]

120 Magaziner (2008: 532); and Takacs (2016: 84).
121 *Mazibuko* (2008), para. 67.
122 Paras 82-89.
123 Paras 105-157.
124 Paras 161-161.
125 Roithmayr (2010: 324).
126 Ibid.
127 Ibid: 325-326; and Couzens (2015: 1169).

Bond[128] argues that the plaintiffs erred in arguing their case with a focus "only upon the consumption needs of low-income residents" and without looking at a wider societal context. He concludes on the need for "as a first step, more coherent critiques of the full range of practices that undermine our ability to perceive and respect water and other aspects of nature as a Commons".[129]

Whilst agreeing with Bond in this regard, this chapter also adopts the position that the existence of a right to water in the South African Constitution already provided the plaintiffs with enough leeway to argue beyond just consumption needs, but the need for water security. Whilst bearing in mind that the 1996 Constitution was adopted years before the concept of water security became popularised, a broader argument geared towards the need for adaptive governance with respect to natural resources like water would perhaps have resulted in the realisation of a more acceptable judgement for the plaintiffs and, therefore, achieve environmental justice for the Phiri residents. Nevertheless, it must also be noted from the *Mazibuko* case that whilst the notion of environmental justice is justified on the basis of distributional justice and equity, it is sometimes limited to the courts ability to apply it.

Thus, despite the Constitutional Court's reluctance to enforce the right to water more aggressively in *Mazibuko*, South Africa presented four documents spanning seventeen years in which lawmakers and policymakers have a blueprint for how government can protect the human right to water to ensure its availability for all.[130] Current South African water laws mentioned above represent a best practice approach that draws upon a range of scientific, technological, social and economic goals,[131] which is what the process of adaptive governance requires. Unfortunately, years after the National Water Act was implemented and enforced, access to water is still highly stratified along racial lines.[132] Kemerink, Ahlersa and van der Zwaag argue that "the dynamics of water politics including water law and rights cannot be understood without also scrutinising the power relations, discourses and discursive practices that guide perceptions of water problems and proposed solutions".[133] Bearing this in mind, it can be argued that the application of adaptive governance to water law reforms in South Africa is effective in the sense that its current law reforms are clearly predicated on explicit distributive justice goals, which define sustainability as a mixture of ecological and human needs.[134] This predication on distributive justice provides the required platform for progressively achieving water security in South Africa within the next few decades.

128 Bond (2013: 141-143); and Couzens (2015: 1168).
129 Ibid.
130 Takacs (2016: 97).
131 Godden (2005: 202).
132 Kemerink et al. (2011: 585).
133 Ibid: 586.
134 Godden (2005: 202).

5 Water security in Nigeria

Nigeria is endowed with adequate freshwater resources with a coastline of about 800 km in the south and also the Lake Chad Basin in the north. It is blessed with large rivers like the Niger, Benue, Kaduna, Anambra, Imo, Gongola, etc., small lakes, streams and ponds in the rural areas. These water resources are sources of livelihood and wealth creation to many families on a daily basis.[135] Despite Nigeria's apparent potential water abundance, Nigerians are in short supply.[136] The Nigerian situation mirrors the sub-Saharan African situation where millions still lack access to safe water supply. Considering that Nigeria is the most populous African nation, it also represents a sizable population of people in sub-Saharan Africa without access to water and sanitation.[137]

In a 2017 report, UNICEF notes that drought and conflict are important factors behind water scarcity in parts of Nigeria.[138] Currently, over 3.6 million people in North-East Nigeria where the Boko Haram insurgency is prevalent, do not have access to basic drinking water as the insurgency has resulted in damage to about 75% of the water and sanitation infrastructure.[139] In these areas, and in other rural parts of Nigeria, hand pumps fitted on bore wells and solar-powered motorised water systems are the two main drinking water sources. Although it is natural to expect that these sources provide uninterrupted water supply to the people,[140] this is not the case in Nigeria. While the concept of water security remains a global one, which should be realised by governments at the national level, water security in North-East Nigeria still appears to be an illusion. This chapter focuses on the apparent lack of water security in North-East Nigeria, as it serves to emphasise why the Nigerian government needs to apply more adaptive governance tactics towards achieving water security.

In North-East Nigeria, particularly in the Borno, Yobe and Adamawa (north) states, the Boko Haram insurgency has ravaged and displaced many people, while drinking water in internally displaced persons' (IDP) camps appears to be inadequate. The absence of financial resources is cited as a key reason why IDPs lack access to water,[141] and priority needs in IDP camps include money to fuel generators to pump water.[142] Other challenges cited include the lack of funds to pay for water from water vendors, the inability to gain access to public water sources and the inability to purchase suitable water containers to store water.[143] In the Borno state, the main water sources are water

135 Federal Ministry of Water Resources (2011: 7).
136 Ibrahim (2012: 71).
137 Henderson & Sundaresan (1982); and UNICEF (2014: 14).
138 *Punch* (2017).
139 Adebowale (2017).
140 UKAID & UNICEF (2017).
141 ACAPS (2016: 4).
142 Ibid: 8.
143 Ibid: 14.

vendors, unprotected wells, rivers and dam water. Unable to pay for water, IDPs often have to beg the host communities for access to wells and boreholes.[144]

If the concept of water security is one that envisages reliable access to, availability and affordability of water, it is evident that North-East Nigeria is a fertile ground for the application of environmental justice. Nevertheless, an examination of water law reforms by the Nigerian government provides an insight into the extent to which existing legislation on water serves to improve water security, particularly but not exclusively in the North-East region of Nigeria.

5.1 Water law reforms in Nigeria

The basis for water law reforms in Nigeria stems from the provision of Section 20 of the Constitution of the Federal Republic of Nigeria (the 1999 Constitution). The provision states that "the State shall protect and improve the environment and safeguard the water, air and land…in Nigeria". This particular provision is contained in Chapter II of the Constitution titled 'Fundamental Objectives and Directive Principles of State Policy.' These fundamental objectives consist of ideals towards which a nation is expected to strive, while the directive principles identify policies, which are expected to be pursued in the nations effort to realise national ideals.[145] This means that while the state has an obligation to safeguard water resources, such obligation is merely aspirational and not justiciable as Section 20 is not housed within the 'Bill of Rights.' Unlike the South African Constitution, which ensures the right to water is contained in its Bill of Rights, the position of Section 20 in the Nigerian Constitution makes it impossible for an individual who does not have the requisite *locus standi* to approach the courts for the enforcement of his/her rights to water or that measures to ensure water security be put in place by government to ensure progressive realisation of such rights.

Nigeria has legislation on water, including the National Water Policy and the Water Resources Act. Nigeria's National Water Policy 2004 and the National Water Resources Draft Policy 2016 are subject to and consistent with the 1999 Constitution in all matters and require that water resources shall be assessed, developed, apportioned and managed in such a manner as to enable all users to have equitable access, taking into account the sustainability of the resource.[146] The Water Resources Act 1993 also vests in the federal government the right to use and control all surface and groundwater and all water in any watercourse affecting more than one state. Thus, any person may take water without charge for his domestic purpose or for watering his livestock from any watercourse to which the public has free access. Any person may use water for

144 Ibid: 15.

145 Nnamuchi (2008: 1).

146 Paragraph 5.3.3 Nigerian National Water Policy (2004).

fishing or for navigation, or may use it from an underground water source without charge for domestic purpose, livestock, personal irrigations schemes if he/she has a statutory right of occupancy over such land.[147]

It should be noted that Nigeria's National Water Policy 2004 was based on the philosophy and principles of the Integrated Water Resource Management (IWRM). Interestingly, the revised National Water Resources Draft Policy 2016 takes into account not only the IWRM, but the underlying philosophy that water is key to sustainable socio-economic development, as it has a direct effect on the population's health conditions, environmental preservation, including the achievement of international development targets.[148] Nevertheless, Nigeria's current water law framework is devoid of detailed regulations. Although administrative structures such as the Federal Ministry of Water Resources exist, there is a lack of efficient personnel to carry out the tenets of water legislation. Weak databases regarding water remain a problem and the overall governmental attitude towards environmental and water issues seems to be lacking political will. The water resource sector also faces the challenge, among others, of unclear roles and responsibilities among the various levels of government, different ministries, departments and agencies at the federal and state levels.[149] Existing legislation set out above fails to inspire litigation relating to enforcement of water rights similar to the *Mazibuko* case in South Africa, as the Constitution precludes the enforcement of a water right in Nigeria. Whilst Nigeria has likewise been an important venue in the fight for environmental justice,[150] this venue has so far only expanded to the extractive sector[151] and not to the water sector.

Key imperatives of the water reform in Nigeria are, *inter alia,* geared towards:[152]

> harnessing the current and potential opportunities and addressing operational challenges within the water resources sector with a view to ascertaining the nature and level of investment required in the sector; and ensuring easy accessibility of supply of water to all Nigerians, including the poor and the most rural.

Nigeria needs 56 billion litres of water supply of potable water per day for domestic use only as well as enough water for industrial and agricultural use.[153] The Nigerian government recognises the need to build commensurate capacity to cope with the level of demand in water and its infrastructure and that policy inconsistency in the sector at

147 Sections 1(1) and 2, Water Resources Act 1993.

148 Federal Ministry of Water Resources (2016: 1).

149 Ibid: 7

150 UNDP (2014: 19).

151 One expression of this has been the plight of local indigenous peoples in the Niger Delta, with increasing community claims of redress for toxic impacts and alleged rights abuses. The Ogoni are one among many indigenous communities in southeast Nigeria, rising to prominence in the environmental justice movement after a massive campaign against large oil multinationals in the Delta, under the umbrella of the Movement for the Survival of the Ogoni People (MOSOP). See UNDP (2014: 19).

152 Federal Ministry of Water Resources (2011: 8).

153 Ibid: 26.

both federal and state government levels has overtime hampered the development of the water resources sector in the country.[154] The attendant consequences have been the abandonment of laudable programmes halfway due to policy somersault[155] or the frequent breakdown or deterioration of water plants due to lack of maintenance.[156]

Consequently, the Nigerian government set long-term goals, which seek to achieve 100% coverage in provision of potable water supply per day for domestic, industrial and agricultural uses by the year 2030.[157] The rationale behind these proposed achievements is reflected in the revised National Water Resources Policy. Such includes, *inter alia*, that no ownership of water but only a right for environmental and basic human needs or an authorisation for its use; and management of water resources shall seek to harmonise human and environmental requirements so that the human use of water does not individually or cumulatively compromise the long-term sustainability of aquatic and associated ecosystems.[158] The government also envisages the support of states to improve the capacity for water resource development, strengthening partnerships and collaboration with stakeholders to increase funding for the water resource sector in all states.[159] Additionally, the National Water Resources Draft Policy 2016 has set out roles and responsibilities of key institutions managing water resources in Nigeria to avoid fragmentation and overlapping of roles.[160]

Whilst these future projections are laudable, this chapter argues that it is imperative for the Nigerian government to apply adaptive governance strategies to its water law reform. Existing water legislation fails to provide an effective basis for the achievement of water security and the absence of a water right in the Nigerian Constitution "serves" as hindrance to environmental justice. Whilst the use of environmental justice should be a means to ensure equity and accessibility to water in Nigeria, this appears to be a non-achievable concord when compared to South Africa, which provides the relevant impetus for environmental justice movements and the basis for adaptive governance in water legislation.

154 Ibid: 27.

155 Ibid.

156 Akali et al. (2014: 3).

157 Federal Ministry of Water Resources (2015 and 2016: 15).

158 Federal Ministry of Water Resources (2016: 12-13).

159 The government also recognises the need to create sustainable funding for the reform and promote private sector participation and collaboration. See Federal Ministry of Water Resources, (2011: 43) and Federal Ministry of Water Resources (2016: 29-31).

160 For an expansion of the roles of these key institutions, see Federal Ministry of Water Resources (2016: 32-40).

6 Conclusion

Water is an important resource for human beings and the environment. Beyond viewing the resource as a paradigm of aid giving and water access, there must be a wider conceptualisation of water[161] as a 'secure' resource in jurisdictions where issues of marginalisation were rampant. Given the magnitude of the resource and the international and national recognition of the right to water, it is clear that the achievement of water security is a key developmental goal for any nation. Whilst many versions of water security exist, it is left for governments at the national level to develop an all-encompassing definition of what constitutes water security within their jurisdiction, bearing in mind the historical inequalities relating to accessibility and affordability of that resource. Nonetheless, increasing attention to water as a socio-ecological system, which requires adaptation to changing circumstances calls for adaptive governance in addressing water issues.

This chapter highlights the South African Constitution's forethought of including a right to water, which is a key driver to achieving water security, and the drawbacks within the Nigerian context stemming from the provisions of the 1999 Constitution. Whilst the full achievement of water security still remains an elusive paradigm in both jurisdictions, there appears to be an achievable concord between environmental justice and water security. Consequently, a key tool towards achieving this concord is for governments to have the political will to apply adaptive governance strategies to water law reform. The implementation of an adaptive governance approach to water security means that governments must exhibit a committed stand towards understanding the drivers of water security as the basis for informed decisions about water law reform and proposed investments for water infrastructure. Another implication requires governments' consciousness of the need for inclusive community/stakeholder participation in dialogues relating to water law reform.

The chapter emphasises the need to ensure water security in jurisdictions like South Africa and Nigeria where specific communities still experience water shortages. Both historical inequalities and extreme poverty hamper environmental justice where developmental policies, legislation and institutions should ensure the progressive realisation of water security for the benefit of present and future generations.

References

ACAPS / The Assessment Capacities Project *Crisis Profile Nigeria* (4-7-2016), at <https://www.acaps.org/sites/acaps/files/products/files/160712_acaps_crisis_profile_north-east_nigeria_b.pdf> (accessed 12-12-2017).

161 Allouche et al. (2011: 168).

Adebowale, N (2017) "Over 180 million people lack drinking water in Nigeria, other countries facing conflicts – UNICEF" *Premium Times* (29-8-2017), at <https://www.premiumtimesng.com/regional/nnorth-east/241897-180-million-people-lack-drinking-water-nigeria-countries-facing-conflicts-unicef.html> (accessed 15-12-2017).

Agyeman, J, R Bullard & B Evans (2002) "Exploring the nexus: bringing together sustainability, environmental justice and equity" 6(1) *Space and Polity* 70-90.

Akali, DM, OT Iorhemen, JA Otun & MI Alfa (2014) "Provision of sustainable water supply system in Nigeria: a case study of Wannune-Benue State" 2(1) *World Journal of Environmental Engineering* 1-5.

Allan C, J Xia & C Pahl-Wostl (2013) "Climate change and water security: challenges for adaptive water management" 5(6) *Current Opinion on Environmental Sustainability* 625-632.

Allouche, J, A Nicol & A Walnycki (2014) "Global environmental justice and the right to water: the case of peri-urban Cochabamba and Delhi" 54 *Geoforum* 158-166.

Allouche, J, A Nicol & L Mehta (2011) "Water securitization: towards the human securitization of water" 12(1) *The Whitehead Journal of Diplomacy and International Relations* 153-171.

Armitage D, F Berkes & N Doubleday (2007) *Collaboration, learning and multi-level governance: adaptive Co-management.*

Backeberg, GR (2005) "Water institutional reforms in South Africa" 7 *Water Policy* 107-123.

Bond, P (2013) "Water rights, commons and advocacy narratives" 29(1) *South African Journal of Human Rights* 125-143.

Chikozho C, L Danga & D Saruchera (2017) "Articulating the history and major departure points evident in post-apartheid South African national water policy and law" 100 *Physics and Chemistry of the Earth* 270-277.

Chiro, G Di (1996) "Nature as community: the convergence of environment and social justice" in W Cronon (ed.) *Uncommon ground: rethinking the human place in nature* 298-320.

Cook, C & K Bakker (2012) "Water security: debating an emerging paradigm" 22 *Global Environmental Change* 94-102.

Cook, C & K Bakker (2016) "Water security: critical analysis of emerging trends and definitions" in C Pahl-Wostl, A Bhaduri & J Gupta (eds) *Handbook on water security* 19-37.

Cooney, R & TF Lang (2007) "Taking uncertainty seriously: adaptive governance and international trade" 18 *European Journal of International Law* 523-551.

Couzens, E (2015) "Avoiding Mazibuko: water security and constitutional rights in southern African case law" 18(4) *Potchefstroom Electronic Law Journal* 1162-1186.

Daniels, R (2006) "Implementation of the right of access to sufficient water through privatization in South Africa" 15 *Pennsylvania State Environmental Law Review* 61-68.

Dietz, T, E Ostrom & PC Stern (2003) "The struggle to govern the commons" 302(5662) *Science* 1907-1912.

DWAF / Department of Water Affairs (2013) *National water resource strategy: water for an equitable and sustainable future* 2nd Ed.

DWAF / Department of Water Affairs and Forestry (1997) *White paper on a national water policy.*

Federal Ministry of Water Resources (2011) Executive summary of the Nigeria water sector roadmap, at <http://awdrop.org/wp-content/uploads/2017/01/water-roadmap.pdf> (accessed 29-12-2017).

Federal Ministry of Water Resources (2015) *Partnership for expanded water supply, sanitation & hygiene (PEWASH) –programmed strategy (2016-2030).*

Federal Ministry of Water Resources (2016) *National water resources policy* final draft.

Folke, C, T Hahn, P Olsson & J Norberg (2005) "Adaptive governance of socio-ecological systems" 30 *Annual Review of Environment and Resources* 441-473.

Foster, S & A MacDonald (2014) "The water security dialogue: why it needs to be better informed about groundwater" 22(7) *Hydrogeology Journal* 1489-1492.

Garrick, D & JW Hall (2014) "Water security and society: risks, metrics, and pathways" 39 *Annual Review of Environment and Resources* 611-639.

Global Water Partnership (2000) *Towards water security: a framework for action.*

Godden, L (2005) "Water law reform in Australia and South Africa: sustainability, efficiency and social justice" 17(2) *Journal of Environmental Law* 181-205.

Gowlland-Gualtieri, A (2007) *South Africa's water law and policy framework - implications for the right to water* IELRC Working Paper.

Grey, D & CW Sadoff (2007) "Sink or swim? water security for growth and development" 9 *Water Policy* 547-548.

Gunderson, L (1999) "Resilience, flexibility and adaptive management – antidotes for spurious certitude?" 3(1) *Conservation Ecology* 7-17.

Hall, J & E Borgomeo (2013) "Risk-based principles for defining and managing water security" *Philosophical Transactions of the Royal Society* A 371, 1-23.

Hardberger, A (2005-2006) "Life, liberty, and the pursuit of water: evaluating water as a human right and the duties and obligations it creates" 4(2) *Northwestern Journal of International Human Rights* 331-362.

Henderson, RH & T Sundaresan (1982) "Cluster sampling to assess immunization coverage: a review of experience with a simplified sampling method" *Bulletin of the World Health Organization*, at <http://www.ph.ucla.edu/epi/rapidsurveys/bulletinwho60(2)253_260_1982.pdf> (accessed 20-12-2017).

Honkonen, T (2017) "Water security and climate change: the need for adaptive governance" 20 *Potchefstroom Electronic Law Journal* 1-26.

Hornstein, DT (2005) "Complexity theory, adaptation, and administrative law" 54 *Duke Law Journal* 929-933.

Humby, T & M Grandbois (2010) "The human right to water in South Africa and the Mazibuko decisions" 51 *Les Cahiers de Droit* 521-540.

Ibrahim, SI (2012) "Water security and good governance in Niger State of Nigeria: challenge for sustainable development" 2(8) *Transitional Journal of Science and Technology* 68-78.

IUCN / International Union For Nature Conservation (2007) *Human rights and the environment: overlapping issues.*

Kasrils, R (Minister of Water Affairs and Forestry) (2003) "Foreword" in D Reed & M Dewit (eds) *Towards a just South Africa: the political economy of natural resource wealth.*

Kaswan, A (2012) "Environmental justice and environmental law" 24(2) *Fordham Environmental Law Review* 149-179.

Keesen, AM & HFMW Van Rijswick (2012) "Adaptation to climate change in european water law and policy" 8(3) *Utrecht Law Review* 38-50.

Kemerink, JS, R Ahlers & P Van der Zwaag (2011) "The struggle for water at catchment level" *Water SA* 585-594.

Langford, M (2005) "The United Nations concept of water as a human right: a new paradigm for old problems?" 21(2) *International Journal of Water Resources Development* 273-282.

Larson, RB (2013) "The new right in water" 70(4) *Washington & Lee Law Review* 2181-2267.

Larson, RB (2017) "Water security" 112(2) *Northwestern University Law Review* 139-200.

MacKay, HM, KH Rogers & DJ Roux (2003) "Implementing the South African water policy: holding the vision while exploring an uncharted mountain" 29(4) *Water SA* 353-358.

Magaziner, AL (2008) "The trickle-down effect: the Phiri water rights application and evaluating, understanding, and enforcing the South African constitutional right to water" 33 *North Carolina Journal of International Law and Commercial Regulation* 512-516.

Mehta L, F Marshall, S Movik, A Stirling, E Shah & A Smith (2007) *Liquid dynamics: challenges for sustainability in water and sanitation* STEPS Working Paper.

Nnamuchi, O (2008) "Kleptocracy and its many faces: the challenges of justiciability of the right to health care in Nigeria" 52(1) *Journal of African Law* 1-42.

Obani, P & J Gupta (2016) "Human security and access to water, sanitation, and hygiene: exploring the drivers and nexus" in C Pahl-Wostl, A Bhaduri, & J Gupta (eds) *Handbook on water security* 201-214.

Oglethorpe, J (2002) *Adaptive management: from theory to practice*.

Onzivu, W (2013) "(Re) invigorating the health protection objective of the Basel Convention on Transboundary Movement of Hazardous Wastes and their Disposal" 33(4) *Legal Studies* 621-649.

Pachova, NI, M Nakayama & L Jansky (2008) *International water security domestic threats and opportunities*.

Pahl-Wostl, C, M Palmer & K Richards (2013) "Enhancing water security for the benefits of humans and nature – the role of governance" 5(6) *Environmental Sustainability* 676-684.

Peart, R & K Govender (2001) "Natural resource policies for the new millennium" 8(1) *South African Journal of Environmental Law and Policy* 39-76.

Perkins, J (2003) "Partitioning water use in South Africa" in Australian Academy of Technological Sciences and Engineering *Proceedings of the 2003 Invitation Symposium, Water the Australian Dilemma* 148.

Pienaar, GJ & E Van der Schyff (2007) "The reform of water rights in South Africa" 3(2) *Law, Environment and Development Journal* 181-194.

Postel, S (1999) *Pillar of sand: Can the irrigation miracle last?*

Punch (2017) "Drought conflict behind water scarcity in Nigeria, others – UNICEF" (22-3-2017), at <https://punchng.com/drought-conflict-behind-water-scarcity-in-nigeria-others-unicef/> (accessed 18-12-2017).

Roithmayr, D (2010) "Lessons from Mazibuko: persistent inequality and the commons" 3(1) *Constitutional Court Review* 317-346.

Ruhl, JB (1997) "Thinking of environmental law as a complex adaptive system: how to clean up the environment by making a mess of environmental law" 34(4) *Houston Law Review* 933-1002.

Ruhl, JB (2009) "Laws complexity: a primer" 24(4) *Georgia State University Law Review* 885-911.

Schlosberg, D (2013) "Theorising environmental justice, the expanding sphere of a discourse" 22(1) *Environmental Politics* 1-48.

Scholz, JT & B Stiftel (eds) (2005) *Adaptive governance and water conflict: new institutions for collaborative planning*.

Schreiner B, B Van Koppen & N Mohapi (2004) "Washing away poverty: water, democracy and gendered poverty eradication" 28(3) *South Africa Natural Resources Forum* 171-178.

Soyapi, C & T Honkonen (2017) "Water security" 20(1) *Potchefstroom Electronic Law Journal: Special Edition* 1-26.

Stein, R (2000) "South Africa's new democratic water legislation: national government's role as public trustee in dam building and management activities" 18(3) *Colorado Journal of International Environmental Law & Policy* 284-295.

Takacs, D (2016) "South Africa and the human right to water: equity, ecology and the public trust doctrine" 34(2) *Berkeley Journal of International Law* 55-108.

Tarlock, D (2008) "Water security, fear mitigation and international water law" 31(3) *Hamline Law Review* 703-728.

Tarlock, D & P Wouters (2009) "Reframing the water security dialogue" 20 *Journal of Water Law* 53-60.

Tewari, D (2009) "A detailed analysis of evolution of water rights in South Africa: an account of three and a half centuries from 1652 AD to present" 35(5) *Water SA* 693-710.

UKAID & UNICEF (2017) *Promising practices in WASH – some case studies of Nigeria*, at <https://www.unicef.org/nigeria/resources_11310.html> (accessed 12-12-2017).

UN-Water (2013) *UN-Water analytical brief water security and the global water agenda*, at <http://www.unwater.org/ water_security_brief.html> (accessed 10-12-2017).

UNDP / United Nations Development Programme (2006) *Beyond scarcity: power, poverty and the global water crisis.*

UNDP / United Nations Development Programme (2014) *Environmental justice – comparative experiences in legal empowerment*, at <http://www.undp.org/content/dam/undp/library/Democratic%20Governance/Access%20to%20Justice%20and%20Rule%20of%20Law/Environmental-Justice-Comparative-Experiences.pdf> (accessed 29-12-2017).

UNHRC / United Nations Human Rights Council (2011) *Study on human rights and the environment* UN Doc. A/HRC/19/34.

UNICEF / United Nations Children's Fund (2014) *Impact evaluation of water, sanitation and hygiene (WASH) within the UNICEF country programme of cooperation, Government of Nigeria and UNICEF 2009-2013*, at <https://www.unicef.org/nigeria/resources_11396.html> (accessed 19-12-2017).

United Nations News "UN united to make the right to water and sanitation legally binding", at <http://www.ohchr.org/en/NewsEvents/Pages/Display-News.aspx?NewsID=10403&LangID=E> (accessed12-12-2017).

United Nations News (2010) "UN united to make the right to water and sanitation legally binding" at <https://newsarchive.ohchr.org/EN/NewsEvents/Pages/DisplayNews.aspx?NewsID=10403&LangID=E> (accessed 12-12-2017).

Vanderwarker, A (2012) "Water and environmental justice" in J Christian-Smith, PH Gleick, H Cooley, L Allen, A Vanderwarker and KA Berry *Twenty-First Century U.S. Water Policy*, 53-89.

Wesson, M (2011) "Reasonableness in retreat? the judgement of the South African Constitutional Court in Mazibuko v City of Johannesburg" 11(2) *Human Rights Law Review* 390-405.

Willis, B, BS Geach, V Pillay, D Versfeld & CM Shackleton (2000) "Review of policies and legislation influencing the sustainable use of South Africa's indigenous woodlands" 7(2) *South African Journal of Environmental Law and Policy* 171-201.

Woodhouse, P (2008) *Water rights in South Africa: insights from legislative reform* BWPI Working Paper No. 36.

Wouters, S, V Vinogradov & BC Magsig (2009) "Water security, hydro solidarity, and international law: A river runs through it" 19 *Yearbook of International Environmental Law* 97-134.

Xia, JLZ, C Lu & J Yu (2007) "towards better water security in north China" 21(1) *Water Resources Management* 233-247.

Zeitoun, M (2013) "Global environmental justice and international transboundary waters: an initial exploration" *The Geographical Journal*, at <http://dx.doi.org/10.1111/j.1475-4959.2012.00487> (accessed 29-12-2017).

Chapter 27:
The Lake Chad Basin Water Charter: strengths and weaknesses

Emmanuel D. Kam Yogo

1 Introduction

Lake Chad, the fourth largest lake in Africa after Lakes Victoria, Tanganyika and Nyassa,[1] poses some challenges to the countries that share its water resources within the context of climate change in the Sahelian zone.[2] These challenges are manifold and have environmental, economic and social implications. In short, they are challenges to sustainable development.

The drying up of the waters is threating the lake according to some sources[3], where drastic and alarming developments have occurred over the last fifty years. The combined actions of the climatic factors and the overexploitation of water resources may, in the short term, profoundly jeopardise fishing, livestock farming and agriculture. The preservation of this regional public property calls for an urgent response.

To overcome these challenges, six surrounding and neighbouring states, namely Cameroon, Central African Republic (CAR), Libya, Niger, Nigeria and Chad resolved to strengthen their cooperation to salvage the lake by adopting a binding legal instrument, the Lake Chad Water Charter (LCWC), in April 2012. This Charter is a conventional framework whose overall objective is to ensure that the Lake Chad Basin (LCB) is sustainably developed through the integrated, equitable and concerted management of the shared water resources and the environment of the Basin. The Charter was adopted within a context characterised by several factors such as: the adoption of the African Water Vision 2025 for the equitable and sustainable use of water for socio-economic development[4] by the African Union (AU) Extraordinary Summit in March 2000; the adoption of the LCB Vision 2025 in 2000 by the Lake Chad Basin Commission (LCBC); the adoption of a sub-regional Action Plan for Integrated Water Resources Management for West Africa[5] in Bamako on 16 December 2000; the creation

1 LCBC (2002: 2).

2 Lake Chad is the largest lake in the Sahel zone.

3 See among others, Lake Chad Vision 2025 (LCBC (2002)), and Lemoalle & Magrin (2014).

4 This LCB Vision 2025 seeks to create a future in which Lake Chad's water resource potential would be fully harnessed to boost and strengthen economic development and social well-being in the region.

5 See Decision A/Dec.12/12/00 of the ECOWAS Heads of State and Government's Summit.

of the permanent framework for the Coordination and Monitoring of the Integrated Water Resources Management in West Africa (PCMF/IWRM/WA);[6] the adoption of the water resources policy for West Africa on 5 December 2008[7]; and the adoption of the general policy of the Economic Community of Central African States (ECCAS) on Environment and Natural Resources Management in March 2007.

According to its provisions, the Charter "falls in line with the Agreement to establish the Lake Chad Basin Commission as specified and supplemented by the Statute of the Commission signed on 22 May 1964 in Fort Lamy".[8] It is in this light that its preamble expressly refers to the legal instruments signed on 22 May 1964 in Fort Lamy and its final provisions stipulate that as follows:[9]

> The present Water Charter shall be ratified by the State Parties to the Agreement in accordance with constitutional rules and procedures and with the 1964 Convention and Statute and shall come into force within thirty days of the deposit of two-thirds of the Member States' ratified instruments. It shall remain in effect until the term of the Convention for the development of the Lake Chad Basin and the Statute of the Lake Chad Basin Commission of 22 May 1964.

This Charter is, therefore, an agreement which supplements the Fort Lamy Convention of 1964, serving as a protocol to this Convention.

The LCWC does not contain any provision defining its relationship with the 1970 Moundou Agreement on the Extraction of the Waters of River Logone for Agricultural Purposes or the 1977 Enugu Agreement on Common Wildlife Regulations. Since the issues handled by these two agreements have largely been addressed by the LCWC for the LCB[10], it suffices to simply note that they will tacitly go extinct when the Charter enters into force in accordance with the provisions of Article 59(1) of the Vienna Convention on the Law of Treaties.[11]

As mentioned above, the overall objective of the LCWC is to ensure that the LCB is sustainably developed, through the integrated, equitable and concerted management of its shared water resources and environment.[12] This overall objective is supplemented by eleven specific objectives: the quantitative management of surface water resources; the qualitative management of wetlands; the management of groundwater

6 See Decision A/Dec.5/12/01.

7 See Additional Acts A/SA.5/12/08 of ECOWAS.

8 See Article 6 of the LCWC.

9 See Article 95 of the LCWC.

10 Articles 14 to 19 of the LCWC deals with the extraction of water (in the 1970 Moundou Agreement), while Articles 28 to 32 borders of the protection of biodiversity (in the Enugu Agreement).

11 According to Article 59(1) of the Vienna Convention on the law of treaties, "a treaty shall be considered as having come to an end where all its contracting parties later sign a treaty on the same subject and: (a) if it appears from the later treaty or if it is otherwise established that according to the intention of the parties the matter must be governed by that treaty; or (b) If the provisions of the later treaty are incompatible with those of the earlier treaty to such an extent that it is impossible to apply the two treaties at the same time". In the same vein, see Daillier et al. (2009: 338-339).

12 See Article 3 of the LCWC.

with the determination of principles and rules for the management of transboundary groundwater; the preservation of ecosystems and their biodiversity; the management of navigation; the determination of navigation principles and rules on the lake and its contributors; and, in particular, the assurance of freedom of navigation for the states of the Basin; the definition of procedures for the examination and approval of new projects that could have a significant quantitative or qualitative impact on the water resources; the dedication of common works and works of common interest; as well as the management of projects for the benefit of the Commission; the determination of responsibilities of national and regional authorities; the sharing of data and information and the participation of the public; the prevention of conflicts, and the assurance of the effective prevention and resolution of interstate conflicts associated with the management of shared water resources; and improvement of the socio-economic conditions of the populations.[13]

The Charter is guided by eighteen further general principles, which include: the sustainable development principle; the principle of prevention; the abstractor-pays principle; the polluter-pays principle; the costs and benefits sharing principle; the principle of subsidiarity; the principle of information and participation; the precautionary principle; the principle of solidarity; the principle of cooperation; the principle of partnership; the principle of equity; the principle of hydrographic sub-basin management; the principle of gender consideration; the principle of accountability; the principle of good governance for the environment; the principle of complementarity; and the principle of progressivity.[14]

By establishing the LCB water statute, the LCWC specifies that the lake, rivers and aquifers and aquatic ecosystems contained in the lake's watershed are declared international waters. These waters thus constitute the common heritage of the LCB member states.[15] It is therefore appropriate to consider whether there is a convergence or divergence between the LCWC and other international legal instruments on water, including the Convention on Wetlands of International Importance, particularly as Waterfowl Habitat of 2 February 1971; the Convention on the Protection and Use of Transboundary Watercourses and International Lakes of 17 March 1992; and the Convention on the Law of the Use of International Watercourses for Purposes other than Navigation of 21 May 1997.

Furthermore, questions arise about the legal relationship between the LCWC and other Water Charters in Africa, in particular, the Niger Water Charter and the Senegal River Charter. What is the relationship between national laws of member states on water management and the LCWC? Do these need to be consistent? Will the LCWC

13 See Article 4 of the LCWC.
14 See Article 7 of the LCWC.
15 See Article 1 of the LCWC.

be a solid legal base for member states to achieve the Sustainable Development Goals (SDGs) relating to water?

While finding the answers to these questions, it is important to analyse how universal principles on international water management are enshrined in the LCWC, and to examine the environmental context of its multi-sectoral character.

2 Universal principles on the management of international waters

The international law relevant to freshwater resources outlines a number of principles enshrined in several universally recognised instruments.[16]

2.1 Integrated management of water resources

Integrated management of water resources is generally defined as a process that promotes the coordinated and rational development and management of water, land and related resources. This is to be done to maximise, in an equitable manner, economic and social well-being without undermining the sustainability of vital ecosystems. This definition is enshrined both in the LCWC[17] and Article 1 of the Niger Basin Water Charter. The Senegal River Water Charter also addresses integrated water resources management taking into account a certain number of parameters.[18] Moreover, according to Agenda 21[19]–

> integrated water resources management is based on the idea that water is an integral part of the ecosystem and constitutes a natural resource and a social and economic good whose quantity and quality determine its distribution. For this purpose, water resources must be protected considering the functioning of aquatic ecosystems and the sustainability of the resource in order to meet or reconcile water requirements with human activities.

Integrated water resources management is also enshrined in the African Convention on the Conservation of Nature and Natural Resources, essentially concerning the fair and reasonable use of water resources and the rationalisation of extraction. However, in explicit terms, national laws of states party to the LCWC do not include integrated water management.

---

16 In this regard, see Boisson de Chazournes & Tignino (2013); and Boisson de Chazournes & Tignino (2011: 245-261).

17 See Article 2 of the LCWC.

18 Article 5(2) of the Senegal River Water Charter.

19 See Chapter 18 of Agenda 21.

2.1.1 Fair and rational use of water resources

The LCWC provides that the state parties shall use the surface water resources and Basin aquifers within their national boundaries in a fair and rational manner in order to ensure optimal and sustainable benefits consistent with the legitimate interests of each Basin state, and with the aim to protect Lake Chad and its watercourses, aquifers and aquatic ecosystems. For ground and surface water, the equitable and rational use is based on the commitment of state parties to respect defined limits.[20]

Since an uncontrolled increase in the extraction of water resources could have significant impacts and lead to a serious reduction in the volume and surface area of the lake, state parties undertake to respect the total volume of water consumed from the lake's inlets, their alluvial groundwater, the lake's aquifers or from the lake itself and should not exceed predefined limits.[21] The LCBC arbitrates the equitable sharing among the state parties by means of providing authorisations for extraction.[22] In addition, state parties undertake to limit groundwater extraction to adapt to the capacity of the transboundary aquifers or aquifer systems of the LCB in order to ensure their sustainable exploitation. States must ensure that they comply with the environmental flows projected at key points in the LCB to conserve aquatic ecosystems and the services they provide. Such compliance may require limiting water extraction by defining maximum volumes.

While enforcing the obligation of fair and sustainable use, states must also take into account the following factors which, for the most part, are also enshrined in the United Nations Convention on the Uses of International Watercourses for Purposes other than Navigation, which was adopted in 1997 and came into force in 2014:[23]

- geographical, hydrographical, hydrological, hydrogeological, climatic, ecological and other natural factors;
- economic and social needs of states parties;
- needs of ecosystems, especially wetlands, and in particular the maintenance of environmental flows to maintain the services provided by ecosystems;
- population relying on Lake Chad or the rivers, aquifers and aquatic ecosystems contained in its watershed;
- effects of the use by a state of Lake Chad or its watershed rivers, aquifers and aquatic ecosystems on other Basin states;
- current and potential uses of Lake Chad and its watershed rivers, aquifers and aquatic ecosystems, including the cumulative impact of extraction and pollution;

---

20 Articles 11 and 12 of the LCWC

21 See Appendix 2 of the LCWC.

22 See Article 17 of the LCWC.

23 Cf. Article 6 of this Convention.

- conservation, protection, enhancement and economy in the use of water resources of Lake Chad or its watershed rivers, aquifers and aquatic ecosystems and the costs of measures taken to this effect;
- other options that may substitute a particular current or envisaged use;
- planning for the development of the LCB;
- sharing of water resources among all users, aquatic systems and associated ecosystems;
- availability of other resources and the cost of a possible substitution;
- avoidance of wasting waters of the LCB;
- the principle of compensating the state that is obliged to forego an activity in order to reconcile divergent uses;
- avoidance of harm likely to be caused by new or extended use;
- recognition of rights of the populations to the LCB's waters;
- the endorheic nature of the lake, which increases the risks of pollution accumulation and cumulative impact on the lake's water levels, water extraction, alluvial aquifers of its inlets and the lake's aquifers;
- inter-basin water transfers that may affect the hydrology and water resources of the lake and associated watercourses; and
- the effects of climate variations and change.

The aforementioned factors equally need to be taken into consideration when it comes to the fulfilment of states' obligations under the 1971 Ramsar Convention on Wetlands of International Importance especially as Waterfowl Habitat.[24]

2.1.2 Rationalisation of water extraction

According to the LCWC, no use of Lake Chad's waters, surface water or groundwater of its watershed, can be considered as a priority in relation to other uses. However, in the event of a conflict between uses, satisfying the basic human needs of the population must be given priority. A state party may not reserve future use of the water resources of the LCB to the detriment of a current fair and rational use since future needs, even if they are to be taken into account in the context of sustainable development (consideration of future generations), should not threaten or relegate current needs. To deprive present generations of water resources would mean to condemn them to death, as water is life.

For the purpose of rationalisation, water extraction from Lake Chad or the surface or ground waters of its watershed, is subject to either an extraction authorisation or a prior declaration in accordance with a predetermined nomenclature. Extraction

24 See, in particular, Article 3 of the Ramsar Convention.

authorisations issued by states to public or private individuals or corporate entities must be subject to the approval of the LCBC and must take into account the availability of water resources and the various uses for which they are intended. The authorisations must also meet the environmental protection and sustainable development requirements prescribed under the LCWC.[25]

Individual and corporate bodies (either private or public), who are granted extraction authorisations have to pay an annual tax as a contribution to the costs of mobilising water resources to meet socio-economic and environmental needs. Such tax is collected by the national authorities in accordance with their financial rules and procedures. The amount and rate of distribution between the state parties and the LCBC are determined by the latter.[26]

Finally, states parties may enter into bilateral or multilateral water-sharing agreements, provided that they comply with the LCWC and that the LCBC is informed of their content. Thus, if for instance Cameroon and Chad desire to sustain the 1970 Moundou Agreement on River Logone Water Extraction for Agricultural Purposes, they will need to renegotiate it in order to ensure that it complies with the provisions of the LCWC. Where state parties use transboundary aquifers or aquifer systems that extend beyond the territorial scope of the LCWC as defined in Article 5, they will have to take the necessary measures to protect the legitimate interests of aquifer states that are not members of the Commission.[27]

2.2 Cooperation between lakeside states

Cooperation between states bordering Lake Chad concerns, *inter alia*, notification, consultation and approval of projects and works. This cooperation is facilitated by the creation of appropriate institutions.

The Charter requires state parties to notify all other Basin states and the LCBC of any natural or man-made disasters affecting the lake or the watercourses, aquifers and aquatic ecosystems of the Basin watershed originating from their territory. Such notification shall provide an indication of the characteristics of the emergency situation, the measures taken by the state party to mitigate its consequences on its territory and any other information that may enable other Basin member states to take the necessary measures to prevent or reduce the consequences of the emergency situation on their territory.

In order to prevent and mitigate emergency situations, member states shall jointly develop and implement contingency and adaptation plans in collaboration with the

25 See Article 17 of the LCWC.
26 See Article 18 of the LCWC.
27 See Article 20 of the LCWC.

LCBC in order to eliminate or reduce harm that may be caused to populations, the environment and the Basin's water resources.[28]

The Basin states shall provide mutual assistance where emergencies arise. Assistance to affected states shall be provided in accordance with the terms and conditions previously agreed upon by the state parties and in accordance with the principles and rules of international law.

Any state party that causes significant harm to another state party, notwithstanding the obligation to prevent transboundary harm, shall immediately enter into consultation with the state affected by that harm in order to eliminate or mitigate the consequences of such harm as soon as possible. State parties shall accordingly consult each other for compensation for significant transboundary harm caused to other state parties by the use of the lake or the surface or ground waters of its watershed within their respective boundaries. Compensation for transboundary damage shall be determined in accordance with international law. Where a state party intends to undertake projects likely to have significant adverse effects beyond its boundaries and where such projects are included in the nomenclature of the proposed compulsory notification measures, it shall notify the other member states through the LCBC. Written notification shall be made in a timely manner and shall include all necessary information and data to enable the LCBC and the recipient states to assess potential transboundary adverse effects of the proposed measure.[29] Upon receipt of the notification, the LCBC shall communicate with state parties in writing as soon as possible, and at the latest one month after receipt of the complete file. The states to which the notification is addressed shall have a period of four months from the date of receipt of the notification to comment on the proposed measures and to communicate their response to the LCBC, which shall in turn inform all state parties thereof. If, at the end of this period, no reaction is received from a state to which the notification had been addressed, it constitutes a tacit consent to the implementation of the proposed measure.[30] Upon expiry of the response time granted to states, the LCBC shall, for the purpose of examining and issuing its opinion, submit to the Committee of Experts on Water Resources and the Committee on Environment, Science and Planning, the notification of the proposed measure along with the observations of state parties. The Committee shall then review the notification with due consideration of all relevant factors and consequences for the Lake Chad Basin.[31] The Committee may draw on the expertise of outside persons in the field of water and environment, and may provide reasoned expert advice.[32]

In the wider context of cooperation, states parties may undertake to construct common works or works of common interest, and may also agree to declare as common

28 Article 38 of the LCWC.

29 Article 54 of the LCWC.

30 Article 55 of the LCWC.

31 Article 56 of the LCWC.

32 Article 56 of the LCWC.

works or works of common interest those already existing in the Basin.[33] The LCBC coordinates the management of any Basin water structures with transboundary impacts. This coordination includes tactical management, seasonal planning, as well as short-term and real-time operational management.

The LCWC provides for a number of institutions that facilitate cooperation among member states. These institutions differ in their political, administrative or technical nature.

Political institutions include the Summit of Heads of State and Government and the Council of Ministers and the Parliamentary Regional Committee. As an administrative institution, there is the Executive Secretariat. Technical bodies include the Technical Committee; the Committee of Experts on Water Resources; the Committee on the Environment, Science and Planning; National Agencies of the LCBC; and the Partners' Forum on the Sustainable Development of LCB.[34]

During the last Summit of the Heads of State of the LCBC member countries, which was held in February and March 2018, the project to transfer water from Ubangi Chari to Lake Chad witnessed tremendous progress. The implementation of this project will strengthen cooperation among state parties to the Charter. Regrettable, however, is the fact that the LCWC does not provide for a specific framework that brings together all the water ministers of the various member countries. In some countries, such as Cameroon, the Minister of the Economy is the official interlocutor to the LCBC, while the Minister of Water often plays no role in the context of LCB cooperation. As a result, ministers from the Basin member states who are not competent on water matters attend the ministerial meetings. In addition, the fact that states belong to different regional blocks also hampers the cooperation efforts between the parties to the LCBC. This is to name but a few weaknesses of the LCWC for the LCB, where integrated water management is so critical.

3 The environmental dimension of the Lake Chad Water Charter

The LCWC contains ambitious provisions relating to environmental protection that provide for environmental impact assessments,[35] environmental audits,[36] strategic environmental assessments[37] and the harmonisation of the environmental assessment laws[38] of the various member states. In more detail, the LCWC contains important

33 Article 67 of the LCWC.
34 Article 82 of the LCWC.
35 Article 45 of the LCWC.
36 Article 46 of the LCWC.
37 Article 47 of the LCWC.
38 Ibid.

provisions in the fight against pollution, the protection of biological diversity and fisheries products, and for the management of risks and natural disasters.

3.1 The fight against pollution

To prevent, control or reduce pollution, LCB member states undertake to:

- control and combat any action likely to significantly modify the characteristics of the lake or the watercourses, aquifers and aquatic ecosystems of its watershed zone, their sanitary and physio-chemical state, biological characteristics and the environment in general;
- take all necessary steps to preserve the quality of the groundwater of the Basin in order to ensure sustainable exploitation; and
- combat pollution at the source.

As general pollution control measures, member states and the LCBC shall identify water quality objectives and criteria, establish techniques and practices for combating pollution from stationary and diffuse sources, and draw up lists of substances and concentrations that should not be introduced into the waters of the Basin or should be limited or subjected to research and monitoring. They shall further preserve the aquatic environments that contribute to the conservation of the good quality of water. Each state shall, in addition, inform the LCBC of any polluting emissions from its territory, that are likely to have significant harmful effects on water resources and/or the environment in other state party's territory.

The LCBC, together with the state parties, establishes standards of pollutants discharge in accordance with the objectives of the LCWC. However, it is important to note that any discharge of radioactive pollutants is forbidden in the Basin.

Any polluting discharge into Lake Chad and the surface or ground waters of its hydrographic basin is subject to either a discharge permit or a prior declaration in accordance with prescribed pollution standards. The nomenclature of samples subject to authorisation or declaration is determined by the LCBC. Any pollutant discharge likely to endanger public health and safety or likely to pose a threat to the biodiversity of the Basin, shall be subject to authorisation.[39] Discharge authorisations are issued by each member state after the approval of the LCBC, which must make its decision within three months. Beyond this deadline, the state party may proceed without the opinion of the LCBC.[40] In any event, authorisations to discharge must take account of the nature of the pollutants, and the hydrological and ecological characteristics of the receiving environment. Furthermore, all parties agree to set up, through the LCBC, a regional

39 Article 24 of the LCWC.

40 Article 25 of the LCWC.

system to regulatory monitor water quality in the Basin. The data produced shall thereafter be integrated into a regional database.

Public or private individuals or corporate entities in possession of any discharge authorisation are subject to payment of an annual tax as a contribution to the cost of pollution prevention, control and abatement measures under taken by public authorities. This is a means of implementing the polluter pays principle as enshrined in the LCWC, which provides that "the cost of pollution prevention, control and abatement measures shall be entirely or partially covered by the polluter".[41]

3.2 Protection of biodiversity and fisheries products

Member states of the LCWC undertake to regularly identify, make inventory of and monitor the biodiversity of aquatic ecosystems of the Basin and to take appropriate measures for their conservation by paying particular attention to endangered species. In addition, members pledge to exploit biological resources of the Basin only in a sustainable manner.[42] These commitments make the LCWC consistent with the universal legal instruments such as the United Nations Convention on Biological Diversity (CBD). The CBD aims to protect biological diversity, to promote the sustainable use of its components, to foster the fair and equitable sharing of the benefits accruing from the exploitation of the genetic resources, including through adequate access to genetic resources and adequate transfer of relevant technologies. It takes into account all rights over the aforementioned resources and technologies, and appropriate funding.[43]

Member states have to take all necessary measures to monitor the introduction of alien or new invasive aquatic fauna or flora that may adversely affect the Basin's ecosystems. Such measures shall contribute to the conservation of the LCB as a natural heritage. It should be recalled here, that the 1972 Convention of the United Nations Educational, Scientific and Cultural Organization (UNESCO) concerning the Protection of World Cultural and Natural Heritage, defines natural heritage as the geological and physiographic formations and strictly delineated areas constituting the habitat of endangered animal and plant species, which are of outstanding universal value from the point of view of science or conservation.[44] Synergies also enfold between the implementation of the provisions of the African Convention on Nature and Natural Resources[45] and the LCWC. It is important to note, however, that the commitments made by member states with regard to biological diversity under the LCWC go beyond the 1977 Enugu Agreement and make the latter virtually obsolete.

---

41 See Article 7(d) of the LCWC.
42 See Article 28 of the LCWC.
43 See Article 1 of the Convention on Biological Diversity.
44 See Article 2 of the 1972 UNESCO Convention.
45 In particular, Article 12 of this Convention.

Member states shall also take appropriate measures to ensure sustainable exploitation of fishery resources in the Basin. In this regard, they are called to establish areas for the conservation of fishery resources by creating fish reserves and by prohibiting areas of the aquatic domain in order to maintain spawning stocks. Harmonisation of national fisheries legislation is being envisaged at the level of the LCWC,[46] despite the difficult nature of such an exercise. This is comparable, for instance, with the experience of the Central African Forest Commission (COMIFAC) in the forest sector where the harmonisation of national forest legislation remains unattained after more than a decade.

3.3 Risk and disaster management

A natural disaster is defined in the LCWC as:[47]

> ... a serious disruption of the functioning of society, which poses a real and widespread threat to life, health, property or the environment, whether arising from an accident, nature, or human activity, whether developing suddenly or as a result of long-term processes, but excluding armed conflict.

Member states of the LCWC are particularly vulnerable to disasters such as floods, earthquakes and tremors, lake lethal gases, volcanic eruptions, rock avalanches, landslides, bushfires and droughts. It is in this light that relevant provisions of the LCWC have expressly identified risk and disaster management as a key area for cooperation between the member states. The LCWC thus stipulates that member states and the LCBC undertake to adopt measures necessary to combat situations that are damaging to the ecosystems of the LCB, such as erosion, riverbank degradations, floods, droughts, desertification and deforestation,[48] and to reduce the deterioration of lands. Furthermore, member states undertake to adopt measures necessary to protect, preserve, sustainably use and rehabilitate the Basin plant cover. Each member state, insofar as it is predisposed to flooding by the lake or its tributaries, or to the extent that its geographical position enables it to predict such risk, is required to:

- identify or map the hazard, vulnerability and risk areas potentially subject to flooding on its territory;
- identify, in a database, remarkable floods and feedbacks on experiences in the management of these occurrences;
- develop and maintain a forecasting and early warning system including rainfall and hydrometric stations; and

46 See Article 34 of the LCWC.

47 See Article 3 of the model act for the facilitation and regulation of international disaster relief and initial recovery assistance.

48 See Article 29 of the LCWC.

- prepare safeguarding plans to define actions to be taken in the event of an alarm or a crisis situation.

Furthermore, during current and future situations of flooding, member states are required to:[49]

- manage hydraulic structures so as to reduce the risk or not to increase it;
- put in place any action likely to alert the population as soon as possible and to minimise the impact of flooding; and
- inform, each year, the population living on the banks of the lake about the maximum level that can be reached on the lake coast, based on the analysis of flood hydrographs of the Chari and Logone rivers.

Member states also undertake to define objective indicators that enable them to qualify and anticipate particularly severe low water conditions that render it impossible to respect the flows defined in Article 12, while abstracting water from the duly authorised flows. They also undertake to define the measures to be taken in such situations by including, among others:[50]

- economical management of demand through water-saving measures and regular checking of abstraction flow rates;
- defining the rules to classify in order of priority the recipients of the water available in the regulation reservoirs and encouraging a careful management of these stocks; and
- actions to reserve the resource available for the distribution of drinking water.

In short, the LCWC commits member states to take specific measures to prevent severe low water levels and drought. It is in this perspective that during the fifteenth Summit of Heads of State of the LCBC held in February 2018, the question of transferring water from the Ubangi-Chari River to Lake Chad was addressed. What is regrettable, however, is that the LCWC does not provide for a direct connection with the United Nations Convention to Combat Desertification (UNCCD) by offering the possibility for the LCBC to effectively subscribe to this UN instrument. Such coupling could effectively lead to a greening of the entire LCB region.

4 The multi-sectoral nature of the Lake Chad Water Charter

The LCWC targets several sectors that are important in achieving its ambitious objectives. Some of the sectors addressed include human rights, peace and economic sectors, which make these ambitions consistent with the following Sustainable Development Goals, in particular, Goals No. 1, No. 2, No. 3, No. 6 and No. 15.

49 See Article 40 of the LCWC.
50 See Article 41 of the LCWC.

4.1 Human rights considerations

The LCWC recognises the right of the people to water and sanitation as a fundamental right necessary for their dignity. Member states must therefore take the necessary normative, institutional and operational measures to ensure the realisation of this right.

The right to information about the environment is also guaranteed. State parties, through public consultation, must ensure that information concerning the state of water resources, the environment and the measures taken or envisaged concerning the Basin are accessible to the population so that they can effectively participate in consultations organised by public authorities as part of the decision-making process in water resources and environmental protection. They must ensure that the people have effective access to administrative and judicial remedies for the implementation of this right. The LCBC establishes a participation plan, which defines the conditions for public information and participation in the management of the Basin's water resources.

State parties undertake to pay particular attention to the needs of women, youth and vulnerable groups in the management of water resources and the environment of the Basin. Cultural rights are also taken into account as member states acknowledge the importance of local techniques and know-how applied in environmental protection, which are consistent with the sustainable management of the Basin's natural resources. They also assure that the role of traditional and customary leaders regarding the protection of the environment and water resources is taken into full consideration. They encourage, in particular, the traditional system of sharing water in the Basin taking necessary measures to ensure the protection of local knowledge, and a greater involvement of customary and traditional authorities in the management of water and the protection of the environment. This provision is similar to that of the African Convention on the Conservation of Nature and Natural Resources, which requires states to take legislative measures in order to ensure that the traditional and intellectual property rights of local communities are respected and that access to and use of traditional knowledge are subject to prior and informed consent of the concerned communities.[51]

The economic rights of livestock farmers are also recognised. The LCWC provides that member states must acknowledge the right of herders in the Basin to exploit pastoral resources, including plant, water and mineral resources to feed their livestock. Member states must also create the conditions necessary for these pastoral rights to be enjoyed in accordance with national laws.

State parties acknowledge and undertake to ensure the right of the local population to participate equitably in the sharing of benefits resulting in particular from the commercial and industrial exploitation of the genetic resources of the Basin in accordance with relevant international agreements. One instrument worth specific mention in this regard is the Nagoya Protocol to the Convention on Biodiversity concerning the

51 See Article 17 of the African Convention.

Access to Genetic Resources and the Fair and Equitable Sharing of Benefits Arising from their Utilisation. This Protocol has been ratified by Cameroon and other member states of the LCB. At the same time, LCB member states adopted national strategies on access to genetic resources and the fair and equitable sharing of benefits arising from their utilisation.

Moreover, member states acknowledge the rights of civil society organisations and legally established grassroots organisations to defend their collective interests in court in matters concerning the environment and water resources.[52] In order to enable the local population to effectively enjoy their rights, the LCBC advocates for the creation of civil society organisations within the Basin area, with national and local agencies. Civil society organisations and grassroots community organisations that contribute to the sustainable management of the Basin shall receive technical and financial support. All these ambitions of the LCWC are equally consistent with the African Convention on the Conservation of Nature and Natural Resources, which stipulates that its member states must guarantee the rights of the people to participate in decision-making, to have access to information on environment and to have free access to justice in environmental matters.[53]

4.2 The need to preserve peace around the Basin

The risks of inter-community and inter-state conflicts in the Basin are a concern to states bordering Lake Chad. Thus, the LCWC has enshrined the principle of solidarity, by which sub-regional inter-state cooperation for the sustainable management of the Basin is founded on the idea that Lake Chad and the watercourses, aquifers and aquatic ecosystems found in its hydrographic basin constitute an asset of "common heritage". In this light, state parties undertake to preserve such assets in the interest of all states to promote peace and development in the sub-region by ensuring political and social cohesion in the Basin, and by supporting the populations and most underprivileged areas in order to gradually eradicate inequalities. State parties agree to peacefully settle any dispute arising from the application or interpretation of the LCWC, in accordance with the United Nations Charter, the Constitutive Act of the African Union and the Declaration on Principles of International Law concerning Friendly Relations and Co-operation among states.

State boundary disputes in the Lake Chad area are on the increase.[54] Thus, in the LCB, "boundaries only exist in the minds of the states and not in the mind of the

52 See Article 77 of the LCWC.
53 See Article 16 of the African Convention on the Conservation of Nature and Natural Resources.
54 Sourna Loumtouang (2014: 1-2).

population who, in their quest for survival, violate them unknowingly".[55] The LCWC has so far failed to provide clear solutions regarding existing border disputes. This is another shortcoming of this legal instrument. We can only assume that in the event of any border dispute erupting between member states within the Basin, the principle of the intangibility of borders inherited from colonisation shall apply. Based on this principle, effective reference has been made in the preamble of the LCWC to the Constitutive Act of the African Union and the United Nations Charter on the Management of Border Disputes. During the settlement of the border dispute between Cameroon and Nigeria, the two member states of the LCB heavily depended on this principle. In the Statement of the Federal Government of Nigeria concerning the ruling of the International Court of Justice (ICJ) regarding the LCB, it stipulates that:[56]

> The Nigerian Local Government Area in the North-East has traditionally provided administrative services and infrastructure for the 60,000 or so Nigerians living in this area. Notwithstanding, the Court ruled that the colonial boundaries are to be respected.

In the event of a dispute between states parties over the interpretation or application of the LCWC, the parties concerned shall seek a solution through direct negotiation. Such negotiation shall be conducted in a climate of good faith with a willingness to reach an agreement. Where state parties fail to reach an agreement through negotiation, they shall resort to the good offices or the arbitration of the LCBC in order to reach a solution acceptable to both parties. Where the LCBC fails to settle the dispute, one of the state parties may seek the good offices or the arbitration of competent regional or subregional organisations. Where all the above dispute settlement mechanisms prove unsuccessful, state parties shall resort to mediation or legal settlement by the ICJ. Where this occurs, state parties are expected for the duration of the dispute settlement period, to abstain from any act that is likely to escalate the situation in the interest of a peaceful and final settlement of the dispute.

A main weakness of the LCWC is its silence on the fight against terrorism. Despite this fact, member states are increasingly organising themselves to face the scourge. Thus, during the fourteenth Ordinary Summit of Heads of State and Government of the LCBC held in Ndjamena in April 2012, a decision was reached to launch a Multinational Joint Task Force made up of troops from Cameroon, Chad, Niger and Nigeria. This initiative has been endorsed by the United Nations Security Council and the African Union Peace and Security Council.

55 Ibid: 11.
56 Olinga (2009: 166).

4.3 Consideration of economic activities

The fight against poverty is a major concern for the states bordering Lake Chad. Some of the specific objectives of the LCWC include to improve of the socio-economic conditions of the population to foster food security in order to guarantee a steady and secured supply of foodstuffs to the population. It also recognises the need to fight poverty and improve the living conditions of the population in order to better the living standards, while ensuring peaceful conditions for collaboration among member states. The LCWC also deals with the principle of complementarity by which member states can, within the framework of regional integration, make the most of complementarities in their economies based on their respective current or potential comparative advantages within the LCBC. Satisfying economic needs of the population is repeatedly reiterated in the LCWC.[57]

5 Conclusion

The LCWC aims to harmonise member states' laws. It thus provides for the harmonisation of laws and institutions on fisheries,[58] the harmonisation of laws on environmental assessment,[59] the harmonisation of fisheries, environment, water and navigation policing[60] and the harmonisation of data collection and processing methods.[61] Harmonisation of laws, as a method of legal integration, should, however, not be mistaken for unification and uniformity. Harmonisation refers to "a simple reconciliation between two or more legal systems"[62] in order to put an end to certain existing contradictions and differences. The LCWC straddles the West Africa sub-regional bloc (Nigeria and Niger), the Central Africa sub-regional bloc (Cameroon, Chad and Central African Republic) and to a certain extent the Maghreb sub-regional bloc (because of Libya). Conducting a harmonisation process in such a complex regional context is extremely difficult. This may constitute another weakness of the LCWC. The geographical location of the LCB, which is shared between several sub-regional blocs (ECOWAS, ECCAS and Maghreb) makes the harmonisation efforts recommended by the LCWC challenging. These challenges to the harmonisation of legislation between countries of the LCB are all the more conceivable in Central Africa in another sub-regional organisation, the Central African Forests Commission (COMIFAC).

---

57 See Articles 5, 13, 14, 18 and 32 of the LCWC.
58 See Article 34 of the LCWC.
59 Article 48 of the LCWC.
60 Article 62 of the LCWC.
61 Article 63 of the LCWC.
62 Cornu (2000: 423).

COMIFAC has to date failed to successfully harmonise forestry legislation.[63] As a harmonisation organisation, COMIFAC did not achieve the expected results in spite of the fact that all its members belong to the same regional bloc, the Economic Community of Central African States (ECCAS). If an organisation which enjoys a unique regional and institutional framework such as COMIFAC fails to achieve its harmonisation objectives, how can one expect any better from an organisation that spans across different sub-regions?

Persistent differences between legal and regulatory frameworks of member states, some of which have not yet internalised the integrated management of water resources, are also a flaw in the LCWC. Added to this are the uncertainties about stable bilateral relations between certain LCB member states. These uncertainties have been observed in the relations between Chad and Nigeria, Chad and the CAR, Cameroon and Nigeria and between post-Kaddafi Libya and other member states. At the judicial level, the LCWC totally disregards other African judicial bodies and refers member states directly to the ICJ when seeking the legal settlement of a dispute. This is another weakness of an instrument adopted in 2012, at a time when Africa was already striving to boost African judicial bodies.

References

Boisson de Chazournes, L & M Tignino (2011) "Gestion internationale de l'eau et développement du droit international" in Le Prestre (ed.) *Vingt ans après : Rio et l'avant-goût de l'avenir* 245-261.

Boisson de Chazournes, L & M Tignino (2013) *Droit international et eau douce.*

Cornu, G (2000) *Vocabulaire juridique.*

Daillier, P, M Forteau, NQ Dinh & A Pellet (2009) *Droit international public.*

LCBC / Lake Chad Basin Commission (2002) *Gestion intégrée de bassin fluvial, les défis du bassin du lac Tchad : Vision 2025.*

Lemoalle, J & G Magrin (2014) *Le développement du lac Tchad: Situation actuelle et futurs possibles.*

Olinga, AD (2009) *L'Accord de Greentree du 12 juin 2006 relatif à la presqu'île de Bakassi.*

Sourna Loumtouang, E (2014) "Les frontières dans le lac Tchad : une notion ignorée ou contestée?" 4(1) *History Rewiew of the University of Sherbrooke* 1-18.

63 Following Article 5 of the Treaty on the Conservation and Sustainable Management of Forest Ecosystems in Central Africa and Establishing the Central African Forest Commission adopted in 2005 in Brazzaville.

PART IV:

REGULATING SOCIAL AND ENVIRONMENTAL IMPACTS

Chapter 28: Making the case for gender and environmental considerations in the regulatory framework relating to the Uganda-Tanzania crude oil pipeline project

Godard Busingye

1 Introduction

Uganda recently started the process of extracting her oil and gas reserves in the Albertine Graben region in the western part of the country. An oil refinery is to be set up at source but Uganda will also export crude oil to other countries through a seaport. Uganda is, however, a landlocked country and can only access the sea routes through a neighbouring country with a coastline. The nearest seaports for Uganda are along the Kenyan and Tanzanian coastlines. Kenya's port of Mombasa has been traditionally preferred by the Ugandan business community, and currently handles much of Uganda's exports and imports.[1] The initial negotiating process for the construction of the crude oil pipeline was between Uganda and Kenya. Construction of the Uganda-Kenya crude oil pipeline would tap into already existing bilateral relations between the two countries.[2] After protracted negotiations, which eventually failed, Uganda started fresh negotiations with the United Republic of Tanzania. The Uganda-Tanzania negotiations yielded positive results. The two countries agreed to construct the pipeline – known as the East African Crude Oil Pipeline (EACOP) – from Uganda to the seaport of Tanga in the United Republic of Tanzania's territory.[3]

Construction of the EACOP raises pertinent environmental and gender issues. It will, of necessity, involve excavation of soil to create a path and this will affect the environment and gender relationships along the way. While EACOP will create employment opportunities for citizens of Uganda and the United Republic of Tanzania as well as those of other countries, there are attendant environmental and social costs. These include pollution of the environment, sexual abuse and exploitation and gender discriminatory practices. This chapter links human rights and the environment focusing particularly on gender equality and the right to a clean and healthy environment. It relies heavily on ecofeminism to analyse the identified concerns. Ecofeminism

1 Nakaweesi (2017).
2 Musisi & Muhumuza (2016).
3 Ibid.

combines environmental, human rights and gender analyses to elicit clear findings and construct succinct conclusions and recommendations that can be relied upon by pipeline countries to address the concerns identified in the construction of the EACOP. Regarding the methodology, the chapter relied on a qualitative desk review approach to obtain information that was analysed using a gender and human rights approach.

1.1 Factual aspects about EACOP

Once completed, the pipeline will transport crude oil from Kabaale in Hoima district, western Uganda to Chongoleani Peninsula near the Port of Tanga in the United Republic of Tanzania.[4] The 24-inch diameter Crude Oil Pipeline will cover a distance of 1,445 km buried pipeline. Only 20%, about 298 km of that distance is in Uganda. It will have six pumping stations, two pressure reduction stations and a marine export terminal at the Port.[5] The pipeline runs from the proposed pumping point at Kabaale through the districts of Kakumiro, Kyankwanzi, Mubende, Gomba, Ssembabule, Lwengo to Rakai at the border of Tanzania.[6] Uganda shall be the source of the crude oil, while the United Republic of Tanzania shall only be used as a conduit to the seaport. The crude oil pipeline will not wholly be operated and managed by the governments of the two countries. It will be constructed and operated by the Government of Uganda through the National Oil Company, a pipeline company with shareholding from the Uganda National Oil Company, the Tanzania Petroleum Corporation and three Oil Companies, namely; CNOOC, TOTAL and Tullow.[7] The private companies shall have commercial interests on account of the hefty sums of money injected in the project in the construction of the crude oil pipeline. Moreover, the governments of the two pipeline countries see the construction of the pipeline as an economic venture that will stir economic development in the countries.[8]

From a political angle, the construction of the EACOP is likely to strengthen the long-standing political ties between the two countries. It will also contribute to the reduction of institutional and legal trans-border bottlenecks between the two countries, non-tariff and tariff barriers and separate legal requirements for environmental and social assessments. The non-tariff barriers likely to be encountered relate to on-spot checkpoints for goods transported between Uganda and the United Republic of Tanzania for the construction and maintenance of the pipeline and free movement of labour between the countries. The tariff barriers include taxes imposed on import and export materials and other goods intended for use in the construction of the EACOP.

4 Kwasiga (2017).
5 Isabalija (2017).
6 Musisi (2017).
7 Kwasiga (2017).
8 Ibid.

With regard to the environment, land degradation, air and water pollution along, and within the vicinity of the pipeline route are likely to occur.

1.2 The problem

The ideal scenario in the construction of the EACOP would have been for the project planning process to have incorporated the involvement of the public in the design and subsequent stages of implementation. This, however, was not the case because of the hasty manner in which the project was moved from the initial Uganda-Kenya route to the Uganda-Tanzania route. It was equally not possible to transfer and apply the results of the feasibility environmental and social assessments conducted for the earlier planned Uganda-Kenya route, because they were route specific, and would not suit the new Uganda-Tanzania route. The possibility of ignoring, at the very initial stage, serious environmental and gender concerns cannot be overlooked in such a situation. Indeed, the hasty manner in which the final agreements were arrived at between the governments implies that key environmental, gender and other social concerns were not adequately taken care of in the project conception. There are political and commercial interests embedded in the project cycle of the EACOP. These need to be catered for without compromising environmental and gender equality standards.

Gender and social concerns related to discriminatory labour practices, sexual abuse and exploitation, resettlement practices, denial of land rights, which must be taken care of in projects like EACOP are not yet clear to those that will be adversely affected by the project. Noteworthy is the fact that oil extraction and transportation endanger the traditional culture and livelihood of indigenous peoples.[9] This is within a context where women are not adequately represented in national and regional levels of governance in the two countries. Their interests could, therefore, not have been fully taken care of in the initial project design, and may continue to be ignored in the implementation of the project.[10]

Compounding the problem at hand is the fact that the two countries do not have similar political ideologies, economic, cultural and social values that could be used as a basis to ensure harmonious progress in the design and implementation of the EACOP. Their environmental and gender policies, laws and institutions regarding aspects of the EACOP differ.[11] The East African Community framework, which would have provided a harmonisation point in this respect, is yet to be fully agreed upon by all partner states.

9 Degteva (2006).
10 Amanda et al. (2006).
11 The harmonisation process of the policies and development strategies in the East African Community has not been achieved as required by the provisions of Article 71(1)(e) of the 1999 Treaty for the establishment of the East African Community.

Lastly, though Uganda's economy is growing, it has a long history of political turmoil from which it aspires to recover very quickly.[12] On the other hand, the United Republic of Tanzania is moving from a nationalised economy to a more liberal economic setup, and is yet to fully come to terms with that changing reality.[13] These factors will affect the implementation of EACOP.

2 Theoretical framework

This chapter relies heavily on ecofeminism to analyse the environmental and gender aspects of the EACOP. Ecofeminism is a preferred paradigm because it combines ecological, social and gender concerns of a project such as EACOP. It is also preferred because of its ability to unravel the negative impacts of the development model crafted within the ambit of capitalism which thrives on the mythology of male dominance. Hoch for instance avers:[14]

> unleashing the father's voice is more threatening to the *status quo* than unleashing the mother's voice not because it is more powerful than the mother's voice – but because of the way patriarchy itself positions mothers and fathers. The mother's situation is viewed first and foremost through the lens of gender. The target of her rage and the focus of her attempts for change is generally the system of male domination. For the fathers, however, the enemy to be organised against is not – initially – so clear.

Based on Hoch's analogy of the male mythology, it becomes clear that the father's enemy is not clear and maybe fear of women's power to influence the situation if given an opportunity. Due to that fear, fathers essentially intimidate and keep women far away from any decision-making arenas concerning the environment they live in. Ecofeminism can be used to unpack and repackage the EACOP project and to shed light on the motivation and underlying concerns of political leaders of the two project countries.[15] Imbuing EACOP with environmental and gender considerations is critical for its successful completion and ultimately, its operation.

It is the central argument of this chapter, therefore, that from a theoretical perspective, only ecofeminism, also known as ecological feminism, can provide clear guidelines and possible solutions to the likely negative effects of the EACOP. Ecofeminism is based on the integration of the ecology and feminism perspectives and their multidimensional approaches into a project cycle. The term ecofeminism was coined in 1974 by Francoise d'Eaudbonne, a French feminist in *Le feminisme ou la mort* (feminism or death). d'Eaudbonne called on women to lead an ecological revolution and

12 Uganda National Planning Authority (2013: 2).
13 Ibhawoh & Dibua (2003).
14 Hoch (2015).
15 Atwijukire (2017).

establish new relationships between humanity and nature as well as men and women.[16] The ideology of ecofeminism as propounded by d'Eaudbonne adopts a methodology that interrogates the socially constructed relationships between men, women and nature. Moreover, it emphasises the ways both nature and women are treated within a patriarchal setting. Patriarchy, the bedrock of the mythology of male dominance, objectifies women and nature and places them in subordinate positions in society.[17] Ecofeminism is based on four pillars: there are vital connections between the oppression of nature and women; understanding these connections is necessary to understanding the two veins of oppression; feminist theory must include an ecological perspective; and ecological problems must include a feminist perspective.[18] Ecofeminism holds that male domination of women parallels the domination of nature by the human race. That undesired domination leads to gender discrimination and environmental destruction.

A clear understanding of the problematic relation between nature and the human race makes it possible for project planners to stress the need for a more interdependent worldview of development, environment and gender. This is very relevant in the construction of the EACOP, which touches the 'nerves' of the two socially dominated aspects – the women and nature.

The governments of Uganda and the United Republic of Tanzania have put in place policies, laws and even invoke principles of international law to mitigate the possible adverse impacts of construction of a crude oil pipeline. That notwithstanding, it cannot be ignored that EACOP will be constructed amidst uncertain agitations for promoting the well-being of the peoples in the region. For example, it is acknowledged in the EAC Vision 2050 that the extractive industry in the region has not been beneficial in promoting the well-being of the people:[19]

> as a result, the mining (extractive) industries contributed a higher percentage of industry's share of GDP of the Partner States. However, this contribution is not equivalent to the value of the products that result from mining activities, nor does it contribute to job creation and employment on an equivalent scale. This is because Africa as a whole, through the multinational corporations that have been given the mining rights, continues to export ores and raw materials instead of finished products. Moreover, the exploitation of mineral resources has historically been a source of disputes instead of being a source of development resources for the region, mainly to the benefit of multinational corporations and their private share.

The realisation of the minimal benefits to be anticipated from the oil and gas exploitation in Uganda, therefore, must be understood against a clear background that exportation of crude oil will largely benefit foreign interests, not those of Ugandans or the people of the United Republic of Tanzania. It is equally clear, at the same time, that the project will inevitably affect the integrity and harmony of the environment along its course. The project will arguably destabilise the social, gender, economic and

16 Ling (2014).
17 Dobscha (1993).
18 Ibid.
19 East African Community (2016).

cultural order of the people living along its route. The pipeline project may equally have similar transboundary impacts in non-project countries far beyond the territorial boundaries. Some of the negative impacts on gender and the environment will fall between the cracks of the policy and regulatory mechanisms made to accommodate the new venture of oil and gas exploitation and transportation because they have not been factored in. Moreover, some adverse impacts are inevitable in the industrialisation and modernisation drives. Ling rightly asserts that:[20]

> with the acceleration of industrialisation and modernisation process, ecological problems have become global problems and key issues which constrain the development of nations. In the internal social ecological systems, gender division and gender inequality have also become important factors that constrain the development. How to effectively overcome the ecological crisis and solve gender conflicts are theoretical problems as well as practical problems.

From a theoretical perspective, therefore, ecofeminism can provide clear guidelines and possible solutions to the likely adverse impacts of EACOP on the environment and gender.

In contrast, the ideology of patriarchy, which portends that nature can be harnessed or controlled and that human beings are separate from, and superior to the environment, is incapable of providing comparable benefits to humanity.[21] The polarised positions taken by adherents of ecofeminism and those of patriarchy regarding the relationship between humanity and nature clarifies why in the EACOP project design, only the dominant view prevails – economic considerations. Being an economic venture, EACOP could not have been fronted from a humanist perspective, because doing so would elicit criticisms on the need to start the project. At whatever cost, the pipeline has to be constructed because it is presented as a project that will improve the wellbeing of the people in the two pipeline countries. The relationship between humanity and nature, which allows humans to do things to the environment that they would not do if they conceived it as being part of the entire system of which humans are only one part, comes on board much later.[22] In this respect, the ecofeminism perspective bridges the gap between humans and the environment within a male-dominated space, where the law, a reflection of the dominant class, and necessarily, patriarchs, becomes a handy tool to be used in the fight for rights of the unsuspecting victims of the EACOP. Moreover, ecofeminism critiques the trends in modern industrial civilisation and tries to rebuild the cultural values of the society so as to obtain the liberation of women and nature from male domination.[23] An analysis of the regulatory framework for the EACOP using an ecofeminism perspective has several advantages. It provides clear avenues through which improvements can be made in the law to ensure that the environment is not degraded wantonly, and secondly, that women, who are equally

20 Ling (2014: 104-108).
21 Broumas (2017).
22 Dobscha (1993: 36-40).
23 Ling (2014: 104-108).

oppressed by the male-dominated society become key players in the design and implementation of the EACOP.

Regarding ventures harnessing the environment on a large scale, ecofeminism becomes a suspicious paradigm, especially because of the symbolic role that women would be asked to play in an ecological crisis emanating from the constructs of the ideology of patriarchy.[24] This would require that the EACOP regulatory framework mainstream gender in all its parameters. Gender mainstreaming, largely advocated for within the realm of ecofeminism is not a mere matter of convenience, it is a human rights issue. In this regard, Williams avers:[25]

> gender mainstreaming is a strategy which aims to bring about gender equality and advance women's rights by infusing gender analysis, gender-sensitive research, women's perspectives and gender equality goals into mainstream policies, projects and institutions. Instead of having segregated activities for women, or in addition to targeted interventions to promote women's empowerment, it brings the focus on women's issues and gender equality into all policy development, research, advocacy, legislation, resource allocation, planning, implementation and monitoring of programs and projects. Gender mainstreaming is intended to be transformative, changing the very definition and discourse of development to include gender equality as a means and an end. With gender fully integrated, therefore, 'the stream' itself will change direction.

From Williams' averments, for EACOP to be successfully undertaken, project designers and planners need to use a properly conceived and crafted gender mainstreaming strategy. The United Nations Economic and Social Council (ECOSOC) defined the strategy for gender mainstreaming:[26]

> in addressing the inequality between men and women in the sharing of power and decision-making at all levels, Governments and other actors should promote an active and visible policy of mainstreaming a gender perspective in all policies and programmes so that before decisions are taken, an analysis is made of the effects on women and men, respectively.

The main elements of the gender strategy are: accountability, results-based management for gender equality, and oversight through monitoring, evaluation, audit and reporting. It also includes: capacity development, coherence, coordination and knowledge information management.[27] According to the ECOSOC, key principles of a gender mainstreaming strategy are:[28]

> issues across all areas of activity should be defined in such a manner that gender differences can be diagnosed – that is, an assumption of gender-neutrality should not be made; responsibility for translating gender mainstreaming into practice is system-wide and rests at the highest levels; accountability for outcomes needs to be monitored constantly; gender mainstreaming also requires that every effort be made to broaden women's participation at all levels of decision-making; gender mainstreaming must be institutionalised through concrete steps, mechanisms and processes in all parts of the system; gender mainstreaming does not replace the need for targeted, women specific policies and programmes or positive legislation, nor does it substitute for gender

24 Dobscha (1993: 36-40).
25 Williams (2004: 3).
26 ECOSOC (1997).
27 United Nations Entity for Gender Equality and the Empowerment of Women (2018).
28 ECOSOC (1997).

> units or focal points; and clear political will and the allocation of adequate and, if need be, additional human and financial resources for gender mainstreaming from all available funding sources are important for the successful translation of the concept into practice.

Implementation of a well-designed gender mainstreaming strategy will help to ensure that EACOP meets its intended objective. That is largely because:[29]

> mainstreaming a gender perspective is the process of assessing the implications for women and men of any planned action, including legislation, policies, or programmes, in all areas and at all levels. It is a strategy for making women's as well as men's concerns and experiences an integral dimension of the design, implementation, monitoring and evaluation of policies, and programmes in all political, economic and societal spheres so that women and men benefit equally and inequality is not perpetuated. The ultimate goal is to achieve gender equality.

From the foregoing narrative, and in order for the EACOP to benefit women and men equally, gender concerns must be institutionalised through concrete steps, mechanisms and processes in whole project design and implementation. There must be political will manifested in the political statements made, and in the actual implementation cycle of the EACOP. All these must be budgeted for and adequate resources allocated in design, implementation and eventually, benefit sharing of the proceeds of the project.[30]

3 The regulatory framework

Construction of the EACOP will be guided by multi-layered environmental and socio-gender regulatory frameworks. The East African Community Treaty as well as other regional and international legal frameworks will also be relevant. The term environment is defined in the Treaty for the Establishment of the East African Community and national laws of Uganda and the United Republic of Tanzania as:[31]

> the natural resources of air, water, soil, fauna and flora, ecosystems, land, the man-made physical features, cultural heritage, the characteristic aspects of the land scape, and the socio-economic interaction between the said factors and any living and non-living organisms.

The East African Community Treaty obligations regarding construction projects and gender concerns will help to fill the gaps in the national regulatory frameworks and act as a monitoring and compliance tool. Moreover, the use of the name 'EACOP' imports a responsibility on part of the East African Community partner states' organs to assume responsibility for overseeing the project's compliance with the Community regulatory framework. Indeed EACOP construction is likely to avoid serious negative effects to the environment and human beings if the two project countries adhere to the normative demands in their national laws as well those in regional and international

29 Ibid.

30 Chief Executives Board for Coordination (2006).

31 Treaty for the Establishment of the East African Community, Article 1 (1999); Section 3 Environment Management Act of the United Republic of Tanzania (2004) and Section 1 of the National Environment Act, Cap. 153, Laws of Uganda.

treaties to which they are a party. Adherence to the law will create a conducive environment for the free movement of goods and services, at least in the short run.[32] In the wildlife protected areas, EACOP will, however, disrupt the free movement of wildlife.[33] It is clear that in case of an oil spill, the spillage will degrade the environment in a manner that is likely to pose a great threat to humanity, the ecosystems and flora and fauna.[34] Oil spillage is a serious problem because its impacts are long-term and recurrent.[35] As much as the construction of the EACOP and its subsequent maintenance are likely to have negative transboundary environmental effects and affect humans, the worst impacts will be felt by vulnerable members of the community such as women. Indeed, the laws of the two project countries require that gender considerations are taken into account. Gender as a concept of social construction:[36]

> describes the social experiences, norms, values, and subjective position that people use to describe their experience of 'masculinity' and 'femininity'. Gender is distinguishable from sex, which refers to biological or bodily traits that distinguish 'men' and 'women'.

On the historical gender imbalances, the Constitution of the Republic of Uganda, 1995 provides:

> Article 32 (1): Notwithstanding anything in this Constitution, the State shall take affirmative action in favour of groups marginalised on the basis of gender...;
>
> Article 33 (5): Without prejudice to article 32 of this Constitution, women shall have the right to affirmative action for the purpose of redressing the imbalances created by history, tradition or custom.

The legal barriers may not have been fully addressed by the two governments as they sought to accommodate the commercial interests of the private companies in the project. These include non-adherence to the requirements of environmental impact assessment for the EACOP and gender concerns in resettlement and employment under the project. Compliance with these requirements is important if EACOP is to provide the anticipated economic and political gains to the peoples of Uganda and the United Republic of Tanzania.

In order to rationalise the political, economic, social, cultural, environmental and gender aspects of the EACOP, Uganda and the United Republic of Tanzania must undertake comprehensive environmental and social reforms that will help them to forestall or mitigate the adverse effects of the project. Environmental and socio-legal reforms may, however, be regarded as irrational by the political and economic actors behind the construction of the oil pipeline because they may delay the implementation of the project. Those legal reforms must, however, be initiated, and operationalised at every stage of the EACOP, including the decommissioning stage. That has to be done

32 Adejoh (2014).
33 WWF & CSCO (2017: 3).
34 Ibid.
35 Adekola & Igwe (2014).
36 Zelvallos (2013).

notwithstanding the fact that from a political and economic angle, such legal reforms may be regarded as concerns of the pessimist environmentalists and feminist protagonists. Regarding pessimism, Pinker asserts:[37] "[I]rrational pessimism is driven by a morbid interest in what can go wrong – and there are always more ways of things to go wrong than to go right".

Indeed, the economic and political domains cannot on their own predetermine what can go wrong with the EACOP without the input of the pessimist environmentalists and ecofeminists. The latter's contribution is very important at an early stage of the construction of the EACOP. The reason for taking this strong position is that oil and gas exploration, extraction and transportation have great potential to endanger the terrestrial and marine environments. They also have potential to disrupt traditional occupations, gender perceptions and roles, culture and livelihood of the indigenous people. The danger of political and economic motivations overriding these considerations should not be underestimated. Such reasonably foreseen danger must be stemmed by the law at the earliest opportune time. The legal framework for EACOP in this chapter is presented at two levels, the national legal frameworks and the transboundary legal framework. The national legal framework is pivotal in this case because Uganda and the United Republic of Tanzania are required under international law to ensure that their activities do not affect areas beyond their territorial boundaries negatively.[38] Uganda being the originator of the crude oil to be transported through the EACOP to the seaport of Tanga in the United Republic of Tanzania, must put in place a strong regulatory framework to contain the anticipated adverse environmental and gender impacts of the pipeline. In similar vein, the United Republic of Tanzania must put in place similar regulatory measures. The regulatory framework advocated for in this chapter is one based on the known international legal principles enshrined in the various environmental and human rights instruments. These principles are discussed in the ensuing sections of this chapter.

3.1 International principles regarding transportation of crude oil through a pipeline

International legal principles regarding sustainable harnessing of the environment include a human rights perspective. For example, the Declaration of the United Nations Conference on the Human Settlement adopted at Paris in 1972 recognises that men (and women) are both the creature and moulder of the environment. It also recognises that humanity derives its physical sustenance, intellectual, moral, social and spiritual

37 Pinker (2018).

38 See the *Trail Smelter* case *(United States v. Canada)*, Arbitral Tribunal, 3 U.N. Rep. Int'l Arb. Awards 1905 (1941).

growth from the environment. States parties to this Declaration recognise the fact that through science and technology, men (and women) have the power to transform the environment in countless ways, and on an unprecedented scale. It is the duty of man (and woman), however, to safeguard the non-renewable resources of the earth. This requires that humanity does not harm the environment when undertaking activities such as the excavation of the soil for construction of the crude oil pipeline.

On its part, the Rio Declaration, adopted at Rio de Janeiro in 1992, establishes a new and equitable global partnership regime. It creates new levels of cooperation among states, key sectors of the global economies, the society and even the people. The Rio process puts in place frameworks that form the basis for future cooperation among states in the field of environmental management.[39] It recognises that humanity has a right to development, but further that such development should be arrived at equitably in order to meet the developmental and environmental needs of the present and future generations.[40] Environmental processes are part of sustainable development advocated for in the Rio Declaration.[41] In regard to the discussion on the transboundary environmental impacts of the EACOP, the Rio Declaration emphasises that developing countries should strive to avoid degradation of their fragile ecosystems. In the case of Uganda and the United Republic of Tanzania, women are identified as being at the centre of environmental degradation.[42] They are also key players in implementing measures to avert the degradation.[43] This recognition is in line with what ecofeminism alludes to – women are best suited to protect nature, because women and nature are vulnerable to abuses by the patriarchal society.

In the Word Conservation Strategy, 1980, states acknowledge that conservation of the environment and development are interdependent, and none ought to be taken a stride ahead of the other. This view was further elaborated in the World Commission on Environment and Development (WCED), also known as Our Common Future in 1987.[44] WCED observed that the concept of sustainable development does not imply absolute limitations on the present state of technology and social organisation. It partly concluded that technology and social organisation ought to be managed and improved to make way for a new era of economic and social transformation, noting that sustainable development is not a fixed state of harmony. Rather, it is a process of change in which the exploitation of resources, the direction of investments, the orientation of technology and institutional change are made consistent with the future. Consequently, the concept of sustainable development becomes a handy tool to the governments of Uganda and the United Republic of Tanzania when constructing the EACOP. The two

39 Preamble, Rio Declaration (1992).
40 Principle 3, Rio Declaration (1992).
41 Principle 4, Rio Declaration (1992).
42 National Environment Management Authority (2006); United Republic of Tanzania (2007).
43 UNDP (2015).
44 WCED (1987).

governments should be mindful of the duty incumbent upon them, and ensure that the construction of the pipeline does not unduly disrupt the integrity and harmony of the environment and the socio-economic activities of the people living on, or near the path of the EACOP. In so doing, they must put in place adequate policy, legal and institutional mechanisms to guide and monitor implementation of the task of construction of the pipeline in a sustainable manner. The latter shall include the obligation not to ignore gender considerations during all phases of the pipeline.

Another important international law principle relevant to the construction of the EACOP is that of permanent sovereignty over natural resources. This principle was adopted by the United Nations General Assembly in its resolution 1803 (XVII), and given prominence in principle two, of the Rio Declaration. The principle states:

> s]ates have, in accordance with the Charter of the United Nations and principles of international law, the sovereign right to exploit their own natural resources pursuant to their own environmental and development policies, and the responsibility to ensure that activities within their jurisdiction and control do not cause damage to the environment of other states or areas beyond the limits of national jurisdiction.

In their activities during the construction of the EACOP, therefore, Uganda and the United Republic of Tanzania should at all times be mindful of their rights and obligations under international law to freely exploit natural resources within their territories. They should be equally mindful, that such a right goes hand in hand with an obligation to ensure that their acts do not injure the ecosystems and flora and fauna in the pipeline area. In practical terms, and within the confines of the concept of sustainable development, Uganda and the United Republic of Tanzania are not only bound not to cause harm to environments beyond their territorial jurisdictions, but are also under a similar obligation not to do so within their territorial jurisdictions. Such obligations stem from the principles of intergenerational and intra-generational equity.

The principle of intergenerational equity and its sister principle of intra-generational equity are premised on an understanding that the present generation owes a duty to its own members and generations yet unborn to preserve the diversity and quality of the planet's life-sustaining environmental resources. These principles were succinctly elaborated upon in the case of *Juano Antonio Oposa and others v. The Honourable Fulgensio S. Factoran and another,* where the court entertained an action by minors on their own behalf and that of generations yet unborn.[45] The action was brought to court through the minors' respective parents together with the Philippine Ecological Network Incorporated, seeking to stop the destruction of the country's forest cover at a rate that would deny both the petitioners and generations yet unborn of the right to benefit from that forest. A discussion of international environmental principles, which are now part and parcel of the national laws of the EACOP countries, cannot be

45 Supreme Court of the Philippines Philippines' Constitutional Rights, Intellectual Rights, Intergenerational Standing G.R No. 101083.

concluded without mentioning the *locus standi* and precautionary principles.[46] Each of these two principles forms the rubric of contemporary environmental law and even the struggle for gender equity in the handling of large projects such as the construction of the EACOP. These principles were tested and elaborated upon in the English case of *R v. Secretary of States and Industry ex parte Duddridge*, where the court came to a conclusion that they are intended to prevent serious harm to the environment in circumstances such as those surrounding the construction of the EACOP.[47] The precautionary principle, in particular, calls for the undertaking of environmental assessments at all stages of a project of the magnitude of the EACOP. Under the Ugandan legal regime for sustainable utilisation of the environment, environmental assessments are mandatory for large projects, whose impacts are likely to fundamentally alter the environment. They are also undertaken to forestall disruption of social, economic and gender roles of the project-affected communities.[48]

3.2 Regional and national regulatory framework for the EACOP

Uganda and the United Republic of Tanzania are founding members of the East African Community which was established in 1999. Article 4(1) of the Treaty for the Establishment of the East African Community, 1999, provides:

> the Community shall have the capacity, within each of the Partner States, of a body corporate with perpetual succession, and shall have power to acquire, hold, manage and dispose of land and other property, and to sue and be sued in its own name.

This form of legal status enables organs of the Community to operate within the territorial jurisdictions of Partner States with limited restrictions. In furtherance of this, Article five, which spells out the objectives of the Treaty *inter alia* provides:

> (3) For purposes set out in paragraph 1 of this Article and as subsequently provided in particular provisions of this Treaty, the Community shall ensure:
>
> (b) the strengthening and consolidation of cooperation in agreed fields that would lead to equitable economic development within the Partner States and which would in turn, raise the standard of living and improve the quality of life of their populations;
>
> (c) the promotion of sustainable utilisation of the natural resources of the Partner States and the taking of measures that would effectively protect the natural environment of the Partner States;

---

46 See Article 50 Constitution of the Republic of Uganda, which gives *locus standi* to any affected person or any other person, to sue for enforcement of rights.

47 *United Kingdom Queen's Bench Division* (4-10-1994).

48 Uganda National Environment Act Cap. 153 (Uganda), Sections 19-23; the Environmental Impact Assessment Regulations, 1998 (Uganda); see also Section 81 of the Environment Management Act (2004) of the United Republic of Tanzania on the rationale for environmental impact assessments.

(e) the mainstreaming of gender in all its endeavours and the enhancement of the role of women in cultural, social, political, economic and technological development.

Objectives of the East African Community Treaty in regard to a shared vision of the partner states are reinforced by the operational principles of the same Treaty. One of the operational principles of the Community provided for in Article 7(1)(g) is the principle of complementarity, whereby partner states undertake to complement each other's endeavours. This form of complementarity is what is exhibited in the construction of the EACOP, where Uganda and the United Republic of Tanzania are working together to promote the well-being of the people in each of the two countries by pooling their resources together for the success of the project. Indeed, in Article 111 of the Treaty, the partner states recognise that development activities, such as the construction of the crude oil pipeline, may have negative impacts on the environment leading to the degradation of the environment and depletion of natural resources and that a clean and healthy environment is a prerequisite for sustainable development. The partner states, therefore:

(a) agree to take concerted measures to foster cooperation in the joint and efficient management and sustainable utilisation of natural resources within the Community;

(b) undertake, through environmental management strategy, to cooperate and co-ordinate their policies and actions for the protection and conservation of the natural resources and environment against all forms of degradation and pollution arising from developmental activities.

National frameworks in each of the partner states reinforce the highlighted provisions of the Treaty for the establishment of the East African Community.

At the national level, in regard to mainstreaming women in all aspects of development, Article 33(4) of the Uganda Constitution provides: "women shall have the right to equal treatment with men and that right shall include equal opportunities in political, economic and social activities".[49] This provides a basis for an integrated environmental and gender consideration commitment. For instance, the Final Draft of Uganda's Revised National Environment Management Policy (NEMP), 2014 provides:[50]

49 See also Article 9(g) of the Constitution of the United Republic of Tanzania, 1997 which provides: "the Government and all its agencies provide equal opportunities to all citizens, men and women alike without regard to their colour, tribe, religion, or station in life".

50 See also Section 105 of the United Republic of Tanzania Environment, 2004 which provides: "(1)Where a mineral or petroleum resource is identified and before specific details are planned or a hydro-electric power station is planned or a major water project is planned, the Ministry responsible for mining, energy or water shall carry out a Strategic Environmental Assessment. (2) The strategic environmental assessment provided for Under sub-section (1), shall assess the area marked for development including the following: (a) baseline environmental conditions and status of natural resources; (b) identification of ecologically sensitive and protected areas; (c) identification and description of communities around the area; (d) existing socio-economic conditions; (e) existing economic activities and infrastructure; (f) power stations; (g) infrastructure and resources required to service these development; potential environmental and social impacts of mining or petroleum development or hydro-electric power or (h) any major water projects; and (i) recommendations for land reclamation and limitations on development in different areas".

> significant achievements have been made during the implementation of the NEMP (1994) some of which include the following:
>
> established a system for sound management of environmental aspects of oil and gas throughout the petroleum value chain through; development of sensitivity atlases, environment monitoring plan, Strategic Environment Assessment (SEA), Environment Impact Assessment (EIA) and Audit processes, public education and awareness, establishment of an office in the Albertine Graben, regular monitoring and inspections, oil waste management and review of environment legislation to include aspects of oil and gas.

It suffices to note that Uganda's first comprehensive environmental management policy was concluded in 1994 long after the process of oil and gas exploration and exploitation had commenced. The policy has, because of that reason, been reviewed to cater for the revived oil and gas activities in the country, which now include transportation. Its ambit, however, does not extend to areas beyond the country's territorial boundaries. It, however, complements efforts in the United Republic of Tanzania and those under the Treaty for the establishment of the East African Community to complete the full picture of environmental assessments for the EACOP.

In regard to avoiding pollution of the area along the EACOP, the Constitution of the Republic of Uganda, 1995, under objective XXVII provides:[51]

> (i) The State shall promote sustainable development and public awareness of the need to manage land, air and water resources in a balanced and sustainable manner for the present and future generations.
>
> (ii) The utilisation of the natural resources of Uganda shall be managed in such a way as to meet the development and environmental needs of present and future generations of Ugandans; and, in particular, the State shall take all possible measures to prevent or minimise damage and destruction to land, air and water resources resulting from pollution or other causes.

In order to ensure that activities such as those related to the construction of the EACOP do not harm the health of Ugandans, the Constitution, under Article 39 provides: "[E]very Ugandan has a right to a clean and healthy environment". This right is justiciable and can be enforced by either the affected person or any other person or organisation under the provisions of Article 50 of the Constitution. Article 50 of the Constitution of Uganda on enforcement of rights and freedoms by courts provides:[52]

> (1) Any person who claims that a fundamental or other right or freedom guaranteed under this Constitution has been infringed or threatened, is entitled to apply to a competent court for redress which may include compensation.
>
> (2) Any person or organisation may bring an action against the violation of another person's or group's human rights.

---

51 See also Section 106(1) of the United Republic of Tanzania Environment, 2004, which provides: "It shall be an offence for any person to pollute or permit any other person to pollute the environment in violation of any standards, prescribed under this Act or any other written law prohibition of pollution regulation a segment of the environment".

52 See also Article 9 of the United Republic of Tanzania's Constitution, 1997, which provides: "The state authority and all its agencies are obliged to direct their policies and programmes towards ensuring – (a) that human dignity and other human rights are respected and cherished; (b) that the laws of the land are upheld and enforced".

(3) Any person aggrieved by any decision of the court may appeal to the appropriate court.

The National Oil and Gas Policy, 2008, which is the operational policy for oil and gas ventures in the country has a key provision on safeguarding the environment. It provides:[53]

> the opportunity to exploit indigenous oil and gas resources means that oil and gas activities are going to become an important sector of development in the country. This sector has the potential to significantly impact the already existing sectors and can be an important engine for poverty reduction and sustainable development. It can also create negative economic and social impacts if not managed properly. Governance, the economy, the environment and subsequently human development will be impacted upon by an emerging oil and gas sector in the country. Many of the areas with the potential for petroleum production in the country also coincide with areas of important biodiversity like national parks, water bodies, game and forest reserves among others. Due consideration will therefore be necessary so as to ensure harmony between developing the country's oil and gas resources and conserving its rich biodiversity.

This policy further recognises that:

> oil and gas activities in the country can impact the environment from several angles. They may affect human beings, wildlife and biodiversity, together with the associated tourism. Transboundary water resources and the economy of the Albertine Graben ecosystem where production is anticipated may also be affected. Furthermore, the corridor in which any pipelines or other transport systems will pass will also be affected. This policy considers environmental protection to include both the physical and social aspects and seeks to mitigate typical forms of environmental damage and hazards associated with oil and gas exploration, development and production.

The Oil and Gas Policy enjoins the Government of Uganda to learn from experiences of other countries in regard to handling the oil and gas resources, particularly in relation to socio-economic, and environmental aspects of the industry. It provides:

> experience from some countries shows that oil and gas producing regions may attract labour and threaten other sources of productivity thus leading to the abandonment and collapse of other sectors of the economy. It is therefore possible that large numbers of people may move to the Albertine Graben where oil and gas activities are likely to be concentrated despite the area being largely a wildlife and biodiversity protected area.

The National Oil and Gas Policy, however, does not specifically mention gender considerations as one of the key areas that need to be taken care in the oil and gas sector. This is a grave omission, because gender considerations are a prerequisite to proper implementation of any policy regarding the management of natural resources as clearly articulated within the ecofeminism perspective. In regard to health concerns, the policy provides: "this policy recognises several potential causes of negative impacts on human health from oil and gas activities. Oil spills can contaminate water sources leading to sickness and disease". This provision provides a firm basis for undertaking environmental and social assessments for the EACOP, within the territorial jurisdictions of Uganda and the United Republic of Tanzania. The Petroleum Supply Act, 2003 for

53 See also the National Petroleum Policy for the United Republic of Tanzania, Draft 2, 2014 which provides: "To explore, produce and utilize the country's petroleum resources in an effective and efficient manner that ensures lasting benefit to the nation as well as minimizing negative impacts to the society and environment".

Uganda, under Section 6(2)(a) empowers the Minister to promote the increase of opportunities for regional petroleum trade and encourage a diversity of supply sources, routes and means of transportation. This provision, read together with those of other petroleum-related policies and laws in Uganda and the provisions of the Treaty for the establishment of the East African Community can be relied on to ensure that construction of the EACOP is undertaken with care and caution to meet the environmental and gender concerns of the peoples of Uganda and the United Republic of Tanzania. Another important law in the oil and gas sector is the Petroleum (Refining, Conversion, Transmission and Midstream Storage) Act, 2013 (Uganda). This Act provides for additional and particular health, safety and environment regulations not sufficiently regulated in other laws. It defines transmission of oil to:

> mean transportation of petroleum products but not for distribution to consumers or retailers or transportation of petroleum commodities through pipelines, including transit pipelines and pipelines originating from outside Uganda connected to and with its inlet or outlet flange at a refinery or gas conversion facility in Uganda.

This definition caters for the EACOP, which is intended to connect Uganda's crude oil from the point source to the port of Tanga, in the United Republic of Tanzania for export.

4 Conclusion

From the foregoing discussion, it is fair to conclude that the EACOP will be constructed largely under the guidance of the political leadership of the two countries. The form of guidance given is motivated by providing improved conditions of living for the peoples in the two countries, which also helps to capitalise on the political gains and capital for the incumbent presidents. The regulatory framework in place is not adequate to handle all aspects of a transboundary nature for the construction of the EACOP. There are, however, good environmental and gender principles in place at the national, regional and international levels, to guide the construction process of the EACOP. The ecofeminism perspective provides a clear theoretical framework to guide the process of mainstreaming gender concerns in the process of constructing the EACOP. Based on this conclusion, the author recommends that the governments of Uganda and the United Republic of Tanzania comprehensively review the regulatory framework of EACOP to include the omitted environmental and gender aspects. The review should seek to identify gaps in the framework and align the project cycle to gender and environmental imperatives to ensure that they are not trumped by industrialisation and modernisation paradigms.

References

Adejoh, OF (2014) "Petroleum pipelines, spillages and the environment of the niger delta region of Nigeria" 4(3) *World Environment* 93-100, at <http://article.sapub.org/10.5923.j.env.20140403.01.html> (accessed 11-11-2017).

Adekola, MO & MC Igwe (2014) "Effects of oil spillage on community development in the Niger Delta Region: implications for the eradication of poverty and hunger (Millennium Development Goal One) in Nigeria" 1(1) *World Journal of Social Science* 27-36, at <http://wjss.sciedupress.com> (accessed 20-11-2017).

Amanda, E, M Claire & BC Mark (2006) *Gender and economic growth in Uganda: unleashing the power of women,* at <http://siteresources.worldbank.org/INTAFRREGTOPGENDER/Resources/gender_econ_growth_ug.pdf> (accessed 11-8-2018).

Atwijukire, D (2017) "Ensure local participation in the oil pipeline" *Daily Monitor* (13-11-2017).

Broumas, A (2017) "The capital-nation-state complex and the environment, transnational institute of social ecology developing analysis, vision and politics" <http://trise.org/2017/11/11/the-capital-nation-state-complex-and-the-environment/> (accessed 28-03-2018).

Chief Executives Board for Coordination (2006) "United Nations system-wide policy on gender equality and the empowerment of women: focusing on results and impact" Second regular session (27-10-2006).

Degteva, A (2006) *Oil industry and reindeer herding: the problems of implementing indigenous rights in the Nenets Autonomous Okrug, Russia* Master of Philosophy in Indigenous Studies, Faculty of Social Sciences University of Tromsø, at <http://library.arcticportal.org/434/1/thesis.pdf> (accessed 11-11-2017).

Dobscha, S (1993) "Women and the environment: applying ecofeminism to environmentally-related consumption" in L McAlister & ML Rothschild (eds) *NA-advances in consumer research* 36-40.

East African Community (2016) *Vision 2050*, at <http://www.africa-platform.org/sites/default/files/resources/eac_vision_2050_february_2016.pdf> (accessed 11-8-2018).

ECOSOC / Economic and Social Council of the United Nations (1997) *Agreed Conclusions, (1997/2)* Excerpt from A/52/3, Chapter IV, at <http://www.un.org/womenwatch/osagi/pdf/ECOSOCAC1997.2.PDF> (accessed 24-04-2018).

Hoch, NJ (2015) "On the threshold: breadwinning, capitalism and the absent/present father in the works of three late 20th-century" Ph.D Thesis, Graduate Center, City University of New York, at <https://academicworks.cuny.edu/gc_etds/975/> (accessed 23-4-2018).

Ibhawoh, B & JI Dibua (2003) "Deconstructing Ujamaa: The legacy of Julius Nyerere in the quest for social and economic development in Africa" *African Journal of Political Science*, at <http://pdfproc.lib.msu.edu/?file=/DMC/African%20Journals/pdfs/political%20science/volume8n1/ajps008001004.pdf> (accessed 22-4-2018).

Isabalija, SR (Permanent Secretary, Ministry of Energy and Mineral Development) (2017) "Commercialisation of Uganda's oil and gas sector: refinery and attendant infrastructure development" ARA Week at the Westin Grand Hotel Cape Town, South Africa.

Kwesiga, P (2017) "Oil firms start detailed plans for production" *New Vision* (7-8-2017), at <https://www.newvision.co.ug/new_vision/news/1459329/oil-firms-start-detailed-plans-production> (accessed 8-8-2018).

Ling, C (2014) "The background and theoretical origin of ecofeminism" 10(4) *Cross-Cultural Communication* 104-108.

Musisi, F (2017) "Uganda to raise Shs300b for crude oil pipeline" *Daily Monitor* (13-12-2017), at <http://www.monitor.co.ug/SpecialReports/Uganda-Shs300b-crude-oil-pipeline-Tanzania/688342-4224138-a944xrz/index.html> (accessed 26-3-2018).

Musisi, F & MK Muhumuza (2016) "The route to Tanga: How big oil deal slipped from Kenya's hands" *Daily Nation* (25-4-2016), at <https://www.nation.co.ke/lifestyle/dn2/How-Kenya-lost-Uganda-pipeline-deal/957860-3174748-rbogomz/index.html> (accessed 28-4-2018).

Nakaweesi, D (2017) "Ugandan traders turn to Dar port as Kenya polls close in" *Daily Monitor* (23-6-2017), at <http://www.monitor.co.ug/Business/Markets/Ugandan--traders---Dar-port--Kenya-elections/688606-3982982-t8fuo0z/index.html> (accessed 28-4-2018).

National Environment Management Authority (2006) *State of environment report for Uganda 2006/07*, at <https://wedocs.unep.org/bitstream/handle/20.500.11822/9237/-State%20of%20the%20Environment%20Report%20-%20Uganda-2007soer_2007.pdf?sequence=3&isAllowed=y> (accessed 11-8-2018).

Pinker, S (2018) "Why we refuse to see the bright side, even though we should" *Time* (15-1-2018), at <http://time.com/5087384/harvard-professor-steven-pinker-on-why-we-refuse-to-see-the-bright-side/> (accessed 11-8-2018).

Uganda National Planning Authority (2013) *Uganda Vision 2040.*

UNDP / United Nations Development Programme (2015) *Tanzania human development report 2014*, at <http://hdr.undp.org/sites/default/files/thdr2014-main.pdf> (accessed 11-8-2018).

United Nations Entity for Gender Equality and the Empowerment of Women (2018) "Intergovernmental mandates on gender mainstreaming", at <http://www.un.org/womenwatch/osagi/intergovernmentalmandates.htm> (accessed 24-4-2018).

United Republic of Tanzania (2007) *National adaptation programme of action (NAPA)*, at <https://www.preventionweb.net/files/8576_tza01.pdf> (accessed 11-8-2018).

WCED / World Commission of Environment and Development (1987) *Our common future*, at <http://www.un-documents.net/our-common-future.pdf> (accessed 23-9-2018).

Williams, M (2004) "IGTN and DAWN, mainstreaming gender perspectives into all policies and programs in the UN System" 3(2) *AWID Spotlight*, at <https://www.awid.org/sites/default/files/atoms/files/spotlight_-_gender_mainstreaming_-_can_it_work_for_womens_rights.pdf> (accessed 24-4-2018).

WWF / World Wildlife Fund & CSCO / Civil Society Coalition on Oil and Gas in Uganda (2017) *Safeguarding people & nature in East African crude oil (EACOP) pipeline project, a preliminary environmental and socio-economic threat analysis*, at <https://d1rirzyrd4ly69.cloudfront.net/downloads/safeguarding_nature_and_people___oil_and_gas_pipeline_factsheet.pdf> (accessed 11-8-2018).

Zelvallos, Z (2013) "Rethinking gender and sexuality, case study of the native American 'Two Spirit' people", at <https://othersociologist.com/2013/09/09/two-spirit-people/> (accessed 22-11-2018).

Chapter 29:
Integrating climate change in the environmental impact assessment process: challenges and prospects in Nigeria

Bibobra Bello Orubebe

1 Introduction

Nigeria comprises an area of approximately 923,853[1] square kilometres with a coastline along the Atlantic Ocean.[2] The country has diverse ecosystems. These include arid and semi-arid lands, savannahs in the north and tropical lowland forest, floodplains, saltwater, freshwater marches, brackish mangrove swamps/forests, sandy beaches, endemic micro-organisms, plants, invertebrates, mammals in the southern part which also has oil and gas deposits. The country is home to a number of threatened and/or endangered species.[3]

Geo-politically, Nigeria shares boundaries with Niger and Chad to the north; the Benin Republic to the west; Cameroon to the east; and Sao Tome/Principe and Equatorial Guinea to the south. In 2017, Nigeria had an estimated population of 180 million people[4] with about 300 ethnic groups,[5] structured into 36 states[6] with Abuja as its capital. The country is further subdivided into 774 local government areas.[7] In theory, Nigeria operates an American style presidential system of government with a bicameral legislature (National Assembly comprised of the Senate and House of Representatives).

Nigeria, although a resource-rich country, is unfortunately still saddled with poverty, misery and unsustainable development. These coupled with several other impediments to development such as corruption, ethnic, religious, cultural, social unrest, and economic mismanagement have pushed Nigeria's population, in the past, to a tipping

1 See <http://www.nationencyclopeadia.com/economies/africa/nigeria.html> (accessed 27-2-2018).
2 Udo (1970: 1-2).
3 Ibid.
4 Nigeria's National Population Commission (1998). Note, however, that in 2018 the Nigeria National Population Commission reviewed this estimate to 198 million people (Nigeria's National Population Commission (2018)).
5 Nigeria's National Population Commission (1998: 23).
6 Constitution of Nigeria (1999) as amended, Section 3(1).
7 Constitution of Nigeria (1999) as amended, Section 4(1).

point with threats of social upheaval and disintegration. Despite these and other deep-seated contradictions, Nigeria is the largest economy in Africa.[8]

It is against this background that some academics argue that one veritable tool Nigeria could use to address these challenges is to explore a science-cum-knowledge driven inter-disciplinary assessment of risks flowing from climate change governed by the correct social and legal framework.[9] Nevertheless, considerable disagreement exists when discussions proceed to question the meaning and effects of climate change,[10] forum and methodology.[11] Axiomatically, this debate includes some vexed issues. What is the right regulatory framework? What is the right objective in terms of scope vis-a-vis analytical methodology in the EIA policy trajectory that deals with climate change best? Will mainstreaming or separate treatment suffice under the current EIA process? Are there identifiable barriers or challenges? Comparatively, is there any best practice evolved elsewhere on the subject that Nigeria and other African countries could imbibe to address the challenges of climate change?

2 The conceptual scope and the problem of defining key terms

The cross-cutting nature and focus of this chapter require that the meaning and context of some key terms such as environmental impact assessment (EIA), greenhouse gasses (GHGs) and climate change (CC) be ascertained from the beginning. In this chapter, EIA means the critical appraisal of the likely effects of a policy, plan, program, project, or activity on the environment.[12] This is a study conducted before the commencement of the actual project. By studying the possible impacts, it is possible to avoid the adverse impacts by either re-designing the project or by taking other mitigating measures with inputs from public participation.[13] The decision-making authority might be a level of government (local, state or federal government) or its agencies. Impacts usually relate to the ecosystem, aesthetic, recreational, archaeological, social, economic and cultural values just as it relates to waste, endangered species and other scientific implications. Climate change is used within the meaning and definition proffered by the United Nations Framework Convention on Climate Change (UNFCCC), namely:[14]

8 *Vanguard* (2016). See also https://www.thecable.ng/world-bank-nigeriasouth-africa-angola-still-largest-economies-continent (accessed 27-2-2018).

9 Orubebe (2009: 161).

10 See <https://www.cigionline.org/multimedia/what-trumps-win-means-climate-change-policy?gclid=EAIaIQobChMI47fiiJa2AIVxBbTCh1iqwa7EAAYAiAAEgLqkvD_BwE> (accessed 19-12-2017).

11 Ibid.

12 Gilpin (2012: 170).

13 Ugandan National Environment Management Authority (2003: 37).

14 Article 1(2) UNFCCC.

> a change of climate that is attributed directly or indirectly to human activity, altering the composition of the global atmosphere. Human activity includes the pollution that arises from industrial activity and other sources that produce greenhouse gases. These gases, such as carbon dioxide, have the ability to absorb the spectrum of infrared light and contribute to the warming of our atmosphere.

The change in terminology from global warming to climate change was introduced to emphasise the fast emerging reality that atmospheric pollution on a global scale could precipitate a variety of extreme weather events, not just warming[15] and the greenhouse effect. The greenhouse effect is the cycle by which these gases become trapped in the atmosphere and heat the planet. The term was coined in 1827 by Joseph Fourier,[16] a French mathematician and physicist, who envisioned that "the warming process of the Earth acted in the same way as a greenhouse traps heat – a process of visible light and invisible radiation, with Earth's atmosphere acting as the glass barrier".[17]

Climate change is used in this context because it is one of the most contentious environmental issues facing Nigeria. In this regard, under the Association of Environmental Law Lecturers in African Universities (ASSELLAU), lawyers from Africa, like their counterparts from elsewhere in the world, are playing an increasing role to help build awareness about this environmental challenge. In terms of causative effects, GHGs are "a group of compounds that are able to trap heat (longwave radiation) in the atmosphere, that keeps the earth surface warmer"[18] than normal. In Nigeria, the major sources of GHGs are carbon emissions from energy, land use change, industry, solvents use, agriculture and waste management, gas flaring, transportation, and electricity generation among others.[19] A critical analysis of Nigeria's initial national communication to the UNFCCC in 1994 reveals that the predominant GHGs in Nigeria

15 Article 1(2) UNFCCC.

16 See <http://mpe.dimacs.rutgers.ed/2013/01/19/the-discovery-of-global-warming> (accessed 5-5-2018).

17 Gilpin (2012: 172).

18 Allison (2010).

19 Federal Republic of Nigeria (2003).

include carbon dioxide,[20] nitrous oxide[21] and methane[22] – gases which occur both naturally and as by-products of human activities. Others such as hydrofluorocarbons, sulphur hexafluorides and perfluoro chlorides[23] are to a large extent man-made.[24] Although these last three substances comprise a comparatively small part of the atmosphere, they have a large impact on the climate due to their potent heat-trapping properties and long residency periods in the atmosphere,[25] spanning in some cases several thousand years.[26]

In Nigeria, the fact that climatic conditions have been changing beyond natural variability is now well established.[27] In fact, evidence accumulated over the past few decades by research centres, particularly geospatial satellite data by foreign-based organisations, indicate that this has intimate links with anthropogenic (human-induced) activities, which are essentially responsible for substantially enhanced levels of emissions of GHGs into the atmosphere. The Intergovernmental Panel on Climate Change (IPCC), established in 1988, has conducted several assessments that show that unless deliberate steps are taken to reduce GHG emissions in the coming decades, irreversible changes will occur in the global climate system. Accordingly –[28]

---

20 Carbon dioxide is produced primarily through the burning of fossil fuels (oil, natural gas, and coal), solid waste, and trees and wood products. Deforestation and soil degradation add carbon dioxide to the atmosphere, while forest regrowth takes it out of the atmosphere. Carbon dioxide's lifetime in the atmosphere cannot be represented with a single value because the gas is not destroyed over time, but instead moves among different parts of the ocean-atmosphere-land system. Natural processes absorb some of the excess carbon dioxide, but some remains in the atmosphere for thousands of years, due to the slow process by which carbon is transferred to ocean sediments. See <http://www.wired.co.uk/article/what-is-climate-change-_Definition-causes-effects>(accessed 19-12-2017).

21 Nitrous oxide is usually emitted during agricultural and industrial activities, as well as during combustion of fossil fuels and solid waste. Its lifetime in the atmosphere stands at 121 years. See <http://www.wired.co.uk/article/what-is-climate-change-Definition-causes-effects> (accessed 19-12-2017).

22 Methane is a gas emitted during the production and transport of oil, coal and natural gas. Methane emissions also result from livestock and agricultural practices and from the anaerobic decay of organic waste in municipal solid waste landfills. Its average lifetime in the atmosphere is 12.4 years. See <http://www.wired.co.uk/article/what-is-climate-change-Definition-causes-effects> (accessed 19-12-2017).

23 Hydrofluorocarbons, Perfluorocarbons, and Sulfur hexafluoride are fluorinated gases, among other chemicals. These gases are emitted from a variety of industrial processes and commercial and household uses and do not occur naturally. They are sometimes used as substitutes for ozone-depleting substances such as chlorofluorocarbons (CFCs). See <http://www.wired.co.uk/article/what-is-climate-change-Definition-causes-effects> (accessed 19-12-2017).

24 See <http://www.wired.co.uk/article/what-is-climate-change-Definition-causes-effects> (accessed 19-12-2017).

25 Ugandan National Environment Management Authority (2003: 37).

26 Schwartz & Randall (2003).

27 Federal Republic of Nigeria (2003).

28 IPCC (2014). According to the report, each of the last three decades has been successively warmer at the Earth's surface than any preceding decade since 1850. The period from 1983 to 2012 was likely the warmest 30-year period of the last 1400 years in the Northern Hemisphere,

> [h]uman influence on the climate system is clear, and recent anthropogenic emissions of greenhouse gases are the highest in history. Recent climate changes have had widespread impacts on human and natural systems.
>
> Warming of the climate system is unequivocal, and since the 1950s, many of the observed changes are unprecedented over decades to millennia. The atmosphere and ocean have warmed, the amounts of snow and ice have diminished, and sea level has risen.

It is important to note that there is substantial evidence that climate change or global warming is likely to accelerate during the 21st century.[29] For Nigeria, its effects will include a rise in sea level, increased desertification, abrupt changes in agricultural production, severe weather conditions, the spread of diseases such as malaria, and the irreversible alteration of critical ecosystems. [30] In recognition of the enormity of the challenge climate change poses, Nigeria signed the Paris Agreement but has not taken coordinated steps to solidify the goals of the agreement as it relates to specific project conceptualisation, planning and implementation. In the meantime, the glaring effects of climate change have already begun to manifest in Nigeria's critical sectors – agriculture and the environment's carrying capacity.[31] Yet, the steps required to promote effective mitigation policies are yet to happen. These include a shift in the development paradigm to focus on the coordinated use of the required technologies in all critical sectors and the commensurate altering of policies to adapt to climate change as a national environmental emergency. The proven antidote to climate change including a strategic national investment in renewable energies, desalination plants, new agricultural practices and improved intergovernmental, inter-agency cooperation aimed at meeting local, regional and national climate resilience goals is absent. Other than white paper agreements, it is difficult to ascertain visible or measurable functional sub-regional, regional or indeed global cooperation between Nigeria and other countries to work toward achieving regulated climate goals. Quite naturally, inadequate or inaccurate impact assessment of climate change conditions would likely lead to aggravated initial effects, as well as ineffective or inadequate mitigation and adaptation with catastrophic consequences.[32]

---

where such assessment is possible (medium confidence). The globally averaged combined land and ocean surface temperature data as calculated by a linear trend show a warming of 0.85°C [0.65 to 1.06] over the period 1880 to 2012, when multiple independently produced datasets exist. In addition to robust multi-decadal warming, the globally averaged surface temperature exhibits substantial decadal and inter-annual variability. During its 45th Session held at Guadalajara, Mexico, 28-31 March 2017, the Panel approved the outline of the *Special Report on the Ocean and Cryosphere in a Changing Climate* (SROCC) to be finalised in September 2019. See <http://www.ipcc.ch/report/srocc/> (accessed 19-12-2017).

29 Schwartz & Randall (2003).

30 Nigeria's initial national communication to the unfccc data bases 1994. https://unfccc.int/resource/docs/natc/nignc1.pdf (accessed 5-5-2018).

31 Federal Republic of Nigeria (2003).

32 Orubebe (2009: 162).

3 The current legal framework for environmental impact assessment (EIA)

The initial legal and policy framework for EIA in Nigeria[33] consisted of the Urban and Regional Planning Decree,[34] the Environmental Impact Assessment Act,[35] the Environmental Impact Assessment Procedure and Environmental Guidelines, and the Standards for the Petroleum Industry.[36] Nigeria's international obligations stem from the United Nations Framework on Climate Change Convention (UNFCCC) which provides in Article 4(f) that:

> All Contracting Parties have responsibilities to take climate change into account..., to minimize adverse effects on the economy, public health, and quality of environment, in projects or measures undertaken to mitigate or adapt to climate change.

This international obligation can only be enforceable in Nigeria after compliance with the provisions of Section 12 of the Nigerian Constitution, which predicates enforceability of all international treaties or conventions upon ratification by the Nigerian National Assembly. Other obligations include the procedural requirements for EIA in the EIA Act and Procedures[37] requiring governmental approval on proposed activities likely to have a significant impact on the environment before or after the incident. This process, although copious and saddled with avoidable bureaucratic bottle-necks, provided guidance on the form and scope of the EIA process; notifications; public participation; consultation; decision-making process; review; and an appeal and monitoring process. The initial administrative authority was vested in the Federal Environment Protection Agency (FEPA) and the Council thereof. Following the repeal of the FEPA Act, the Federal Ministry of Environment is now vested with the administrative authority over EIA.

The current EIA process is saddled with inadequacies and shortcomings.[38] Notwithstanding these critical reservations expressed by critics and environmental scholars,[39] the federal authorities only acknowledged the inadequacies in July 2017 during a workshop of stakeholders in Abuja. At this workshop, the Federal Minister of Environment, for the first time, admitted the shortcomings of the Nigerian EIA process. According to Shehu Mahmud Usman (a Federal Permanent Secretary) who read the Minister's address:[40]

---

33 Oludayo (2004: 544).

34 Nigerian Urban and Regional Planning Act, formerly Decree No. 82 of 1992.

35 Nigerian Environmental Impact Assessment Act, Cap. E 12 (2004).

36 Environmental Guidelines and Standards for the Petroleum Industry (2000).

37 Nigerian Environmental Impact Assessment Act, Cap. E 12 [2004].

38 These include a lack of public participation, the poor quality in the commenting process, inadequate funding, corruption by officials involved in the EIA process, and the poor state of equipment.

39 Orubebe (2009: 175-181).

40 See <https://fmic.gov.ng/ministry-environment-holds-stakeholders-forum-review-eia-guidelines/> (accessed:19-12-2017).

> The Federal Ministry of Environment is hosting this stakeholders' workshop to enable it to develop new robust guidelines on EIA issues in line with global best practices. The review exercise underscores the Federal Government's commitment to the Principles of Sustainable Development and good governance as well as the creation of an enabling environment that will ensure that her citizens live within environmental limits and standard that will promote healthy living. 25 years ago, Decree No. 86 (now known as EIA Act CAP E 12 LFN) was promulgated by the Federal Government in order to achieve sustainable development in Environmental Impact Assessment. This law keeps evolving and unfortunately our existing guidelines do not have the capacity to incorporate climate smart decisions that will adequately address this phenomenon. That with these new trends and emerging global environmental issues, it has become imperative for Nigeria to review the existing EIA Act which has been in operation for the past two decades and address the shortcomings in order to bridge the gaps and ensure conformity with international standards especially against the backdrop of the dynamics of Nigeria's environment.

On 6 July 2017, the Federal Government of Nigeria issued 15 new EIA guidelines which include the EIA procedural guidelines, guidelines for strategic environmental assessment, EIA guidelines and standards on social impact assessment, EIA guidelines for health impact assessment, and EIA guidelines for oil and gas upstream (large volumes, base deports, tank farms, terminals and flow stations).[41] A careful perusal of the Nigerian Federal Government's new EIA guidelines shows no meaningful progress because it is difficult to identify any significant provision in the details aimed at addressing the fundamental environmental challenge of climate change within the EIA process.

4 Theoretical difficulties, analytical gaps and barriers in the Nigerian EIA process

EIA is a multidisciplinary land-use, planning, decision-making and sustainable soil management tool for environmental governance, through which climate change could potentially be addressed. For EIA efficacy, there is a need to harmonise theory and practice. In other words, the challenge is to find the best way to address climate change through EIA effectively and address the analytical gaps and barriers in the current Nigerian EIA process. There is evidence that suggests that specific climate change related regulation and guidelines are required in each step of the EIA process.[42] In addition, the current procedural and substantive legal regime that governs EIA in Nigeria needs to be synchronised with other instruments such as strategic and sustainability assessments, broader economic instruments[43] and other land use and planning policies before it can adequately address climate change. In this regard, the steps taken so far by Nigeria are at best an attempt aimed at putting in place new EIA regulations, but these fall short of putting in place climate specific guidance capable of integrating, or better

41 See <http://punchng.com/fg-produces-15-new-environmental-guidelines-reviews-others/> (accessed 19-12-2017).

42 Sok et al.(2011: 1).

43 Ibid.

still incorporating, climate change issues within the EIA process. This appears to be an important first step in tackling this global environmental issue.[44] In addition to this shortcoming, there exist classical theoretical difficulties in the Nigerian governments' effort aimed at integrating EIA and climate change. These include scientific uncertainty and confusion about the analytical nexus between climate change and climate variability.

4.1 Scientific uncertainty and stationarity

The concept of stationarity in natural environmental management means that "natural systems fluctuate within an unchanging envelope of variability".[45] This, according to Milly:[46]

> is the best basis for managing the environment and natural resources and can be captured through the historical record of system behaviour. It implies that any variability (for example, annual stream flow or annual Flood peak) has a time-invariant (or one-year-periodic) probability density function, whose properties can be estimated from scientific records....

Regardless of one's ideological bent, the scientific controversies associated with scholarly views of this nature cannot be ignored. However, the concept of stationarity appears to underpin the efficacy of legal frameworks and management approaches, including the EIA[47] process in Nigeria and most African countries. It assumes that the surrounding environment of plans and projects is stable, stationary or constant and thus their environmental impacts are predictable and can be tracked through historical records.[48]

4.2 Analytical nexus between climate change and climate variability

Currently, regardless of an environmental law lecturer's ideological bent, the search for science-based solutions that integrate climate change into the EIA process is fraught with overwhelming analytical difficulty associated with a science-based solution. *A fortiori*, the Nigerian EIA law and the ensuing regulations and related policies tend to highlight the impacts of plans/projects on the environment without

44 Ibid.

45 Milly et al. (2008: 573). Note that this view was also espoused within the context of environmental management process by He (2013).

46 Milly et al. (2008: 573).

47 Ibid.

48 He (2013).

investigating the impacts of the environment on proposed plans/projects.[49] For example, according to Xiangbai:[50]

> during the environmental baseline investigation stage – an indispensable step of EIA, climate change impacts, such as rising temperature, sea level rise, or the intensity and frequency of extreme weather events, are not assessed.

There is a real difficulty for the environmental law lecturer in this respect because climate change related facts are uncertain, unpredictable and complex.[51] Besides, the growing uncertainty cannot be tracked through existing databases or records. Thus the uncertainty and complexity associated with –[52]

> climate change may exceed the boundaries of environmental stationarity and have a significant impact on the performance of EIAs, predetermined development objectives. Scientific uncertainty concerning climate change means that human systems cannot predict and be thoroughly prepared for climate change due to imperfect knowledge about the probability, magnitude, timing and location of climate change impacts. This could lead to difficulties in assessing climate change impacts in EIA due to lack of specifics on individual projects.

In Nigeria, practical reality of this difficulty occured in 2012 when the Niger Delta region was flooded by the Forcados, Ramos, Niger rivers and their tributaries. Almost all major communities living in the Niger Delata region were flooded. A large portion of the major East-West Road under construction by the federal government of Nigeria was destroyed. The ethnic minority populations were temporarily resettled and all schools in the affected areas were closed. Some oil and gas facilities in the region were also shut down due to the hazards posed by the flood. During the flood, economic, political, social and cultural activities were paralysed. A critical review revealed that several EIAs were purportedly carried out in the region from 1956 to 2011 on Nigeria's unsustainable exploitation of oil and gas resources. One curious finding in ongoing research[53] is the observation that in most of the EIAs, GHGs have been considered in the proposed oil and gas drilling, pipelines and infrastructure proposals. However, under the current Nigerian EIA process, these projects are usually regarded as separate. The Federal Ministry of the Environment and the current EIA legal framework view them simply from the environmental decision-making tool perspective, namely plan/project design approval and implementation. It is imperative to note that although almost all the EIAs purported to address GHG emissions pursuant to the current Nigerian legal framework, with the goal of reducing potential adverse environmental effects, the said oil and gas facilities, the minority ethnic populations and the environment were all negatively impacted by the 2012 floods. This is against the background that climate change has already gone beyond scientific debate both at the international

49 Ibid. See also the broader dialectical expose by Xia et al. (2011).
50 He (2013); and Xia et al. (2011).
51 Ibid.
52 Ruhl (2011). See also Arvai et al. (2006: 217).
53 Novena University (undated).

and domestic levels and is now regarded as a fact resulting from anthropogenic GHG emissions.[54]

The above scenario concerning Nigeria explains today's environmental reality, which is the continuous pursuit of the narrow objective of the EIA process. This has several implications. Firstly, the current process is limited to only plan/project design approval and implementation based on land use and planning criterion. This is by all standards a far cry from what is required. Secondly, the current Nigerian EIA process allowed all these projects' EIAs to proceed without identifying, assessing and mitigating climate change. Thirdly, it is a deducible fact that the authorities claimed to have addressed GHG emissions under the current EIA regime – to reduce potential adverse environmental effects in the following terms:[55]

> The values of air quality measurements from this study were all within regulatory limits before commencement of the project. Marine transportation is known to produce obnoxious gases that could lead to atmospheric pollution. Some of these air pollutants are carbon monoxide (CO), nitrogen dioxide (NO_2), particulate matter (PM), and sulphur dioxide (SO_2). Greenhouse gases including carbon dioxide (CO_2) can also be emitted.

This paragraph, which appears in almost all the EIAs, for the period in question and up till now, is not supported by the facts. There are no data or facts to justify the claim that under the current EIA regime potential adverse environmental effects of GHG emissions have been reduced. These and other mischaracterisations of the facts[56] explain why Nigeria's current EIA process requires reform.

The critical environmental issue here is that the various EIAs conducted in the Niger Delta region in the period referred to above did not envisage or document the fact that the shrinking canals, silting lakes and rivers are warming, precipitation patterns are changing, and extreme events such as flooding are becoming more frequent and severe. If these persist, education, energy supply, health care, disease control, and road infrastructure will be negatively impacted upon. In fact, under the current Nigerian EIA process, impact assessment has been treated as an effective approach to control pollution and prevent environmental degradation. The potential pollution generated by these projects was the major consideration in determining whether an EIA was needed or not. In other words, pollution was also regarded as the most important criterion to assess whether these proposed projects would have significant environmental impacts (mainly pollutant discharge),[57] and the extent of their environmental impacts.

Fourthly, there is a difference between climate change and traditional environmental problems. It is the basis for integrating climate change in the EIA process. At a higher level of jurisprudential analysis, the integration of the two without a flexible, yet clear and precise step-by-step point for integration or consideration of climate

54 IPCC (2007).

55 Shell Petroleum Development Company of Nigeria Limited (2015: 209).

56 Ibid.

57 He (2013).

change, could create additional theoretical and implementation challenges.[58] In spite of the fact that climate change is one of the most complex and perhaps overwhelming environmental challenges for Nigeria in the 21st Century, the Nigerian government, private and public officials (planners and regulators inclusive) have not paid the attention that it requires. This is as a result of some apparent barriers, namely:

- the inadequacy of the Nigerian Government's EIA law, policy and incentive or commitment to climate change;
- the misconception on the part of government officials and the leadership of the country who at best view climate change and other environmental challenges as issues for minorities, particularly the Niger Delta's ethnic minorities;
- the lack of political will and capacity in all tiers of government to address climate change as a life-threatening and impending environmental catastrophe;
- the current Nigerian EIA framework and process, including the scoping process, that does not address climate change impacts in biodiversity, sustainability, cumulative impacts, disaster risk reduction (DRR), climate mitigation and adaptation; and
- the lack of coordinated yet flexible tools or strategies and the requisite expertise to deal with the challenge of climate change.

In addition to the above, there exist other vexed issues such as poor institutional arrangements, the lack of political will, inadequate budgetary provisions and corruption in the EIA process. Commenting on these shortcomings, Zagi, an official of the Nigerian Department of Petroleum Resources, affirmed in a study that:[59]

> EIA has become a standard practice in environmental and project planning on some major exploration and project development activities. However, our experiences in Nigeria suggest that not much is achieved despite the increase in the number of EIA studies being carried out. The reason for this is not farfetched since it is universally accepted that EIA as a planning tool is saddled with so many weak points. Some of the major weak points associated with EIA in Nigeria include the sparsity of baseline information against which the environmental impacts are measured; lack of budgetary allocations from the operators to implement mitigative measures and monitoring plans; lack of human resources and political commitment to enforce the environmental management plan amongst others. Consequently, oil operators carried out EIA in Nigeria to a larger extent, to satisfy regulatory requirements for the obtention of environmental permits.

It is noteworthy that in Nigeria, corruption has been linked to the EIA process in several respects and stages. For example, in the screening stage, the decision on whether an EIA needs to consider climate change can be unduly influenced by either the project proponents or government officials. While it is difficult to link corruption and the EIA process on the surface, investigative studies[60] affirm that corruption is possible in

58 Wang et al. (2003: 543).
59 Zagi (2002).
60 Williams & Dupuy (2017).

Nigeria because most environmental laws on EIA are unclear. Furthermore, they also grant unfettered discretionary power to government authorities. In fact, "some reports suggest that corruption has resulted in the Nigerian environmental ministry openly disregarding the country's EIA regulations".[61] Thus "some project proponents may bribe government officials to determine that a proposed project does not require EIA"[62] or government officials may solicit bribes from project proponents under the guise of transportation, welfare, accommodation and other 'payments'. All these are aided by vague EIA and climate change legislation. Another weakness of Nigeria's EIA regime is the non-transparent process of appointing experts. This is currently the prerogative of the Nigerian Federal Ministry of Environment. Unfortunately, this explains why the authorities have not deemed it fit to appoint ASSELLAU members in Nigeria or leading environmental lawyers as truly independent experts, rather defaulting to experts who appear to uphold the interests of project proponents. These and other unwholesome practices have led to allegations that:[63]

> ...during the scoping process, project proponents' may bribe the individuals responsible for carrying out an EIA to consider or ignore certain issues and impacts (climate change), or appoint arm chair experts who may bribe or extort project proponents for the fraudulent and falsified data collection...or even manipulate data collection and presentation... Perpetuate fraud through bribes, extortion, or kickbacks in order to collect needed data to include particular types of data or interpret it favorably. Sometimes fraud, kickbacks, and embezzlement take the form of procurement, contracting, billing, wages during public hearing where local communities are bribed to give their consent to projects, or to provide false data or permit/approve projects during report submission....

This said, however, the Nigerian government has declared its intention to establish a Climate Change Commission.[64] This idea is laudable, but the government must address the barriers noted above. Looking at the provisions of the Climate Change Bill, some progress has been made in providing a legal framework for mainstreaming climate change responses and actions into government policy formulation and implementation.[65] This includes the establishment of a Council to coordinate climate change governance in the country.[66] A careful perusal of the legislation, however, reveals that Section 6, which deals with functions, is silent on mainstreaming or integrating climate change into the EIA process. The Climate Change Bill also fails to address the need for a robust strategy to deal with barriers and challenges in the current Nigerian EIA

61 Ibid.

62 Ibid.

63 Ibid.

64 Bill for an Act to Establish the National Climate Change Commission and other Matters Connected therewith (2017), at <https//www.vanguardngr.com/2017/11/reps-pass-climate-change-bill/> (accessed 18-5-2018).

65 Sections 1(1) and (2), 2, 3 and 6, Bill for an Act to Establish the National Climate Change Commission and other Matters Connected therewith (2017).

66 Section 3, Bill for an Act to Establish the National Climate Change Commission and other Matters Connected therewith (2017).

process. Even where the right objectives are encapsulated, the Bill falls short of an enforceable broad-based right of citizens to sue and claim damages from corporations whose activities cause climate change. These *lacunae* need to be addressed if the proposed Climate Change Commission is to achieve its expected objectives. It has to be recognised that the "law does not operate in a vacuum. It operates in a social, economic and political context".[67] Consequently, it is not yet time for Nigerians to celebrate and in this regard, it is worth noting that although the National Assembly passed the Bill on 8 November 2017,[68] the President has not yet signed it into law.

5 What Nigeria needs to do to move forward

Moving forward, Nigeria needs to integrate climate change considerations into the EIA process. One of the strategies is mainstreaming and/or incorporating climate change-related concerns within the EIA process at both the strategic and regional policy interface, and specific project level. In addition to this, Nigeria needs to develop a mechanism that will identify climate change concerns early on in the EIA process. The Federal Ministry of Environment and other relevant authorities and stakeholders also need to develop consensus on the scope of GHG assessments. There is also a need to be clear about climate change scenarios used in the EIA process. This requires the highlighting of potential areas of contention and other relatively grey areas for better input. In addition, there is also the urgent need for specialised spatial data facilities with the capability to deal exhaustively with climate change mitigation; climate change adaptation and the identification of ecosystem degradation; loss and degradation of habitats within determined baselines; and the determination of trends in key indicators, particularly, thresholds/limits. Key areas that may be adversely affected by worsening environmental trends, such as protected or designated areas, require special attention.

The Nigerian EIA process needs to be adapted to isolating critical interdependencies, for example, water supply and sewage treatment systems, flood defences, energy/electricity supply and communication networks. Climate change vulnerability assessment needs to be built into the analysis of the baseline environment and the consideration of alternatives. Major infrastructure projects, in particular, are likely to be vulnerable. Accordingly, the Nigerian government must take into account the fact that, when developing the baseline against which projects are to be evaluated, it is important to acknowledge uncertainty as an inevitable consequence of climate change, and that this usually increases for large-scale projects. Such uncertainty can be accommodated or properly factored into the climate risk matrix using terms such as 'strongly

67 Kameri-Mbote & Nzomo (2004: 21).

68 See <https://www.vanguardngr.com/2017/11/reps-pass--climate-change-bill/>(accessed 18-5-2018).

suspected' and 'suspected' as recommended by the IPCC in its recent Assessment Report. The Federal Ministry of Environment needs to encourage environmental law experts and climate scientists to develop more detailed guidance on expressing climate uncertainty or risks.

Another important issue that needs to be addressed relates to benefits and losses that climate change integration will bring to the EIA process. In this regard, the question of which stakeholders accrue benefits and which do not becomes a challenge. At the moment, there is no fast and rigid EIA rule on what constitutes beneficial and adverse impacts. In practice, impacts are often not proportionally distributed within society – changes in ecosystems affect some population groups and economic sectors more seriously than others. This reasoning informs the proposed four functional steps and modalities for the EIA process.

Figure 1 and Figure 2 below are guides to assist EIA practitioners in specifically paying attention to possible alternatives and mitigation measures early in the EIA process. In the early stages of the process, alternatives are essentially different ways through which the developer can feasibly meet the project's objectives. This can be done by, for example, carrying out a different type of activity, choosing a different location or adopting a different technology or design for the project. This reality emphasises the need always to consider the no-go option (that is taking no action at all) while addressing climate change risk in an EIA. A practical approach to avoid maladaptation of climate-related variables in the EIA process is considering the no-go option as a specific alternative and developing baseline climate resilience data early in the process. At a more detailed level of analysis, alternatives may also merge into mitigation measures, where specific changes are made to the project design or to methods of construction or operation to prevent, reduce and where possible offset any significant adverse effects on the environment.

Many alternatives and mitigation measures that are important from the point of view of biodiversity and climate change should be addressed at strategic levels, in a strategic environmental assessment (SEA). For example, to avoid problems associated with flooding risk, planners should prevent projects from being developed on floodplains or areas of flood risk, or promote land management to increase water retention capacity. To avoid or minimise effects on areas of high biological value located near motorways or railway projects, it is necessary to assess the sitting corridors within the assessemnt of alternatives. Figures 1 and 2 summarise the four steps required.

Figure 1: Assessing climate change risks within the EIA process

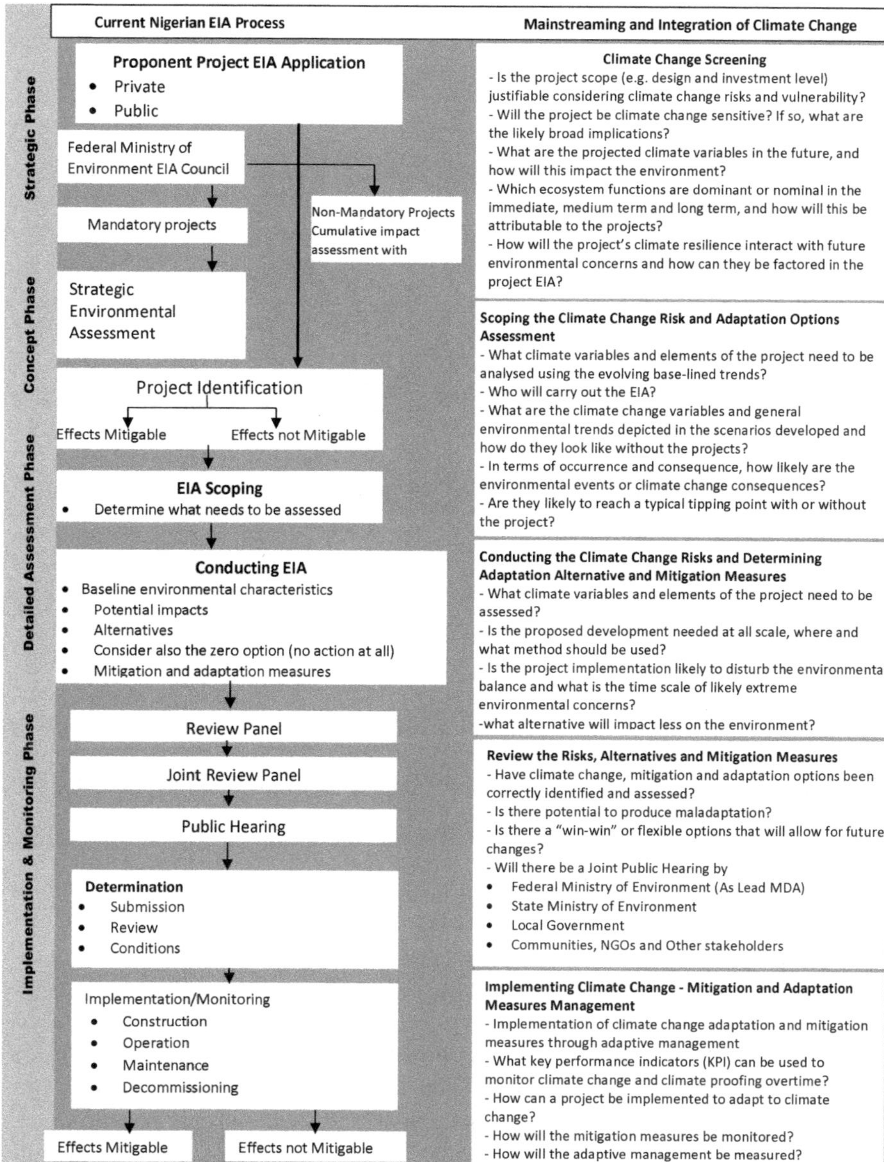

Figure 2: Mainstreaming and integrating climate change into the current Nigerian EIA process

STEP 1 Screen for climate sensitivity	**STEP 2** Obtain climate data and projections	**STEP 3** Prepare climate change risk and adaptation options assessment	**STEP 4** Develop a flexible science based risk matrix for assessment
• Review project brief to identify all project aspects including design elements. • Broad level discussion with key designers and project manager to identify project aspects which are climate sensitive • Develop a template that deals with the essential ingredients such as: ✓ A schedule of activities to be carried out; ✓ Provision for legislative oversight; ✓ Adequate environmental data base; ✓ Assemble high competent team inter disciplinary approach; ✓ Clear allocation of responsibilities; ✓ Avenues for citizens to appeal against decisions; ✓ Opportunity of individuals to request review in a public hearing; ✓ Ready availability to the public of all documents; ✓ Agreeing on how to deal with annual reporting and how to deal with trans boundary regional environmental plans, state & Local issues, etc.	• Source data set from the Bureau of Meteorology& specialised organisations to characterise the average climate change. • Liaise with the various specialised organisations/Ministries, Departments and Agencies (MDAs) to obtain climate projections at the fines possible scale. Providing Geographic Positioning System coordinates of the proposed development usually does this. Specialised organisations/MDAs typically provides climate projections for a high resolution at least 1 metre 1° x 1° grid centred on the appropriate coordinates • Review published state guidelines and policies for the considered area (e.g. Niger Delta) Authenticated Records on – rainfall, Sea Level Rise, etc.	• Using the risk framework and the climate data, determine the likelihood and consequences of the climate risks to the proposed project. • Validate these draft findings in a working session with the key designers and project manager. • Discuss any risk reduction measure, buffer zone, and design flexibility already in place, how they address the identified climate change risks and how they can be expanded or amended to reduce these risks.	• Link climate variability to cumulative impact assessment and disaster risk reduction assessment. • Ensure that the risk matrix input emphasizes occurrence and consequence including likelihood, almost certain, possible, unlikely, rare. • Develop risk-rating charts using the matrix and the climate resilience impact. • Develop risk scenario and link same with climate variables describing in phases the risk flows and rate all into immediate, medium and distant.

6 Importance of using social and strategic impact assessment to integrate climate change

In general, social impact assessment (SIA) is a tool that deals with the assessment of the impact of major policies, plans, programmes, activities and developments on people and society on a large scale. Social impacts or effects are those changes in social relations between members of a community, society or institution, resulting from external change.[69] The changes might be physical or psychological involving social cohesion, general lifestyle, cultural life, attitudes and values, social tranquillity, relocation of residents and severance or separation as is usually the case with huge infrastructural development such as the construction of large hydro-electricity dams or major railway lines in which large populations are relocated into unfamiliar environments.[70] The consequences include social discontent, unhappiness, increased illness

69 Gilpin (2012: 172).
70 Ibid.

and loss of productivity and income.[71] EIA does not only apply to individual projects, but to policies, plans, programmes, activities and regional land-use objectives.[72] There is a growing perception that climate change and related risks are matters that cannot be adequately dealt with in the course of one EIA because some of the risk elements have already been documented and, by necessary implication, factored into the cumulative effects of other projects within the same or related programmes in a particular region. This is the intertwining link between major infrastructural programmes, namely transportation, road infrastructure, rail infrastructure and energy infrastructure. Project decisions are often significantly influenced by preceeding broad policy-based decisions relating to road and infrastructure energy generation, climate change and natural resource conservation and management.[73]

Including climate change considerations in EIA typically results in multiple mitigation and adaptation plans. The adaptation plans need to be developed at regional levels, often beyond the boundaries of an individual project.[74] To have an effective cumulative impact assessment (CIA) at a regional scale requires an adaptation and mitigation plan that incorporates multiple projects in a region. CIA usually starts with regional EIA (REIA) and SEA.[75] In practice, some scholars, in an attempt to coordinate general EIA policy, insist that:[76]

> The mitigation plans on the emergent situations, the EMPs need to be accompanied by the Disaster Management Plan (DMP). Once CC considerations are included, adaptation and mitigation elements get factored and the DMP assumes a form of a Disaster Risks Assessment which is an integral part of the project in question.

Be that as it may, these expanded requirements raise questions of cost sharing, but these can be dealt with in a coordinated fashion with shared responsibilities without distorting the purpose of EIA law and policy in the course of integration of climate change. In the case of Nigeria, the country's current EIA process does not enjoy the benefit and insight that is usually associated with SEA and CIA. These tools are not only necessary, but through their robust public participation elements, they provide legitimacy and act as important milestones in overall project acceptability and risk management in the EIA process.

71 Ibid.
72 Ibid.
73 Ibid.
74 Agrewala et al. (2010: 24-32).
75 Ibid.
76 Ibid.

7 Conclusion

This chapter argues that Nigeria needs a paradigm shift in its EIA process to integrate climate change effectively. The reform required must be holistic and capable of unleashing the advantages of climate change mitigation and adaptation. One approach would be to reform the legal and policy guidelines on EIA. This should enable Nigeria to address the resources and capacity challenges associated with generating the requisite data that captures climate change impacts at regional and project-specific scales. In this process, good science must be the basis for the development of climate change vulnerability or risk models with accurate sector-specific scenarios developed on the basis of long-term environmental data. This must be predicated on functional vulnerability and climate resilient templates with implementable mitigation and adaptation measures. The outcome of such scientific and inter-disciplinary EIAs is the pathway, and requisite tool Nigeria can use to address climate change associated risks. Nigeria and the African continent and, indeed the world, need to collaborate to avail humanity with the advantages of best practices on integrating climate change considerations within the EIA process.

References

Agrewala, SA, M Kramer, G Prudent-Richard & M Sainsbury (2010) *Incorporating climate change impacts and adaptation in environmental impact assessments opportunities and challenges* OECD Environmental Working Paper No. 24.

Allison, I (2010) *The science of climate change: questions and answers.*

Arvai, J, G Bridge, N Dolsak, R Franzese, T Koontz, A Luginbuhl, P Robbins, K Richards, K Smith Korfmacher, B Sohngen, J Tansey & A Thompson (2006) "Adaptive management of the global climate problem: bridging the gap between climate research and climate policy" 78(1) *Climate Change* 217-225.

Federal Republic of Nigeria (2003) *Nigeria's first national communication under the UNFCCC*, at <https://unfccc.int/resource/docs/natc/nignc1.pdf> (accessed 11-8-2018).

Gilpin, A (2012) *Environmental impact assessment (EIA) cutting edge for the twenty-first century.*

He, X (2013) "Integrating climate change factors within china's environmental impact assessment legislation: new challenges and developments" 9(1) *Law, Environment and Development Journal* 50-67.

IPCC / Intergovernmental Panel on Climate Change (2007) *Climate change 2007: the physical science base* Contribution of Working Group I to the Fourth Assessment report: Summary for Policymakers, at <https://www.ipcc.ch/pdf/assessment-report/ar4/wg1/ar4-wg1-spm.pdf> (accessed 11-8-2018).

IPCC / Intergovernmental Panel on Climate Change (2014) *Climate change 2014 – synthesis report*, at http://www.ipcc.ch/pdf/assessment-report/ar5/syr/AR5_SYR_FINAL_Front_matters.pdf (accessed 11-8-2018).

Kameri-Mbote, P & M Nzomo (2004) The coverage of gender issues in the Draft Bill of the Constitution of Kenya Review Commission 2002: have the hens finally come home to roost for Kenyan women? 2(1) *University of Nairobi Law Journal* 1-21.

Milly, P, J Betancourt, M Falkenmark, RM Hirsch, ZW Kundzewicz, DP Lettenmaier & RJ Stouffer (2008) "Stationarity is dead: whither water management?" 319(5863) *Science* 574-574.

Nigeria's National Population Commission (1998) *1991 Census report.*

Nigeria's National Population Commission (2018) *Statement on sustainable cities, human mobility and international migration (national experience) at the 51st session of commission on population and development (CPD)*, at <http://www.un.org/en/development/desa/population/pdf/commission/2018/country/AgendaItem3/en_nigeria.pdf> (accessed 12-8-2018).

Novena University (undated) *Environmental survey 2017* on file with the author.

Oludayo, AG (2004) *Environmental law and practice in Nigeria.*

Orubebe, BB (2009) *Environmental legal implications of oil and gas exploration in the Niger Delta of Nigeria.*

Ruhl, JB (2011) "General design principles for resilience and adaptive capacity in legal systems: applications to climate change adaptation law" 89 *North Carolina Law Review* 18.

Schwartz, P & D Randall (2003) *An abrupt climate change scenario and its implications for United States national security*, at <http://www.futurebrief.com/dod-climate.pdf> (accessed 11-8-2018).

Shell Petroleum Development Company of Nigeria Limited (2015) *Environmental impact assessment (EIA) of Dodo North Non-Associated Gas (NAG) wells development project in Ekeremor local government area, Bayelsa State*, at <https://www.shell.com.ng/sustainability/environment/environment-impact-assessments/_jcr_content/par/textimage.stream/1481187683953/a7335b526e774eb9ce0d3a88d314e6d42f0a4011ffb4749596839fbd03c0b13e/report-dodo-north-non-associated-gas-project-eia.pdf> (accessed 11-8-2018).

Sok, V, J Bryan, BJ Boruff & A Morrison-Saunders (2011) *Addressing climate change through environmental impact assessment: international perspectives from a survey of IAIA members.*

Udo, RK (1970) *Geographical regions of Nigeria.*

Ugandan National Environment Management Authority (2003) *Handbook on the practice of environmental law in Uganda.*

Vanguard (2016) "Nigeria remains Africa's biggest economy – IMF" *Vanguard* (19-10-2016), at <https://www.vanguardngr.com/2016/10/nigeria-remains-africas-biggest-economy-imf/> (accessed 11-8-2018).

Wang, Y, RK Morgan & M Cashmore (2003) "environmental impact assessment of projects in the People's Republic of China: new law, old problems" 23(5) *Environment Impact Assessment Review* 543-579.

Williams, A & K Dupuy (2017) "Deciding over nature corruption and environmental impact assessments" 65 *Environmental Assessment Revue* 118-124, at <https://www.cmi.no/publications/file/6225-deciding-over-nature.pdf> (accessed 11-8-2018).

Xia, J, CZ Liu & GY Liu (2011) "Opportunity and challenges of the climate change impact on the water resource" 26(1) *Advance in Earth Science* 1-12.

Zagi, MM (2002) "Environmental impact assessment and the Nigerian oil industry: a review of experiences and learnings" SPE International Conference on Health, Safety and Environment in Oil and Gas Exploration and Production, 20-22 March, Kuala Lumpur, Malaysia, at <https://www.onepetro.org/conference-paper/SPE-74074-MS> (accessed 18-5-2018).

Chapter 30: The Environmental Management Act (2011): a basis for the growth of an environmental ethos and good environmental governance in Zambia?

Pamela Towela Sambo

1 Introduction

The Republic of Zambia is located in south-central Africa. It is bordered to the north by Tanzania and the Democratic Republic of Congo; the west by Angola; the south by Namibia, Botswana and Zimbabwe; and east by Malawi and Mozambique. With a total land surface area of 751,610 square kilometres and a population of 16.8 million people, the population density in Zambia is among the lowest in sub-Saharan Africa, representing one of the most land resource abundant countries in the region. It therefore follows that this vast stretch of land is home to a huge variety of natural resources that are accordingly exploited for their benefit to the human populace. Zambia, however, also has one of the highest rates of urbanisation in sub-Saharan Africa that has led to numerous attendant challenges such as the proliferation of shanty settlements, which in turn present numerous other environmental problems. With a high population growth rate and human development dependent on the surrounding natural environment, the depletion of natural resources is ever on the increase. Against this background, it is a recognised common task to advance environmental law to ensure that it aids in arresting national, regional and global environmental degradation.

This chapter critically evaluates the development of environmental legislation in Zambia with a view to assessing whether, and how, it is catalytic in the development of an 'environmental ethos' in the country. Central questions addressed include 'what is an environmental ethos' and 'what are some of its constituent elements'? The chapter begins by analysing the historical development of the now repealed Environmental Protection and Pollution Control Act (1990) (EPPCA) and its successor the Environmental Management Act[1] (2011) (EMA). The purpose of this analysis is to identify the key environmental themes that these two laws embody, and it extends to consider the relevance of the legal provisions towards shaping the environmental discourse in Zambia. The chapter then briefly discusses some aspects of the constitutional framework

1 Act 12 of 2011.

within which EMA, as an Act of parliament, operates. Thereafter, the chapter proceeds to evaluate these key environmental themes with a view to understanding their practical impact on the development of an environmental ethos in Zambia.

2 History of environmental regulation in Zambia

This section discusses environmental legislation in three general phases: pre-1990; post-1990; and post-2011. These phases are segmented on the basis that the pre-1990 phase had no clear-cut environmental legislation; while the other two phases are defined by two clear pieces of environmental framework legislation, the EPPCA and EMA respectively. These phases accordingly merit segmented discussion with a view to understanding the specific issues characterising each phase.

2.1 Pre-1990 phase

The conservation of natural resources in Zambia has existed since the 1950s.[2] It has been argued by some commentators that pre-political independence legislation in Zambia was preoccupied with preserving colonial practices that ensured that resource allocation and exploitation were maintained as opposed to the sustainable use of environmental resources.[3] These views lend credence to the argument that at this stage of Zambia's political development, the understanding of environmental issues including the sustainable use of natural resources was rather rudimentary. With the advent of various environmental challenges, such as desertification and other environmental health problems, the need to develop policies and strategies to protect the environment and human health arose.

Although Zambia has been independent since October 1964, it was only in the late 1980s that tangible legislative efforts were taken to promote environmental protection. It can be argued that one reason for this was the 'hangover' from the pre-political independence era that focused on preserving a colonial approach towards resource allocation and exploitation.[4] The launch of the National Conservation Strategy (NCS) for Zambia in 1985 can be viewed as a key preliminary step towards protecting the environment. This was the country's first attempt to develop an environmental policy and laid the groundwork for national legislation and administrative structures dealing with environmental issues.[5] The NCS also recommended, amongst other issues: the

2 Phiri (2006); and Bass (1998: 8).
3 Mulonda (2000: 1-3); and Jere (1999: 1-6).
4 Aongola et al. (2009: 32).
5 Ibid: 34.

enactment of a comprehensive environmental law framework; the development of environmental input in development planning processes through the environmental assessment of projects; and the promotion of community participation in natural resources management.[6] These recommendations resulted in the enactment of the EPPCA.

2.2 Post-1990 phase

The enactment of the EPPCA in 1990 provided a single and comprehensive national legislative and administrative structure for environmental protection in Zambia. This milestone made the country one of the few in Southern Africa at the time with a comprehensive environmental law and relevant institutional structures. The EPPCA was divided into 12 parts that focussed, amongst other things, on the protection and control of pollution and the establishment of the Environmental Council of Zambia (the main body to realise the objectives of the EPPCA).

It can be argued that the aim of the EPPCA was to harmonise the needs of human beings and the environment by reducing damage to the environment. During this period, environmental damage was mainly due to mining activities especially in the Copperbelt mining towns. Before the enactment of the EPPCA, each industry or authority was responsible for monitoring pollution associated with its activities or those undertaken in their area.[7] In reality, however, this did not occur and in 1992, the government formed the Ministry of Environment and Natural Resources, which in itself, demonstrated the importance of coordinated environmental efforts by the government. The implementation of the EPPCA, however, was to be one of the biggest challenges. The economic crisis in Zambia at the time resulted in environmental issues remaining relegated to the background in spite of the declared policy of the government.[8]

In 1994, the National Environmental Action Plan (NEAP) was developed as a comprehensive plan to curtail growing environmental degradation in the country. The NEAP updated the provisions and aspirations of the NCS by introducing the right of citizens to a clean and healthy environment, local community and private sector participation in natural resources management and mandatory environmental impact assessments (EIAs) for major development projects in all sectors.[9] The overall objective of the NEAP was to integrate environmental concerns into the social and economic development planning processes of the country. The NEAP identified key

6 Saidi (2010: 6).

7 For instance, the Mines and Mineral Act, the Factories Act and the Town and Country Planning Act were to guide respective organisations in the monitoring and controlling levels of pollution.

8 See generally: Kakonge (2009); and Adams (1990).

9 Ministry of Environment and Natural Resources (1994: 31-33).

environmental problems and issues, such as water, air and land pollution particularly that stemming from the mining and manufacturing sectors.[10]

Building on the NCS and NEAP, the government developed the National Policy on Environment (NPE) in 2007 to "harmonise various strategies, and rationalise legislation relating to the use and management of the environment in order to attain an integrated approach towards development".[11] The NPE was developed through a comprehensive research and consultative process that sought to integrate decentralisation, community participation and privatisation as components of sustainable development in Zambia. The express purpose of the NPE was to create "a comprehensive framework for effective natural resource utilization and environmental conservation which would be sensitive to the demands of sustainable development".[12] The NPE had seven specific objectives, most of which have found expression in Zambia's contemporary environmental legislation. These were as follows:

1. Promote the sound protection and management of Zambia's environment and natural resources in their entirety, balancing the needs for social and economic development and environmental integrity to the maximum extent possible, while keeping adverse activities to the minimum.
2. Manage the environment by linking together the activities, interests and perspectives of all groups, including the people, non-governmental organisations and government at both the central and decentralised local levels.
3. Accelerate environmentally and economically sustainable growth in order to improve the health, sustainable livelihoods, income and living conditions of the poor majority with greater equity and self-reliance.
4. Ensure broad-based environmental awareness and commitment to enforce environmental laws and to the promotion of environmental accountability.
5. Build individual and institutional capacity to sustain the environment.
6. Regulate and enforce environmental laws.
7. Promote the development of sustainable industrial and commercial processes having full regard for environmental integrity.

2.3 Post-2011 phase

EMA was enacted on 15 April 2011 and introduced innovative provisions in line with global and integrated environmental management principles. Part I of EMA states that the law takes precedence over other sector-specific legislation. It furthermore includes: a right to a clean, safe and healthy environment; a duty on citizens to protect the environment; and a set of principles that govern environmental management in Zambia. These aspects are explained more fully below.

---

10 Chipungu & Kunda (1994: 51).
11 Ministry of Environment and Natural Resources (1994: 31-33).
12 Chabwela (2005).

Part I includes the Preamble that outlines the purpose of the law as facilitating "…the implementation of international environmental agreements and conventions to which Zambia is a party". This means that the practice of environmental law and management in Zambia must be in substantial conformity with international agreements to which Zambia is a party. This read together with the provisions of Section 3 of EMA confirms that environmental well-being should take precedence over other considerations.

Section 3 of EMA provides that subject to the Constitution, where there is any inconsistency between the provisions of EMA and the provisions of any other written law relating to environmental protection and management, which is not a specific subject related to law on a particular environmental element, the provisions of EMA shall prevail to the extent of the inconsistency.

Section 4(1) of EMA provides for a right to a clean and healthy environment. The right is enshrined subject to the Constitution. Section 4(3) provides that "a person may, where the right in subsection (1) is threatened or is likely to be threatened as a result of an act or omission of any person, bring an action against the person whose act or omission is likely to cause harm to human health or the environment". The construction of this provision emphasises that a person may bring an action where the right to a clean, safe and healthy environment is threatened or is likely to be threatened. The import of this construction is that any juridical person may commence an action in the event of both threatened and actual environmental damage. It may also be argued that this provision does not refer to any actual damage being suffered by the person seeking to utilise the right. The action by the affected person, "may seek to prevent, stop or discontinue any activity or omission which threatens, or is likely to cause harm to, human health or the environment".[13] Section 4 provides other remedial measures such as compelling a public officer to take certain steps to prevent the contravention,[14] undertake an environmental audit of offending activities or omissions,[15] and take other appropriate measures.[16] Interestingly, Section 4(3) raises debates about locus standi in environmental proceedings, an issue that will be dealt with later in this chapter.[17]

Sections 5 and 6 of EMA present further innovations in remarked departure from the erstwhile EPPCA. Section 5 imposes upon 'every person' a duty to safeguard and enhance the environment and to inform the Zambia Environmental Management Agency (ZEMA) of anything that 'affects' or 'may affect' the environment. This innovation is welcome, although the provision remains unclear as to whether there would be any sanction for a person who does not fulfil the prescribed duty. This lack of clarity on sanctions for non-compliance is likely to affect enforcement of the otherwise

13 Section 4(4)(a) of EMA.
14 Section (4)(4)(b) of EMA.
15 Section (4)(4)(c) of EMA.
16 Section 4(4)(d-f) of EMA.
17 See part 3.1 below.

innovative provisions.[18] Further, the realisation of the aspiration in this provision is lost against the backdrop of insufficient environmental awareness in Zambia. Section 6 of EMA introduces principles that must govern environmental management in Zambia with a view to achieving its overarching purposes.[19]

Part II of EMA creates ZEMA as a corporate body with the function of carrying out "all such things as are necessary to ensure the sustainable management of natural resources, protection of the environment and prevention and control of pollution".[20] This part of EMA also makes provision for the powers of inspectors and prosecutors,[21] which include powers of arrest without a warrant of persons reasonably believed to have committed an environmental offence.[22] Inspectors appointed under EMA are granted immunity from acts performed in good faith in the exercise of any of the powers, functions or duties conferred upon them.[23] Arguably, the rationale for such a provision is that the inspectors should not be hindered in the performance of their official environmental duties by considerations that may render them potentially liable for wrongdoing in their individual capacity.

Integrated environmental management (IEM) is provided for in Part III of EMA. IEM is defined as "a philosophy that is concerned with finding the right balance (sometimes called the 'golden mean') between development and the environment in a holistic manner with acknowledgement of interconnections in both the physical and human systems".[24] This means that IEM is holistic in terms of both the mode and manner of addressing the vast range of environmental issues in a jurisdiction. Sections 20-30 of EMA make provision for two main techniques for achieving IEM in Zambia, namely reporting[25] and environmental assessments.[26]

Part IV of EMA is dedicated to environmental protection and pollution control. An integrated pollution prevention and control approach is promoted throughout this part

---

18 See generally on the use of civil or criminal sanctions to ensure compliance in environmental law: Dimento (1993); Öberg (2011); China ASEAN Environmental Cooperation Centre and United Nations Environment Programme (2014); Kidd (2002); Gunningham (2011); Lambrechts (2016); and Watson (2005).

19 Notable amongst these principles are: the environment is the common heritage of present and future generations; the polluter pays principle; the precautionary principle; access to information; and community participation.

20 Section 9(1) of EMA.

21 Section 15 of EMA.

22 Section 16(1)(a) of EMA.

23 Section 19 of EMA.

24 See generally on IEM: Margerum & Born (2000: 5-7); Margerum (1999: 151); Cairns (1991: 7); and Retief & Sandham (2001).

25 According to Sections 20 and 21 of EMA, the main reports and plans provided for are the State of the Environment Report (every five years) and the National Environmental Action Plan (every ten years).

26 Section 23 of EMA provides for strategic environmental assessments in relation to policies, programmes and plans that could have an adverse effect on environmental management or the sustainable management and use of natural resources.

of the Act. This approach looks at environmental protection and pollution control from the perspectives of land, water, air, ionising radiation, noise, pesticides and toxic substances. There is also provision for emergency preparedness and the declaration of environmental emergency situations.[27] Furthermore, this part of EMA canvasses natural resources management and makes specific mention of mechanisms to promote the protection of hills and landscapes, promote the conservation of natural resources and prohibit the import and introduction of invasive alien species.[28]

Part V of EMA addresses international matters in environmental protection and covers international agreements and transboundary environmental management programmes. These provisions relating to international matters are especially important in any transboundary environmental issue that the country may from time to time be engaged in.

Parts VI and VII of EMA deal with issues related to promoting environmental democracy,[29] namely: access to environmental information (including its analysis, research and dissemination); and public participation in environmental decision-making through public reviews and hearings. Part VIII of EMA creates the Environment Fund, which according to Section 97, the purpose of which is to, inter alia, mitigate or restore environmental degradation and facilitate research. It is unclear from this provision how and by whom use of the Environment Fund may be made.

Enforcement provisions are provided for under Part IX of EMA and include environmental audits and monitoring.[30] Other enforcement mechanisms provided for are prevention measures, protection measures, environmental restoration measures, compliance measures and cost orders. A protection order may require the person on whom it is served to, inter alia, take any measures to: avoid, remedy or mitigate any adverse effects and to stop the activity that is resulting, or is likely to result, in an adverse effect; control the activity; assess the actual or anticipated extent of the adverse effect; remedy any adverse effects caused by the activity; or prevent a recurrence of the activity.[31] Sections 107, 108, 110 and 111of EMA are relevant with regard to the general issue of access to environmental justice and it can be argued that these provisions reflect the need to embrace community participation in ensuring environmental wellbeing.

According to Section 108, a person may initiate the issue of an order by the Director-General of ZEMA by setting out factual details disclosing the need for remedial measures to be undertaken in the environmental interest. Section 109 of EMA makes provision for prosecutions to be initiated by the public. In the event that the Director-General decides not to commence the prosecution provided for under this section, a

27 Sections 41 and 42 of EMA.

28 Sections 74-83 of EMA.

29 See generally on environmental democracy: Jasanoff (1996); and Wates (2005).

30 Sections 101 and 102 of EMA.

31 Sections 103-107 of EMA.

member of the public may proceed to do so.[32] In such a case, EMA provides that no costs shall be awarded by the courts against the person initiating the proceedings unless "the court finds that the primary motivation for the prosecution was not a concern for the public interest or the enhancement, protection and conservation of the environment".[33] In a similar vein to the provision on granting immunity to environmental inspectors, this section ensures that members of the public do not abuse the leeway given by EMA to initiate legal proceedings for the mere purpose of settling other scores unrelated to environmental wellbeing.

Section 110(1) of EMA provides for the initiation of a civil matter for damages by any person where there is an act or omission in contravention of the Act. Pursuant to this section, a person may also sue for damages in respect of an act or omission that constitutes a contravention of EMA or that is likely to have an adverse effect, whether or not that person or any other person has suffered, or is likely to suffer, any loss or harm from the act or omission.

Part X provides for administrative mechanisms such as reviews and appeals. Under Sections 112–114, appeals against decisions made by ZEMA lie to the ZEMA Board. Sections 115 and 116 of EMA provide for appeals against the ZEMA Board to the Minister. This is an innovation that was not available under the EPPCA. EMA has also introduced provisions for an aggrieved party to seek review, first with the ZEMA Board, then the Minister and ultimately to the High Court.[34] In contrast, the EPPCA reposed the power to review in the Minister. The current provisions of EMA recognise ZEMA as a legally constituted environmental regulator that takes technical environmental concerns into consideration; in contrast to the Minister, who may be more likely to base an environmental decision on political expediency.

Part XI provides for environmental offences relating to a broad array of issues including environmental impact assessment, environmental standards, biological diversity, hazardous waste materials, chemicals, radioactive substances and protected areas. Part XII contains general provisions on confidentiality, civil damages and the imposition of penalties.

In summary, the provisions of EMA have introduced innovations in environmental regulation in Zambia, which can properly be termed as the development of an environmental ethos. In order to have a better understanding of the implementation of EMA, it is important to give some background to the provisions of Zambia's supreme law, the Constitution.

---

32 Section 109(4) of EMA.
33 Section 109(6) of EMA.
34 Sambo (2012: 203-204).

2.4 Constitution of Zambia

The Constitution of Zambia (Amendment) Act (2016)[35] (the Constitution) is the supreme law in Zambia. The provisions of EMA are accordingly subservient thereto. The Constitution has important provisions for environmental regulation, despite not containing a right to a clean, safe and healthy environment.[36]

The Constitution provides that "a citizen shall protect and conserve the environment and utilise natural resources in a sustainable manner and maintain a clean and healthy environment".[37] This duty to protect and conserve the environment is bestowed upon each and every citizen. Without meaningful support, however, the role that a citizen can play in the momentous task of environmental management cannot be achieved. Article 255 of the Constitution provides for the general management and development of the environment and natural resources and prescribes adherence to a number of environmental principles, also provided for in EMA, which include the following: polluter pays principle; equitable sharing of environmental benefits and natural resources; the need to ensure that natural resources have an environmental, economic, social and cultural value and the reflection of this in their use; precautionary principle; the conservation and protection of ecologically sensitive areas, habitats, species and other environment shall be done in a sustainable manner; respect for the integrity of natural processes and ecological communities; effective participation of people in the development of relevant policies, plans and programmes; and access to environmental information to enable people preserve, protect and conserve the environment. Furthermore, Article 256 provides that:

> ... a person has a duty to co-operate with state organs, state institutions and other persons to:
>
> (a) Maintain a clean, safe and healthy environment;
>
> (b) Ensure ecologically sustainable development and use of natural resources;
>
> (c) Respect, protect and safeguard the environment; and
>
> (d) Prevent or discontinue an act which is harmful to the environment.

This provision needs to be read together with Article 43(1) which mandates citizens to protect and conserve the environment. Article 256 requires a person to cooperate in maintaining a clean, safe and healthy environment and generally respect, protect and safeguard the environment. Implicit in this obligation is that a person must have the awareness that this is required of them and also the means to carry out the obligation. It is arguable that this is a very fluid legal provision that needs to be elucidated if it is

35 Act 2 of 2016.

36 The Bill of Rights currently in force in Zambia is that contained in the Constitution of Zambia, Act 18 of 1996. This is as a result of the failure to pass the 2016 National Referendum to adopt a new Bill of Rights.

37 Article 43(1)(c) and (d) of the Constitution.

to serve a meaningful and practical purpose. Article 257 of the Constitution further provides that:

> …the State shall, in the utilisation of natural resources and management of the environment –
>
> (a) protect genetic resources and biological diversity;
>
> (b) implement mechanisms that minimise waste;
>
> (c) promote appropriate environment management systems and tools;
>
> (d) encourage public participation;
>
> (e) protect and enhance the intellectual property in, and indigenous knowledge of, biodiversity and genetic resources of local communities;
>
> (f) ensure that the environmental standards enforced in Zambia are of essential benefit to citizens; and
>
> (g) establish and implement mechanisms that address climate change.

This provision focuses on the role of the state in using natural resources and managing the environment. This means that the state has a duty to facilitate overall sustainable use of natural resources by protecting genetic resources and biological diversity and also carrying out all the obligations listed in this provision. These state duties encompass the full breadth of environmental regulation and governance. This chapter is unable to provide evidence that the state has fulfilled these obligations following the enactment of the Constitution.

In general, this section of the chapter has shown that the Constitution has clear and progressive provisions regarding environmental management. The question that begs an answer, however, is whether these provisions are adhered to. In a country with relatively poor levels of environmental awareness, the state can hardly be held accountable.

3 Enter an 'environmental ethos' beyond pollution control

As highlighted above, EMA is the current framework environmental legislation in Zambia. Read together with the relevant constitutional provisions, the Act reveals that there are key environmental themes that are likely to have a positive impact on environmental regulation and the development of an environmental ethos in Zambia. The question to be resolved, however, is whether these relatively good provisions are contributing, if at all, to the creation of an environmental ethos that has practical benefits.

According to the Oxford English Dictionary, the word ethos is defined as "the characteristic spirit of a culture, era or community as manifested in its attitudes and aspirations".[38] The Collins Dictionary defines an ethos as "the set of ideas and attitudes that is associated with a particular group of people or a particular type of activity".[39]

---

38 See <www.en.oxforddictionaries.com> (accessed 2-5-2018).

39 See <www.collinsdictionary.com> (accessed 2-5-2018).

Therefore, this chapter advances the definition of 'environmental ethos' as the set of ideas and attitudes towards the environment that are informed by relevant education, awareness and enforcement of legislative provisions. Environmental education in general addresses education about the environment, which involves building awareness, understanding and skills necessary for developing a world population that is aware of, and concerned about, the environment and its associated problems; and which has the knowledge, skills, attitude, motivation and commitment to work individually and collectively towards forging solutions to current problems and the prevention of new ones.[40] It is the hypothesis of this chapter that the development of an environmental ethos is dependent on the availability of opportunities for enhanced environmental education. This education needs to be approached from a multidisciplinary perspective to ensure that all aspects of the environment are adequately covered. In this vein, the cooperation of environmental lawyers with other environmental specialists seems essential.

3.1 Environmental law practice and *locus standi*

Locus standi is the right one has to bring an action before a court of competent jurisdiction. To do so a person generally must be affected by the matter and there must be a case that can be resolved by legal action. Environmental cases can push the bounds of *locus standi* because people may often not hold individual, immediate or exclusive interests in the thing harmed. Environmental concerns are often collective or shared in nature, implicit in the definition of the environment – that it is everything around us.

Section 4(3) of EMA regulates *locus standi* in environmental matters. This concept is referred to as the *action popularis*, which means an action to obtain a remedy by a person or a group in the name of the general public, without the necessity of representation authorisation from the victims of the harm.[41] The *locus standi* provision in EMA is universal in the sense that any person can bring the action, whether or not they are directly affected. This is a departure from the past practice where the right to bring an action was based on actual harm or injury being occasioned to the person bringing the action. This new position is recognition that environmental matters are matters of general public interest, and further that the general public should have a right to seek redress for environmental law wrongs. The nature and scope of the remedies that can be sought are alive to both the general harmful effects of pollution on the environment and the possible harm caused to the individual.

Section 109 of EMA empowers a member of the public to request in writing the Director-General to investigate an alleged contravention of the legislative provisions.

---

40 See generally: Woock (1972); and Maina-Okori et al. (2017).

41 Aceves (2003: 360).

Where the Director-General decides not to investigate the said matter, the person who made the request may lay a charge and prosecute. This shows that members of the public are not hindered from accessing the courts by the legal technicality of *locus standi*. In a similar manner, Section 110(1) of EMA provides that:

> A person may sue for damages in respect of an act or omission that constitutes a contravention of the Act or that is likely to have an adverse effect whether or not that person or any other person has suffered or likely to suffer any loss or harm from the act or omission.

This provision makes it clear that the issue to consider for one who intends to sue for damages for acts or omissions contravening EMA, is the likelihood of suffering harm and not whether the harm has actually been suffered, thereby enhancing a person's *locus standi*.

Since the enactment of EMA, the rights and duties of citizens in environmental matters have been clearly laid out. However, with literacy and awareness levels being low, these otherwise progressive provisions remain unutilised.[42]

Despite the recognition of the right to a clean, safe and healthy environment in EMA, and the creation of various offences in several laws governing environmental management and conservation, water management and mining and mineral processing activities, there is still a dearth of judicial decisions on these matters. One reason for this is that the public has not taken steps to test the waters in enforcing the right to a clean and healthy environment using the progressive provisions in both EMA and the Constitution.

In the case of *James Nyasulu & 2000 Others v. Konkola Copper Mines (KCM) Plc., Environmental Council of Zambia & Chingola Municipal Council*[43] (*Nyasulu* case), instituted in the Lusaka High Court in 2007 but only decided in 2011, the court ordered the first defendant to pay a total of K10 billion as general and punitive damages to the 2000 plaintiffs who had suffered personal and environmental injury as a result of the first defendant discharging effluent from its mining operations into Kafue River, the main source of water for the plaintiffs' livelihood.

The *Nyasulu* case could well be referred to as a success in enforcing environmental rights. It must be noted that this case was argued on the basis of the provisions of the now repealed EPPCA. This is one case in which the courts missed an opportunity for judicial activism. Despite the court establishing that the actions of the first defendant caused harm to fish, frogs, crocodiles, hippos, aquatic plants and people who used the water for drinking purposes, the defendant was not punished for the harm caused to the environment. The court could have taken this opportunity to address the wider environmental harm caused by the pollution instead of focusing solely on the personal loss suffered by the plaintiffs.

42 See generally: Sambo (2012).

43 *James Nyasulu and Others v. Konkola Copper Mines Plc and Others* (2007/HP/1286) (unreported).

In the *Nyasulu* case, the Environmental Council of Zambia (the then equivalent of ZEMA and the second defendant in the case), was exempted from liability by the court on the grounds that it operated under difficult circumstances since it was a government agency not insulated from political control. According to the provisions of the now repealed EPPCA, the agency was indeed a government agency tasked with ensuring that the provisions of the legislation were adhered to.

The plaintiffs in this case argued that the Environmental Council of Zambia had neglected its duty by failing to prosecute the first defendant, enforce the licence conditions and to protect the community. Accordingly, the court's decision can be said to have been misguided in that it failed to give effect to clear legislative provisions for unknown reasons. Arising from the *Nyasulu* case, it is arguable that there is a continued need for public environmental education and awareness with regard to environmental rights and the duties and obligations of both state and private individuals in relation to environmental management.

Whilst great strides have been made toward widening the scope of access to environmental justice in Zambia, a lot still remains to be done. Mere legal pronouncements without deliberate efforts to enhance their enforcement serve no practical purpose. More concerted efforts are needed to raise public awareness and access to environmental information. Further, measures such as establishing special courts or tribunals to deal with environmental matters and aimed at lowering the costs of instituting and undertaking environmental litigation need to be implemented to encourage public participation in environmental litigation and ensure true access to justice.

3.2 Environmental good governance

Good governance in all sectors of a country is a process and not an occasion. Environmental good governance refers to the processes of decision-making involved in controlling and managing the environment and natural resources,[44] and has been the subject of numerous scholarly writings. The concept is now firmly established both in international and domestic law.[45] Environmental good governance also includes the manner in which decisions are made.

According to Article 8 of the Constitution, there are national values and principles that must be followed in Zambia. Specifically, Article 8(c), (e) and (f) call for democracy and constitutionalism, good governance, integrity and sustainable development. These principles are important in every sector of the economy and governance. Article 9 buttresses the provisions of Article 8 by emphasising that the national values and principles shall apply to the interpretation of the Constitution, enactment and

44 Esty (1999).

45 Feris (2010); and Bernstein (2004).

interpretation of the law, and the development and implementation of state policy. The necessity of these national values and principles in environmental governance cannot be overemphasised.

Environmental governance encompasses "adherence to values such as transparency, accountability, public participation in decision-making and freedom of association".[46] Environmental governance should also involve a social element. The aspiration towards establishing a society based on social justice is important.

In the context of South Africa, some of the key pointers as to what constitutes good environmental governance are that: governance should be responsible and accountable; regulations should be enforced; mechanisms and structures that facilitate participation should be clearly laid out; environmental issues should be 'mainstreamed' through all sectors of the economy; and access to information should be prevalent.[47] In addition, international measures of environmental governance can also be useful in measuring various aspects of national environmental governance relative to other countries.[48]

Using the South African key pointers of good environmental governance as a basis for a rudimentary comparison with Zambia reveals that almost all these pointers are provided for in EMA and the Constitution as has been shown in the discussion relating to the specific legislative provisions above.[49]

3.3 Greening the Zambian judiciary

The history of global environmental law has repeatedly demonstrated the importance of the judiciary in ensuring that "ordinary citizens can, through the legal process, make their governments protect the environment when that may be the last thing their governments want to do".[50] The judiciary is the bedrock of the rule of law and good governance in any society. In order to ensure that these values permeate the environmental sector, it is essential that the judiciary as a neutral arbiter is equipped with environmental consciousness. This raises the argument for specialised environmental courts. An environmental court is defined as "any government judicial or administrative body specialising in resolving disputes about environment, natural resources, land use, or related issues".[51] The creation of such specialised courts is a necessary part of the

46 Feris (2010: 76).
47 Fakier et al. (2005); and Hassan (2001: 11).
48 Fakier et al. (2005).
49 See parts 2.3 and 2.4 above.
50 Houck (2010: 9).
51 Pring & Pring (2016: 54).

concept of 'greening the judiciary'. From the South African perspective, Kidd has argued that:[52]

> …it would appear that the judges' performance is rather 'chequered' in environmental cases, which suggests that the judiciary needs to become more attuned to environmental law. I call this process, for purposes of this note, 'greening the judiciary'. What I mean by this is not that judges must decide all environmental cases in a way that favours the environment, but that they must correctly consider, interpret and apply the relevant environmental law, and give environmental considerations appropriate deliberation. This note aims to identify, in admittedly somewhat general terms, the current state of environmental decision-making by judges and to suggest what needs to happen for such decisions to be improved.

The issues brought out in this argument are pertinent to Zambia. The performance of judges in environmental cases does indeed suggest that there is need for continuous training. The author agrees that the critical consideration is not whether judges decide all environmental matters in favour of the environment, but rather that some balance must be struck between developmental needs that necessitate projects and the preservation of the environment. It is important that the judges are aware through routine training that there is a need to look beyond rendering traditional or default judgments that only focus on promoting the socio-economic aspect of development.

It has been argued that a number of courts around the world have used "environmental provisions in national constitutions to break new legal ground in an effort to respond to contemporary environmental problems, such as climate change".[53] For instance, in India the courts have created a system of public interest litigation with very broad *locus standi* for interested members of the public to bring environmental cases.[54] The question that might be asked is what the advantages of having environmental courts are. One advantage is that the efficiency with which environmental cases are handled may improve. Further, specialist environmental judges can over time develop greater expertise.

Flowing from a critical analysis of South African environmental law cases, Kidd concludes that:[55]

> … these judicial shortcomings are, in all likelihood, not solely the fault of the judges however. It is probable that the reason why these provisions were not considered is that counsel did not bring them to the courts' attention. In light of this, I would argue strongly that the greening of the judiciary is not achievable, certainly not in any comprehensive sense, unless legal practitioners also are more closely exposed to the burgeoning body of environmental law, which is beginning to permeate many more 'traditional' areas of law.

---

52 Kidd (2006: 3).

53 Percival (2017: 1).

54 *M.C. Mehta v. Union of India (Taj Trapezium)* 1998 (2) SCALE 7 (SP) [268]. M.C. Mehta has been the top public interest environmental lawyer. He petitioned the Supreme Court to take action to protect the Taj Mahal from the ravages of air pollution. Relying on Article 21 of the Indian Constitution that creates a "right to life", which the court has interpreted to imply a right to a healthy environment, the court ordered that polluters who were harming the Taj Mahal had to cease doing so or relocate.

55 Kidd (2006: 8).

This conclusion highlights that judges cannot be held to shoulder the blame alone on judicial shortcomings in environmental matters. The author agrees with this observation especially that cases presented before courts must be well prepared by legal practitioners. A judiciary well-informed of the rapidly expanding boundaries of environmental law and law in the field of sustainable development, and sensitive to their role and responsibilities in promoting the rule of law in regard to environmentally friendly development, would play a critical role in the vindication of the public interest in a healthy and secure environment through the interpretation, enhancement and enforcement of environmental law. Kidd further argues that in order for judges to arrive at sound environmental decisions, they must be "guided by arguments raised by counsel and it is therefore critical that environmental lawyers embrace the scientific dimensions of environmental decision-making as well...".[56] With the emergence of new global environmental challenges, it is necessary to ensure that the almost limitless boundaries of science and technology are employed in enunciating effective environmental law and policy in Africa.

4 Conclusion

It has been shown that the enactment of EMA in 2011 gifted Zambia a robust and forward-looking environmental regime, with the exception that there is no constitutional environmental right to a clean, safe and healthy environment. The constitutional protection of environmental rights has been proved world over to be an important mechanism for securing individual environmental rights and promoting environmental and ecological sustainability. This lack of constitutional force in the quest to uphold environmental integrity is one drawback towards developing a meaningful environmental ethos in Zambia. With an enforceable constitutional environmental right in Zambia, the key themes towards good environmental governance are likely to be more easily achieved. Environmental education encompassing awareness, access to information, meaningful public participation, enhanced access to (environmental) justice are all important concepts that are given adequate prominence in the legislation. As noted throughout this chapter, however, these innovative legal provisions are yet to be exploited for the environmental good. These innovative legislative provisions need to be exploited to the fullest if real change is to be seen in the management of the country's environment and natural resources.

In 2012, a recommendation with regard to the practice of environmental law in Zambia highlighted the following:[57]

56 Ibid: 11.
57 Sambo (2012: 217).

> The courts in Zambia need to have a good understanding of environmental law principles in order to arrive at informed decisions which are necessary in the sound environmental management and dispensation of environmental justice. In addition, legal practitioners in Zambia need to be equipped with the necessary interest, knowledge and skills to conduct environmental litigation which is important in resolving environmental injustices.

Six years down the line, the position remains the same, notwithstanding forward-looking legislation. It can be argued that adequate environmental law provisions combined with a 'green' judiciary are likely to make a significant contribution towards the development of an environmental ethos and good environmental governance in Zambia. These two factors, however, are by no means significant in themselves. With the aid of other research methodologies, it would merit further research to understand how some jurisdictions are making progress towards entrenching environmental considerations in governance models.

References

Aceves, W (2003) "Actio Popularis – the class action in international law" *University of Chicago Legal Forum* 353-402.

Adams, MW (1990) *Green development: environment and sustainability in a developing world.*

Aongola, L, I Liayo, D Ndopu, S Bass, J Makumba, I Nyambe, J Chileshe, M Maimbolwa, A Pope, J Daka, K Munyinda, M Sichilongo, B Dalal-Clayton & N Munyinda (2009) *Creating and protecting Zambia's wealth: experience and next steps in environmental mainstreaming.*

Bass, S (1998) "National conservation strategy Zambia" in C Conroy & M Litvinoff (eds) *The greening of aid.*

Bernstein, S (2004) "Legitimacy in global environmental governance" *Journal of International Law and International Relations* 139-166.

Cairns, J (1991) "The need for integrated environmental systems management" in J Cairns & TV Crawford (eds) *Integrated environmental management* 5-20.

Chabwela, H (2005) *Provincial environmental policy situation analysis – Eastern Province of Zambia.*

China ASEAN Environmental Cooperation Centre and United Nations Environment Programme (2014) *Enforcement of environmental law: good practices from Africa, central Asia, ASEAN countries and China.*

Chipungu, PD & DM Kunda (eds) (1994) *State of environment in Zambia.*

Dimento, JF (1993) "Criminal enforcement of environmental law" 575 *The Annals of the American Academy of Political and Social Science* 134-146.

Esty, D (1999) "Toward optimal environmental governance" 74(6) *New York University Law Review* 1495-1574.

Fakier, S, A Stephens & J Tholin (2005) *Environmental governance* Background Research Paper for the South Africa Environment Outlook Report.

Feris, L (2010) "The role of good environmental governance in the sustainable development of South Africa" 13(1) *Potchefstroom Electronic Law Journal* 73-99.

Gunningham, N (2011) "Enforcing environmental regulation" 23(2) *Journal of Environmental Law* 169-201.

Hassan, P (2001) "Elements of good environmental governance" 16(1) *Asia Pacific Journal of Environmental Law* 1-11.

Houck, OK (2010) *Taking back Eden: eight environmental cases that changed the world.*

Jasanoff, S (1996) "The dilemma of environmental democracy" 13(1) *Issues in Science and Technology* 63-70.

Jere, PD (1999) "Executive summary on gaps, inconsistencies and conflicts in environmental and related legislation in Zambia" Harmonisation Workshop (Ministry of Legal Affairs).

Kakonge, JO (2009) *Environmental planning in sub-Saharan Africa: environmental impact assessment at the crossroads* Yale School of Forestry and Environmental Studies Working Paper No. 9.

Kidd, M (2002) *The protection of the environment through the use of criminal sanctions: a comparative analysis with specific reference to South Africa* PhD Thesis, University of Natal.

Kidd, M (2006) "Greening the judiciary" 19(3) *Potchefstroom Electronic Law Journal* 1-15.

Lambrechts, D (2016) "Environmental crime in sub-Saharan Africa – a review and future challenges" 43(2) *South African Journal of Political Studies* 155-158.

Maina-Okori, M, J Koushik & A Wilson (2017) "Reimagining intersectionality in environmental and sustainability education: a critical literature review" *Journal of Environmental Education* 1-11.

Margerum, DR (1999) "Integrated environmental management: the foundations for successful practice" 24(2) *Environmental Management* 151-166.

Margerum, DR & MS Born (2000) "A co-ordination diagnostic for improving integrated environmental management" 43(1) *Journal of Environmental Planning and Management* 5-21.

Ministry of Environment and Natural Resources (1994) *National environmental action plan.*

Mulonda, P (2000) *Implementation and enforcement of environmental law in Zambia – a legal perspective.*

Öberg, J (2011) "Criminal sanctions in the field of EU environmental law" 2(4) *New Journal of European Criminal Law* 402-425.

Percival, R (2017) *The 'greening' of the global judiciary* University of Maryland Francis King Carey School of Law Legal Studies Research Paper.

Phiri, JA (2006) *Political history of Zambia from the colonial period to the Third Republic.*

Pring, G & C Pring (2016) *Environmental courts and tribunals: a guide for policymakers.*

Retief, LA & FP Sandham (2001) "Implementation of integrated environmental management (IEM) as part of integrated development planning" 8(1) *South African Journal of Environmental Law and Policy* 77-94.

Saidi, AT (2010) *Environmental impact assessment as a policy tool for integrating environmental concerns in development* AISA Policy Brief No. 19.

Sambo, PT (2012) *A conceptual analysis of environmental justice approaches: procedural environmental justice in the EIA process in South Africa and Zambia* PhD Thesis, University of Manchester.

Wates, J (2005) "The Aarhus Convention: a driving force for environmental democracy" 2(1) *Journal for European Environmental and Planning Law* 2-11.

Watson, M (2005) "The enforcement of environmental law: civil or criminal penalties?" 17(1) *Environmental Law and Management* 3-6.

Woock, A (1972) "Goals and objectives of environmental education" 4(2) *Journal of Environmental Education* 61-62.

Chapter 31: Regulating environmental impacts associated with mining in Uganda

Emmanuel Kasimbazi

1 Introduction

According to Uganda's Constitution (Amendment) Act (2005) and the Mining Act (2003), a mineral is defined as any substance, other than petroleum, whether in solid, liquid or gaseous form, occurring naturally in or on the earth, formed by or subject to a geological process. This definition excludes clay, murram, sand or any stone commonly used for building or similar purposes. With the favourable business climate in Uganda for over two decades, many mining companies have taken up licences in the mining sector. Over the last 10 years, the sector has been growing positively peaking at 19.4% in FY 2006/2007. In FY 2009/2010, the sector grew by 12.8%. In terms of licences granted, 66 licences were issued in 1999 in the exploration and mining licence categories combined; while a total of 517 licences were issued by the beginning of 2010.[1]

The production, conversion, transportation and final use of minerals have direct and indirect environmental and social impacts.[2] The significant impacts of a mining project include water pollution, air pollution and noise pollution. Mining also causes direct and indirect damage to wildlife, contamination of soils, deforestation, land degradation, displacement of communities and disruption of livelihoods. Mining causes poverty through damaging subsistence agriculture, increases social inequality between those who benefit and those who do not, and promotes economic dependency that leads to vulnerability when mines scale down or close.

The regulatory framework for environmental protection in Uganda is scattered among various laws. The Constitution of Uganda (1995), as amended, requires Parliament to provide for measures to protect and preserve the environment. The Mineral Policy (2004) aims to minimise and mitigate the adverse social and environmental impacts associated with mineral exploitation. The National Environment Management Policy (1994) establishes a more comprehensive and integrated approach to environmental issues. The National Environment Act Cap 153 is the main law for conservation and management of the environment. The Mining Act (2003) regulates the distribution

1 Musoke (2015).
2 National Environment Management Authority (2004).

of rights and benefits relating to mining. The Land Act Cap 227 provides for the land tenure systems, ownership, management, use and the compulsory acquisition of land. The Water Act Cap 152 guides the acquisition of the right to use water for mining activities. The National Forest and Tree Planting Act (2003) provides for the conservation, sustainable management and development of forests. The Mining Regulations (2004) provide for environmental protection in mining areas. The National Environment (Environmental Impact Assessment) Regulations (1998) apply to all projects for which and environmental impact assessment (EIA) is required. The National Environment (Minimum Standards for Discharge of Effluents into Water or Land) Regulations (1999) control the discharge of effluent or waste on land or into the aquatic environment.

Environmental protection is the responsibility of several institutions. The Ministry of Energy and Mineral Development directs and controls the mining sector. The Ministry of Water and Environment develops, manages and regulates water and environmental resources. The National Environment Management Authority (NEMA) coordinates, monitors, regulates and supervises environmental management in the country. The local governments are responsible for the protection of the environment at the district level. The Environmental Protection Police Unit enforces environmental laws and prevents the degradation of protected areas.

There are several challenges facing environmental protection in the mining sector. These include limited enforcement measures in support of the environmental and social regulatory framework, informality, and marginalisation of artisanal and small-scale miners. This chapter analyses the effectiveness of the environmental and social regulatory framework for the protection of the environment in the mining sector in Uganda.

2 Overview of the mining sector in Uganda

Uganda has mineral resources in different parts of the country. There are several potential mineral formations, most importantly: gold in the Karamoja Region and other areas; copper in Kasese; extensive marble formations in Moroto in the eastern part of the country; phosphates in Tororo; and huge deposits of iron ore in central Uganda. New iron smelting factories are being set up. The Government's negotiation for iron ore mining is underway and commercialising this mineral is a key government priority for 2018.

Uganda's mining sector is a mix of large-scale mining with officially registered mining companies (both local and international) and artisanal small-scale miners. Artisanal and small-scale mining (ASM) in Uganda provides a source of livelihood for almost 200,000 men and women, over half of whom are engaged in production of industrial minerals to serve the construction demands of the country's rapidly growing population (3.3% per annum).[3] At least 20,000 of these miners are engaged in gold mining through artisanal and small-scale gold mining (ASGM), which has become a relatively important economic activity, mostly in the regions of Busia and Karamoja in the east and northeast, as well as in the Kigezi and Buhweju goldfields across the west and southwest of the country. Over the past decade, escalating gold prices, coupled with high population density and resultant land pressures (across the west and southwest), and prolonged droughts, tribal conflict and loss of traditional pastoral livelihoods (in the northeast) are rapidly attracting growing numbers into ASGM. The gender dimension of ASGM also seems to be shifting, depending on local circumstances. Only 10-25% of miners are women in ASGM areas in the west and southwest where farming continues to thrive. However, in the comparatively impoverished northeast, women's participation increases to approximately 50-60% and is as high as 90% at some ASGM sites.

ASM is unsufficiently regulated and hazardous.[4] While ASM has the potential to contribute to more sustainable livelihoods, the strategies, poor working conditions, accidents and diseases that are associated with ASM can reduce worker productivity and income for dependents, burdening families and communities. Artisanal and small-scale miners are usually engaged in heavy and precarious manual labour and frequently use rudimentary or unsafe mining and mineral processing techniques. In addition, the impacts of ASM activities often extend beyond the miners themselves to their families and communities who are exposed to environmental pollution and hazards either through their participation in various parts of the mining commodity chain or because of their residential proximity to mining activities.

Undoubtedly, the single most pressing issue impacting health and safety in the ASM sector is the use of mercury by artisanal and small-scale gold miners, due to its harmful effects on both human health and the environment. The lack of reliable data and regulatory oversight of ASM activities present obvious obstacles to improving conditions where the health and safety of miners, their communities and the environment are at risk.[5]

3 Environmental impacts of mining

Mining has direct and indirect impacts on the environment from the exploration to the closing stage. The direct impacts are through the value chain activities such as prospecting, exploration, site development, ore extraction, mineral dressing, smelting, refining/metallurgy, transportation and post-mining activities. The indirect impacts are

3 UNEP (2012: 6).
4 Maier et al. (2014: 86).
5 Hentschel (2002: 41).

through the changes in the socio-cultural aspects of communities surrounding mining areas.

3.1 Adverse environmental impacts

3.1.1 Impacts on water resources

Perhaps the most significant impact of a mining project is its effects on water quality and availability of water resources within the project area. Key questions are whether surface and groundwater supplies can remain fit for human consumption and whether the quality of surface waters in the project area can remain adequate to support indigenous aquatic life and terrestrial wildlife. The specific impacts of mining are described below.

3.1.1.1 Acid mine drainage and contaminant leaching

The potential for acid mine drainage is a key issue. Acid mine drainage is considered one of mining's most serious threats to water resources. Acid mine drainage refers to the outflow of acidic water from a mining site.[6] In most cases, this acid comes primarily from oxidation of iron sulfide (FeS2, also known as pyrite or 'fool's gold'), which is often found in conjunction with valuable metals. A mine with acid mine drainage has the potential for long-term devastating impacts on rivers, streams and aquatic life. Acid mine drainage is a concern at many metal mines, because metals such as gold, copper, silver and molybdenum are often found in rock with sulfide minerals. When the sulfides in the rock are excavated and exposed to water and air during mining, they form sulfuric acid. This acidic water can dissolve other harmful metals in the surrounding rock. If uncontrolled, the acid mine drainage may run off into streams or rivers or leach into groundwater. The abandoned Kilembe copper mine in western Uganda is a source of contaminants, mobilised from mine tailings into the River Rukoki flowing through a belt of wetlands into Lake George. In Kilembe, the mining of copper left a legacy of metalliferous material (tailings, rock fill and rock waste) dumped within a mountain river valley. Up to 15 million tonnes of waste were generated during the processing of the copper-cobaltiferous pyrite ores. The exposure of the sulfidic components in the wastes to an oxic environment (especially under tropical weathering conditions) leads to complex oxidation processes, resulting in a marked increase of acidity.[7] Acid mine drainage may be released from any part of the mine where sulfides

6 David (2010).
7 Owor & Muwanga (2007: 1065).

are exposed to air and water, including waste rock piles, tailings, open pits, underground tunnels and leach pads. If mine waste is acid-generating, the impact on fish, animals and plants can be severe. Many streams impacted by acid mine drainage have a pH value of 4 or lower – similar to battery acid. Fish, animals and plants are unlikely to survive in streams such as this.

3.1.1.2 Erosion of soils and mine wastes into surface waters

Land use without adequate soil erosion control measures is continuously increasing the risk of soil erosion by water in Uganda.[8] For most mining projects, the potential of soil and sediment eroding into and degrading surface water quality is a serious problem. Because of the large area of land disturbed by mining operations and the large quantities of earthen materials exposed at sites, erosion can be a major concern at hard rock mining sites. The mining and processing of copper in Kilembe, Western Uganda, from 1956 to 1982 left over 15 metric tonnes of tailings containing cupriferous and cobaltiferous pyrite dumped within a mountain river valley. A pilot study was conducted to assess the nature and extent of risk to local populations from metal contamination arising from these mining activities. The results showed that tailings, containing higher concentrations of carbon monoxide (Co), copper (Cu), and nickel (Ni) as compared with world average crust values, had eroded and contaminated local soils. Local water supplies were contaminated, with Co concentrations that exceeded Wisconsin (US) thresholds in 25% of domestic water supplies and 40% of Nyamwamba River water samples.[9] Major sources of erosion/sediment loading at mining sites can include open pit areas, heap and dump leaches, waste rock and overburden piles, tailings piles and dams, haul roads and access roads, ore stockpiles, vehicle and equipment maintenance areas, exploration areas and reclamation areas.

Beyond the potential for pollutant impacts on human and aquatic life, increased velocities and run-off volumes lead to downstream flooding, scouring of stream channels, and removal of vegetation and soil from the affected area. Once the soils have been removed, it is difficult for the slope to be revegetated either naturally or with human assistance.

8 Karamage et al. (2017: 1).
9 Mwesigye et al. (2016: 366).

3.1.1.3 Impacts of tailing impoundments, waste rock, heap leaching, and dump leaching facilities

The impact of wet tailings impoundments, waste rock, heap leaching and dump leaching facilities on water quality can be severe.[10] These impacts include contamination of groundwater beneath these facilities and surface waters. Toxic substances can leach from these facilities, percolate through the ground, and contaminate groundwater, especially if the bottom of these facilities is not fitted with an impermeable liner. When wet tailings impoundments fall, they release large quantities of toxic water that can kill aquatic life and poison drinking water supplies for many miles downstream of the impoundment.

3.1.1.4 Impacts of mine dewatering

When an open pit intersects the water table, groundwater flows into the open pit. For mining to proceed, mining companies must pump and discharge this water to another location. Pumping and discharging mine water causes a unique set of environmental impacts. Impacts from ground water drawdown may include reduction or elimination of surface water flows; degradation of surface water quality and beneficial uses; degradation of habitat; reduced or eliminated production in domestic supply wells; and water quality/quantity problems associated with discharge of the pumped groundwater back into surface waters downstream from the dewatered area. Dewatering from rock faces in mine shafts, quarries or gravel pits often contains abrasives such as sand, clay particles, drill cuttings and other potentially damaging objects, and the pH value is usually very low. The impacts can last for many decades.

10 Tailings impoundments are ponds used to store the waste made from separating minerals from rocks. Waste rock is the primary and most prevalent waste generated by many mining operations and consists of rock and target minerals in concentrations too low for economic recovery, and is removed along with the ore. Heap leaching is the process of extracting precious metals like gold, silver, copper and uranium from their ore by placing them on a pad (a base) in a heap and sprinkling a leaching solvent, such as cyanide or acids over the heap. Dump leaching is carried out on rejected low grade material that during normal mining has been put aside in big dumps at the mine site. The particle size of the material is generally big and the ore is processed for many years by sprinkling acidified water on the dump surface. The leach solution percolates through the dump and is collected in ditches at the base of the dump. This might become a source of environmental pollution if leach escapes collection and flows into natural water-supplies.

3.1.2 Impacts of mining projects on air quality

Mining operations mobilise large amounts of material, and waste piles containing small-size particles that are easily dispersed by the wind. The largest sources of air pollution in mining operations are:

- Particulate matter transported by the wind as a result of excavations, blasting, transportation of materials, wind erosion (more frequent in open-pit mining), fugitive dust from tailings facilities, stockpiles, waste dumps and haul roads.
- Gas emissions from combustion of fuels in power generation installations, and drying, roasting and smelting operations. Many producers of precious metals smelt metal on site, prior to shipping to off-site refineries.
- Mobile sources of air pollutants include heavy vehicles used in excavation operations, cars that transport personnel at the mining site, and trucks that transport mining materials. Even though individual emissions may be relatively small, collectively these emissions can be of real concern.

According to the World Health Organisation, more than 8 million people die around the world each year as a result of living in a polluted environment. Pollution is the biggest killer in developing countries. Contaminated air claims millions of lives every year. In Uganda, the effects of air pollution are becoming more and more noticeable. Air pollution has become one of the biggest challenges facing the country, and mining is among the leading causes of air pollution. Therefore, air pollution can cause serious damage to people's health and to the environment.[11]

3.1.3 Noise pollution

Noise pollution associated with mining may include noise from vehicle engines, loading and unloading of rock into steel dumpers, chutes, power generation and other sources. Cumulative impacts of shovelling, ripping, drilling, blasting, transport, crushing, grinding and stock-piling can significantly affect wildlife and nearby residents. Machine operations associated with Limestone mining at the Dura Quarry site in Queen Elizabeth National Park, Kamwenge District, generate significant noise. In addition, the quarry management run four pumps that operate 24 hours a day generating much noise, beyond the permissible levels. This threatens the animal populations, causing migrations and disturbance to animal breeding, among other impacts.[12]

Vibrations are associated with many types of equipment used in mining operations, but blasting is considered the major source. Vibration has affected the stability of infrastructure, buildings and homes of people living near large-scale open-pit mining

11 Serginho (2015).
12 National Association of Professional Environmentalists (2015).

operations. According to a study commissioned in 2000 by the European Union,[13] shocks and vibrations as a result of blasting in connection with mining can lead to noise, dust and collapse of structures in surrounding inhabited areas. The animal life, on which the local population may depend, might also be disturbed.

3.1.4 Impacts of mining projects on wildlife

Wildlife is a broad term that refers to all plants and any animals (or other organisms) that are not domesticated. Mining affects the environment and associated biota through the removal of vegetation and topsoil, the displacement of fauna, the release of pollutants and the generation of noise.

3.1.4.1 Habitat loss

Wildlife species live in communities that depend on each other. Survival of these species can depend on soil conditions, local climate, altitude and other features of the local habitat. Mining causes direct and indirect damage to wildlife. The impacts stem primarily from disturbing, removing and redistributing the land surface. Some impacts are short-term and confined to the mine site. Others may have far-reaching and long-term effects. In Uganda, Hima Cement (U) Ltd operates the Dura Quarry that is located in Queen Elizabeth National Park. The large disturbances caused by mining in the Dura Quarry have disrupted the environment around the quarry, adversely affecting the aquatic habitats (streams and rivers), terrestrial habitats (grasslands and forests) and riverine wetlands[14] that many organisms rely on for survival.

3.1.4.2 Habitat fragmentation

Habitat fragmentation occurs when large areas of land are broken up into smaller and smaller patches, making dispersal of native species from one patch to another difficult or impossible, and cutting off migratory routes. Isolation may lead to the local decline of species or lead to behaviour that has genetic consequences, such as inbreeding.

---

13 MINEO Consortium (2000).

14 Riverine wetlands are those systems that are contained within a channel (such as a river, creek or waterway) and their associated streamside vegetation.

3.1.5 Impacts of mining projects on soil quality

Mining can contaminate soils over a large area. Agricultural activities near a mining project may be particularly affected. Mining operations routinely modify the surrounding landscape by exposing previously undisturbed earthen materials. Erosion of exposed soils, extracted mineral ores, tailings and fine material in waste rock piles can result in substantial sediment loading to surface waters and drainage ways. In addition, spills and leaks of hazardous materials and the deposition of contaminated windblown dust can lead to soil contamination.

Environmental soil-related risks generally fall into two categories, namely contaminated soil resulting from windblown dust and soils contaminated by chemical spills and residues. The inherent toxicity of the dust depends upon the proximity of environmental receptors and the type of ore being mined.

In Uganda, mining activities generate wastes that are usually deposited on the surface and abandoned after closure of the mines. Owing to pollution, the soils close to wastes are usually degraded. Near Queen Elizabeth Conservation Area (QECA), 1.13 million metric tonnes of pyrite materials were dumped from 1956 to 1982 to form a large cobaltiferous stockpile. which has remained devoid of vegetation since the suspension of mining activities in 1982. This has led to the wide dispersal of pyrite materials laden with heavy metals into gardens and surrounding aquifers at Kilembe and into the QECA.[15] Therefore, soils contaminated by chemical spills and residues at mine sites may pose a direct contact risk when these materials are misused as fill materials, or for ornamental landscaping and soil supplements.

3.1.6 Deforestation

With open cast mining the overburden, which may be covered in forest, must be removed before the mining can commence. Although the deforestation due to mining may be small compared to the total amount, it may lead to species extinction if there is a high level of local endemism.

Reducing deforestation to conserve biodiversity and regulate climate is a globally significant goal,[16] yet deforestation rates remain high.[17] Demand for minerals also poses significant risks, particularly where mineral resources and forests co-exist in developing countries that seek revenue from mining but lack regulatory oversight and enforcement capability.[18] Mining causes deforestation both within and beyond lease

15 Ssenku et al. (2014: 191-198).
16 Foley (2015: 570-574).
17 Hansen (2013: 850-853).
18 Murguía et al. (2016: 409).

boundaries. Within leases, forests are cleared for mineral extraction, processing and infrastructure development.[19] However, deforestation may extend for substantial distances beyond lease boundaries, due to the combined effects of land-use displacement, urban expansion, development of commodity supply chains, and concerns over mine waste discharge and spills. It is essential to understand and mitigate mining-induced deforestation if tropical forests are to be conserved, yet the full extent of these impacts is yet to be quantified.

3.1.7 Land degradation

The mining and processing of mineral resources generally has a considerable impact on land. Despite the fact that Uganda has a large percentage of arable land, land degradation is a substantial problem in the country. It is estimated that 4-12% of gross national product is lost as a result of environmental degradation. The percentage of land affected by degradation ranges from 90% in Kabale to 20% in Masindi.[20] Land degradation tends to extend beyond the excavation and surface plant areas of both surface and sub-surface mines. Large mining operations disturb the land by directly removing material in some areas and dumping waste in others, thus changing the topography.[21] Mining tends to increase the susceptibility of the land to erosion, and increase the occurrence of landslides, mudflow and slumps as a result of the exploration, processing and miscellaneous mining activities.[22]

The extraction of minerals especially by the open cast process leaves undesirable effects on the land surface. Indeed, mining operations have been envisaged by environmentalists and conservationists alike as causing some of the most devastating and far-reaching consequences to the environment, especially land degradation.[23]

3.2 Adverse social impacts of mining

3.2.1 Displacement of communities and disruption of livelihoods

The displacement of settled communities is a significant cause of resentment and conflict associated with large-scale mineral development. Entire communities may be uprooted and forced to shift elsewhere, often into purpose-built settlements not necessarily of their own choosing. Besides losing their homes, communities may also lose

19 Alvarez-Berríos & Aide (2015).
20 Olson & Berry (2003: 3).
21 Mbaya (2013: 145).
22 Ibid.
23 Ibid.

their land, and thus their livelihoods. Community institutions and power relations may also be disrupted. Displaced communities are often settled in areas without adequate resources or are left near the mine, where they may bear the brunt of pollution and contamination.

While Uganda's mining laws require a surface rights agreement to be negotiated with landowners prior to active mining and payments of royalties to lawful landowners once revenues flow, the law does not require any communication or consent from the local population during exploration work. Despite Uganda's land laws recognising customary land ownership, the Land Board is hesitant to grant any such certificates anywhere in the country. Several extractives companies have gone to Karamoja in northeastern Uganda to seek natural resources, particularly gold and marble, but these companies have consistently failed to secure the free, prior and informed consent from the local communities before they start operations on communal lands. This has led to displacement of communities and disruption of livelihoods.[24] Community displacement can be particularly disastrous for indigenous communities who have strong cultural and spiritual ties to the lands of their ancestors, and who may find it difficult to survive when these are broken.

3.2.2 Increased poverty through damaging subsistence agriculture

There is concern about the increased competition between mining and agriculture. Mining gradually destroys agricultural lands as well as crop production, resulting in a net food deficit. The fast shift of labour from agriculture to mining has consequently led to a fall in the general level of food production. In Lubaali-Kayonza-Kitumbi Sub County – Mubende District, most people were subsistence farmers who used to earn their livelihood from growing maize, beans, sweet potatoes and cassava. The area has turned into a settlement for artisanal miners whose population comprises thousands of people – women, men, teenage girls and boys, and a few babies.[25] Farmlands in such areas are usually taken over by estate developers as well as mining support companies who have also acquired vast lands for construction and other purposes. The result is that there is always a reduction in food production in those areas and the need for food to be brought from distant areas at exorbitant prices leading to poverty.

24 Emerson (2014).
25 *The Independent* (2016).

3.2.3 Increased inequalities

Mining increases inequality within communities between those who benefit directly from the mine and those who do not. There is an inherent tension between local and national rights to mineral wealth and the other benefits brought about by mining. People living near mines or adversely affected by them demand that they should be compensated for any inconvenience, hardship or loss of opportunity suffered. But the question is, should they receive a larger share of the benefits? If so, how should that share be determined?

In Uganda, mining revenues are generated through a mix of consistently applied corporate income taxes and competitive royalties. Royalties are shared between national and local budgets. A variable tax rate based on profit addresses the unique nature of mineral profits. However, royalty payments often do not reach landowners, and payment problems are compounded by the complex nature of land ownership. Royalty payments are distributed with limited transparency via the national budget and the revenue from mining generally does not translate into long-term social and economic development in communities located near mining projects.[26] Sustainable development of the local community requires an equitable sharing of benefits. If there is obvious inequity, there will be strife, which impedes the development process.

3.2.4 Economic dependency

Mining causes economic dependency that makes local communities vulnerable when the mines close or scale down operations. In addition, all mines have a finite life span, and it is difficult to sustain the direct benefits they bring to communities in terms of wages and improved welfare after mine closure. The infrastructure that develops with a mine may be scaled down or neglected when the mine closes unless provision has been made for maintenance and upkeep well in advance. Communities are particularly vulnerable where linkages with other sectors of the economy are weak.

4 Regulatory framework for environmental and social protection in the mining sector

Uganda's regulatory framework for environmental and social protection in the mining sector is contained in policies, acts, regulations and guidelines.

26 Crawford et al. (2015: 32).

4.1 Environmental and social policy framework for the mining sector

There are key policies that provide guidance for environmental and social aspects in the mining sector. The first one is the Mineral Policy (2001) that is the main policy informing mining in Uganda. Its main aim is to develop the mineral sector to enable it to contribute to sustainable economic and social growth by creating gainful employment and income, particularly to the rural population.[27] It has a specific section on social and environmental assessment. Under Objective 4 of the Policy, it seeks to minimise and mitigate the adverse social and environmental impacts of mineral exploitation. The strategies relating to this objective include the following: strengthening the environmental monitoring unit of the Ministry; carrying out sensitisation of the society on the impact of mining on the environment; promoting the application of environmentally friendly technologies and methods in mineral exploitation; ensuring health and safety in all stages of mineral development through regulations and education; and undertaking responsibility for the clean-up operations of past negative mining environmental impacts.

The second policy is the National Environment Management Policy (1994), which is being revised. The Policy recognises that Uganda faces a number of environmental issues including: soil degradation; deforestation; loss of biodiversity; increasing pollution; and environmentally-related diseases as a result of mining. These problems are compounded by poverty, low environmental awareness and low levels of technology. The Policy aims to address these issues by establishing a more comprehensive and integrated approach to environmental issues. The Policy, therefore, creates an effective monitoring and evaluation system to track the impacts of mining on the environment; attempts to promote a new sustainable conservation culture; and aims to harmonise local and national policy efforts in respect of environmental issues.

The Policy provides strategies to guide and assist decision makers and resource users in determining priorities in the national context and also at the sectoral, private sector and individual level. It provides for integration of environmental concerns in the national socio-economic development planning process, avenues for intersectoral cooperation, and comprehensive and coordinated environmental management. As a result, environmental management is now a key criterion for national socio-economic development decisions.

The objective of the Policy is to control the pollution of water, land and air from domestic, industrial and other emissions and discharges, and to promote environmentally sound management of wastes and hazardous materials. The strategies include establishing environmental standards for permissible levels of pollution; strengthening institutional and technical capacities for waste management; enhancing institutional

27 Ministry of Energy and Mineral Development (2001).

coordination; and maintaining regular environmental audits to ensure the adoption of environmentally sound practices.

4.2 Legal framework for environmental and social regulation in the mining sector

4.2.1 Ugandan legal framework for environmental and social regulation in the mining sector

The legal framework provides different mechanisms for regulating mining in Uganda. The major ones are described below.

4.2.1.1 Public trust doctrine

The public trust doctrine refers to the responsibility of the state to hold property rights in trust for the benefit of the citizens of the state. This doctrine is important as a shield for protecting the environment and linking environmental protection of the biotic community with resource utilisation. The Constitution of Uganda (1995) (as amended) recognises the public trust doctrine. The National Objective XIII imposes an obligation on the Government to protect important natural resources, including land, water, wetlands, minerals, oil, fauna and flora on behalf of the people of Uganda.[28] Article 237(2)(b) provides that the Government, or a local government as determined by Parliament by law, shall hold in trust for the people and protect natural lakes, rivers, wetlands, forest reserves, game reserves, national parks and any land to be reserved for ecological and tourist purposes for the common good of all citizens. Further, Article 244 specifically provides for the public trust doctrine in relation to minerals. It states that subject to Article 26 of the Constitution, the entire property in, and the control of, all minerals and petroleum in, on or under any land or waters in Uganda are vested in the Government on behalf of the Republic of Uganda. The article also provides that, Parliament shall make laws regulating: (i) the exploration of minerals and petroleum; (ii) the sharing of royalties arising from mineral and petroleum exploration; (iii) the conditions for payment of indemnities arising out of exploration of minerals and petroleum; and (iv) the conditions regarding the restoration of derelict lands. It is further provides that minerals, mineral ores and petroleum shall be exploited taking into account the interest of the individual landowners, local governments and the Government.

The Mining Act, which is the main act for regulating mining, also provides for the public trust doctrine. Under Section 3, the entire property in and control of all minerals

28 Constitution of the Republic of Uganda (1995).

in, on or under any land or waters in Uganda are vested in the Government, notwithstanding any right of ownership of or by any person in relation to any land in, on or under which any such minerals are found.

The public trust doctrine is further emphasised under Section 44 of the Land Act that provides that the Government or a local government shall hold in trust for the people and protect natural lakes, rivers, groundwater, natural ponds, natural streams, wetlands, forest reserves, national parks and any other land reserved for ecological purposes for the common good of the citizens of Uganda.

4.2.1.2 Environmental and social assessment

As noted above, mining activities can have adverse effects on the environment. Therefore, any type of mining activity demands an environmental and social impact assessment (ESIA) to assess potential for both positive and negative impacts to the environment and to use the produced results to mitigate the negatives and optimise the positives. Uganda has specific laws that require ESIA for activities, such as mining, that have an impact on the environment.

Section 19 of the National Environment Act Cap 153 requires that an EIA be undertaken by a developer of a project described in the Third Schedule to the Act (including mining),[29] and requires the developer to submit a project brief to the lead agency, in the prescribed form and giving the prescribed information. An EIA is to be undertaken by the developer where the lead agency, in consultation with the executive director, is of the view that the project may have an impact on the environment; is likely to have a significant impact on the environment; or will have a significant impact on the environment.

The details on how an EIA is to be conducted are provided under the National Environment (Environmental Impact Assessment) Regulations (1998). These Regulations apply to all projects for which an EIA is required (all projects included in the Third Schedule to the National Environment Act Cap. 153),[30] including mining. Mining includes quarrying and open-cast extraction of precious metals, diamonds, metalliferous ores, coal, phosphates, limestone and dolomite, stone and slate, aggregates, sand and gravel, clay and exploration for the production of any form of petroleum.

Regulation 3(2) prohibits any developer from implementing a project for which an EIA is required unless the EIA has been concluded in accordance with the Regulations. The Regulations also require every licensing authority in Uganda to request the

---

29 Projects to be considered for EIA under the Third Schedule include mining; which includes quarrying and open-cast extraction of precious metals, diamonds, metalliferous ores, coal, phosphates, limestone and dolomite.

30 Regulation 3(1)(a).

production of a certificate of approval of EIA from any developer before issuing a licence for any project. An inspector is authorised to enter any land, premises or other facility at any reasonable time to determine whether a project has complied with the requirements for EIA.

Regulation 5(1)(h) provides that a developer must prepare a project brief stating in a concise manner: the environmental effects of the materials, methods, products and by-products of the project; and how they will be eliminated or mitigated.

Where it is discovered that a proposed mining project will have no significant impact on the environment, or that the project brief discloses sufficient mitigation measures to cope with the anticipated impacts, the project may be approved. However, where it is discovered that the project will have significant impacts on the environment and that the project brief discloses no sufficient mitigation measures to cope with the anticipated impacts, the developer is required to undertake an environmental impact study.[31]

The Regulations promote public participation within the environmental impact study. Regulation 12 provides that the developer of a mining project must take all measures necessary to seek the views of the people in the communities that may be affected by the project during the process of conducting the study. The developer is required to: publicise the intended project, its anticipated effects and benefits through the mass media in a language understood by the affected communities for a period of not less than 14 days; hold meetings with the affected communities to explain the project and its effects; and ensure that the venues and times of the meetings are convenient for the affected persons and the local council leaders.

Section 108 of the Mining Act (2003) requires every holder of an exploration licence or a mining lease to carry out an EIA for his or her proposed operations in accordance with the National Environment Act Cap 153. A holder of the licence or mining lease must commence with the proposed operations only after securing a certificate of approval of his or her proposed operations from NEMA. The holder of the licence or mining lease is required to carry out an annual environmental audit and to keep records describing how far the operations conform to the EIA. Section 109 provides that in every mining licence and lease there must be a condition requiring the licence holder to take all necessary steps to uphold environmental standards and to take the necessary steps to ensure the prevention and minimisation of pollution of the environment. The licence or mining lease holder is required to submit to the Commissioner and the Executive Director of NEMA an environmental management plan indicating the type and quality of wastes to be generated from any exploration and mining operations, and the method of its final disposal.

The Mining Regulations (2004) made under Part XI of the Mining Act provide for environmental protection in mining areas. Regulation 64(1)(e) requires a holder of an

31 Regulation 9.

exploration licence to prepare a project brief before commencement of work, indicating the likely environmental effects of the materials to be used, the products and by-products to be generated, the duration of the environmental effects, and measures ensuring their prevention and mitigation.

The Regulations provide for the review of project briefs in a manner specified under the guidelines for EIA in the mineral sector developed by NEMA.[32] Where the environmental impacts are likely to be significant and the mitigation measures are not readily prescribed, the Commissioner consults with NEMA and then calls on the holder of the exploration licence in question to carry out an EIA.

Under Regulation 66, there is a requirement for the submission of a costed environmental restoration plan. The holder of an exploration licence or a mining lease is required to submit to the Commissioner a costed environmental restoration plan, which addresses restoration of worked-out areas. The holder of an exploration licence or a mining lease may be requested to deposit with the Commissioner an environmental bond commensurate with the cost of implementing the environmental restoration plan submitted to the Commissioner. The holder of an exploration licence or mining lease cannot commence development under his or her exploration licence or mining lease unless approval of the environmental restoration plan is granted.

The regulations make it a requirement to include in every exploration licence or mining lease granted under the Act, a condition that the holder of the exploration licence or mining lease shall submit a self-monitoring plan of the project implementation and the environmental quality of the surroundings of the project.[33] Where the impacts are worse than anticipated, the holder of the exploration licence or the mining lease shall propose to the Commissioner and the Executive Director of NEMA new mitigation measures for improved environmental conservation. The Commissioner, after consultation with the Executive Director of NEMA, shall advise the holder of the exploration licence or mining lease on the necessary remedies to correct any negative impacts of the activities on the environment. NEMA can demand that applicants undertake an environmental and social impact assessment whereby they have to show evidence of an agreement or the consent of the landowner before they are issued with NEMA certificates that are a pre-requisite to obtaining a mining lease to undertake mining.

Section 38 of the National Forestry and Tree Planting Act requires a person intending to undertake a project or activity, which may, or is likely to have, a significant impact on a forest, to undertake an EIA. Section 54(1)(g) empowers the National Forestry Authority, in conjunction with other regulatory authorities, to control and monitor industrial and mining developments in central forest reserves for their protection.

32 Regulation 65(3).
33 Regulation 67(1).

4.2.1.3 Land acquisition and compensation

The right of government to acquire land compulsorily for public purposes, including but not limited to mining purposes, is commonly recognised in most jurisdictions. Equally recognised is the obligation to compensate the deprived landowners adequately for the loss of their land. Access to land for the purpose of mineral exploration and mining continues to be an issue for the mining industry in Uganda.

Article 26(2) of the Constitution of Uganda (1995) (as amended) empowers the Government to acquire private land in a compulsory manner, provided that the following conditions are satisfied:

- (a) the taking of possession or acquisition is necessary for public use or in the interest of defence, public safety, public order, public morality or public health; and
- (b) the compulsory taking of possession or acquisition of property is made under a law which makes provision for –
  - (i) prompt payment of fair and adequate compensation, prior to the taking of possession or acquisition of the property; and
  - (ii) a right of access to a court of law by any person who has an interest or right over the property.

Section 2 of the Land Acquisition Act (1965) empowers the responsible Minister to authorise a person to ascertain the suitability of any land acquisition for a public purpose. The Government is required to pay compensation to any person who suffers damage as a result of the land acquisition process, and any dispute as to the compensation payable is referred by the Attorney General to the court for a decision.

Section 82 of the Mining Act (2003) clearly spells out the need for adequate compensation of surface right owners before mining starts. The landowner is entitled to compensation for financial loss, hardship or inconvenience resulting from exploration through an exploration licence. This may be negotiated directly between the landowner and operator, or be determined by a government valuer. It is only when the surface right owner fails to cooperate or if an agreement cannot be reached that the Government opts for compulsory acquisition in national interest. It is a last resort after failed negotiations and it is done in the public interest because minerals are national resources needed to develop the economy for everyone to benefit.

The provisions above imply that a prospecting licence holder is required to obtain a social permit in addition to the mining lease prior to commencing their operations.

4.2.1.4 Restoration order

A restoration order is a measure directing a person to restore the environment to its prior condition before it was degraded. The Mining Act[34] provides for environmental restoration plans to be included in every exploration licence or mining lease for the exploration or mining of areas that may be damaged or adversely affected by exploration or mining operations. These plans must be submitted to the Commissioner and should be consistent with the local physical, environmental and climatological conditions. The Commissioner[35] is empowered under Section 111 to direct the person who was the last holder of an exploration licence or mining lease to protect the environment by giving effect to any conditions in his or her environmental restoration plan. If a person without reasonable excuse fails or neglects to comply with the Commissioner's order, he or she is liable on conviction to pay a fine of not less than 100 currency points or to imprisonment for a term not less than two years or both; and, in the case of a corporate body, to a fine of not less than 500 currency points.

Section 67 of the National Environment Act provides NEMA with the power to issue an environmental restoration order requiring a person to restore the environment to the condition it was in before the damage causing activity commenced. The restoration order may also be issued to prevent a person from taking any action that may harm the environment; or to levy a charge on a person that represents a reasonable estimate of the cost of any action taken by an authorised person to restore the environment to its previous condition.[36] This order can be used by NEMA to restore the environment to the condition it was in before mining activities commenced.

4.2.1.5 Maintenance of water quality and pollution control

The Constitution of Uganda (1995) (as amended) provides for the right to a clean and healthy environment.[37] Therefore, it is the duty of each person to protect the environment and this includes bringing an action for breach of the right to a clean and healthy environment. The Constitution provides that the violation of any human right entitles any person to sue for the redress of such violation, even if the violation did not affect the plaintiff personally.[38]

The Water Act Cap. 152 prevents pollution of water by mining activities. Section 20 provides that a holder of a permit issued under the Act must not cause or allow any

34 Section 110 of the Mining Act (2003).

35 According to Section 2 of the Mining Act (2003), Commissioner means "the Commissioner for the Geological Survey and Mines Department appointed under Section 13 of this Act".

36 Section 67 of the National Environment Act, Cap 153.

37 Article 39.

38 Article 50.

water to be polluted; shall prevent damage to the source from which water is taken or to which water is discharged after use; shall take precautions to ensure that no activities on the land where water is used result in the accumulation of any substance that may render water less fit for the purpose for which it may be reasonably used; shall observe conditions prescribed by regulations made under the Act; and shall observe any special condition that may be attached to the permit.

The Water Act also creates sanctions applicable to the pollution of water by mining activities. Section 31 provides that a person who pollutes water or causes water to be polluted; commits an offence and is liable to pay the cost of remedying the damage caused and reinstating the environment, as far as is possible, to the condition that would have existed if the damage was not caused.

The National Environment (Minimum Standards for Discharge of Effluents into Water or Land) Regulations (1999) made under the Water Act deter pollution in the mining areas. They prohibit discharge of effluent or waste on land or into the aquatic environment contrary to established standards and without a waste discharge permit. Regulation 3 provides that before effluent or waste water is discharged into water or on land it must comply with the standards prescribed in the Schedule to the Regulations. The Schedule lists the maximum permissible limits of effluent or waste water that may be discharged into water or on land. The Executive Director or other duly authorised person is given authority to issue guidelines and recommend the method of effluent discharge for industries or establishments so as to ensure assimilation by the water or land into which the effluent is discharged.

The Regulations also create a general obligation to mitigate pollution.[39] Every industry or establishment is required to install, at its premises, anti-pollution equipment for the treatment of effluent chemical discharge emanating from the industry or establishment. The anti-pollution equipment installed should be based on the best practicable and environmentally sound practice or other guidelines, as the Executive Director may determine.

The National Environment Act Cap. 153 prohibits pollution that is contrary to established standards. According to Section 57, no person is allowed to pollute or lead any other person to pollute the environment contrary to the prescribed standards or guidelines. Sections 58 and 59 require every person who wishes to carry out any activity that is likely to pollute the air, water or land in excess of any standards or guidelines to acquire a pollution licence prior to doing so.

39 Regulation 4 of the National Environment (Minimum Standards for Discharge of Effluents into Water or Land) Regulations (1999).

4.2.1.6 Controlled use of water

The use of water for mining activities requires a permit. Section 31 of the Mining Act (2003) confers an exclusive right on a holder of an exploration licence to carry on exploration operations in the area of land and extract the mineral to which the licence relates. Section 6 of the Mining Act provides that the holder does not acquire any rights to use water or to construct or operate any works unless authorised under Part II of the Act. Thus, unless a person is an occupier of land on which surface water exists, water may not be used for any purpose without the approval of an authority. The general rights to use surface water are limited to domestic use and fire fighting, once again indicating the importance attached to water supply for domestic purposes. Section 18 of the Mining Act makes it clear that a person may not construct or operate any works unless he or she has a permit granted for that purpose by the director, Directorate of Water Resources Management (DWRM). It is therfore illegal to use water for mining activities without a water permit granted by DRWM.

4.2.2 International legal framework for environmental and social regulation in the mining sector

While the primary regulatory mechanisms are mainly under national environmental law, an international regulatory framework is increasingly becoming important in the mining sector. The key instruments are listed below.

4.2.2.1 The Safety and Health in Mines Convention 1995

The United Nations International Labour Organisation's Safety and Health in Mines Convention (1995) is an international convention to protect the health and safety of mine workers. Adopted in 1995,[40] the Convention sets out a framework for countries to create a safe mining environment, with duties for companies/employers and rights for workers. Article 7 requires employers to take all necessary measures to eliminate or minimise the risks to safety and health in mines under their control. Article 10 requires the employer to ensure that adequate training and retraining programmes and comprehensible instructions are provided to workers, at no cost to them, on safety and health matters as well as on work assigned.

The Convention makes governments responsible for the domestic implementation of its framework. Article 3 of the Convention requires states to formulate, carry out and periodically review a coherent policy on safety and health in mines, particularly

40 Uganda has signed but not ratified the Convention.

with regard to the measures to give effect to the provisions of the Convention, taking into consideration the national conditions and practice and after consultation with the most representative organisations of employers and workers concerned.

The most important aspect of the Convention is the right of workers to participate in workplace safety through independent safety representation, and the right to refuse unsafe work. This gives unions space to organise. Article 13 provides that national laws and regulations should provide for workers' rights to: obtain information relevant to their safety and health, held by the employer or the competent authority; remove themselves from any location at the mine when circumstances arise which appear, with reasonable justification, to pose a serious danger to their safety or health; and to collectively select safety and health representatives to represent workers on all aspects of workplace safety and health, such as monitoring and investigating safety and health matters, and consulting with the employer in a timely fashion on safety and health matters, including policies and procedures.

Article 15 requires states to take measures in accordance with national laws and regulations, to encourage cooperation between employers and workers and their representatives to promote safety and health in mines.

This Convention is important because it requires state parties to pass domestic laws to make sure that mines are as safe as possible.

4.2.2.2 The Safety and Health in Mines Recommendation 183 (1995)

The provisions of the Safety and Health in Mines Recommendation 183 (1995) supplement those of the Safety and Health in Mines Convention 1995 and are applied in conjunction with them.[41]

Provision 3 of the Recommendation advocates for consultations with the most representative organisations of employers and workers on the effect of the length of working hours, night work and shift work on workers' safety and health. After such consultations, it urges the state to take necessary measures relating to regulating working time and, in particular, to set maximum daily working hours and minimum daily rest periods. Under the Employment Act (2006) employees' total working time should not exceed 10 hours per day and 50 hours per week; and, where employees work in shifts, the average working time over a period of three weeks should not exceed 10 hours per day or 56 hours per week. Where the daily working time is at least eight hours, a 30-

41 Recommendations are often intended to offer guidelines for action by member states. Recommendations will elaborate upon the provisions of a Convention on the same subject. Member states have certain important procedural obligations in respect of recommendations – namely, to submit the texts to their legislative bodies, to report on the action resulting and to report occasionally at the request of the Governing Body on the measures taken or envisaged to give effect to the provisions.

minute break should be given to the employees daily. Any overtime hour should be remunerated at a minimum rate of one and a half times the hourly rate on normal working days, and two times the hourly rate if the overtime is worked on gazetted public holidays.[42]

Provision 15 of the Recommendation requires all mine works to be ventilated in an appropriate manner to maintain an atmosphere in which working conditions are adequate. Provision 25 requires employers, where appropriate, to provide and maintain at no cost to the worker: sufficient and suitable toilets, showers, wash-basins and changing facilities that are, where appropriate, gender-specific; adequate facilities for the storage, laundering and drying of clothes; adequate supplies of potable drinking-water in suitable places; and adequate and hygienic facilities for taking meals. These two requirements are reflected in the Occupational Safety and Health Act (2006), which provides that the employer must ensure: proper ventilation and circulation of free air in working premises;[43] suitable lighting;[44] provision of adequate sanitary conveniences with separate accommodation for each gender;[45] adequate wholesome drinking water;[46] adequate and suitable clock rooms;[47] facilities for sitting down;[48] and facilities for meals.[49]

Provision 31 provides that the measures to encourage cooperation as provided for in Article 15 of the Convention should include the consultation of workers and their representatives by the employer in establishing safety and health policy and procedures; and the inclusion, by the employer, of workers' representatives in the investigation of accidents and dangerous occurrences, as provided in Article 10(d) of the Convention. In Uganda, it is the duty of every employer to consult a safety representative in the making and maintenance of arrangements which enable the employer and the workers to cooperate effectively in promoting the development of measures to ensure the safety and health of employees.[50]

Provision 33 requires that due regard should be given to the possible impact of mining activities on the surrounding environment and on the safety of the public. In particular, this should include the control of subsidence, vibration, fly-rock, harmful contaminants in the water, air or soil, the safe and effective management of waste tips and the rehabilitation of mine sites. Under Section 108 of the Mining Act (2003), every holder of an exploration licence or a mining lease is required to carry out an EIA for his or her proposed project; to follow environmental protection standards by taking all

42 Section 53 of the Employment Act (2006).
43 Section 47 of the Occupational Safety and Health Act (2006).
44 Section 48 of the Occupational Safety and Health Act (2006).
45 Section 49 of the Occupational Safety and Health Act (2006).
46 Section 50 of the Occupational Safety and Health Act (2006).
47 Section 51 of the Occupational Safety and Health Act (2006).
48 Section 52 of the Occupational Safety and Health Act (2006).
49 Section 53 of the Occupational Safety and Health Act (2006).
50 Section 15 of the Occupational Safety and Health Act (2006).

the necessary steps to ensure the prevention and minimisation of pollution of the environment;[51] and to submit an environmental restoration plan of the exploration or mining area that may be damaged or adversely affected by the exploration or mining operations.[52]

These provisions of the Safety and Health in Mines Recommendation 183 of 1995 supplement those of the Safety and Health in Mines Convention 1995 and are applied in conjunction with them and the recommendations guide states in drafting legislation that regulates the impacts of mining.

4.2.2.3 International Finance Corporation Performance Standards

The International Finance Corporation (IFC) Performance Standards are an international benchmark for identifying and managing environmental and social risk. They have been adopted by many organisations as a key component of their environmental and social risk management. IFC's Environmental, Health and Safety (EHS) Guidelines are technical reference documents with general and industry specific examples of Good International Industry Practice (GIIP).[53]

The EHS Guidelines contain the performance levels and measures that are generally considered to be achievable in new facilities by existing technology at reasonable costs. Application of the EHS Guidelines to existing facilities may involve the establishment of site-specific targets, with an appropriate timetable for achieving them.

The applicability of the EHS Guidelines should be tailored to the hazards and risks established for each project on the basis of the results of an EIA in which site-specific variables, such as host country context, assimilative capacity of the environment and other project factors, are taken into account. Potential environmental issues associated with mining activities may include management of water use and quality, wastes, hazardous materials, land use and biodiversity, air quality, noise and vibrations, energy use, and visual impacts.

---

51 Section 109 of the Mining Act (2003).

52 Section 110 of the Mining Act (2003).

53 Defined as the exercise of professional skill, diligence, prudence and foresight that would be reasonably expected from skilled and experienced professionals engaged in the same type of undertaking under the same or similar circumstances globally. The circumstances that skilled and experienced professionals may find when evaluating the range of pollution prevention and control techniques available to a project may include, but are not limited to, varying levels of environmental degradation and environmental assimilative capacity as well as varying levels of financial and technical feasibility.

5 Institutional framework for environmental protection in mines

5.1 Ministry of Energy and Mineral Development

The direction and control of the mining sector is the responsibility of the Ministry of Energy and Mineral Development (MEMD). The mandate of the Ministry is to promote, develop, strategically manage and safeguard the rational and sustainable use of energy and mineral resources for economic and social development. Through the various agencies and departments, the MEMD has the overall responsibility for the energy sector, dealing specifically with policy formulation, policy implementation, and licensing, monitoring and regulatory control. The Directorate of Energy and Mineral Development under the Ministry oversees three technical departments responsible for energy resources, petroleum exploration, and production and mineral resources.

The Geological Survey and Mines Department of the Directorate is technically responsible for the administration and management of the mineral sector. The Department is mandated to promote and ensure rational development and use, in a safe and sustainable environment, of mineral resources for the socio-economic enhancement of the people of Uganda. Specifically, the Department has the mandate to: (i) collect, collate, process, analyse, archive and disseminate geosciences data; (ii) monitor operators and enforce regulations in the sector; and (iii) develop and retain professionals capable of generating and utilising the available geosciences data.

Therefore, the Ministry of Energy and Mineral Development ensures the fulfilment of the energy needs of Uganda's population for social and economic development in an environmentally sustainable manner.

5.2 Ministry of Water and Environment

The Ministry of Water and Environment (MWE) was established in 2007. It has the overall responsibility of developing, managing and regulating water and environment resources in Uganda.[54] It aims to provide sound and sustainable management of the environment for optimum social and economic benefits for present and future generations. The Ministry is also responsible for: initiating legislation; formulating policy; setting standards; inspecting; monitoring; coordinating; and backing up technical support in relation to the water and environment subsectors.

A multidisciplinary team representing stakeholders and constituting the Water Policy Committee advises the Minister on the functions mentioned above and is mandated to initiate revisions to legislation and regulations.

54 See <http://www.mwe.go.ug/mwe/about-ministry> (accessed 27-3-2018).

The Ministry has several divisions that assist in fulfilling its mandate. The Directorate of Water Development is in charge of promoting the rational management and use of water resources of Uganda by coordinating and regulating activities that may have an impact on water quality and quantity. Quality and quantity of water in watercourses is monitored and regulated by the Directorate of Water Resources Management, which also issues permits for water abstraction and effluent disposal. The Wetland Inspection Department is another technical unit in the Ministry that advises Government on technical matters and policies related to sustainable wetland conservation and management. The Department of Meteorology is responsible for providing climate and weather information to any stakeholders engaged in national development activities in Uganda.

5.3 The National Environment Management Authority

NEMA, a semi-autonomous institution, was established in May 1995 under the National Environment Act Cap. 153. It became operational in December 1995, as the principal agency in Uganda charged with the responsibility of coordinating, monitoring, regulating and supervising environmental management.

NEMA advises Government and spearheads the development of environmental policies, laws, regulations, standards and guidelines; and guides Government on sound environmental management in Uganda. NEMA's activities are focused on providing support to Government's main goal of ensuring sustainable development through the National Development Plan (NDP), in accordance with the policy framework of the Government of Uganda and the Sustainable Development Goals (SDGs).

NEMA's enforcement branch is the Department of Monitoring and Compliance. This Department is responsible for ensuring that enterprises comply with the various environmental regulations and standards. NEMA has appointed environmental inspectors whose powers and duties are spelled out in Section 81 of the National Environmental Act. These include closing down any activity that pollutes or is likely to pollute the environment and is contrary to the National Environment Act, for a period of not more than three weeks. The environmental inspector may also issue an improvement notice requiring an operator of any activity to cease any activities deleterious to the environment and which are contrary to the Act. NEMA has the power to prosecute environmental offenders in respect of offences committed under the National Environment Act, and may impose fines and prison sentences on the offender. NEMA is responsible for approving EIAs and reports for mining projects, in coordination with mineral agencies.

5.4 District local governments

Local governments are responsible for the protection of the environment at the district level. The districts receive and forward applications for various mineral rights, arbitrate on compensation, resolve disputes and grant licences for those minerals not administered under the Mining Act and goldsmith licences. This implies that local governments have a big role to play in mining activities to be carried out within their jurisdiction and on matters that affect the environment.

The districts regulate the impacts of mining through District Environment Committees. Section 14 of the National Environment Act Cap 153 provides that NEMA shall, in consultation with the district council, provide guidelines for the establishment of a committee on the environment for each district (District Environment Committee). The functions of the District Environment Committee include the following: ensuring that environmental concerns are integrated in all plans and projects approved by the District Council; assisting in the development and formulation of by-laws relating to the management of the environment; promoting the dissemination of information about the environment through education and outreach programmes; coordinating with the authority on all issues relating to environment management; and preparing a district state of the environment report every year.

5.5 The Environmental Police Protection Unit

In 2011, the Ministry of Water and Environment set up the Environmental Protection Police Unit (EPPU) to enforce environmental laws and prevent the degradation of protected areas. The Government also commissioned 153 policemen to police lakes, forests and wetlands that are threatened by encroachment. The policemen were also tasked to sensitise members of the public on environmental laws.[55]

According to a recent report submitted by the EPPU to Uganda Police, it has recorded 1,127 environment-related cases, arrested over 1,000 suspects and confiscated 1,065 tools used by degraders. The tools include music equipment confiscated during operations against noise pollution, power saws used for illegal logging and others used in wetland reclamation. The EPPU has significantly contributed to the protection of the environment against degradation and the impacts of mining activities.[56]

---

55 *Uganda Radio Network* (2013).
56 *The New Vision* (2014).

6 Key challenges in environmental and social protection

6.1 Gaps in the legal and institutional framework

There are some gaps in the legal and institutional framework that affect effective regulation of mining activities in Uganda. Under the Mining Act (2003), the duty and roles of the Minister, Commissioner and Inspector of Mines are not clearly defined. There is furthermore no provision for the independent oversight of the Commissioner, Inspector of Mines, or other public officers in the exercise of their duties, although there may be additional provisions under other legislation applicable to public officers in Uganda. There are no clear limits to the discretion that may be exercised by the Minister and the Commissioner.

The Commissioner is empowered to take a number of key decisions, including those relating to the granting of licences[57] and certain environmental issues, without needing to consult the Cabinet, other relevant agencies or an independent commission. No clarification is provided as to the separate roles and functions of the Inspector of Mines and the Commissioner in relation to inspections. Similarly, the relationship between the Commissioner and the Executive Director of NEMA is unclear. There is only limited provision for the review of decisions made by the Commissioner.

Furthermore, there are weak laws on policies relating to ASM. The legal framework does not provide adequate licencing regimes for ASM or measures protecting environmental and social rights in the context of ASM. As a result, ASM communities are vulnerable and marginalised.[58]

At the institutional level, the EPPU is poorly funded and, as a result, has a mere 153 officers. This is an insufficient number to undertake patrols and surveillance across the entire country and investigate all environmental cases thoroughly.

6.2 Limited enforcement of environmental regulations

There is limited enforcement of the relevant law owing to a lack of knowledge of environmental law, management and monitoring expertise, and equipment and facilitation. This is in addition to political interference that undermines law enforcement.

57 Section 43(3) of the Mining Act (2003).
58 Buxton (2013: 8).

7 Conclusion and recommendations

The activities in the mining value chain have direct and indirect environmental and social impacts. These include water pollution; air pollution; noise pollution; harm to wildlife; contamination of soils; deforestation; land degradation; displacement of communities and disruption of livelihoods; damage to subsistence agriculture; social inequality; and economic dependency. Although Uganda has a regulatory and institutional framework for environmental protection during the mining value chain, there are a number of challenges that undermine environmental protection efforts. These challenges include some gaps in the legal regime and the inadequate enforcement of the existing regime. To address these challenges, a number of recommendations are proposed. Firstly, it is necessary to revise the legislation to recognise the international best practices for protection of the environment and human rights in mining areas. Such practices include: involvement of all stakeholders; regulation of artisans and small-scale miners; inclusion of gender elements in the mining sector; safety and health; and resettlement and compensation standards. Secondly, there is a need to strengthen capacity to ensure monitoring and enforcement of environmental standards at all stages of the mining cycle. Lastly, it is important to raise the awareness of the local communities so that they know their rights relating to the elimination of the vulnerability and marginalisation of communities.

References

Alvarez-Berríos, NL & TM Aide (2015) "Global demand for gold is another threat for tropical forests" 10(1) *Environmental Research Letters* 1-11.

Buxton, A (2013) *Responding to the challenge of artisanal and small-scale mining. How can knowledge networks help?*, at <https://womin.org.za/images/impact-of-extractive-industries/women-and-artisanal-mining/IIED>, accessed 27 March 2018.

Crawford, A, K Disney & M Harris (2015) *Supporting implementation of the mining policy framework in member states of the intergovernmental forum on mining, minerals, metals and sustainable development; Uganda: assessment of implementation readiness*, at <https://www.iisd.org/sites/default/files/publications/mpf-uganda-assessment-of-implementation-readiness.pdf> (accessed 12-4-2018).

David, C (2010) "Acid mine drainage" (29-10-2014) at <http://www.groundtruthtrekking.org/Issues/MetalsMining/AcidMineDrainage.html> (accessed 20-3-2018).

Emerson, J (2014) *How can we survive here? The impact of mining on human rights in Karamoja, Uganda*, at <https://www.hrw.org/report/2014/02/03/how-can-we-survive-here/impact-mining-human-rights-karamoja-uganda> (accessed 15-4-2018).

Foley, JA (2015) "Global consequences of land use" 309 *Science* 570-574.

Hansen, MC (2013) "High-resolution global maps of 21st-century forest cover change" 342 *Science*, 850-853.

Hentschel, T, F Hruschka & M Priester (2002) *Global report on small-scale mining international institute for environment and development* (IIED) and World Business Council for Sustainable Development (WBCSD) Working Paper No. 70.

Karamage, F, C Zhang, L Tong, A Maganda & A Isabwe (2017) "Soil erosion risk assessment in Uganda" 8(52) *Forests* 1-20, at <https://pdfs.semanticscholar.org/4adb/2a599e94689df3472bfb56ecf6be2d207f13.pdf> (accessed 15-4-2018).

Maier, RM, F Díaz-Barriga, JA Field, J Hopkins, B Klein & M Poulton (2014) "Socially responsible mining: the relationship between poverty, human health and the environment" 29(1-2) *Reviews of Environmental Health* 83-89.

Mbaya, RP (2013) "Land degradation due to mining: the Gunda scenario" 2(12) *International Journal of Geography and Geology* 144-158.

MINEO Consortium (2000) *Review of potential environmental and social impact of mining*, at <http://www2.brgm.fr/ mineo/UserNeed/IMPACTS.pdf> (accessed 22-3-2018).

Ministry of Energy and Mineral Development (2001) *Mineral policy of Uganda*, at <http://energyandminerals.go.ug/downloads/minpol00.pdf> (accessed 1-5-2018).

Murguía, DI, S Bringezu & R Schaldach (2016) "Global direct pressures on biodiversity by large-scale metal mining: spatial distribution and implications for conservation"180 *Journal for Environmental Management* 409-420.

Musoke, E (2015) "Mining and mineral exploration opportunities in Uganda", at <https://www.linkedin.com/pulse/mining-mineral-exploration-opportunities-uganda-evans-musoke> (accessed 19-3-2018).

Mwesigye, A, S Young, B Elizabeth & S Tumwebaze (2016) "Population exposure to trace elements in the Kilembe copper mine area, Western Uganda: a pilot study" 573 *Science of the Total Environment* 366-375, at <http://eprints.nottingham.ac.uk/36061/1/Mwesigye%20et%20al%202016.pdf> (accessed 10-4-2018).

National Association of Professional Environmentalists (2015) "Environmental costs related to Limestome mining at the Dura Quary site in Queen Elizabeth National Park, Kamwenge" *NAPE Blog* (18-8-2015), at <http://www.nape.or.ug/blogs/environmental-costs-related-to-limestome-mining-at-the-dura-quary-site-in-queen-elizabeth-national-park-kawenge> (accessed 15-4-2018).

National Environment Management Authority (2004) *Environmental impact assessment guidelines for the energy sector*, at <http://archive.resourcegovernance.org/sites/default/files/Uganda,%20enviro%20impact%20assessment%20guidelines.pdf> (accessed 26-3-2018).

Olson, J & L Berry (2003) *Land degradation in Uganda: its extent and impact*.

Owor, M & A Muwanga (2007) "Impact of tailings from the Kilembe copper mining district on Lake George, Uganda" 51(6) *Environmental Geology* 1065-1075.

Serginho, R (2015) "Pollution is silent killer in Uganda" *VoA News* (18-2-2016) at <https://www.voanews.com/a/pollution-is-silent-killer-in-uganda/2648372.html> (accessed 15-4-2018).

Ssenku, JE, M Ntale & HO Origa (2014) "Physico-chemical characteristics of copper tailings and pyrite soils in Western Uganda: implication for phytoremediation" 2(4) *International Journal of Environmental Monitoring and Analysis* 191-198, at <http://www.cns.mak.ac.ug/sites/default/files/publications/10.11648.j.ijema_.20140204.12.pdf> (accessed 15-4-2018).

The Independent (2016) "Inside Mubende's golden villages" *The Independent* (1-11-2016), at <http://allafrica.com/stories/201611010300.html> (accessed 12-4-2018).

The New Vision (2014) "Environmental police too broke to enforce laws" *The New Vision* (13-5-2014), at <https://www.newvision.co.ug/new_vision/news/1340644/environmental-police-broke-enforce-laws> (accessed 25-3-2018).

Uganda Radio Network (2013) "Environmental police struggles to enforce laws" *Uganda Radio Network* (8-5-2013), at <https://ugandaradionetwork.com/story/environmental-police-struggles-to-enforce-laws> (accessed 25-3-2018).

UNEP / United Nations Environment Programme (2012) *Analysis of formalization approaches in the artisanal and small-scale gold mining sector based on experiences in Ecuador, Mongolia, Peru, Tanzania and Uganda*, at <https://wedocs.unep.org/bitstream/handle/20.500.11822/11611/Case_Study_Uganda_June_2012.pdf> (accessed 19-3-2018).

Chapter 32: An analysis of environmental impacts of timber exploitation on indigenous communities' land in Cameroon

Esther Effundem Njieassam

1 Introduction

Cameroon is known by different monikers as 'Africa in miniature' (because of its diversity in landscapes); 'Mecca of African soccer' (because of its legendary performance in soccer); and 'Africa's crossroads between west and east Africa'(because of its strategic location).[1] These appellations are fuelled by its ethnic, ecological, climatic, cultural, linguistic, and religions diversity.[2] The country stretches from 2°N to 13°N latitude between 8°25'E and 16°20'W longitude, covering an area of 475,440 square km.[3] The moist tropical rainforest area of Cameroon is positioned in Central Africa, precisely in West Africa on the Gulf of Guinea.[4] The country is surrounded by other African countries: to the north by Chad, to the east by the Central African Republic, to the south by the Democratic Republic of Congo, Republic of Congo, Gabon and Equatorial Guinea.[5] To the west is the Federal Republic of Nigeria.[6] With a population of over 22 million people, it comprises over 250 ethnic groups that speak over 270 different languages whose speakers exhibit various cultural practices and institutions to which indigenous peoples are inclusive. The official languages are English and French.[7] English is spoken in the southern part of Cameroon, while French is the dominant language used in the eastern part of the country.

The rich and diverse ecosystem surrounding the tropical rainforest in Cameroon has attracted plenty of attention at the international and national levels, owing to its climatic conditions and biological diversity. Among the vast and assorted forest resources is the lowland humid timber rainforest consisting of 58% of the total surface area of the country, where the Baka, Bakola and Bagyéli indigenous communities have

1 Gross (2003: xv).
2 Amungwa (2011: 53-54).
3 Sunderland-Groves et al. (2003: 1-2).
4 Amungwa (2011: 54).
5 Sayer et al. (1992: 110).
6 Ibid.
7 Echu (2013: 19).

resided over decades.[8] In these areas of moist forest zones, the majority of logging activities in the country take place. Timber plays a vital role in the country's economy and contributes over 10% of its GDP. Timber is considered one of the most important sources of income for economic growth.[9] To this end, timber has been rated second in terms of export after oil. Timber offers between 45,000 and 70,000 jobs to the population.[10]

The rainforest area is home to many indigenous peoples (Pygmies) serving them as a source of food, water, shelter, clothing, cultural identity and spiritual survival.[11] Until colonisation, timber was solely used for carvings, canoe construction and the building of bridges. Little commercial value was initially attached to this important resource.[12] This changed with the colonial system of divide and rule, resulting in severe disruptions to the traditional ways of life and the environment of indigenous peoples.[13] European traders not only exploited the area in search of fertile and vacant lands but also harvested natural resources such as timber.[14] After independence, the post-colonial government of Cameroon failed to meet the socio-economic and environmental needs of indigenous peoples and local inhabitants. Land and environmental laws adopted were still influenced by European ideology of private ownership, resource exploitation and management.[15] This contributed to an increase in illegal acquisition of land and unsustainable resource exploitation.[16] This in turn contributed to further destruction of the environment and marginalisation of indigenous communities in Cameroon.[17]

This chapter assesses the deleterious effects that timber exploitation has caused to the environment of indigenous communities in Cameroon. It is argued that the excessive rate of timber exploitation on indigenous peoples' land have had disastrous impacts on the environment and the peoples' well-being. The extraction of timber from the rich, dense forests prompted the government to enact some sectoral laws at the national level. These are the Forestry Law[18] and its Decree of implementation,[19] including Law No. 96/12 relating to environmental management regulating forestry activities in order to ensure environmental sustainability in the country. Despite the enactment of these laws, the rate of illegal timber exploitation and its environmental impacts on land occupied by indigenous peoples remains overwhelming. This chapter

8 Beauchamp & Ingram (2011: 402); and Amungwa (2011: 54).
9 Alemagi & Kozak (2010: 554-555).
10 Ibid; Mbatu (2010: 444-445).
11 Mbatu (2010: 444-445).
12 Amariei (2005: 7-8).
13 Dersso (2010: 32-33); see also Dersso (2012).
14 Ardener (1962: 342).
15 Amungwa (2011: 54).
16 Alemagi & Kozak (2010: 554-556).
17 Ibid.
18 No. 94-01 of 20 January 1994.
19 Decree No. 95-531 of 23 August 1995 was laid down to determine the implementation process of Forestry, Wildlife and Fisheries regulations (also referred to as the Forestry Decree).

uncovers the underlying causes of recurrent negative environmental impacts caused by timber exploitation on indigenous peoples' lands. For this matter, the chapter critically examines the rate of exploitation of timber on indigenous lands, highlighting the devastating environmental impacts on affected communities. It also evaluates international, regional and national legal frameworks regulating environmental protection relevant to Cameroon, assessing whether the national government and extractive industries adhere to international standards. The chapter concludes with some suggestions for policy and legal reform.

2 The exploitation of timber on indigenous peoples' lands in Cameroon

The rich, dense forest of Cameroon consists of 20 million hectares which constitute about 42% of the national territory.[20] The tropical rainforest comprises two types, although the dense forest area estimated at 17 million hectares is the largest in comparison to the other.[21] About three quarters (75%) of the country's evergreen tropical forest is situated in the southern part of the country forming part of the Congo Basin forest.[22] This forest area is ranked the second largest ecosystem in the world after the Amazonia, which has attracted multinational corporations (MNCs) and extractive industries from different parts of the globe.[23]

Given the wide range of Cameroon's natural resources, one would expect a certain level of socio-economic and infrastructural development including a stable economy and a high standard of living for indigenous communities. Ironically, this is not the case. The situation is similar to most other African countries, where despite the abundance of natural resources, the people are still entrapped by a myriad of challenges including chronic poverty and environmental degradation. As Ross[24] posits, resources are at times more a 'curse than a blessing', since they easily instigate conflicts in low and middle-income countries, especially if the resources are located within areas occupied by indigenous peoples. This observation is affirmed by some scholars. For example, Frankel[25] opines that natural resources do not boost economic growth as is the case in resource-rich countries like Angola, Nigeria, Sudan and Congo, where despite the vast amount of oil, diamonds, petroleum and other mineral resources, living standards and per capita income remain extremely low. The host communities where these

20 Mbatu (2016: 467).
21 Ernst et al. (2012: 25).
22 Mbatu (2016: 467).
23 Oyono (2005: 321).
24 Ross (2015: 240).
25 Frankel (2012: 4).

resources are extracted live in abject poverty and are often confronted with environmental and other socio-economic challenges. Scholars have further argued that:[26]

> The overlap in the functions of the Ministry of Environment and Nature Protection, charged with the duty to articulate, execute, and evaluate government policy in relation to environmental protection and the Ministry of Forestry and Wildlife that enact, assess and implement policies regarding the forest sector makes it difficult to safeguard a sustained environment. This is particularly true when it comes to environmental impact assessment following developmental projects to be executed in indigenous peoples' territories.

The exploitation of forests and other natural resources dates back to the colonial period when European settlers and traders such as the Germans, British and French implemented a policy of indirect rule. This practice enabled them to manage all land and forest resources in Cameroon. Commercial logging was introduced in the country during the German colonial rule in the 19th century. It was later adopted by Britain and France shortly after the First World War. These colonial masters saw the vast resources in Cameroon as a source of income essential for the development of their country, to the detriment of the local population. This relegated indigenous communities to a periphery position, as the management and control of natural resources was centralised in the hands of the colonial administration.[27] It is estimated that by 1920, close to 59,000 tons of timber had been exported to France.[28] This amplified by 1948, when the Anglo-Franco administration of Cameroon at the time managed to secure logging concessions over a period of 25 years within an area of 714,000 hectares of forest land.[29] Indigenous peoples were reduced to mere cheap labourers on the lands they traditionally occupied over time.

Prior to this period, over 70% of the population of Cameroon depended on agricultural products for subsistence.[30] Related studies reveal that agricultural products contributed to about 40% of the GDP, as against 20% of the industrial sector and 36% generated from the civil service.[31] The severe economic recession that affected the world in the late 1980s led to a drastic fall in the prices of agricultural products and the country's GDP declined by 6% between 1986, 1988 and 1989 respectively, resulting in social unrest and economic instability.[32] To this end, internal and external pressures from western financial institutions forced the government of Cameroon to embark on a number of internal economic restructuring projects such as the Structural Adjustment Programme spurred by the International Monetary Fund (IMF).

Efforts to recover from the effects of the economic crisis caused the government to focus on the exploitation of timber for export to enhance the living conditions of the

26 Alemagi & Kozak (2010: 557-558); and Alemagi (2011: 70).
27 Fonjong et al. (2010: 159).
28 Biesbrouck (2002: 56).
29 Oyono et al. (2005: 358).
30 Ibid.
31 Djontu (2009: 10).
32 Wunder (2003: 183).

population. In fact, timber exploitation became a primary source of income, especially after the significant price decline of oil, cocoa, coffee and cotton.[33] Reports from the Ministry of Environment and Forestry,[34] indicate that the country had a steady increase in the demand for timber resources during this period.[35] This was possible with the advent of globalisation, which facilitated the free movement of goods and services from one country to the other. As a result, the government resorted to timber extraction for export as a means to generate income and increase economic growth through taxes.[36]

Notwithstanding the significant contribution of timber to the economy, the country experienced a high rate of depletion of the rain forests. The forest sector contains important biodiversity with a variety of species relevant in the context of climate change and environmental sustainability.[37]

It is estimated that between 1990 and 2010, the country experienced a deforestation rate of about 0.9% per year, constituting approximately 4,400,000 hectares (1.8%).[38] According to Atyi et al.,[39] out of the 105 companies involved in timber exploitation in Cameroon, 90 have obtained logging rights while 15 are involved in timber processing and export. There is a substantial amount of documented evidence of illegal logging activities and bad practices by large European (French) and Asian (Chinese) companies, including the violation of concession rules, exploitation in prohibited areas and extinction of protected species.[40] This was inter alia due to the lack of effective monitoring mechanisms and inconsistency in the functions and implementation of government policies by responsible ministries.[41]

Companies such as Rougier and Pallisco (both French-owned companies), operating in Cameroon have accumulated vast lands in Lomié (a district in the Upper Nyong division in the East Province of Cameroon) where the Baka indigenous peoples (Pygmies) are located.[42] These MNCs and their logging activities have forcefully displaced the Baka and Bagyeli people from their traditionally owned lands to the roadside where

---

33 Ibid.

34 Decree No. 92/069 of 9 April 1992 laid down by the Ministry of Environment and Forestry (MINEF) in 1992, which has been changed to Ministry of Forestry and Wildlife (MINFOF) following the passing of the Forestry Law with an implementing Decree aimed at regulating the forestry sector in Cameroon.

35 Ekoko (2000: 133).

36 Ibid: 134.

37 Djeukam (2013: 108).

38 Mbatu (2016: 467).

39 Atyi et al. (2013: 43).

40 Cerutti et al. (2013: 540). Although the Forestry Law of 1994 has made provision for all logging companies to obtain legal documents before operating on a given area, this has not been the actual situation on ground.

41 Ibid.

42 The estimated surface area occupied by them amounts to 625,253 ha and 388,949 ha respectively. This is way beyond the minimum amount prescribed by the Forestry Law of 1994, which only provides for 200,000 ha.

they were forced to adopt a sedentary lifestyle. This can be seen as a violation of their fundamental human right to a safe and healthy environment, access to land and natural resources, health care, food security and the right to existence as a people. It can also be seen as a violation of Section 23 of the Forestry Law 1994.[43] The government of Cameroon in collaboration with the MNCs, greatly neglected and failed to protect indigenous peoples' fundamental human rights as reiterated in several international instruments. Indigenous communities are disgruntled not just because the government has permitted illegal logging operations on their lands, but also by allowing activities that cause substantial damage to the environment. On 12 September 2017, 50 Baka and Bagyeli indigenous communities signed a declaration requesting for the respect and recognition of their rights to land and natural resources as well as a safe and healthy environment.[44] They indicated that:[45]

> We, the forest indigenous peoples, have increasingly experienced serious violations of our human rights, because of agro-industrial activities, mining, forestry concessions, and because of the creation of protected areas on our ancestral lands. This disturbing situation foreshadows a future where we as indigenous peoples will no longer have land. If we continue to lose our lands and forests, the very survival of our cultures and peoples' is at risk.

Based on the above declaration, it is unfortunate to note, that the same people who are bestowed with the responsibility of protecting indigenous peoples' interests are the very perpetrators allowing the violation of their fundamental human rights. It is also worth noting that the government and extractive industries work to safeguard their own selfish interest, leaving indigenous communities to deal with the consequences of timber exploitation on their ancestral lands.[46] The discussion that follows is an assessment of the legal framework regulating environmental protection in Cameroon.

3 Legal framework regulating environmental protection in Cameroon

3.1 International framework

The increasing global concern for the health and environment of the world's forest-dependent people has caused Cameroon to become actively involved in the

---

43 Section 23 of the Forestry Law provides that: "…management of a permanent forest means the carrying out of certain activities and investments, based on previously established objectives and on a plan, for the sustained production of forest products and services, without affecting the primitive value or compromising the future productivity of the forest nor causing any damage to the physical and social environment".

44 Reuters (2017).

45 Declaration on land rights from the Gabandi Platform, Cameroon, at <http://www.forestpeoples.org/en/rights-land-natural-resources/news-article/2017/declaration-land-rights-gbabandi-platform-cameroon> (accessed 10-3-2018).

46 Cultural Survival (2017).

development of international instruments protecting the environment. Studies reveal that by 2013 the government of Cameroon had signed and ratified a multitude of international environmental agreements.[47] Although this might reflect the government's commitment to guarantee a safe and healthy environment for its citizens, the situation on the ground presents a rather different picture. Nevertheless, a few of the aforementioned instruments, especially those relevant to indigenous peoples are discussed below.

3.1.1 The Convention on Biological Diversity

The 1992 Convention on Biological Diversity (CBD) also aims to safeguard the conservation of forest biodiversity. As is stipulated in Article 1, CBD aims at "the conservation of biological diversity, the sustainable use of its component and the fair and equitable sharing of the benefits arising out of the utilisation of genetic resources". Based on these objectives, states in accordance with their particular capabilities are under the obligation to develop national strategies, plans and programmes, which enhance the conservation and sustainable use of biological diversity.[48] Contracting parties are also encouraged to adopt measures that serve as incentives for the sustainable use of natural resources.[49] Besides, states are to identify and monitor components of biological diversity that demand immediate conservation measures and have the potential for sustainable use.[50] States are also expected to identify processes and activities that might have adverse effects on the conservation and sustainable use of these resources as well as to monitor their effects through sampling and other techniques.[51] These processes aim to preserve and protect the rainforest and other natural resources from future depletion.

One important aspect of CBD is that it explicitly recognises indigenous peoples' traditional knowledge. It requires states to enact national legislation and policies that respect, preserve and maintain indigenous peoples' traditional lifestyles vital for the conservation and sustainable use of biological diversity.[52] This is in line with Steven's argument that indigenous peoples as polytheistic and self-ascribed human beings are the best caretakers of the environment.[53] This is attributed to the close affinity they have with their ancestral lands coupled with their collective pattern of management

47 Mitchell (2003: 434-436).
48 Article 6 of the Convention on Biological Diversity (CBD) 1760 UNTS 79, 31 ILM 818 (1992).
49 Article 7(a) CBD.
50 Article 7(b) CBD.
51 Article 7(c) CBD.
52 Article 8(j) CBD.
53 Stevens (1997: 49).

and ability to preserve and transmit these lands to younger generations.[54] Environmentalists and conservationists are expected to work together with indigenous peoples rather than to cast them into the role of environmental villains and dispossess them from their traditionally owned lands.[55]

Besides, regarding developing countries, states are obliged to cooperate, as appropriate, directly or through competent international organisations to provide financial support and establish programmes for scientific and technical education. They are also required to provide training opportunities that seek to promote and encourage research that contributes to the conservation and sustainable use of biological diversity.[56] It is the responsibility of states to formulate suitable measures like impact assessments and to provide notifications and exchange information on activities that might cause serious harm to the environment and promote public participation to help mitigate such effects.[57] Given that indigenous peoples are also likely to suffer more from the adverse effects of climate change, it is important to involve them in impact assessment programmes to help minimise the grave effects of climate change that remain a pertinent environmental challenge in Cameroon.

States must take into consideration legislative and administrative national programmes that encourage methods of cooperation that promote the use of technologies, indigenous knowledge and traditional technologies, provided they are in line with the objectives of the CBD, especially those that do not cause substantial damage to the environment.[58] Cameroon is a party to the CBD, which shows the country's willingness to ensure environmental sustainability for its population. The worrying question is whether the country is living up to international standards, especially owing to gross environmental harms caused by MNCs and other extractive companies on indigenous peoples traditionally owned lands.

The answer to this question is simple. A closer look at the activities of timber exploiting companies and the serious effects on the environment and well-being of indigenous peoples reveals that the country is not honouring its international or national obligations in safeguarding a safe and healthy environment for the population. The excessive destruction of the ecosystem, soil, plants, pollution of water sources and air caused by the process of timber extraction as discussed below reflecting the government's inability to comply with the normative expectation of the CBD.

---

54 Ibid.
55 Colchester (2000: 1365).
56 Article 12 CBD.
57 Article 14 CBD.
58 Articles 16, 17 and 18 CBD.

3.1.2 The Convention on International Trade in Endangered Species of Wild Fauna and Flora

Unlike the CBD and the United Nations Framework Convention on Climate Change (UNFCCC), the Convention on International Trade in Endangered Species of Wild Fauna and Flora (CITES) is an international instrument with binding force on member states. CITES is the brainwork of a draft resolution of the 1963 meeting of members of the International Union for the Conservation of Nature. Signed on 3 March 1973 and entered into force on 1 July 1975, CITES has been operational for 43 years. As an international instrument that combines wildlife and trade, CITES aims at promoting the conservation and sustainable use of species, including timber. Its main objective is to ensure that wildlife, fauna and flora in international trade are exploited in a sustainable manner such that they are prevented from extinction.[59]

As a country endowed with a variety of natural resources including timber, Cameroon signed CITES in June 1981 and ratified it in September of the same year. This gesture also shows the country's commitment to protect the environment and to improve on persistent environmental degradation resulting from continuous resource extraction and pollution.[60] Most importantly, the government seeks to ensure that growing international trade in CITES-listed timber species is consistent with sustainable management and conservation policies in the country.[61]

CITES provides that prior to the exportation of any specimen of species, the scientific and management authority of the state has a responsibility to ensure that such activity does not have a substantial impact on the survival of species.[62] A species is also not to be obtained contrary to the laws that protect the fauna and flora in the country.[63] Articles VIII and XIV require member states to adopt appropriate and stricter measures at domestic levels to safeguard future violations in relation to species that prohibit trade, possession and transportation. While Cameroon has maintained an impressive record of memberships to several international multilateral environmental agreements to eradicate pressing environmental issues in the country, it is worth noting, that the enforcement and monitoring mechanisms remain a challenge. This is attributed to ineffective and weak government policies coupled with the absence of an efficient monitoring system to control the activities of MNCs and other extractive industries. Government officials in charge of ensuring that logging companies adhere to and respect government policies and contracts are often incapable of performing their duties as extractive companies bribe their way through the process.

59 Article II of the Convention on International Trade in Endangered Species of Wild Fauna and Flora (CITIES) 27 UST 1087, TIAS 8249, 993 UNTS 243.

60 Mbatu (2016: 470).

61 Amougou et al. (2009: 15).

62 Articles III and IV CITIES.

63 Article V CITIES.

3.1.3 The United Nations Framework Convention on Climate Change

The growing concern about the impacts of human activities on the environment resulting from climate change called for the adoption of an international framework to respond to the changing climate. The negotiations around the UNFCCC were spurred during the 1992 United Nations Conference on Environment and Development (UNCED) in Rio de Janeiro, Brazil following deliberations regarding the development of the forest principles in Chapter 11 of Agenda 21. Even though the UNCED did not impose an obligation on member states to address forest loss and related issues in its forest principles, the framework was applauded for establishing the UNFCCC.[64] As its main objective, the UNFCCC seeks to "stabilise greenhouse gas concentrations in the atmosphere so as to prevent dangerous anthropogenic interference with the climate system",[65] as well as to ensure sustainable economic development and sufficient food production in the state. The UNFCCC in its Articles 3 and 4 obligates parties to protect the climate system to the advantage of present and future generations and to address the specific and special needs of those groups that are particularly vulnerable to its effects. It also obliges states to take precautionary measures through national policies to anticipate, prevent and mitigate the effects of climate change as well as to promote international economic systems that will enhance sustainable development in developing countries to improve their endogenous capacities and capabilities.[66] The development and implementation of educational and public awareness programmes, access to information as well as public participation in addressing climate change issues through training of scientific, technical and managerial personnel is equally the responsibility of member states.[67]

Recognised as one of the achievements of UNFCCC to minimise the effects of climate change, UNFCCC is a programme intending to reduce emissions from deforestation and forest degradation (REDD+). As a global initiative that seeks to preserve the world's remaining forest, REDD+ also aims at protecting the rights, needs and aspirations of indigenous peoples.[68] Considering that Cameroon is a party to the UNFCCC with a variety of diverse ecosystems, Cameroon has the potential to protect the forest ecosystem, improve the environment and livelihood of indigenous peoples and to enhance their right to a forest and the resources therein. It is on this basis that the government adopted the REDD+ readiness programme as part of its national policy to combat forest degradation in the country.

---

64 Mbatu (2016: 479).

65 Artcile 2 of the United Nations Framework Convention on Climate Change (UNFCCC) 1771 UNTS 107, S.Treaty Doc No. 102-138, U.N. Doc. A/AC.237/18 (Part II)/Add.1, 31 ILM 849 (1992).

66 Article 3 of the UNFCCC.

67 Article 5 of the UNFCCC.

68 Savaresi (2013: 4-5).

Viewed as a framework to promote the voluntary efforts of developing countries to mitigate climate change, to promote conservation and the sustainable management of the forest, the government of Cameroon has embarked in the process of establishing crucial technical, institutional and policy competencies for REDD+.[69] This includes the REDD+ Steering Committee established on 13 June 2012 through a Ministerial Decree.[70] Chaired by a Committee under the Ministry of Environment, Nature Protection and Sustainable Development and assisted by the Minister of Forestry and Wildlife, the main objective of this Committee is to approve and pilot activities that aim at enhancing REDD+ programmes.[71]

The major way of realising the REDD+ process in the country is to ensure the full participation, prior consent and information sharing which enable indigenous peoples to be informed and be involved in the management process. Unfortunately, the process has not been effectively implemented.[72] It is argued that indigenous peoples are not fully involved or represented in the REDD+ process and no measures are prescribed for redress at the national level in cases of violation of their rights.[73] Studies reveal that the REDD+ process has in fact intensified indigenous peoples marginalisation by putting them under pressure and limiting their rights.[74] This explains why indigenous peoples continue to suffer the consequences of climate change in their various communities.

It is significant to note, that despite all efforts to ensure compliance and commitment with regards to climate change, the UNFCCC and the Kyoto Protocol omitted indigenous peoples rights in relation to a healthy environment.[75] Though it is widely observed that indigenous peoples are the ones most affected by the impacts of climate change, most international instruments do not provide for adequate adaptation mechanisms specifically designed for indigenous peoples.[76] Policymakers should thus revisit international and national frameworks regulating climate change and environmental protection with a stronger focus on indigenous peoples.

4 Regional framework

Environmental protection has a longstanding history in Africa.[77] The Organisation of the African Unity (OAU) and its successor the African Union (AU) have developed

69 Alemagi et al. (2014: 711).
70 Decree No. 103/CAB/PM.
71 Alemagi et al. (2014: 711).
72 Savaresi (2013: 12-14).
73 Hansungule & Jegede (2014: 287).
74 Cultural Survival (2018).
75 Hansungule & Jegede (2014: 283).
76 World Bank (2010: 128).
77 Erinosho (2013: 378).

several legal instruments to enhance environmental protection on the African continent both through 'soft law' (non-binding) and 'treaty law' (binding).[78] The most prominent of these treaties is the African Convention on Nature and Natural Resources (African Convention), adopted in Algiers in 1968 and entered into force in 1969.[79] It is considered as one of the first multilateral efforts at the regional level to regulate and preserve the natural environment. It has been revised following the adoption of the Stockholm Declaration of 1972, the Rio Declaration of 1992 and in 2003 in Maputo within the framework of the African Union. Cameroon is yet to ratify the Convention, which has the main goal to foster cooperation with other international environmental instruments and to implement measures that enhance environmental protection on the African continent.

These principles are stated in the Preamble, which recognises the significance of the natural environment and natural resources to humankind with an obligation on states to harness natural and human resources in a way that improves the well-being of the population. It affirms that the conservation of the African environment is the primary responsibility of all human beings.[80] This implies that all segments of the population, including governments and foreign investors, have the responsibility to ensure that their activities pose no threats to the natural environment and the people living close by. The Convention has as a key objective to enhance environmental protection and foster the conservation and sustainable use of natural resources through the harmonisation and coordination of policies. The African Convention emphasises on the right of all people to a satisfactory environment and calls on states to implement preventive measures that prohibit land degradation and guarantee the effective management of forests and other natural resources to ensure sustainable development.[81]

Interestingly, the African Convention reiterates the need to adopt effective legislative and regulatory measures that aim at providing a coherent means of disseminating information to the general public to enable them to participate in decisions regarding potential environmental impacts within their natural habitats.[82] The African Convention equally obliges member states to enact legislative measures that promote indigenous peoples' traditional rights. This includes access to indigenous knowledge through prior informed consent as well as active participation in the planning and management of programmes relating to natural resources.[83] Despite the fact, that Cameroon is not a signatory to the African Convention, the participation of indigenous peoples in forest management can help preserving the environment for future generations.

78 Van der Linde (2002: 33).
79 African Convention on Nature and Natural Resources (African Convention) 1001 UNTS 3.
80 Paragraphs 1, 2, 3 and 4 of the Preamble to the African Convention.
81 Articles II, III, IV, VI, VII, VIII, XIV of the African Convention.
82 Article XVI of the African Convention.
83 Article XVII of the African Convention.

4.1 The African Charter on Human and Peoples' Rights

It is observed that efforts made by the African Union to safeguard environmental protection have resulted in a rights-based approach to environmental protection ushered by the African Charter on Human and Peoples' Rights (the Banjul Charter) in its Article 24.[84] While most African countries are endowed with a wide variety of natural resources, the continent is encountering numerous environmental problems. These problems range among others from the pollution of waterways, deforestation, desertification, loss of biodiversity, climate change to the destruction of the soil.[85] It is against this background that the Banjul Charter adopted in 1981 has embarked on protecting the environment to secure a better standard of living especially for forest-dependants. The Banjul Charter stipulates in its Article 24 that "[a]ll peoples shall have the right to a general satisfactory and healthy environment favourable to their development". Although it does not directly refer to indigenous peoples, the wording "all peoples" can be interpreted to mean all categories of human beings in the society, including indigenous peoples, whose survival is strongly tied to the natural environment. Based on the above provision, it is established that a healthy environment is crucial to all human beings to enable them to live a healthy and dignified life, vital for realising sustainable development.

As a binding legal instrument, the Banjul Charter is widely known for incorporating categories of rights such as solidarity rights, the right to a satisfactory environment and the right to development as reiterated in Articles 22 and 24 respectively.[86] Evidently, the present condition of indigenous peoples in Cameroon is quite frustrating, where the ever-increasing over-exploitation of timber is undermining their rights by reducing their prospects of realising environmental sustainability. In fact, it seems more than important that states adopt appropriate national measures aimed at safeguarding the environment in favour of those communities that rely on natural resources for their subsistence. Regrettably, this has not been the case in Cameroon and other African countries.

The landmark case of *Social and Economic Rights Action (SERAC) and Centre for Economic and Social Rights (CESR) v. Nigeria*[87] deals with a violation by the Nigerian government and the oil company Shell of the rights to health and a clean environment of the Ogoni people residing in the Niger Delta. It was submitted that the government of Nigeria did not only fail in its duty to carry out studies that might determine potential environmental threats on the said area; it also participated in perpetrating the contamination of water sources, pollution of air, destruction of soil and the natural

84 Strydom (2015: 37).
85 Colchester (2000: 1366-1367).
86 Scholtz (2015: 104).
87 Communication No. 155/96 African Commission on Human and Peoples' Rights.

environment of the Ogoni people. In deciding this case, the African Commission on Human and Peoples' Rights invoked the provision of Article 24 of the Banjul Charter, which guarantees everyone a satisfactory and healthy environment. The Commission found that the Nigerian government has failed to take necessary measures to monitor, regulate and mitigate the activities of the oil consortium company in the Niger Delta, with a view to minimising the adverse effects of these activities on the Ogoni peoples' land. This case demonstrates the significance of a healthy environment for indigenous communities. States are obliged to take reasonable measures within their national legislation to ensure that the activities of extractive industries do not jeopardise the health and natural environment of indigenous peoples. In addition, actions should be taken at all stages of development processes to mitigate such effects. Unfortunately, this is not happening in Cameroon, as it is submitted that despite the persistent outcry by indigenous communities following multiple spills from the Chad-Cameroon Pipeline Project, in Kribi, at the country's coast, the government is more concerned with the financial gains than the welfare of indigenous communities residing in that area.

For instance, prior to the project, oil companies had promised to improve the living conditions of indigenous peoples as well as to ensure that their natural environment is not altered. However, none of these promises has been kept. Instead, affected communities are left to battle with social and environmental challenges, such as the destruction of flora and fauna, dispossession of land, contamination of water sources, pollution and poisoning of natural habitats and plants, and the destruction of ecological and cultural structures.[88] It is therefore submitted that economic development projects have been driven by ideological and economic agendas as opposed to national and international models of sustainable development.[89]

5 Cameroon's legal framework

The urgent need to address the alarming environmental problems caused by extractive companies triggered the adoption of environmental policies to minimise its impacts at the national level. These policy and legal frameworks are examined below.

88 Swing et al. (2012: 257-273).

89 For a better understanding of this argument in general, see Swing et al. (2012).

5.1 The Constitution of the Republic of Cameroon

Owing to human rights concerns and the need for environmental sustainability, the Constitution of Cameroon provides for the enforcement of environmental interests. The provision stipulates as follows:[90]

> Every person shall have a right to a healthy environment. The protection of the environment shall be the duty of every citizen. The State shall ensure the protection and improvement of the environment.

A cursory analysis of this provision prompts an impression that environmental protection in Cameroon is a collective commitment to the entire population. This constitutional provision requires the state to ensure that all segments of the population, including indigenous peoples, enjoy a satisfactory, safe and healthy environment essential for their development. This is in line with the government's promise to "ensure the protection of minorities and preserve the rights of the indigenous population".[91] This being said, one would least expect recurrent instances of environmental degradation within the areas occupied by indigenous peoples. Closer scrutiny into the country's activities reveals, however, the possibility of a contradictory notion. For instance, government activities in collaboration with extractive companies constantly violate and undermine indigenous peoples' rights to a clean, safe and healthy environment. In addition, the sophisticated machines used for timber exploitation together with toxic chemicals have had a great toll on the nature, including animals, crops, plants and the soil, leaving indigenous communities in a destitute state. This is attributed to the lack of adequate protection and recognition of indigenous peoples in the national Constitution. It is observed that the government usually refers to indigenous peoples as 'marginalised populations' or 'vulnerable groups'. Unfortunately, the Constitution also fails to specifically define, which groups constitute indigenous peoples in the country.[92] Worse is the fact, that the Constitution fails to state clearly, which groups of people deserve the special protection as reiterated in paragraph 5(2) of the Constitution.[93]

The aforementioned shortcomings can be explained in a sense where Cameroon, like most African countries, is reluctant to acknowledge the existence of indigenous peoples maintaining that in fact the entire population is indigenous.[94] The Cameroonian legal system is hesitant to adopt a definition of the indigenous population as provided in international law, which refers to those people who have unique identities and organised societies, distinct from the broader society, who were the original

90 Paragraph 5(22) of the Preamble of the Constitution of the Republic of Cameroon Law No. 96-06 of 18 January 1996 to amend the Constitution of 2 June 1972.

91 Paragraph 5(2) of the Constitution of the Republic of Cameroon, 1996.

92 Nguh (2013: 8); and Pelican (2013: 13-14).

93 Pelican & Maruyama (2015: 49-50); and Pelican (2013: 13-14).

94 Ibid.

inhabitants of and have a special relationship with their ancestral land. As the latter is of course vital for their collective, physical and cultural survival as peoples, many such groups experience a state of subjugation, marginalisation, dispossession, exclusion or discrimination as a result of their unique and distinct traditional lifestyle.[95]

Under Cameroonian law, the term indigenous population is thus applied in a broader sense to include all categories of people in the country. This assertion is confirmed by the provision of Article 57(3) of the Constitution, which allows an indigene of a region to be elected as a member of the Regional Council. Based on this provision, it is observed that the term 'indigene' is used to refer to all categories of people in Cameroon and does not specifically refer to 'indigenous populations' as defined in international law. This controversy in the application of the term has deterred the full recognition and protection granted to indigenous peoples by international instruments. Yet, it is significant to note, that scholars have established that the term 'indigenous peoples' as used in international instruments has a different connotation to 'natives', 'first inhabitants' or 'aboriginal' referred to by colonial masters in African states.[96] It is therefore important for the Cameroonian government to review its stand regarding the definition of indigenous peoples, so as to enable them to enjoy the special recognition and protection accorded to them by international law.

Even though the right to a healthy environment is only mentioned in the Preamble to the Constitution, the same Preamble also has a provision that affirms the country's commitment to human rights and fundamental freedoms such as those contained in the Universal Declaration of Human Rights, the Charter of the United Nations, the Banjul Charter and all duly ratified international instruments relating to environmental protection.[97] In support of the above provision, Article 45 provides that all "duly approved or ratified treaties and international agreements shall, following their publication override national laws, provided the other party implements the said treaty or agreement".[98] This implies that indigenous peoples could seek recourse through these international instruments in cases of violation or failure to adequately protect their right to a healthy environment.

In line with the Constitution, the government has also developed some sectoral legislation at the national level to regulate environmental management. This happened shortly after the establishment of the UNCED, which emphasised the global need for a holistic approach to environmental management. It is on this basis that Law No. 94/01 of 20 January 1994 relating to Forestry, Wildlife, and Fisheries and Law No. 96/12 of 5 August 1996 relating to environmental management were adopted to ensure efficient forestry management and environmental protection in the country. The above

95 Wessendorff (2002: 4).

96 Anaya (2010: 27); and Gilbert & Couillard (2011: 62).

97 Article 5 of the Constitution of the Republic of Cameroon.

98 Article 45 of the Constitution of the Republic of Cameroon.

laws, main objectives are to ensure the principles of precaution, prevention and corrective measures, of public participation and the polluter pays responsibility. They lay down a framework for environmental sustainability in the country and advocate for environmental impact assessment (EIA), especially on projects that have the potential of causing severe harm to the environment. The next section examines these legal frameworks.

5.2 The Forestry Law

The Forestry Law and its Decree of implementation enacted in Cameroon, are part of the government strategy to regulate the exploitation of forestry (timber) activities and to ensure the sustainable conservation and proper management of such resources and the ecosystem in the country.[99] It is argued, that an increase in human population and the growing need for natural resources have rendered the forest vulnerable to poachers and extracting companies, who exploit resources indiscriminately and on a day to day basis.[100] In Cameroon, the management and protection of the forest, which is not limited to importation, exploration and exploitation to safeguard against environmental degradation is the sole responsibility of the state.[101] By implication, the state is in charge of managing the forest and making decisions regarding all activities taking place therein. The main reason for this is to combat the excessive rate of illegal timber exploitation and the unequal distribution of forest benefits in a way that indigenous peoples may share in the proceeds and ensure that they are involved in the forest management and related decision-making processes. Such forest management shall also take the needs of the younger generations into account.[102] It should enable indigenous peoples to take part in decisions relating to the use, control, management and development of the land and resources as well as suggest possible measures to mitigate environmental degradation therein.

The Forestry Law prohibits any development project that has the potential of destroying the forest or the aquatic environment. This is particularly relevant, where the creation or maintenance of a permanent forest cover is considered essential for soil preservation, protection of river banks to control water flows, or preserving biodiversity as the area might be declared ecologically fragile.[103] This implies that no exploitation is allowed to take place within that area in order not to damage the ecosystem or to pollute the soil and water sources.[104] In addition, the Forestry Law classifies the

99 Section 1 of the Forestry Law No. 94/01 of 20 January 1994.
100 Rusko (2015: 125-126).
101 Part II Sections 11 and 13 of the Forestry Law.
102 Alemagi et al. (2013: 8-9).
103 Sections 16(2) and 17(1) of the Forestry Law.
104 Section 17(2) of the Forestry Law.

forest into two parts, namely the permanent forest and the non-permanent forest. The permanent forest is land used exclusively for forestry and wildlife habitat, while non-permanent forests include forest land also used for other purposes.[105] The permanent forest is also referred to as state or council forest and comprises 30% of the national territory, which is the private property of the state and exclusively managed by the state.[106] The non-permanent forest, also known as unclassified forest, includes communal and community forest belonging to private individuals.[107] Although this portion of land has been handed to local communities and requires them to manage woodland areas, it is interesting to note that the state still has absolute control over this portion of land.[108] This is the reason why most timber exploited in the country comes from the communal forests, that is, areas inhabited by indigenous communities.

More so, the Forestry Law provides that exploitation activities require a legal approval by means of a licence authorising the exploitation of timber within a specific period.[109] It also entails that the exploitation of certain volumes of standing timber may not exceed the annual logging potential renewable for fifteen years and assessed every three years.[110] In addition, Section 49 clearly stipulates that the total forest area to be granted to a licence-holder will depend on the potential of the forest concession. This is usually calculated on the basis of sustainability and lasting yield and the capacity of the said extractive industry not exceeding 200,000 hectares. This is granted to large-scale logging companies over a long-term period of fifteen years. Thus, no extracting company in whatever case is allowed to exploit an area of more than 200,000 hectares. Section 55 of the Forestry Law authorises the exploitation of timber from a communal forest following a sale of standing volume not exceeding 25,000 hectares for a non-renewable period of three years. This is usually at the expense of indigenous peoples as most often extractive companies violate their rights and exploit beyond the specified limits resulting in their dispossession of natural habitats.

As previously mentioned, the management of forests is the responsibility of the state, specifically the Ministry of Forestry and Wildlife. As prescribed in Section 23 of the Forestry Law, the state is under the duty to ensure that the exploitation of timber is done in a sustainable manner. It is also essential that timber is exploited in a way that does not alter the traditional values of local inhabitants or compromise the future productivity of the forest. Nor shall it cause any substantial damage to the physical and social environment. In this regard, emphasis is laid on aspects pertaining to inventory,

105 Part III Section 20 of the Forestry Law.
106 Chapter I Sections 21-33 of the Forestry Law.
107 Chapter II Section 34 of the Forestry Law.
108 Sections 37 and 38 of the Forestry Law.
109 Sections 41 to 44 of the Forestry Law.
110 Sections 45 to 46 of the Forestry Law.

re-afforestation, natural or artificial regeneration, sustained forestry exploitation and infrastructure.[111]

A reading of Section 63 places a responsibility on the state and other bodies in charge of managing forest products to ensure that prior to the issuance of exploiting licences and drafting of contracts, an inventory is carried out on the specific area to be allotted to exploiting companies. They must also ensure that while the prescribed area is under exploitation, there is a replacement of younger trees in the exploited area and that extracting activities are done in a way that does not jeopardise the needs of future generations. In other words, forest exploitation must be carried out in a manner that does not exceed production, to enable the forest to continue growing such that there remain sufficient forest resources for unborn generations.[112] Furthermore, as specified in Section 61, extractive industries must embark on infrastructural developments such as the construction of roads, the building of bridges, health centres, schools and other social amenities that help in developing indigenous communities. There is a salient need for stakeholders, the government, civil society and extractive companies to be proactive in improving the living standards of indigenous peoples, and in promoting and protecting the ecological forest where these people live. It is worth noting that the recent normative approach to forest management and environmental protection in Cameroon has failed to generate viable results. This is because logging activities are usually attained in grave disregard of existing laws, indigenous peoples' environment and well-being.

5.3 Environmental management

Law No. 96/12 lays down the general framework regulating environmental management in Cameroon.[113] Conscious of the fact that the environment is a common heritage, its protection and the rational management of resources therein are of prime importance given its significance to human beings.[114] The Law guarantees everyone the right to a sound environment and calls on both public and private institutions to include programmes in their activities that sensitise and provide knowledge about environmental concerns in the country.[115] The provision implies that information about the state of the environment where indigenous peoples reside is essential for them. In line with the above assertion, Section 7 provides for the right to be informed of the activities that might have adverse effects to the environment, livelihood and possible measures put in place to mitigate these effects. To this end, the state has an obligation to ensure

111 Section 63 of the Forestry Law.
112 Alemagi (2011: 66).
113 Section 1 of Law No. 96/12 of 5 August 1996.
114 Section 2 of Law No. 96/12 of 5 August 1996.
115 Section 6 of Law No. 96/12 of 5 August 1996.

that all population, especially indigenous peoples who are most often affected, have information about dangerous substances and activities that have adverse effects to their health and the environment.[116] The Law also requires that forest-dwellers be consulted prior to any decisions relating to their environment.[117] This shall enable them to challenge policies that have the potential to destroy the environment and alter their traditional way of life.

The state is also obliged to develop, coordinate and implement strategies that safeguard air, water and soil pollution, which may have a detrimental impact on indigenous peoples' health and environment.[118] Further efforts to safeguard the environment require the government to develop a national environmental management plan and set up an environmental information system that obliges the authorities concerned to ensure that all environmental issues relating to land are respected at all levels.[119]

The law on environmental management also makes provision for environmental impact assessment (EIA). This requires that – prior to the execution of any development project – the state, together with the extractive industries, should carry out an EIA on the area where the project is to be executed. This process shall enable the state to assess the nature of the impact on the physical environment and the host communities likely to be affected by the project in question.[120]

Based on Principle 17 of Agenda 21 of the UNCED, the government of Cameroon has adopted the EIA policy as an essential requirement prior to the execution of development projects, which can instigate environmental degradation on the lands of indigenous peoples. It is argued that this process is far from being effective as often, the conditions laid down for the EIA, are those designed by funding institutions that tend to undermine national policies on EIA.[121] In many instances the national environmental management plan, which aims at ensuring environmental management is ignored. In the absence of proper consultation, host communities that are potentially affected have no means of public participation and possible effects on socio-political aspects of the local population are often not clearly addressed.[122] A practical example is the procedure used in carrying out an EIA on the Mokong Dam Project (Waza-Logone Project, 1995).[123] Situated 42 kilometres west of Maroua in the Far North Region of Cameroon, the Mokong Dam construction required an EIA prior to the execution of the project in order to assess its biophysical and socio-economic impacts on the environment surrounding the Waza National Park and River Longone. The EIA was

116 Section 9(e) of Law No. 96/12 of 5 August 1996.
117 Section 9(e) (iv) of Law No. 96/12 of 5 August 1996.
118 Section 10(1)(2) of Law No. 96/12 of 5 August 1996.
119 Sections 13, 14 and 15 of Law No. 96/12 of 5 August 1996.
120 Section 17 of Law No. 96/12 of 5 August 1996.
121 Bitondo (2000: 33-35).
122 Ibid: 37-38.
123 Ibid: 35-36.

conducted by some Cameroonian experts in collaboration with a Brazilian expert. The reports revealed that the Dam construction would have serious repercussions on the biophysical, economic and social well-being and environment of local communities. However, following the absence of specific clarifications of its impacts to the general public coupled with irregularities in conducting and handling of the report and the lack of prior consultation with the affected communities, the government suspended the project and embarked on employing alternative measures in developing the region.[124]

It is submitted that economic development projects have ideologically and economically driven agendas as opposed to national and international models of sustainable development and resource extraction.[125] These practices have caused many conflicts between the state, logging companies and indigenous communities over government's failed policies to guarantee a sustainable environment for its population.[126] As such, indigenous peoples' livelihoods are endangered as they fear that increased exploitation of natural resources and destruction of their traditional lands could ultimately reduce their chances of survival, increase poverty, food insecurity and complete destruction of their living environment.

6 The impact of timber exploitation on indigenous peoples' environment

Unsustainable logging activities threaten the rainforest biodiversity in Cameroon. Alemagi[127] has noted that these logging operations left a plethora of challenges to the environment and indigenous peoples' survival.

6.1 Environmental degradation

Environmental degradation is provoked by considerable deforestation rates by multinationals who pay little attention to the long-term sustainability of the wood.[128] Indigenous peoples are of the opinion that government symbolises an alien that threatens their land and resource security leaving them with little or no economic benefits or employment opportunities.[129] Instead, they have to deal with the environmental consequences left behind which undermine their subsistence base.

Inefficient and weak government policies and the absence of effective monitoring and enforcement mechanisms have caused MNCs and other extractive companies to

124 Ibid.
125 Ibid.
126 Alemagi (2011: 69-70).
127 Ibid: 65.
128 Shearman (2012: 18-19).
129 Glastra (1999: 70).

exploit the situation to their advantage. To this end, indigenous communities in Cameroon are unable to retain their traditional sustainable ways of life, land use and environmental management.[130] The adverse effects of timber exploitation on the forest ecosystem of indigenous peoples remain visible and alarming, posing a substantial threat to food security and their survival. Moreover, forest exploitation has resulted in the development of large-scale trade in bush meat, which indigenous communities use as their primary source of protein.

6.2 Climate change

Climate change is a human influence identified by several scholars as a global environmental challenge affecting millions of forest-dependent communities.[131] Lenzerini and Piergentili argue that climate change is also a major cause of biodiversity loss.[132] Instigated by greenhouse gas emissions, climate change has serious repercussions on the poor rural and forest-dweller communities who depend solely on agriculture and forest products for their economic subsistence.[133] Although the adverse effects of climate change are not specific to indigenous peoples, their close affinity to land makes their case significant and requires immediate redress.[134] From this perspective, the destruction caused by timber extractive companies in areas inhabited by indigenous peoples have gravely disrupted their societies and lifestyle.

Between 1972-1973, 1982-1983 and 1987-1988 severe droughts affected the Sahelian northern part of Cameroon with dry spells, predominantly caused by timber exploitation and excessive deforestation.[135] The overall impacts included food shortages, hunger, famine, malnutrition and high mortality rates.

The hot climatic conditions caused by climate change conditions have resulted in drying streams leading to the disappearance of some species of fish (*Nwahka*), which the Baka indigenous communities use for traditional rituals, such as during the initiation of young girls upon maturity for marriage and womanhood.[136] Both mushroom, *tre larvae* and bush yam (*Bahh*), which serve as their staple food have gradually disappeared from the forest due to the harsh and changing climatic conditions.[137]

Additionally, the severity of climate shocks has aggravated hunting activities due to the prolonged absence of rainfall. Indigenous hunters usually trace the footprints of

130 Sikod (2010: 75).
131 Jegede (2016: 35).
132 Lenzerini & Piergentili (2016: 159).
133 Abate & Kronk (2013: 3).
134 Jegede (2016: 3).
135 Molua & Lambi (2007: 8).
136 Animatua et al. (2010).
137 Ibid.

animals left behind during rains in order to trap them. The continuous droughts have, however, rendered this practice impossible, thereby intensifying the suffering and vulnerability of indigenous communities.[138] More important is the fact that crop yields, especially cash crops have significantly decreased due to unstable rainfall.[139] The changes in climatic conditions trick indigenous women to plant food crops at the sight of early rains, which only last for a couple of days, the excessive sun that follows afterwards destroys the crops that had managed to germinate.[140] This situation has both a direct and indirect influence on the survival and resilience of indigenous peoples and poses serious threats to their health and existence. In fact, the increase rate of sicknesses such as malaria, ulcers, skin rashes and subsequent death is attributed to the absence of nutritious food, which fortifies the immune system, coupled with high temperatures and the absence of frequent rainfalls.[141]

6.3 Pollution of water sources, air and soil

Pollution refers to the degradation of the quality and quantity of natural resources.[142] Air pollution, in particular, is a common cause of environmental degradation as it emits contaminations into the environment that may damage or kill plants and animal species.[143] Moreover, the method of timber extraction produces dust (sawdust) and smog, thereby polluting the air. As such dust particles are inhaled by local inhabitants living around the area, it affects their eyes, causing allergies, blindness, persistent flu and lung infections, which subsequently result in tuberculosis.

The indiscriminate and unsustainable extraction of timber on local indigenes lands has left detrimental effects on water sources leading to serious health issues such as respiratory infections, heart diseases and lung cancer. The process of timber extraction requires the use of fuelled engine saws and other sophisticated machines, which cause fuel spills that pollute the ground and local streams, thereby poisoning the only source of water which indigenous peoples use for drinking, cooking, bathing and other household chores. Once this water is consumed, it leads to severe health problems and at times subsequent death. When the soil is contaminated by spillage substances, it loses its quality and fertility level, resulting in decreased crop productivity, famine and poverty. In some cases, crops that manage to survive contain poisonous substances from the chemicals, which might lead to serious health complications when consumed. It is submitted that although the forest is a sink for carbon dioxide and the major gas

138 Molua & Lambi (2007: 8-9).
139 Animatua et al. (2010).
140 Ibid.
141 Bele et al. (2011: 373).
142 Tyagi et al. (2014: 1492).
143 Ibid: 1493.

enhancing greenhouse effects, the immense timber exploitation process has caused a decline in environmental services that are only provided by the forest.[144]

6.4 Destruction of ecosystems

It is widely established that logging companies are first and foremost interested in the economic value of timber for income and profit and care little about their impact on the environment and well-being of host communities. In fact, the common notion of "grab-it-and-run" as described by 20th-century European geographers aims at exploiting the rich timber species within a short period without regard to environmental sustainability.[145] Even though it is argued that specific logging (clear-cut logging) prevents large-scale damage to the forest, the process has the potential to cause direct and indirect environmental effects. For example, in a bid to search for preferred species, MNCs construct roads into large portions of the forest. This activity destroys ecosystems and peasant fields and exposes the forest to poachers, thereby decimating rare and wild animals such as forest elephants and lowland gorillas.[146] It is maintained that the extraction of each cubic metre subsequently results in massive destruction leading to a substantial change of the ecosystems diversity.[147]

7 Conclusion

This chapter examined the exploitation of timber and its environmental impact on indigenous peoples' lands in Cameroon. It observed that – despite the significant contribution of timber to the country's economy – forest activities have the potential to cause substantial damage to the ecosystem, flora and fauna, including rivers and other water catchments. Extensive timber exploitation activities have placed the country on the map as foreign investors keep invading the country's rich, dense forest in search of timber. Besides, in assessing the country's commitment to environmental protection, it was revealed that Cameroon, like many African countries, has been quite active in promoting international, regional and national instruments that enhance environmental sustainability. Yet, weak government policies, the absence of efficient monitoring and implementation mechanisms, the lack of an integrative participative management system has, however, rendered the rich, diverse rainforest vulnerable to environmental degradation, depletion, pollution and the consequent extinction of flora and fauna. It

144 Djeukam (2013).
145 Ibid: 10.
146 Samndong & Vatn (2012: 217-219).
147 Djeukam (2013: 115).

is suggested that a key starting point to improved environmental protection in Cameroon is to develop an effective monitoring system with the aim to impose serious penalties for perpetrators in cases of violations. For example, if the licences of perpetrators are suspended for a certain period of time, the current status quo in the country could be significantly improved. An inclusive system of participative governance should be encouraged to enable indigenous peoples to become part of the policy formulations, decision-making processes and in the management of environmental resources. In fact, the Cameroonian government should consult and collaborate with indigenous peoples on issues relating to forest management prior to the execution of development projects within the areas they occupy. There is also a need to review environmental laws especially the Forestry Law and Law No. 96/12 relating to environmental management. The Forestry Law should be revisited to ensure that indigenous peoples have absolute control over the communal and community forest. The fact that the Forestry Law has made the state the sole manager of the forest has permitted the state to make decisions on the portions of land allocated to indigenous peoples without their informed consent. Since indigenous peoples are the best custodians of the land, Law No. 96/12 on environmental management should be revised to include indigenous peoples as part of the EIA committee. This would go a long way in mitigating environmental harms and in ensuring environmental sustainability on indigenous peoples' lands.

References

Abate, RS & EA Kronk (2013) "Commonality among unique indigenous communities: an introduction to climate change and its impact on indigenous peoples" in RS Abate & EA Kronk (eds) *Climate change and indigenous peoples: the search for legal remedies* 3-18.

Alemagi, D (2011) "Sustainable development in Cameroon's forestry sector: progress, challenges, and strategies for improvement" 5(2) *African Journal of Environmental Science and Technology* 65-72.

Alemagi, D & R Kozak (2010) "Illegal logging in Cameroon: causes and the path forward" 12(8) *Forest Policy and Economics* 554-561.

Alemagi, D, PA Minang, M Feudjio & L Duguma (2014) "REDD+ readiness process in Cameroon: an analysis of multi-stakeholder perspectives" 14(6) *Climate Policy* 709-733.

Alemagi, D, R Hajjar, Z Tchoundjeu & R Kozak (2013) "Cameroon's environmental impact assessment decree and public participation in concession-based forestry: an exploratory assessment of eight forest-dependent communities" 6(10) *Journal of Sustainable Development* 8-24.

Amariei, L (2005) *Legal compliance in the forestry sector case study: Cameroon* Final Report, at <http://www.fao.org/forestry/195800b266e69b6880da012e1a1875f2319a15.pdf> (accessed 26-12-2017).

Amougou, A, JL Betti, I Bindzi, P Bilong, M Tchatat, N Ndam, M Onana, N Mbarga, J Belinga, D Koulbout, J Tieguhong & S Assembe (2009) *Non-detriment findings report on PERICOPSIS ELATA (FABACEAE) in Cameroon* Report Prepared for the National Forest Development Agency (ANAFOR), at <http://www.itto.int/files/user/cites/cameroon/NDF%20Report_Cameroon_December%202009.pdf> (accessed 16-12-2017).

Amungwa, FA (2011) "The evolution of conflicts related to natural resource management in Cameroon" 35(1) *Journal of Human Ecology* 53-60.

Anaya, SJ (2010) "The evolution of the concept of indigenous peoples and its contemporary dimensions" in S Dersso (ed) *Perspectives on the rights of minorities and indigenous peoples in Africa* 23-42.

Animatua G, R Yasmine & G Bamboye (2010) *Indigenous women and climate change in South and North-West Cameroon*, at <http://www/cameroon%201%.pdf> (accessed 29-3-2018).

Ardener, E (1962) "The political history of Cameroon" 18(8) *The World Today* 341-350.

Atyi, RE, S Assembe-Mvondo, G Lescuyer & P Cerruti (2013) "Impacts of international timber procurement policies on Central Africa's forestry sector: the case of Cameroon" 32 *Forest Policy and Economics* 40-48.

Beauchamp, E & V Ingram (2011) "Impacts of community forest on livelihoods in Cameroon: lessons from two case studies" 13(4) *International Forestry Review* 389-403.

Bele, MY, O Somorin, DJ Sonwa, JN Nkem & B Locatelli (2010) "Forests and climate change adaptation policies" 16(3) Mitigation and Adaptation Strategies for Global Change 369-385.

Biesbrouck, K (2002) "New perspectives on forest dynamics and the myth of 'communities': reconsidering co-management of rainforests in Cameroon" 33(1) *IDS Bulletin* 55-64.

Bitondo, D (2000) "Environmental assessment in Cameroon: state of the art" 18(1) *Impact Assessment and Project Appraisal* 33-42.

Cerutti, PO, L Tacconi, G Lescuyer & R Nasi (2013) "Cameroon's hidden harvest: commercial chainsaw logging, corruption, and livelihood" 26(5) *Society & Natural Resources: An International Journal* 539-553.

Colchester, M (2000) "Self-determination or environmental determination for indigenous peoples in tropical forest conservation" 14(5) *Conservation Biology* 1365-1367.

Cultural Survival (2018) *Observations on the state of indigenous human rights in Cameroon*, at <https://www.culturalsurvival.org/sites/default/files/UPR-report-Cameroon-2017.pdf> (accessed 11-8-2018).

De Schutter, O (2014) *International human rights law: cases, materials and commentary* 2nd Ed.

Dersso, SA (2010) "Introduction" in SA Dersso (ed.) *Perspectives on the right of minorities and indigenous peoples in Africa* 3-22.

Dersso, SA (2012) *Taking ethno-cultural diversity seriously in constitutional design*.

Djeukam, R (2013) "Forestry and communities in Cameroon" in H Healy, J Martínez-Alier, L Temper, M Walter & JF Gerber (eds) *Ecological economics from the bottom-up* 108-137.

Djontu, GA (2009) *AG Influence of NGOs, World Bank and Members of Parliament on the Cameroon Forestry Law: A Contribution to Good Forest Governance* Doctoral Thesis Faculty of Forestry, Albert-Ludwigs-Universität Freiburg im Breisgau.

Echu, G (2013) "The language question in Cameroon" 18(1) *Linguistik Online* 19-33 <http://www.linguistik online.de/18_04/echu.html> (accessed 14-2-2018).

Ekoko, F (2000) "Balancing politics, economics and conservation: the case of cameroon forestry law reform" 31 *Development and Change* 131-154.

Erinosho, BT (2013) "The Revised African Convention on the Conservation of Nature and Natural Resources: prospects for a comprehensive treaty for the management of Africa's natural resources" 21(3) *African Journal of International and Comparative Law* 378-397.

Ernst, C, A Verhegghen, P Mayaux, M Hansen & P Defourny (2012) "Cartographie du couvert forestier et des changements du couvert forestier en Afrique Centrale" in C De Wasseige (ed.) *Les forêts du Bassin du Congo – état des forêts 2010* 23-42.

Fonjong, L, I Sama-Lang & FL Fon (2010) "An assessment of the evolution of land tenure system in Cameroon and its implications on women's land rights and food security" 9 *Perspectives on Global Development and Technology* 154-169.

Frankel, JA (2010) *The natural resource curse: a survey of diagnoses and some prescriptions* HKS Faculty Research Working Paper Series, at <https://dash.harvard.edu/bitstream/handle/1/8694932/rwp12-014_frankel.pdf?sequence=1> (accessed 11-8-2018).

Gilbert, J & V Couillard (2011) "International law and land rights in Africa: the shift from states' territorial possessions to indigenous' people's ownership rights" in R Home (ed.) *Essays in African land law* 47-68.

Glastra, R (ed.) (1999) *Cut and run: illegal logging and timber trade in the tropics.*

Gross, JG (2003) *Cameroon: politics and society in critical perspectives.*

Hansungule, M & AO Jegede (2014) "The impact of climate change on indigenous peoples land tenure and use: the case for a regional policy in Africa" 21 *International Journal of Minority and Group Rights* 256-291.

Henkin, L (1990) *The age of rights.*

Jegede, AO (2016) *The climate change regulatory framework and indigenous peoples' lands in Africa: human rights implications.*

Lenzerini, F & E Piergentili (2016) "A double-edge sword: climate change, biodiversity and human rights" in O Quirico & M Boumghar (eds) *Climate change and human rights: an international and comparative law perspective* 159-172.

Mbatu, R (2010) "Deforestation in the Buea-Limbe and Bertoua Regions in southern Cameroon (1984-2000): modernisation, world-systems, and neo-malthusian outlook" 75(5) *GeoJournal* 443-458.

Mbatu, R (2016) "Linking the global to the national: an application of the international pathways model to examine the influence of international environmental agreements on Cameroon's Forest Policy" 16(4) *International Environmental Agreements* 465-492.

Mitchell, RB (2003) "International environmental agreements: a survey of their features, formation, and effects" 28(2) *Annual Review of Environmental Resources* 429-461.

Molua, EL & CM Lambi (2007) *The economic impact of climate change on agriculture in Cameroon* The World Bank Development Research Group Research Working Paper, at <https://openknowledge.worldbank.org/bitstream/handle/10986/7362/WPS4364.pdf?sequence=1> (accessed 26-12-2017).

Ntoubandi, S & R Adjovi (2016) "A wider human rights spectrum to fight climate change" in O Quirico & M Boumghar (eds) *Climate change and human rights: an international and comparative law perspective* 256-269.

Oyono, PR (2005) "Profiling local-level outcomes of environmental decentralisation: the case of Cameroon's forests in the Congo Basin" 14(3) *The Journal of Environment and Development* 317-324.

Oyono, PR, C Kouna & W Malla (2005) "Benefits of forests in Cameroon. global structure, issues involving: access and decision-making hiccoughs" 7 *Forest Policy and Economics* 357-368.

Pelican, M (2013)"Insights from Cameroon: five years after the declaration on the rights of indigenous peoples" 29(3) *Anthropology Today* 13-16.

Pelican, M & J Maruyama (2015) "The indigenous rights movement in Africa: perspectives from Botswana and Cameroon" 36(1) *African Study Monographs* 49-74.

Reuters (2017) "Cameroon forest people: land rights abuses threaten survival" *Voice of Africa* (13-9-2017), at <https://www.voanews.com/a/cameroon-forest-people-say-land-rights-abuses-threaten-survival/4027761.html> (accessed 11-8-2018).

Ross, ML (2015) "What have we learned about the resource curse?" 18 *Annual Review of Political Science* 239-259.

Rusko, M (2015) "Environmental and quality management systems in the context of sustainable development" 23(36) *The Journal of Slovak University of Technology* 125-132.

Samndong, RA & A Vatn (2012) "Forest related conflicts in South East Cameroon: causes & policy options" 14(2) *International Forestry Review* 213-226.

Savaresi, A (2013) "REDD+ and human rights: addressing synergies between international regimes" 18(3) *Ecology and Society* 5-13.

Sayer, JA, CS Harcourt & NM Collins (1992) *The conservation atlas of tropical forest: Africa.*

Scholtz, W (2015) "Human rights and the environment in the African Union context" in W Scholtz & J Verschuuren (eds) *Regional environmental law: transregional comparative lessons in pursuit of sustainable development* 103-127.

Shearman, P, J Bryan & WF Laurance (2012) "Are we approaching 'peak timber' in the tropics?" 151(1) Biological Conservation 17-21.

Shelton, DL (2002) "Protecting human rights in a globalised world" 25 *International and Comparative Law Review* 273-322.

Sikod, F (2010) "Poverty and environmental degradation in Cameroon" in S Del Campo, T Hamada, G Barbieri-Masini, PN Nkwi, O Sichone & A Momoh (eds) *Social and economic development* Volume VII 72-88.

Stevens, S (ed.) (1997) *Conservation through cultural survival: indigenous peoples and protected areas.*

Strydom, H (2015) "Introduction to regional environmental law of the African Union" in W Scholtz & J Verschuuren (eds) *Regional environmental law: transregional comparative lessons in pursuit of sustainable development* 21-50.

Sunderland-Groves, JL, TCH Sunderland, JA Comiskey, JSO Ayeni & M Mdaihli (2003) "Takamanda: the biodiversity of an African rainforest" in JA Comiskey & TCH Sunderland (eds) *Takamanda Forest Reserve*, Cameroon 1-8.

Swing, K, V Davidov & S Brendan (2012) "Oil development on traditional lands of indigenous peoples: coinciding perceptions on two continents" 28(2) *Journal of Developing Societies* 257-280.

Tyagi, S, N Garg & R Paudel (2014) "Environmental degradation: causes and consequences" 81(8-2) *European Researcher* 1491-1498.

Van der Linde, M (2002) "A review of the African Convention on Nature and Natural Resources" 2 *African Human Rights Law Journal* 33-59.

Wessendorff, K (2002) *The indigenous world 2001/2002.*

World Bank (2010) *World development report*, at <https://openknowledge.worldbank.org/handle/10986/4387> (11-8-2018).

Wunder, S (2003) Oil wealth and the faith of the forest: a comparative study of eight tropical countries.